IN

Servlets, Struts, JavaMail, EJB, JSP, Hibernating, RMI, JDBC-ODBC, JSF, JNDI, Java Security, Sockets

Himalaya

# Java EE
## : from trainee to trained

**Ravi Majithia**

Assistant Professor

Department of Computer Science

Deogiri College,

**Aurangabad (M.S.) – 431005.**

MUMBAI • NEW DELHI • NAGPUR • BENGALURU • HYDERBAD • CHENNOPAI • PUNE • LUCKNOW
AHMEDABAD • ERNAKULAM • BHUBANESWAR • INDORE • KOLKATA • GUWAHATI

Inspite of best efforts taken to present the book without mistakes, some mistakes may have inadvertently crept in. So we do not take any legal responsibility for them. If they are brought to our notice, corrections will be done in the next edition.

**First Edition : 2015**

**Published by** : Mrs. Meena Pandey
for **HIMALAYA PUBLISHING HOUSE PVT. LTD.,**
"Ramdoot", Dr. Bhalerao Marg, Girgaon, Mumbai - 400 004.
Phones: 23860170, 23863863, Fax: 022-23877178.
**Email: himpub@vsnl.com**
**Website: www.himpub.com**

**Branch Offices:**

**New Delhi** : "Pooja Apartments", 4-B, Murari Lal Street, Ansari Road, Darya Ganj, New Delhi-110 002. Phones: 23270392, 23278631, Fax: 011-23256286

**Nagpur** : Kundanlal Chandak Industrial Estate, Ghat Road, Nagpur - 440 018. Phones: 2738731, 3296733 Telefax: 0712-2721216.

**Bengaluru** : No. 16/1 (Old 12/1), 1st Floor, Next to Hotel Highlands, Madhava Nagar, Race Course Road, Bengaluru - 560 001. Phones: 22281541, 22385461, Telefax: 080-22286611.

**Hyderabad** : No. 3-4-184, Lingampally, Besides Raghavendra Swamy Matham,Kachiguda, Hyderabad - 500 027. Phones: 040-27560041, 27550139.

**Chennai** : No. 85/50, Bazullah Road, T. Nagar, Chennai - 600 017. Phones: 044-32463737, 42124860.

**Pune** : First Floor, "Laksha" Apartment, No. 527, Mehunpura, Shaniwarpeth, (Near Prabhat Theatre), Pune - 411 030. Phones: 020-24496323, 24496333.

**Lucknow** : House No. 731, Shekhupura Colony, Near B.D. Convent School, Vikas Nagar, Aliganj, Lucknow - 226022. Mob: 09307501549.

**Ahmedabad** : 114, "SHAIL",1st Floor, Opp. Madhu Sudan House, C.G.Road, Navrang Pura, Ahmedabad - 380 009. Phone: 079-26560126.

**Ernakulam** : 39/176 (New No: 60/251) 1ST Floor,Karikkamuri Road,Ernakulam, Kochi - 682011, Kerala. Tel : (91) (0484) 2378012, 2378016.

**Bhubaneswar** : 5 Station Square, Bhubaneswar (Orissa) - 751 001. Phone: 0674-2532129,9338746007.

**Kolkata** : 108/4, Beliaghata Main Road, Near ID Hospital, Opp. SBI Bank, Kolkata - 700 010. Phone: 033-32449649.

**Guwahati** : House No. 15, Behind Pragjyotish College Near Sharma Printing Press, P.O. Bharalumukh, Guwahati-781 009 (Assam). Mobile: 09883055590/36.

**DTP by** : Prasad (HPH, Nagpur)

**Printed at** : Geetanjali Press Pvt. Ltd., Nagpur on behalf of H.P.H.

# Dedication

*To my wife, Chandrika, and our little deployment project, Jaineel.*

*You've both been very tolerant of the time I've spent*

*on the computer, either working on the book*

*or on Java itself.*

# Preface

A lot has happen to Java platform since its first release. It has achieved remarkably prevalent use in very short time. The broad acceptance of Java reflects Java's technical strength and feature-set, such as: platform neutrality, dynamism, garbage collection, security, concurrency, robustness and internet sense. The Java language has established itself as a strong, mature, general-purpose and standard programming language which has wide spectrum of application development.

In this book, I focus on developing high-end applications in Java using **NetBeans IDE**. For beginners, even I have included a preparatory chapter teaching basic exercise of Java NetBeans IDE. It teaches how to develop applications and how to properly use its tools. This book is an attempt to teach java to a certain depth, which I believe is best covered in a book in its own right.

In designing this book, I have strived to achieve three goals. **First**, to produce a concise introductory text, free from unnecessary verbosity, so that even beginners can develop a good understanding of the language in a short period of time. **Second**, I have tried to combine a tutorial style (based on explanation of concepts through examples) with a reference style (based on a flat structure). As a result, each chapter consists of a list of relatively short sections with examples and screenshots. This, I hope, further simplifies the reader's task. **And Third**, I have consciously avoided trying to present an absolutely complete description of core Java. While no important topic has been omitted, descriptions of some of the minor idiosyncrasies have been avoided for the sake of clarity and to avoid overwhelming beginners with too much information. Experience suggests that *any small knowledge gaps left as a result, will be easily filled over time through self discovery.*

While writing this book, I have assume that you have basic knowledge of core Java including object oriented features and java standard class libraries. Albeit, I begin with history and outlines of java programming to sum up. For application development we start with understanding applet & GUI programming and go up to RMI, Collections Framework and Security. At the end of this book I have also included some sample java projects that will help you to echo into your projects. Hence, this book covers enormous amount of view of J2EE and this will be very much helpful for professional programmers and students.

Special thanks to **Mr. Rakesh Jain, Mr. Kaushik Deoda, Mr. Kiran Sakla, Mr. Deepak Toshniwal, Mr. Kartik Khanapurkar** and **Mr. Nitin Pinkurwar** for their implications and liveliness that helped me to complete this book.

I am also very much thankful to **Shri. G. N. Pandey (Director, Himalaya Publishing House, Nagpur)** and **Dinesh Dhawane** (Area Manager) for the encouragement and support they have extended. I am also thankful to all staff members of **Himalaya Publishing House** for their efforts to make this book as helpful as it is.

We have jointly made attempts to eliminate all errors in this book. However if you find any, please let us know, that will help us to improve further.

# Contents

## Part I: Java History



## Part II: Java EE Overview

## Part III: Creating GUI Applications

## Part V: Surplus to Java EE



## Part VI: Farewell

# Part I

# Java History

1. The Roots of Java

2. Outlines of Java

# Chapter 1

# The Roots of Java

In January of 1991, Bill Joy, James Gosling, Mike Sheradin, Patrick Naughton, and several other individuals met in Aspen, Colorado for the first time to discuss the ideas for the Stealth Project. The goal of the Stealth Project was to do research in the area of application of computers in the consumer electronics market. The vision of the project was to develop "smart" consumer electronic devices that could all be centrally controlled and programmed from a handheld-remote-control-like device. According to Gosling, *"The goal was to build a system that would let us do a large, distributed, heterogeneous network of consumer electronic devices all talking to each other."* With this goal in mind, the stealth group began work. Members of the Stealth Project, which later became known as the Green Project, distributed project tasks among them and gifted a new language to the world. It took 18 months to develop the first working version of this new language which was initially known as **oak** but was renamed as **Java** in 1995.

## 1.1 Birth of Java

The trouble with C and C++ (and most other languages) is that they are designed to be compiled for a specific target. Although it is possible to compile a C++ program for just about any type of CPU, to do so requires a full C++ compiler targeted for that CPU. The problem is that compilers are expensive and time-consuming to create. An easier and more cost efficient solution was needed. In an attempt to find such a solution, Gosling and others began work on a portable, platform-independent language that could be used to produce code that would run on a variety of CPUs under differing environments. This effort ultimately led to the creation of Java.

The original thrust of java was not for internet...! But it was originated as a platform independent language that could be used to create software to be embedded in various electronic devices like remote controls, set-top boxes, ovens etc. In attempt to find such solution, Gosling and his team, began working and as a result they came out with Java.

Java derives much of its characteristics from C and C++. The Java team knew that using syntax of C and continuing object oriented features of C++ would make their language easier for the C / C++ programmers to understand. In addition to that java has added many new concepts which took java such high. Most importantly java is tested by the professional programmers, which adds the real experience of using java programming in different applications. Java gives full controls to the programmers. If you program well, your program reflects it. If you program poorly then also program reflects well...! Make a note that, java is not for learning purpose but it is for professional programmers.

## 1.2 History of Java

This section gives a short history of Java's evolution. Java goes back to 1991, when a group of Sun engineers, led by Patrick Naughton James Gosling, wanted to design a small computer language that could be used for consumer devices like cable TV switchboxes. Because these devices do not have a lot of power or memory, the language had to be small and generate very tight code. Also, because different manufacturers may choose different central processing units (CPUs), it was important that the language not be tied to any single architecture. The project was code-named "Green."

The requirements for small, tight, and platform-neutral code led the team to resurrect the model that some Pascal implementations tried in the early days of PCs. Niklaus Wirth, the inventor of Pascal, had pioneered the design of a portable language that generated intermediate code for a hypothetical machine. (These are often called virtual machines—hence, the Java virtual machine or JVM.) This intermediate code could then be used on any machine that had the correct interpreter. The Green project engineers used a virtual machine as well, so this solved their main problem.

The Sun people, however, come from a UNIX background, so they based their language on C++ rather than Pascal. In particular, they made the language object oriented rather than procedure oriented. But, as Gosling says in the interview, "All along, the language was a tool, not the end." Gosling decided to call his language "Oak" (presumably because he liked the look of an oak tree that was right outside his window at Sun). The people at Sun later realized that Oak was the name of an existing computer language, so they changed the name to Java. This turned out to be an inspired choice.

In 1992, the Green project delivered its first product, called "*7." It was an extremely intelligent remote control. (It had the power of a SPARCstation in a box that was 6 inches by 4 inches by 4 inches.) Unfortunately, no one was interested in producing this at Sun, and the Green people had to find other ways to market their technology. However, none of the standard consumer electronics companies were interested. The group then bid on a project to design a cable TV box that could deal with new cable services such as video on demand. They did not get the contract. (Amusingly, the company that did was led by the same Jim Clark who started Netscape—a company that did much to make Java successful.)

The Green project (with a new name of "First Person, Inc.") spent all of 1993 and half of 1994 looking for people to buy its technology—no one was found. (Patrick Naughton, one of the founders of the group and the person who ended up doing most of the marketing, claims to have accumulated 300,000 air miles in trying to sell the technology.) And the first Person was dissolved in 1994.

While all of this was going on at Sun, the World Wide Web part of the Internet was growing bigger and bigger. The key to the Web is the browser that translates the hypertext page to the screen. In 1994, most people were using Mosaic, a noncommercial web browser that came out of the supercomputing center at the University of Illinois in 1993. (Mosaic was partially written by Marc Andreessen for $6.85 an hour as an undergraduate student on a work-study project. He moved on to fame and fortune as one of the cofounders and the chief of technology at Netscape.)

In the SunWorld interview, Gosling says that in mid-1994, the language developers realized that "We could build a real cool browser. It was one of the few things in the client/server mainstream that needed some of the weird things we'd done: architecture neutral, real-time, reliable, secure—issues that weren't terribly important in the workstation world. So we built a browser."

The actual browser was built by Patrick Naughton and Jonathan Payne and evolved into the HotJava browser. The HotJava browser was written in Java to show off the power of Java. But the builders also had in mind the power of what are now called applets, so they made the browser capable of executing code inside web pages. This "proof of technology" was shown at SunWorld '95 on May 23, 1995, and inspired the Java craze that continues today.

Sun released the first version of Java in early 1996. People quickly realized that Java 1.0 was not going to cut it for serious application development. Sure, you could use Java 1.0 to make a nervous text applet that moved text randomly around in a canvas. But you couldn't even print in Java 1.0. To be blunt, Java 1.0 was not ready for prime time. Its successor, version 1.1, filled in the most obvious gaps, greatly improved the reflection capability, and added a new event model for GUI programming. It was still rather limited, though.

The big news of the 1998 JavaOne conference was the upcoming release of Java 1.2, which replaced the early toy like GUI and graphics toolkits with sophisticated and scalable versions that come a lot closer to the promise of "Write

Once, Run Anywhere"™ than their predecessors. Three days after (!) its release in December 1998, Sun's marketing department changed the name to the catchy Java 2 Standard Edition Software Development Kit Version 1.2.

Besides the "Standard Edition," two other editions were introduced: the "Micro Edition" for embedded devices such as cell phones, and the "Enterprise Edition" for server-side processing. This book focuses on the Standard Edition.

Versions 1.3 and 1.4 of the Standard Edition are incremental improvements over the initial Java 2 release, with an ever-growing standard library, increased performance, and, of course, quite a few bug fixes. During this time, much of the initial hype about Java applets and client-side applications abated, but Java became the platform of choice for server-side applications.

Version 5.0 is the first release since version 1.1 that updates the Java language in significant ways. (This version was originally numbered 1.5, but the version number jumped to 5.0 at the 2004 JavaOne conference.) After many years of research, generic types (which are roughly comparable to C++ templates) have been added—the challenge was to add this feature without requiring changes in the virtual machine. Several other useful language features were inspired by C#: a "for each" loop, autoboxing, and metadata. Language changes are always a source of compatibility pain, but several of these new language features are so seductive that we think that programmers will embrace them eagerly. Following table shows the growth of the Java library over the years. As you can see, the size of the application programming interface (API) has grown tremendously.

| Version | Numbers of library classes and interfaces |
|---|---|
| 1.0 | 211 |
| 1.1 | 477 |
| 1.2 | 1524 |
| 1.3 | 1840 |
| 1.4 | 2723 |
| 1.5 | 3270 |

## 1.3 Area of Applications of some famous Programming Languages

In current world there are many languages which led the computer technology to the highest peak. Here is a small list of some famous programming languages with their area of applications.

### 1.3.1 C Language

C language was developed by Dennis Ritchie in 1970. C was originally developed to provide compatibility to operating systems so that an operating system can run on any hardware platform. Right from creating small console applications up to writing codes for UNIX and Windows, uses of C language is everywhere. Here is a small list of different applications of C.

- Operating Systems
- Language Compilers
- Assemblers
- Text Editors
- Print Spoolers
- Network Drivers
- Modern Programs
- Data Bases
- Language Interpreters
- Chip Designing

In recent years C has been used as a general-purpose language because of its popularity with programmers. It is not the world's easiest language to learn, but must learn C as your first programming language! C is trendy - many well established programmers are switching to C for all sorts of reasons, but mainly because of the portability that writing standard C programs can offer.

### 1.3.2 C++

In 1983 Bjarne Stroustrup has developed C++. It was initially called as CWC (C With Classes) and then renamed as C++ (Increment in C). C++ is one of the famous Partially Object Oriented Programming Language. C++ has clearly set a stage for developing Java. Some of the applications of C++ are mentioned below.

- Computer Aided Design systems
- Animation related software (Like Maya, Alias, Wavefront, etc.)
- IOKit device drives.
- Kernal designing of operating systems (Like, Apple OS X)
- Multiprocessor multimedia designing (Like BeOS)
- Software plug-ins and web browsers (Like Google Chrome)
- Designing the statistics source code analysis tools (Like Coverity)
- Internet Management System (IMS) and IP Based network management applications.

As the best one, the main telephone transmission nodes Germany and France are written in C++.

### 1.3.3 VB.net

VB.net is an updated version of Visual Basic which is combined with .net technology. It is simply a collection of framework class library to solve different programming needs in much simpler and smaller way. It is an object oriented programming language which uses systematic and a wide collection of built-in classes and objects. VB programs are mainly algorithmic in nature, different applications of VB.net are

- Creating windows applications.
- MDI applications
- Console applications
- Graphical and GUI based applications
- Cross-platform and open source development (C# is more suitable for open source development)

VB.net is totally even driven, imperative and object oriented programming.

### 1.3.4 PHP

PHP is a server-side scripting language whose primary purpose is to generate HTML content. Its creator, Rasmus Lerdorf defines it as "a cross-platform, HTML-embedded, server-side web scripting language". With the current direction of the Web, it is easily being adapted to writing out all forms of XML content as well. The most recent version of PHP is PHP 4. PHP is used for

- Database accessing, File accessing, Application Controlling
- Graphics
- Online project management tools
- Building an online community
- Parsing XML files
- Image processing and Generation
- Creating dynamic websites (Most of the code of Facebook.com is written in PHP)

Three things make PHP popular. The first is that it is easy: easy to implement, easy to learn, and easy to use. The second is that it is free. The third is that it runs on almost any Web server on almost any platform currently available.

## 1.4 Java Bytecodes

The problems related to security and portability is solved by providing the concept of bytecodes. Java bytecodes are a highly optimized set of instructions designed to be executed by the Java run-time system, which is called the **Java Virtual Machine (JVM)**. That is, in its standard form, the JVM is an interpreter for bytecodes. Most modern languages are designed to be compiled, not interpreted—mostly because of performance concerns. However, the fact that a Java program is executed by the JVM, which solves the major problems associated with downloading programs over the Internet.

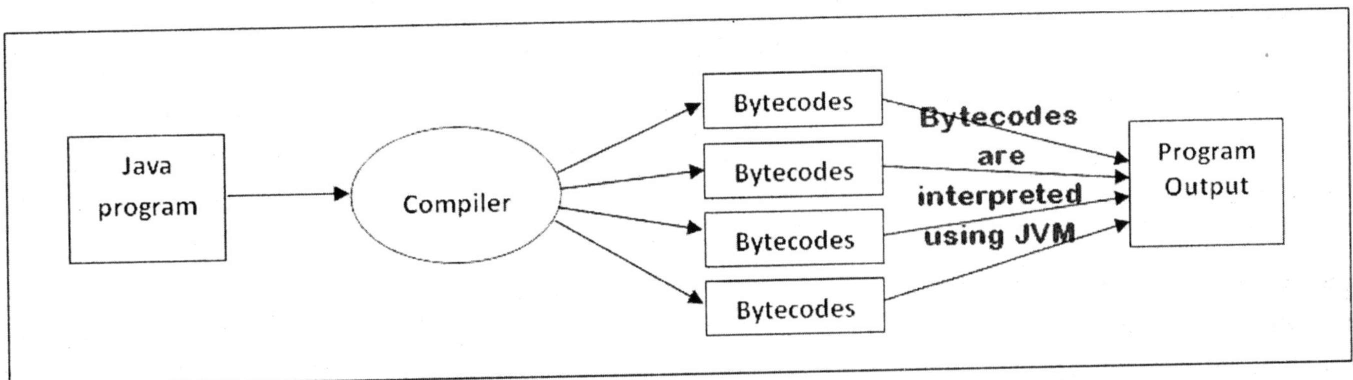


Above diagram displays that, a compiler distributes a java program into number of bytecodes and then bytecodes are combined and interpreted using JVM. Another major advantage of these bytecodes is it can be interpreted on any platform.

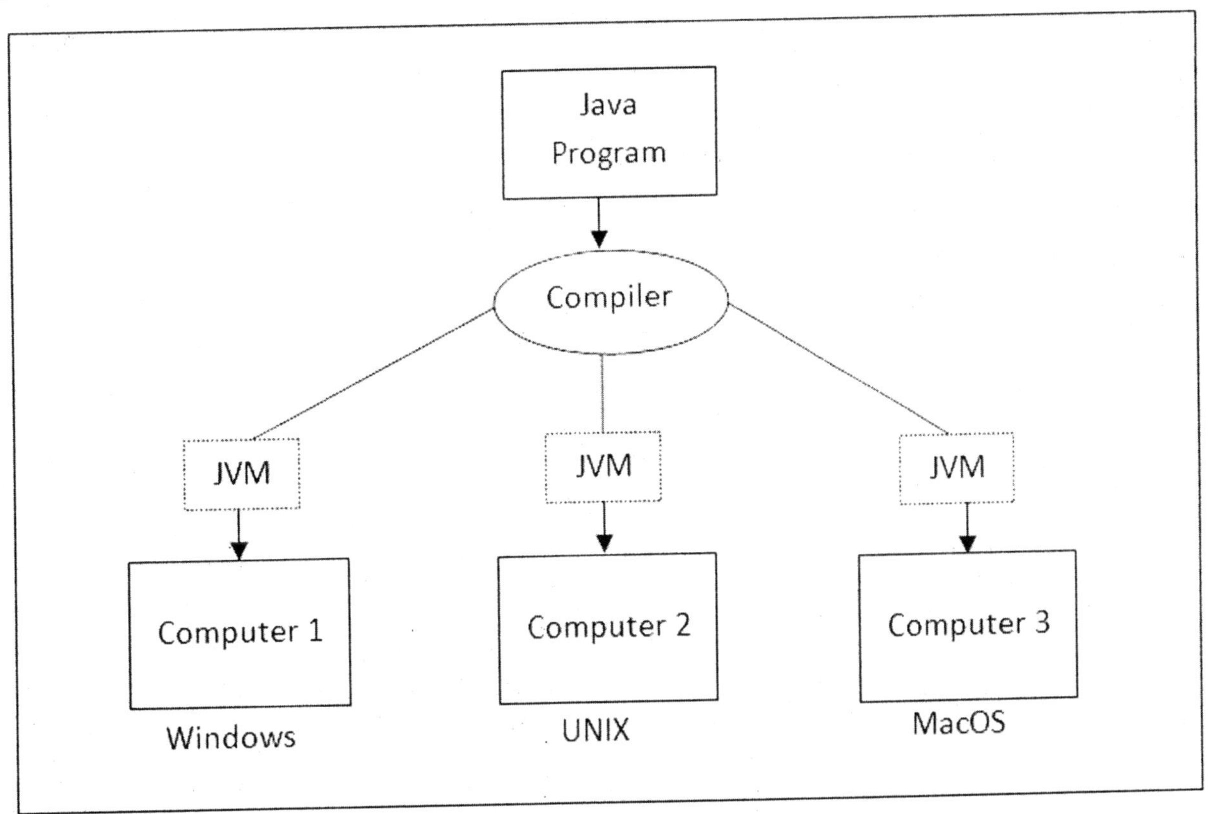


The fact that a Java program is interpreted also helps to make it secure. Because the execution of every Java program is under the control of the JVM, the JVM can contain the program and prevent it from generating side effects outside of the system. As you can see, above diagram is demonstrating that, each platform is using its own supportive JVM and can run same application everywhere.

> Note: Bytecodes is not a new idea. More than 20 years ago, original implementation of Pascal and the UCSD Pascal system used the same technique.

Many people think that java program interprets much slower than a normally interpreted language because of distribution into bytecodes and then conquering them again. However, with Java, the differential between the two is not so great. The bytecodes and JVM are designed in such a way that the Java run-time system interprets a program much faster than you might expect.

Not all the new programming languages use the concept of bytecodes for speed and accuracy. In **.net technology** there is a concept of **just-in-time (JIT) compilers**. These work by compiling the bytecodes into native code once, caching the results, and then calling them again if needed. This approach speeds up commonly used code tremendously because one has to do the interpretation only once. Although still slightly slower than a true native code compiler, a just-in-time compiler can give you a 10 or even 20 fold speedup for some programs and will almost always be significantly faster than an interpreter. This technology is being improved continuously and may eventually yield results that cannot be matched by traditional compilation systems.

Since so long we are discussing about bytecodes, these bytecodes are actually distribution of a program according to the user defined classes and interfaces, defined in it. Java compiler creates separate files with **.class** extensions. These .class files are called as bytecodes and they are provided the same name as of classes and interfaces of that program. During the interpretation, role of JVM is to search and conquer required .class files and interpret them as a single unit. (Refer above diagrams)

## 1.5 Java Runtime Environment (JRE) and its architecture

Java Runtime Environment (JER) contains JVM, class libraries and other supporting components. As we know that Java source code is compiled into bytecode by java compiler. This bytecode will be stored as .class files. During runtime, these bytecodes will be loaded and verified. The JVM interprets the bytecode into machine code which will be executed in the machine in which the Java program runs.

A Java Runtime Environment performs the following main tasks respectively.

1. Loads the class : This is done by the class loader
2. Verifies the bytecode : This is done by bytecode verifier.
3. Interprets the bytecode : This is done by the JVM

These tasks are described in detail in the subsequent sessions. A detailed Java architecture is shown below.

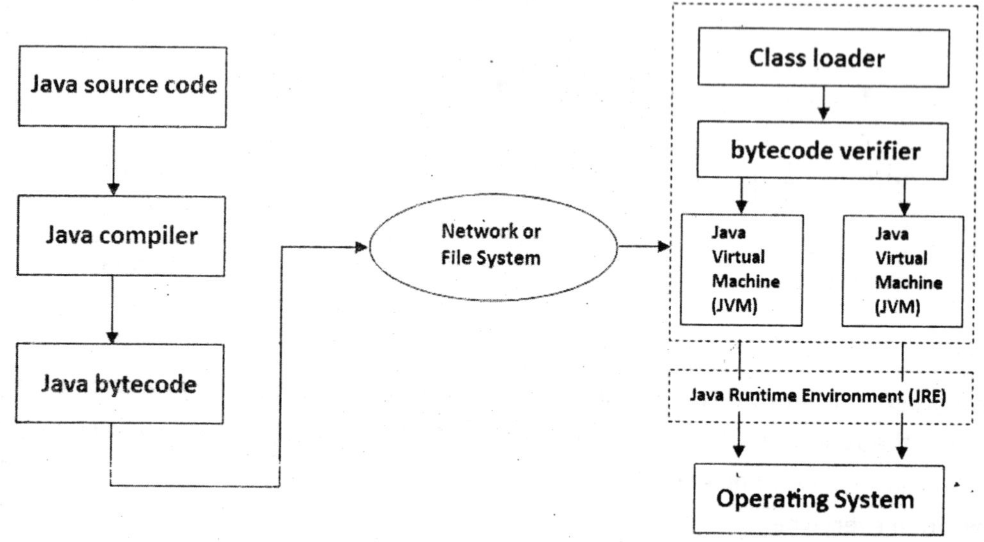

### Class loader :

Class loader loads all the class files required to execute the program. Class loader makes the program secure by separating the namespace for the classes obtained through the network from the classes available locally. Once the bytecode is loaded successfully, then next step is bytecode verification by bytecode verifier.

### Bytecode verifier :

The bytecode verifier verifies the bytecode to see if any security problems are there in the code. It checks the byte code and ensures the followings.

- The code follows JVM specifications.
- There is no unauthorized access to memory.
- The code does not cause any stack overflows.
- There are no illegal data conversions in the code such as float to object references.

### JVM :

Once this code is verified and proven that there is no security issues with the code, JVM will convert the bytecode into machine code which will be directly executed by the machine in which the Java program runs.

## 1.6 Java platforms

Java platform consists of a **Java Virtual Machine (JVM)** and **Class libraries**. Sun Microsystems refers their implementation of the Java platform as the **Java Runtime Environment (JRE)**. To develop the applications for different types of systems, there are now three versions of the Java platform (JRE). They are:

- Java Platform, Micro Edition (Java ME)
- Java Platform, Standard Edition (Java SE)
- Java Platform, Enterprise Edition (Java EE)

### Java Platform, Micro Edition (Java ME)

Java ME is a Java platform designed for embedded systems. It is a collection of Java APIs for the development of software for resource-constrained devices such as PDA, cell phones and consumer products such as Air conditioner, Fridge, Microwave oven and embedded devices such as set-top boxes.

There are more than 2.1 billion Java ME enabled mobile phones and PDAs. Although it's not used on some of today's newest mobile platforms (e.g. iOS, Windows Phone 8 and newer, BlackBerry 10, Android). It was also used on the BADA OS and on Symbian OS along with native software.

### Java Platform, Standard Edition (Java SE)

Java SE is a Java platform designed for many portable applications for desktop and server environments. It is a collection of Java APIs for developing general purpose software applications for desktop PCs, servers and similar devices.

Java SE provides a purely object oriented programming environment with a large number of ready to use classes filled in API packages and also includes the Java Language Specification and the Java Virtual Machine Specification. One of the most well-known implementations of Java SE is Oracle Corporation's Java Development Kit (JDK).

**Java Platform, Enterprise Edition (Java EE)**

Java EE is Oracle's enterprise Java computing platform. The platform provides an API and runtime environment for developing and running enterprise software, including network and web services, and other large-scale, multi-tiered, scalable, reliable, and secure network applications.

The Java EE includes Enterprise Java Beans (EJB), Java Server Pages (JSP), Servlets and a variety of interfaces for linking to the information resources in the enterprise. Java EE also includes several API specifications such as JDBC, RMI, JavaMail, Web services, XML and also defines how to organize them.

## 1.7 Java vs. C++

During the late 1970s and early 1980s, C became the dominant computer programming language, and it is still widely used today. Since C is a successful and useful language, you might ask why a need for something else existed. The answer is *complexity*. Throughout the history of programming, the increasing complexity of programs has driven the need for better ways to manage that complexity. C++ was a response to that need. C++ was invented by Bjarne Stroustrup in 1982 – 83, as an object oriented programming language. OOP is a programming methodology that helps organize complex programs through the use of inheritance, encapsulation, and polymorphism. While comparing C++ and Java, there are endless areas of programming and technology which can show importance of both of these. This topic intends to provide *technical insights* into *differences between the Java and C++ programming languages*. (Knowledge of C++ is assumed.)

- **Object oriented programming tactic:** C++ is a partially object oriented programming language, i.e. in C++ it is optional to define class in a program. Even when we talk about built in methods, all of those are also not defined in any library class. Where in java, it is compulsory to define at least one class in each program. In java, main( ) method must define inside a class. All the library methods are provided under specific library class. (Refer above mentioned numbers of library classes and interfaces.)
- **Memory models:** Java allocates all its objects on the *heap* (all managed by the garbage collector); C++ additionally offers *stack* based instantiation, and static instantiation. Stack objects are automatically deleted, when they go out of scope, so a programmer has to assure no references are kept further. Instantiation order with static instantiation is difficult to predict, and therefore error-prone, less portable, and restricted. Due to Java's memory model, no copy constructor and assignment operator are needed, and therefore can't become a source of bugs. Due this memory model, Destructor code is not needed in Java. *Garbage collection* prevents the types of *memory leaks* found in C++.
- **Expression evaluation order:** Evaluation order within expression is stricter defined in Java, leading to more deterministic behavior, and avoiding a specific source of problems. C++ compiler however may allow options to warn about undefined semantics outside of sequence points.
- **Garbage collection:** Java's *garbage collector* largely avoids the need for manual referencing of instances. Unreferenced / unreachable objects are not occurring in Java. Garbage-collected environments allow copy-on-write data structures, which are useful for fast implementations of concurrent algorithms. C++ do not have garbage collector therefore programmers have to give references for all the instances.
- **Code optimization:** (*Optimizability affects performance and space requirements.)* Due to being *optionally* less dynamic, C++ is more optimizable. C++ allows more control over *compile-time optimization*, whereas Java depends on the specific runtime optimization used. In C++ such optimizations are often done by providing many platform-specific dynamic libraries; however, code has to be compiled with a set of different platform dependent options.
- **Safety:** These safety issues affect program reliability and the cost to make software work. C++ programs crash where Java issues useful diagnostic information. Many of the contents make problem analysis harder in C++. Undetected error conditions data input cause security problems, and vulnerabilities. There are many other reasons which make java a more reliable option of for programming. Such as, no uninitialized pointers and data, array bounds checks, null pointer handling, type cast checks, explicit Boolean type, memory model strictly defined, etc.

- **Design Considerations:** Java incorporates some design decisions that make the language simpler or more comfortable to use. Some of them are single-rooted classes, useful root class methods, no global data, multilevel break and continue no reference parameters, nested classes and inner classes, etc.
- **Portability:** Java provides portability to other computer platforms and to other programming languages too. Java provides serializable and composed classes and data types. Such serializable container classes make it easy to ship complex data across platforms.

## 1.8 Java availability

One of the benefits of Java SE or Java EE as a platform is that it is possible to get started with little or no cost. The Java SDK for implementing Java SE or Java EE application is available from many websites for free. There are also many open source tools available to simplify development. Such as,

- **NetBeans IDE** : A full-featured integrated environment for Java Developers
- **Eclips** : Eclipse is a kind of universal tool platform - an open extensible IDE for anything and nothing in particular.
- **jEdit** : jEdit is a mature and well-designed programmer's text editor that has been in development for over 5 years.
- **DrJava** : DrJava is a lightweight development environment for writing Java programs. It is designed primarily for students, providing an intuitive interface and the ability to interactively evaluate Java code. It also includes powerful features for more advanced users.
- **BlueJ** : BlueJ is an integrated Java environment specifically designed for introductory teaching.
- **EasyEclips** : EasyEclipse 1.2.1 has been released! EasyEclipse packages together Eclipse, the open-source software development platform, and selected open source plug-ins. This new version is based on Eclipse 3.2.1 Callisto.
- **tIDE** : tIDE is a Java integrated development environment(IDE). tIDE is a small, powerful, quick, efficient, easy and open framework to create 100% Java applications.
- **Junit** : A framework for automatic unit tests.
- **Apache Tomcat** : A servlet / JSP web server.

*****

# Chapter 2

# Outlines of Java

Java is a **high level, object oriented programming language**. Object-oriented programming is at the core of Java. In fact, all Java programs are object oriented (hence, java is purely object oriented programming language) – this isn't an option as it was, in C++. OOP is so important to Java that you must understand its basic principles before you can write even simple Java programs. Therefore, this chapter begins with a discussion of the theoretical aspects of OOP.

## 2.1 Object oriented concepts

Object oriented programming is an approach to program's development and organization which attempts to eliminate some of the pitfalls of common programming methods. It is a new way of organizing and developing programs and has nothing to do with any particular language. However not all the languages are able to implement OOP concepts easily, and which implements it, becomes Object Oriented Programming Language.

Concepts of OOP – which forms the spirit of Java – are described in brief here.

**Classes and Objects:** A class is a template which is set of data members and member functions. In other words class is a blue print for which an individual object is created. An object is defined in many ways, an object is copy of class, or an object is an instance entity, or an object is set of instances, or an object is an instance of class that contains real values instead of variables. This book contains a separate chapter on which describes role of classes and objects more significantly.

**Abstraction:** Abstraction is a process of identifying the relevant qualities and behaviors of an object. Let's take an example to understand abstraction. A car consists of many complex but manageable pieces. From the outside, the car is a single object but from inside you can see that the car consists of several subsystems like breaks, steering, seat belts, sound system, and so on. The intrinsic details are invisible. Think about if you would have to call to the engineer who knows all details of the car before operating it. This would have highly expensive as well as not easy to use. So here the car is an object that is designed to hide complexity of its subsystems and you can easily judge the relevant quality and behavior of that car by identifying its each subsystem.

Consider if you need to write a block of software to track the student's details of a school, you may probably need to create student's objects. People comes in all different backgrounds, educational qualifications, locations, hobbies, ages and have multiple religion, language but in terms of application, a student is just a name, age, class and roll number, while the other qualities are not relevant to the application. Determining what other qualities (background, qualifications, location, hobbies etc) are in terms of this application is abstraction.

In object-oriented software, complexity is managed by using abstraction. Abstraction is a process that involves identifying the critical behavior of an object and eliminating irrelevant and complex details. A well thought-out abstraction is usually simple, and easy to use in the perspective of the user, the person who is using your object.

**Encapsulation:** Encapsulation is a process of binding the data together -- for protecting data from unwanted access – in an object where it is only accessible through that object's interface. Many people refer encapsulation as information hiding, but both are different. In fact, information hiding is actually the result of Encapsulation. Encapsulation makes it possible to separate an object's implementation from its original behavior.

It is the mechanism by which Abstraction is implemented. In other words you can say that it is the result of the Encapsulation. For example, a car is an object that encapsulates many technologies / machineries that might not be understood clearly by most people who use it.

**Inheritance:** Inheritance is the ability to define a new class or object that inherits the behavior & functionality of another existing class(s). The new class or object is called a child or subclass or derived class while the original class is called parent or base class. The main concept behind inheritance is extensibility and code reusability. This book contains a detailed chapter on inheritance which will describe it very deeply.

**Polymorphism:** As name suggests, Polymorphism means an ability to assume different forms at different places. In OOP, it is a language's ability to handle objects differently based on their runtime type and use. Polymorphism is briefly described as "one interface, many implementations". Polymorphism is a characteristic of being able to assign a different meaning or usage to something in different contexts - specifically, to allow an entity such as a variable, a function, or an object to have more than one form.

There are two types of polymorphism.

1. Compile time polymorphism - It is achieved by overloading functions and operators.
2. Run time polymorphism - It is achieved by overriding virtual functions.

## 2.2 Java is a strongly typed language

In strongly typed language, variables have a type and they will always remain in that type. We cannot assign value of one type to variable of another type. In a weakly typed language, variables don't have a type. We can assign anything to them.

Java is a strongly typed language. It is statically typed, because you always have to declare your variables before you use them. It is strongly typed, because a variable of type **int** will always hold int values. You can't assign booleans to them. All assignments, whether explicit or via parameter passing in method calls, are checked for type compatibility. There are no automatic conversions of conflicting types as in some languages. The Java compiler checks all expressions and parameters to ensure that the types are compatible. Any type mismatches are errors that must be corrected before the compiler will finish compiling the class.

If you are from C / C++ background, note that Java is more strictly typed than any other language. For example, in C / C++ we can assign a floating-point value to an integer. In Java, we cannot. Also, in C there is not necessarily strong type-checking between a parameter and an argument during compilation. In Java, there is. You might find Java's strong type-checking a bit tedious at initial, but in the long run it will help reduce the possibility of errors in your code.

## 2.3 Java Naming Conventions

A naming convention is rule to follow as you decide what to name your identifiers (e.g. class, package, variable, method, etc.). When choosing a name for an identifier make sure it's meaningful. For instance, if your program deals with customer accounts then choose names that make sense to dealing with customers and their accounts. Don't worry about the length of the name. A longer name that sums up the identifier perfectly is preferable to a shorter name that might be quick to type but ambiguous.

Java has following 4 notations which are applied to its built in contents.

- **Lowercase** is where all the letters in a word are written without any capitalization (e.g., while, if, mypack).
- **Uppercase** is where all the letters in a word are written in capitals. When there are more than two words in the name use underscores to separate them (e.g., MAX_HOURS, FIRST_DAY_OF_WEEK).
- **CamelCase** (also known as Upper CamelCase) is where each new word begins with a capital letter (e.g., CamelCase, CustomerAccount, PlayingCard).
- **Mixed case** (also known as Lower CamelCase) is the same as CamelCase except the first letter of the name is in lowercase (e.g., hasChildren, customerFirstName, customerLastName).

Standard naming conventions for built in contents are shown below.

| Built-in Content | Naming convention |
|---|---|
| packages | Lower case letters.(e.g. util, io, applet, awt) |
| classes | CamelCase notation.(Thread, Exception, Frame) |
| interfaces | CamelCase notation.(Runnable, Servlet) |
| methods | Mixed case notations.(readLine, parseInt, getText, setAlignment) |
| constants | Uppercase letters.(MAX_PRIORITY, MIN_PRIORITY, EXIT_ON_CLOSE) |
| objects | Lower case letters.(in, out. err) |
| keywords | Lower case letters.(extends, implements, while, class, interface) |

**Note: all above naming conventions are given to help you in recall them while using in a program. But there is no such naming rule for user defined contents.**

## 2.4 Java Keywords

Keywords are the reserve words whose meanings are already known to the language. The 50 Java keywords have specific meanings within the language and we can't make up new meanings for those words. You cannot use any of the following as identifiers in your programs. The keywords `const` and `goto` are reserved, even though they are not currently used. `true`, `false`, and `null` might seem like keywords, but they are actually literals; you cannot use them as identifiers in your programs.

| | | | | |
|---|---|---|---|---|
| abstract | Continue | for | new | switch |
| assert | Default | goto | package | synchronized |
| boolean | Do | if | private | this |
| break | Double | implements | protected | throw |
| byte | Else | import | public | throws |
| case | Enum | instanceof | return | transient |
| catch | Extends | int | short | try |
| char | Final | interface | static | void |
| class | Finally | long | strictfp | volatile |
| const | Float | native | super | while |

**Note: As we discussed earlier java is a highly case sensitive programming language. Remember that all the keywords are in lower case letters.**

## 2.5 JDK tools:

JDK stands for Java Development Kit. JDK has different tools which are useful in developing a java application in different ways. Before understanding each of JDK tools let us begin with different available versions of JDK with their special features in it.

| Version | Released Date | Features |
|---|---|---|
| JDK 1.0 | January 1996 | • First stable version 1.0.2 is called as Java.<br>• private and protected together to create another form of protection that would restrict access to methods and data members. |

| | | |
|---|---|---|
| JDK 1.1 | February 1998 | • retooling of the AWT event model<br>• inner classes<br>• JavaBeans<br>• JDBC<br>• RMI<br>• No modification at runtime was possible. |
| JDK 1.2 | December 1998 | • stricrtfp keyword<br>• Swing graphical API was integrated<br>• equipped with a JIT compiler for the first time<br>• Java plug-in |
| JDK 1.3 | May 2000 | • HotSpot JVM included<br>• RMI was modified to support CORBA<br>• JavaSound<br>• Java Naming and Directory Interface (JNDI) included<br>• Synthetic proxy classes |
| JDK 1.4 | February 2002 | • Language changes<br>• assert keyword<br>• Library improvements<br>• regular expressions modeled<br>• exception chaining allowed<br>• Internet Protocol version 6 (IPv6) support<br>• image I/O API for reading and writing images<br>• Integrated XML parser and XSLT processor.<br>• integrated security and cryptography extensions (Like JCE, JSSE, JAAS)<br>• Java Web Start included<br>• Preferences API |
| JDK 1.5 | September 2004 | • Generics: Provides compile-time type safety for typecasts.<br>• Metadata: allows classes and methods to be tagged with additional data.<br>• Autoboxing/unboxing: Automatic conversions between primitive types and primitive wrapper classes.<br>• Enumerations: The enum keyword.<br>• Enhanced for each loop. |
| JDK 1.6 | December 2006 | • Support for older Win9x versions dropped.<br>• Scripting Language Support.<br>• Dramatic performance improvements for the core platform and Swing.<br>• Improved Web Service support through JAX-WS.<br>• JDBC 4.0 support.<br>• New algorithms and upgrades to existing garbage collection algorithms and start up processes. |
| JDK 1.7 | July 2011 | • JVM support for dynamic languages.<br>• New file I/O library<br>• New platform APIs for the graphics features<br>• Support for new network protocols and sockets. |

**There is also expected releases of JDK 1.8, 1.9 and 1.10 in September 2013, May 2015 and January 2017, respectively. Most importantly JDK 1.10 has rumor of removing primitive data types and move towards 64-bit addressing.**

Here is a list of tools which are the foundation of the Java Development Kit. They are the tools you use to create and build applications.

| JDK Tool | Description |
|---|---|
| **javac** | The compiler for the Java programming language. |
| **java** | The launcher for Java applications. Used to execute java program. |
| **javadoc** | API documentation generator. |
| **appletviewer** | Run and debug applets without a web browser. |
| **jar** | Manage Java Archive (JAR) files. |
| **jdb** | The Java Debugger. |
| **javah** | C header and stub generator. (Used to write native methods.) |
| **javap** | Class file disassemble. |
| **extcheck** | Utility to detect Jar conflicts. |

## 2.6 Wrapper Classes

Wrapper classes in java the classes which are with same name as of a datatype. Wrapper classes are provided to convert the primitive datatypes into objects. We will study further about Vectors, which cannot handle primitive datatypes and for such vectors we need to create objects of wrapper classes. Ultimately, for example, a wrapper class converts an **int** value into an **integer object.** Here is a table showing wrapper class list for primitive datatypes and their parameterized constructors.

| Primitive Datatype | Wrapper Class | Constructor |
|---|---|---|
| int | Integer | Integer( int ) // converts int variable into Integer object |
| long | Long | Long( long ) // converts long variable into Long object |
| short | Short | Short( short ) // converts short variable into Short object |
| byte | Byte | Byte( byte ) // converts byte variable into Byte object |
| char | Character | Character( char ) //converts char variable into Character object |
| float | Float | Float( float ) // converts float variable into Float object |
| double | Double | Double( double ) // converts double variable into Double object |
| boolean | Boolean | Boolean( boolean ) // converts boolean variable into Boolean object |

Wrapper classes are also used in input statements of Java. Wrapper classes have built-in static methods which are explained below along with their signature.

| parse( ) methods | valueOf( ) methods | Description |
|---|---|---|
| int = Integer.parseInt(str) | int = Integer.valueOf(str) | converts and returns string into int variable |
| float = Float.parseFloat(str) | float = Float.valueOf(str) | converts and returns string into float variable |
| long = Long.parseLong(str) | long = Long.valueOf(str) | converts and returns string into long variable |

Similarly these methods are applicable to **double, byte, short** and **char** too. Remember that java accepts everything by default in String format. Use of wrapper class is to convert input string into required datatype variable.

## 2.7 API Packages

In java, API stands for **Application Programming Interface**. A package is group of classes and interfaces. Java provides built-in packages which are called as API packages. As java is a purely object oriented programming language, it's all the library functions are present into related library classes and all the library classes are into library packages. Refer following diagram.

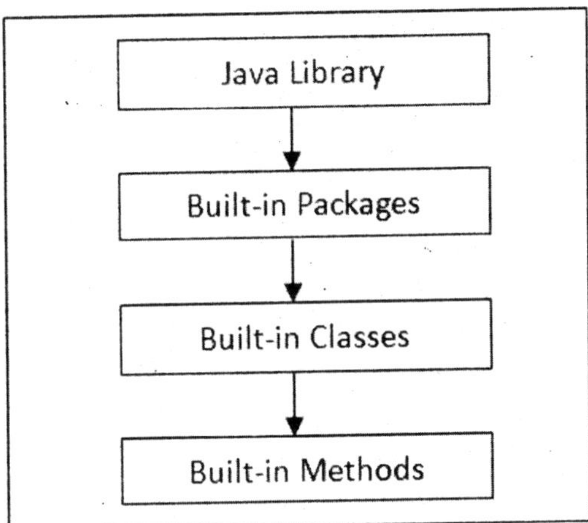


In JDK 1.5 library, there are 13 most widely used built-in hierarchy packages come under Java library. They are shown in table here.

| Package | Primary Function |
|---|---|
| java.applet | Supports construction of applets. |
| java.awt | Provides capabilities for graphical user interfaces. |
| java.awt.color | Supports color spaces and profiles. |
| java.awt.datatransfer | Transfers data to and from the system clipboard. |
| java.awt.dnd | Supports drag-and-drop operations. |
| java.awt.event | Handles events. |
| java.awt.font | Represents various types of fonts. |
| java.awt.geom | Allows you to work with geometric shapes. |
| java.awt.im | Allows input of Japanese, Chinese, and Korean characters to text editing components. |
| java.awt.im.spi | Supports alternative input devices. |
| java.awt.image | Processes images. |
| java.awt.image.renderable | Supports rendering-independent images. |
| java.awt.print | Supports general print capabilities. |
| java.beans | Allows you to build software components. |
| java.beans.beancontext | Provides an execution environment for Beans. |
| java.io | Inputs and outputs data. |
| java.lang | Provides core functionality. |
| java.lang.annotation | Supports annotations (metadata). |
| java.lang.instrument | Supports program instrumentation. |
| java.lang.management | Supports management of the execution environment. |
| java.lang.ref | Enables some interaction with the garbage collector. |
| java.lang.reflect | Analyzes code at run time. |
| java.math | Handles large integers and decimal numbers. |
| java.net | Supports networking. |
| java.nio | Top-level package for the NIO classes, Encapsulates buffers. |
| java.nio.channels | Encapsulates channels, which are used by the NIO system. |
| java.nio.channels.spi | Supports service providers for channels. |
| java.nio.charset | Encapsulates character sets. |

| | |
|---|---|
| java.nio.charset.spi | Supports service providers for character sets. |
| java.rmi | Provides remote method invocation. |
| java.rmi.activation | Activates persistent objects. |
| java.rmi.dgc | Manages distributed garbage collection. |
| java.rmi.registry | Maps names to remote object references. |
| java.rmi.server | Supports remote method invocation. |
| java.security | Handles certificates, keys, digests, signatures, and other security functions. |
| java.security.acl | Manages access control lists. |
| java.security.cert | Parses and manages certificates. |
| java.security.interfaces | Defines interfaces for DSA (Digital Signature Algorithm) keys. |
| java.security.spec | Specifies keys and algorithm parameters. |
| java.sql | Communicates with a SQL (Structured Query Language) database. |

Above table do not completely describe all the packages but it just gives a short summary on each of them. Remember that, all those packages are under Java library and some of them also include some inner / nested packages. We will study some of them later in this book. The **java.lang** package is by default imported in each java program.

As above diagram demonstrates that, all the library classes and interfaces are under specific package. In case of using any of the built-in classes and their methods we need to import related API package in our program by using keyword *import*. (It is same as we are including header files in C / C++.) To import built-in classes and interface, general syntax is:

*import* package_name . class_name ;

For example: *import* java.io.DataInputStream;

*import* java.util.Vector;

Another way of importing is to replace class name with * mark, which imports all the classes and interface present under specified package.

For example: *import* java.io.*; // imports all the classes and interfaces under java.io

*import* java.applet.*; // imports all the classes and interfaces present under java.applet

## 2.8 Java Datatypes

Based on the datatype of a variable, the operating system allocates memory and decides what can be stored in the reserved memory. There are 8 primitive datatypes in java. Refer following tree structure to understand the category and subcategory of datatypes.

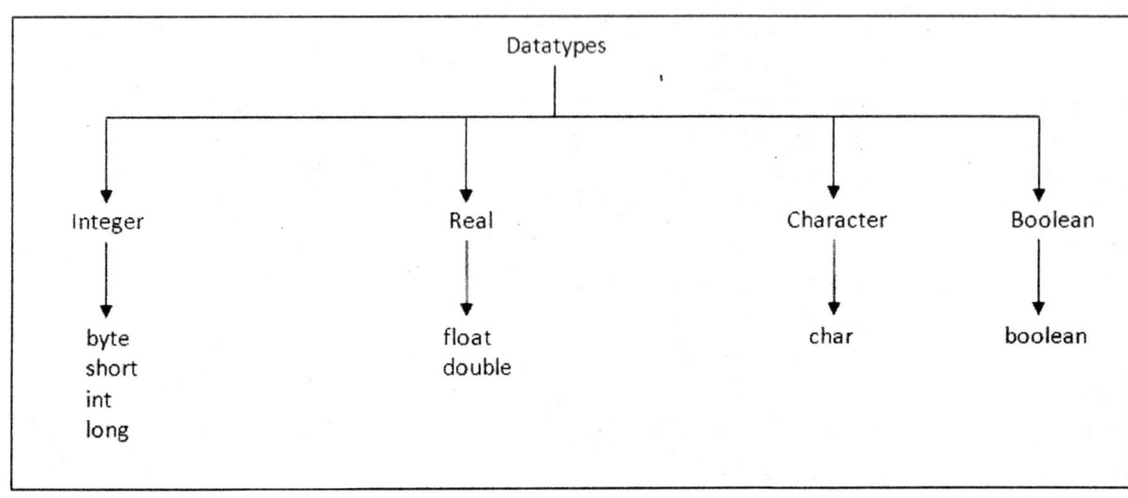

Let's understand these groups first, one by one.

**Integer**: Integer values means values without decimal point i.e. wholevalued signed values. This group includes *byte, short, int* and *long* as subcategory.

**Floating-point (real) values**: This group contains real values i.e. values with decimal point. This group includes *float* and *double* as subcategory.

**Character**: This category has one subcategory *char*. We can store any single alphabet, special symbol or digit as a character.

**Boolean**: Its *boolean* subcategory is used for representing true / false values.

There are eight primitive data types in Java. These data types are predefined. Let us study them in detail.

**byte:**

- Byte data type occupies 8-bit (1 byte) of memory.
- Range : -128 to +127
- Byte data type is used to save space in large arrays, mainly in place of integers, since a byte is four times smaller than an int.
- Example : byte a = 100 , byte b = -50;

**short:**

- Short data type occupies 16-bit (2 byte) of memory.
- Range : -32,768 to +32,767
- Short data type can also be used to save memory as byte data type.
- Example : short s= 10000 , short r = -20000;

**int:**

- Int data type occupies 32-bit (4 byte) of memory.
- Range : - 2,147,483,648 to +2,147,483,647
- Int is generally used as the default data type for integral values unless there is a concern about memory.
- Example : int a = 100000, int b = -200000;

**long:**

- Long data type occupies 64-bit (8 byte) of memory.
- Range : -9,223,372,036,854,775,808 to +9,223,372,036,854,775,807
- This type is used when a wider range than int is needed.
- Differentiate long values by applying 'L' at the end of value.
- Example : long a = 100000L, long b = -200000L;

**float:**

- Float data type is a single-precision 32-bit (4 byte) floating point value.
- Approximate Range : 1.4e -045 to 3.4e +038
- Float is mainly used to save memory in large arrays of floating point numbers.
- Float data type is never used for precise values such as currency.
- Differentiate float values by applying 'f' at the end of value.
- Example : float f1 = 234.5f;

**double:**

- double data type is a double-precision 64-bit (8 byte) floating point value.
- Approximate Range : 4.9e -324 to 1.8e +308

- This data type is generally used as the default data type for decimal values. Generally the default choice.
- Double data type should never be used for precise values such as currency.
- Example : double d1 = 123.4;

**char:**

- char data type is a single 16-bit (2 byte) Unicode character.
- It is a unification of dozens of character sets, such as Latin, Greek, Arabic, Cyrillic, Hebrew, Katakana, Hangul, and many more.
- Char data type is used to store any single alphabet, special symbol or digit.
- Example : char ch ='A';
- Remember that, we compare and assign character value in single quotes. (' ')

**boolean:**

- boolean data type represents one bit of information.
- There are only two possible values: true and false.
- This is the type returned by all relational operators, such as **a < b**. boolean is also the type required by the conditional expressions that govern the control statements such as **if** and **for**.
- This data type is used for simple flags that track true/false conditions.
- In Java, default boolean value is **false**.
- In C++, true and false are keywords. Here in Java, they are not.
- Example : boolean flag = true;

**Note: All above listed subcategories are java keywords.**

*****

# Part II

# Java EE Overview

- Introduction to J2EE
- Working with Java NetBeans IDE

# Chapter 3

# Introduction to J2EE

## 3.1 Java platforms

Java is the widest programming language that has its roots in almost all the technological areas; including software related to websites, web servers, consumer electronic devices, medical resources, medicinal resources, etc.

All these technological areas are distributed and have different java platforms called as JRE (Java Runtime Environment). JRE has two main components and can be shown by using following diagram.

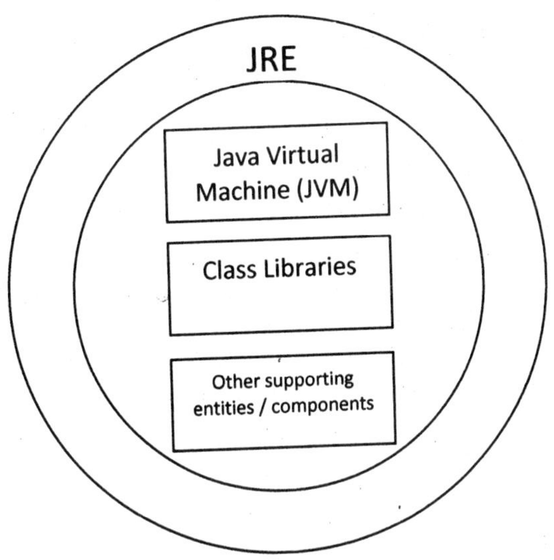


The complete java language has total 3 platforms (JREs).

1. **Java SE – Java platform, Standard Edition**
   Java Platform, Standard Edition or Java SE is a widely used platform for development and deployment of portable applications for desktop and server environments. Java SE uses the object-oriented Java programming language. This JRE is the most basic and it is suitable for desktop and laptop client systems. Strictly speaking, Java SE is a platform specification. It defines a wide range of general purpose APIs—such as Java APIs for the Java Class Library and also includes the Java Language Specification and the Java Virtual Machine Specification. One of the most well-known implementations of Java SE is Oracle Corporation's Java Development Kit (JDK).
2. **Java EE – Java platform, Enterprise Edition**
   Java Platform, Enterprise Edition or Java EE is Oracle's enterprise Java computing platform. The platform provides an API and runtime environment for developing and running enterprise software, including network and web services, and other large-scale, multi-tiered, scalable, reliable, and secure network applications. Java EE extends the Java Platform, Standard Edition (Java SE), providing an API for object-relational mapping, distributed and multi-tier architectures, and web services. The platform incorporates a design based largely on modular components running on an application server. Software for Java EE is primarily developed in the Java programming language. The platform emphasizes Convention over configuration and annotations for configuration. Optionally XML can be used to override annotations or to deviate from the platform defaults.

3. **Java ME – Java platform, Micro Edition**

   Java Platform, Micro Edition, or Java ME, is a Java platform designed for embedded systems (mobile devices are one kind of such systems). Target devices range from industrial controls to mobile phones (especially feature phones) and set-top boxes. Java ME has a minimized JVM to fit on the embedded systems with limited memory.

   There are more than 2.1 billion Java ME enabled mobile phones and PDAs. It is popular in sub devices such as Nokia's Series 40. It was also used on the **Bada** operating system and on **Symbian** OS along with native software. Also, there are implementations for Windows CE, Windows Mobile, Maemo, MeeGo and Android available for separate download.

## 3.2 Introduction to J2EE

J2EE is a standard and a JRE develop to create a high end tools that use different types of distribution technologies. As discussed earlier, large-scale, multi-tiered, scalable, reliable, and secure network applications. J2EE has a separate JRE; it has two main components i.e.

**Standard API i.e. Class libraries**: contains standard library classes and interfaces, used to develop enterprise level applications. The J2EE library is the largest library available in Java. In this complete book we will study the APIs of J2EE one by one.

**JVM**: Java itself is implemented as JVM, which is the application that executes in the Java program. In other words, a JVM installed on a computer allows you to run java programs. Therefore, Java programs do not need to be self sufficient and do not need all the machine-level code that runs on the computer. Instead, a program is first *compiled* and then translated into *bytecodes*. Then JVM reads and interprets these bytecodes to run the program. You should note that, when you run a Java applet on a web page, you are actually running a bytecode file.

J2EE applications architecture has three main layers / parts that get distributed. It is

1) Presentation Layer /GUI Layer
2) Logical Layer /Business Logic Layer
3) Data Layer /Storage Layer

**Presentation Layer /GUI Layer:** This part/layer of the application is the actual appearance or visible or usable part that directly interacts with end users. All the forms and GUI pages that appear to end users are these layers. This layer ultimately interacts with user in predefined format and takes data to/from other application layers.

**Logical Layer /Business Logic Layer:** This layer contains the code that executes either locally or remotely. This is the actual code written in programming language that handles all logical statements and interact with other layers.

**Data Layer /Storage Layer:** This layer contains the data bases (RDBMS, OODBMS). This layer interacts with the business logic layer and responds on different request on business layer.

## 3.3 EE Architecture Types

Java developers select a suitable enterprise architecture type for an application according to their and the application's requirements. Based on role and place of above specified layers, J2EE application has following four architectures.

1) One-tier architecture
2) Two-tier architecture
3) three-tier architecture
4) n-tier architecture

Let's now discuss these different types of architecture in the following section.

- **One-tier Architecture**

In this architecture system of J2EE application presentation layer, business logic layer and database are present on a single or one system. Following figure shows single-tier / one-tier architecture.

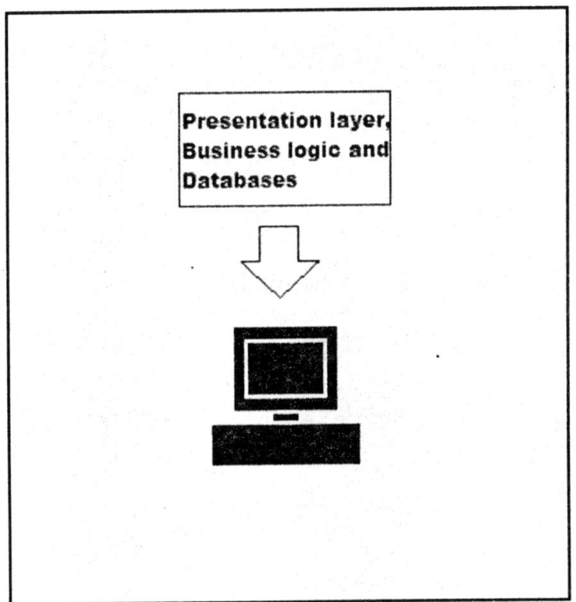


Applications created on the single-tier architecture are comparatively easy to manage and implement data consistency, as data is stored in same location. A student level project, operating system and other installed applications are present on a single or one system. However, they also have some disadvantages. Singletier systems do not scale to handle multiple users, and they do not provide an easy means of sharing data across an enterprise. Think of the word processor on your personal computer: It does an excellent job of helping you to create documents, but the application can be used by only a single person. Also, while you can share documents with other people, only one person can work on the document at a time.

- **two-tier ArchitecturE**

In this architecture system or J2EE application presentation layer is present on one system (for interacting with end users) and business logic layer and database are present on another system. Following figures shows two-tier architecture.

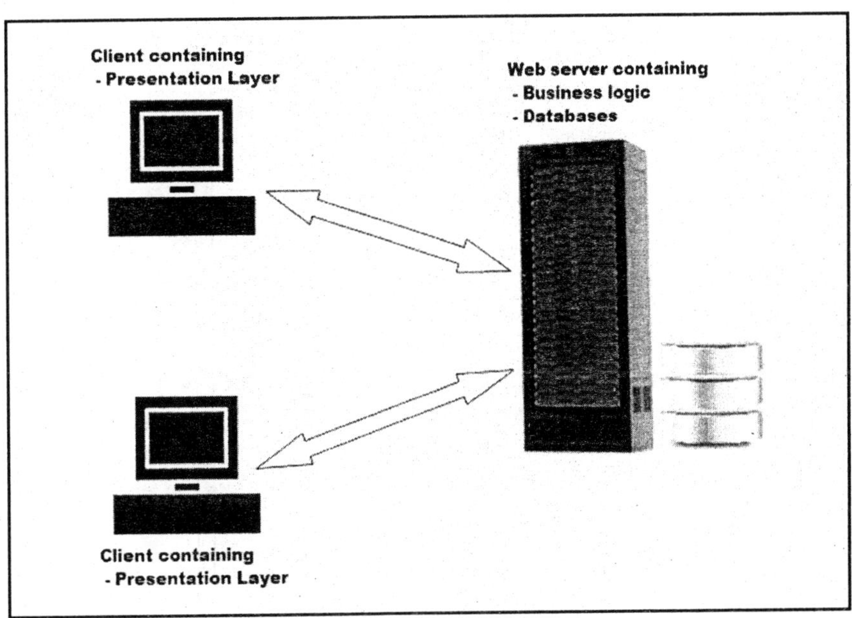


The applications developed using the two-tier application programming model have a **user-friendly interface**. These applications **can support only a few users** and allow data to be shared within a homogeneous environment. All client server architecture system work's on this architecture system.

- **Three-tier Architecture**

In this architecture system or J2EE application. Presentation layer is on one system (for interacting with user). Business logic layer is present on another system (called as web server) and the database is present on different system (to manage database systems called as database servers). Following diagram shows three-tier architecture.

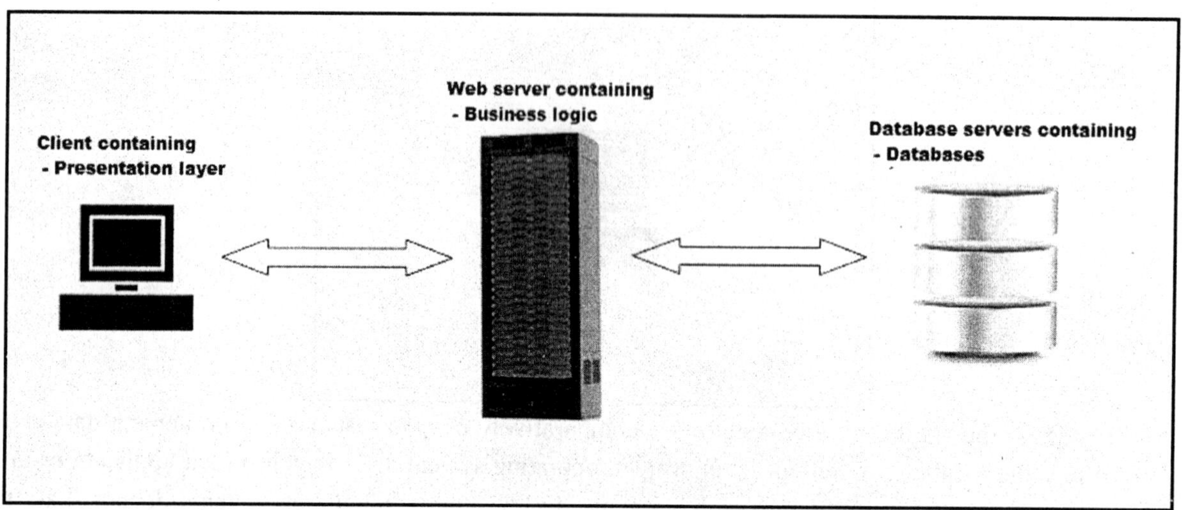


Almost all the web sides use three-tier architecture where client or end users requests to web servers and web servers generates a requests by using server application (servlets) to database servers. In response database server response to web servers and web servers' response to client.

- **n-tier Architecture**

In this architecture system of J2EE application business logic is distributed on different layer. These layers are either java beans or use defined protocols. Following figure shows the n-tier architecture.

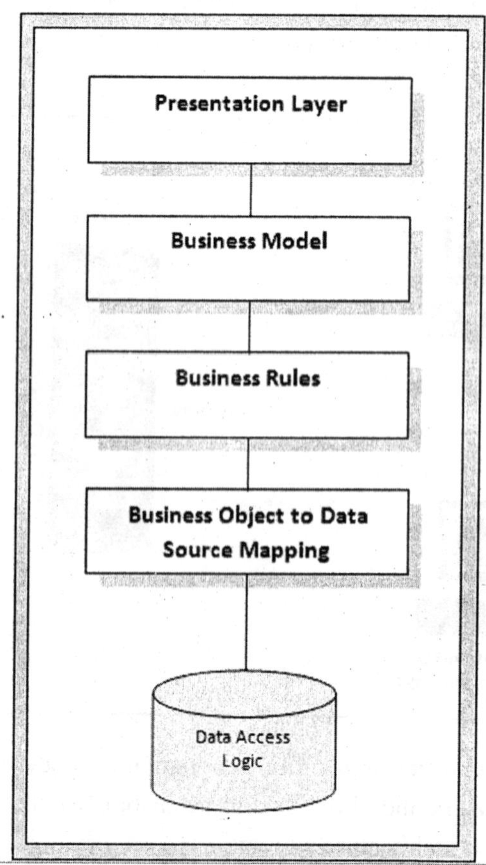


All the websites containing user's private data and many social networking web sides use this architecture system.

## 3.4 Features of Java EE application

Till now, we have discussed the need of enterprise programming and briefly introduced the latest Java platform for large scale development. There are many other paths that drove a program to develop an enterprise application, one is towards Microsoft's .net technology and another is towards Sun Microsystem's (Oracle's) EE platform. Apart from these technologies there are BEA and IBM which helps to host enterprise solutions as well. Although the programmers have such a variety of choices then also Java continues to be a popular choice to them. To understand the reason for such popularity, let's look at following a feature that boosts programming architecture and use of different components of J2EE. These features are:

- Managed Object
- Modularity
- Platform Independence
- Reusability
- Enhanced Web Services
- Simplified Enterprise Java Beans (EJB)
- Support for Web 2.0

Let's discuss them in brief.

**Managed Objects**

J2EE architecture or application creates numbers of object during runtime. J2EE provide a great managed and simplified environment for programming. This environment enables in developers to easily create server side and client side applications.

Another important properties of J2EE application is the simplicity and easy to modify the program. Most of the developer uses Java NetBeans IDE to developed J2EE application. That provides users a great reusability concept such as JavaBeans.

**Modularity**

When we develop a complete server side application, the program becomes very large and complex. J2EE application allows to be distributed into number of module with each of this module responsibility of performing specific tasks decrease this makes a java application "Easy to maintain".

The modularity of J2EE application is beneficial because we break the application into modules and use any of its architecture suitable for our application.

**Platform Independency**

We all know that, java is a platform independent programming language. A J2EE application is also platform independent because there are no exact requirements to develop and run such high end application. Any of the layers of J2EE application can easily be developed and run on any platform. At the end we have swing, hibernating and beans. These contents jointly makes any client side and /or server side application platform independence.

A J2EE application never demands specific tools, environment, platform or other services which makes it platform independence.

**Reusability**

Each J2EE application creates a package which automatically generates a scope to re-use its contents. J2EE has Beans, JSP-pages, hibernating which also help the developer to achieved re-usability. Even because of purely object oriented model of java reusability of method, classed and code automatically apply to developers mind and can develop easy to maintain reusable code.

We know that reusability of any programming language decides its power. Java is having the highest contains/ entities that can be reused in the same or another project.

**Enhanced web services**

J2EE has a great support for web services because it has a huge library classes to built high end server based applications. J2EE provides concept of Servlets, Strut, JSF and AJAX (Asynchronous Java and XML) tools that improves Java's use to develop web application.

**Simplified EJB**

Java Beans is the most powerful entities that simplify reusability. Java uses POJO (Plain Old Java Objects) classes that provide huge libraries that simplified EJB programming. To connect EJB with databases a new concept has arrived called as *EJB 2.0 + POJO + Hibernating*. That makes a Bean more powerful and easy to maintain.

**Support for web 2.0**

Web 2.0 is a new technology allows maintaining a number of users on World Wide Web (WWW). Web 2.0 is that latest technology that can store centralized information with multiple users. J2EE application use JSF (Java Server Faces), AJAX tools and JSTL (Java Standard Tag Library) that fully supports web 2.0 applications.

## 3.5 J2EE container

J2EE application mostly follows three-tier architecture system (and n-tier architecture for web servers). This three tier architecture system contains following layers / parts.

- **Presentation system** : Present on client system
- **Business logic** : Present on server system
- **Data layer** : Present on database server system

J2EE focus on the three-tier architecture system, where each of these layers requires different services. The J2EE provides *various services* in the form of container. These services are actually external services required by that specific component / files. Refer following diagram

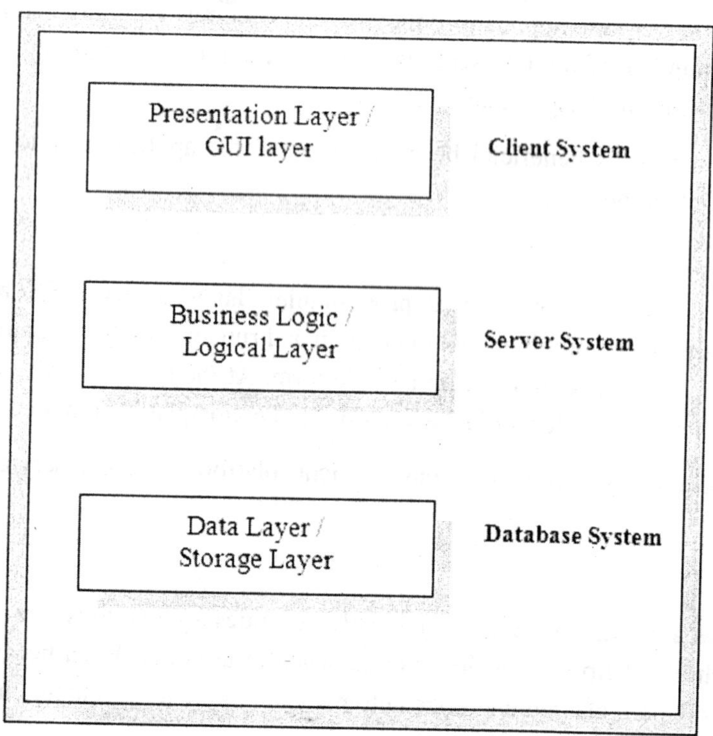

The containers are a run time interface between the application component and platform specific functionality. Here platform means the system (either client system or server system or database server) on which that component runs.

The containers are necessary, so that developer has to focus only on code. The container provides many facilities such as deployment, thread management, execution support, memory management etc. J2EE containers are available on all the system for all the files. Following diagram show types of files present on different system of J2EE architecture.

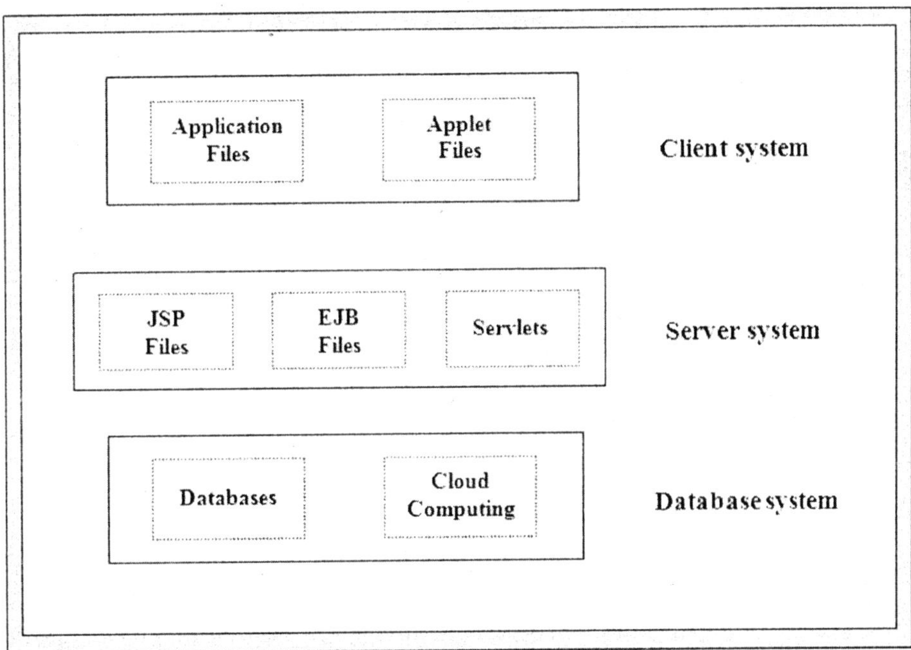


During the deployment of a Java EE application, the components of the application are installed in the Java EE containers available in the Java EE server. The Java EE server is used to execute the application, which contains EJB and Web components. Java EE containers can be categorized as follows.

**Web container :** This container provides external support for executing all servlet application and JSP application.

**Application container/client container :** This container provides external support to execute the application file or executable file or GUF file on the client machine (Microsoft framework is example of application container).

**EJB container/Bean container :** This container provides external support to execute all Java enterprise beans.

**Applet container :** This container allows executing an applet. It is a combination of web browser and Java plug-ins.

## 3.6 Components of container

The Java EE container consists of 4 components.

- Component contract
- Service APIs
- Declarative services
- Other supporting services

Following diagram shows the components of EE container.

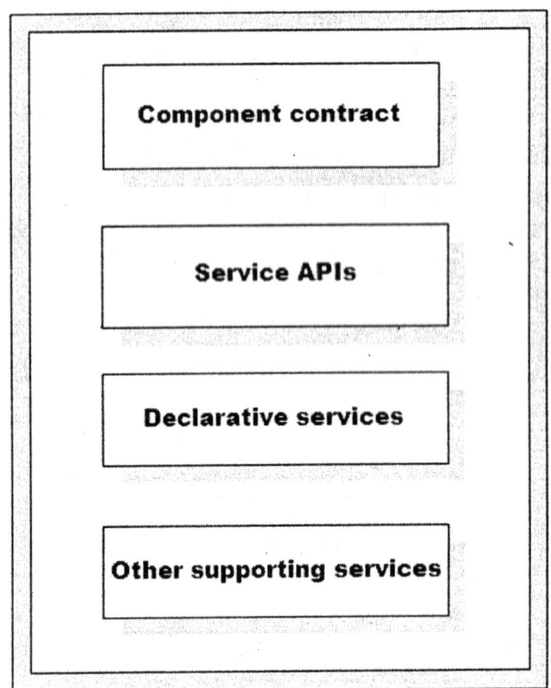


**Component contract**

Component contracts are rules, stored in the form of APIs, which application components must extend of implement. A Java EE container acts as a runtime environment to manage application components. At runtime, the instances of these application components are invoked within the JVM of the container. This tool maintains specific rules that provide privacy, security and availability. This tool automatically extends eternal classes and implements internal interfaces to follow certain rules.

**Service API**

These are the API's which all the application need to use in the program the basic protocols are also comes under this services APIs. This is how you use JDBC (Java Database Connectivity), JNDI (Java Naming Directory Interface), JMS (Java Massaging Services), JTS (Java Transaction Services) in the container. All above packages provides group of classes that are minimum required by any three-tier or n-tier application.

**Declarative services**

This includes the declaration services that allow using Deployment Descriptors (DD). These DD are use to specify configuration and other setting while deploying requests. Various elements used to customize Java EE 6 services are configured in DD, which allows a Java EE container to interpose the new service before the transfer of a request to the application component. The advantage of this approach is that you can interpose new services without changing the application component.

**Other supporting services**

The other container supporting services includes following services.

- To maintain life system of allocation
- Allocating and deal locating run time memory.
- Distributing different multiple request.
- Loading and unloading component object and establishing local connections with local files.
- Keeping track of execution process.
- Maintaining request load on same application (using load balancing)

## 3.7 Web server v/s Application server

### Web server

In a web application, the physical or virtual machine that responds to multiple client requests is web server. It is also central system from where different web pages get available to the client on a request.

The apache tomcat server is the web server that can virtually makes a system as a web server. You can deploy and run Java Web applications on the Tomcat Server, which is an open source web server introduced by **Apache**. The Apache Tomcat Server also contains WEB-INF file which is an xml file and store servlet name, and servlet mapping and server URL. The web server's duty is to select appropriate servlet according to the request and load into memory for execution. Apache tomcat server 6.0 is the latest version. The main objective of web server is to deal with servlet and JSP. By default, the Tomcat Server uses port 8080 to run Web applications. After installing Tomcat, you can start or stop the Tomcat Server by using its windows service installed on your computer (appears in system tray).

### Application server:-

An application server is a server program that provides business logic for an application. In other words, the application server provides a GUI to run three – tier application. The application server acts similar to an extended virtual machine used to run application and handle databases. The following are some remarkable application servers used to deploy Java EE applications.

- WebLogic application server
- WebSphere application server
- JBoss application server
- Glassfish application server

### WebLogic application server

This is developed by oracle system. The web logic application server mainly runs on middle tier. It is the leading online transaction processing transaction used to connect multiple user system. The web logic is based on J2EE and use different types of connecters to connect multiple clients.

### Web sphere application server

This is developed by IBM. The web sphere works with various web services such as HTTP servers, enterprise server and Microsoft IIS (Internet information Service).

### JBoss application server

This is developed by JBoss (Java Bean Open Source Software) software foundation. It is mainly use to deploy, pack and run various J2EE applications that are mainly open source. Currently JBoss is own by Red Hat services which is also one of the open source system.

### Glassfish application server

This is developed y Sun-Micro system and it is first preferred application server. Java's net bean IDE by default provides glass fish server. It is capable two manage server side application and even manage many web services. The latest version is glass fish 3.0.

## 3.8 Java EE Technologies

Java EE is a set of coordinated technologies that reduces the complexity of developing, deploying and managing multi-tier and server-centric enterprise applications. These technologies help to build stable and secure Web and Enterprise applications. Lets discuss these EE technologies in brief as their introduction.

### JDBC ODBC

It is the basic database connectivity option that provides storage into basic databases such as MS-Access, SQL server, MySQL and Oracle. It has *java.sql* as it package and we use its related classes and interfaces. In Java Standard Edition we have already studied about JDBC ODBC connectivity.

There are 4 types of JDBC drivers which are used according to the database and application architecture. JDBC ODBC uses SQL queries to interact with databases.

### Hibernating

Hibernating is another option for database connectivity where different types of database are supported such FoxPro, PostGREs etc. Hibernate is an open source framework that enables a developer to work easily with relational databases in an enterprise application. Hibernating generates HQL (Hibernating Query Language) queries through XML tags which automate the process of handling result sets.

For hibernating we create a separate .hbm which is an xml file with tag. This file requires **dialect** and **database Name**. When this file is created, it automatically generates on xml tag skeleton containing drivers.

### Struts

J2EE supports an application architecture called as MVC architecture (Model View Controller). The task of creating Model, View and Controller of a web application has been simplified by the evolution of struts. The struts provide various tags. You can use these tags to simplify the implementation of various functionalities, such as validations. The Struts 2.0 is the latest technology of struts.

### Servlets

Java servlet, a platform technology, provides a component – based, platform – independent approach to create web applications. Java EE provides servlet 3.0 with new features such as annotations, to develop a servlet class.

In a web application, client details such as logging information need to be maintained across multiple web pages to implement session handling. Previously, this task was done by using URL rewriting, hidden form fields and cookies. But Java servlet provides an API to implement the session handling mechanism to retain a client's state till long.

### JSP (Java Server Pages)

The JSP technology is an extension of the Java servlet technology and has been created to support embedding of Java code in HTML pages. The duty of JSP pages is to provide dynamic content. It has the power to incorporate and xml tags with java statements which run time generate dynamic content by using **scriplets**. The focus of Java EE 6 has been to simplify the development of web or enterprise application by using Java annotations. JSP 2.1 extends this impetus of Java and allows the use of annotations for dependency injection on JSP tag handlers and context listeners.

### JSF (Java Server Faces)

In many large scale applications developer's has to code for page navigation, validating user's input, type casting, using streams and converting many string input into java objects. All these code will divert developers mind from actual code of developing business logic. JSF is the technology that minimizes the developer's task to focus on such small task. Using JSF we can directly provide validation, page navigations, type casting and use of streams.

### AJAX (Asynchronous JavaScript and XML)

Earlier, while access a web page, client had to wait for a long time after refreshing a page or clicking on a link. While refreshing a web page, the browser first sends the request to the web server, which then performs the required operations. After all operations, the response is provided to the client. However, now all this has changed. AJAX, with the help of JavaScript, provides asynchronous client and server interaction. All these operations are performed by using the AJAX engine.

**EJB (Enterprise Java Beans)**

Stands for Enterprise Java Beans. Previously java uses "*JavaBeans*" to mainly develop business logic. The java bean provides user interface component but do not provide services such as transaction management, transaction security required for developing robust and secure application. This is the reason of developing new version of JavaBeans called as EJB. The EJB provide services and security and ORM (Object Relation Mapping) services. EJB is a common business logic that can be reused for web application or stand alone application. EJB are more secure to deal with databases using JDBC or hibernating.

**Spring**

We know that EJB is called as a layered technology, where business logic is distributed into layer for reusability and ease of maintenance. Spring is the technology that helps to manage these layers of EJB. it is actually a kind of framework that helps to create client and remote interfaces between beans.

**JCA (Java EE Connector Architecture)**

This is stands for Java Connector Architecture. JCA is the technology that is used by spring to connect multiple beans we know that beans are reusable business logic block which main present n different server. The Spring technology uses JCA to connect and create an architecture system to provide interaction between local and remote beans.

**JAAS (Java Authentication & Authorization Services)**

It is mainly responsible for providing security services in web and enterprise applications. The role of JAAS is to authorise and authenticate client requests.The programmatic security can also be provided by developing business focus from which again diverts developers focus from the actual development. Hence JAAS is a technology and authentication service.

**JavaMail**

JavaMail is introduced to implement the functionality of sending and receiving mails in an enterprise application. JavaMail provides the JavaMail API, which contains the classes and interfaces required to develop mail and messaging applications. The JavaMail API provides a protocol independent platform to send and receive mails.

*****

# Chapter 4

# Working with Java NetBeans IDE

NetBeans is an Integrated Development Environment (IDE) for developing applications primarily with Java, but also with other languages, in particular PHP, C/C++, and HTML 5. It is also an application platform framework for Java desktop applications and others. The NetBeans Platform allows applications to be developed from a set of modular software components called modules. Applications based on the NetBeans Platform can be extended by third party developers and can run on Windows, OS X, Linux, Solaris and other platforms supporting a compatible JVM.

All the functions of the IDE are provided by modules. Each module provides a well defined functionality, such as editing, providing support, checking errors and exception, providing containers and components, etc. NetBeans contains all the modules needed for Java development in a single installation, allowing the user to start working immediately. New features, such as support for other programming languages, can be added by installing additional modules. Currently there are many other IDEs such as Sun Studio, Sun Java Studio Enterprise, and Sun Java Studio Creator, etc that are based on NetBeans IDE.

There are many versions available for NetBeans IDE which improves functionalities and adds new features in each version. The latest version release is **Java NetBeans IDE 8.0 (Released in 18 March 2014)**. You can download the different versions of NetBeans IDE from Oracle's official website for free. Then also we have provided you following links to download it.

https://netbeans.org/downloads/ or from

http://www.oracle.com/technetwork/java/javase/downloads/index.html

Well, in this chapter we will guide you through the NetBeans IDE **only to create (not working with)** the different types of projects and adding required components (such as servlet, XML file, JSP file, EJB modules, Hibernate files, Java class, Java package, struts actions, etc) to it. In fact we have to study all above components in detail in related chapters.

**Note: In this complete chapter I have given screenshots of NetBeans IDE 7.2.1 Hence it is possible that the screenshots may not be exactly as on your IDE's version. (However, I am sure that only graphical appears may change, not entirely).**

## 4.1 History

NetBeans began in 1996 as **Xelfi**, which was a student project at Charles University in Prague. In 1997 **Roman Stanek** formed a company around this project and start producing commercial versions of the NetBeans IDE until it was bought by Sun Microsystems in 1999. Sun made the NetBeans IDE as an Open source in June 2000. Since then, the NetBeans community has continued to grow worldwide. In 2010, Sun was acquired by Oracle and thus NetBeans also belongs to Oracle.

## 4.2 Getting started with NetBeans IDE

In this section you will be introduced with NetBeans IDE startup page. This startup page will help you to find the easy way to start the proceedings with it. Following screenshot shows the startup page and describes its three tabs.

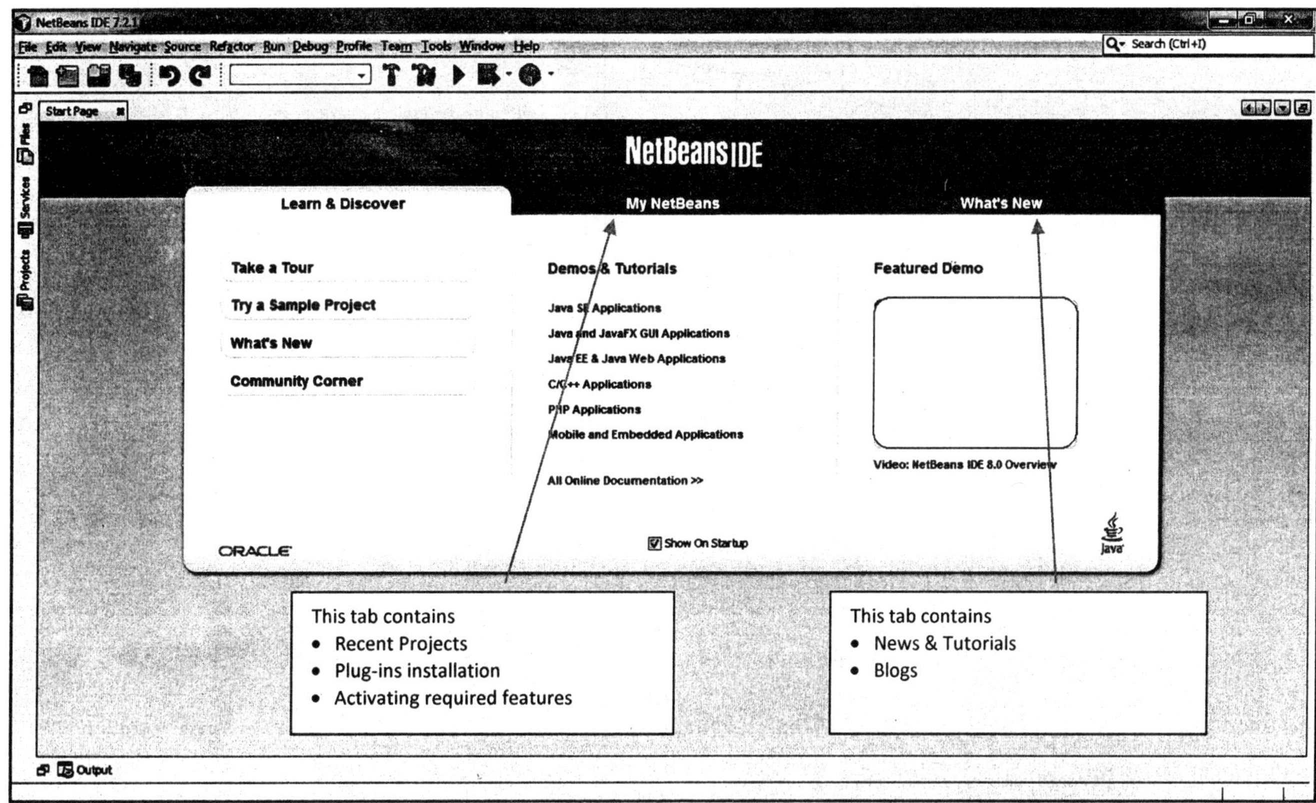


Here is above figure, what you are seeing is the startup page with open first tab **Learn & Discover,** menus, toolbars, project pane, files pane, runtime pane, navigator pane, and other panes.

## 4.3 Creating a Project

To be able to successfully build programs using NetBeans IDE, it is recommended the intended procedure. First to create a new project, follow the following steps.

Step 1: Open "File" menu → select "**New Project**"

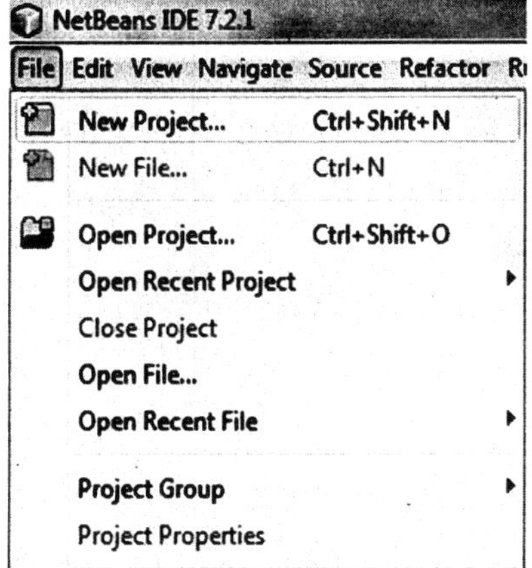

<u>Step 2</u>: You will see a "**New Project**" window will appear. Select type of project, you want to build and click "**Next**".

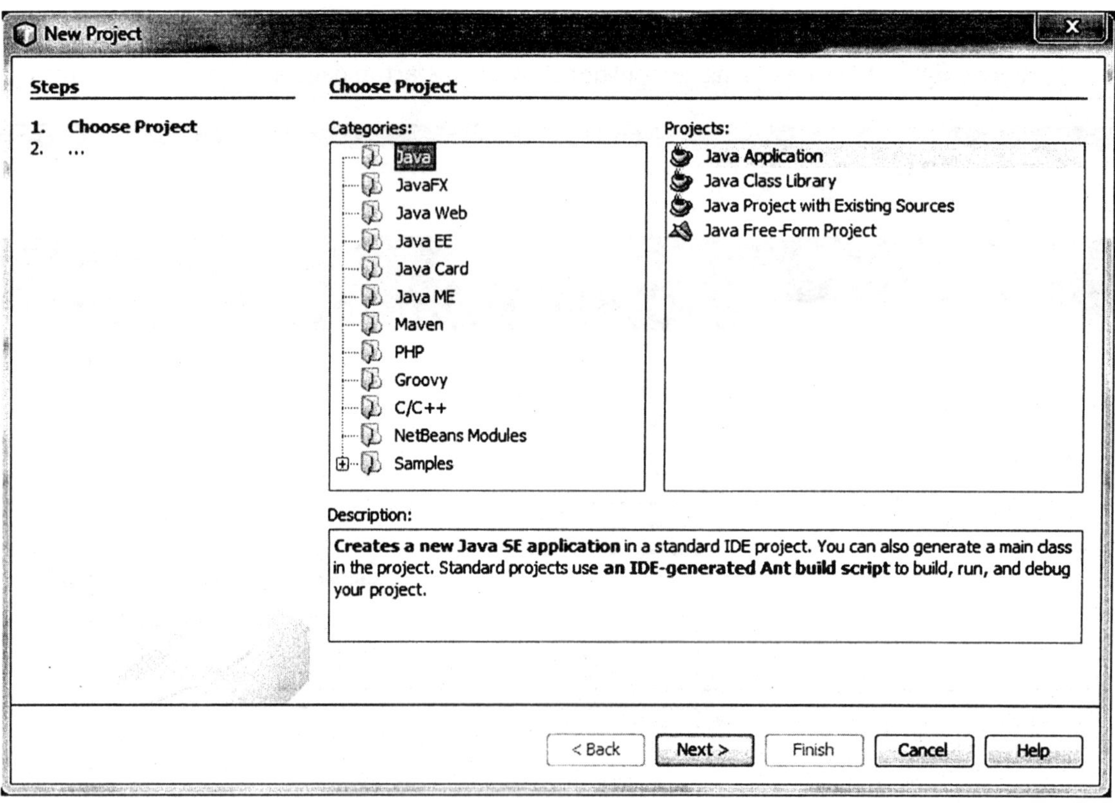


<u>Step 3</u>: A new window will appear, give project name and click "**Finish**". You will get the required *environment* and *program skeleton* according to the selected project type.

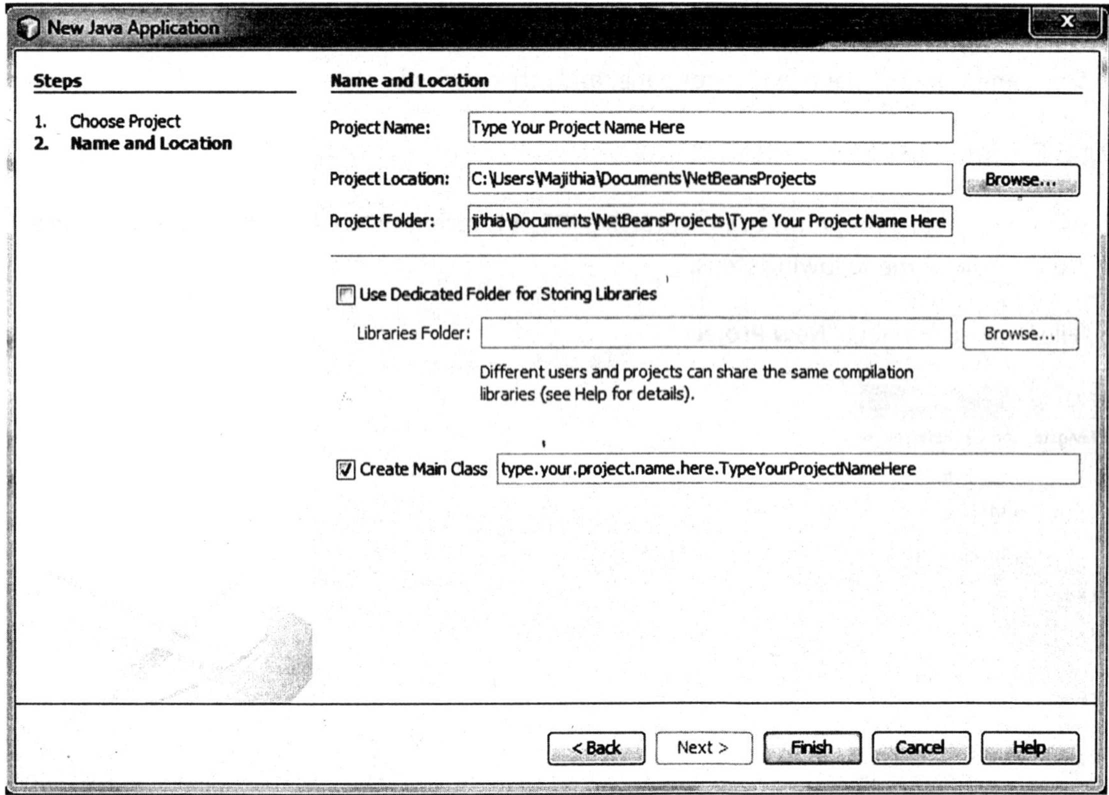

## 4.4 Executing a Project

The projects created in NetBeans IDE are executed by three easy ways.

1) Open "**Run**" menu → click on "**Run Project (Project Name)**" or press **F6** directly.

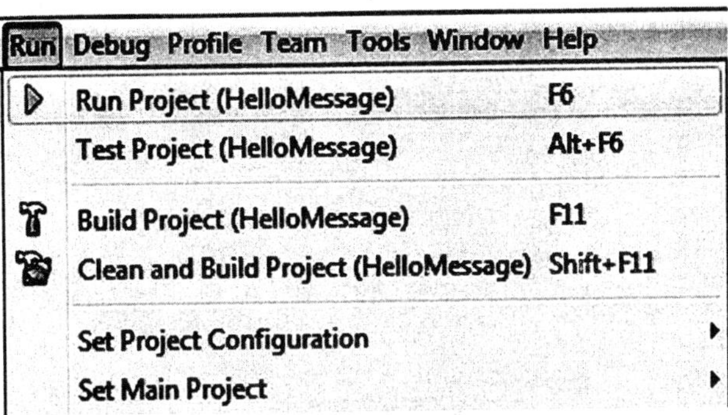


2) Click on "**Run Project**" shortcut present on toolbar.

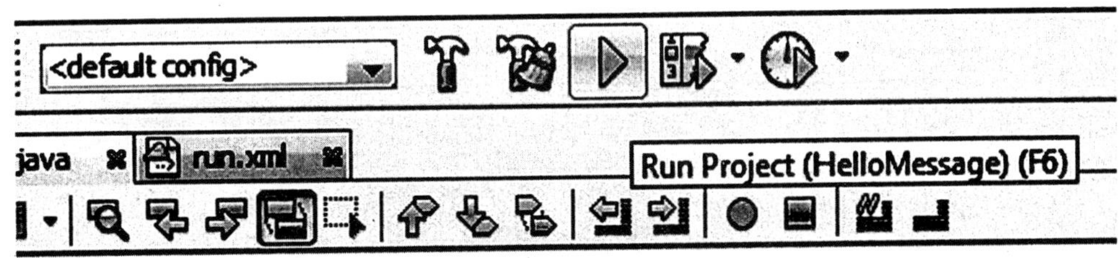


3) Open "**Project Pane**" on left side of your screen. Then Right click on the project you want to run and click on "Run"

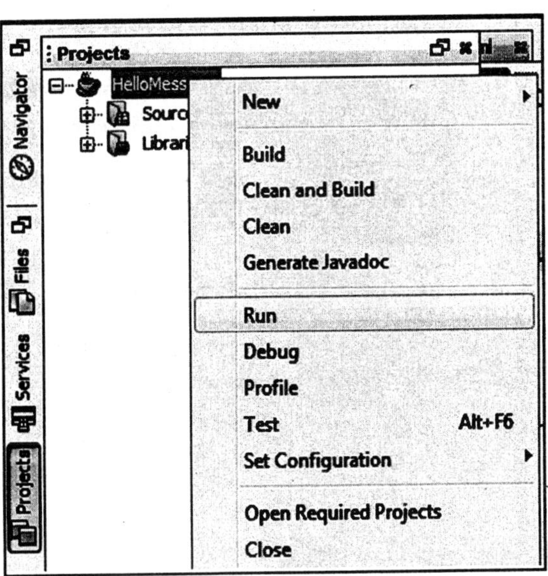


## 4.5 Creating a Java console application

In Java console application, you can create main class with console Java programming statements. To create a Java console applications, follow the following steps.

Step 1: Open "File" menu → select "**New Project**".

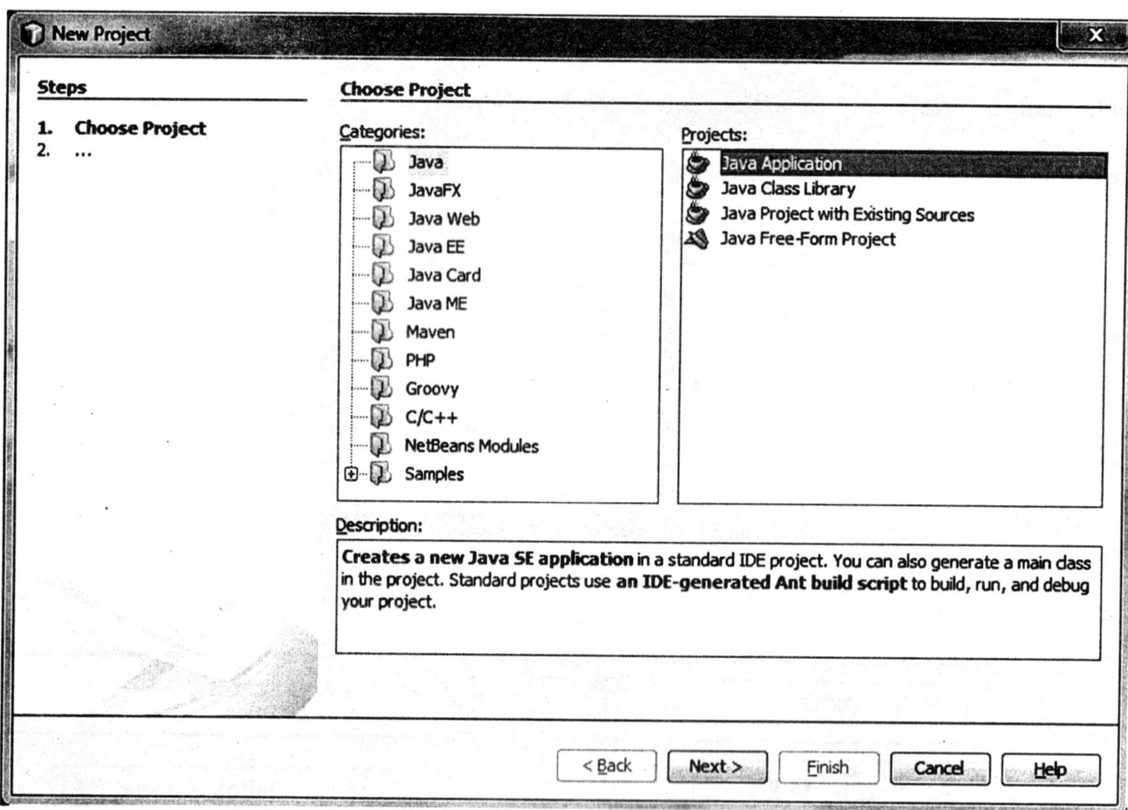


Step 2: Select "**Java**" from categories and select "**Java Application**" and click "**Next**" You will see following window.

New Java Application

Steps
1. Choose Project
2. Name and Location

Name and Location
Project Name: HelloMessage
Project Location: C:\Users\Majithia\Documents\NetBeansProjects Browse...
Project Folder: C:\Users\Majithia\Documents\NetBeansProjects\HelloMessage
Use Dedicated Folder for Storing Libraries
Libraries Folder: Browse...
Different users and projects can share the same compilation libraries (see Help for details).
Create Main Class hellomessage.HelloMessage
< Back Next > Finish Cancel Help

Step 3: Give project name and give "**Finish**". You will see a generated HelloMessage.java page with default skeleton.

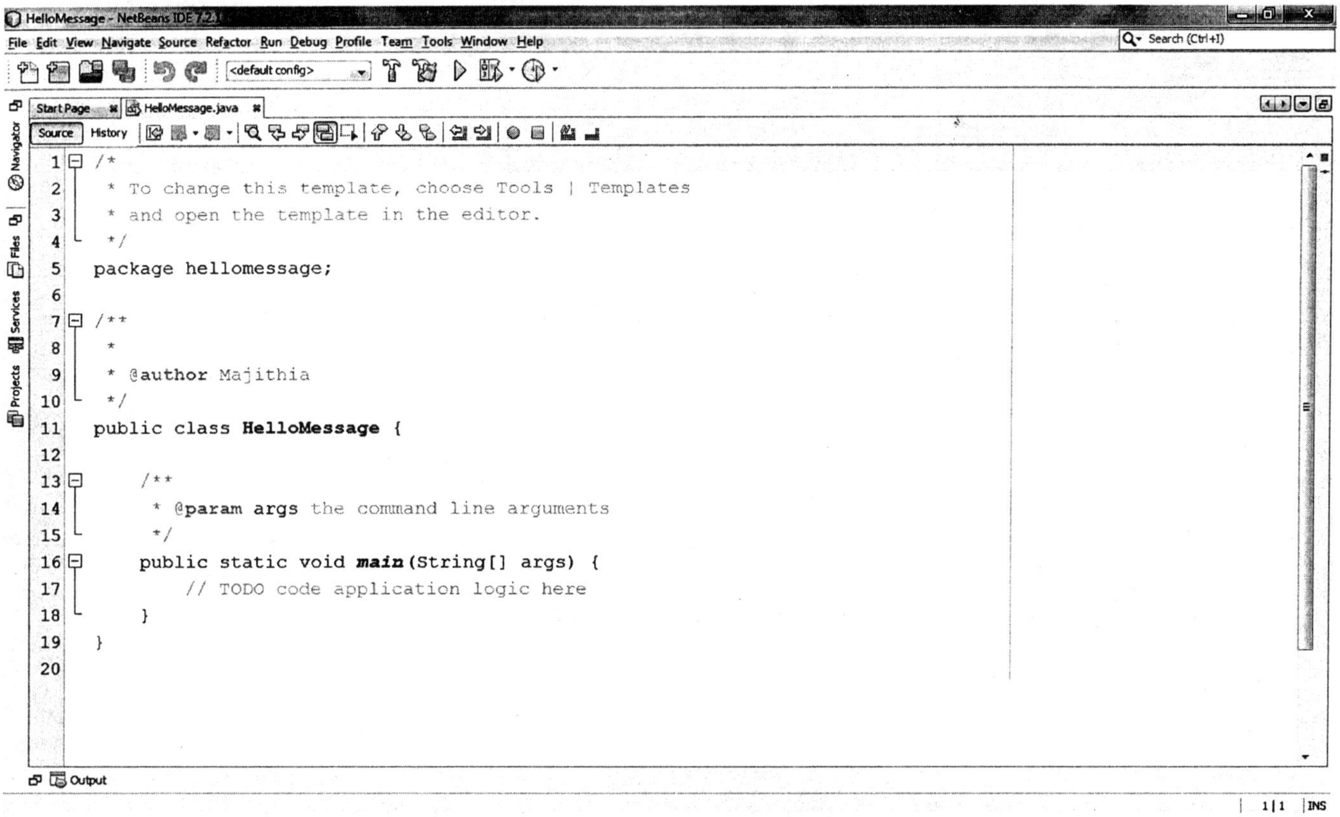

HelloMessage - NetBeans IDE 7.2.1

File Edit View Navigate Source Refactor Run Debug Profile Team Tools Window Help

Start Page | HelloMessage.java

Source | History

```
/*
 * To change this template, choose Tools | Templates
 * and open the template in the editor.
 */
package hellomessage;

/**
 *
 * @author Majithia
 */
public class HelloMessage {

    /**
     * @param args the command line arguments
     */
    public static void main(String[] args) {
        // TODO code application logic here
    }
}
```

Output

1 | 1 INS

You can see that above skeleton contains a **public class** and **main( )** method. You can write other console statements and even add other user defined methods, classes and interfaces. Here is a small program that is written and executed in NetBeans IDE.

```
package hellomessage;
public class HelloMessage
{
        public static void main(String[] args)
        {
                System.out.println("Hello all from Java NetBeans IDE");
        }
}
```

To execute the project, follow the instructions given under section 3.3 (Executing a Project). After executing above project, you will see following output.

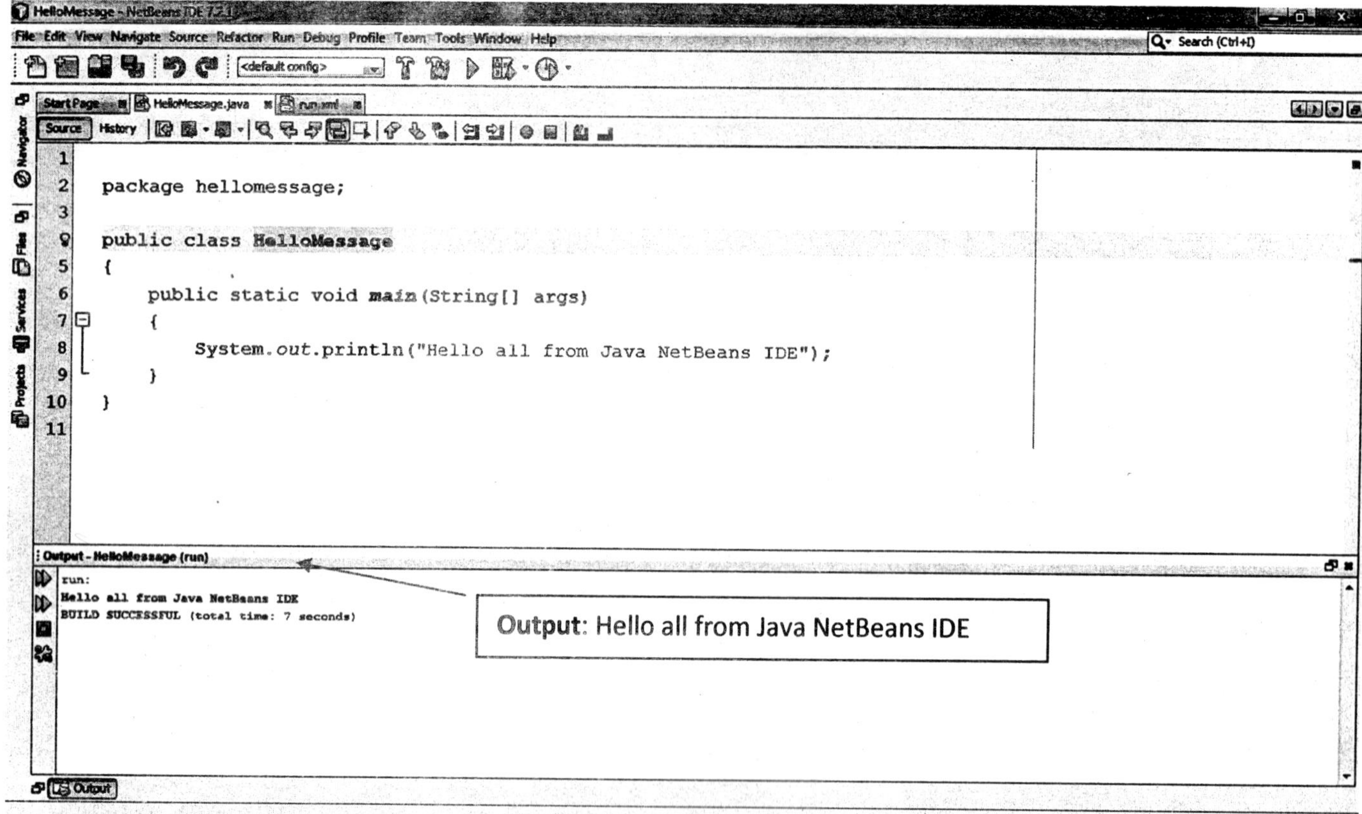


## 4.6 Creating GUI using JFrame

To create a GUI Frame for stand-alone GUI application, follow the following steps.

Step 1: Open "File" menu → select "**New Project**".

Step 2: Select "**Java**" from categories and select "**Java Class Library**" and click "**Next**"

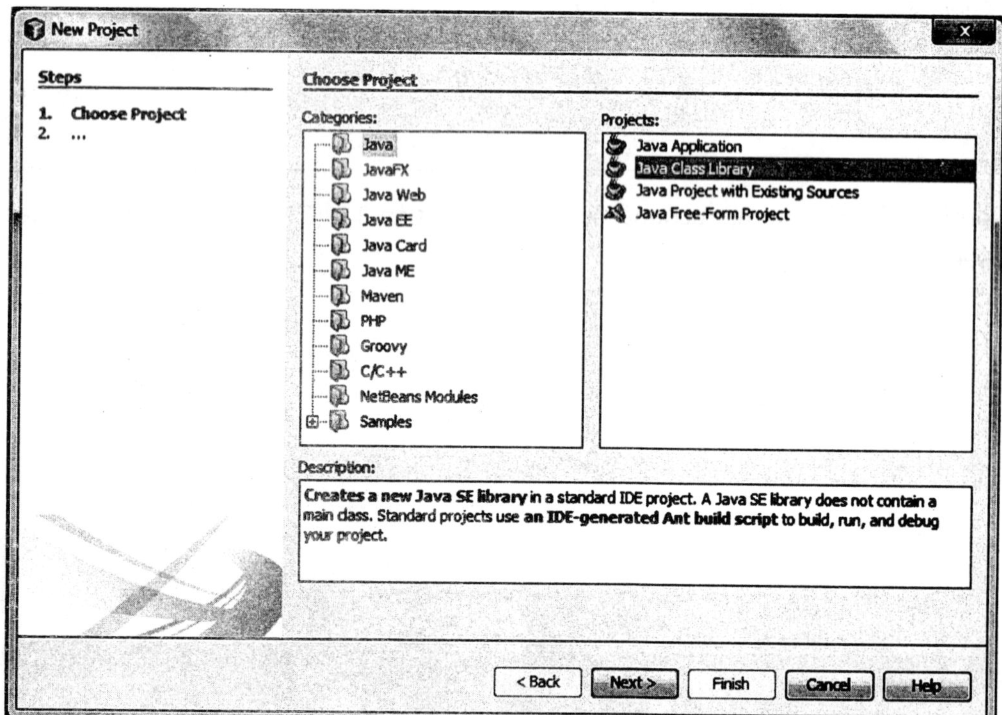

Step 3: Give project name and give "**Finish**".

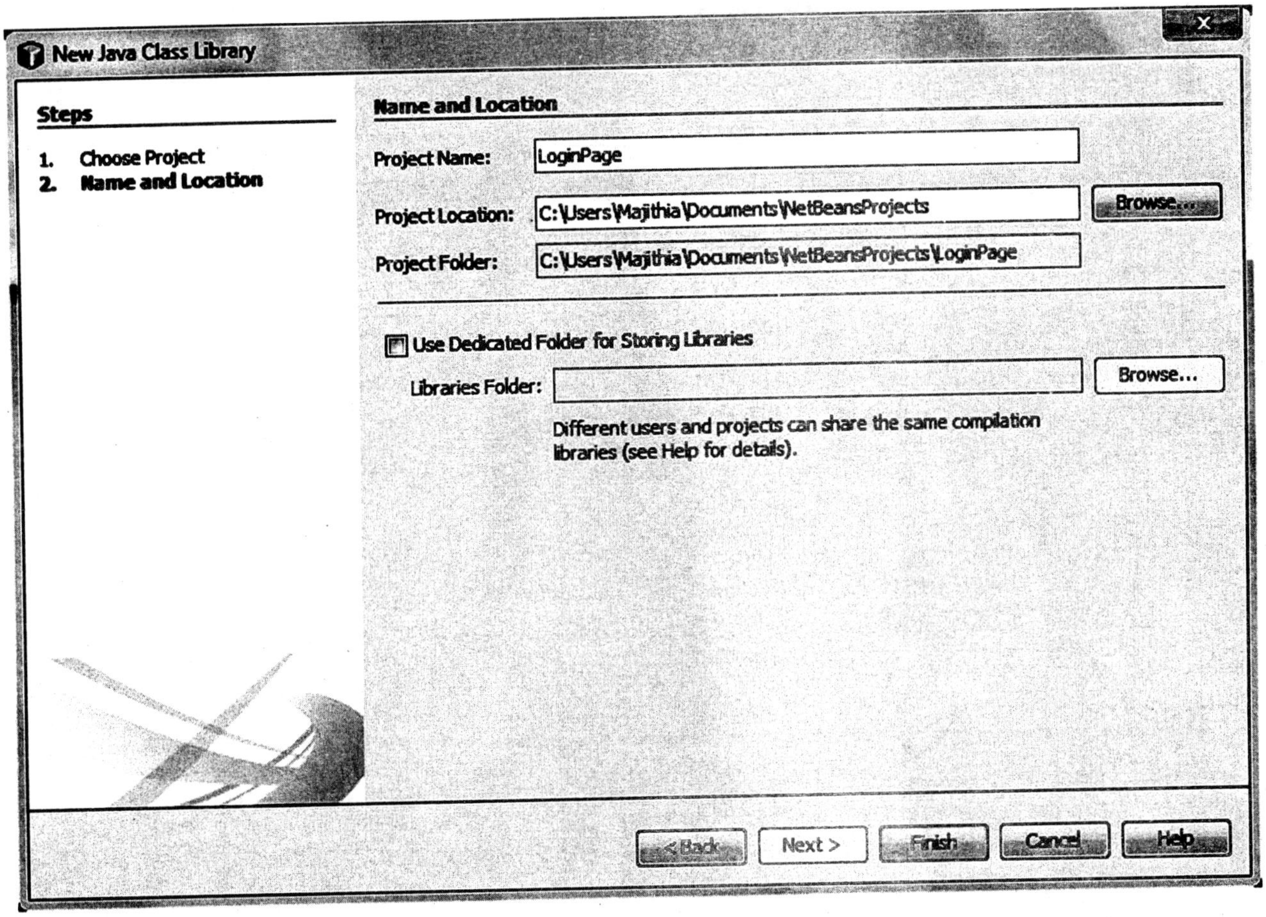

New Java Class Library
Steps
1. Choose Project
2. Name and Location
Name and Location
Project Name: LoginPage
Project Location: C:\Users\Majithia\Documents\NetBeansProjects
Project Folder: C:\Users\Majithia\Documents\NetBeansProjects\LoginPage
Browse...
Use Dedicated Folder for Storing Libraries
Libraries Folder:
Browse...
Different users and projects can share the same compilation libraries (see Help for details).
< Back
Next >
Finish
Cancel
Help

Step 4: You will see "**LoginPage**" project appears in "**Project Pane**" (No default class or skeleton appears). *Right click* on project name and click on "**New**" → "**JFrame Form**".

Projects
New
Build
Clean and Build
Clean
Generate Javadoc
Run
Debug
Profile
Test
Alt+F6
Set Configuration
JFrame Form...
Servlet...
Struts Action...
JApplet Form...
Java Class...
Java Package...
Java Interface...
JPanel Form...
Entity Class...
Entity Classes from Database...
Web Service Client...

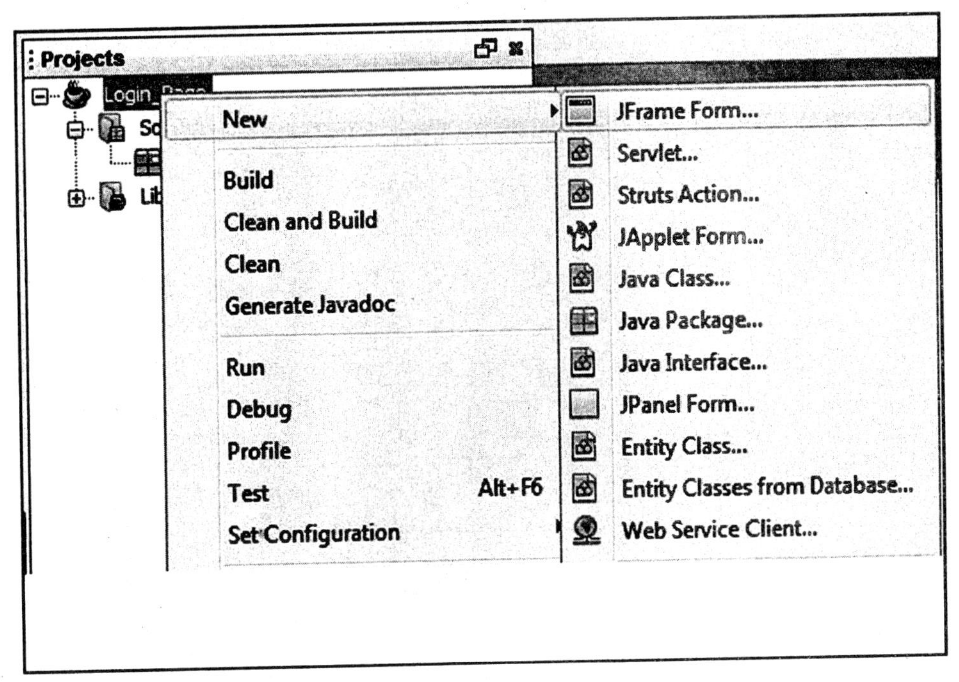

Step 5: A "**New JFrame Form**" window will appear. Give the JFrame class name and Package name and then click "**Finish**"

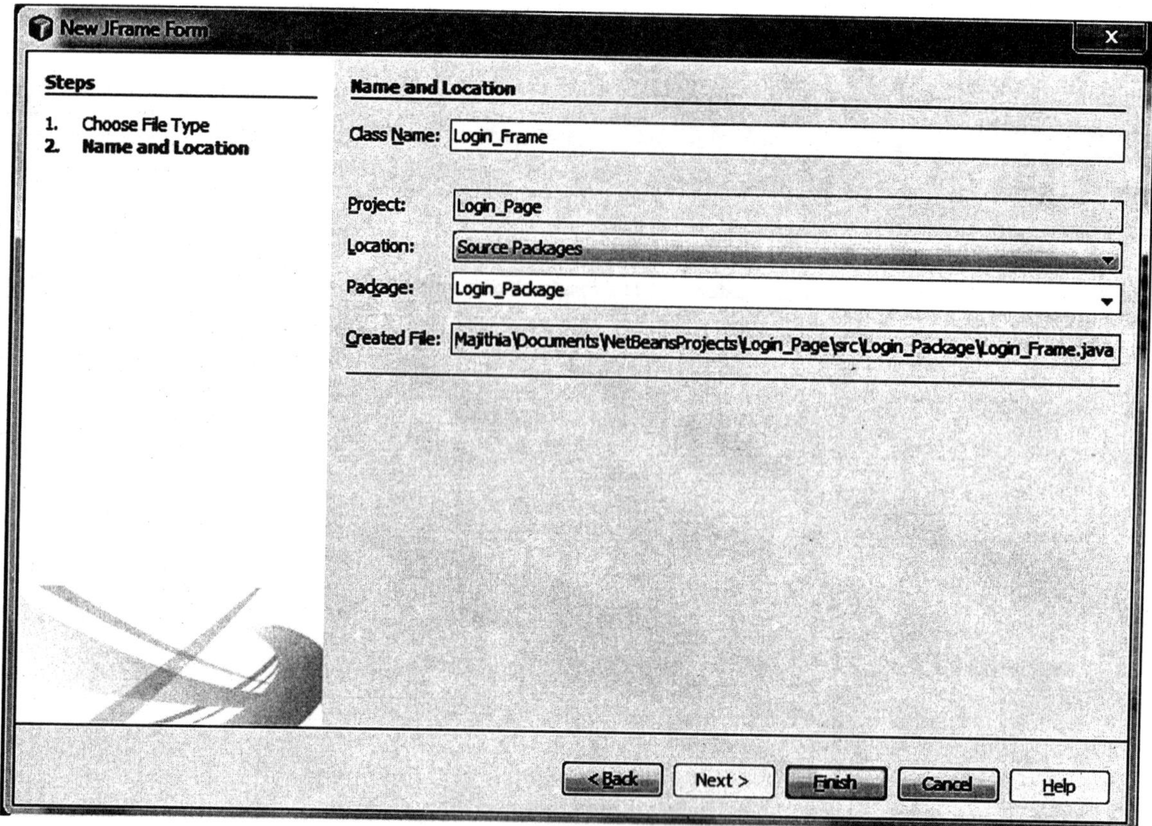


Step 6: You will see a blank JFrame and two new panes "**Palette**" and "**Properties**" on right side of the IDE environment.

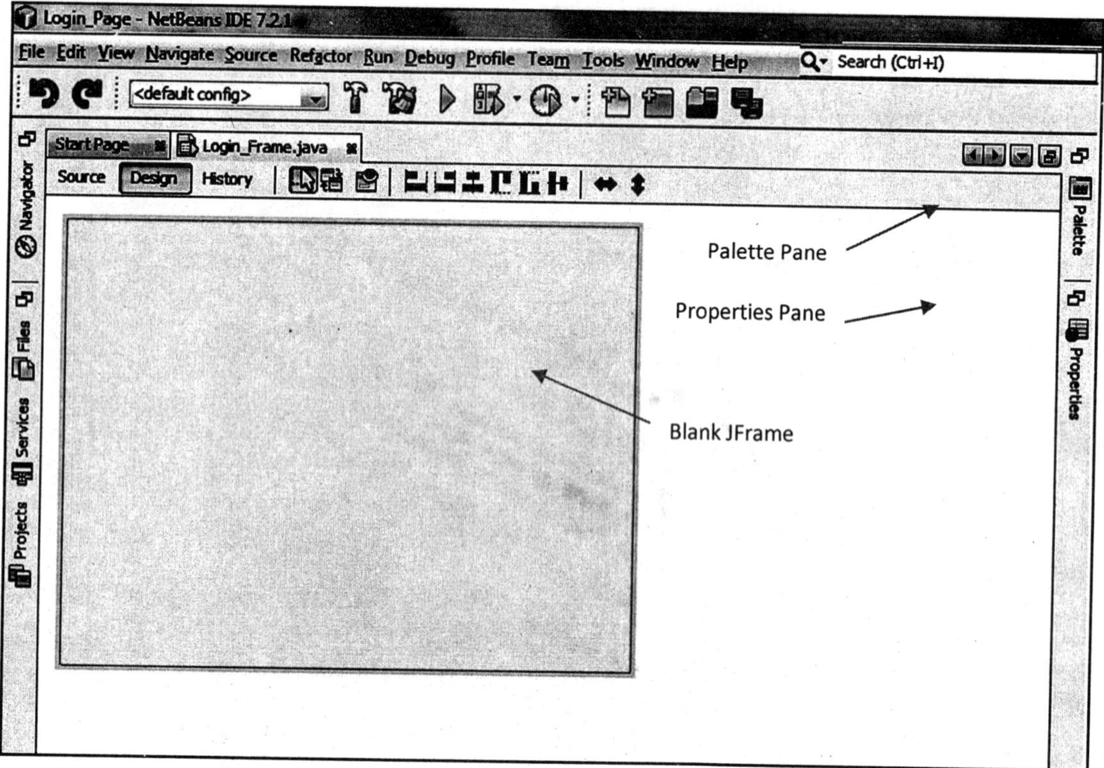


Step 7: You can drag and drop required components from "**Palette Pane**" into the JFrame and put the GUI as you want.

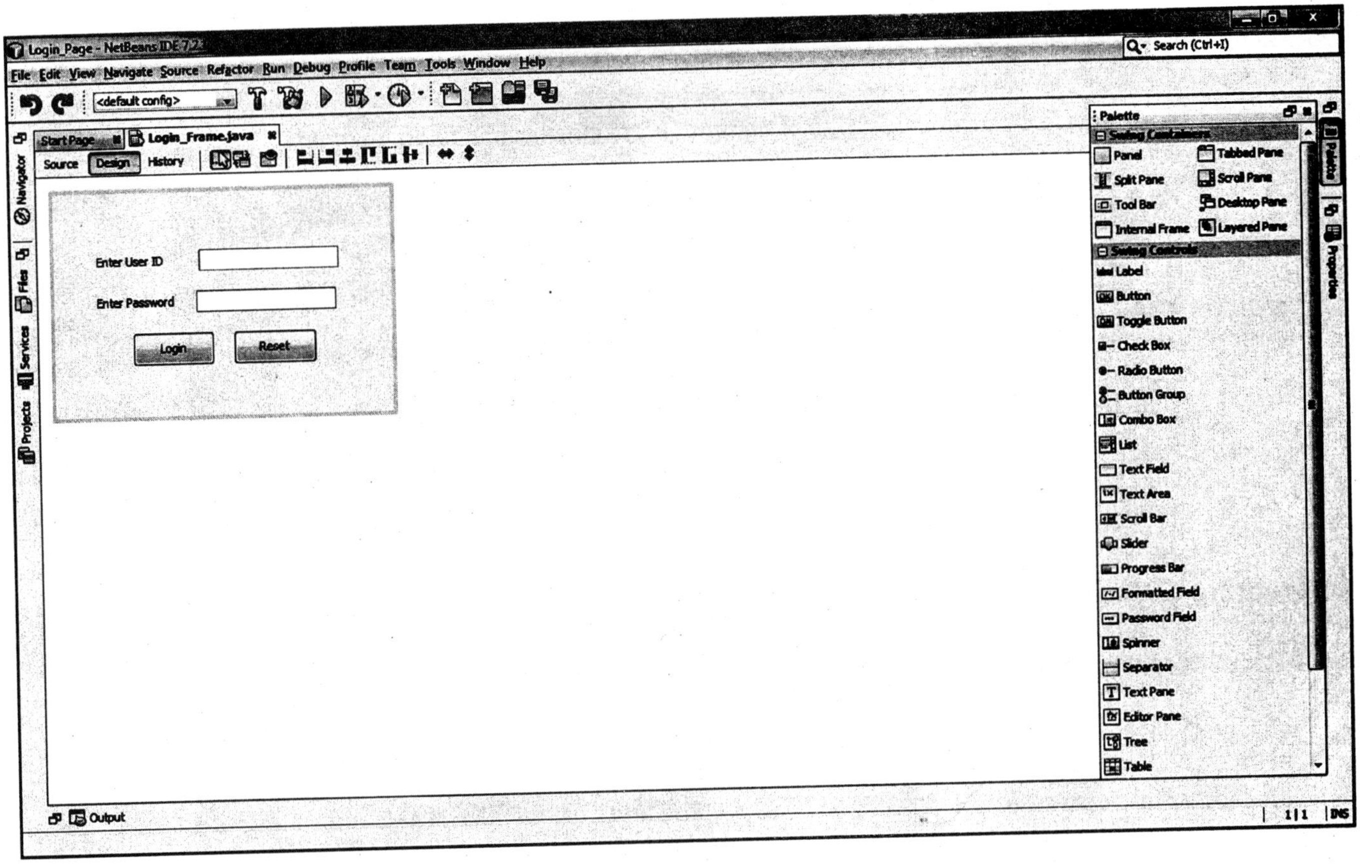

Login_Page - NetBeans IDE 7.2.1
File Edit View Navigate Source Refactor Run Debug Profile Team Tools Window Help
Search (Ctrl+I)
<default config>
Start Page
Login_Frame.java
Source Design History
Enter User ID
Enter Password
Login
Reset
Palette
Panel
Tabbed Pane
Split Pane
Scroll Pane
Tool Bar
Desktop Pane
Internal Frame
Layered Pane
Label
Button
Toggle Button
Check Box
Radio Button
Button Group
Combo Box
List
Text Field
Text Area
Scroll Bar
Slider
Progress Bar
Formatted Field
Password Field
Spinner
Separator
Text Pane
Editor Pane
Tree
Table
Navigator
Files
Services
Projects
Properties
Output


Step 8: Change the properties of different components from the "**Properties pane**"

Step 9: To deal with **event handling**, simply **double click** on any component for which you want to handle the event, and you will get the class with implemented interfaces and empty event handling methods.

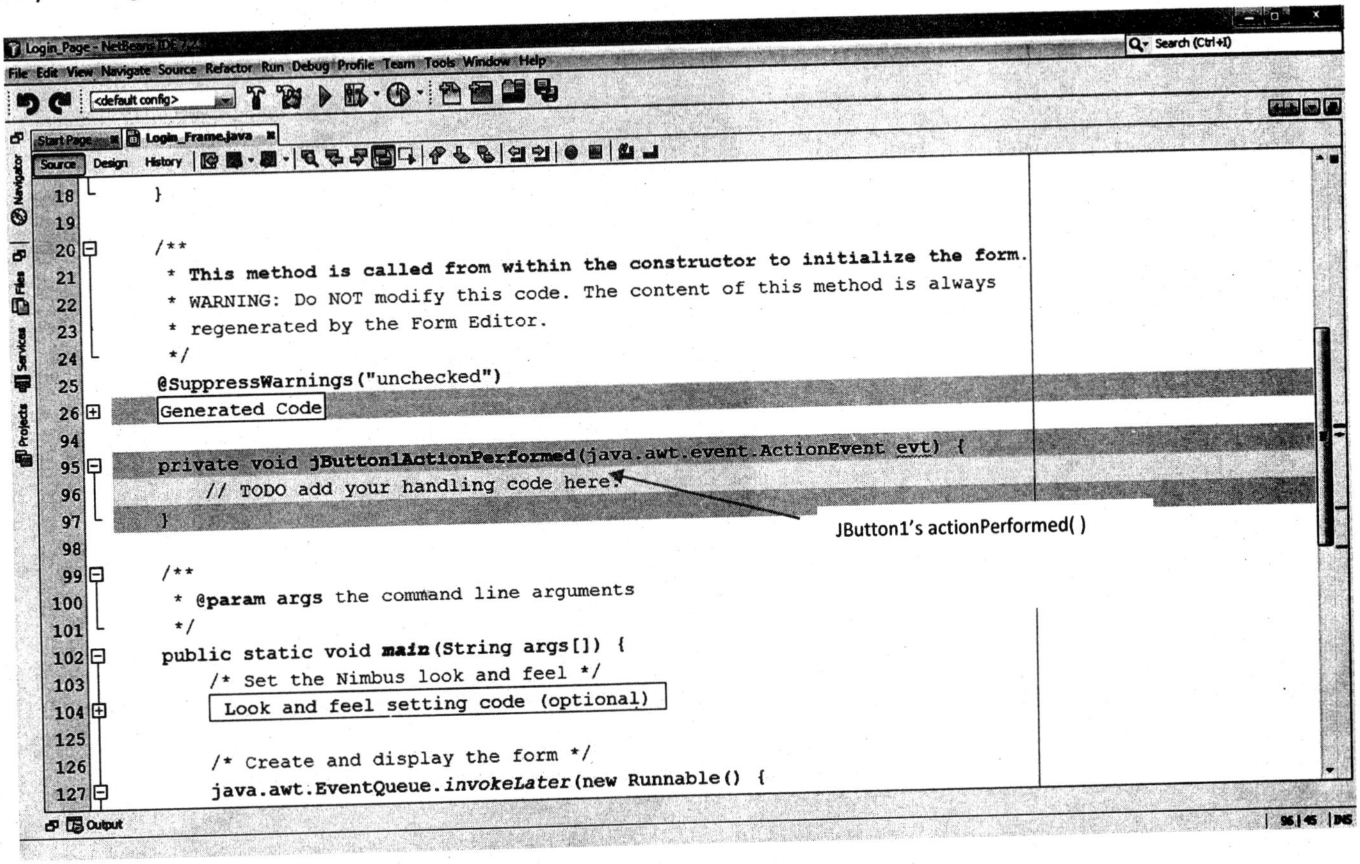

Login_Page - NetBeans IDE 7.2.1
File Edit View Navigate Source Refactor Run Debug Profile Team Tools Window Help
Search (Ctrl+I)
<default config>
Start Page
Login_Frame.java
Source Design History
}
/**
* This method is called from within the constructor to initialize the form.
* WARNING: Do NOT modify this code. The content of this method is always
* regenerated by the Form Editor.
*/
@SuppressWarnings("unchecked")
Generated Code
private void jButton1ActionPerformed(java.awt.event.ActionEvent evt) {
// TODO add your handling code here:
}
JButton1's actionPerformed( )
/**
* @param args the command line arguments
*/
public static void main(String args[]) {
/* Set the Nimbus look and feel */
Look and feel setting code (optional)
/* Create and display the form */
java.awt.EventQueue.invokeLater(new Runnable() {
Output

Step 10: Run the project and you will see following window as output.

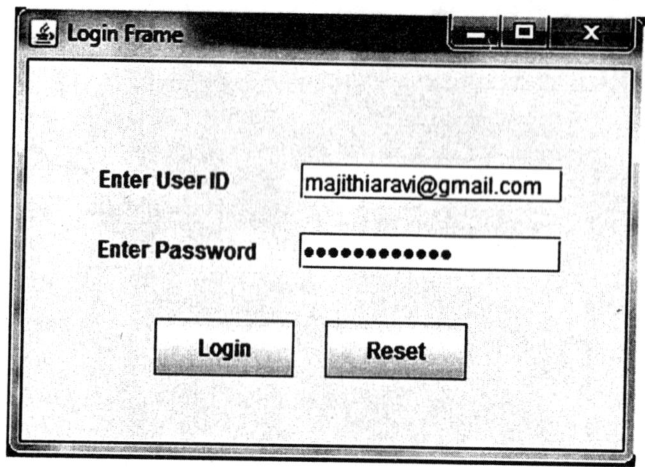


## 4.7 Creating GUI using JApplet

To create a GUI application using JApplet, follow the following steps.

Step 1: Open "File" menu → select "**New Project**".

Step 2: Select "**Java**" from categories and select "**Java Class Library**" and click "**Next**"

Step 3: Give project name and give "**Finish**".

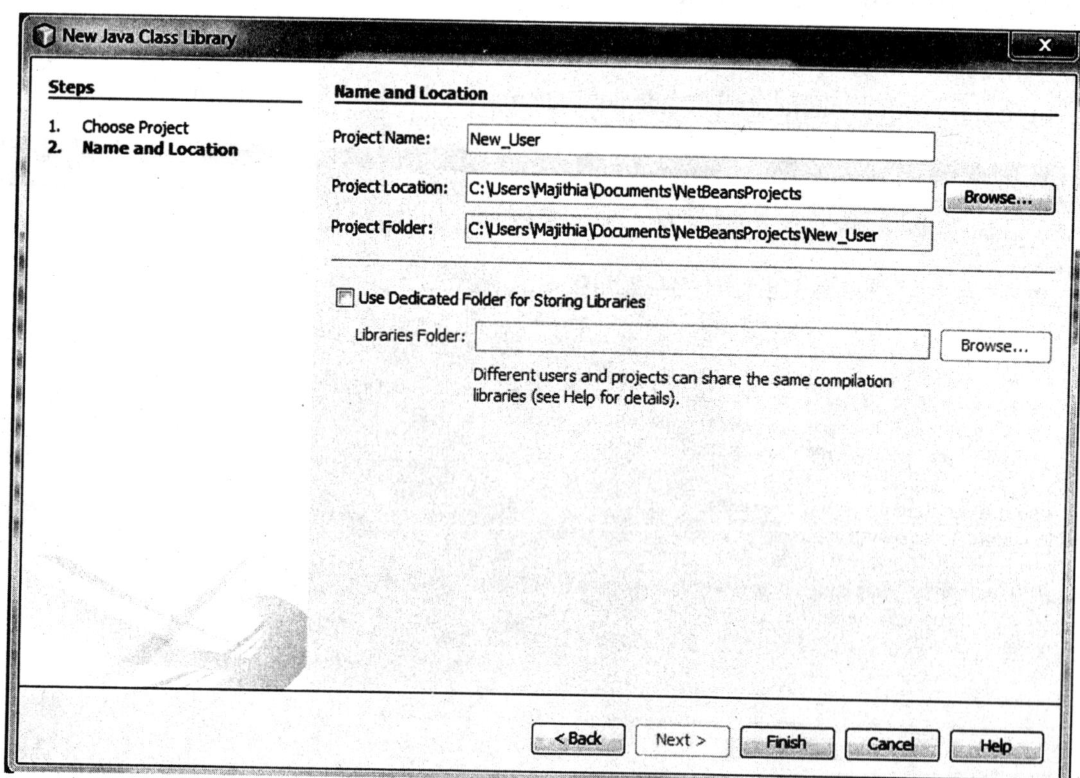


Step 4: You will see "**New_User**" project appears in "**Project Pane**" (No default class or skeleton appears). *Right click* on project name and click on "**New**" → "**JApplet Form**".

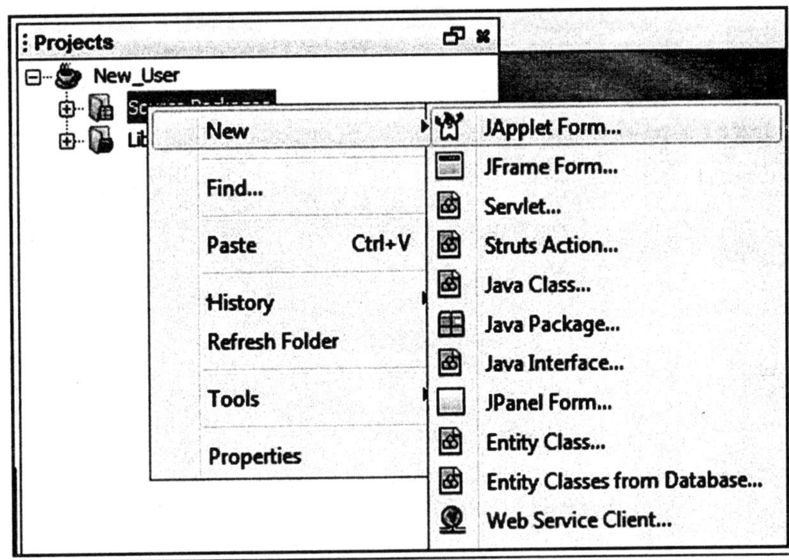


Step 5: A "**New JApplet Form**" window will appear. Give the JApplet class name and Package name and then click "**Finish**"

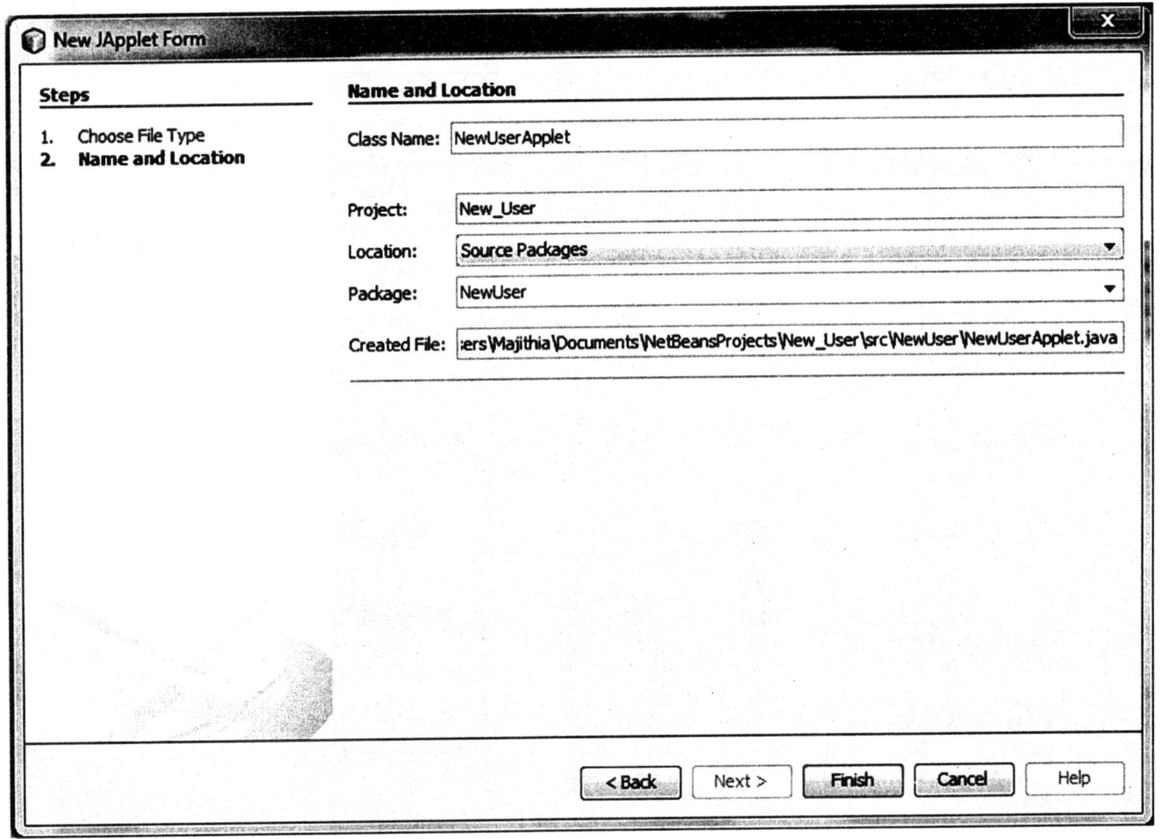


Step 6: You will see a blank JApplet and two new panes "**Palette**" and "**Properties**" on right side of the IDE environment.

Step 7: You can drag and drop required components from "**Palette Pane**" into the JApplet and put the GUI as you want.

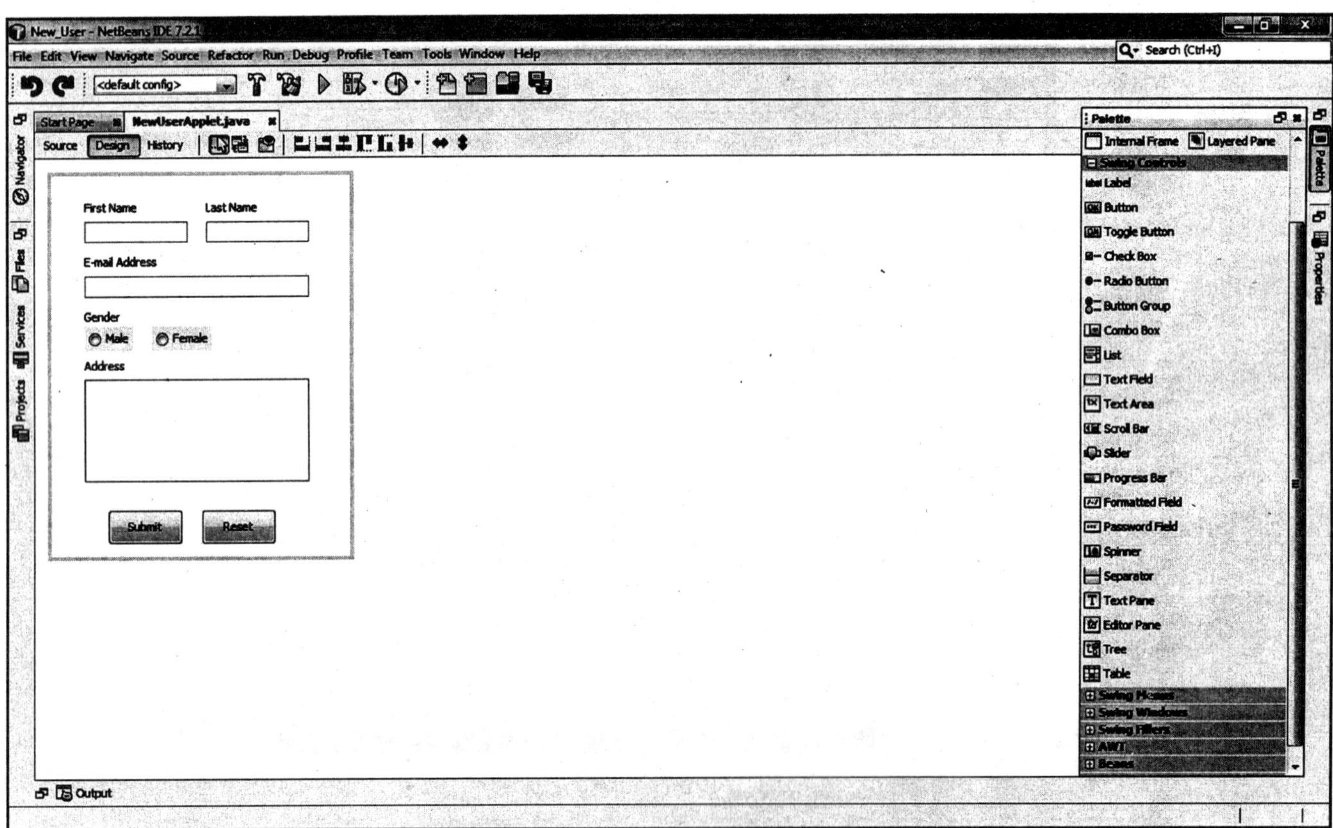


Step 8: To deal with **event handling**, simply **double click** on any component for which you want to handle the event, and you will get the class with implemented interfaces and empty event handling methods.

Step 8: Run the JApplet from "**Project Pane**" and you will see following output.

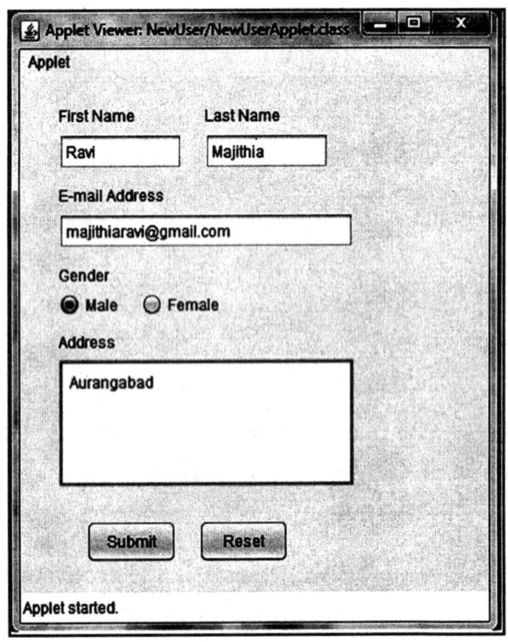


## 4.8 Creating a Servlet

Lets create a servlet application that accepts user's name and submits it to servlet follow the following steps.

Step 1: Open "File" menu → select "**New Project**".

Step 2: Select "**Java Web**" from categories and select "**Web Application**" and click "**Next**"

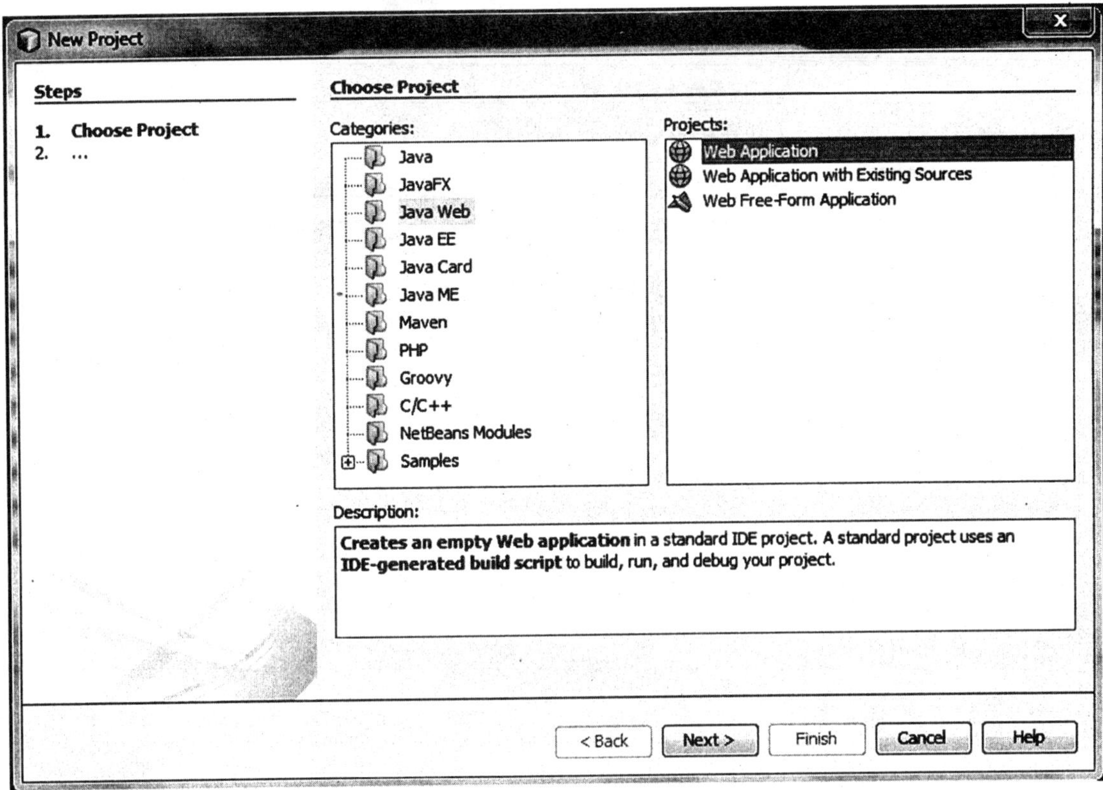


Step 3: Provide project name and click "**Next**".

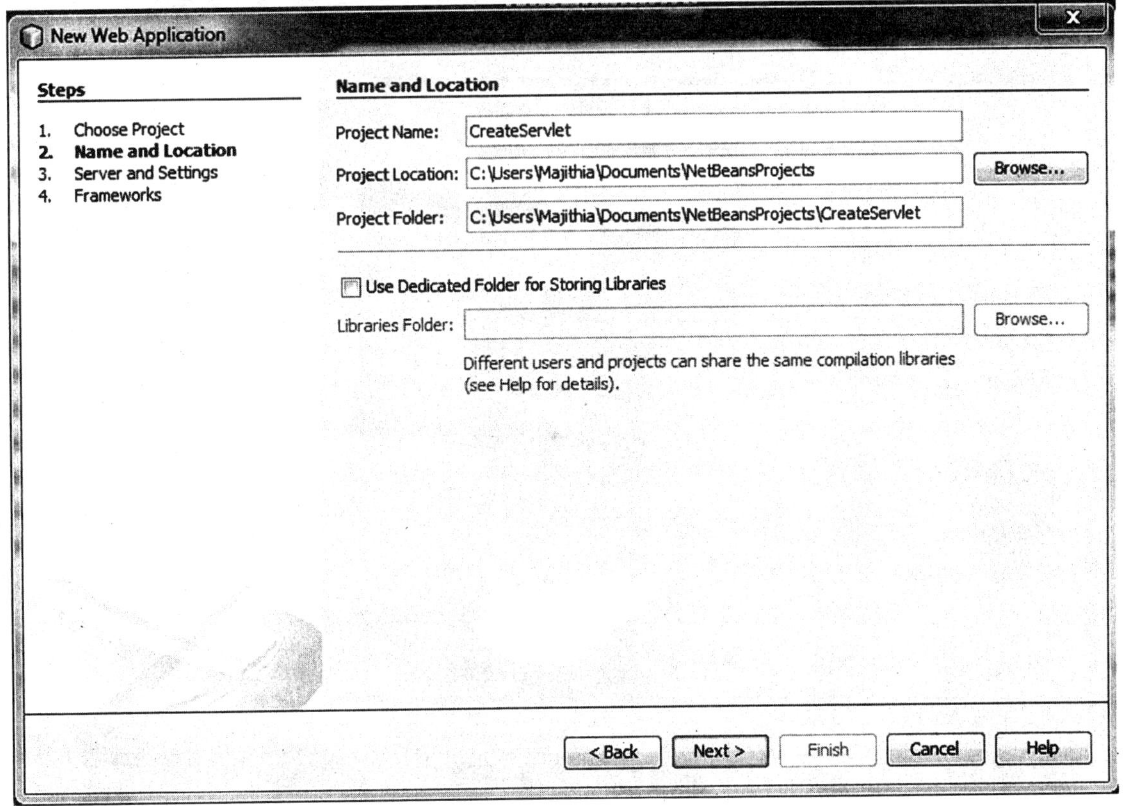


Step 4: You will be asked for "**server and settings**". Select "**GlassFish Server**" any version and click "**Next**".

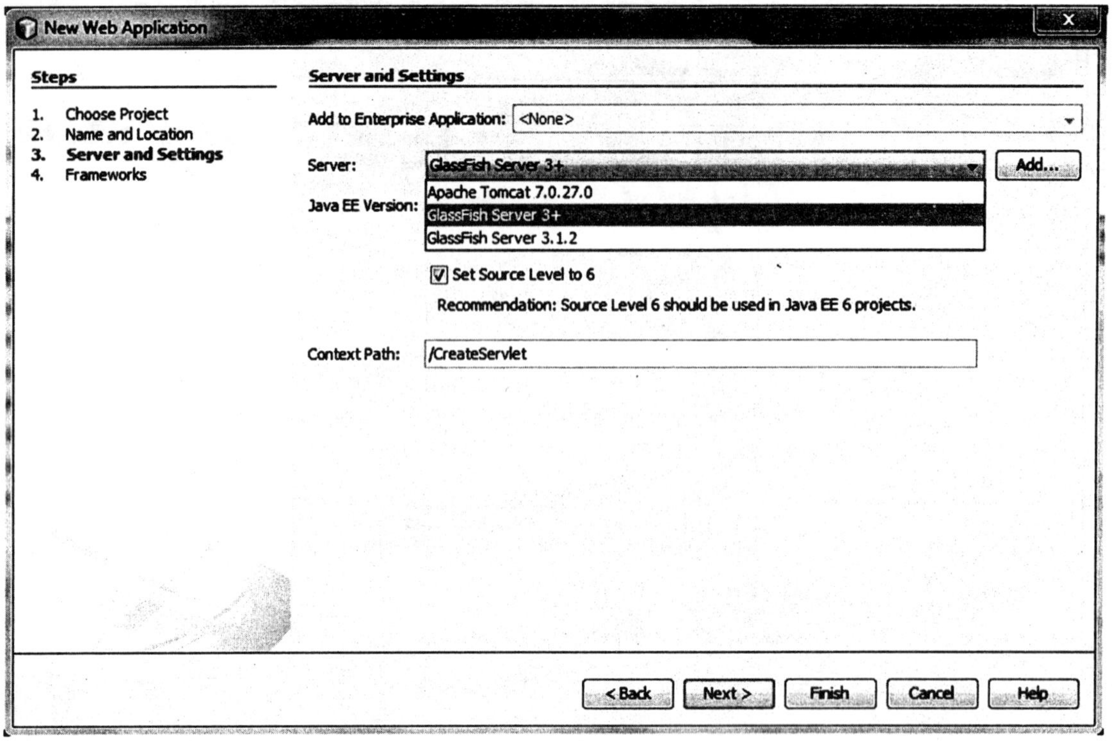

New Web Application
Steps
1. Choose Project
2. Name and Location
3. Server and Settings
4. Frameworks
Server and Settings
Add to Enterprise Application: <None>
Server: GlassFish Server 3+
Add...
Apache Tomcat 7.0.27.0
GlassFish Server 3+
GlassFish Server 3.1.2
Java EE Version:
Set Source Level to 6
Recommendation: Source Level 6 should be used in Java EE 6 projects.
Context Path: /CreateServlet
< Back
Next >
Finish
Cancel
Help

Step 5: You will be asked to choose framework. *Do not check* any Framework and click "**Finish**".

New Web Application
Steps
1. Choose Project
2. Name and Location
3. Server and Settings
4. Frameworks
Frameworks
Select the frameworks you want to use in your web application.
Spring Web MVC
JavaServer Faces
Struts 1.3.10
< Back
Next >
Finish
Cancel
Help

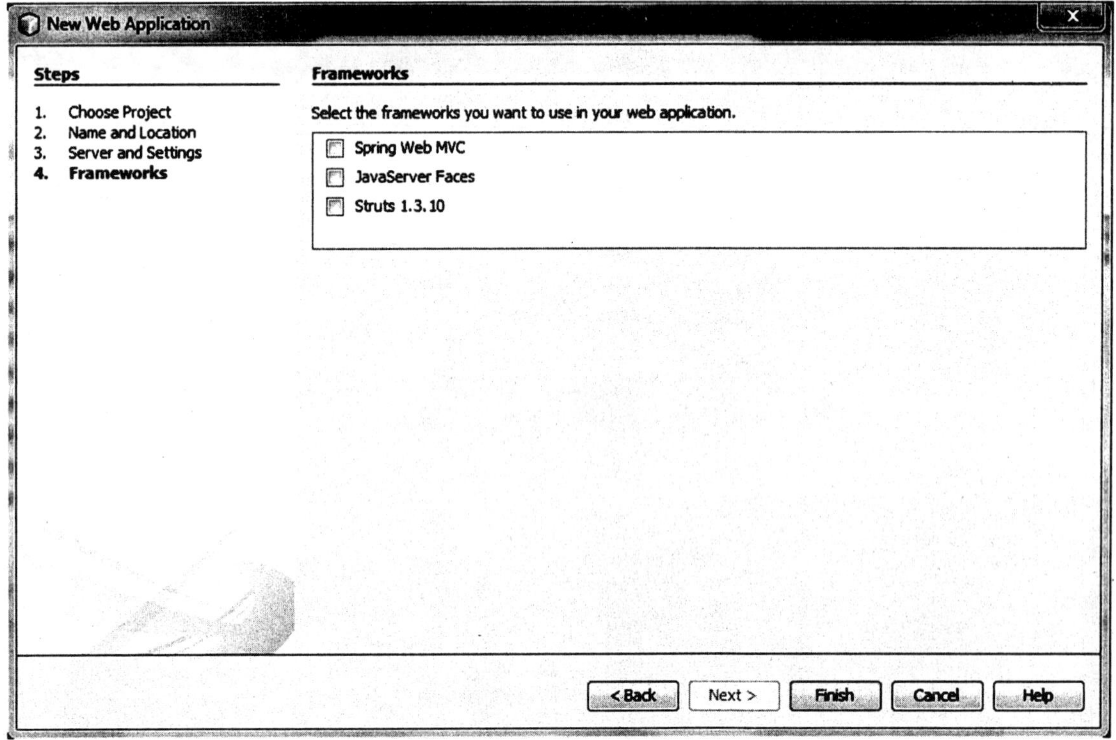

Step 6: The **index.jsp** page will appear. You can design the page using HTML tags and add the servlet file to it.

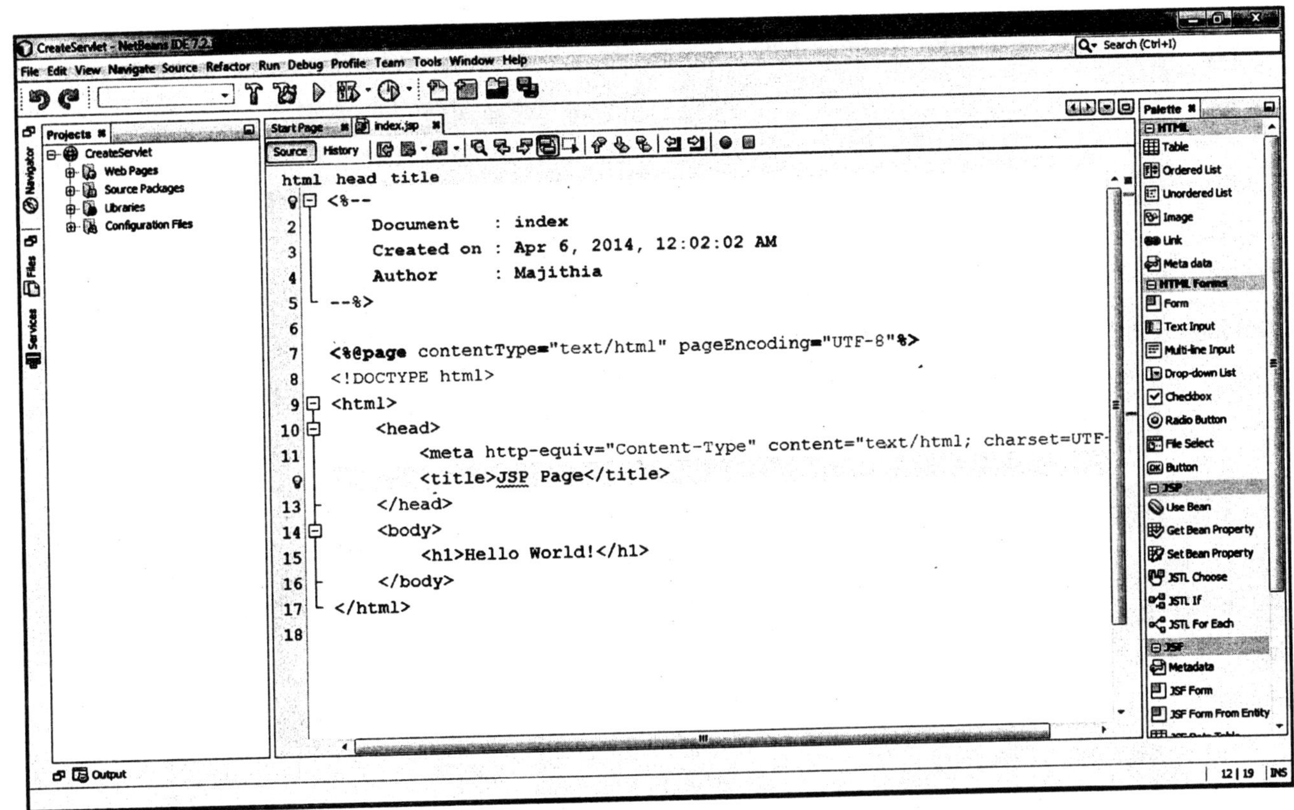

Step 7: Modify above index.JSP file as follows.

```
<%--
  Document   : index
  Created on : Apr 6, 2014, 12:02:02 AM
  Author     : Majithia
--%>

<%@page contentType="text/html" pageEncoding="UTF-8"%>
<!DOCTYPE html>
<html>
  <head>
    <meta http-equiv="Content-Type" content="text/html; charset=UTF-8">
  <title>Welcome to my first servlet example page</title>
</head>
  <body>
 <h1>A Welcome application</h1>
    <form method="POST" action="WelcomeServlet">
      <label title="Enter your name here">Enter your name :</label>
      <input type="text" id="txtname"/><br><br>
      <input type="submit" value="Submit"/>
    </form>
 </body>
</html>
```

Step 8: Open "**Project Pane**", right click on project name and select "**New**" → "**Servlet**"

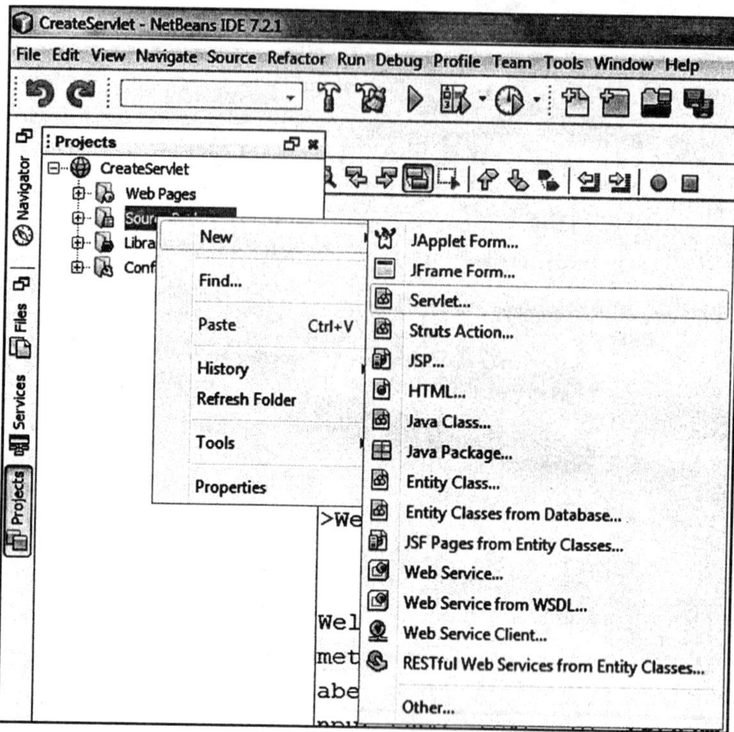


Step 9: A "**New servlet**" window will appear, give class name as "**WelcomeServlet**" and package name as "**FirstServlet**" and click "**Next**"

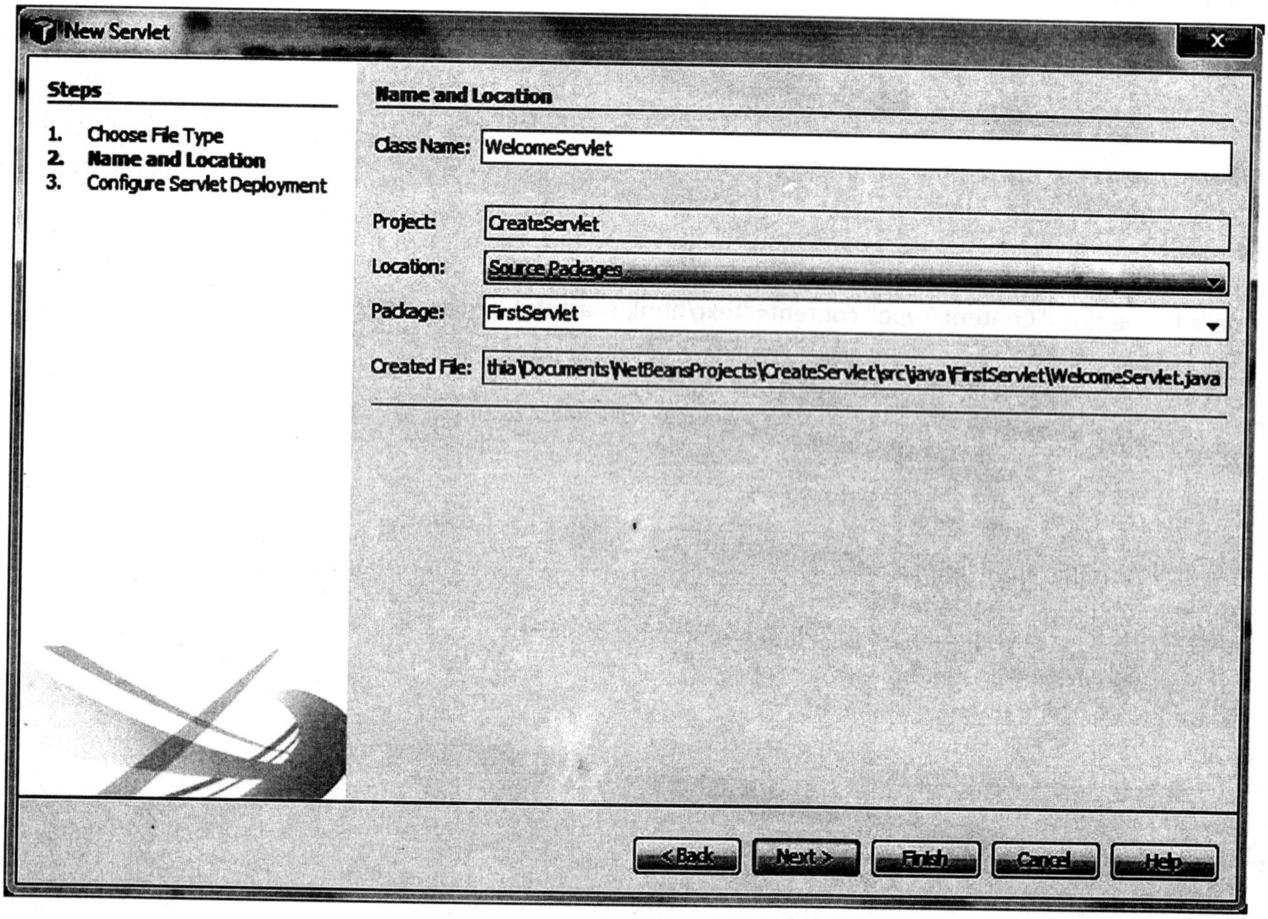

New Servlet

Steps

1. Choose File Type
2. **Name and Location**
3. Configure Servlet Deployment

**Name and Location**

Class Name: WelcomeServlet

Project: CreateServlet

Location: Source Packages

Package: FirstServlet

Created File: thia\Documents\NetBeansProjects\CreateServlet\src\java\FirstServlet\WelcomeServlet.java

< Back | Next > | Finish | Cancel | Help

Step 10: A "Configure Servlet Deployment" window will appear, simply check the checkbox that appears in front of *"Add information to deployment descriptor (web.xml)"* and click "**Finish**"

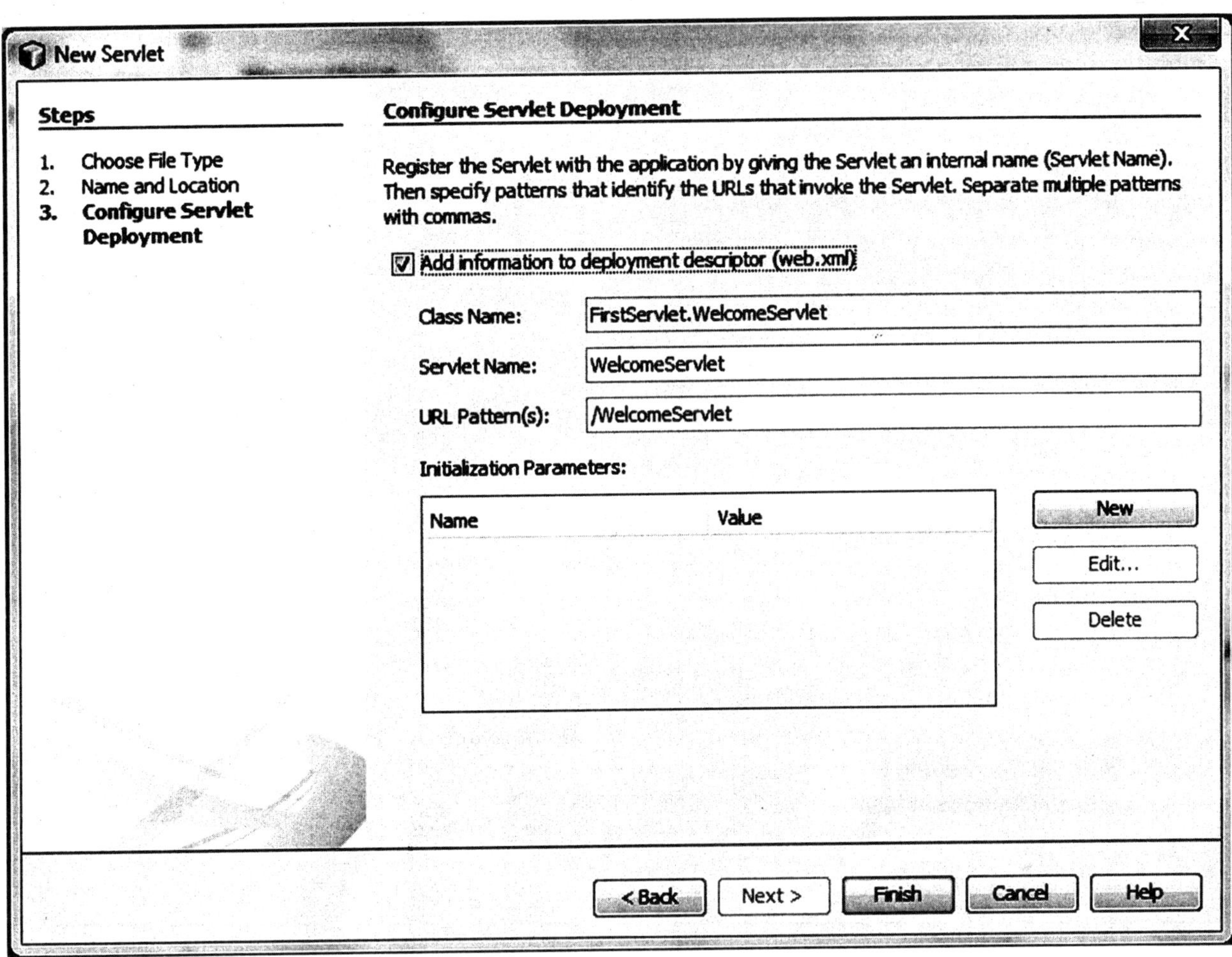


Step 11: The servlet named "**WelcomeServlet.java**" is created with default skeleton. You can also see another file called "web.xml" is created and that is because you checked the checkbox that appeared in last step(deployment descriptor).

Note: If you did not check that checkbox then the web.xml will not be created but instead you will see an annotation line added above the servlet class definition as:

```
@WebServlet ( name = "WelcomeServlet" , urlpattern = {"/WelcomeServlet"} )
```

Step 12: Type the following code into that servlet class.

```
package FirstServlet;

import java.io.IOException;
import java.io.PrintWriter;
import javax.servlet.ServletException;
import javax.servlet.http.HttpServlet;
import javax.servlet.http.HttpServletRequest;
import javax.servlet.http.HttpServletResponse;

public class WelcomeServlet extends HttpServlet
{
    @Override
    protected void service(HttpServletRequest request,HttpServletResponse response) throws
ServletException,IOException
    {
        PrintWriter pw = response.getWriter();
        response.setContentType("text/html;charset=UTF-8");
        pw.println("<html><head>");
        pw.println("<title>This is reponse from servlet</title></head>");
        pw.println("<body>");
        String s = request.getParameter("txtname");
        pw.println("<h1>Welcome <u>" + s + "</u> to the servlet page</h1><br><br>");
        pw.println("<a href='index.jsp'>Click here to return to home page</a>");
        pw.println("</body></html>");
    }
}
```

After building and running this application, you will get following output.

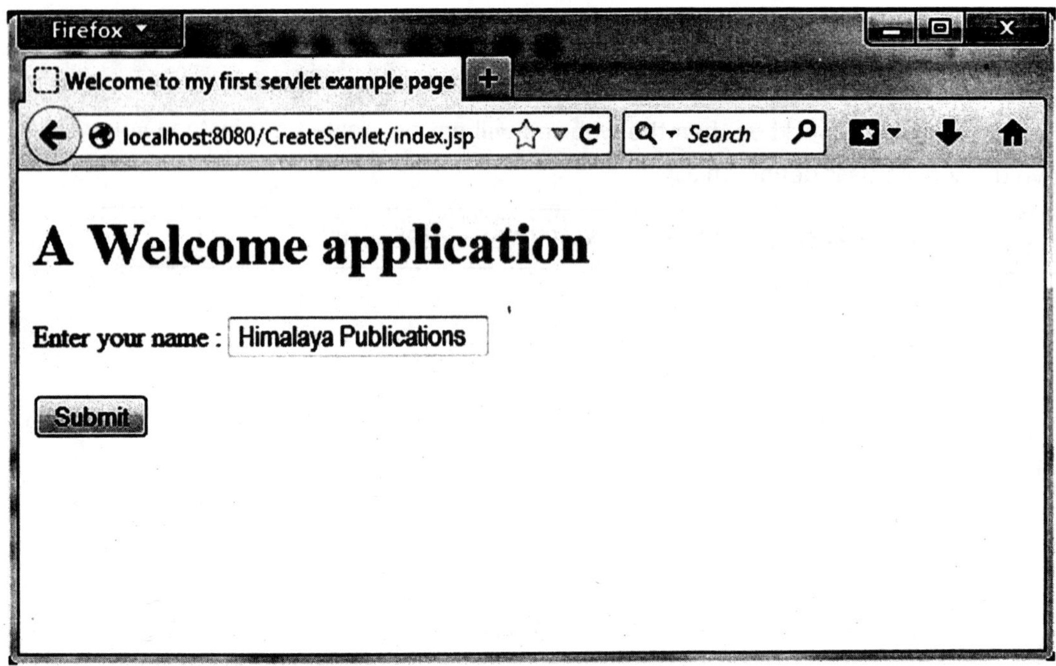

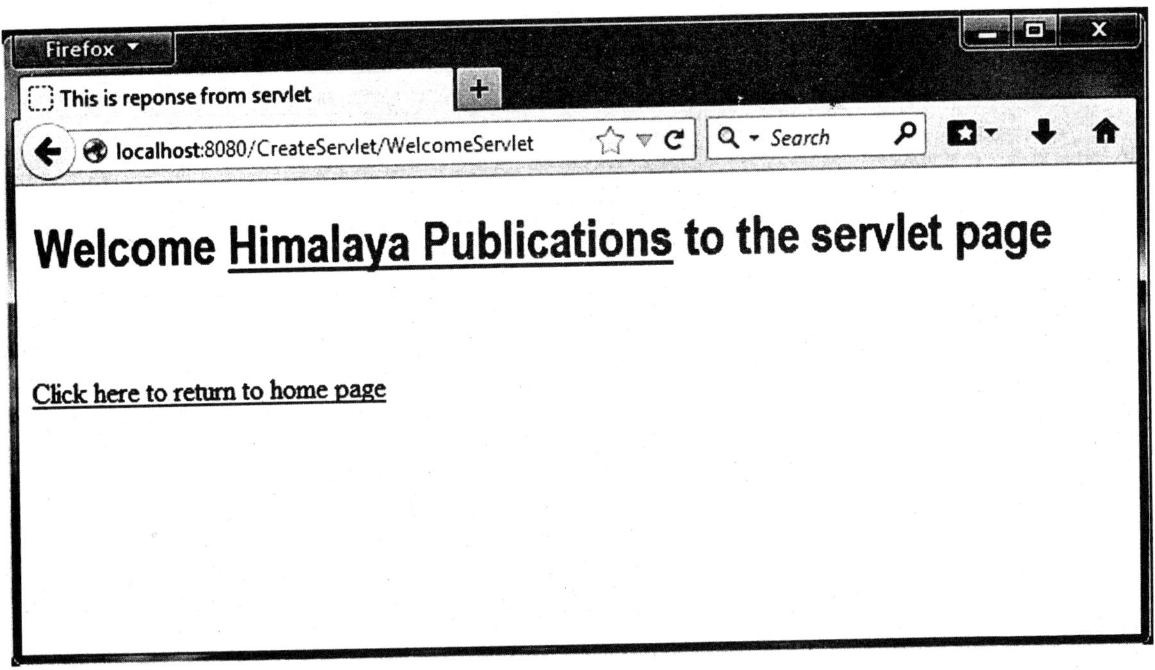


## 4.9 Creating Filter

Actually filters are not servlets and therefore they are not responsible for response. Filters provide universal functions which can be attached to any servlet or JSP. Filters are pre-processors of servlet requests and post-processors of servlet responses.

To create a filter and add it to current servlet, follow the following steps.

Step 1: Create a servlet as shown in above section 3.6. Here I am continuing above created servlet project "**CreateServlet**".

Step 2: Open "**Project Pane**", right click on "**Source Package**". Select "**New**" and then "**other..**"

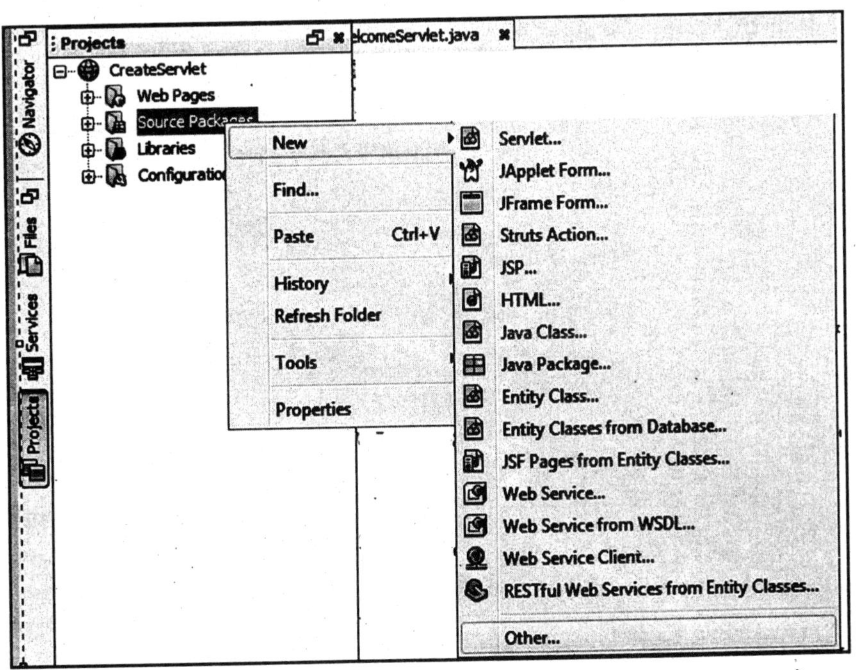


Step 3: A "**New File**" window will appear. Select "**Filter**" from "**File Types**" and click "**Next**"

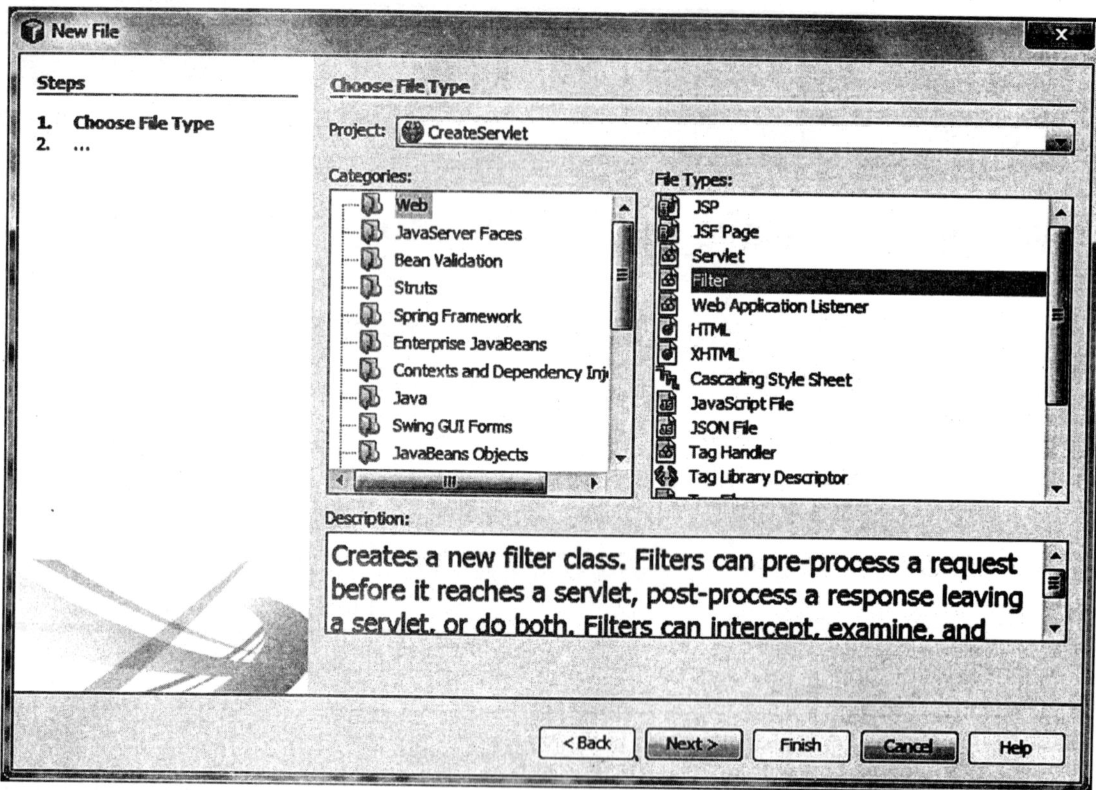


Step 4: A "New Filter" window will appear. Give *class name* and *package name*. Then click "**Next**".

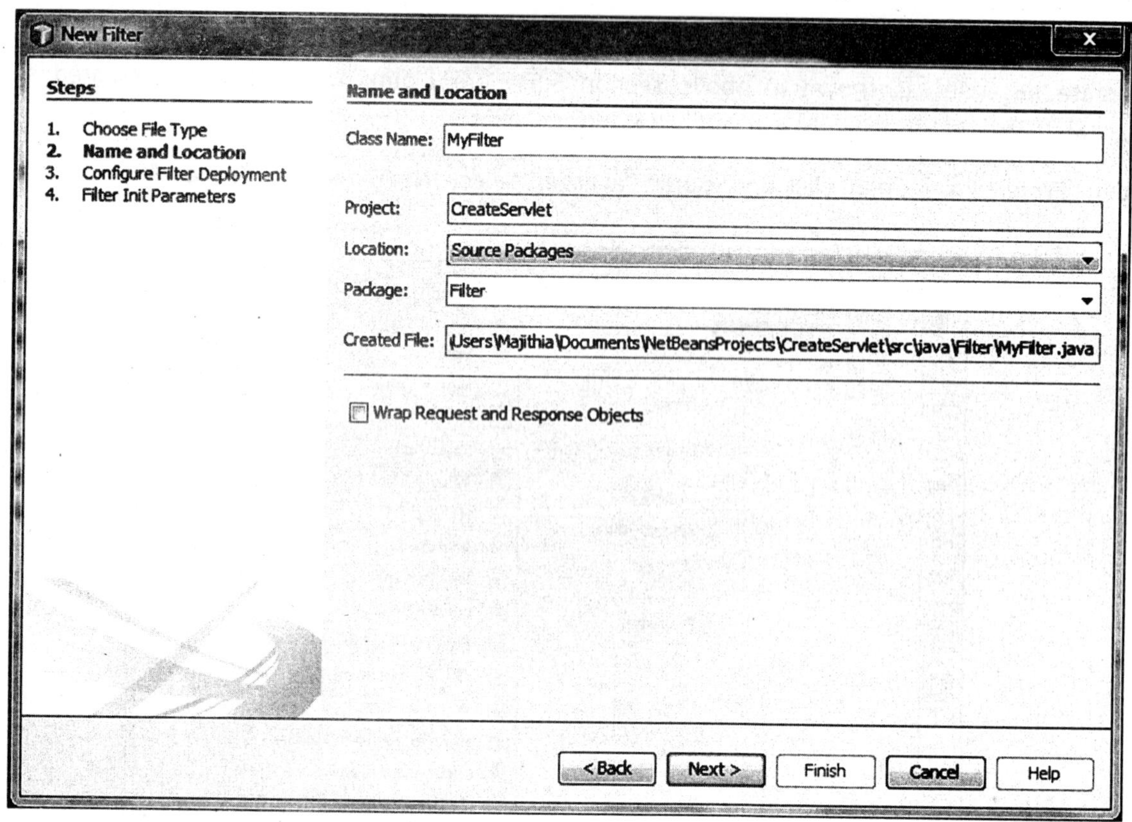


Step 5: A "**Configure Filter Deployment**" window will appear. Check the checkbox in front of "*Add information to deployment descriptor (web.xml)*". Then click "**Next**".

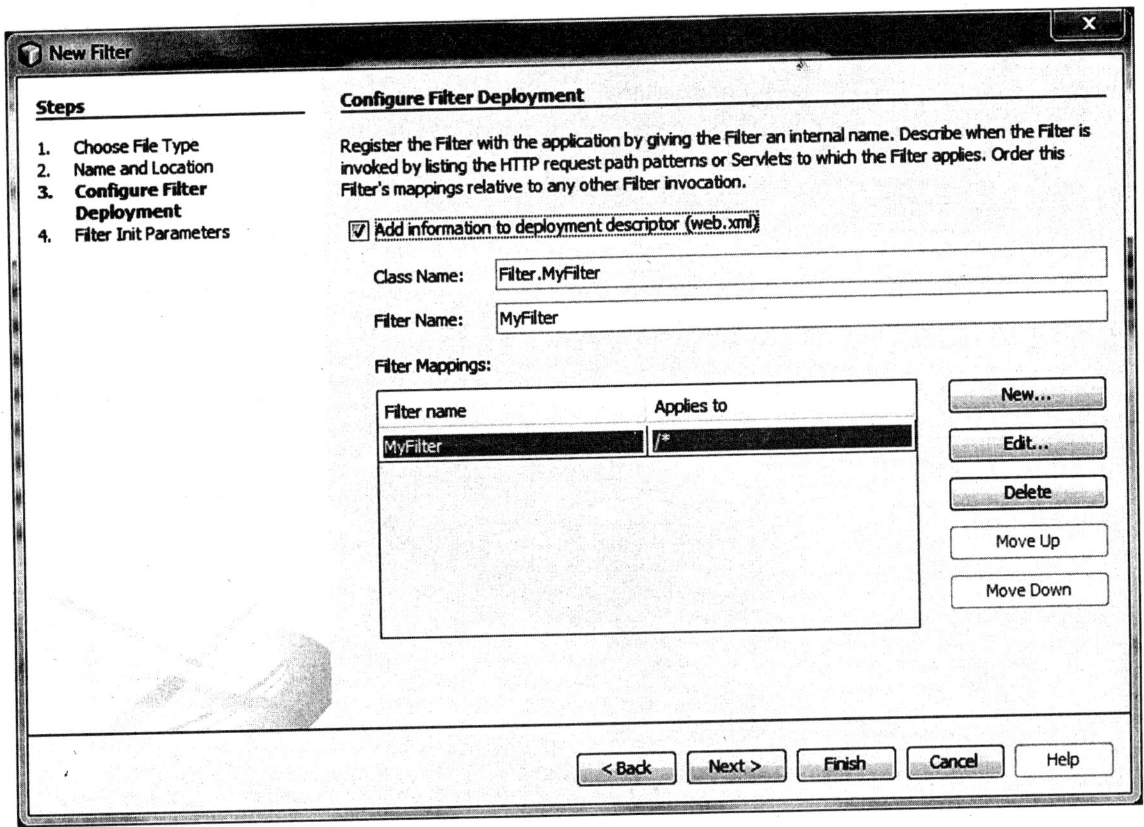


Here you can see "**Filter Mapping**" option. At this time, keep the defaults as it is. In case if you want to change the filter mapping, then click on "**New**". You will see a filter mapping dialog box.

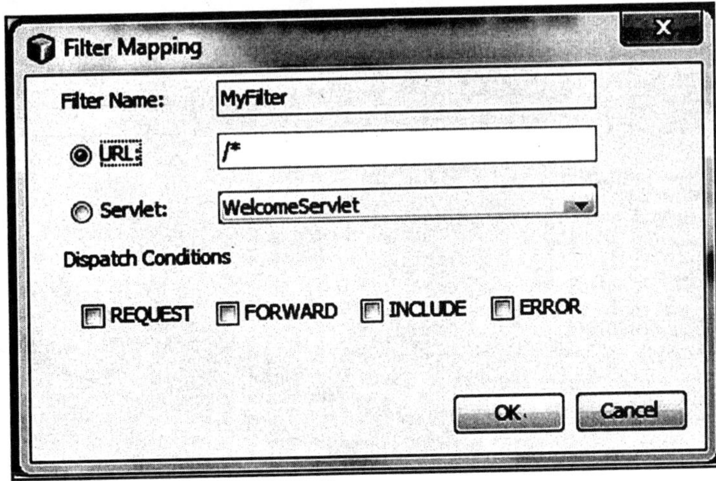


Change any parameters if you want to and click "**OK**".

Step 6: Now you will see the "**Filter Init Parameters**" window. Since the basic application does not deal with init parameters, it is better to skip this section. Click "**Finish**" to complete the configurations.

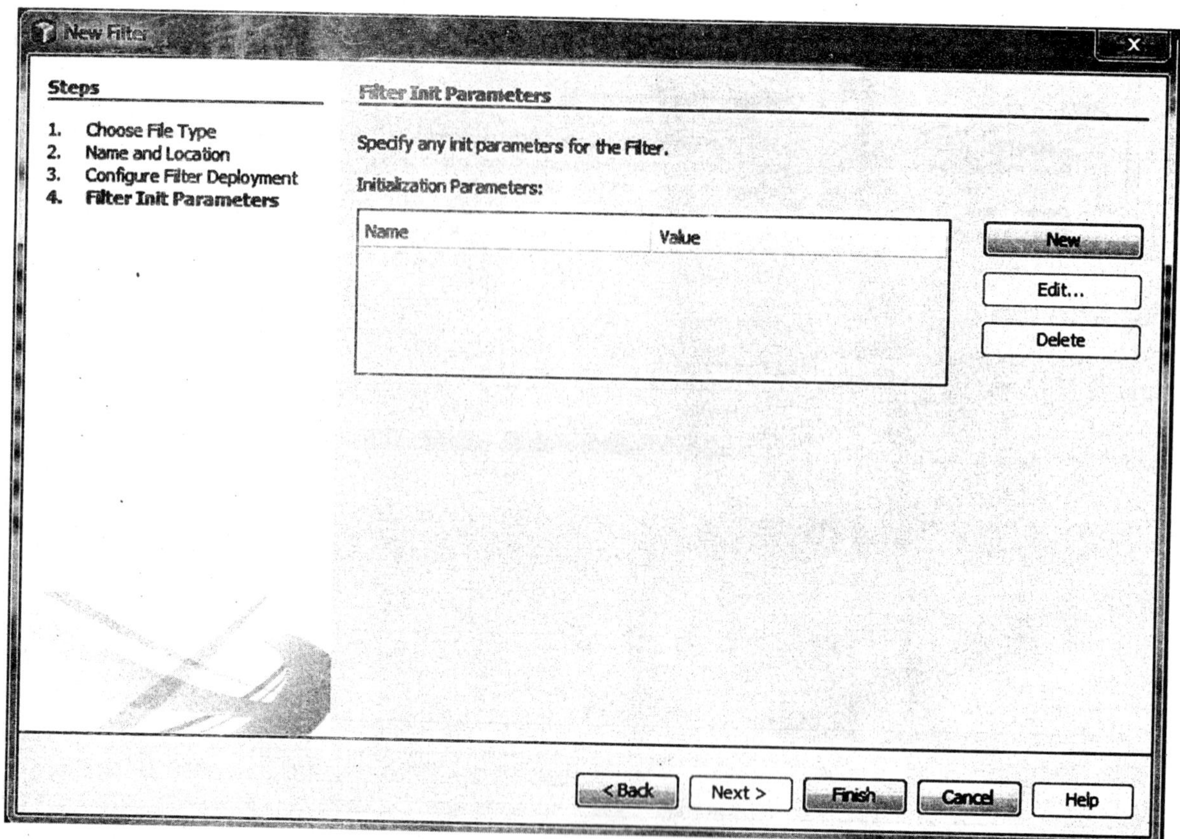


Step 7: You will see the filter named "**MyFilter.java**" is created in the package "**Filter**".

```
package Filter;

import java.io.IOException;
import java.io.PrintStream;
import java.io.PrintWriter;
import java.io.StringWriter;
import javax.servlet.Filter;
import javax.servlet.FilterChain;
import javax.servlet.FilterConfig;
import javax.servlet.ServletException;
import javax.servlet.ServletRequest;
import javax.servlet.ServletResponse;

public class MyFilter implements Filter
{
    private static final boolean debug = true;
    private FilterConfig filterConfig = null;

    public MyFilter()
    {

    }

```

## 4.10 Adding JSP page to project

To add a new JSP page to any project, follow the following steps.

Step 1: Create a servlet as shown in above section 3.6. Here I am continuing above created servlet project "**CreateServlet**".

Step 2: Open "**Project Pane**", right click on "**Source Package**". Select "**New**" and then "**JSP**"

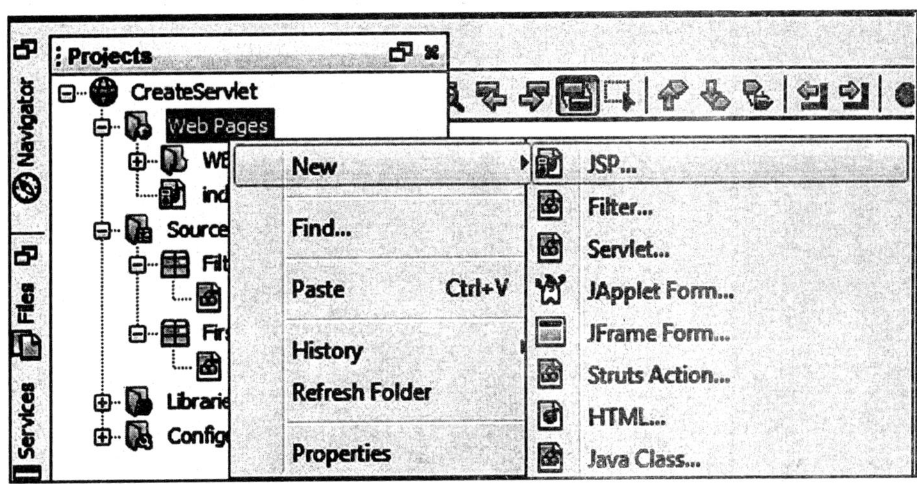


Step 3: A "New JSP" window will appear. Apply *File name* and *folder name*. You will also see two radio buttons under "Options" section. Check the "**JSP File (Standard Syntax)**" if you want to make a standard ***.jsp** file and check "**JSP document (XML Syntax)**" if you want to make a JSP document as ***.jspx**. Then click "**Finish**".

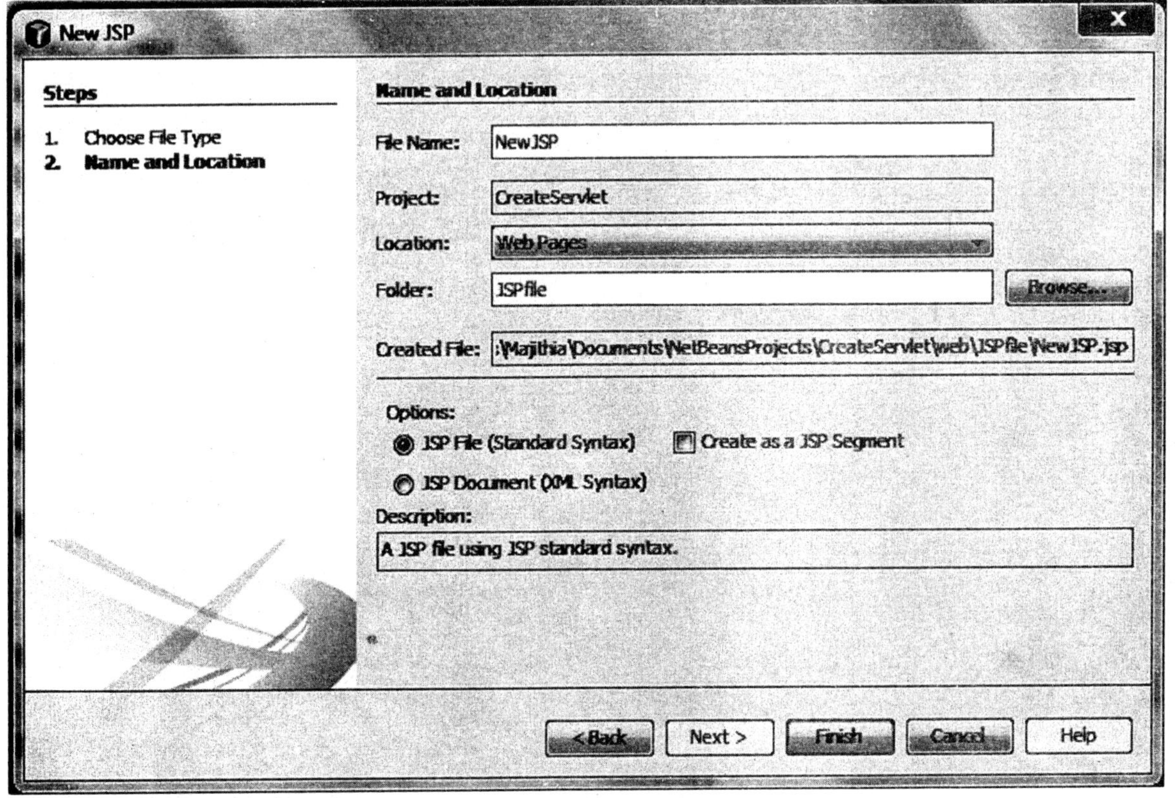


Step 4: You will see the JSP file named "**NewJSP.jsp**" with default skeleton.

```
<%--
    Document   : NewJSP
    Created on : Apr 7, 2014, 3:22:08 PM
    Author     : Majithia
--%>

<%@page contentType="text/html" pageEncoding="UTF-8"%>
<!DOCTYPE html>
<html>
    <head>
        <meta http-equiv="Content-Type" content="text/html; charset=UTF-8">
        <title>JSP Page</title>
    </head>
    <body>
        <h1>Hello World!</h1>
    </body>
</html>
```

Modify above JSP file as required and run the project.

## 4.11 Adding Deployment Descriptor (web.xml)

During a servlet page, if you did not check the checkbox that appears in front of *"Add information to deployment descriptor (web.xml)"* then the web.xml file will not be generated. Now in case if you required to manually add the deployment descriptor (web.xml) then follow the following steps.

Step 1: Open "**Project Pane**", right click on "**Source Package**". Select "**New**" and then "**Other..**"

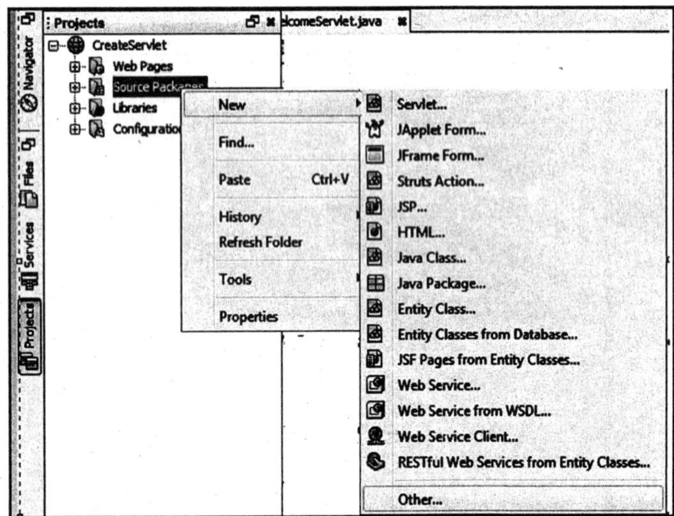


Step 2: A "New File" window will appear. Select "**Web**" from categories and select "**Standard Deployment Descriptor (web.xml)**" form the File Types. Then click "**Next**".

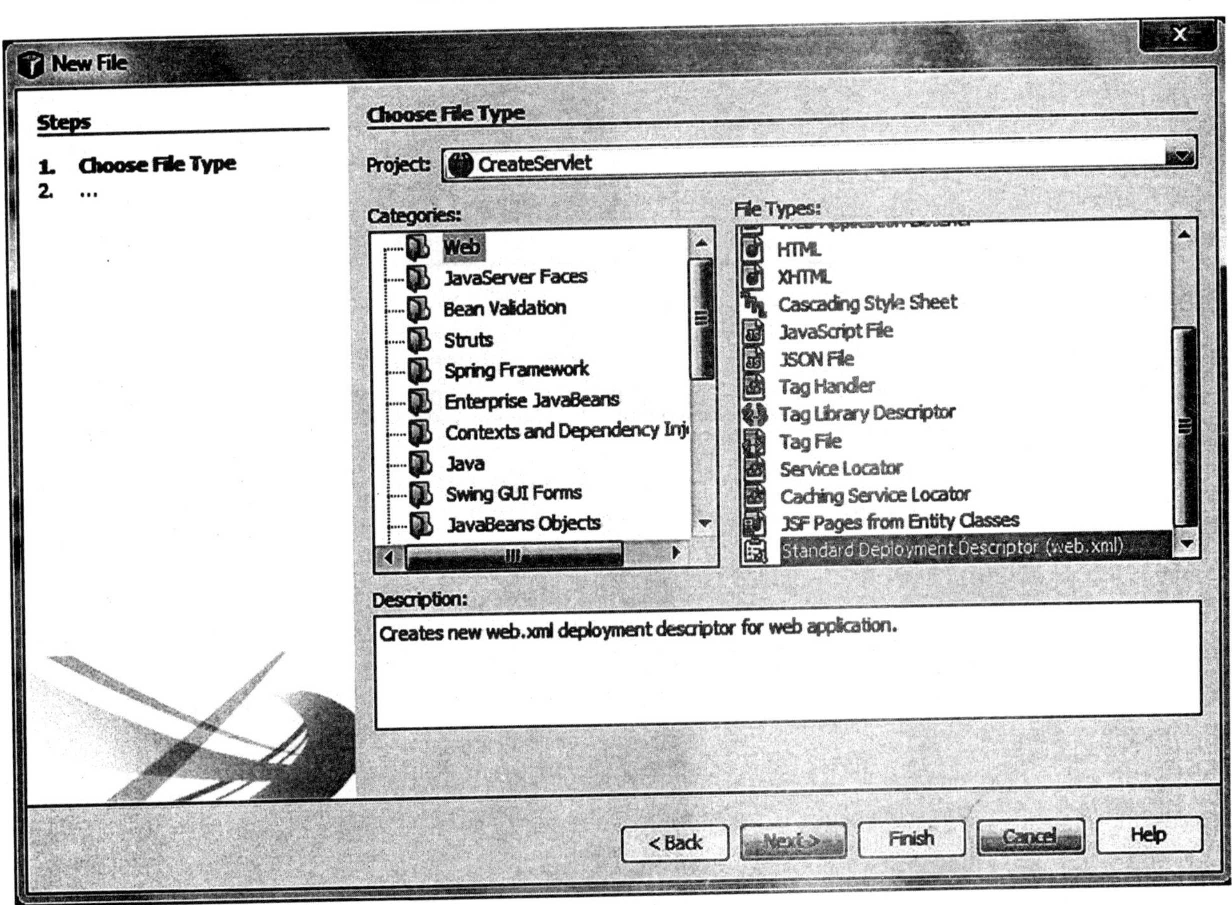


Step 3: A "New Standard Deployment Descriptor (web.xml)" window will appear. You cannot change the file name. If the web.xml is *already exists* in your project, then it will not be created. (See following diagram). If the web.xml *does not exists* in your project, then only "**Finish**" button will be enabled.

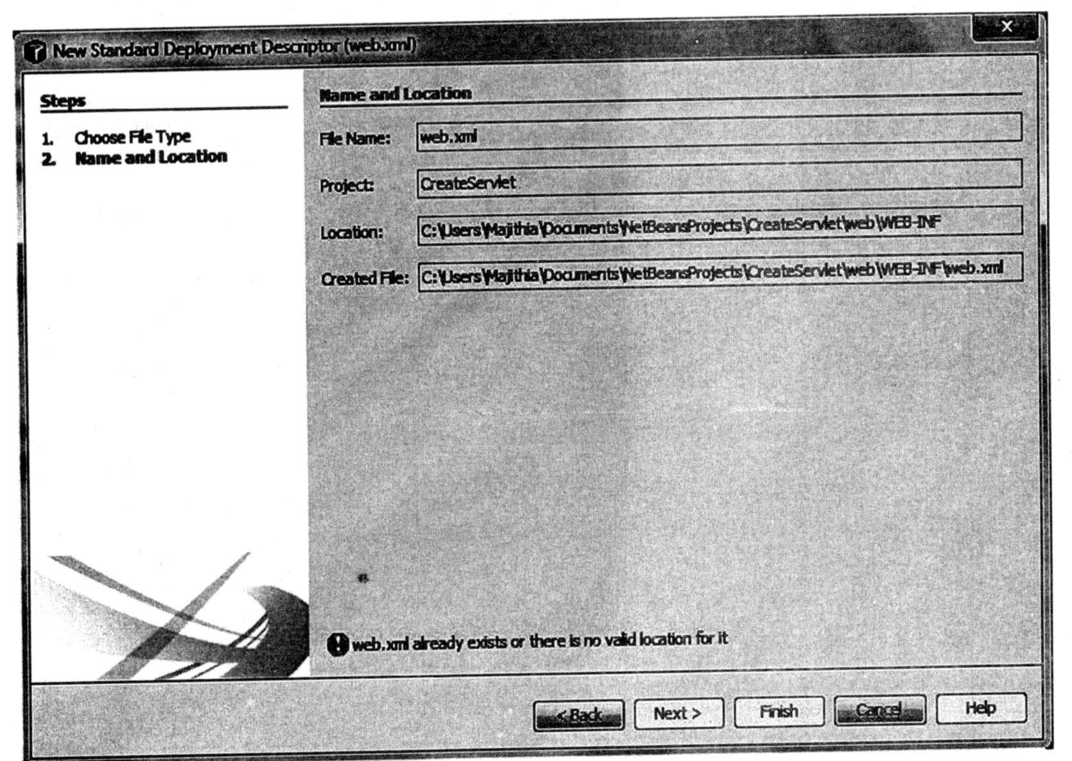


Step 4: Click "**Finish**" and you will see the **web.xml** will be added into your project with default skeleton.

## 4.12 Adding JSF Pages

The JSF pages are added into the project by two simple ways. First is to directly select **Java Server Faces** from the "**New Web Application**" window.

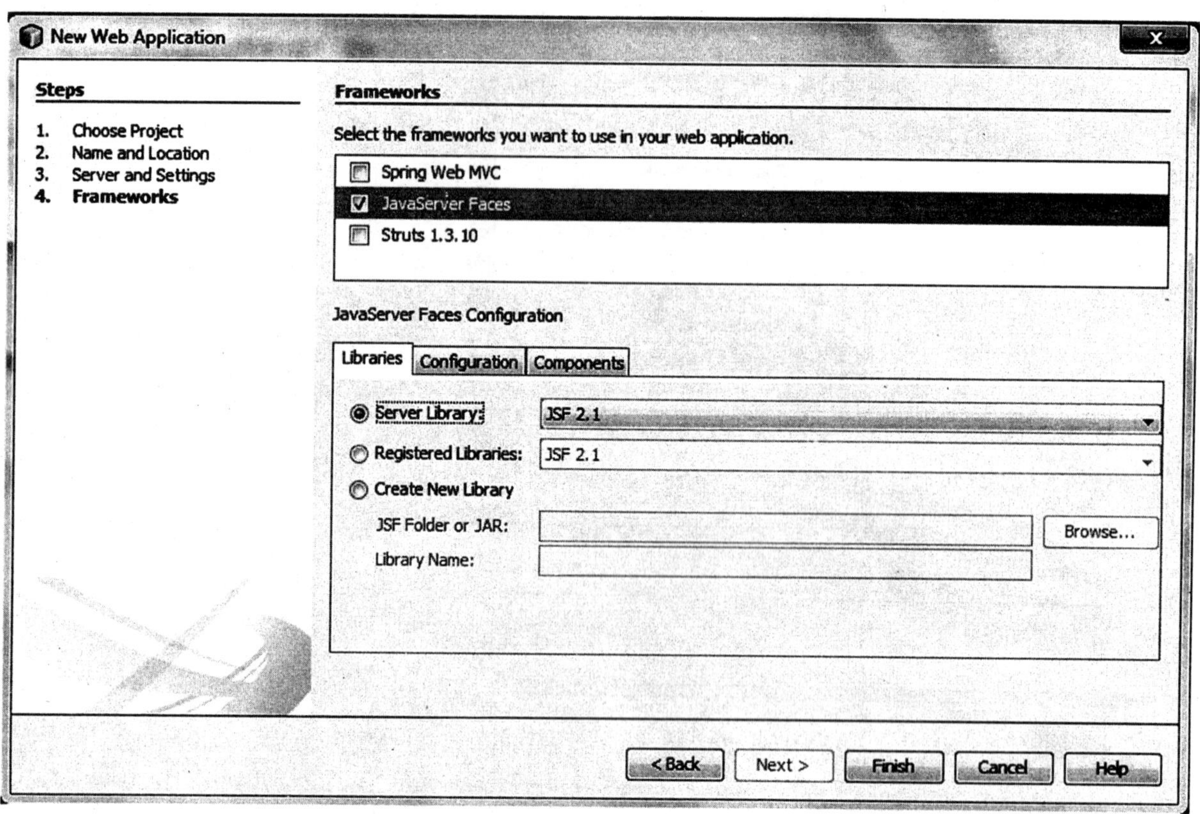


Then click "**Finish**" and you will see the JSF skeleton (see following step 4). Another way is shown in following steps.

<u>Step 1</u>: Open "Project Pane", right click on project → Select "**New**" → and click on "**other..**"

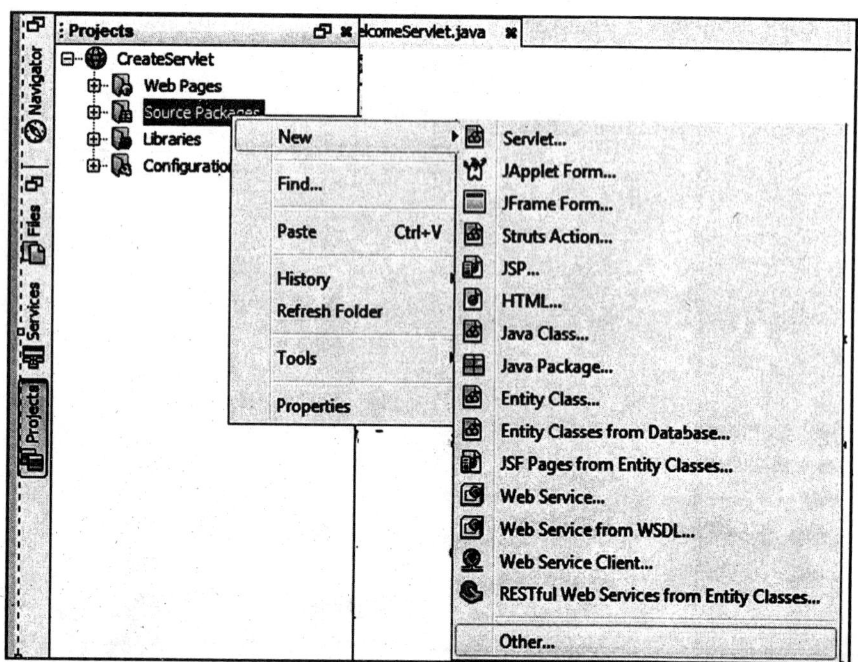


<u>Step 2</u>: Select "**Java Server Faces**" from *Categories* and select "**JSP page**" from *File Types*. Then click "**Next**"

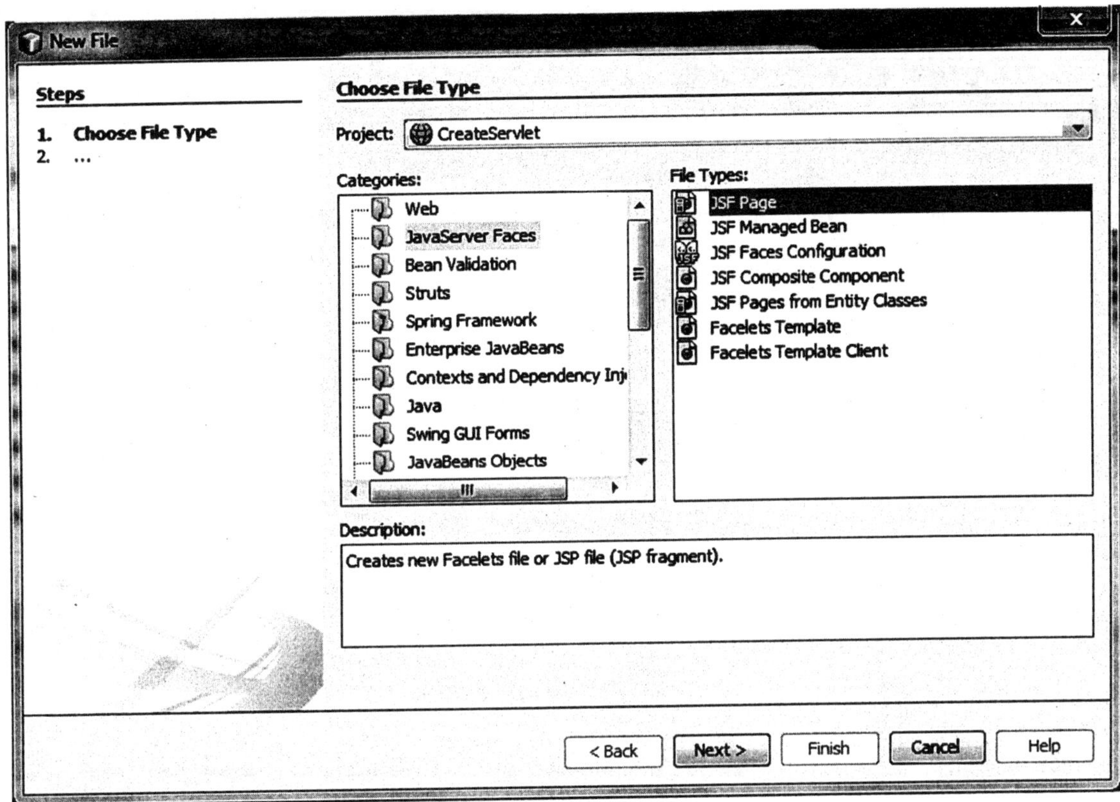


Step 3: A New JSP Page window will appear. Type *File name* and *Folder name*, select "**Facelets**" from the options. Then click "**Finish**".

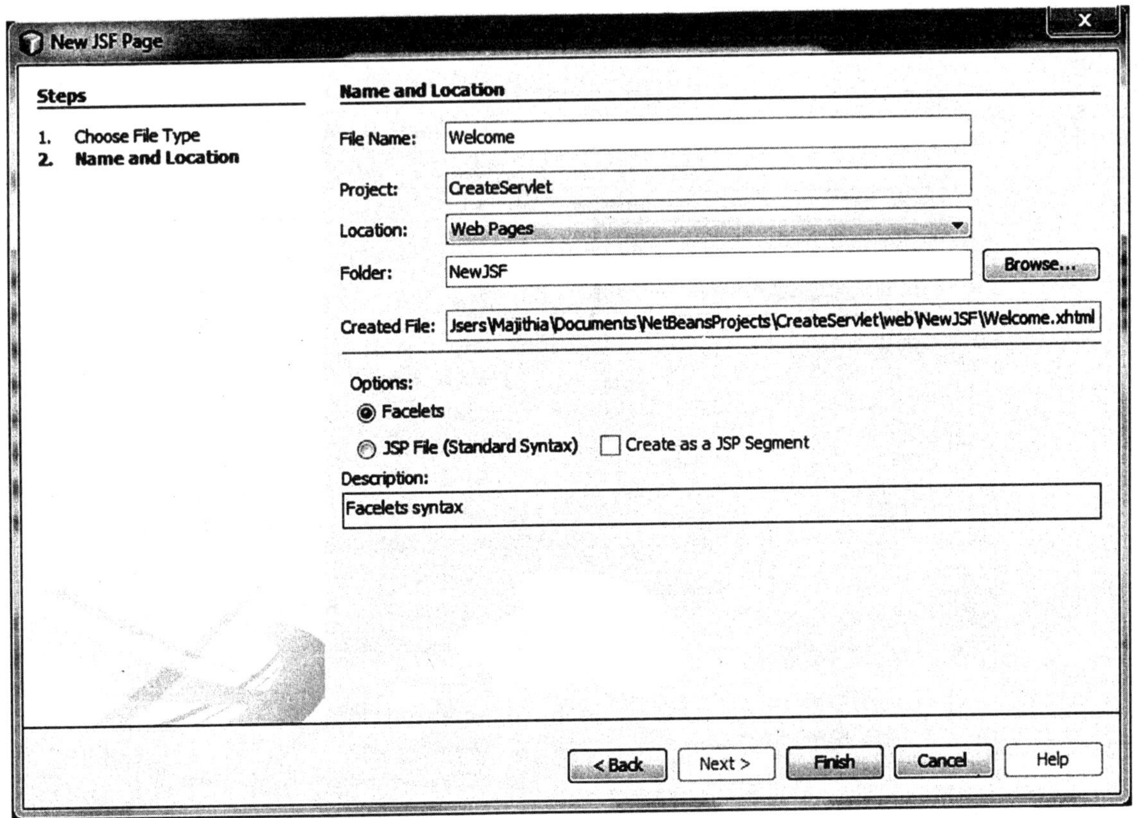


Step 4: After clicking "**Finish**" you will see the JSF page skeleton.

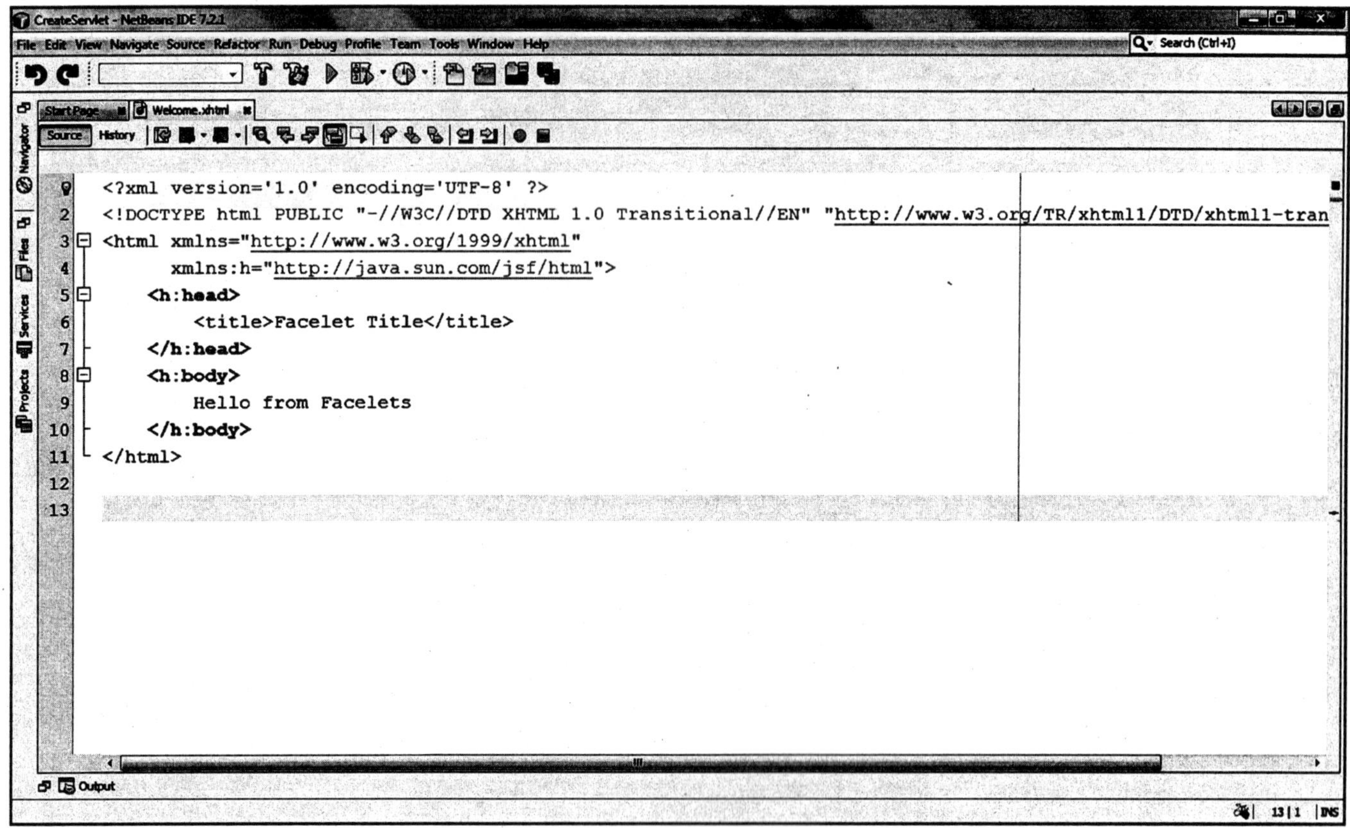


## 4.13 Adding JSF Managed Beans

Once the JSF pages are created, the next step is to create a managed bean. To create the managed bean, follow the following steps.

<u>Step 1</u>: Open "Project Pane", right click on project → Select "**New"** → and click on "**other..**"

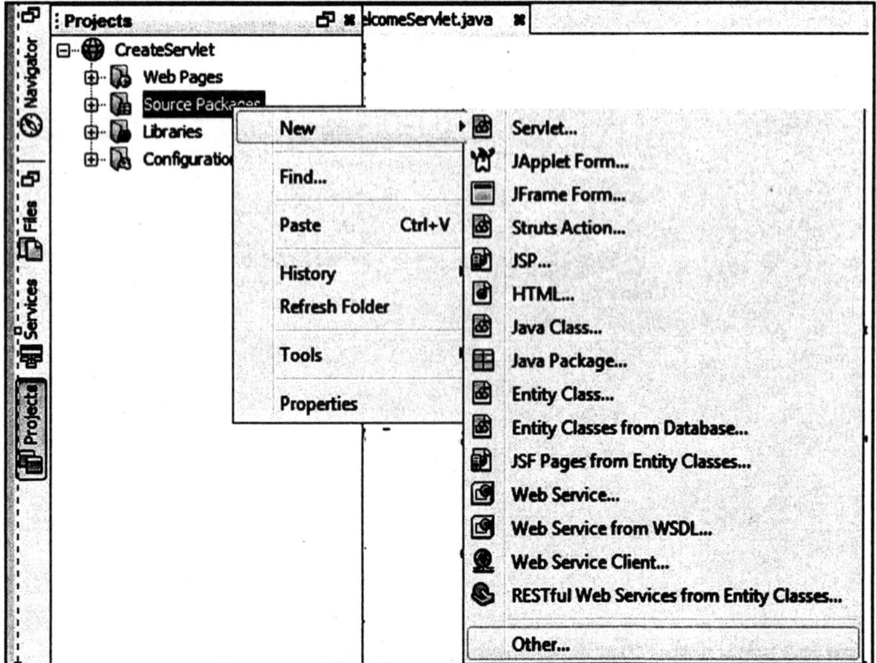


<u>Step 2</u>: Select "**Java Server Faces**" from *Categories* and select "**JSP Managed Bean**" from *File Types*. Then click "**Next**"

New File
Steps
1. Choose File Type
2. ...
Choose File Type
Project: CreateServlet
Categories:
Web
JavaServer Faces
Bean Validation
Struts
Spring Framework
Enterprise JavaBeans
Contexts and Dependency Inj
Java
Swing GUI Forms
JavaBeans Objects
File Types:
JSF Page
JSF Managed Bean
JSF Faces Configuration
JSF Composite Component
JSF Pages from Entity Classes
Facelets Template
Facelets Template Client
Description:
Creates a new managed bean class.
< Back
Next >
Finish
Cancel
Help

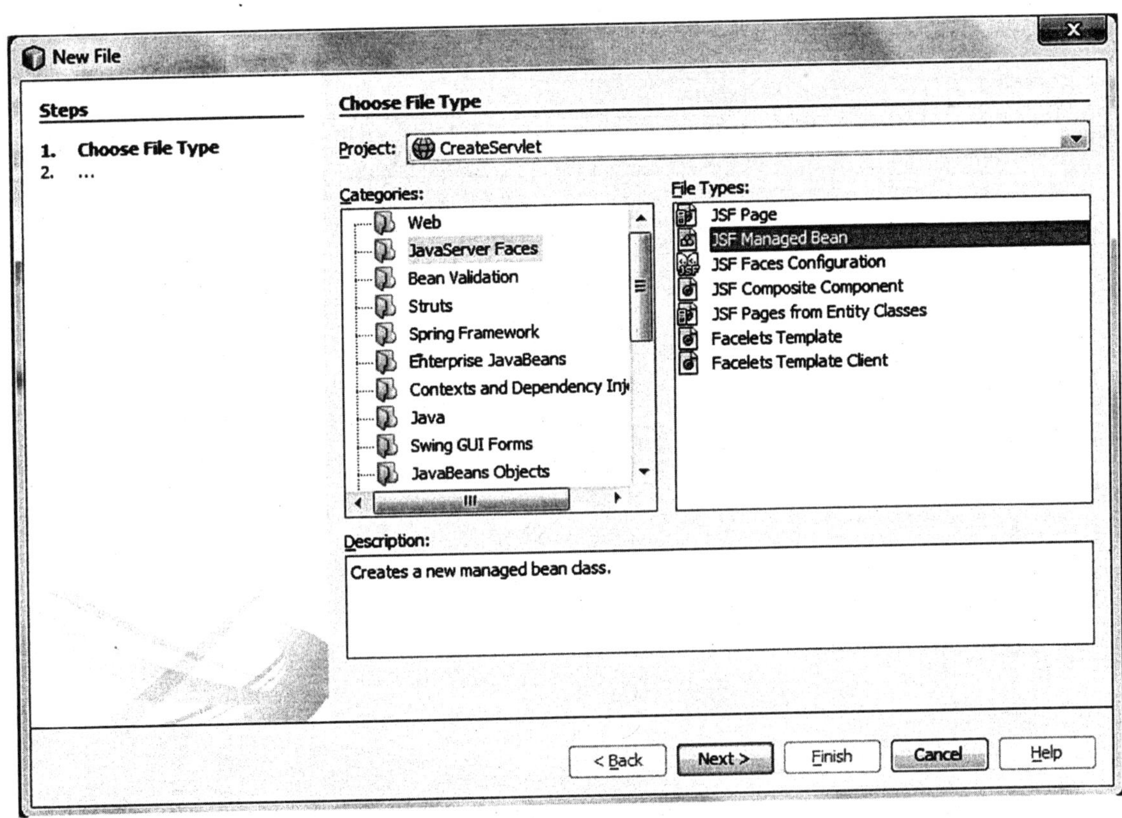

Step 3: You will see a "**New JSF Managed Bean**" window. Provide class name and package name as required then click "**Finish**".

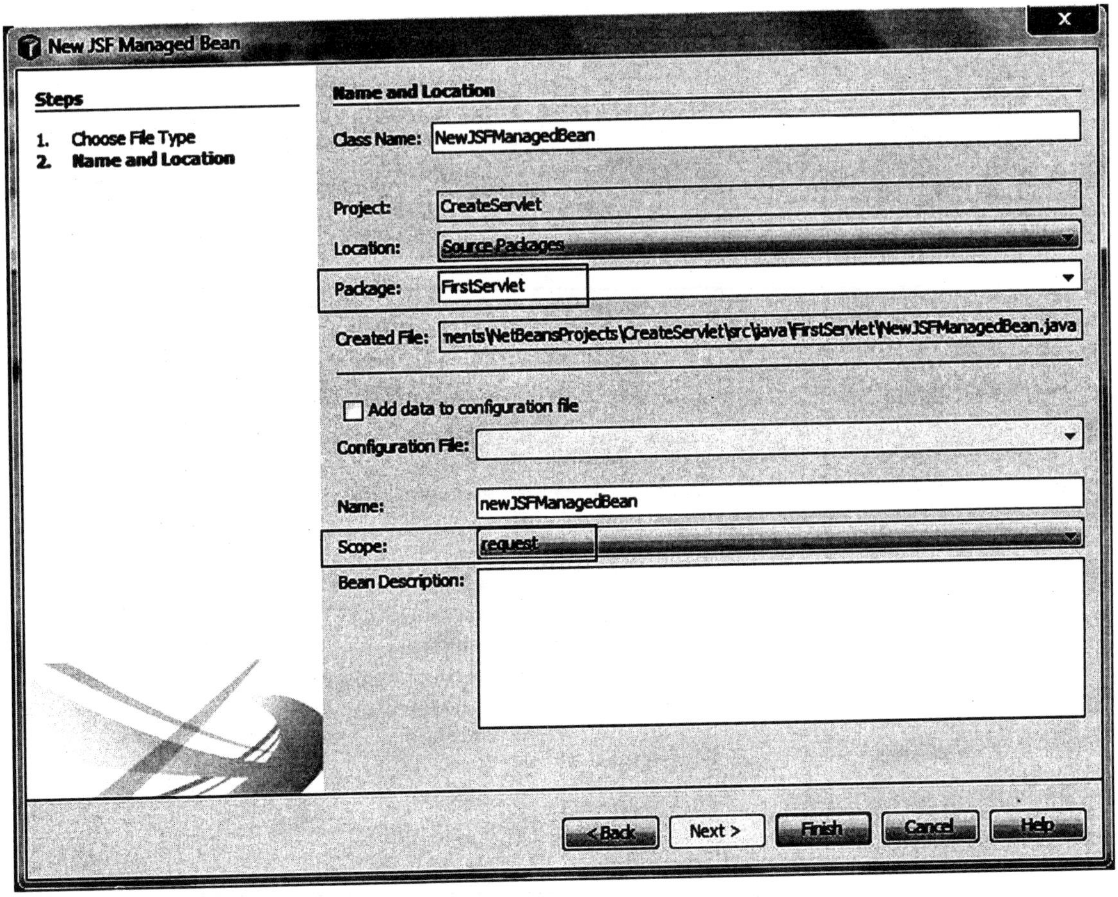

New JSF Managed Bean
Steps
1. Choose File Type
2. Name and Location
Name and Location
Class Name: NewJSFManagedBean
Project: CreateServlet
Location: Source Packages
Package: FirstServlet
Created File: ments\NetBeansProjects\CreateServlet\src\java\FirstServlet\NewJSFManagedBean.java
Add data to configuration file
Configuration File:
Name: newJSFManagedBean
Scope: request
Bean Description:
< Back
Next >
Finish
Cancel
Help

Step 4: You will see a class **NewJSFManagedBean** and its skeleton.

```java
import javax.faces.bean.RequestScoped;

/**
 *
 * @author Majithia
 */

@ManagedBean
@RequestScoped
public class NewJSFManagedBean
{
    /**
     * Creates a new instance of NewJSFManagedBean
     */
    public NewJSFManagedBean()
    {

    }
}
```

## 4.14 Adding Enterprise JavaBean

The JavaBean are reusable files of any project that can be attached to any web application or stand alone application. Here are the steps to create Enterprise JavaBean.

Step 1: create a web application.

Step 2: Open "Project Pane", right click on project → Select "**New**" → and click on "**other..**"

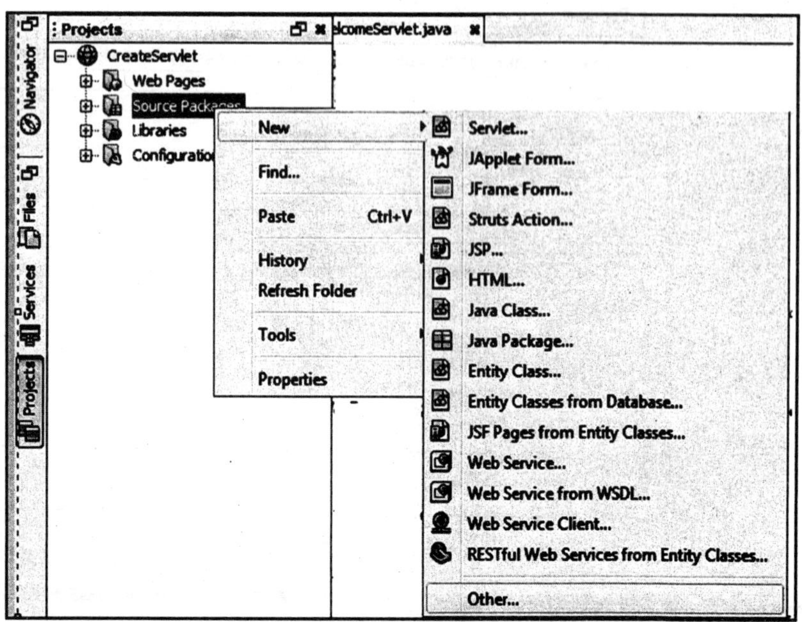


Step 3: Select "**Enterprise JavaBeans**" from *Categories* and select "**Session Bean**" from *File Types*. Then click "**Next**".

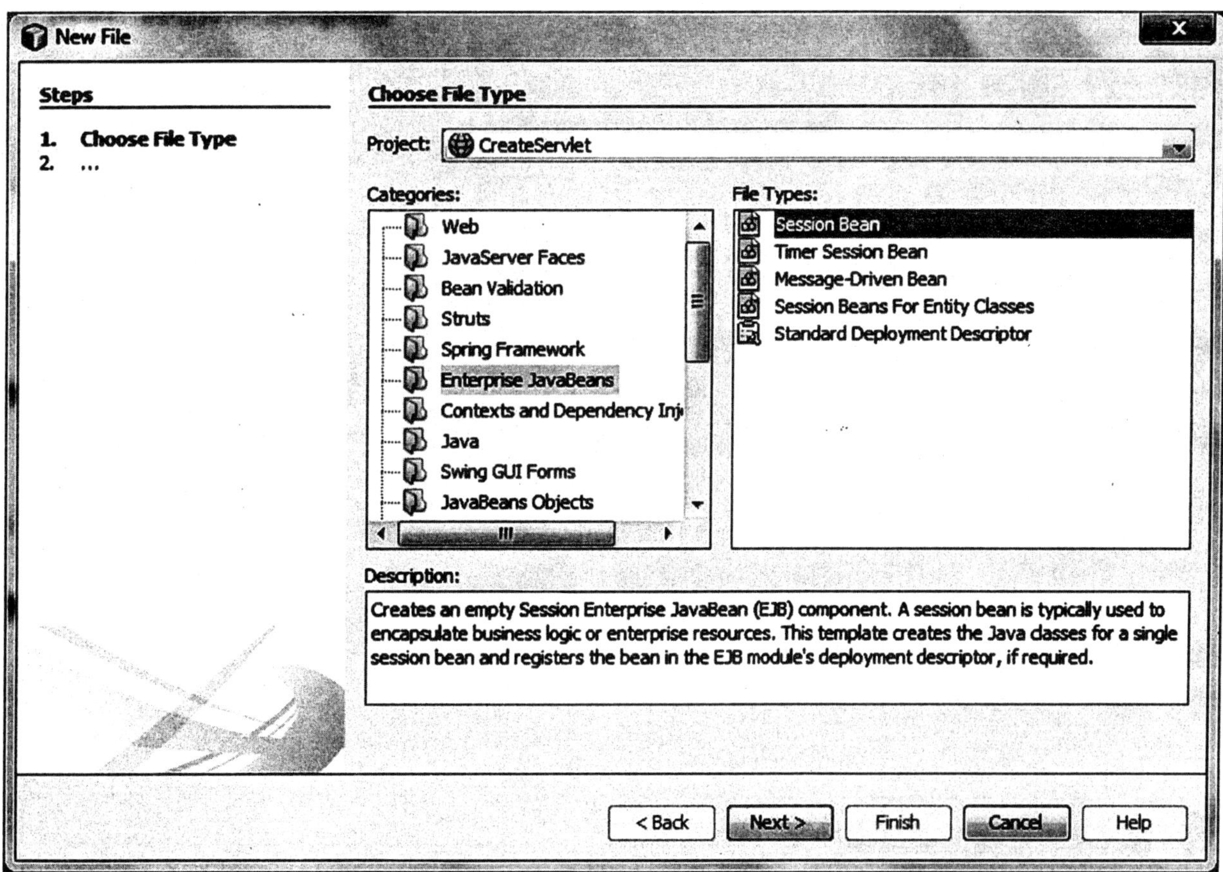


Step 4: A "**New Session Bean**" window will appear. Provide *EJB Name* and *Package name*. Select required *Session Type* and *Interface*. Then click "**Finish**".

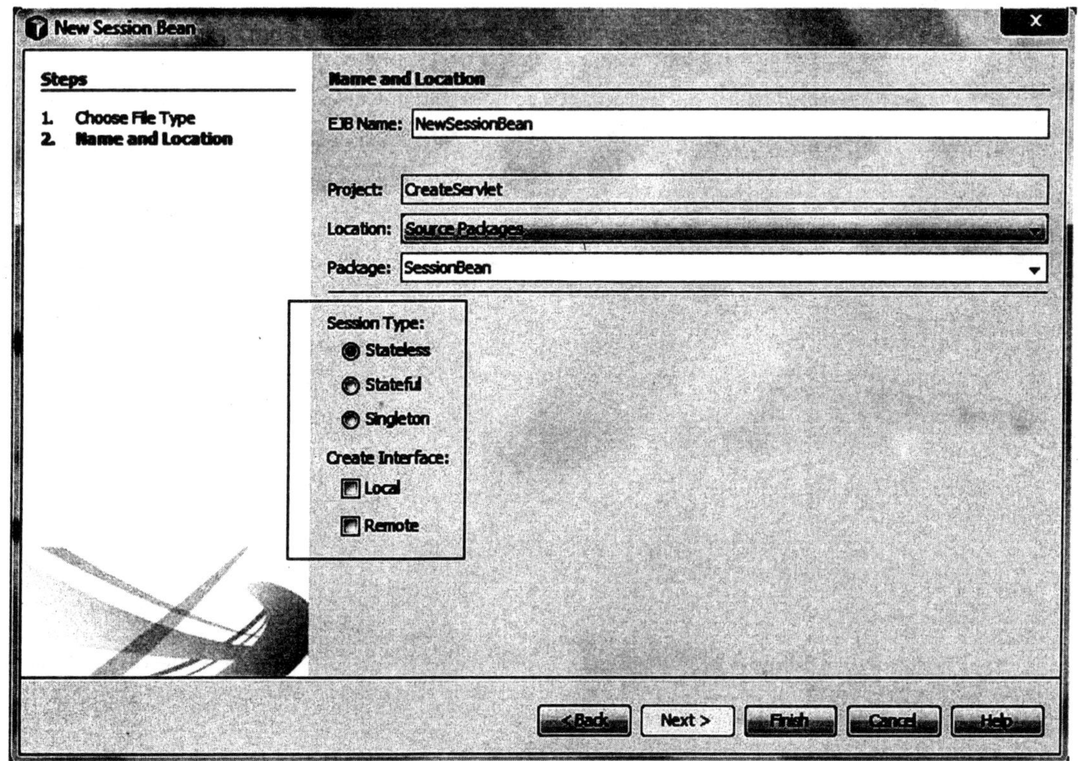


Step 5: You will see a stateless bean file **NewSessionBean.java.**

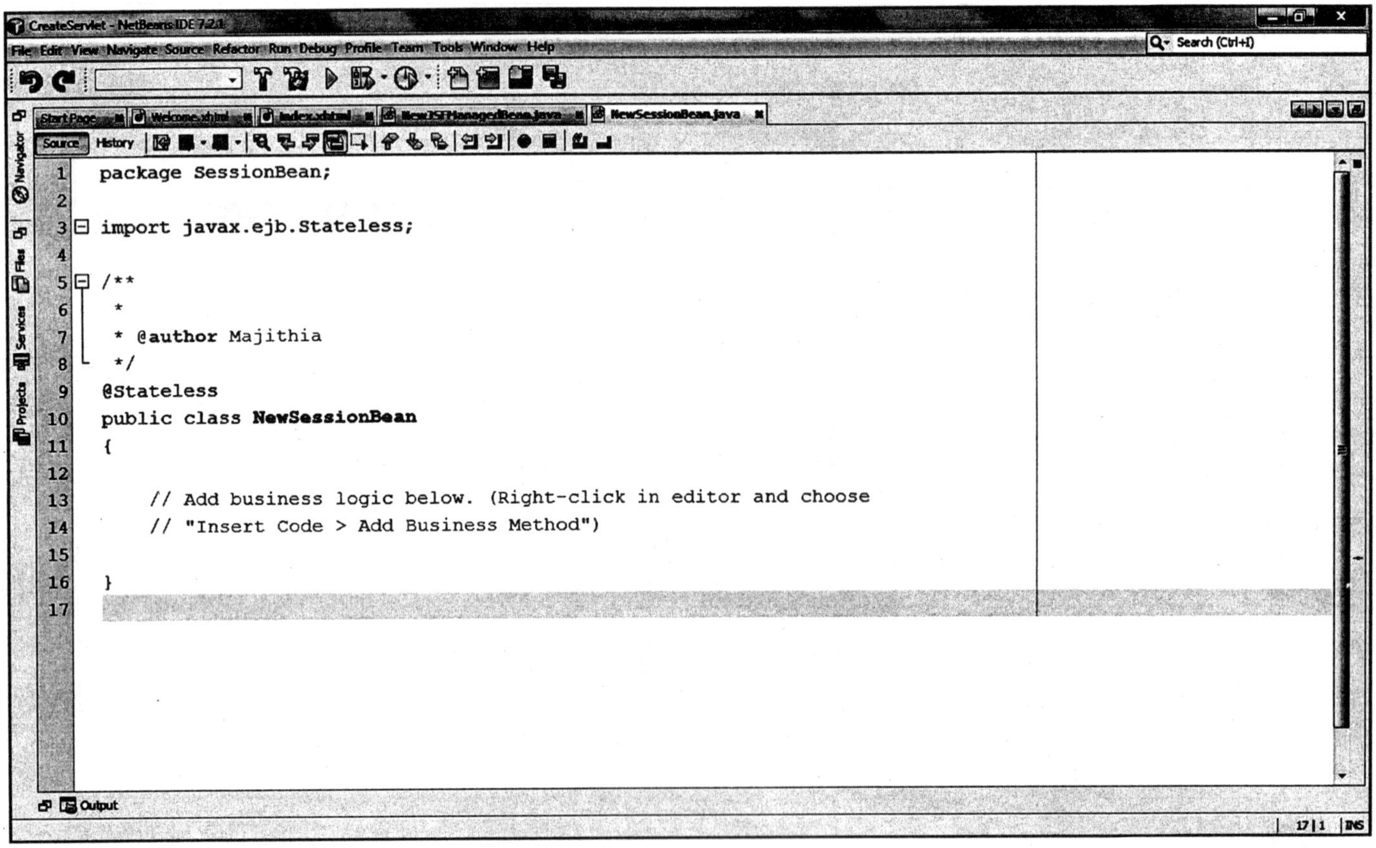
CreateServlet - NetBeans IDE 7.2.1
File Edit View Navigate Source Refactor Run Debug Profile Team Tools Window Help
Search (Ctrl+I)
Start Page
Welcome.xhtml
index.xhtml
NewJSFManagedBean.java
NewSessionBean.java
Source
History
package SessionBean;
import javax.ejb.Stateless;
/**
*
* @author Majithia
*/
@Stateless
public class NewSessionBean
{
// Add business logic below. (Right-click in editor and choose
// "Insert Code > Add Business Method")
}
Output
17 | 1
INS

## 4.15 Adding Hibernating Configuration File

Hibernating is a more advanced content to deal with databases and resource mapping. Here are the steps to create hibernate configuration file.

**Step 1**: create a web application.

**Step 2:** Open "Project Pane", right click on "Libraries" and select "**Add JAR/Folder**". Search and add following JAR files into the project.

- hibernate3.jar
- antlr-2.7.6.jar
- jta-1.1.jar
- javassist-3.9.0.GA.jar
- commons-collections-3.1.jar
- dom4j.jar
- slf4j-api-1.5.8.jar
- cglib-2.2.jar
- log4j.jar

According to your NetBeans version, may be the jar file version is different. After adding the required JAR files, it will appear under "**Libraries**" root in "**Project Pane**"

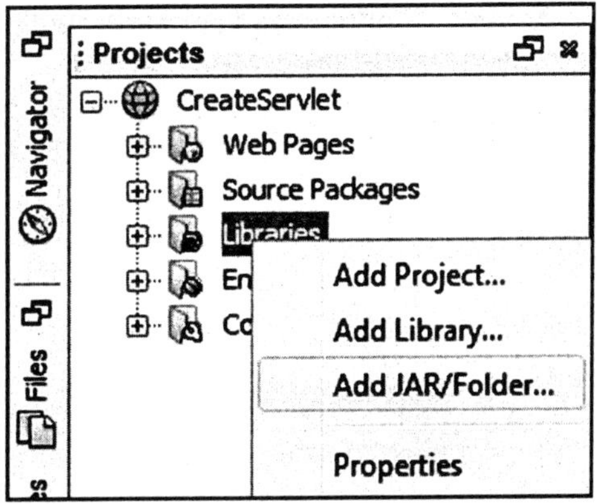


**Step 3**: Now open "**Project Pane**", right click on project → Select "**New**" → and click on "**other**"

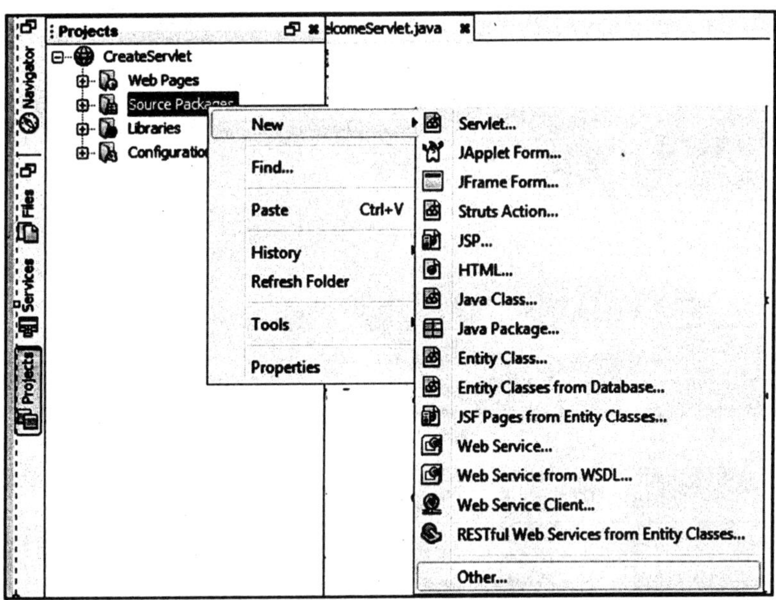


**Step 4**: Select "**Hibernate**" from *Categories* and select "**Hibernate Configuration Wizard**" from *File Types*. Then click "**Next**"

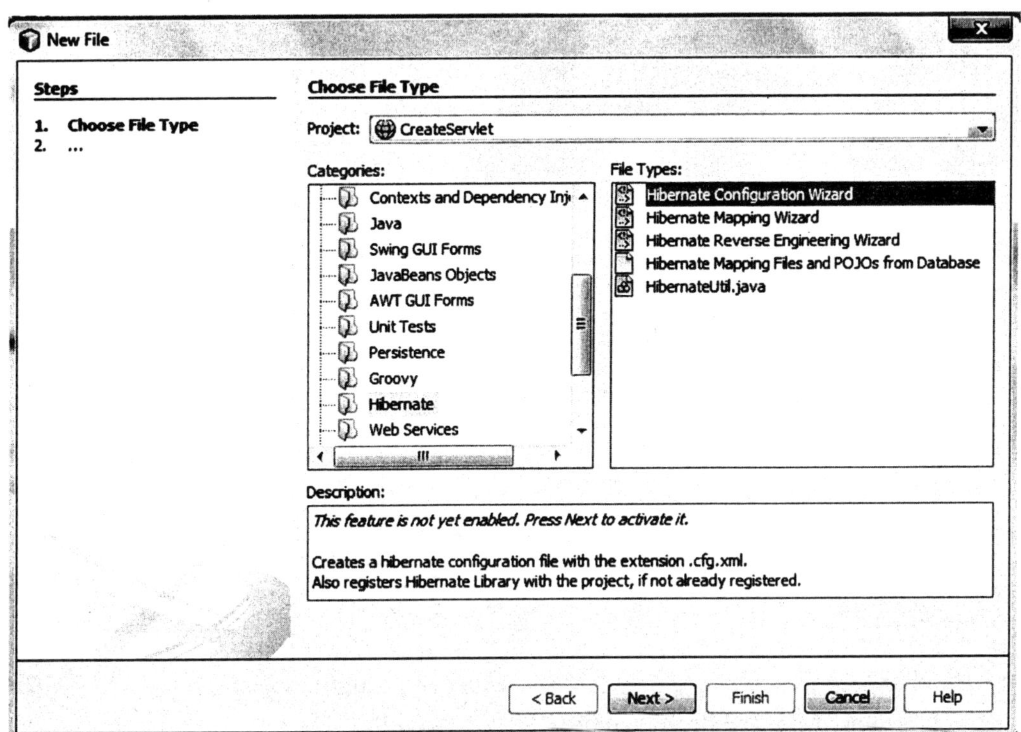

**Step 5**: A "**New Hibernate Configuration Wizard**" window will appear. Provide *File Name* and click "**Next**".

New Hibernate Configuration Wizard
Steps
1. Name and Location
2. Select Data Source
Name and Location
File Name: hibernate.cfg
Project: CreateServlet
Folder: src\java
Browse...
Created File: :\Users\Majithia\Documents\NetBeansProjects\CreateServlet\src\java\hibernate.cfg.xml
< Back
Next >
Finish
Cancel
Help

**Step 6**: Select *Database Connection* and *Database Dialect*. Then click "**Next**".

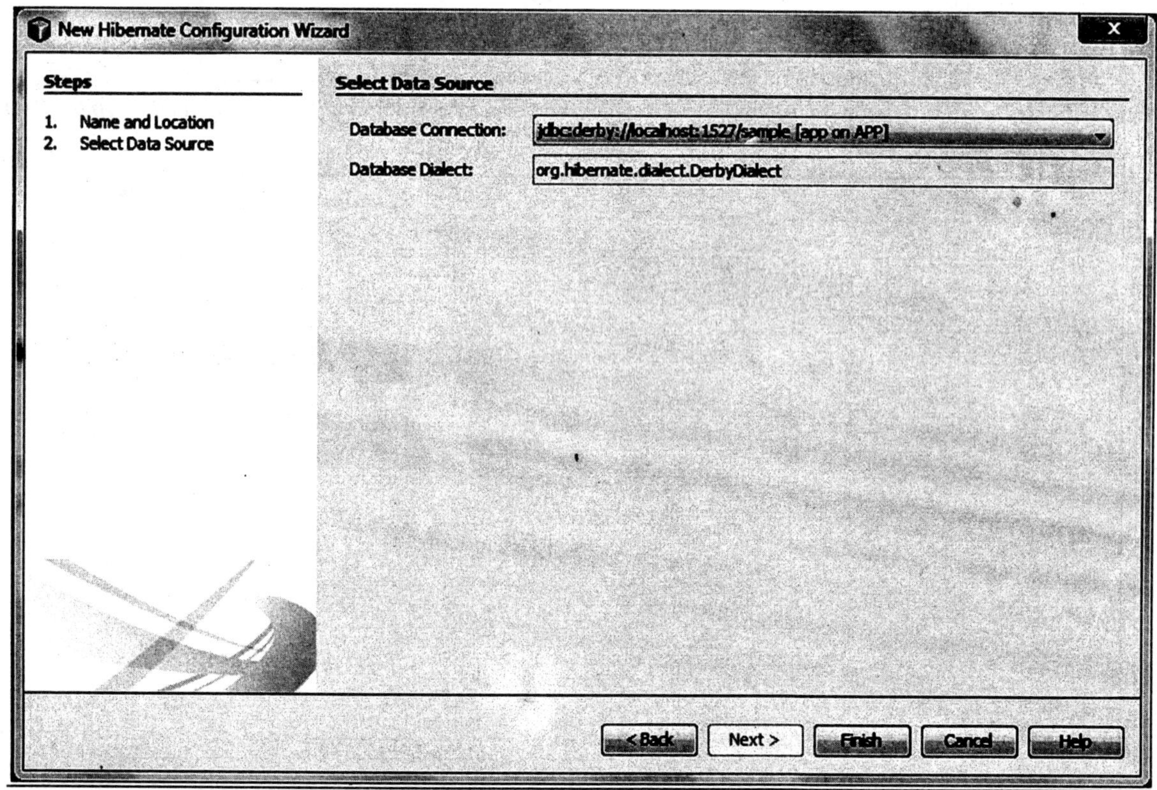


Step 7: Select "**New Database Connection**" from *Database Connection* dropdown list. You will see a "**New Connection Wizard**" window. Select "**Driver**" from the dropdown list.

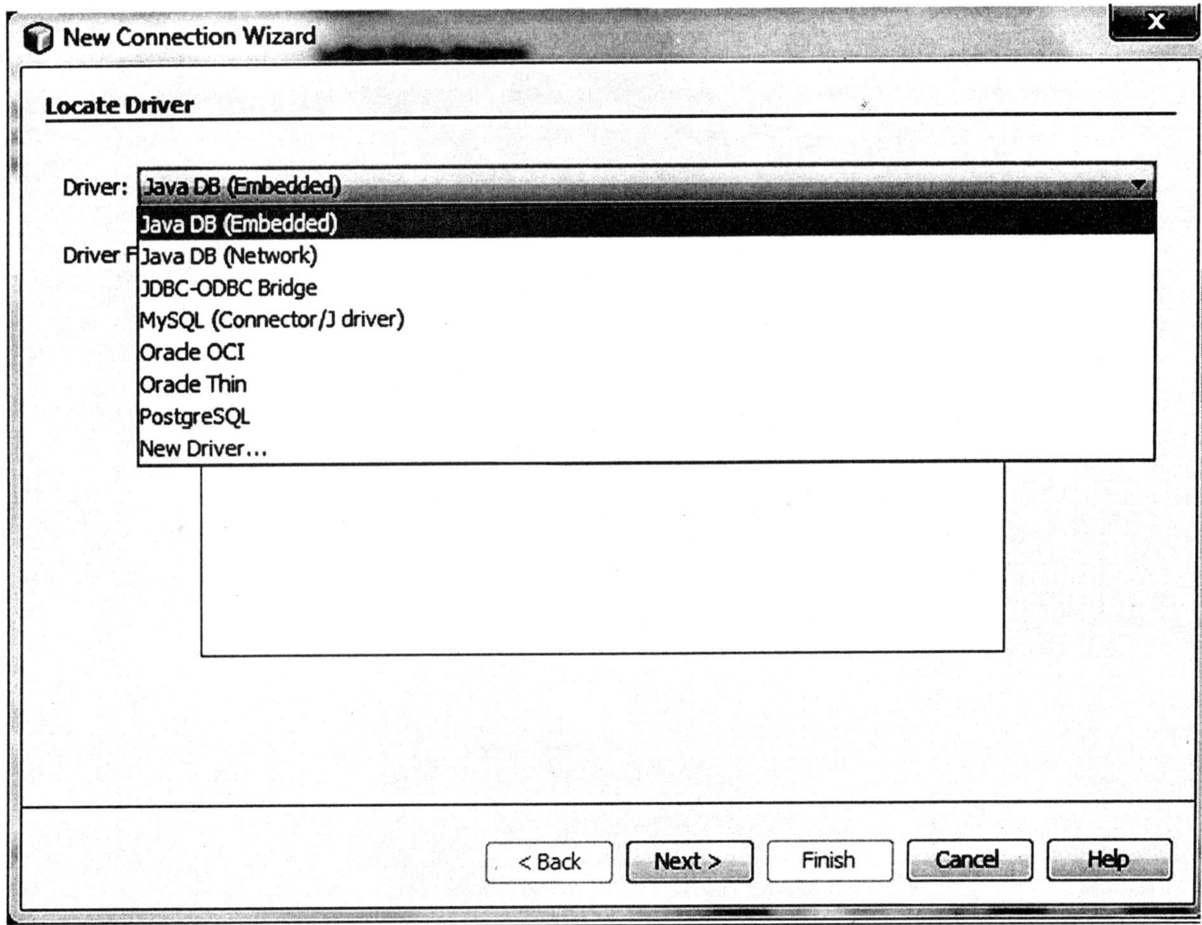


Step 8: A "New Connection Wizard" window will appear, Provide required fields to **customize connection**. Then click "**Finish**"

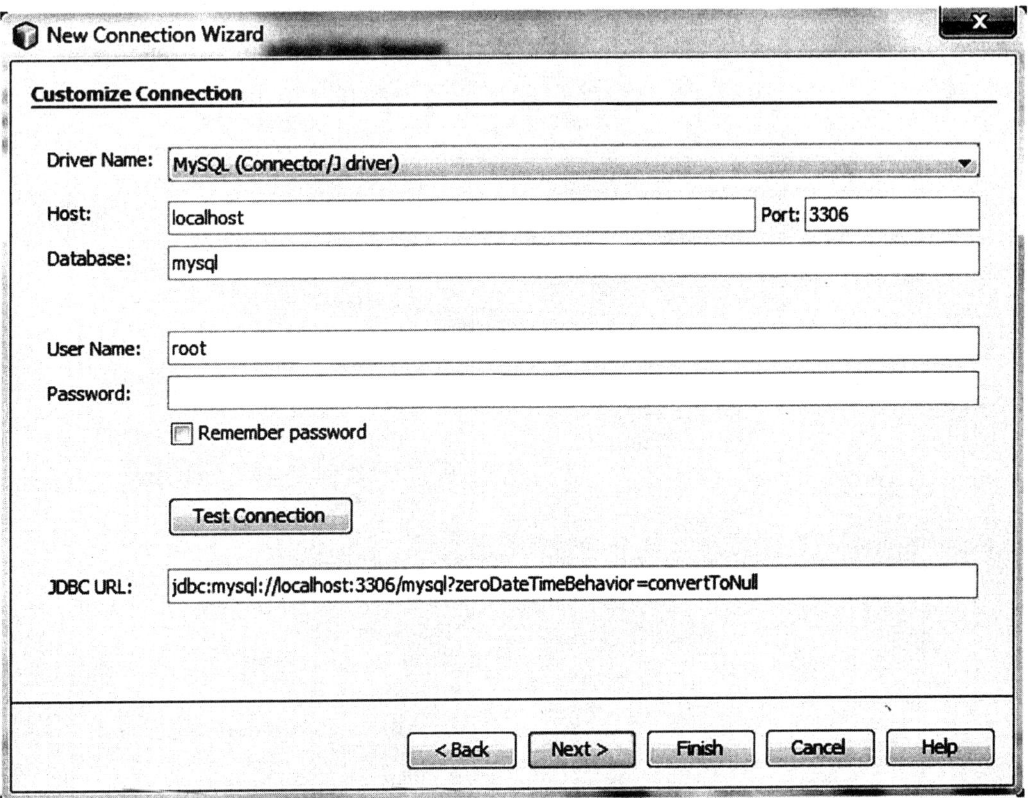

Step 9: Click "**Finish**" to complete the wizard and you will see the "**hibernate.cfg.xml**" file

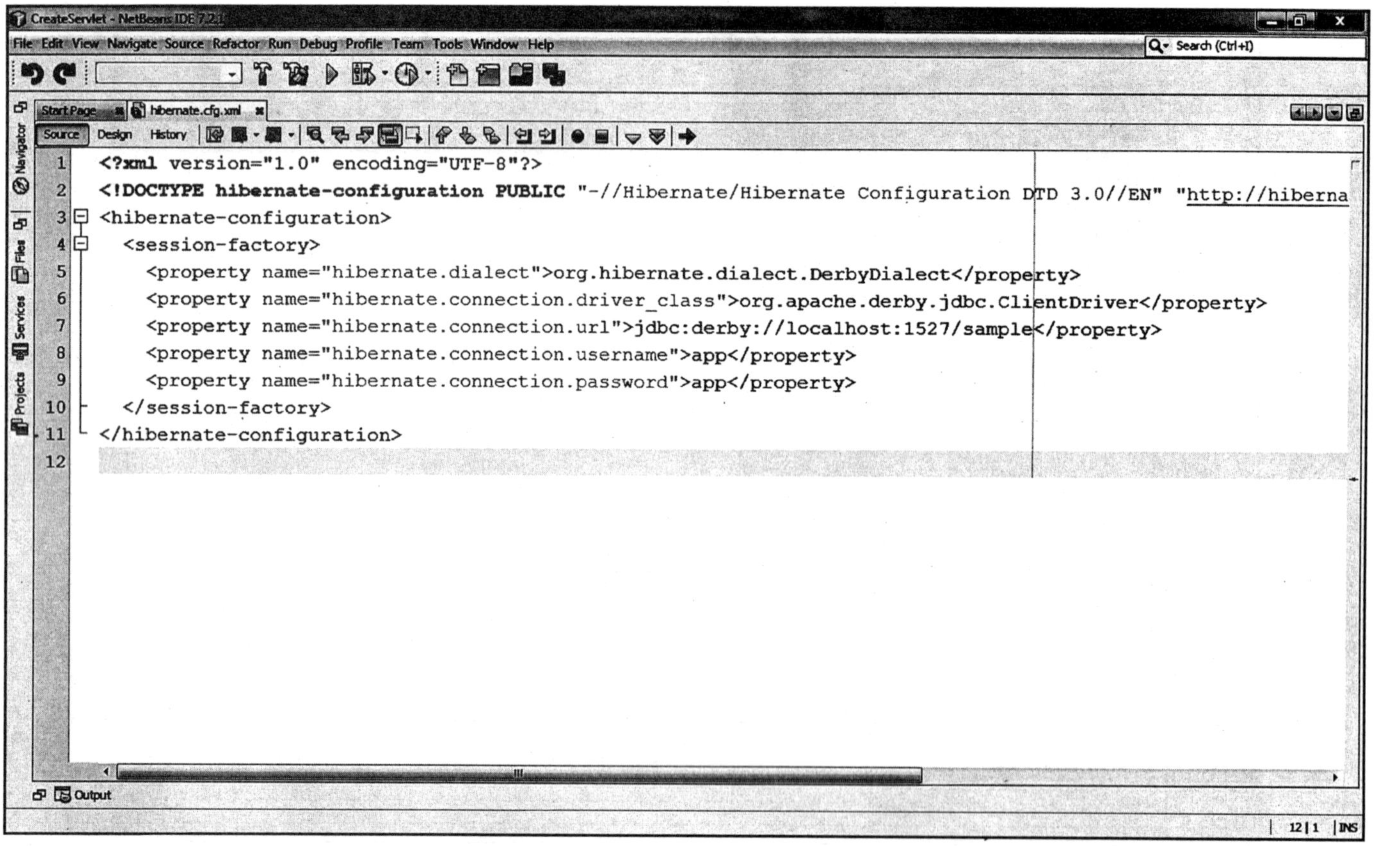

CreateServlet - NetBeans IDE 7.2.1

File Edit View Navigate Source Refactor Run Debug Profile Team Tools Window Help

Start Page | hibernate.cfg.xml

Source Design History

```
<?xml version="1.0" encoding="UTF-8"?>
<!DOCTYPE hibernate-configuration PUBLIC "-//Hibernate/Hibernate Configuration DTD 3.0//EN" "http://hiberna
<hibernate-configuration>
  <session-factory>
    <property name="hibernate.dialect">org.hibernate.dialect.DerbyDialect</property>
    <property name="hibernate.connection.driver_class">org.apache.derby.jdbc.ClientDriver</property>
    <property name="hibernate.connection.url">jdbc:derby://localhost:1527/sample</property>
    <property name="hibernate.connection.username">app</property>
    <property name="hibernate.connection.password">app</property>
  </session-factory>
</hibernate-configuration>
```

Output

## 4.16 Adding Hibernate Mapping File

After adding hibernate configuration file, you should add hibernate mapping file to map the objects with database. To add hibernate mapping file, follow the following steps.

**Step 1**: Open "**Project Pane**", right click on project → Select "**New**" → and click on "**other**"

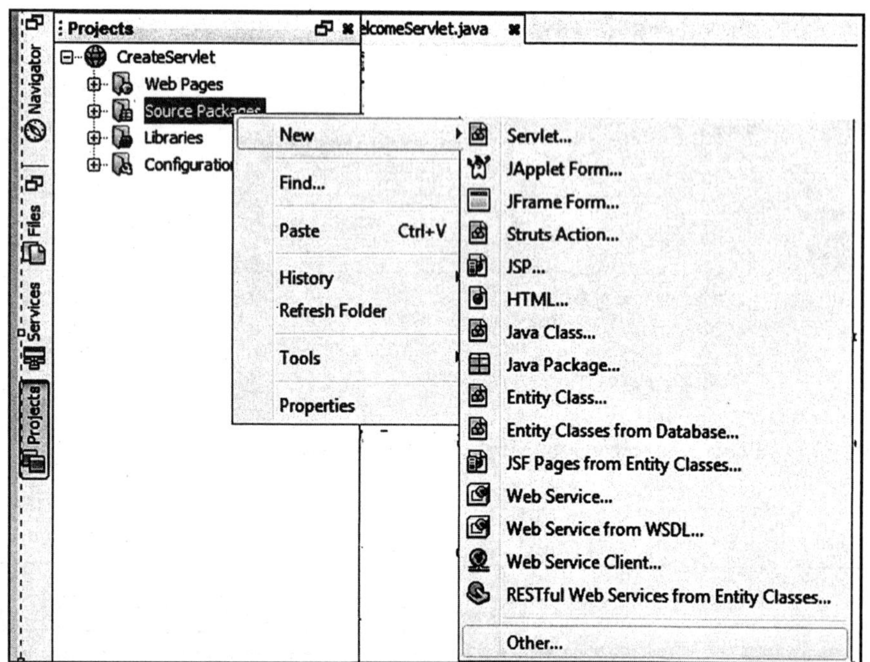

**Step 2**: Select "**Hibernate**" from *Categories* and select "**Hibernate Mapping Wizard**" from *File Types*. Then click "**Next**"

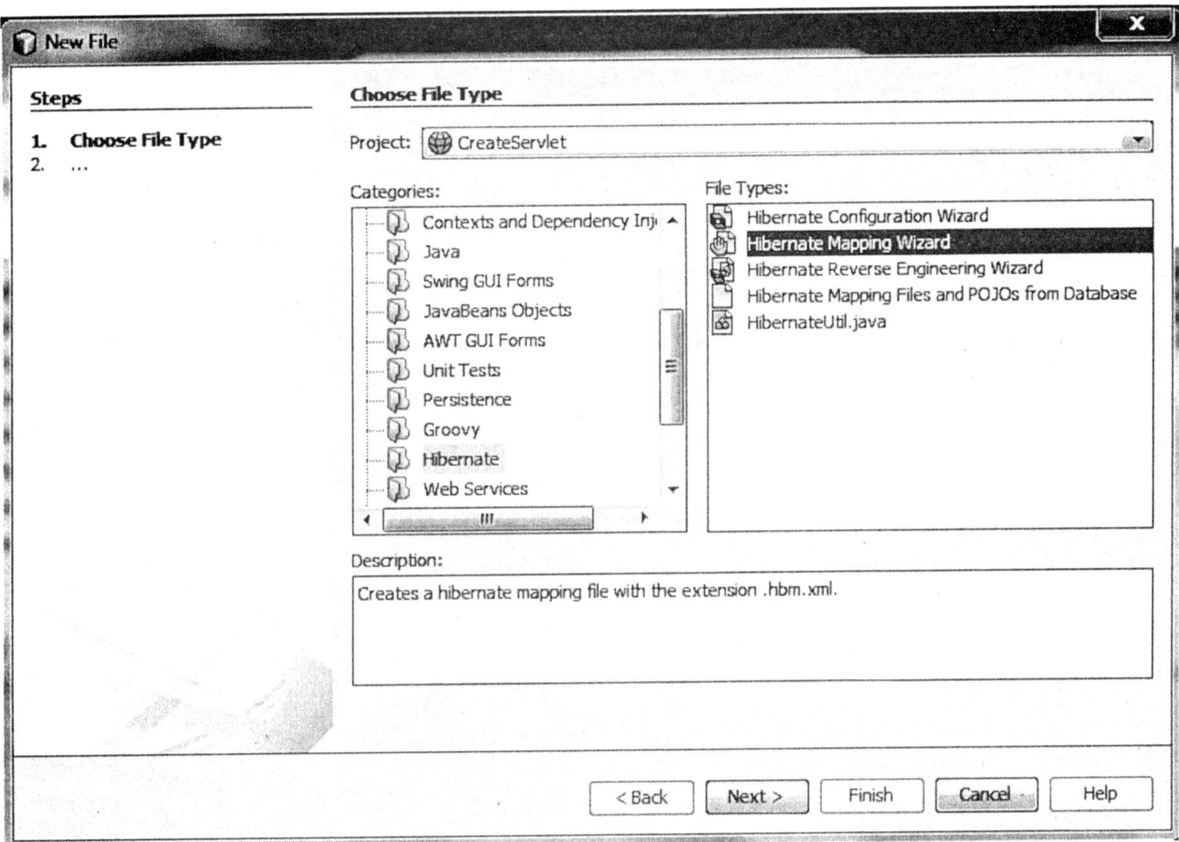


**Step 3:** Provide Hibernate Mapping file name and click "**Next**".

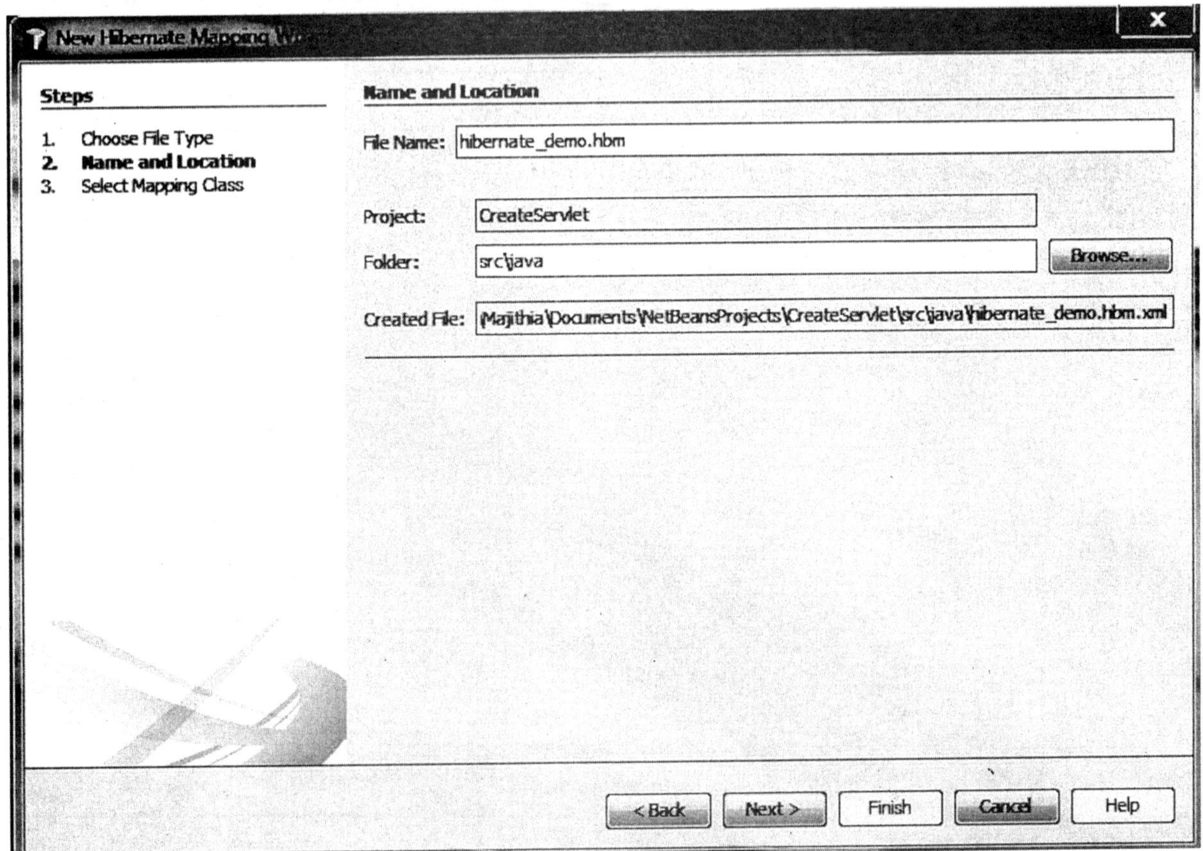

**Step 4:** Provide class to map with (Generally it is a bean or POJO class) and select database table name. Then click "**Finish**"

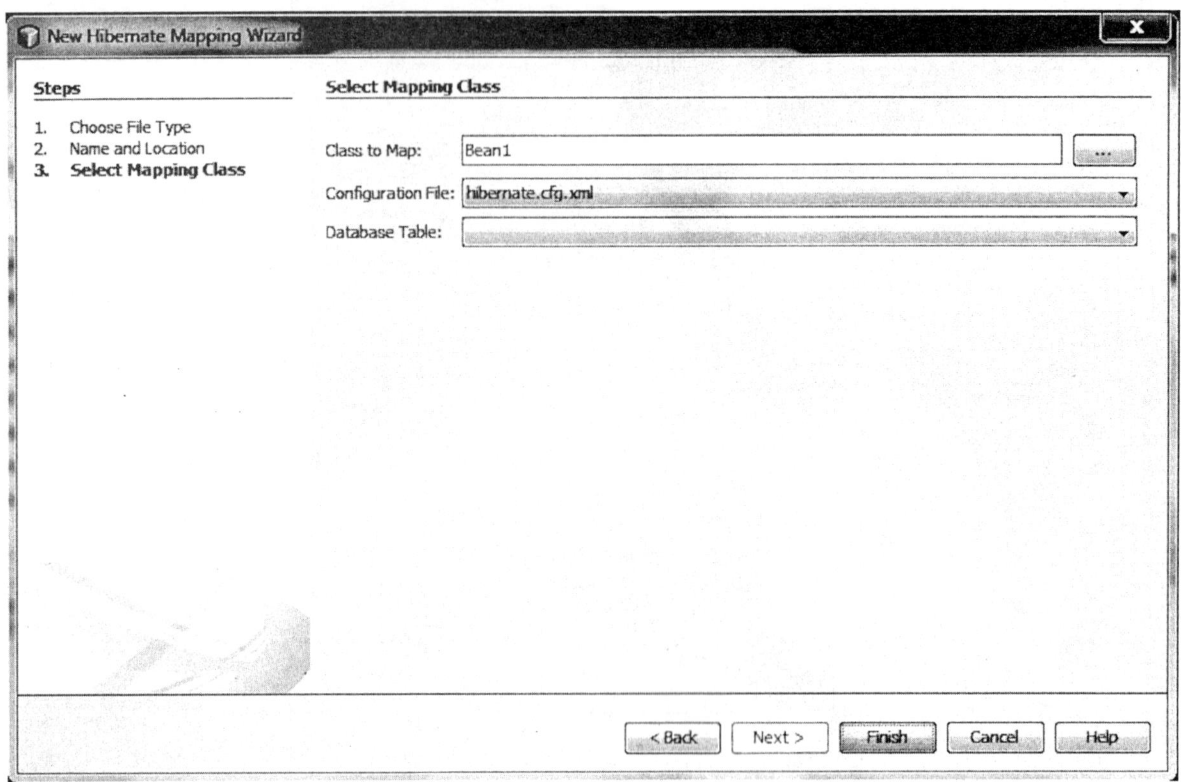


**Step 5:** You will get the Hibernate Mapping file with default skeleton as shown in following screenshot.

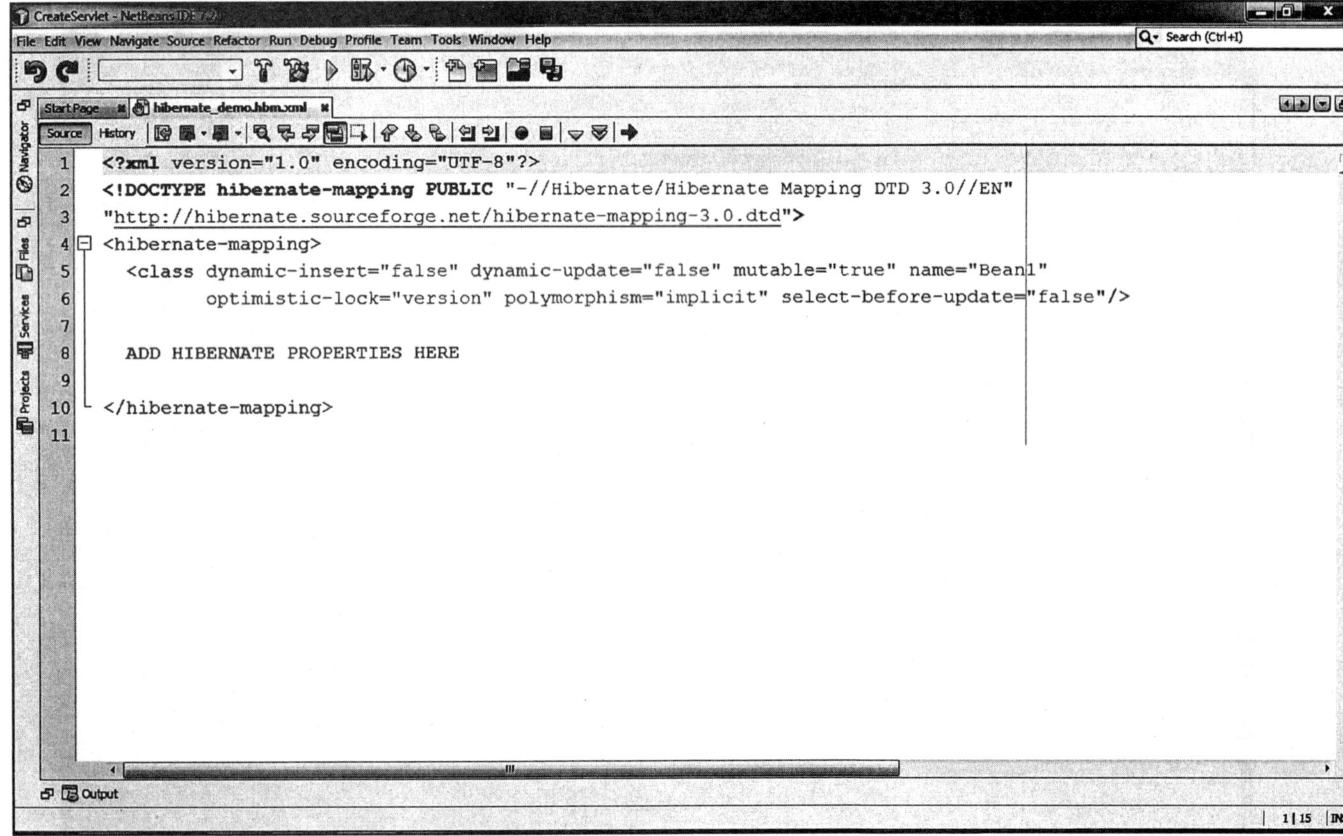

## 4.17 Getting Help in NetBeans

At any instance in NetBeans IDE, you can get help by following these steps.

**Step 1:** Go to "**Help**" menu -> select "**Help Contents**".

CreateServlet - NetBeans IDE 7.2.1
File Edit View Navigate Source Refactor Run Debug Profile Team Tools Window Help
Start Page
web.xml
Source
General
Servlets
Filters
Pages
References
Navigator
Files
Help Contents
Online Docs and Support
Keyboard Shortcuts Card
Report Issue...
Javadoc Index Search Shift+F1
Javadoc References
Check for Updates
Start Page
About

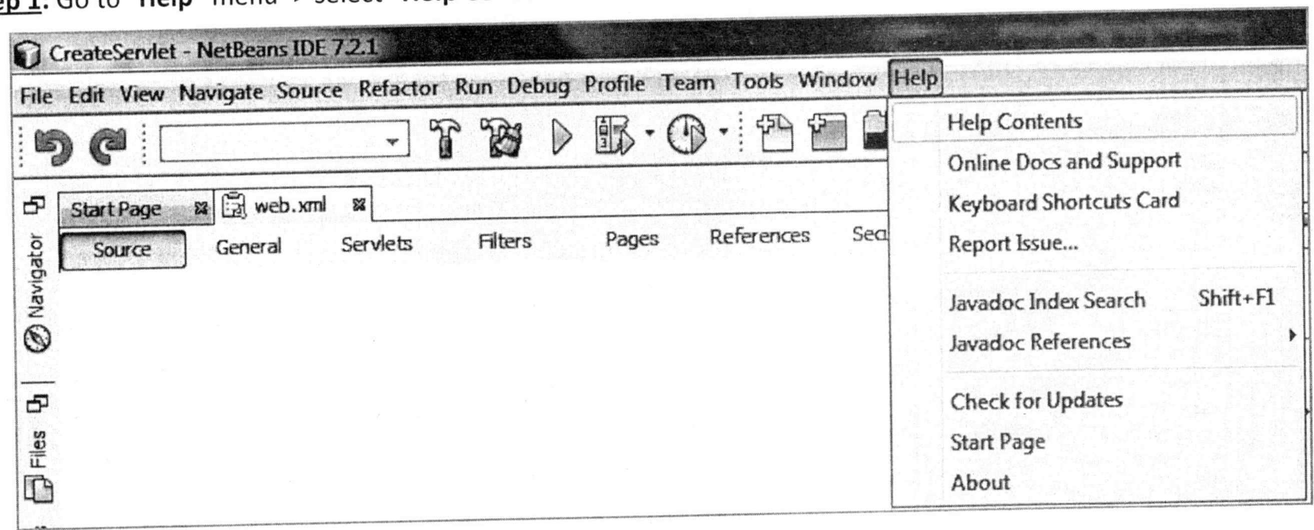

**Step 2:** A Help window will appear. From left panel, expand to the tree to select the required contents on which you want to get help.

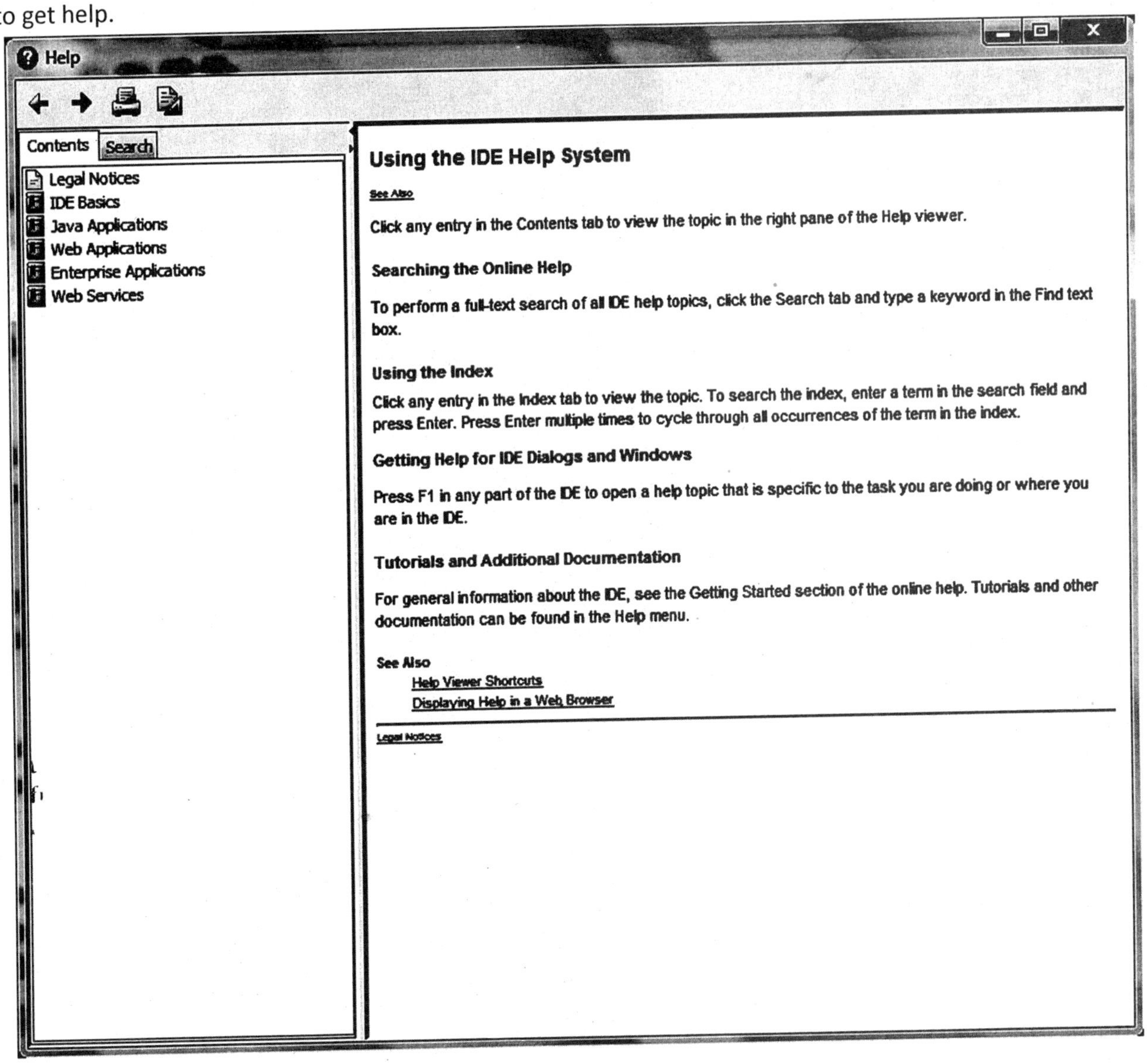

Help
Contents
Search
Legal Notices
IDE Basics
Java Applications
Web Applications
Enterprise Applications
Web Services
Using the IDE Help System
See Also
Click any entry in the Contents tab to view the topic in the right pane of the Help viewer.
Searching the Online Help
To perform a full-text search of all IDE help topics, click the Search tab and type a keyword in the Find text box.
Using the Index
Click any entry in the Index tab to view the topic. To search the index, enter a term in the search field and press Enter. Press Enter multiple times to cycle through all occurrences of the term in the index.
Getting Help for IDE Dialogs and Windows
Press F1 in any part of the IDE to open a help topic that is specific to the task you are doing or where you are in the IDE.
Tutorials and Additional Documentation
For general information about the IDE, see the Getting Started section of the online help. Tutorials and other documentation can be found in the Help menu.
See Also
Help Viewer Shortcuts
Displaying Help in a Web Browser
Legal Notices

**Step 3:** The selected help will appear in right panel.

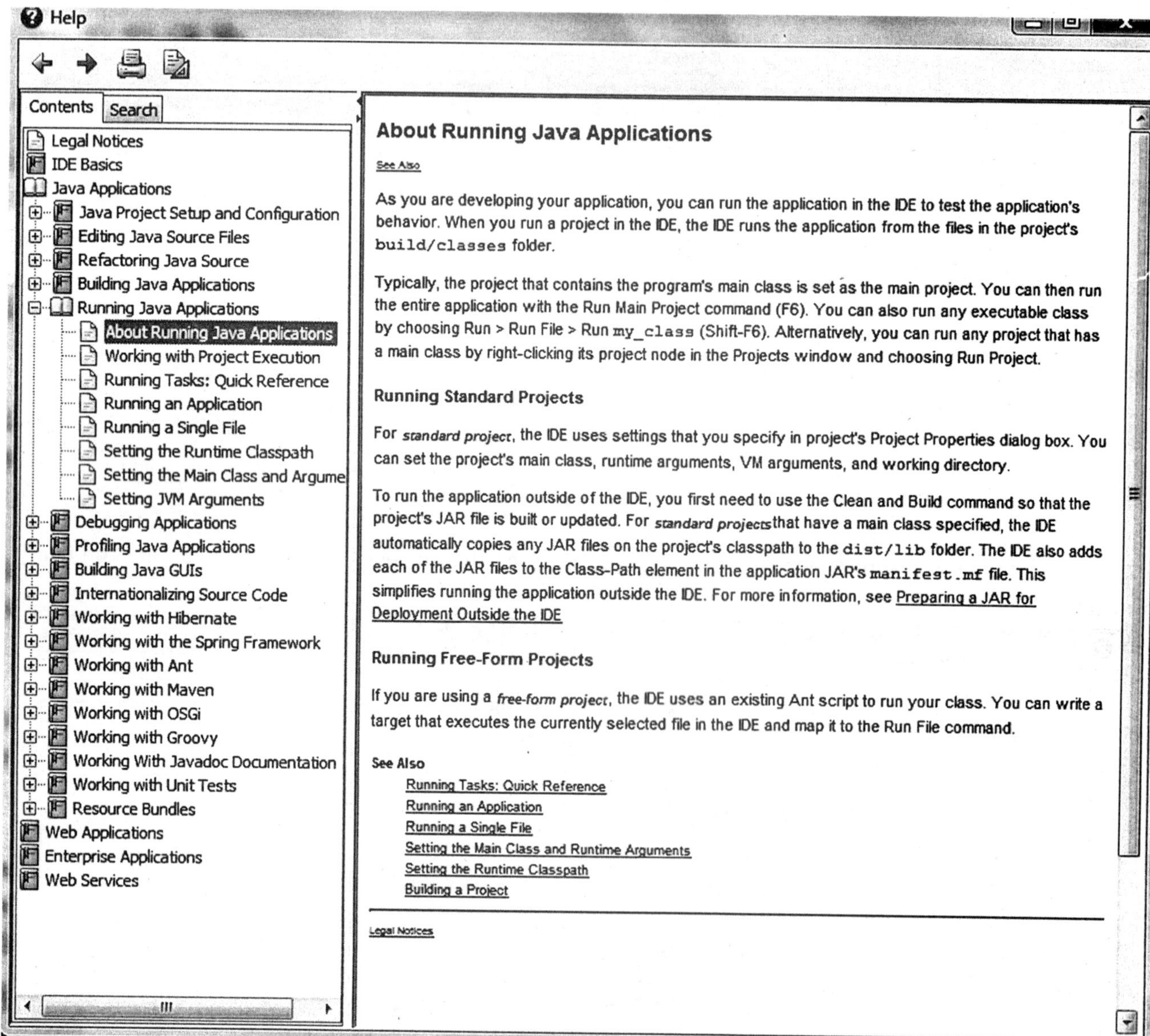


*****

# Part III

# Creating GUI Applications

- Applet & GUI Programming
- Swings
- Event Handling
- Database connectivity using JDBC
- Networking and Socket Programming

# Chapter 5

# Applet & GUI Programming

In previous chapters, many times we discussed that java's major application is in internet programming. Applets are smart programs that are used for internet programming. In this chapter we will study about applet, AWT components and event handling. These all topics are jointly used to prepare internet applications. We will study all these in detail and also study how all these applications are developed and executed over the internet.

## 5.1 Applet Essential

Applets are small programs that are used to prepare web applications and run over the internet. To start with applet, first of all remember that **Applet** is a library class which comes under **java.applet** and we also need to import **java.awt** packages. Remember that applets are not like console programs that executes with command based runtime interpreter. Applets are programs specially designed for web applications and rather executed using a web browser or appletviewer.

An applet program do not have **main( )** method to start execution but there are some applet methods which are needed to be overridden in a user defined class that extends Applet class. Execution sequence of these applet methods is fixed. We will study these all methods in applet's life cycle. As applet do not concern with console programming, hence the input and output statements we used till now are not applicable now onwards. Instead of that we will use AWT components for that purpose. AWT stands for *Abstract Window Toolkit*.

Once an applet program is compiled, it is executed by using a web browser or appletviewer. To execute an applet program we have to set up APPLET tag in the same program - **as a comment** or **by providing a separate HTML file**. This APPLET tag is shown in following example.

<applet code = "*applet_class_name.**class***" width = "*width_in_pixels*" height = "*height_in_pixels*">

</applet>

As mentioned above, either place this tag in the same program as a multiline comment (/* ...... */) or create a separate HTML file containing this tag. Both the execution processes are discussed in this chapter.

## 5.2 Applet class and methods

To create an applet first of all we have to extend a user defined class with library class Applet by using keyword *extends*. For example,

```
class apl1 extends Applet
{
        ------------        // define applet methods here
        ------------
}
```

Here, the class apl1 is inheriting the library class Applet and hence has to override Applet class' methods. The Applet class contains actually 24 methods. We can override them in our class as per requirement. Some of them are shortly discussed here.

| Method | Description |
|---|---|
| void init( ) | Will be executed when an applet begins its execution. This is the first method of an applet to be executed. |
| void start( ) | This method will be executed automatically after init( ) method. |
| void paint(Graphics *obj*) | This method redraws the applet output. Generally used to draw graphical objects in the applet. |
| void stop( ) | This method will be called by the browser to suspend the execution of the applet. Once an applet is stopped, it will begin from start( ) method. |
| void destroy( ) | Called after stop( ) to perform any cleanup before destruction of the applet. |
| String getAppletInfo( ) | Returns a string containing information of applet. |
| URL getCodeBase( ) | Returns the URL concern with the invoking applet. |
| boolean isActive( ) | Returns **true** if applet is started, otherwise **false**. |
| void play(URL *url*) | plays an audio clip, if present at specified *url*. |
| void resize(int *w*, int *h*) | resizes the applet with specified width *w* and height *h*. |

## 5.3 Applet Life Cycle

An applet, during its execution, goes through following stages.

- Initialization state
- Running state
- Idle state
- Dead / Destroyed state

Following diagram will show you the states and the series of changes in these states.

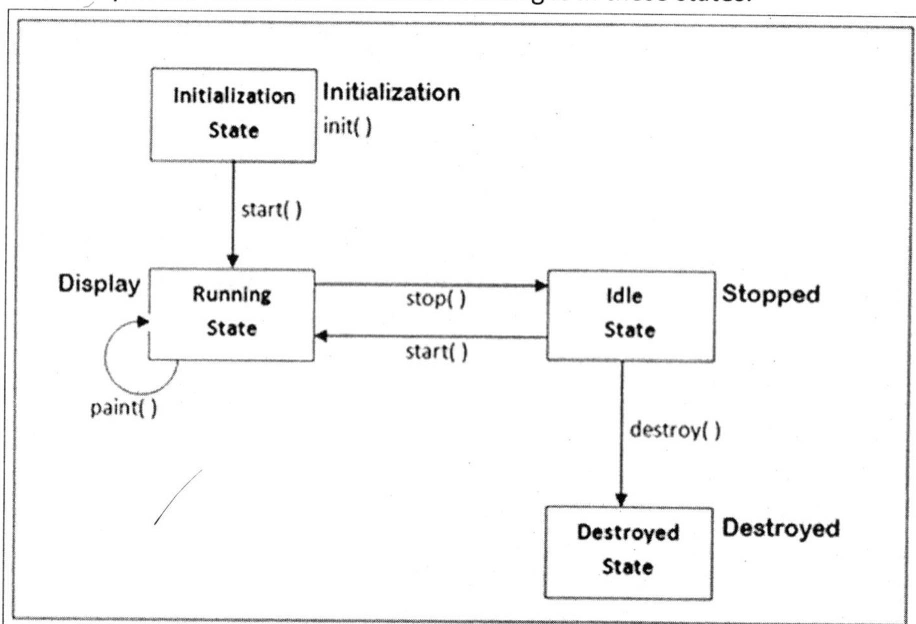


Let us study these states one by one.

**Initialization state:** Applet executes init( ) method when it enters in initialization state. This init( ) method is executed only first time when applet is first time loaded. *In init( ) method we can perform initial settings like creating objects, connecting and opening databases, setting fonts and colors, initialize variables, etc.*

**Running state:** Running state of an applet begins when start( ) method is executed. This method will be called automatically after init( ) method and executes each time when applet's contents are displayed. *start( ) method generally contains all executable and event related statements, handling databases and files, starting threads, playing audio / video files, calling other methods, animations, etc.*

**Idle state:** An applet is in idle state when it is stopped from running. Stopping occurs automatically when we leave current running applet and jump to another applet. This can also be performed manually by using stop( ) method. *stop( ) method is generally used to stop a thread, disconnecting database connections, stopping an audio / video clip, animation, etc.*

**Destroyed state:** An applet is in dead / destroyed state when it is completely removed from the memory. This occurs when we quit the browser. This can be manually done by using destroy( ) method. This is the last mthod to be executed for the applet. *In destroy( ) method we release the used object or threads.*

As we discussed earlier, an HTML file with <APPLET> tag require for running an applet. Let us discuss the steps involved to create and run an applet.

1. Create a **.java** file with a user defined applet class.
2. Compile this file and create its bytecode (.class file)
3. Design an HTML file containing <APPLET> tag
4. Run this .html file using appletviewer.

In apple life cycle we have discussed about applet states. It is also important to understand the methods which are responsible for change in these states. Here is the brief discussion about the most useful methods.

**init( ) :** The init( ) method is the first method of applet to be executed. init( ) method will be executed only once, i.e. first time when an applet is loaded. General form of init( ) method is:

```
void init( )
{
        -----------          // statements here
        -----------
}
```

**start( ) :** This method will be called after init( ). This method will be executed each time when an applet is displayed. General form of start( ) is:

```
void start( )
{
        -----------          // statements here
        -----------
}
```

**paint( ) :** This method is used to draw graphical objects on applet page. This method will be executed whenever the applet must redraw its output, paint( ) method is called. paint( ) method has one parameter which is object of class **Graphics**. This object provides graphical environment in which applet is running. Graphics class comes under **java.awt** package. The definition of paint( ) is:

```
void paint(Graphics obj)
{
        -----------          // statements here
        -----------
}
```

**stop( ) :** stop( ) method will be called when the browser leaves a page and jumps to another page. After stopping a thread, using start( ) we can restart the execution. It begins execution from start( ) method instead of init( ). Definition of stop( ) method is:

```
void stop( )
{
        -----------            // statements here
        -----------
}
```

**destroy( ) :** The destroy( ) method will be executed when we exit from a browser or when browser environment determines that your applet is no longer useful. Hence the destroy method is the last method to be executed for the applet. This method is defined as:

```
        void destroy( )
{
        -----------            // statements here
        -----------
}
```

Here is a small program demonstrating applet's skeleton. Call this program **appl_demo.java**

```
import java.awt.*;
import java.applet.*;
public class appl_demo extends Applet
{
        public void init( )
        {
                // this method executes first and only first time when applet is initially loaded.
        }
        public void start( )
        {
                // this method will be called second, after init( ) method and called each time.
        }
        public void paint(Graphics g)
        {
                // used to draw graphical objects using object g.
        }
        public void stop( )
        {
                // executes when applet is stopped or when controls leaves a page.
        }
        public void destroy( )
        {
                // executes after stop( ). This is the last method to be executed.
        }
}
```

## 5.4 Executing Applet using appletviewer

We have discussed about Applet class, steps to be followed for applet programs, applet life cycle and its states, <APPLET> tag. These all are required to understand applet programming. Now we will learn to execute applets using **appletviewer**. appletviewer is a tool provided by JDK to execute an applet. Here is the HTML file containing <APPLET> tag. This HTML file is linked with above program.

```
<html>
<body>
<applet code = "appl_demo.class" height = "300" width = "300"> </applet>
</body>
</html>
```

Let us call this file as **one.html**. This file is connected with "appl_demo.class" file using <APPLET> tag. This taga has total 8 different attributes; out of them here we used 3. They are

[CODE = "applet's .class file"]
[HEIGHT = "height of appletviewer in pixel"]
[WIDTH = "width of appletviewer in pixel"]

Other attributes are: [CODEBASE, ALT, NAME, ALIGH, VSPACE]

Refer following screenshot and study the execution process.

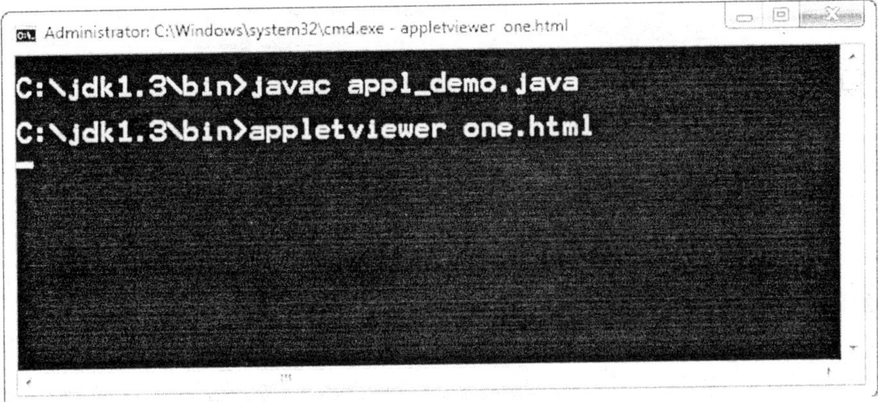


Although, above program is not able to display any output contents, but still you can see this appletviewer screen as output.

Note: Do not forget to make the applet class as public. If you forget it, then in the same appletviewer screen, you will see "Applet not initialized" at the bottom.

## 5.5 Passing parameters to Applet

We can pass user defined parameters to an applet using <PARAM> tag. (PARAM is a short form of PARAMETER). This tag has two important attributes NAME and VALUE. Refer following syntax:

<PARAM NAME = "parameter name" VALUE = "value of parameter">

This <PARAM> tag must be inside <APPLET> tag. This passed parameter is received in Java program by using **getParameter( )** method. This method is defined as:

String getParameter(String *parameter_name*)

This *parameter_name* represents the parameter name passed from applet and the value of that parameter will fetched from applet and returned as string. Following example demonstrates use of **<PARAM> tag** and **getParameter( )** method.

Following program shows the use of getParameter( ). Call this program as **param_demo.java**

```
import java.awt.*;
import java.applet.*;
public class param_demo extends Applet
{
        String st;
        public void init()
        {
                st=getParameter("argument");
                st = "Hello " + st +"!";
        }
        public void paint(Graphics g)
        {
                g.drawString(st,100,100);
        }
}
```

Now, lets create HTML file containing <PARAM> tag. Call this file as **two.html**

```
<html>
<head>
<title>PARAM tag demo</title>
</head>
<body>
<applet code="param_demo.class" width="300" height="300">
<param name = "argument" value = "James">
</applet>
</body>
</html>
```

After executing above html file using appletviewer we can get following output.

## 5.6 Applet's Graphics Methods

We can write java applets that can draw lines, different graphical objects, images and text contents in different fonts, colors and sizes. Every applet has its own area of the screen where these objects are drawn, it is called as *canvas*. First of all see following figure showing coordinate system of java's applet.

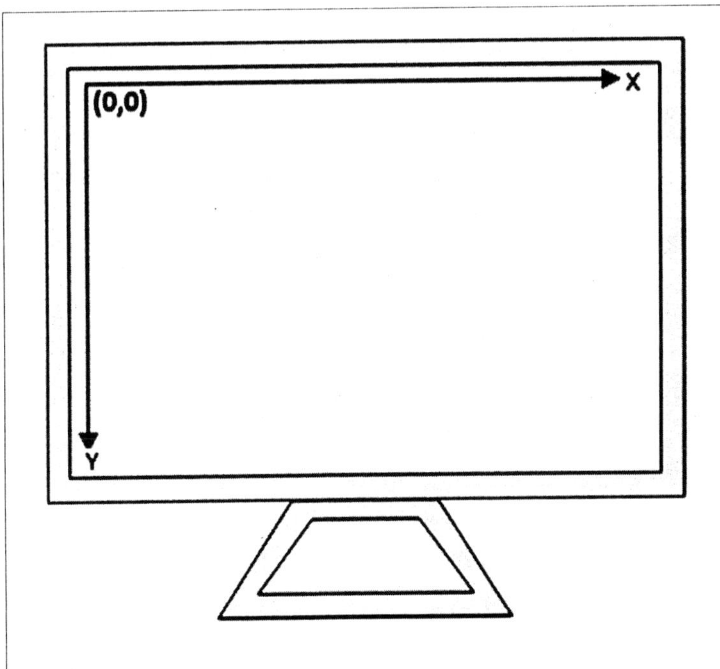


Above diagram, shows that (0,0) coordinates are in top left corner of your screen. Here are some of the methods required to study. Remember that, all these methods are member functions of library class **Graphics** and draw them in paint( ) method, defined in applet class.

### 5.6.1 Displaying String

A string can also be displayed on the screen as a graphical object. It is done by using **drawstring( )** method. General form of this method is:

void drawString(*"String message"* , int *x* , int *y*)

This method displays *string message* starting from specified *x* and *y* coordinates. Following program demonstrates use of this method.

```
import java.awt.*;
import java.applet.*;
public class string_demo extends Applet
{
        public void paint(Graphics g)
        {
                g.drawString("Himalaya Publications",60,100);
        }
}
```

Output of above applet will be:

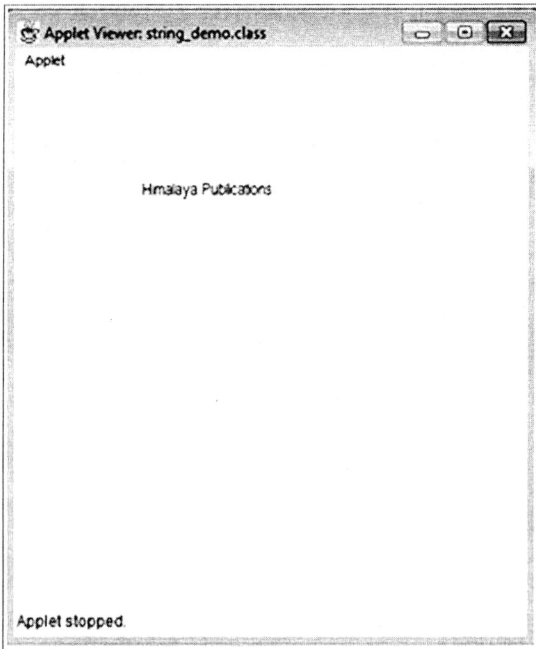


### 5.6.2 Drawing line

Line is the simplest drawing shape that we can draw using graphical methods. The method **drawLine( )** is used for drawing a straight line. The general form of **drawLine( )** is:

void drawLine(int *start*X, int *start*Y, int *end*X, int *end*Y)

This method will draw a line that begins at *start*X – *start*Y and ends at *end*X – *end*Y by using current drawing color. For example,

g.drawLine(40 , 75 , 110 , 190);

Following program draws several lines in different colors. You can also study the coloring method.

```
import java.awt.*;
import java.applet.*;
public class line_demo extends Applet
{
        public void paint(Graphics g)
        {
                g.drawLine(40,75,110,190);
                g.setColor(Color.red);
                g.drawLine(140,100,200,290);
                g.setColor(Color.blue);
                g.drawLine(25,65,150,210);
                g.setColor(Color.green);
                g.drawLine(70,90,130,135);
                g.setColor(Color.yellow);
                g.drawLine(95,125,175,230);
        }
}
```

Above program will show following output in appletviewer.

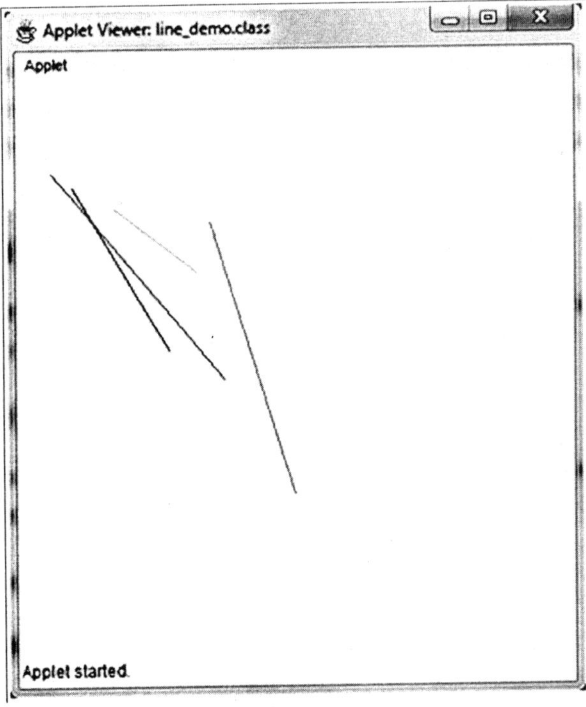


### 5.6.3 Drawing Rectangles

We can also draw rectangles using drawing methods. There are four methods related to drawing a rectangle: **drawRect( )**, **fillRect( )**, **drawRoundRect( )**, **fillRoundRect( )**.

**drawRect( )** and **fillRect( )** methods draws an outline and filled rectangle using current drawing color, respectively. Their general forms are:

void drawRect(int *start*X, int *start*Y, int *width*, int *height*)
void fillRect(int *start*X, int *start*Y, int *width*, int *height*)

These methods create a starting point at *start*X – *start*Y and dimensions are specified by *width* and *height*.

Another methods are **drawRoundRect( )** and **fillRoundRect( )**. These methods are same as above two but they just require two additional arguments. Their general forms are:

void drawRoundRect(int *startX*, int *startY*, int *width*, int *height*, int *Xdiam*, int *Ydiam*)
void fillRoundRect(int *startX*, int *startY*, int *width*, int *height*, int *Xdiam*, int *Ydiam*)

Here is an applet demonstrating rectangle methods.

```
import java.awt.*;
import java.applet.*;
public class rect_demo extends Applet
{
        public void paint(Graphics g)
        {
                g.drawRect(10, 10, 60, 50);
                g.fillRect(110, 90, 40, 30);
                g.drawRoundRect(190, 10, 60, 50, 15, 15);
                g.fillRoundRect(60, 170, 140, 100, 30, 40);
        }
}
```

Above program will show following output.

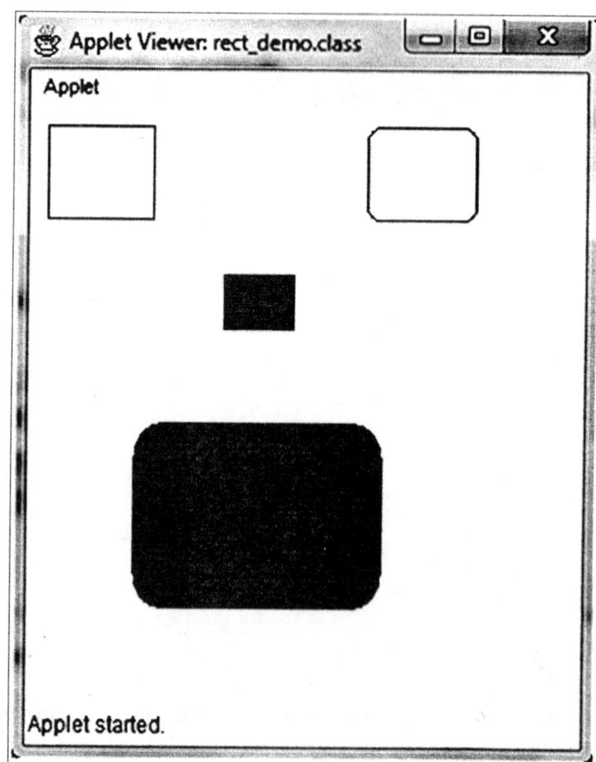


Tip: To draw a perfect rectangle, keep the width and height equal.

### 5.6.4 Drawing Ellipses and Circles

To draw ellipses and circles we have **drawOval( )** and **fillOval( )** mehods. The general form of these methods are:

void drawOval(int *startX*, int *startY*, int *width*, int *height*)
void fillOval(int *startX*, int *startY*, int *width*, int *height*)

The general syntax of drawing oval is same as of drawing rectangle. These methods, first generate a bounding rectangle and join midpoint points of each side and draw an oval. Following applet demonstrates drawing & filling ellipses & circles with different colors.

```
import java.awt.*;
import java.applet.*;
public class oval_demo extends Applet
{
        public void paint(Graphics g)
        {
                g.drawOval(10, 10, 60, 60);
                g.fillOval(110, 90, 40, 40);
                g.drawOval(190, 10, 60, 60);
                g.fillOval(60, 170, 140, 60);
        }
}
```

After successful compilation and executing using appletviewer, output of above program will be:

Tip: To draw a perfect circle, keep the width and height equal.

### 5.6.5 Drawing Arcs

Arcs can also be drawn and filled by using graphical methods. General syntax to draw and fill arc is:

void drawArc(int *start*X, int *start*Y, int *width*, int *height*, int *start*Angle, int *sweep*Angle)

void fillArc(int *start*X, int *start*Y, int *width*, int *height*, int *start*Angle, int *sweep*Angle)

These methods also generates a bounding rectangle and the arc is drawn from startAngle through the angular distance specified by *sweep*Angle. We specify the angles in terms of *degree*. The negative angle draws arc clockwise and positive angle draws arc counterclockwise. The following applet draws several arcs.

```
import java.awt.*;
import java.applet.*;
public class arc_demo extends Applet
{
        public void paint(Graphics g)
        {
                g.drawArc(10, 40, 70, 70, 0, 75);
                g.setColor(Color.cyan);
                g.fillArc(100, 40, 70, 70, 0, 75);
                g.setColor(Color.pink);
                g.drawArc(10, 100, 70, 80, 0, 175);
                g.setColor(Color.black);
                g.fillArc(100, 100, 70, 90, 0, 270);
                g.setColor(Color.magenta);
                g.drawArc(200, 80, 80, 80, 0, 180);
        }
}
```

Above applet program will show following applet output.

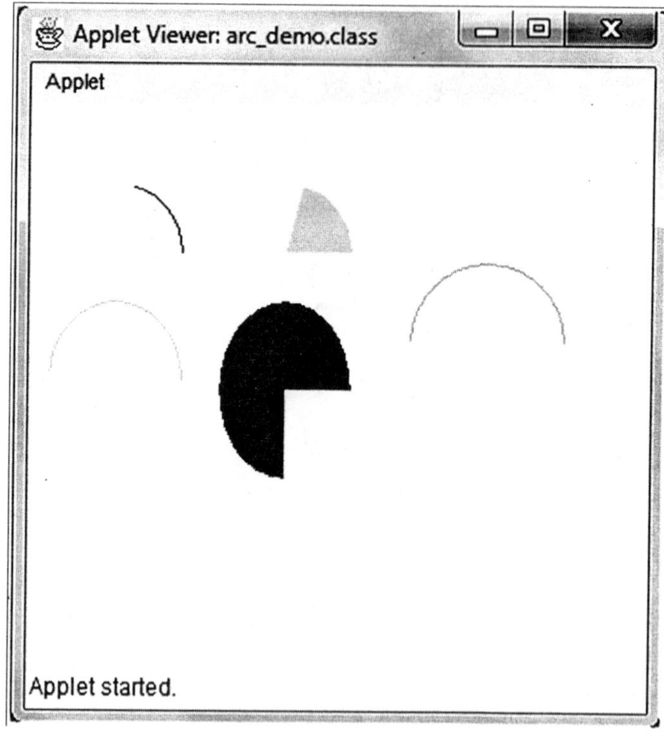


### 5.6.6 Drawing Polygons

Java also provides methods to draw and fill polygons using **drawPolygon( )** and **fillPolygon( )**. General form of these methods are:

void drawPolygon(int *x*[ ], int *y*[ ], int *numpoints*)
void fillPolygon(int *x*[ ], int *y*[ ], int *numpoints*)

Polygon's endpoints are specified by providing arrays for x and y coordinates along with specifying the numbers of points defined by x and y array. Here is the program drawing polygons.

```
import java.awt.*;
import java.applet.*;
public class poly_demo extends Applet
{
        public void paint(Graphics g)
        {
                int x1[]={30,200,30};
                int y1[]={30,30,200};
                int x2[]={200,200,30};
                int y2[]={30,200,200};
                g.drawPolygon(x1,y1,3);
                g.fillPolygon(x2,y2,3);
        }
}
```

Above program will produce following output.

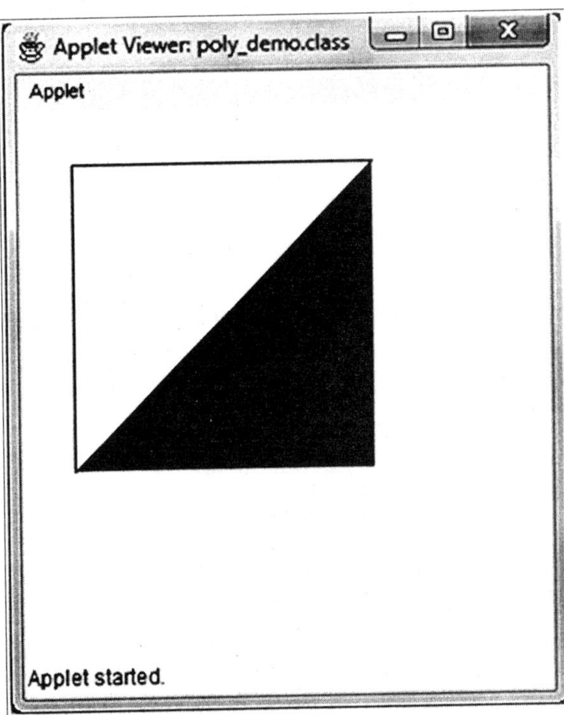


## 5.7 Introduction to AWT Component Classes

AWT (Abstract Window Toolkit) contains large number of built-in classes, interfaces and methods which allows creating and managing window applications. The AWT classes and interfaces are actually component classes which are helpful to design a window application and a web application as well. Using AWT classes we can design windows controls such as textbox, label, button, list, menu, choice, radio button, checkbox, etc. In this topic we will cover the most commonly used component classes and its methods along with setting fonts and colors.

The AWT component classes can be used for both, i.e. in **Applet class** to create **web applications** and in **Frame class** to create **stand alone windows application** that run in a GUI (Graphical User Interface) environment.

## 5.8 AWT Component Classes

All the AWT classes and interfaces are under **java.awt** package. (*applet's Graphics class also belongs to this package.*) Here is a list of AWT classes which we are going to study in this chapter.

| Class | Description |
|---|---|
| Button | Creates a command button / push button. |
| Checkbox | Creates a checkbox control for multiple selections. |
| Choice | Creates a pop up list. |
| Color | Class for managing different colors. |
| Label | Creates a label that displays a string as instruction. |
| TextField | Creates a textbox for taking input. |
| TextArea | Creates a multiline textbox for paragraphs. |
| List | Creates a list box from which the user can choose. |
| Scrollbar | Creates a scrollbar for a component. |
| Menu | Creates a pull down menu which has MenuItems in it. |
| MenuBar | Creates a menu bar, which has different Menus in it. |
| MenuItem | Creates a menu item which is selected for an event. |
| Dialog | Creates a window dialogue box. |
| Font | Deals with different font families, size and font styles. |
| Frame | Creates a window that can have menu-bar, title-bar, sizing corners, and white work area. |
| Panel | A subclass of Container which forms a group of components for multiple uses. |
| FlowLayout | The default Layout. This arranges the components from left to right, top to bottom. |
| CardLayout | This layout emulates index cards, i.e. only one on the top will be shown. |
| BorderLayout | This layout arranges the layout on five positions: East, West, North, South and Center. |
| GridLayout | Arrange the components in two dimensional grid. |

All these components are AWT components, achieved by creating object of associated class. Refer following hierarchy diagram, which describes the relation and functionality of each class with each level.

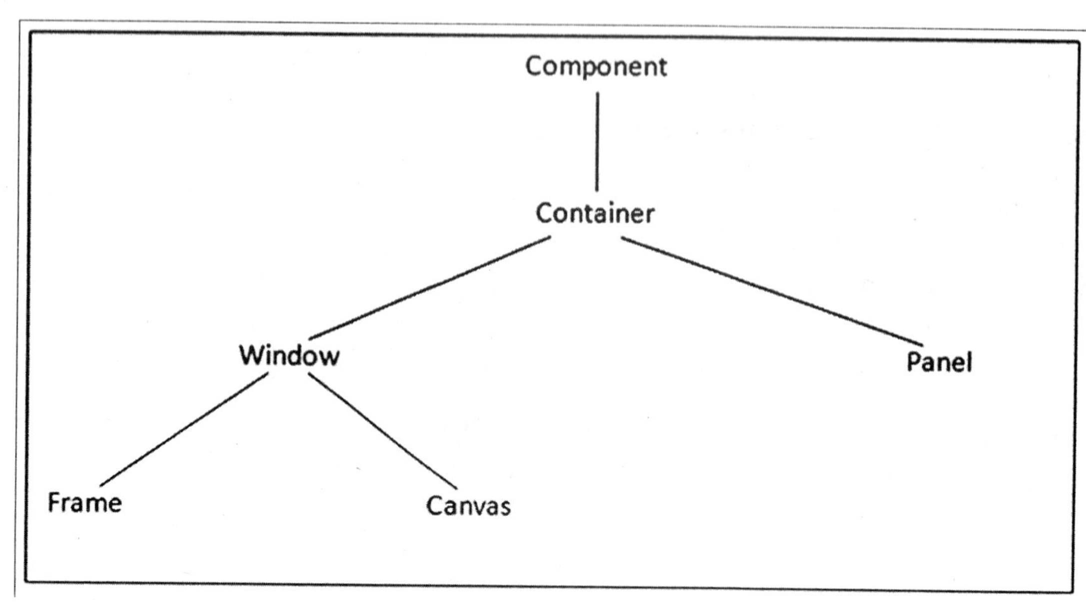

Let us discuss about these built-in classes in brief.

**Component**: Component class is the hierarchy class for all the AWT components. This is an abstract class that contains all the classes and methods of windows component. This class also defines Event classes and Listener interfaces that are responsible for managing different events (such as window, mouse, key, input, etc.), placing and resizing components, setting colors and fonts, etc. This class has important methods like **setLocation( )**, **setSize( )** and **setBounds( )** for positioning and resizing components, after they are added. These methods are defined as:

```
void setLocation(int x_position, int y_position)
void setSize(int width, int height)
void setBounds(int x_position, int y_position, int width, int height)
```

Remember, these methods will work after a component is added into the window and Layout is set to be **null.**

**Container**: This class is a subclass of Component class. Container class is mainly responsible for positioning components on a window by using different layout managers. This class provides the facility of nesting of one object into another. Container class has **add( )** method to add components in a window and **remove( )** method to remove components from a window. These methods are defined as

```
void  add(Component object)
void  remove(Component object)
```

**Window**: This class is base class for two top-level-window classes; **Panel** and **Frame**. We cannot place any component objects into Window class. Generally, we create Panel or Frame class' objects as top-level-window and place different components into them.

**Panel**: This panel class implements **Container**. A panel is group of components which is used recursively and nested inside a Frame or Applet class. A panel does not have any border, titlebar and menubar. This is where it differs from a Frame. We simply add components into a panel and then add this panel into a Frame or Applet by using **add( )** method.

**Frame**: Frame is the actual stand-alone-window that has border, titlebar, menubar and resizing corners. It is a top level window that has component objects in it. Role of a Frame is same as Forms in VB.

**Canvas**: Canvas is the blank window on which we can draw different graphical objects.

### 5.8.1 Frame

As discussed above, Frame is the top-level-window in which we can add component objects to create stand-alone applications. A Frame is created by extending a normal class with built-in class Frame. For example,

```
class fr_demo  extends  Frame
{
        ------------
        ------------
}
```

Object of above class actually creates a window, during the output. Here are the constructors of Frame class.

```
Frame( )
Frame(String str)
```

First form creates a Frame without any title and second form creates a Frame with specified *str* as its title. There are several methods which are useful while working with a Frame. They are discussed here in brief.

**setSize( )** method is used to set the dimensions of a window. This dimensions should be its width and height. General form of this method is:

void setSize(int *width*, int *height*)
void setSize(Dimension *obj*)

New width and height is specified as two int arguments or it can be specified by providing object of Dimension class. Remember, the dimensions should be in pixels.

**setTitle( )** method is used to set the title of the Frame. This method is defined as:

void setTitle(String *title*)

Here specified string will be the new title of the Frame.

**setVisible( )** method is used to make a Frame visible or invisible. The Frame is by default invisible and it will not be visible until you make it visible. This method is defined as:

void setVisible(boolean *state*)

If Frame will be visible if the specified *state* is **true**, otherwise it will be hidden.

**Closing a Frame** is important because by default we cannot close a Frame window by clicking on **close control** of your window. We have to call **setVisible(false)** method in **windowClosing( )** event of **WindowListener** interface. This example will be seen in event handling.

Here is a program to demonstrate Frame.

```
import java.awt.*;
import java.applet.*;
class fr_demo extends Frame
{
	public fr_demo()
	{
		// create AWT component objects here
	}
	public static void main(String ar[])
	{
		fr_demo fr1 = new fr_demo();
		fr1.setSize(200,200);
		fr1.setTitle("Frame Demo");
		fr1.setVisible(true);
	}
}
```

Above program will show following output. In this program **applet is initially executed** using appletviewer and from this applet's start( ) method, we are creating and making the Frame visible.

Many of the following components are demonstrated in Frame. The process of executing a Frame and an applet is different.

### 5.8.2 Button

The most widely used component is Button. A button is also called as *push button*. The button class defines following two constructors.

```
Button( )
Button(String str)
```

First constructor creates a button without any label on it. Second constructor creates a button with a label on it. For example,

```
Button  bt1 = new  Button( );
Button  bt2 = new  Button("Click Me");
```

In first example, button object **bt1** is creates a push button without any label and second object **bt2** creates a push button with "Click Me" as label on it.

The Button class has following methods which are helpful while handling events of button.

```
void  setLabel(String str)
String  getLabel( )
```

First method sets the specified *label* on the button object used. Second method returns the label of button object.

Here is a program to demonstrate Button in Applet.

```
import java.awt.*;
import java.applet.*;
public class button_demo extends Applet
{
        public void init()
        {
                Button bt1 = new Button();
                Button bt2 = new Button("Click Me");
                add(bt1);
                add(bt2);
        }
}
```

Above program will show following applet.

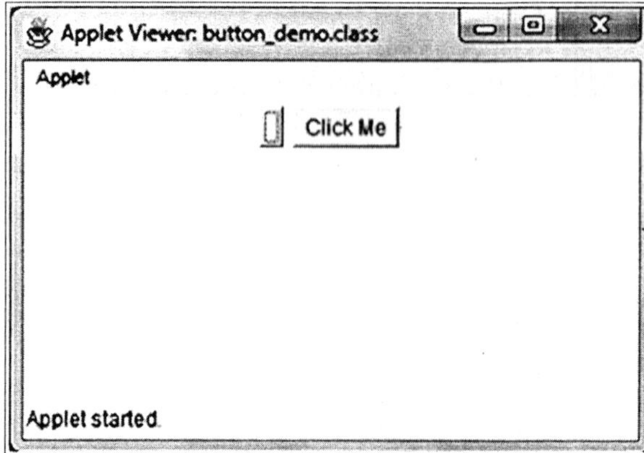


First button bt1 is without any label and second button has a label "Click Me" on it. Here **add( )** method is used to add bt1 and bt2 in the applet.

### 5.8.3 Label

Label is a string which is used to interact with the user. Label class has following three constructors.

Label( )
Label(String *str*)
Label(String *str*, int *how*)

First constructor creates a blank label. Second constructor creates a label with specified text on it. Third constructor creates a label with specified text and the alignment specified by *how*. The allowed value for *how* must be one of these static constants: **Label.LEFT**, **Label.RIGHT** or **Label.CENTER**. Following are the methods used with Label object.

void setText(String *str*)
String getText( )
void setAlignment(int *how*)
int getAlignment( )

As their names suggest, **setText( )** method is used to set or modify the text of specified label object. **getText( )** method is used to retrieve text of invoking label object. **setAlignment( )** method is used to set alignment of label by using one of the above mentioned static constants. **getAlignment( )** method is used to retrieve the type of alignment we set for invoking label object. Here is a program demonstrating label.

Following program demonstrates use of Label in an Applet.

```
import java.awt.*;
class label_demo extends Applet
{
	public void init( )
	{
		Label lb1 = new Label("Himalaya Publications");
		Label lb2 = new Label("Enter User ID : ");
		add(lb1);
		add(lb2);
	}
}
```

After compiling and executing using appletviewer, above program will show following output.

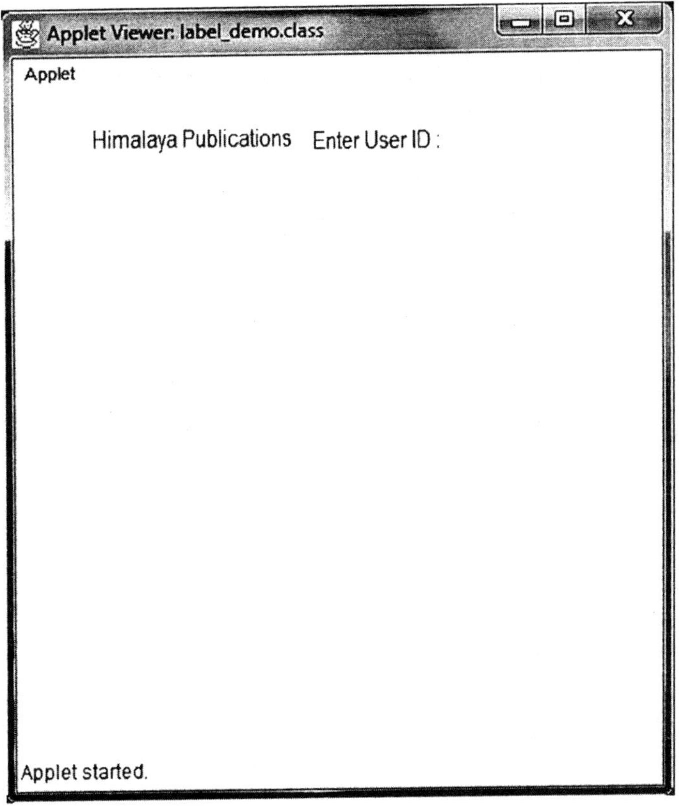


### 5.8.4 Checkbox

Checkbox is used to check multiple options among a group. A checkbox can be checked or unchecked to change its state. Here are the constructors of Checkbox class.

> Checkbox( )
> Checkbox(String *str*)
> Checkbox(String *str*, boolean *state*)
> Checkbox(String *str*, boolean *state*, CheckboxGroup *obj*)

First form of constructor creates a checkbox without any label and whose initial state is false i.e. unchecked. Second form of constructor creates a checkbox with a label specified by *str* and initially unchecked. Third form of constructor creates a checkbox with *str* as its label and specified state. If state is true then it initially appears checked and if state is false then it initially appears unchecked. Fourth constructor creates a checkbox whose label is specified by *str* whose state is mentioned and group is specified by CheckboxGroup *obj*. (CheckboxGroup is described in next session.)

Following are the methods of Checkbox class which are helpful during handling the events.

> void setLabel(String *str*)
> String getLabel( )
> void setState(boolean *state*)
> boolean getState( )

**setLabel( )** method is used to set the label of checkbox specified by *str*. **getLabel( )** method returns the label of invoking object of checkbox as String. **setState( )** method is used to set the state of checkbox by specifying *state*. To retrieve the current state of checkbox, call **getState( )** method that returns boolean value.

If a checkbox is already with label, then **setLabel( )** will overwrite its older label with new string passed. Same is applicable for **setState( )** method.

Following program demonstrates the checkboxes in applet.

```
import java.awt.*;
import java.applet.*;
public class checkbox_demo extends Applet
{
        public void init( )
        {
                Checkbox chb1 = new Checkbox("Pizza");
                Checkbox chb2 = new Checkbox("Hot-Dog");
                Checkbox chb3 = new Checkbox("Burger",true);
                Checkbox chb4 = new Checkbox("Pastry");
                add(chb1);
                add(chb2);
                add(chb3);
                add(chb4);
        }
}
```

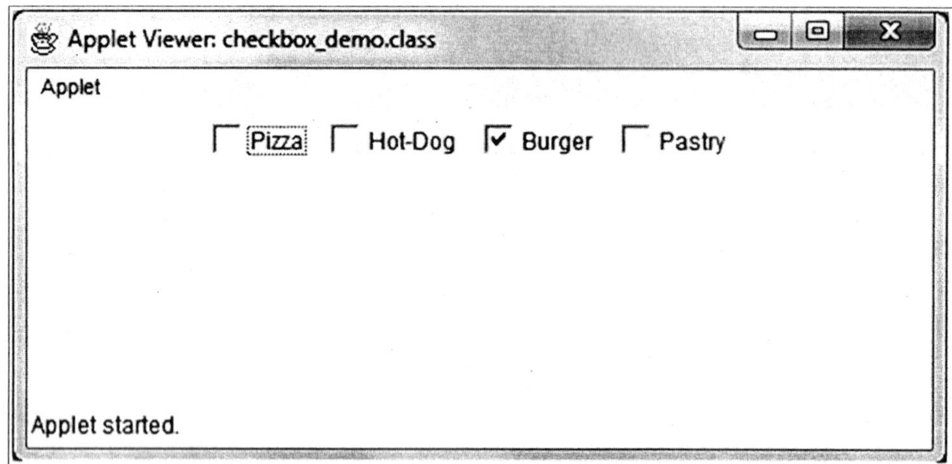


### 5.8.5 CheckboxGroup

*ChecboxGroup converts a checkbox into radio-button.* Fourth constructor of Checkbox class uses CheckboxGroup object. This class has only one constructor which is its default constructor i.e.

```
CheckboxGroup( )
```

CheckboxGroup class has a method, used to determine which checkbox is currently checked.

```
Checkbox getSelectedCheckbox( )
```

Following example demonstrates CheckboxGroup

```
import java.awt.*;
import java.applet.*;
public class checkboxgroup_demo extends Applet
{
        public void init()
        {
                CheckboxGroup cbg = new CheckboxGroup();
                Checkbox chb1 = new Checkbox("Pizza",false,cbg);
                Checkbox chb2 = new Checkbox("Hot-Dog",true,cbg);
                Checkbox chb3 = new Checkbox("Burger",false,cbg);
                Checkbox chb4 = new Checkbox("Pastry",false,cbg);
                add(chb1);
                add(chb2);
                add(chb3);
                add(chb4);
        }
}
```

Above programs shows following output.

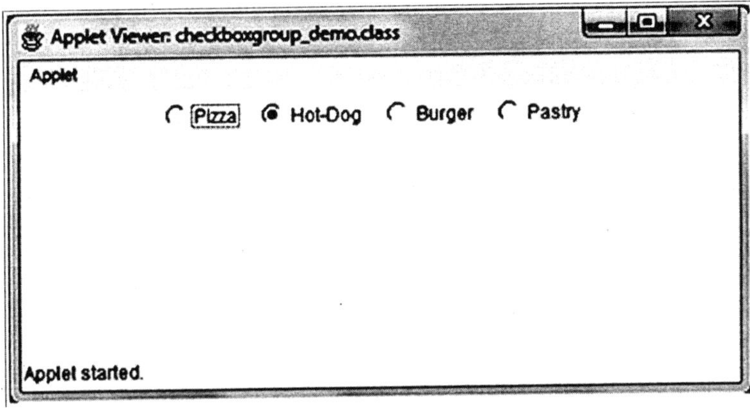


### 5.8.6 Choice

Choice class object provides a list of items to be selected. Choice is like a pop-up list and only one item of the list can be selected. This class has only one constructor which is its default constructor i.e.

```
Choice( )
```

When user clicks on the choice control, the whole list of choices pops up and user can select one item among the list. Each item in the list is a string, added by **add( )** method. It is defined as,

void add(String *item*)

The items are added and appear in the choice list as the add( ) method is called. To determine which item is currently selected, we have

```
String getSelectedItem( )
int getSelectedIndex( )
```

The **getSelectedItem( )** method returns selected item's name as a string. **getSelectedIndex( )** method returns the index number of selected item.

Other useful methods of Choice class are as follows.

int getItemCount( )
void select(int *index*)
void select(String *item*)
String getItem(int *index*)

The **getItemCount( )** method returns the total numbers of items added in the choice list. The overloaded **select()** method sets the initial selected item by specifying *index* or string *item*. **getItem( )** method returns item name present at specified *index*. Here is a program to demonstrate Choice.

```
import java.awt.*;
import java.applet.*;
public class choice_demo extends Applet
{
        public void init( )
        {
                Choice ch1 = new Choice( );
                Choice ch2 = new Choice( );
                ch1.add("Pizza");
                ch1.add("Hot dog");
                ch1.add("Burger");
                ch1.add("Pastry");
                ch2.add("Breakfast");
                ch2.add("Lunch");
                ch2.add("Dinner");
                add(ch1);
                add(ch2);
        }
}
```

Ouput of above applet program will be:

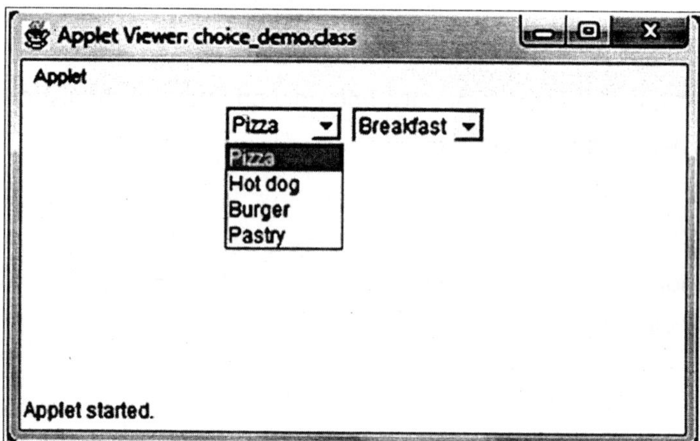


### 5.8.7 List

An object of this class provides a list with multiple selection option and scrollbars. List class has following constructors. A list control shows any numbers of items as choice in an open-visible block.

List( )
List(int *visible_rows*)
List(int *visible_rows*, boolean *multi_select*)

First form of constructor creates a list control that allow to select only one item at a time. Second constructor creates a list control in which *visible_rows* specified numbers of entries in the list that will always be visible and other items can be viewed by scrolling. Third form of constructor specified visible rows and multiple selections option. If boolean value is **true** then user can select multiple options and if it is false then only one item can be selected. This class has **add( )** method to add items into the list. For list, **add( ) method is overloaded** and has following two forms.

```
void add(String item)
void add(String item. int at_index)
```

First form adds specified item into the list and second form adds specified item into the list at specified index. Here is a list of methods related with List class.

```
String getSelectedItem( )
int getSelectedIndex( )
String[ ] getSelectedItems( )
int[ ] getSelectedIndexes( )
int getItemCount( )
void select(int index)
String getItem(int index)
```

The **getSelectedItem( )** method returns the selected item of list. If multiple selections are made or no item is selected then it returns **null. getSelectedIndex( )** method returns index of selected item. It returns -1 if multiple selections are made or no item is selected. When multiple selection is made **getSelectedItems( )** returns all the selected items as a String array and **getSelectedIndexes( )** returns indexes of all the selected items as an integer array. **getItemCount( )** method returns total numbers of items in the list. The **select( )** method sets the currently selected item specified by index. **getItem( )** method obtains the item name present at specified *index*. Here is a program demonstrating List control.

```
import java.awt.*;
import java.applet.*;
public class list_demo extends Applet
{
	public void init()
	{
		List ls1 = new List(4);
		List ls2 = new List(5,true);
		ls1.add("India");
		ls1.add("China");
		ls1.add("Australia");
		ls1.add("America");
		ls2.add("Andhra Pradesh");
		ls2.add("Karnataka");
		ls2.add("Gujarat");
		ls2.add("Maharashtra");
		ls2.add("Bihar");
		ls2.add("J & K");
		add(ls1);
		add(ls2);
	}
}
```

Above applet will show following output containing two list boxes.

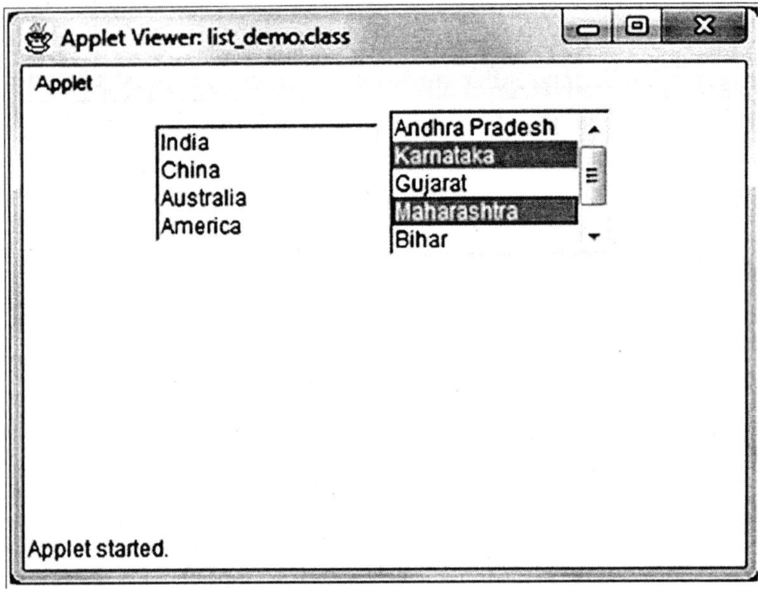


### 5.8.8 Scrollbar

Scrollbar provides horizontal and vertical movement of a component or window. Scrollbars may be oriented horizontally or vertically. Scrollbar class defines following three constructors.

> Scrollbar( )
> Scrollbar(int *type*)
> Scrollbar(int *type*, int *initial_value*, int *thumb_size*, int *min_value*, int *max_value*)

First form of constructor creates vertical scrollbar only. Second and third form of constructor allows to specify the type of scrollbar by using **Scrollbar.VERTICAL** and **Scrollbar.HORIZONTAL**. The initial value of scrollbar is passed through *intial_value*. The number of units of height of the thumb is specified by *thumb_size*. The minimum and maximum value for the scrollbar is specified by *min_value* and *max_value*. All the values can also be set by using

> void setValues(int *initial_value*, int *thumb_size*, int *min_value*, int *max_value*)

Minimum and maximum values can be retrieved by using **getMinimum( )** and **getMaximum( )** methods, respectively. They are defined as:

> int getMinimum( )
> int getMaximum( )

To obtain current value of scrollbar, call **getValue( )** method. To set the current value of scrollbar, call **setValue( )** method. They are defined as:

> int getValue( )
> void setValue(int *value*)

Here is a program demonstrating Scrollbars.

```
import java.awt.*;
import java.applet.*;
public class scroll_demo extends Applet
{
        public void init( )
        {
                Scrollbar sb1 = new Scrollbar(Scrollbar.VERTICAL,0,1,0,50);
                Scrollbar sb2 = new Scrollbar(Scrollbar.HORIZONTAL,0,1,0,50);
                add(sb1);
                add(sb2);
        }
}
```

output of above program scroll_demo.java is as follows.

### 5.8.9 TextField

An object of TextField class provides a single line textbox control, generally used to take input value from the user. TextField class defines following constructors.

TextField( )
TextField(int *max_chars*)
TextField(String *str*)
TextField(String *str*, int *max_chars*)

First constructor creates a TextField without any initial text in it. Second constructor creates a TextField that can have maximum numbers of characters specified by *max_chars*. Third form of constructor creates a TextField with initial text specified by *str*. Fourth constructor creates a TextField with initial text as *str* and maximum numbers of character as *max_chars*. TextField is a derived class of **TextComponent** class. Following is a list of member function of TextField class.

String getText( )
void setText(String str)
String getSelectedText( )
void select(int *start_index*, int *end_index*)
boolean isEditable( )
void setEditable(boolean *editable*)
void setEchoChar(char *ch*)
boolean echoCharIsSet( )
char getEchoChar( )

The **getText( )** method returns the text currently present in invoking TextField object. **setText( )** method sets initial text in the TextField specified by *str*. **getSelectedText( )** method returns selected text of TextField as a string. select( ) method selects the characters beginning at *start_index* and ends at *end_index-1*. Modification of contents of a TextField depends on value of **setEditable( )**. We can determine whether a TextField is editable or not by using **isEditable( )** method.

The TextField used for taking password, should be defined by calling **setEchoChar( )** method which disables the echoing of the characters as they are typed. This method requires a character which will be displayed as a mask on typed characters. You can also determine whether echo character is set or not by calling **echoCharIsSet()** method. You can also retrieve the echo character by calling **getEchoChar( )**. Following program demonstrates TextField in an applet.

```
import java.awt.*;
import java.applet.*;
public class textfield_demo extends Applet
{
        public void init( )
        {
                TextField tf1 = new TextField("Himalaya Publications");
                TextField tf2 = new TextField("Password");
                tf2.setEchoChar('*');
                add(tf1);
                add(tf2);
        }
}
```

Above program will show following output.

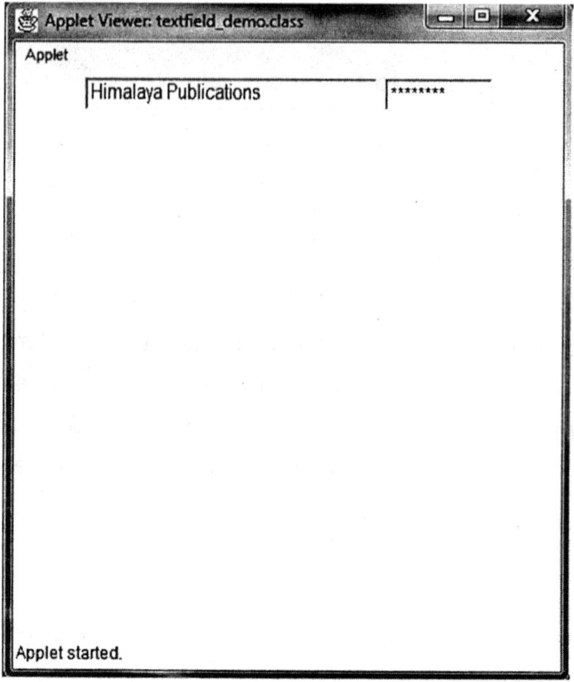


### 5.8.10 TextArea

TextArea is a multiline TextField. A TextArea is used to provide a paragraph or multiple lines as input. TextArea has following constructors.

TextArea( )
TextArea(int *max_lines*, int *max_rows*)
TextArea(String *str*)
TextArea(String *str*, int *max_lines*, int *max_rows*)
TextArea(String *str*, int *max_lines*, int *max_rows*, int *scrollbar_type*)

First constructor creates a TextArea without any initial string and with default settings. Second constructor creates a TextArea specifying maximum numbers of lines and maximum numbers of characters in each line. Third constructor initializes a TextArea with specified string *str*. Fourth constructor specifies initial string, maximum numbers of lines and maximum numbers of characters in each line. Fifth constructor allows adding *scrollbar type*. The values for scrollbar type are static constants. They are,

SCROLLBAR_BOTH
SCROLLBAR_VERTICAL_ONLY
SCROLLBAR_NONE
SCROLLBAR_HORIZONTAL_ONLY

TextArea is derived class of **TextComponent** class therefore the following methods are common.

String getText( )
void setText(String *str*)
String getSelectedText( )
void select(int *start_index*, int *end_index*)
boolean isEditable( )
void setEditable(boolean *editable*)

TextArea has added following methods.

void append(String *str*)
void insert(String *str*, int *index*)
void replaceRange(String *str*, int *start_index*, int *end_index*)

**append( )** method appends the string *str* at the end of current text of TextArea. **insert( )** method inserts string *str* at specified *index*. **replaceRange( )** method replaces the characters from *start_index* to *end_index-1* with specified string *str*.

Remember that TextArea class do not deals with passwords; therefore methods related to echo character are not allowed with this.

Here is a program to demonstrate TextArea.

```
import java.awt.*;
import java.applet.*;
public class textarea_demo extends Applet
{
	public void init()
	{
		TextArea ta1 = new TextArea("This is a multiline textbox\nWe can place new lines also.",10,65);
		add(ta1);
	}
}
```

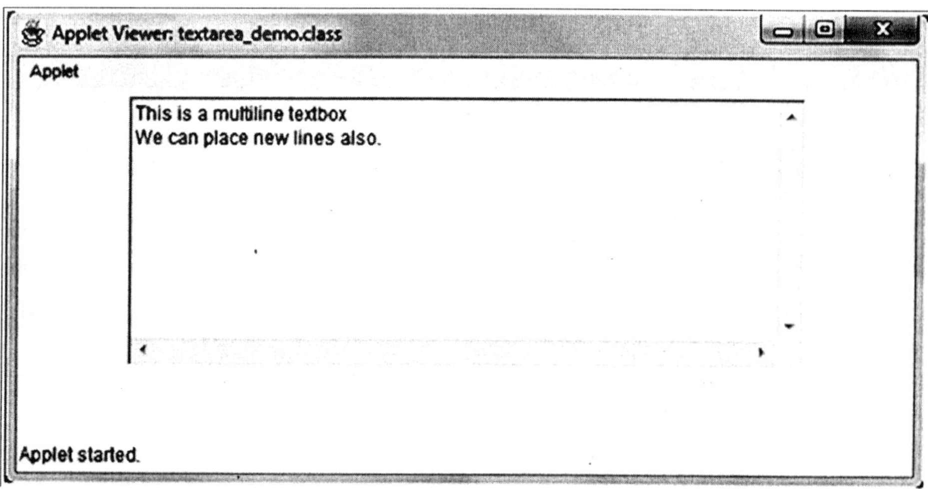


## 5.9 Menu, MenuBar and MenuItem

A menubar is most useful component. A menubar is associated with top-level- window only. i.e. *only a Frame class can have menubar*. In java, menubar is generated by coupling three different classes: **Menu**, **MenuBar** and **MenuItem**. Usually, a MenuBar object contains different Menus. Each Menu object contains list of MenuItems. MenuItem object represents something that can be selected by the user to perform certain task. MenuItems can also be replaced by objects of **CheckboxMenuItem** objects; which contains checkable menu-items. (For example, **Word Wrap** option under **Format** Menu, in Notepad.)

Let us study these classes one by one with their constructors and methods.

To create a menu bar, first of all create an object of class **MenuBar**. This class has only one constructor i.e. its default constructor, because MenuBar do not requires any parameters, title or settings. That constructor is

MenuBar( )

Next is Menu class. Its object provides a menu option under which many MenuItems are fabricated. **Menu** class has following Constructors.

Menu( )
Menu(String *menu_title*)
Menu(String *menu_title*, boolean *is_removable*)

First constructor creates a Menu without any title and by default it is not removable. Second form of constructor creates a Menu with specified *menu_title* on it. Third form of constructor creates a Menu with specified string as *menu_title* and removable option. If *is_removable* option is **true**, then pop-up menu can be removed and allowed to float free in MenuBar; for **false**, it will remain attached to the MenuBar.

MenuItem class has following three constructors.

MenuItem( )
MenuItem(String *item_title*)
MenuItem(String *item_title*, MenuShortcut *key*)

First constructor creates a MenuItem without any title on it. Second constructor creates MenuItem containing *item_title* as title. Third form of constructor creates a MenuItem with *item_title* and menu shortcut key for this item. MenuItem class has following methods.

void setEnabled(boolean *enable*)
boolean isEnable( )
void setLabel(String *item_title*)

String getLabel( )

**setEnable( )** method is used to enable or disable the MenuItem. The value **true** means enable and **false** means disabled. **isEnable( )** method returns whether that MenuItem is enabled or not. If it is enabled then it returns **true** else returns **false**. **setLabel( )** method is used to change the title of invoking MenuItem object. **getLabel( )** method returns the current title of invoking MenuItem object.

As mentioned earlier, MenuItem can be replaced by **CheckboxMenuItem** object. It has following constructors.

CheckboxMenuItem( )
CheckboxMenuItem(String *title*)
CheckboxMenuItem(String *title*, boolean *checked*)

CheckboxMenuItem actually toggles i.e. each time on clicking, its state changes. Default state is false i.e. unchecked. First constructor creates a CheckboxMenuItem without any title on it. Second form of constructor creates a CheckboxMenuItem with a *title* on it. Third constructor creates a CheckboxMenuItem object with a *title* and *checked state*.

This class has two methods to get and set the states of invoking CheckboxMenuItem object. They are,

void setState(boolean *checked*)
boolean getState( )

The MenuBar, Menu and MenuItem class; all three classes has **add( )** method to add its descendent object into it. Once we have created a Menu, place it in MenuBar using **add( )** method. MenuItems are added into specific Menu by using **add( )** method. For nested MenuItems, MenuItems can be added under another MenuItem by using **add( )** method. Following program demonstrates Menubar, Menu, MenuItem and CheckboxMenuItem.

```
import java.awt.*;
class menu_demo extends Frame
{
	public menu_demo( )
	{
		MenuBar mb = new MenuBar();
		Menu m1 = new Menu("File");
		Menu m2 = new Menu("Edit");
		Menu m3 = new Menu("Format");
		Menu m4 = new Menu("Open");
		MenuItem mi1 = new MenuItem("New");
		MenuItem mi2 = new MenuItem("Save");
		MenuItem mi3 = new MenuItem("Save As");
		MenuItem mi4 = new MenuItem("Cut");
		MenuItem mi5 = new MenuItem("Copy");
		MenuItem mi6 = new MenuItem("Paste");
		MenuItem mi7 = new MenuItem("Font");
		MenuItem mi8 = new MenuItem("File 1");
		MenuItem mi9 = new MenuItem("File 2");
		CheckboxMenuItem cmi1 = new CheckboxMenuItem("Word Wrap",true);
		mb.add(m1);
		mb.add(m2);
		mb.add(m3);
		m1.add(mi1);
```

```
                m1.add(mi2);
                m1.add(mi3);
                m1.add(mi4);
                m2.add(mi5);
                m2.add(m4);
                m2.add(mi6);
                m2.add(mi7);
                m3.add(cmi1);
                m4.add(mi8);
                m4.add(mi9);
                setMenuBar(mb);
        }
        public static void main(String ar[ ])
        {
                menu_demo m = new menu_demo( );
                m.setTitle("Menu Demo");
                m.setSize(300,300);
                m.setVisible(true);
        }
}
```

Above frame program is compiled and executed as normal program because it contains main( ) to begin the execution and role of main( ) is to make the Frame visible.

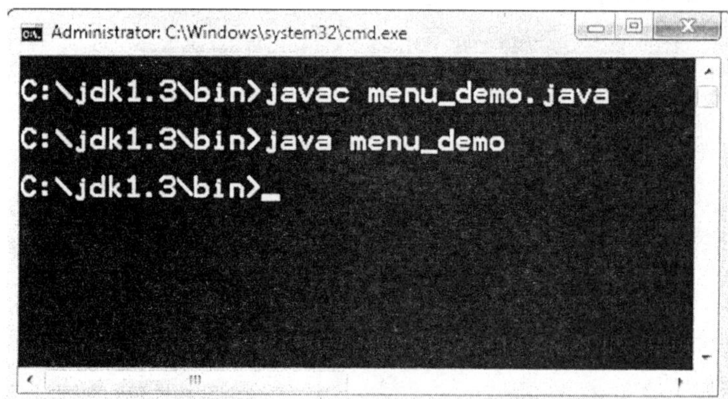


Output of above program will be as follows.

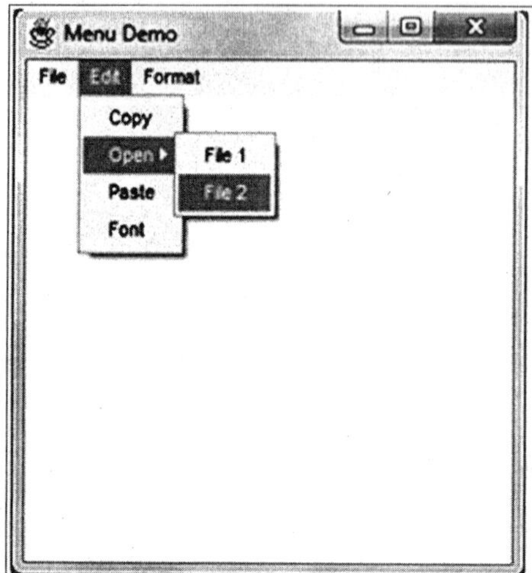


**setMenuBar( )** method is used to set menubar in the Frame window.

## 5.10 Dialog Boxes

Dialog boxes and Panels are child windows of top-level window that contain set of related controls. Panel and Dialog boxes cannot have MenuBar. We add different component objects into the Dialog boxes and Panel same as other top-level windows i.e. by using add( ) method. A Dialog box is created by extending a user defined class with built-in class **Dialog**. Dialog class has following methods.

void setTitle(String *title*)
void setSize(int *width*, int *height*)
void setVisible(boolean *visible*)
void dispose( )

**setTitle( )** method sets the title of the dialog box. **setSize( )** method sets the size of dialog box. **setVisible( )** method makes the dialog box visible and invisible. When a call to **displose( )** method is made, it frees all the system resources associated with the invoking Dialog box object.

Dialog class has following two constructors.

Dialog(Frame parent_window_object, boolean visibility)
Dialog(Frame *parent_window_object*, String *title*, boolean *visibility*)

Here is a program to demonstrate dialog box.

```
import java.awt.*;
import java.applet.*;
import java.awt.event.*;
class dialogbox extends Dialog
{
        public dialogbox(Frame fr,String st)
        {
                super(fr,st,true);
                Label lb1 = new Label("This is in Dialog box");
                add(lb1);
                setSize(300,200);
        }
        public void paint(Graphics g)
        {
                g.drawString("This is in the dialog box", 10, 70);
        }
}

class open_dialog extends Frame implements ActionListener
{
        Frame f1;
        public open_dialog()
        {
                setLayout(null);
                Button bt = new Button("Show Dialog");
                add(bt);
                bt.setBounds(50,100,90,35);
                bt.addActionListener(this);
        }
```

```
        public void copy(Frame f)
        {
                f1=f;
        }
        public void actionPerformed(ActionEvent ae)
        {
                dialogbox d = new dialogbox(f1,"Dialog box Title Here");
                d.setVisible(true);
        }
}

public class dialog_demo extends Applet
{
        public void init()
        {
                open_dialog d1 = new open_dialog();
                d1.copy(d1);
                d1.setSize(400,400);
                d1.setTitle("Frame showing Dialog box");
                d1.setVisible(true);

        }
}
```

Output of above program will be:

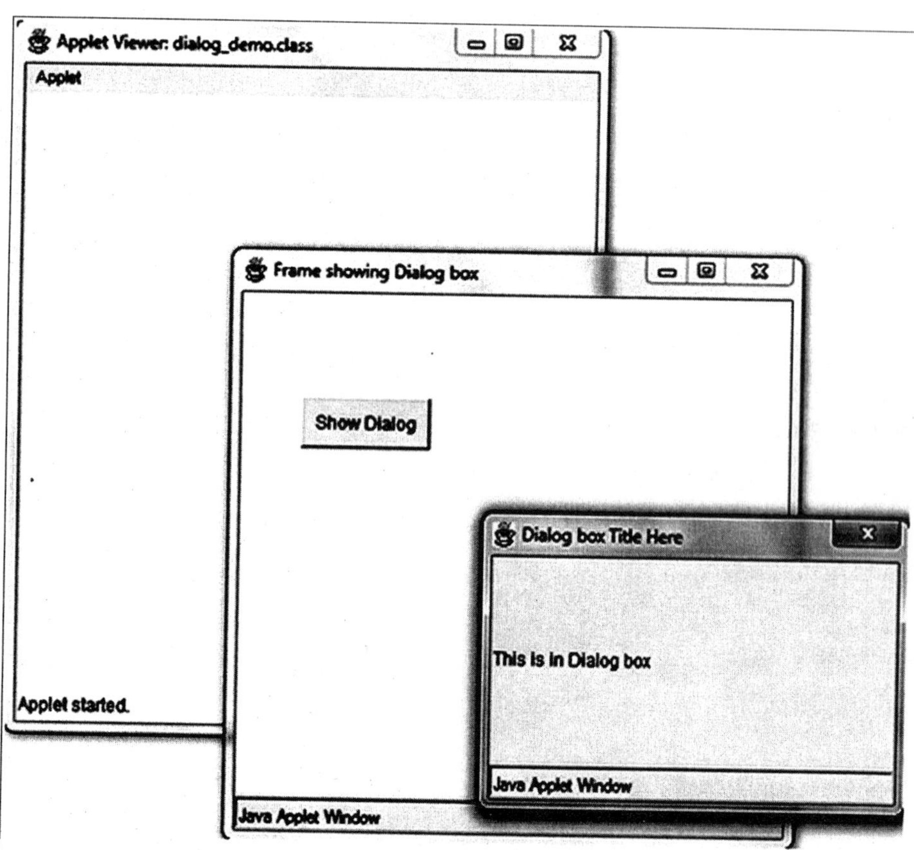


Execution of above program begins with Applet, which sets visibility of frame. The dialog box appears when the button "Show Dialog" is clicked. Handling such clicks is part of **event handling mechanism**. It is explained later in this chapter.

## 5.11 Using Panel

As discussed above Panel class is a child window of top-level window. Consider a group of component objects, which is needed to be appeared on multiple frames or applets. It is not feasible solution to create all those component objects on all the frames or applets. For such task, Panel class is a good option. To create a panel, extends a user defined class with built-in class Panel and add components using constructor of that class. For example,

```
class  pnl extends Panel
{
        public  pnl( )
        {
                ------------            // declare and add components for panel
                ------------
        }
}
```

A Panel actually works *as a container which contains multiple component objects* and even *as a component which is added into the Frame or Applet classes* using **add( )** method. Following program demonstrates Panel.

```
import java.awt.*;
import java.applet.*;
class pnl extends Panel
{
        public pnl()
        {
                Label lb1 = new Label("This is from Panel");
                Button bt1 = new Button("Panel");
                add(lb1);
                add(bt1);
        }
}

public class panel_demo extends Applet
{
        public void init()
        {
                pnl p1 = new pnl();
                Checkbox ch1 = new Checkbox("From Applet");
                add(p1);
                add(ch1);
                fr f1 = new fr();
                f1.setTitle("Frame showing Panel");
                f1.setSize(400,300);
                f1.setVisible(true);
        }
}


class fr extends Frame
{
        public fr()
```

```
    {
            setLayout(null);
            pnl p2 = new pnl();
            Checkbox ch1 = new Checkbox("From Frame");
            add(p2);
            add(ch1);
            p2.setBounds(50,50,200,50);
            ch1.setBounds(200,200,100,20);
    }
}
```

Output of above program will be:

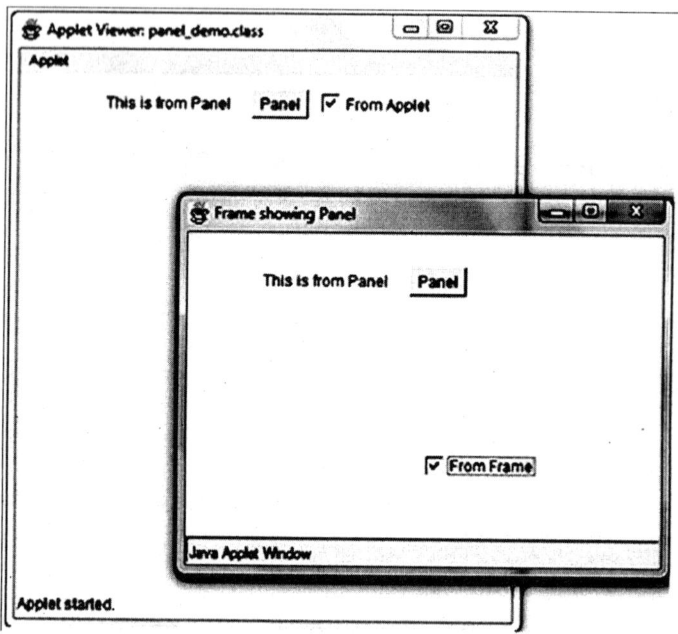


We can see that Label and Button is from panel and both the windows contains a checkbox provided by each class. Similarly we can add any number of components and use it for multiple top-level windows. Remember that, a Panel can be nested in another Panel too, as a component.

## 5.12 Managing fonts

Java supports different fonts to make an application more attractive. To deal with fonts, java provides a built-in class **Font**. This Font class has three important variable arguments. They are: **name, size** and **style**. To select a new font, you must create an object of Font class with all required parameters. Its constructor is:

Font(String *font_name*, int *font_style*, int *font_size*)

Here *font_name* specifies name of the desired font. Remember before applying any font, check whether that font is available with your operating system or not. *font_size* describes size of font in points. The style of font is specified by using three static constants: **Font.PLAIN**, **Font.BOLD**, **Font.ITALIC.** To combine styles, use OR (|). For example **Font.BOLD | Font.ITALIC.**

After defining specified Font object, apply the font by using **setFont( )** method. It is defined as,

void setFont(Font *obj*)

We can also retrieve current font by using **getFont( )** method. Its signature is:

```
Font  getFont( )
```

We can also retrieve all the available fonts by using getAllFonts( ) method defined under **GraphicsEnvironment** class. It is called by using object of **GraphicsEnvironment** class. It is defined as:

```
Font[ ] getAllFonts( )
```

This program will show you all the available fonts with your operating system.

```
import java.awt.*;
import java.applet.*;
public class font_ extends Applet
{
	public void paint(Graphics g)
	{
		String list = "";
		String f[ ];
		GraphicsEnvironment ge = GraphicsEnvironment.getLocalGraphicsEnvironment( );
		f = ge.getAllFonts();
		for(int i = 0; i < f.length; i++)
		{
			list = list + FontList[i] + " ";
		}
		g.drawString(list, 10, 15);
	}
}
```

Here is another program demonstrating font.

```
import java.awt.*;
import java.applet.*;
public class font_demo extends Applet
{
	public void init()
	{
		Font f1 = new Font("Serif",Font.ITALIC,25);
		setFont(f1);
		Label lb1 = new Label("This is Label 1");
		Label lb2 = new Label("This is Label 2");
		add(lb1);
		add(lb2);
	}
}
```

## 5.13 Layout Managers

It is very tedious job to align all the components on a window. All the components which we have studied so far appears on the screen by using **add( )** method. These components are by default positioned on screen by using default layout manager. Role of layout manager is to position these components using different alignment algorithms.

If you have observed each output screenshots carefully, you can see that all the components are not aligned properly. If we are programming for a GUI application then it is essential to align all the components, because most of success of an application depends on its easy and eye-catching design. Hence it is necessary to understand layout managers and align the components properly.

The layout manager is set by using **setLayout( )** method, comes under **LayoutManager** interface. This method is defined as:

void setLayout(LayoutManager *obj*)

Here, *obj* is an object of desired layout manager. If you want to disable the layout manager then **pass "null" to setLayout( )** method and align the components manually by using **setBounds( )** method. Normally to avoid headache of aligning components manually, we use layout managers. Java has four built-in LayoutManager classes. They are discussed here in brief.

### 5.13.1 FlowLayout

FlowLayout is the default layout manager. All the previous examples have used this layout. This is the simple layout which arranges the components as they are added. When no more components fit on a line, it begins with next line. By default it keeps space of **5 pixels** between vertical and horizontal components. To create an object of this layout manager, we have following constructors.

FlowLayout( )
FlowLayout(int *alignment*)
FlowLayout(int *alignment*, int *horizontal_gap*, int *vertical_gap*)

First constructor creates an object which by default leaves gap of 5 pixels and aligns center. Second constructor requires to specify *alignment* of each line. It is done by using three static constants: **FlowLayout.LEFT**, **FlowLayout.RIGHT**, **FlowLayout.CENTER**. Third constructor requires alignment and horizontal and vertical gap between components. Here is a program demonstrating FlowLayout manager.

```
import java.awt.*;
import java.applet.*;
public class flowlayout_demo extends Applet
{
	public void init()
	{
		FlowLayout fl = new FlowLayout();
		setLayout(fl);
		Label l1 = new Label("Enter User ID :");
		Checkbox ch1 = new Checkbox("Pizza");
		TextField tf1 = new TextField("This is textbox");
		Label l2 = new Label("Enter Password :");
		add(l1);
```

```
            add(ch1);
            add(tf1);
            add(l2);
    }
}
```

Above program will show following output.

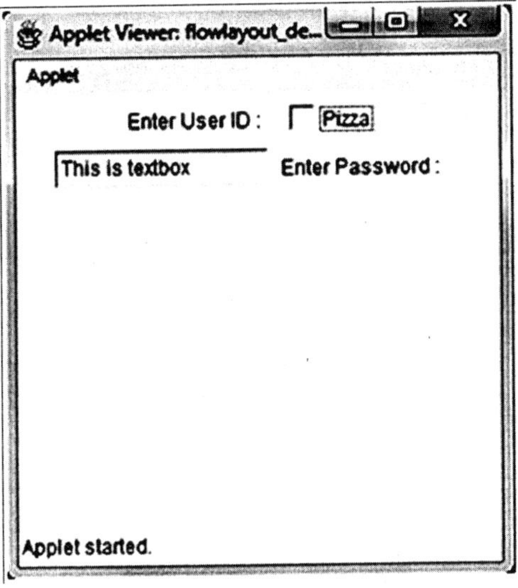


We can see that components are by default aligned center and TextField is placed in second line because of insufficient space.

### 5.13.2 BorderLayout

BorderLayout is with four sides and one center area. Its sides are referred as north, south, east and west. The middle area is called as center. We can place fixed width components at the edges. Here is a list of constructors of BorderLayout.

BorderLayout( )
BorderLayout(int *horizontal_gap*, int *vertical_gap*)

First constructor creates a default BorderLayout object with default settings. Second constructor allows us to specify horizontal and vertical space between components.

While adding components using BorderLayout, use following add( ) method.

add(Component *object*, int *region*)

here, *region* specifies where the components is to be placed. BorderLayout specifies these region related constants: **BorderLayout.CENTER**, **BorderLayout.SOUTH**, **BorderLayout.EAST**, **BorderLayout.WEST**, **BorderLayout.NORTH**.

Refer following program to demonstrate BorderLayout.

```
import java.awt.*;
import java.applet.*;
import java.util.*;
public class borderlayout_demo extends Applet
{
        public void init()
        {
                setLayout(new BorderLayout());
                Button bt1 = new Button("TOP HEADER - NORTH");
                add(bt1,BorderLayout.NORTH);
                add(new Button("BOTTOM FOOTER - SOUTH"),BorderLayout.SOUTH);
                Button bt3 = new Button("RIGHT - EAST");
                add(bt3, BorderLayout.EAST);
                add(new Button("LEFT - WEST"), BorderLayout.WEST);
                String S = "This program shows another\n"
                +"way of creating and\n"
                +"adding a components\n";
                add(new TextArea(S), BorderLayout.CENTER);
        }
}
```

Output of above program will be:

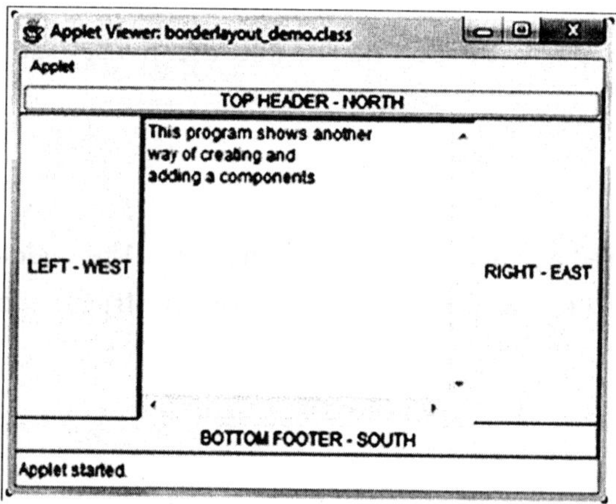


### 5.13.3 GridLayout

GridLayout position the components in two dimensional grid. Here is the list of constructors of GridLayout.

> GridLayout( )
> GridLayout(int *rows*, int *columns*)
> GridLayout(int *rows*, int *columns*, int *horizontal_gap*, int *vertical_gap*)

First constructor creates a default GridLayout with single row and column. Second constructor allows specifying numbers of rows and columns. Third form requires numbers of rows and columns as well horizontal and vertical space between components. Following program creates a mobile keypad.

```
import java.awt.*;
import java.applet.*;
public class gridlayout_demo extends Applet
{
```

```
        public void init()
        {
                setFont(new Font("SansSerif", Font.BOLD, 24));
                GridLayout gl = new GridLayout(4,3);
                setLayout(gl);
                for(int i = 1;i <=9; i++)
                {
                        add(new Button("" + i));
                }
                Button bt1 = new Button("*");
                Button bt2 = new Button("0");
                Button bt3 = new Button("#");
                add(bt1);
                add(bt2);
                add(bt3);
        }
}
```

Above program will show following output.

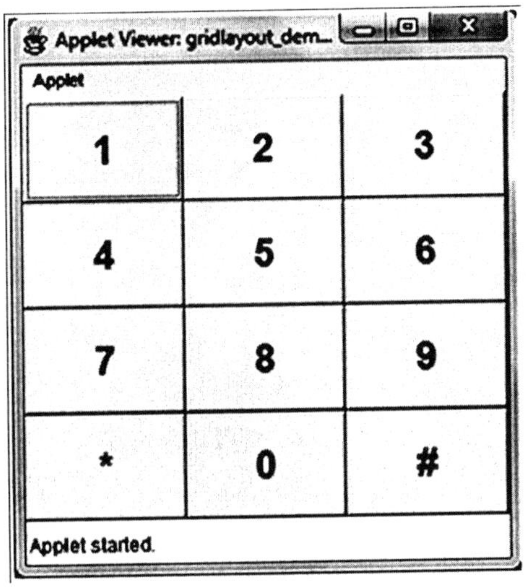

| Applet Viewer: gridlayout_dem... | | |
|---|---|---|
| 1 | 2 | 3 |
| 4 | 5 | 6 |
| 7 | 8 | 9 |
| * | 0 | # |

Applet started.

### 5.13.4 CardLayout

The card layout is a unique layout among other layout manager classes. Different CardLayout object can have different layouts. A CardLayout manger object should be held in an object of Panel. We can have multiple Panel objects and any one object can be on the top. Other Panel objects can be made visible and invisible as per user's input. Here are the constructors of CardLayout.

CardLayout( )
CardLayout(int *horizontal_gap*, int *vertical_gap*)

Use of CardLayout requires more work than other layout managers. You must create a **Panel** that contains the deck and a Panel for each card in the deck. Then you add to the appropriate panel that contains components. Then add these panels to the main panel to which **CardLayout** is set. This looks a bit complicated but when you practice this, it becomes a normal process for you. To add cards to the panel, add( ) method is used. Its general form is:

void add(Component *obj*, Panel *obj*)

This method adds specified component object into specified panel object. CardLayout has following methods which shifts between different decks.

void first(Container *deck*)
void last(Container *deck*)
void next(Container *deck*)
void previous(Container *deck*)
void show(Container *deck*, String *card_name*)

Here *deck* is a **Panel object** that holds the cards. The method **first( )** shows first card in the deck. **last( )** method shows last card in the deck. **next( )** method shows next card in the deck. **previous( )** method shows previous card in the deck. **show( )** method displays specified *card_name* in specified *deck*. Following program demonstrates CardLayout.

```
import java.awt.*;
import java.applet.*;
import java.awt.event.*;
public class cardlayout_demo extends Applet implements ActionListener
{
        Checkbox ch1, ch2, ch3, ch4;
        Panel pnl1;
        CardLayout cl;
        Button btn1, btn2;
        public void init( )
        {
                btn1 = new Button("Colours");
                btn2 = new Button("Flavours");
                add(btn1);
                add(btn2);
                cl = new CardLayout();
                pnl1 = new Panel();
                pnl1.setLayout(cl);
                ch1 = new Checkbox("Blue");
                ch2 = new Checkbox("Red");
                ch3 = new Checkbox("Vanilla");
                ch4 = new Checkbox("Strawberry");
                // Adding Color checkboxes to panel-2
                Panel pnl2 = new Panel();
                pnl2.add(ch1);
                pnl2.add(ch2);
                // Adding Flavour checkboxes to panel-3
                Panel pnl3 = new Panel();
                pnl3.add(ch3);
                pnl3.add(ch4);
                // Adding panels to card deck panel-1
                pnl1.add(pnl2, "Colors");
                pnl1.add(pnl3, "Flavours");
                // Adding panle-1 to applet
                add(pnl1);
                // registering buttons for event
                btn1.addActionListener(this);
                btn2.addActionListener(this);
        }
```

```
        public void actionPerformed(ActionEvent ae)
        {
                if(ae.getSource() == btn1)
                {
                        cl.show(pnl1, "Colors");
                }
                else
                {
                        cl.show(pnl1, "Flavours");
                }
        }
}
```

Output of above program will be:

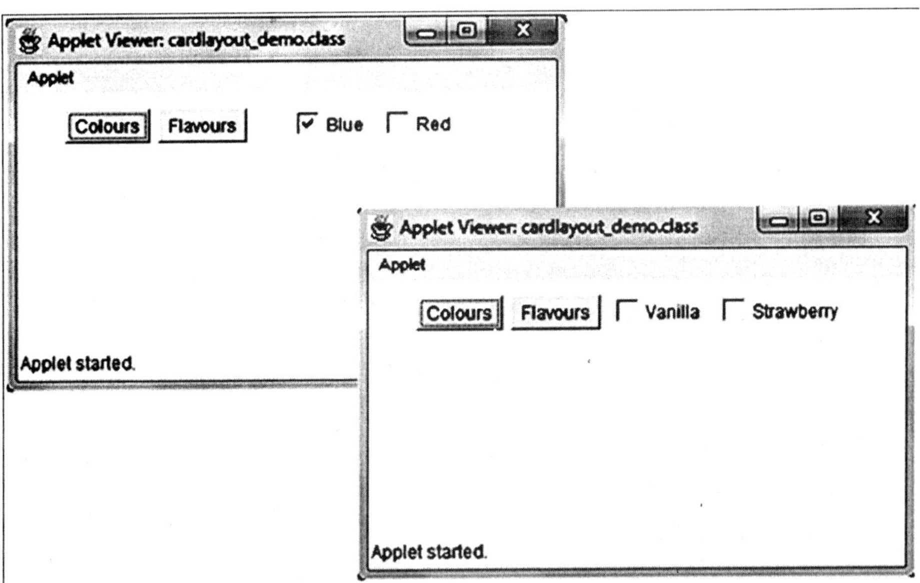


When a button is clicked, its related panel is shown by using **show( )** method.

## 5.14 Color class and methods

Java supports the highest numbers of colors among all other programming languages. Java's color system allows you to specify any color you want. Java has many color constants to specify common colors. We can also create our own colors by using constructor of **Color** class. The most commonly used forms are mentioned here:

> Color(int *red*, int *green*, int *blue*)
> Color(int *rbg_value*)
> Color(float *red*, float *green*, float *blue*)

The first constructor specifies a color which is blend of red, green and blue color. These values must be in-between 0 to 255. Second constructor contains a single integer value that contains the mix of red, green and blue packed into an integer. Third constructor generates a color which is combination of red, green and blue color. These float values must be between 0.0 to 1.0

Once you have defined a color object, you can use it with coloring methods.

```
void setForeground(Color obj)
void setBackground(Color obj)
```

**setForeground( )** method is used to set font color and **setBackground( )** method is used to set background color. You can also retrieve coloring values of red, green and blue color separately, by calling following methods.

int getRed( ) - returns red color component found in invoking color object.
int getGreen( ) - returns green color component found in invoking color object.
int getBlue( ) - returns blue color component found in invoking color object.

We can also retrieve current color combination by using:

Color getColor( )

Here is a program demonstrating colors in Applet.

```
import java.awt.*;
import java.applet.*;
public class color_demo extends Applet
{
	public void paint(Graphics g)
	{
		Color c1 = new Color(100,100,255);
		Color c2 = new Color(150,200,100);
		Color c3 = new Color(120,120,20);
		g.setColor(c1);
		g.fillRect(20,20,110,220);
		g.setColor(c2);
		g.fillOval(150,150,100,160);
		g.setColor(Color.red);
		g.drawLine(75,30,200,250);
		g.setColor(c3);
		g.fillRoundRect(190,10,160,150,15,15);
	}
}
```

Output of above program will be:

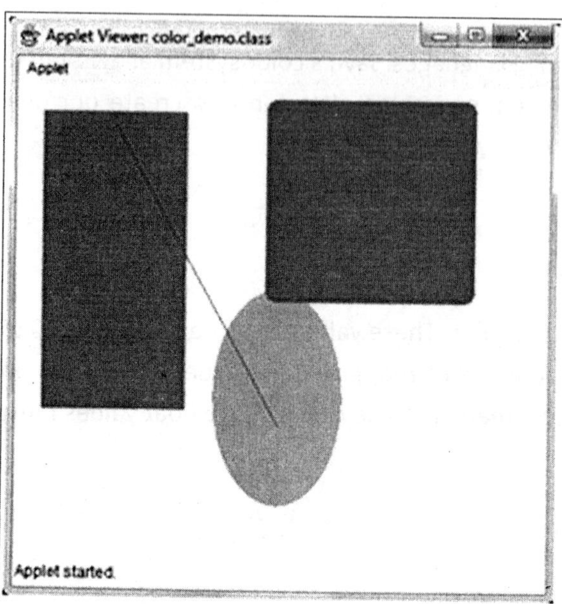

## 5.15 Difference between Applet and Application

All Java programs can be classified as **Applications** and **Applets**. The striking difference between them is about main( ) method. Applications contain main( ) but Applets do not. One more difference is, Applets create web applications and Applications create stand alone applications. Following table shows the basic visible differences between applet and application.

| Feature | Applet | Application |
|---|---|---|
| **main( ) method** | Not required. | Required. |
| **Security** | Security Manager provided by browser. Remote code is untrusted. | No default Security Manager. All code is trusted by default |
| **Execution Privileges** | Runs in the context of a browser | Runs standalone |
| **Container** | Browser | None |
| **Communication** | Inter-applet communication limited by browser | No restrictions. |
| **Lifecycle** | Controlled by browser | Controlled by user. |
| **Peer** | Created and assigned by the Browser | No default. Must be created by the application. |
| **Network Access** | May only open a socket connection to the host it was loaded from | No restrictions |
| **Invoke Native Methods** | No | Yes |
| **Support** | Applet is portable and can be executed by any JAVA supported browser. | Need JDK, JRE, JVM installed on client machine. |

## 5.16 Understanding Swing

Till now we have studied different AWT components. But here we will have a little discussion on its alternate called as *swing*. Swings are more **powerful**, **flexible** and **light-weight** components as compare to AWT components. In addition to the familiar components of AWT, such as Button, TextField, TextArea, Checkbox, List, Label, etc. swing provides several exciting additions to it, such as Tabbed Panes, Radio Buttons, Scroll Panes, Trees, Tables, Combo Boxes, etc. Swing also provides additions in methods, data members, properties, and constructors of component classes.

Here is a list of swing classes with a small description.

| Class | Description |
|---|---|
| JButton | swing edition of command button / push button. |
| JCheckbox | swing edition of Checkbox. |
| JLabel | swing edition of Label. |
| JTextField | swing edition of TextField. |
| JTextArea | swing edition of TextArea. |
| JList | swing edition of List. |
| JFrame | swing edition of Frame. |
| JPanel | swing edition of Panel. |
| JApplet | swing edition of Applet. |
| JTabbedPane | shows different tabs in a window. |
| JTree | shows hierarchy view. |
| JTable | shows a table. |
| JRadioButton | shows a radio button. |
| JComboBox | shows a combobox: combination of TextField and List. |

Remember that, all these swing component classes are under **javax.swing** package. We cannot study all these components at this stage. But here is a program which demonstrates swing components.

```
import javax.swing.*;
import java.awt.*;
public class swing_demo extends JApplet
{
	public void init()
	{
		Container ct = getContentPane( );
		ct.setLayout(null);
		JLabel lb1 = new JLabel("This is label");
		JButton bt1 = new JButton("Click Me");
		JTextField tf1 = new JTextField();
		ct.add(lb1);
		ct.add(bt1);
		ct.add(tf1);
		lb1.setBounds(20,20,100,30);
		bt1.setBounds(20,70,150,30);
		tf1.setBounds(20,120,90,30);
	}
}
```

Here is the output of above program.

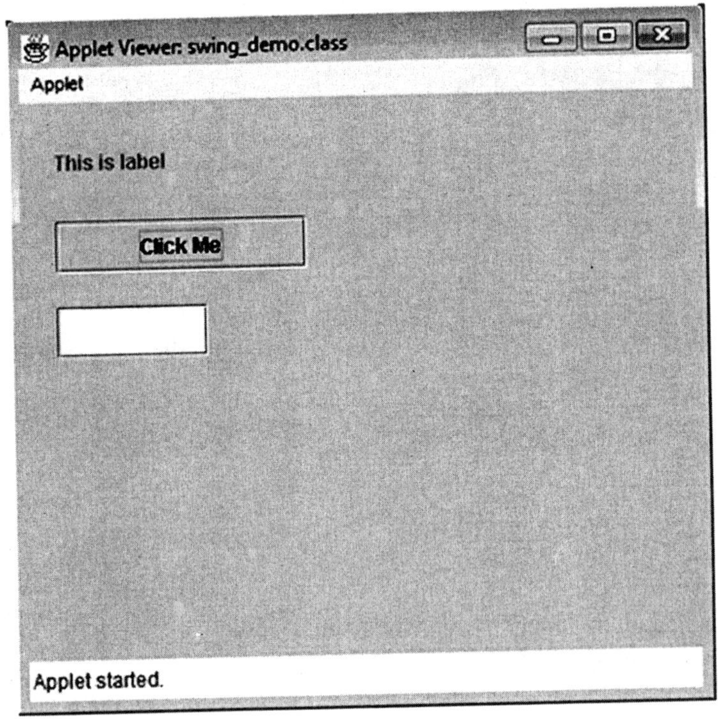


Note the difference between **add( )** method, used to add components on the window. JApplet very much differs from basic AWT Applet. It is rich in functionalities. JApplet supports various **Panes**, like content pane, glass pane and root pane. We cannot directly add a component into the JApplet. We have to create an object of **required Pane** and add the component into that Pane. Refer the statement:

```
Container ct = getContentPane( );
```

Here, **ct** is an object of Container class which gets the permission to add into the content pane. The method getContentPane( ) is defined as:

```
Container getContentPane( )
```

The same method is used to add components into the Frame.

*****

# Chapter 6
# Swings

The last section of previous chapter described quite a few core concepts related to swing. Now in this chapter we will study the swing components and their relative advantages of AWT components. Swing implements a set of GUI components that build on AWT technology and provide a pluggable look and feel. Swing is implemented entirely in the Java programming language, and is based on the **JDK 1.1 Lightweight UI Framework**.

Swing features include:

- All the features of AWT.
- 100% Pure Java certified versions of the existing AWT component set (Button, Scrollbar, Label, etc.).
- A rich set of higher-level components (such as tree view, list box, and tabbed panes).
- Pure Java design, no reliance on peers.
- Pluggable Look and Feel.

Swing components do **not depend on peers** to handle their functionality. Thus, these components are often called **"lightweight" components**.

In general, AWT components are appropriate for simple applet development that targets a specific platform (i.e. the Java program will run on only one platform).

For most any other Java GUI development you will want to use Swing components. Also note that the Borland value-added components included with JBuilder, like dbSwing and JBCL (Java Borland Class Library), are based on Swing components so if you wish to use these components you will want to base your development on Swing.

## 6.1 The origin of Swing

In first version of Java, the swing actually was not present. As and when the developers started using AWT components, they realize the deficiencies in AWT's GUI system. We know that, AWT defines a basic set of components, window, menus, dialogue boxes, applets. But AWT components has limited graphical interface. The look and feel of AWT components are purely platform based. The reason behind this is, AWT components uses native code resources. Hence they are referred to as **heavy-weight components**.

Actually the use of native code requires native peers. These native peers generate the problem. Such as:

- Because of difference in Operating system environments; look, feel and activity of components changes.
- The use of AWT components causes some boundaries to developers. (Such as shape of each component is fixed; either rectangular or opaque.)
- Look and feel of each component is fixed. (Due to Operating System dependency)

Now, the Java team requires a serious solution to these problems of heavy-weight components. Hence, in 1997 swing components were introduced. It was initially available in Java 1.1 as a separate library(called JFL : Java Foundation Library), but in Java 1.2, it was fully merged with Java Class Libraries.

## 6.2 Swing is built on AWT

As we have discussed that, limitation of AWT components are overcame by Swing components and eliminated many drawbacks. Now many users wonder, "why AWT is still part of Java?". Actually, Swing does not replace AWT. Instead, Swing is based on the foundation of AWT. That is why still AWT is a vital part of Java.

The swing components use same event handling mechanism as of AWT. Therefore a basic understanding of event handling is necessary. In this book, **chapter 6** teaches event handling system. It contains some examples related to AWT and some to swings.

## 6.3 Key features of Swing

As discussed in above **section 6.1**, swing has eliminated many limitations of AWT. It is mainly because of its two features.

- Swing components are lightweight
- Swing supports a pluggable look and feel

The swing components are entirely written in Java and hence not platform-specific. This makes swing as light-weight components. Swing components are more efficient and more flexible.

Pluggable look and feel gives some advantages. When swing components appear on screen, it gives default look and feel called as **metal**. Swing has three built-in look and feel (like Operating System themes): **Metal**, **Motif** and **Nimbus**. We can also create a custom look and feel.

## 6.4 The MVC architecture

The MVC architecture is the most adopted component architecture that effectively contains: Model – View – Controller. Any component has three major phases:

1. The information/properties associated with that component.
2. The way that the component looks when submitted on the screen.
3. The way that the components reacts to user.

There are many other architectures used to implement a component, and all contains above three phases. But the MVC is the most adopted component architecture.

The MVC architecture is successful because **each** component corresponds to all phases. In MVC architecture, **the model** represents the information/properties associated with the component, **the view** represents the way that component is displayed, and **the controller** represents how the component reacts to user. For example, in case of a Listbox, **the model** controls the properties containing collection of items of Listbox, **the view** controls how it is displayed and which item is initially kept as selected, **the controller** controls the reactions of Listbox on user clicks.

**Note: Actually swing uses a modified version of MVC architecture, that combines view and controller into a single entity called as UI. Hence MVC architecture for swing is called as Model-Delegate architecture or the Separable Model architecture.**

## 6.5 Components and Containers

Swing's User Interface is distributed into two items: **components** and **containers**. As we already studied in previous chapter, that **component** is an independent individual visual control and **container** is the area where components are grouped or placed. We can also say that *a container is also one of the components.* In order to display any component, it must be held within a container. A *container can also hold other containers* and create hierarchy of containers. The components and containers are described here in brief.

## 6.6 Component classes

JComponent class is the hierarchy/root class of all swing component classes. JComponent is the class that provides pluggable look and feel. JComponent class gives visual GUI to swing components. JComponent class inherits AWT's Component class. Hence, we can say that swing components are built on AWT classes. Following is the list showing swing component classes.

| JApplet | JFrame | JWindow | JPanel |
|---|---|---|---|
| JButton | JSpinner | JRadioButton | JRadioButton |
| JRadioButtonMenuItem | JInternalFrame | JRootPane | JDialog |
| JLayer | JComponent | JDesktopPane | JEditorPane |
| JFileChooser | JFormattedTextField | JPasswordField | JLayeredPane |
| JColorChooser | JLabel | JList | JOptionPane |
| JPopupMenu | JProgressBar | JComboBox | JScrollBar |
| JScrollPane | JSeparator | JSlider | JSplitPane |
| JTabbedPane | JTable | JTextArea | JTextField |
| JTextPane | JToolBar | JToolTip | JTogglebutton |
| JMenu | JMenuItem | JMenuBar | JTree |
| JViewport | | | |

Remember that, all swing component classes are under **javax.swing** package. These all class names begin with capital letter 'J'.

## 6.7 Containers

Swing defines two types of containers.

1. Heavyweight containers
2. Lightweight containers

The heavyweight containers are top-level containers that do not inherit JComponent. The heavyweight swing containers are **JFrame**, **JApplet**, **JWindow** and **JDialog**. As the name implies a top level container must be at top of control hierarchy. The most commonly used top-level containers are JFrame for standalone applications and JApplet for web application.

The lightweight containers do inherit JComponent. The lightweight container supported by swing is **JPanel, JLayeredPane** and **JRootPane**. It is a general purpose container. The lightweight containers are often used to organize and manage groups of related components because a lightweight container can be contained within another container (i.e. can be nested). Thus, we can use lightweight containers such as JPanel to create subgroups of related controls that are contained within an outer container.

## 6.8 The Top-Level Container Panes

Each top level container defines a set of panes. Swing's top level containers provide three panes. These panes are managed by lightweight container JRootPane. It also helps to manage the menu bar.

1. glass pane
2. content pane
3. layered pane

The **glass pane** is the top-level pane and covers all other panes. By default, it is a transparent instance of JPanel. For example, the glass pane enables us to manage mouse events that affect the entire container or to paint over any other component. In most cases, we won't need to use the glass pane directly, but it will be available if we need it.

The **layered pane** is an instance of JLayeredPane. The layered pane allows components to be given a depth value. This value determines which component overlays another. Thus, the layered pane lets you specify a Z-order for a component, although this is not something that we usually need to do. The layered pane hold the content pane and menu bar.

The **content pane** is the pane with which your application will interact the most, because this is the pane to which you will add visual components (AWT or swing). In other words, when you add a component, such as a button, to a top-level container, you will add it to the content pane. By default, the content pane is an opaque instance of JPanel.

## 6.9 The Swing Packages

The swing is a very large sub system. It contains many packages and sub-packages. Following table shows the swing packages available till this release.

| Package | Description |
|---|---|
| **javax.swing** | Provides a set of "lightweight" (all-Java language) components that, to the maximum degree possible, work the same on all platforms. |
| **javax.swing.plaf** | Provides one interface and many abstract classes that Swing uses to provide its pluggable look-and-feel capabilities. |
| **javax.swing.plaf.basic** | Provides user interface objects built according to the Basic look-and-feel. |
| **javax.swing.plaf.multi** | Provides user interface objects built according to multi- platform look-and-feel. |
| **javax.swing.plaf.metal** | Provides user interface objects built according to the ``metal" look-and-feel. |
| **com.sun.java.swing.plaf.motif** | Provides user interface objects built according to the ``Motif" look-and-feel. |
| **com.sun.java.swing.plaf.windows** | Provides user interface objects built according to the ``Windows" look-and-feel. |
| **javax.accessibility** | Defines a contract between user-interface components and an assistive technology that provides access to those components. |
| **javax.swing.border** | Provides classes and interface for drawing specialized borders around a Swing component. |
| **javax.swing.colorchooser** | Contains classes and interfaces used by the JColorChooser component. |
| **javax.swing.event** | Provides for events fired by Swing components. |
| **javax.swing.filechooser** | Contains classes and interfaces used by the JFileChooser component. |
| **javax.swing.table** | Provides classes and interfaces for dealing with java.awt.swing.JTable. |
| **javax.swing.text** | Provides classes and interfaces that deal with editable and noneditable text components. |
| **javax.swing.text.html** | Provides the class (HTMLEditorKit) and supporting classes for creating HTML text editors. |
| **javax.swing.tree** | Provides classes and interfaces for dealing with java.awt.swing.JTree. |
| **javax.swing.undo** | Provides support for undo/redo capabilities in an application such as a text editor. |

Among these, the javax.swing is the most commonly used package that contains the swing component classes for push buttons, labels, textfields, checkboxes and radio buttons.

## 6.10 A Simple Swing Application using JFrame

We know that swing programs are very much different from AWT based programs and console based programs. Using swing we can create desktop applications and web applications. To study more on swing, it is better to understand a swing program and discuss. Refer following program that uses JFrame as top-level window and JLabel as its component.

```
import javax.swing.*;

        import java.awt.*;
        class jframe_demo extends JFrame
        {
                public jframe_demo ( )
                {
                        Container ct = getContentPane( );
                        JLabel jl = new JLabel("Swing has pluggable look and feel");
                        ct.add(jl);
                }
                public static void main(String ar[ ])
                {
                        jframe_demo sd = new jframe_demo ( );
                        sd.setTitle("Demonstrating Swing");
                        sd.setSize(300,300);
                        sd.setDefaultCloseOperation(JFrame.EXIT_ON_CLOSE);
                        sd.setVisible(true);
                }
        }
```

Let's call above program as *jframe_demo.java*

Swing programs are compiled and executed in the same way as other AWT programs. Hence compile above program as:

*javac jframe_demo.java*

and run this program as:

*java jframe_demo*

On successful compilation the swing program also generates bytecodes (.class files). When above program is executed it shows following output.

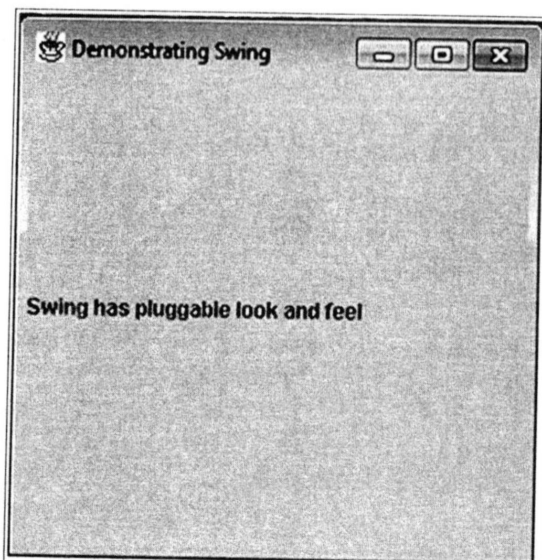


As above program contains some core swing concepts, we will discuss this one by one, line by line.

*import javax.swing.*;*

imports javax.swing classes. Here we import it for JFrame and JLabel.

*import java.awt.*;*

imports java.awt classes. Here we import it for Container.

*Container ct = getContentPane();*

creates a container object *ct* to add swing components into it. The getContentPane( ) method returns a container object. It is defined as : ***Container getContentPane( )***

*JLabel jl = new JLabel("Swing has pluggable look and feel");*

creates *jl* as JLabel object with text as "Swing has pluggable look and feel".

*ct.add(jl);*

adds *jl* into container *ct*.

*jframe_demo sd = new jframe_demo ();*

creates *sd* as object of user defined JFrame class.

*sd.setTitle("Demonstrating Swing");*

sets title for frame. This method is defined as : **void setTitle (String title)**

sd.setSize(300,300);

sets size for frame in numbers of pixels. This method is defined as : **void setSize (int width,int height)**

sd.setDefaultCloseOperation( )

sets default close operation for frame. An AWT Frame cannot be closed by closing that window. We have to additionally use window events to close it. But here in JFrame we can directly close a JFrame window by using this mehthod. This method is define as : **void setDefaultCloseOperation (int operation)**

This close operation is specified by three static constants of **WindowConstants interface** declared in javax.swing and this is implemented by JFrame class. Their name reflects their actions. They are :

EXIT_ON_CLOSE
HIDE_ON_CLOSE
DO_NOTHING_ON_CLOSE

sd.setVisible(true);

By default a frame is not visible; we have to call this method and apply it true, to make it visible. This statement makes a frame window visible. This method is defined as : **void setVisible(boolean visibility)**

## 6.11 A Simple Swing Application using JApplet

The second type of application that commonly uses the swing components is the JApplet. Swing based JApplet is same as AWT based Applet. Simply we need to extend **JApplet** instead of **Applet** and create Container object to add components into it. A swing JApplet extends AWT Applet and hence the life cycle of JApplet is same as the life cycle of Applet and all the functionalities found in AWT Applet is achieved in swing's JApplet.

As described earlier the JApplet is also a top-level window and contains various panes. Hence object of Container is required to add components into it. Here is a modified version of above program that extends JApplet and executes using web browser or appletviewer.

```
import javax.swing.*;
import java.awt.*;
public class japplet_demo extends JApplet
{
        public void start( )
        {
                Container ct = getContentPane( );
                JLabel jl = new JLabel("Demonstrating swing components in JApplet");
                ct.add(jl);
        }
}
```

Let's call above program japplet_demo.java

JApplet program are compiled and executed in the same way as we did for AWT applet programs. Hence compile above program as:

*javac japplet_demo.java*

and to run this program create html file with <applet> tag as:

```
<html>
<body>
<applet code="japplet_demo.class" width="400" height="400"></applet>
</body>
</html>
```

Let's call above program as one.html and run this using *appletviewer* as :

*appletviewer one.html*

When above program is executed it shows following output.

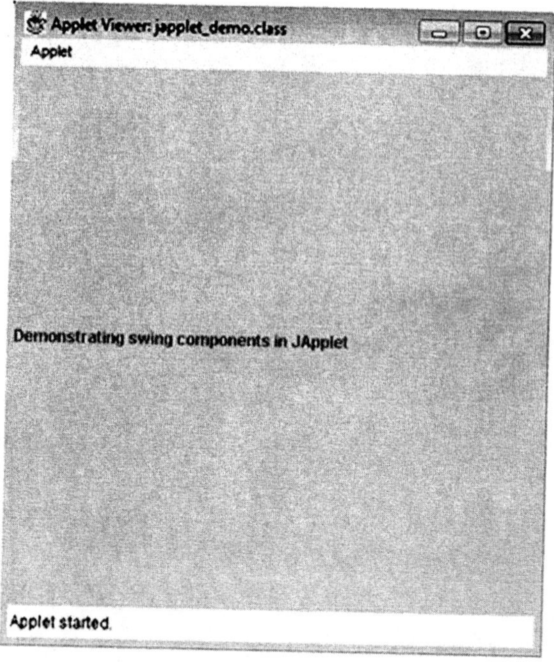

Swing's applets use the same four lifecycle methods as described in previous chapter : init( ), start( ), stop( ) and destroy( ). Of course, you need override only those methods that are needed by your applet. Painting is accomplished differently in Swing than it is in the AWT, and a Swing applet will not normally override the paint( ) method.

## 6.12 Swing Component classes

This section continues the discussion of Swing by presenting an overview of several Swing components, such as buttons, check boxes, trees, and tables. The Swing components provide rich functionality and allow a high level of customization. Because of space limitations, it is not possible to describe all of their features and attributes. Rather, the purpose of this overview is to give you a feel for the capabilities of the Swing component set.

The Swing component classes described in this section are shown here:

| | | | |
|---|---|---|---|
| ImageIcon | JLabel | JTextField | JButton |
| JToggleButton | JRadioButton | JRadioButton | JTabbedPane |
| JScrollPane | JComboBox | JTree | JTable |

### 6.12.1 JLabel and ImageIcon

Using an ImageIcon is the easiest way of applying an image to any image supporting component. The ImageIcon implements Icon interface provided by swing. There are many swing classes that supports providing Image by applying ImageIcon object as argument. There are several ways to provide an Image, including reading it from file, downloading from a URL or invoking from local system. The most commonly used ImageIcon constructors are:

```
ImageIcon(String filename)
ImageIcon(url URL)
```

First constructor obtains the image from specified file name and second constructor downloads the image from specified url.

The ImageIcon class defines three methods that are actually declared in Icon interface. They are:

```
int getIconHeight( )
int getIconWidth( )
void paintIcon(Component comp, Graphics g, int x, int y)
```

The first method returns the height of the icon in pixels. Second method returns the width of the icon in pixels. Third method paints the icon at position *x*, *y* on the graphics context *g*.

The instance of JLabel class creates labels, used to provide instructions and information. This class has following overloaded constructors

```
JLabel(ImageIcon obj)
JLabel(String text)
JLabel(String text, ImageIcon obj, int alignment)
```

Here first constructor assigns specified icon, second constructor assigns specified text for the label. Third constructor assigns text, image and alignment. This alignment is provided by **LEFT**, **RIGHT**, **CENTER**, **LEADING** or **TRAILING**. These constants are defined in the **SwingConstants** interface with many others used by swing components.

The JLabel class provides following methods to handle text and icons associated with it.

> void setIcon(ImageIcon *obj*)
> ImageIcon getIcon( )
> void setText(String *text*)
> String getText( )

The following example illustrates how to create and display a label containing both an icon and a string. The applet begins by getting its content pane. Next, an **ImageIcon** object is created for the file **india.gif**. This is used as the second argument to the **JLabel** constructor. The first and last arguments for the **JLabel** constructor are the label text and the alignment. Finally, the label is added to the content pane.

```
import javax.swing.*;
import java.awt.*;

/*
<applet code="jlabel_demo" width=300 height=300>
</applet>
*/

public class jlabel_demo extends JApplet
{
        public void start( )
        {

                // getting content pane
                Container ct = getContentPane( );

                //creating an icon. Place india.gif in local directory.
                ImageIcon ii1 = new ImageIcon(" india.gif ");

                //creating JLabel instance.
                JLabel jl1 = new JLabel("India",ii1,JLabel.CENTER);

                //adding it to container.
                ct.add(jl1);
        }
}
```

Output of this applet is shown here.

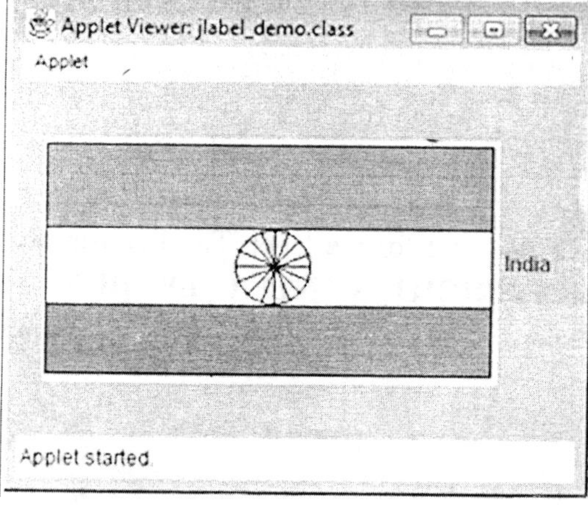

### 6.12.2 JTextField

JTextField is the most simplest and widest used swing component. The JTextField allows to edit one line of text used as input component for application. The JTextField is derived from JTextComponent class. Following are some of the overloaded constructors of JTextField.

JTextField( )
JTextField(String *text*)
JTextField(int *cols*)
JTextField(String *text*, int *cols*)

Here text is the string that is to be initialized and cols is numbers of columns. If first constructor is used then textfield initially appears empty.

The following example demonstrates JTextField in JApplet. Again same start( ) method is overridden and JTextField object is added in content pane.

```
import javax.swing.*;
import java.awt.*;

/*
<applet code="jtextfield_demo" width=300 height=300>
</applet>
*/

public class jtextfield_demo extends JApplet
{
        public void start( )
        {
                // getting content pane
                Container ct = getContentPane( );

                //setting flow layout.
                ct.setLayout(new FlowLayout( ));

                //creating textfield object.
                JTextField jtf1 = new JTextField("You can type here",15);

                //adding to content pane
                ct.add(jtf1);
        }
}
```

Output of above program will be:

### 6.12.3 JButton

Swing provides four types of buttons derived from AbstractButton class. They are **JButton**, **JToggleButton**, **JRadioButton** and **JRadioButton**. Here we will discuss about JButton and remaining are in forthcoming sections.

The JButton is very much different from AWT Button in many respects. Following are the overloaded constructors of JButton class.

> JButton(String *label*)
> JButton(ImageIcon *obj*)
> JButton(String *label*, ImageIcon *obj*)

JButton class has following methods to deal with its *label* and *icon*.

> void setLabel(String *label*)
> *String* getLabel( )
> void setIcon(ImageIcon *obj*)
> *ImageIcon* getIcon( )

The base class AbstractButton also contains some methods that allows us to control behavior of buttons. These methods are :

> void setDisabledIcon(Icon *obj*)
> void setPressedIcon(Icon *obj*)
> void setSelectedIcon(Icon *obj*)
> void setRolloverIcon(Icon *obj*)

Here purpose of each method is indiated by its name. All the AbstractButtons invokes many events but all are discussed in next chapter.

Following is the program that demonstrates JButton with icon and label on it.

```
import javax.swing.*;
import java.awt.*;

/*
<applet code="jbutton_demo" height="200" width="300">
</applet>
*/

public class jbutton_demo extends JApplet
{
public void start( )
{
        Container ct = getContentPane( );
        ct.setLayout(new FlowLayout( ));
        ImageIcon ii1 = new ImageIcon("india.gif");
        JButton jbt1 = new JButton("India",ii1);
        ct.add(jbt1);
}
}
```

Output of above program will be

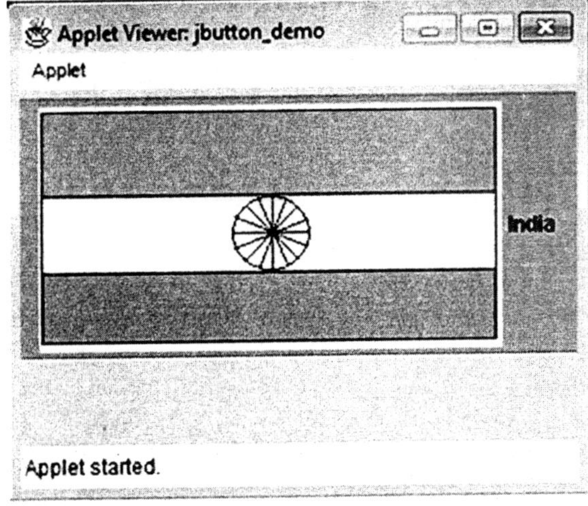


## 6.12.4 JToggleButton

A toggle button looks same like a push button, but it works differently. It has two states: pushed and released. When a toggle button is pressed, it remains pressed rather than popping back up. When you push it second time, it pops back up and comes to normal situation. Hence each time it toggles between two states. JToggleButton is the superclass two derived classes: **JCheckBox** and **JRadioButton** which also provides two state buttons. Some of its overloaded constructor is:

> JToggleButton(String *label*)
> JToggleButton(ImageIcon *obj*)
> JToggleButton(String *label*, InageIcon *obj*)

Here, *label* refers to the string and *obj* is the icon that appears on toggle button. By default any toggle button appears off.

The JToggleButton class has following methods:

void setLabel(String *label*)
*String* getLabel( )
void setIcon(ImageIcon *obj*)
*ImageIcon* getIcon( )
*boolean* isSelected( )

The easiest way to determine a toggle button's state is by calling the isSelected( ) method. It returns true if button is selected otherwise false.

Following is the example that shows a toggle button.

```
import javax.swing.*;
import java.awt.*;
/*
<applet code="jtoggle_demo" height="200" width="300">
</applet>
*/

public class jtoggle_demo extends JApplet
{
public void start( )
{
        Container ct = getContentPane( );
        ct.setLayout(null);
        JToggleButton jtb = new JToggleButton("On / Off");
        ct.add(jtb);
        jtb.setBounds(30,50,80,30);
}
}
```

Following is the output of above program.

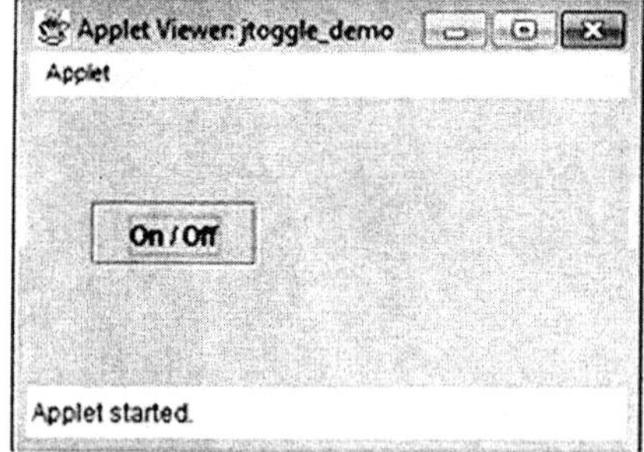


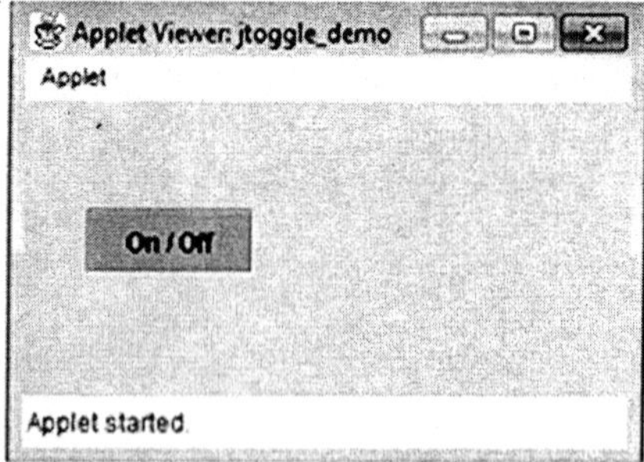


### 6.12.5 JCheckBox

JCheckBox is the immediate derived class of JToggleButton which provides two stated button. It is swing version of AWT Checkbox which provides the facility to insert images also. Following are some of the overloaded constructors of JCheckBox.

JCheckBox(ImageIcon*obj*)
JCheckBox(ImageIcon*obj*, boolean*state*)
JCheckBox(String *text*)
JCheckBox(String *text*, boolean*state*)
JCheckBox(String *text*,ImageIcon*obj*)
JCheckBox(String *text*, ImageIcon*obj*, boolean*state*)

Here *obj* is the object of ImagIcon and *text* is the string that appears on checkbox and state specifies initial checked state. If state is true then checkbox initially appears selected otherwise not.

To handle different events on JCheckBox we have following JCheckBox methods.

voidsetText(String *text*)
String getText( )
voidsetIcon(ImageIconobj)
ImageIcongetIcon( )
voidsetSelected(boolean state)
booleanisSelected( )

Here, setSelected( ) is to change the state of invoking JCheckBox object. It returns true if checkbox is checked otherwise returns false.

Following is the example that shows a toggle button.

```
importjavax.swing.*;
importjava.awt.*;

public class JCheckBox_demo extends JFrame
{
        publicJCheckBox_demo( )
        {
        Container ct = getContentPane( );
        ct.setLayout(null);
        JCheckBox ch1 = new JCheckBox("Option 1",true);
        JCheckBox ch2 = new JCheckBox("Option 2");
        JCheckBox ch3 = new JCheckBox("Option 3");
        JCheckBox ch4 = new JCheckBox("Option 4",true);
        ct.add(ch1);
        ct.add(ch2);
        ct.add(ch3);
        ct.add(ch4);
        ch1.setBounds(30,50,100,30);
        ch2.setBounds(150,50,100,30);
        ch3.setBounds(30,100,100,30);
        ch4.setBounds(150,100,100,30);
        }

        public static void main(String ar[])
        {
        JCheckBox_demo fr1 = new JCheckBox_demo();
        fr1.setTitle("Demonstrating JCheckBox");
        fr1.setSize(300,300);
        fr1.setDefaultCloseOperation(JFrame.EXIT_ON_CLOSE);
        fr1.setVisible(true);
        }
}
```

Following is the output of above program.

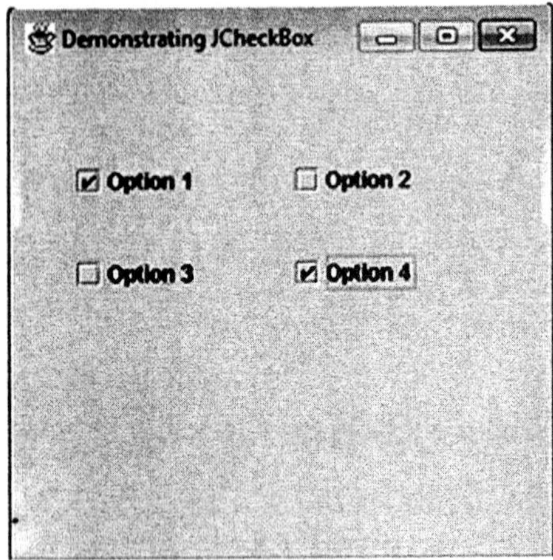


### 6.12.6 JRadioButton

JRadioButton is the immediate derived class of JToggleButton which provides two stated button. It is swing version of AWT Radio button which provides the facility to insert images also. Following are some of the overloaded constructors of JRadioButton.

> JRadioButton(ImageIcon *obj*)
> JRadioButton(ImageIcon *obj*, boolean *state*)
> JRadioButton(String *text*)
> JRadioButton(String *text*, boolean *state*)
> JRadioButton(String *text*, ImageIcon *obj*)
> JRadioButton(String *text*, ImageIcon *obj*, boolean *state*)

Here *obj* is the object of ImagIcon and *text* is the string that appears on radio button and state specifies initial checked state. If state is true then radio button initially appears selected otherwise not.

Radio buttons must be configured into a group. Hence, only one of the radio button can be checked from a group at any time. If user selects a radio button then automatically previously selected radio button will get deselected. For this, create object of **ButtonGroup** class with default constructor. Use add( ) method of ButtonGroup class to add radio button objects into a group.

> .void add(JRadioButton *obj*)

The following example shows how to use radio button and add them into a group.

```
import java.awt.*;
import javax.swing.*;

/*
<applet code="jradiobutton_demo" height="200" width="400">
</applet>

*/

public class jradiobutton_demo extends JApplet
{
public void start()
{
```

```
            Container ct = getContentPane();
            ct.setLayout(null);

            //creating radio buttons
            JRadioButton rb1 = new JRadioButton("Male");
            JRadioButton rb2 = new JRadioButton("Female");
            JRadioButton rb3 = new JRadioButton("Internet Explorer");
            JRadioButton rb4 = new JRadioButton("Mozill Firefox");
            JRadioButton rb5 = new JRadioButton("Google Chrome");

            //adding radio buttons to content pane
            ct.add(rb1);
            ct.add(rb2);
            ct.add(rb3);
            ct.add(rb4);
            ct.add(rb5);

            //aligning components
            rb1.setBounds(30,50,100,30);
            rb2.setBounds(150,50,100,30);
            rb3.setBounds(30,100,100,30);
            rb4.setBounds(150,100,100,30);
            rb6.setBounds(270,100,100,30);

            //crating button groups
            ButtonGroup bg1 = new ButtonGroup();
            ButtonGroup bg2 = new ButtonGroup();
            bg1.add(rb1);
            bg1.add(rb2);
            bg2.add(rb3);
            bg2.add(rb4);
            bg2.add(rb5);
      }
}
```

Following is the output of above program.

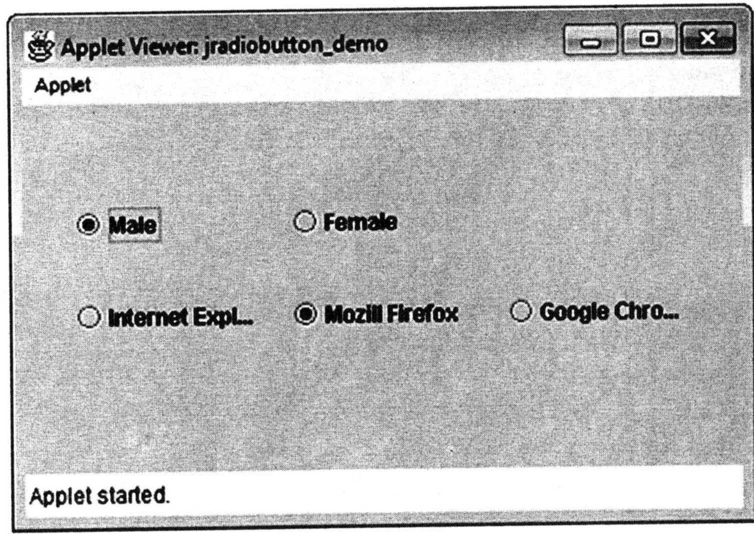

## 6.12.7 JComboBox

Swing provides JComboBox class that creates a combo box. The combo box is combination of text field and a drop-down list. By default it shows a drop-down list box that allows user to select one item but user can also type his selection into the text filed. Following are two overloaded constructors of JComboBox class.

JComboBox( )
JComboBox(Vector *obj*)

First constructor creates an empty combo box and second constructor fills vector items into the combo box. Items can be added manually into the combo box by using addItem( ) method, it is defined as:

void addItem(Object *obj*)

The following example creates a combo box into the frame and displays country list into it.

```
import java.awt.*;
import javax.swing.*;

public class jcombobox_demo extends JFrame
{
        public jcombobox_demo()
        {
                Container ct = getContentPane( );
                ct.setLayout(null);

                // Creating combo box
                JLabel jl = new JLabel("Select Country :");
                JComboBox jc = new JComboBox( );
                jc.addItem("France");
                jc.addItem("Germany");
                jc.addItem("Italy");
                jc.addItem("Japan");

                //adding combo box to content pane
                ct.add(jl);
                ct.add(jc);

                //aligning components
                jl.setBounds(30,50,100,30);
                jc.setBounds(150,50,100,30);
        }

        public static void main(String ar[ ])
        {
                jcombobox_demo fr1 = new jcombobox_demo( );
                fr1.setTitle("Demonstrating combo box");
                fr1.setSize(300,400);
                fr1.setDefaultCloseOperation(JFrame.EXIT_ON_CLOSE);
                fr1.setVisible(true);
        }
}
```

Following will be the output of above program.

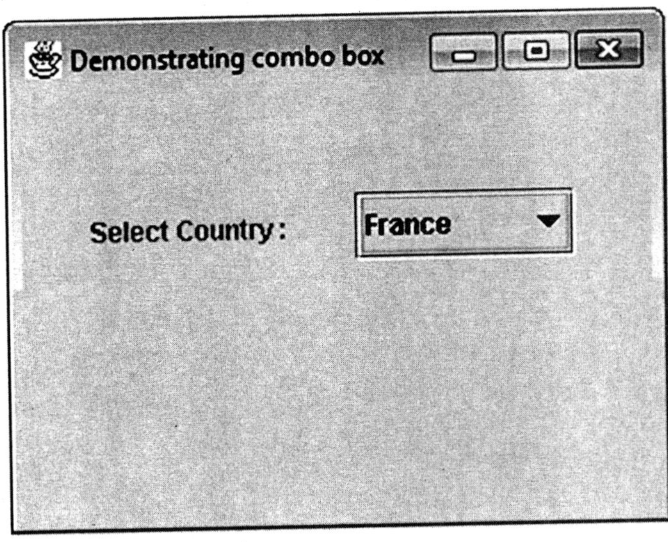


### 6.12.8 JTabbedPane

JTabbedPane is a component which appears as a group of multiple tabs, each containing a title and a panel as group of components. When user selects a tab, its contents becomes visible and user can interact it's with the contents. The main purpose of tabbed panes is to provide configuration related options. (For example windows explorer → tools menu → Folder options)

We create the object of JTabbedPane using it's default constructor and add different tabs under it using addTab( ) method. This method is defined as:

void addTab(String *title*, Component *obj*)

Here, *title* is the title for the tab, and *obj* is the component that should be added to the tab. Typically, a **JPanel** or a subclass of it is added.

The procedure to use a tabbed pane is as follows.

1. define required numbers of panel classes with components in it.
2. create JTabbedPane object.
3. call its addTab( ) method with a title and related panel object.
4. add the tabbed pane into the container of JApplet or JFrame.

The following example shows how to create tabbed pane using JPanel.

```
import java.awt.*;
import javax.swing.*;

/*
<applet code="jtab_demo" height="200" width="400">
</applet>
*/
class pnl1 extends JPanel
{
        public pnl1()
        {
                JCheckBox jcb1 = new JCheckBox("Red");
                JCheckBox jcb2 = new JCheckBox("Blue");
```

```
                JCheckBox jcb3 = new JCheckBox("Green");
                JCheckBox jcb4 = new JCheckBox("Yellow");
                add(jcb1);
                add(jcb2);
                add(jcb3);
                add(jcb4);
        }
}

class pnl2 extends JPanel
{
        public pnl2()
        {
                JButton jbt1 = new JButton("Chocolate");
                JButton jbt2 = new JButton("Vanilla");
                JButton jbt3 = new JButton("Str");
                JButton jbt4 = new JButton("Pineapple");
                add(jbt1);
                add(jbt2);
                add(jbt3);
                add(jbt4);
        }
}

class pnl3 extends JPanel
{
        public pnl3()
        {
                JComboBox jcb = new JComboBox();
                jcb.addItem("Circle");
                jcb.addItem("Oval");
                jcb.addItem("Rectangle");
                jcb.addItem("Square");
                add(jcb);
        }
}

public class jtab_demo extends JApplet
{
        public void start()
        {
                Container ct = getContentPane();
                JTabbedPane jtp = new JTabbedPane();
                jtp.addTab("Colors",new pnl1());
                jtp.addTab("Flavours",new pnl2());
                jtp.addTab("Shapes",new pnl3());
                ct.add(jtp);
        }
}
```

Above program contains a tabbed pane with three tabs in it.

Colors : having four checkboxes with color options.
Flavours : having four buttons with flavor options.
Shapes : having a combobox with shape options.

output of above program will be:

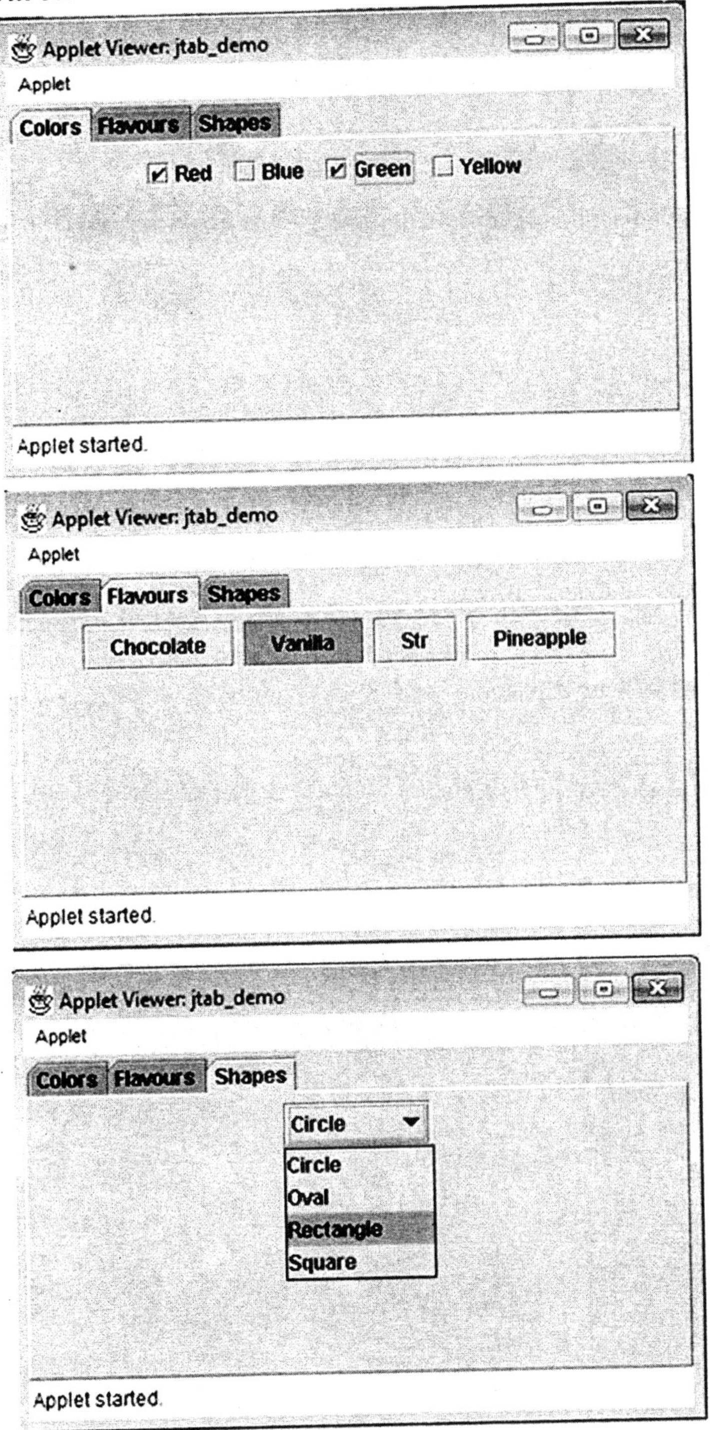


## 6.12.9 JScrollPane

JScrollPane is the class that provides a rectangular scrollable area in which a component can be viewed. Horizonal and/or vertical scrollbar may be provided if required. Some of its overloaded constructors are:

> JScollPane(Component *obj*)
> JScollPane(int *vertical*, int *horizontal*)
> JScollPane(Component *obj*, int *vertical*, int *horizontal*)

Here, *obj* is the component object which is required to be placed in scroll pane. *vertical* and *horizontal* are the **int** constants that defines type of horizontal and vertical scrollbar defined in **ScrollPaneConstants** interface. These constants are:

HORIZONTAL_SCROLLBAR_ALWAYS
HORIZONTAL_SCROLLBAR_AS_NEEDED
VERTICAL_SCROLLBAR_ALWAYS
VERTICAL_SCROLLBAR_AS_NEEDED

Their names specifies their appearance.

Following is the program that demonstrates a scroll pane controlling a text area.

```
import java.awt.*;
import javax.swing.*;
/*
<applet code="jscrollpane_demo" width=300 height=250>
</applet>
*/
public class jscrollpane_demo extends JApplet
{
        public void start( )
        {
                Container ct = getContentPane( );
                String s="This is text area\n" + "displayed in a scroll pane\n" + "appears
                with horizontal and\n"  +  "vertical scrollbar";

                //scroll pane constants.
                int h = ScrollPaneConstants.HORIZONTAL_SCROLLBAR_ALWAYS;
                int v = ScrollPaneConstants.VERTICAL_SCROLLBAR_ALWAYS;

                //creating text area.
                JTextArea jt = new JTextArea(s);

                //creating scroll pane and applying text area with scrollbars
                JScrollPane sp = new JScrollPane(jt,v,h);

                //adding scroll pane to content pane
                ct.add(sp);
        }
}
```

Output of above program will be:

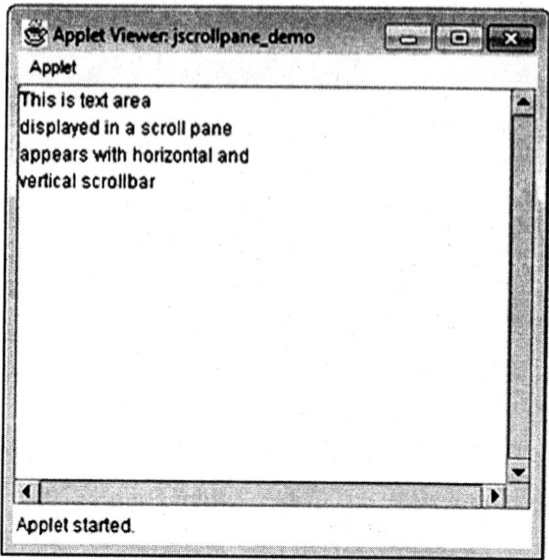

### 6.12.10 JTrees

A JTree is an expandable and collapsible component containing sub-trees to display. Some of the JTree constructors are:

JTree(Hashtable *obj*)
JTree(Object *obj*[ ])
JTree(TreeNode *obj*)
JTree(Vector *obj*)

Here, each obj is object of respective components.

A JTree generates event when it gets expanded or collapsed. The **TreeNode** interface declares methods that obtain information about a tree node. For example, it is possible to obtain a reference to the parent node or an enumeration of the child nodes. The **MutableTreeNode** interface extends **TreeNode**. It declares methods that can insert and remove child nodes or change the parent node. The **DefaultMutableTreeNode** class implements the **MutableTreeNode** interface. It represents a node in a tree. One of its constructors is shown here:

DefaultMutableTreeNode(Object *obj*)

Here, *obj* is the object to be enclosed in this tree node. The new tree node doesn't have a parent or children. To create a hierarchy of tree nodes, the **add( )** method of **DefaultMutableTreeNode** can be used. Its signature is shown here:

void add(MutableTreeNode *child*)

Here, *child* is a mutable tree node that is to be added as a child to the current node. Following is the program that demonstrates creation of tree.

```
import java.awt.*;
import javax.swing.*;
import javax.swing.tree.*;

/*
<applet code="jtree_demo" width=400 height=200>
</applet>
*/

public class jtree_demo extends JApplet
{
        public void start( )
        {
                // Get content pane
                Container ct = getContentPane();

                // Set layout manager
                ct.setLayout(new BorderLayout( ));

                // Create top node of tree
                DefaultMutableTreeNode root = new DefaultMutableTreeNode("Options");

                // Create subtree of "A"
                DefaultMutableTreeNode a = new DefaultMutableTreeNode("A");
                root.add(a);
                DefaultMutableTreeNode a1 = new DefaultMutableTreeNode("A1");
                a.add(a1);
                DefaultMutableTreeNode a2 = new DefaultMutableTreeNode("A2");
                a.add(a2);
```

```
            // Create subtree of "B"
            DefaultMutableTreeNode b = new DefaultMutableTreeNode("B");
            root.add(b);
            DefaultMutableTreeNode b1 = new DefaultMutableTreeNode("B1");
            b.add(b1);
            DefaultMutableTreeNode b2 = new DefaultMutableTreeNode("B2");
            b.add(b2);
            DefaultMutableTreeNode b3 = new DefaultMutableTreeNode("B3");
            b.add(b3);

            // Create tree
            JTree tree = new JTree(root);

            // Add tree to a scroll pane
            int v = ScrollPaneConstants.VERTICAL_SCROLLBAR_AS_NEEDED;
            int h = ScrollPaneConstants.HORIZONTAL_SCROLLBAR_AS_NEEDED;
            JScrollPane jsp = new JScrollPane(tree, v, h);

            // Add scroll pane to the content pane
            ct.add(jsp, BorderLayout.CENTER);
      }
}
```

Output of above program will be:

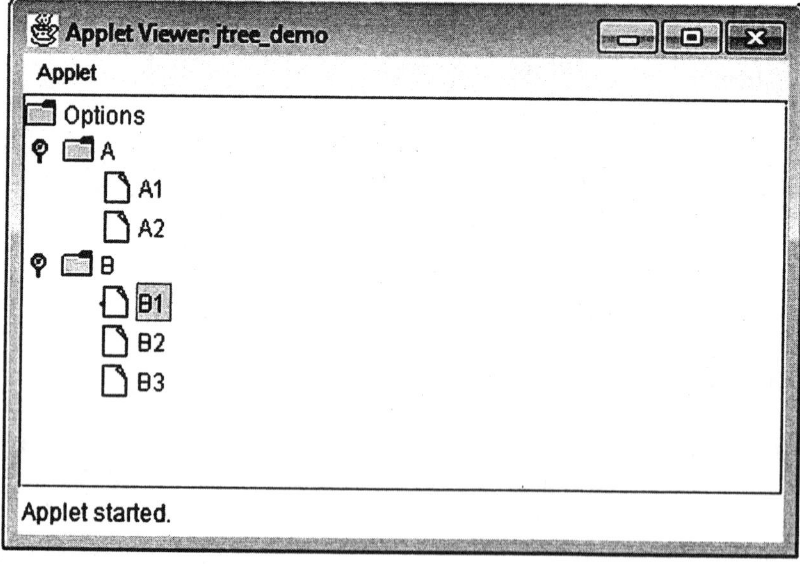


### 6.12.11 JTable

A JTable is a component that displays rows and columns of data. You can drag the cursor on column boundaries to resize columns. You can also drag a column to a new position. One of its constructors is shown here:

JTable(Object *data*[ ][ ], Object *colHeads*[ ])

Here, *data* is a two-dimensional array of the information to be presented, and *colHeads* is a one-dimensional array with the column headings.

Here are steps to create a table in scroll pane.

1. create JTable object with data and column titles.
2. create JScrollPane object and provide the table into it.
3. add the scroll pane into the content pane.

The following example shows how to create a table.

```
import java.awt.*;
import javax.swing.*;

/*
<applet code="jtable_demo" width=400 height=200>
</applet>
*/

public class jtable_demo extends JApplet
{
        public void start( )
        {
                // Get content pane
                Container ct = getContentPane( );

                // Set layout manager
                ct.setLayout(new BorderLayout( ));

                // Initialize column headings
                final String[] colHeads = {"Roll", "Name", "city", "phone"};

                // Initialize data
                final Object[ ][ ] data = {
                { "1", "Amit", "Ahmedabad", "559847" },
                { "2", "Ketan", "Rajkot", "756655" },
                { "3", "Vivek", "Junagadh", "563458" },
                { "4", "Mahendra", "Rajkot", "734592" },
                { "5", "Ankita", "Surat", "123733" },
                { "6", "Jayesh", "Baroda", "565614" },
                { "7", "Rajshree", "Jamnagar", "567221" },
                { "8", "Suresh","Surat", "674142" },
                { "9", "Hiren", "Rajkot", "902375" }
                };

                // Create the table
                JTable table = new JTable(data, colHeads);

                // Add table to a scroll pane
                int v = ScrollPaneConstants.VERTICAL_SCROLLBAR_AS_NEEDED;
                int h = ScrollPaneConstants.HORIZONTAL_SCROLLBAR_AS_NEEDED;
                JScrollPane jsp = new JScrollPane(table, v, h);

                // Add scroll pane to the content pane
                ct.add(jsp, BorderLayout.CENTER);
        }
}
```

Output of above program will be:

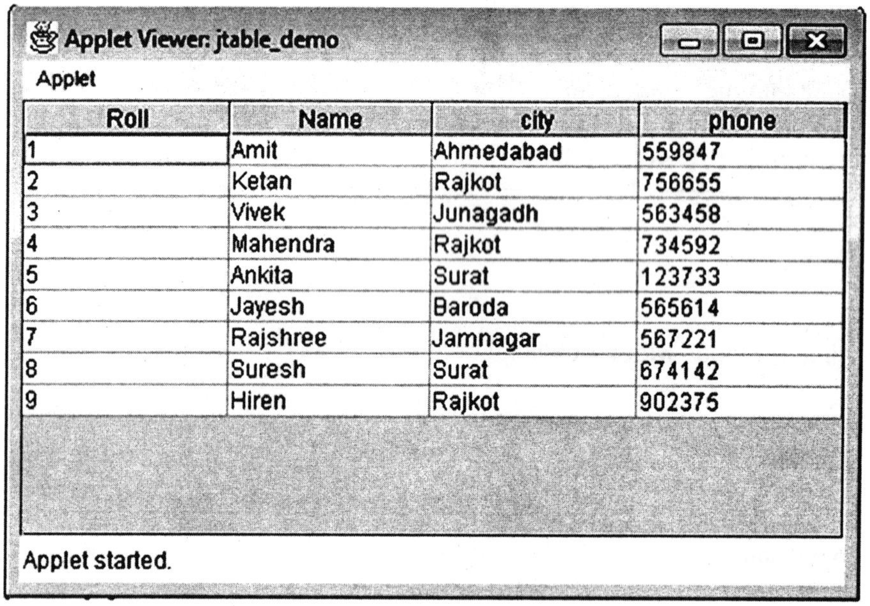

Applet Viewer: jtable_demo

Applet

| Roll | Name | city | phone |
|---|---|---|---|
| 1 | Amit | Ahmedabad | 559847 |
| 2 | Ketan | Rajkot | 756655 |
| 3 | Vivek | Junagadh | 563458 |
| 4 | Mahendra | Rajkot | 734592 |
| 5 | Ankita | Surat | 123733 |
| 6 | Jayesh | Baroda | 565614 |
| 7 | Rajshree | Jamnagar | 567221 |
| 8 | Suresh | Surat | 674142 |
| 9 | Hiren | Rajkot | 902375 |

Applet started.

*****

# Chapter 7

# Event Handling

In previous chapter we studied AWT component classes and Applet class. The knowledge of previous chapter will let you to design the application forms / pages using different AWT components. In this chapter we will study the basic concepts of even handling.

Event handling is the core part of any application. In the beginning of this chapter, we will study the event mechanism, and then event related classes and interfaces, inner classes, extending component classes and finally handling keyboard, mouse and window events.

## 7.1 The Delegation Event Model

To begin our study with event, first of all we have to understand how events are handled? The delegation event model defines the standard background mechanism to process on generated event. The mechanism of delegation event model is: the *source* generates an *event* and sends it to multiple *listeners*. Now let us understand each of these parameters one by one.

**Event** *is an action performed on any source*. Event is a result of user's action which changes the state of a source. Therefore event is also defined as *change of state of any source*. Some of the examples of events are: clicking on a push button, pressing a key from keyboard, clicking mouse button, selecting an item from a list, check or uncheck a checkbox, etc.

**Source** *is the component object on which action is performed.* A source can generated more than one type of events. It is necessary that a source must register listener in order to generate event. Each event has its own registration method which registers listener. For example: **addKeyListener( )** method registers keyboard keys with event listener, **addActionListener( )** method registers any select action with event listener. Similarly, we can also remove the registration of listener by using **removeKeyListener( )** and **removeActionListener( )** methods. Hence, **add** and **remove** methods are responsible for registering and removing a source with event listener.

**Listener** *is the object which gets notified when an event occurs*. There are several methods which are defined in set of interfaces found in **java.awt.event**. For example: **MouseListener** interface defines methods related to mouse clicked, pressed, released, dragged, moved, entered, exited. **KeyListener** interface defines methods related to keyboard's key pressed, released and typed. Remember that, listener must have been registered with one or more sources to receive notifications.

## 7.2 Event classes

Event classes are at the core of Java's event handling mechanism. All the listeners and its methods are also encapsulated with event classes. All the event classes are present under **java.awt.event** package. Here is a table showing most used event classes with a small description on it.

| Event Classes | Description |
|---|---|
| ActionEvent | Generated when mouse button is pressed, MenuItem is selected or List item is double clicked. |
| AdjustmentEvent | Generated when a scrollbar is manipulated. |
| ComponentEvent | Generated when a component object is hidden, shown, moved or resized. |
| ContainerEvent | Generated when a component object is added or removed from a container. |
| FocusEvent | Generated when a component gains or losses focus. |
| InputEvent | Abstract base class for all component input event classes. |
| ItemEvent | Generated when a checkbox or list item is clicked or CheckboxMenuItem is checked or unchecked. |
| KeyEvent | Generated when keyboard key is pressed. |
| MouseEvent | Generated when the mouse is dragged, moved, clicked, pressed, released, enters or exits from a component object. |
| MouseWheelEvent | Generated when mouse wheel is moved. |
| TextEvent | Generated when the value of a TextArea or TextField is changed. |
| WindowEvent | Generated when a window is activated, deactivated, closed, opened, iconified, deiconified, or about to be closed. |

These all classes are responsible for all events and an essential ingredient in all listeners. All these event classes contains a list of member functions which are discussed later in this chapter in issue no 7.4

## 7.3 Sources of Event

As discussed earlier, sources are the component objects which can generate event. Almost all the components, discussed in previous chapter, are sources of event. Here is a table which shows a list of sources with a description saying when it can generate event.

| Source | Description |
|---|---|
| Button | Generates event when the button is pressed. |
| Checkbox | Generates event when checkbox is checked or unchecked. |
| Choice | Generates event when a choice is changed. |
| List | Generates event when an item is selected. |
| MenuItem | Generates event when a MenuItem is selected. |
| CheckboxMenuItem | Generates event when a CheckboxMenuItem is checked or unchecked. |
| TextArea & TextField | Generates event when text is typed in it. |
| Window | Generates event when a window is minimized, maximized, activated, deactivated, iconified, deiconified, opened or closed. |

All here listed component objects behaves as source and generates event, but only if it is registered as a source for specific listener.

## 7.4 Event Listeners

As discussed earlier, listener is an object which recognizes occurrence of an event. All the events are based on two objects: source and listener. In java, listeners are the interfaces, which contain methods related to different possibilities of events that can be performed on a source. Following is the table showing all the listeners and member functions defined under it with a small description.

| Listener Interface | Member Functions | Description |
|---|---|---|
| ActionListener | void actionPerformed(ActionEvent ae) | When mouse button is pressed, MenuItem is selected or List item is double clicked. |
| AdjustmentListener | void adjustmentValueChanged(AdjustmentEvent ae) | When scroll bar is manipulated. |
| Component Listener | void componentResized(ComponentEvent ce)<br>void componentMoved(ComponentEvent ce)<br>void componentShown(ComponentEvent ce)<br>void componentHidden(ComponentEvent ce) | When any component is resized.<br>When any component is moved.<br>When any component is made visible.<br>When any component is hidden. |
| ContainerListener | void componentAdded(ContainerEvent ce)<br>void componentRemoved(ContainerEvent ce) | When any component is added to the container.<br>When any component is removed from the container. |
| FocusListener | void focusGained(FocusEvent fe)<br>void focusLost(FocusEvent fe) | When any component gains focus.<br>When any component loses focus. |
| ItemListener | void itemStateChanged(ItemEvent ie) | When state of any checkable component is changed. |
| KeyListener | void keyPressed(KeyEvent ke)<br>void keyReleased(KeyEvent ke)<br>void keyTyped(KeyEvent ke) | When a keyboard key is pressed.<br>When a keyboard key is released.<br>When a keyboard key is typed. |
| MouseListener | void mouseClicked(MouseEvent me)<br>void mouseEntered(MouseEvent me)<br>void mouseExited(MouseEvent me)<br>void mousePressed(MouseEvent me)<br>void mouseReleased(MouseEvent me) | When mouse button is clicked.<br>When mouse enters a component.<br>When mouse exits from a component.<br>When mouse button is pressed.<br>When mouse button is released. |
| MouseMotionListener | void mouseDragged(MouseEvent me)<br>void mouseMoved(MouseEvent me) | When mouse is dragged.<br>When mouse is moved. |
| MouseWheelListener | void mouseWheelMoved(MouseWheelEvent mwe) | When mouse wheel is moved. |
| TextListener | void textChanged(TextEvent te) | When text of any TextField or TextArea is changed. |
| WindowFocusListener | void windowGainedFocus(WindowEvent we)<br>void windowLostFocus(WindowEvent we) | When window gets focus.<br>When windows loses focus. |
| WindowListener | void windowActivated(WindowEvent we)<br>void windowClosed(WindowEvent we)<br>void windowClosing(WindowEvent we)<br>void windowDeactivated(WindowEvent we)<br>void windowDeiconified(WindowEvent we)<br>void windowIconified(WindowEvent we)<br>void windowOpened(WindowEvent we) | When a window is activated.<br>When a window is closed.<br>When a window is about to close.<br>When a window is deactivated.<br>When a window is deiconified.<br>When a window is iconified.<br>When a window is opened. |

Study and remember above interfaces and its methods.

## 7.5 MouseListener

Here is a program to demonstrate **MouseListener** to respond to mouse events.

```
import java.awt.*;
import java.applet.*;
import java.awt.event.*;
public class mouse_demo extends Applet implements MouseListener
{
        public String st="";
        public void init( )
        {
                addMouseListener(this);          //registering MouseListener
        }
                public void mouseClicked(MouseEvent me)
        {
                st="Mouse is clicked";
                repaint( );
        }
        public void mouseEntered(MouseEvent me)
        {
                st="Mouse Entered";
                repaint();
        }
        public void mouseExited(MouseEvent me)
        {
                st="Mouse Exited";
                repaint();
        }
        public void mousePressed(MouseEvent me)
        {
                st="Mouse Button Pressed";
                repaint();
        }
        public void mouseReleased(MouseEvent me)
        {
                st="Mouse Button Released";
                repaint();
        }
        public void paint(Graphics g)
        {
                g.drawString(st,20,20);
        }
}
```

Here, **MouseListener** interface is implemented to handle mouse related events. It is registered for events by using **addMouseListener( )** method. Each time when an event occurs, value of String changes and repaint( ) method is used to call paint( ) method manually, whenever required. Whenever mouse event is performed, the MouseListener recognize the type of event and call to related method. Here is the output of above program.

## 7.6 KeyListener

Here is a program demonstrating **KeyListener,** that handles keyPressed( ), keyReleased( ) and keyTyped( ) events.

```
import java.awt.*;
import java.applet.*;
import java.awt.event.*;
public class key_demo extends Applet implements KeyListener
{
        String st = "";
        public void init( )
        {
                addKeyListener(this);
        }
        public void keyPressed(KeyEvent ke)
        {
                showStatus("Key Down");
        }
        public void keyReleased(KeyEvent ke)
        {
                showStatus("Key Up");
        }
        public void keyTyped(KeyEvent ke)
        {
                st = "You typed : " + ke.getKeyChar( );
```

```
            repaint( );
        }
        public void paint(Graphics g)
        {
            g.drawString(st,20,20);
        }
}
```

Here, **KeyListener** interface is implemented to handle Key related events. It is registered by using addKeyListener( ) method. The **showStatus( )** method is used to display any user defined message on the statusbar. The **getKeyChar( )** method returns the character which is pressed for performing that event. Here is the output of above program.

## 7.7 Component events examples

### 7.7.1 Demonstrating event on Button using ActionListener

Let's perform one program containing three buttons "SQUARE", "CUBE" and "FACTORIAL" to perform operations on the value entered on first textbox and displays result in second textbox.

```
import java.awt.event.*;
import java.awt.*;
import java.applet.*;

/*
<applet code = "arithmatic_opera2" width="400" height="400">
</applet>
*/

public class arithmatic_opera2 extends Applet implements ActionListener
{
        TextField tf1,tf2;
        Button btn1,btn2,btn3;
        public void start()
        {
```

```
                setLayout(null);
                tf1=new TextField( );
                tf2=new TextField( );
                btn1=new Button("SQUARE");
                btn2=new Button("CUBE");
                btn3=new Button("FACTORIAL");
                add(tf1);
                add(btn1);
                add(btn2);
                add(btn3);
                add(tf2);
                tf1.setBounds(120,50,200,30);
                tf2.setBounds(120,150,200,30);
                btn1.setBounds(70,100,80,30);
                btn2.setBounds(180,100,80,30);
                btn3.setBounds(290,100,80,30);
                btn1.addActionListener(this);
                btn2.addActionListener(this);
                btn3.addActionListener(this);
        }
        public void actionPerformed(ActionEvent ae)
        {
                String s=ae.getActionCommand();
                int a,b,i;
                a=Integer.parseInt(tf1.getText());
                if(s.equals("SQUARE")==true)
                {
                        b=a*a;
                        tf2.setText(" "+b);
                }
                if(s.equals("CUBE")==true)
                {
                        b=a*a*a;
                        tf2.setText(" "+b);
                }
                if(s.equals("FACTORIAL")==true)
                {
                        int f=1;
                        for(i=1;i<=a;i++)
                        {
                                f=f*i;
                        }
                        tf2.setText(" "+f);
                }
        }
}
```

In above program, getActionCommand( ) method is member function of **ActionEvent** class. It returns the label of the button which is clicked. It is defined as :

*String getActionCommand( )*

Based on its returned string, we take decision what logical operations is to perform. Following is the output of above program.

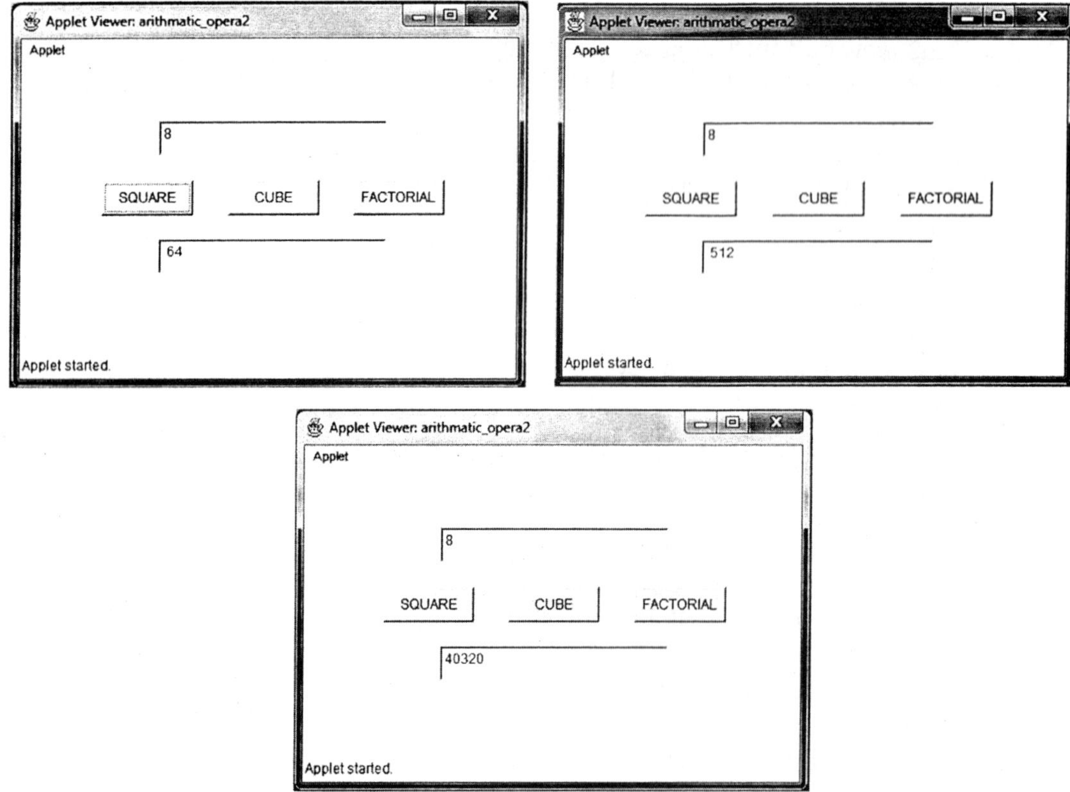

### 7.7.2 Demonstrating event on TextField using TextListener

Lets perform one program that copy the text of one textbox into another textbox as and when text of first textbox modifies.

```
import java.awt.event.*;
import java.applet.*;
import java.awt.*;

/*
<applet code="textcopy" width="400" height="400">
</applet>
*/

public class textcopy extends Applet implements TextListener
{
        TextField tf1,tf2;
        public void start()
        {
                setLayout(null);
                tf1 = new TextField();
                tf2 = new TextField();
                add(tf1);
                add(tf2);
                tf1.setBounds(50,80,200,30);
```

```
                tf2.setBounds(50,130,200,30);
                tf1.addTextListener(this);
        }
        public void textValueChanged(TextEvent te)
        {
                tf2.setText(tf1.getText());
        }
}
```

Above program uses TextEvent and TextListener that invokes its textValueChanged( ) as and when text of TextField tf1 changes. We grab the text of TextField tf1 and set it as text of TextField tf2. Hence only TextField tf1 is registered for TextListener. Following is the output of above program.

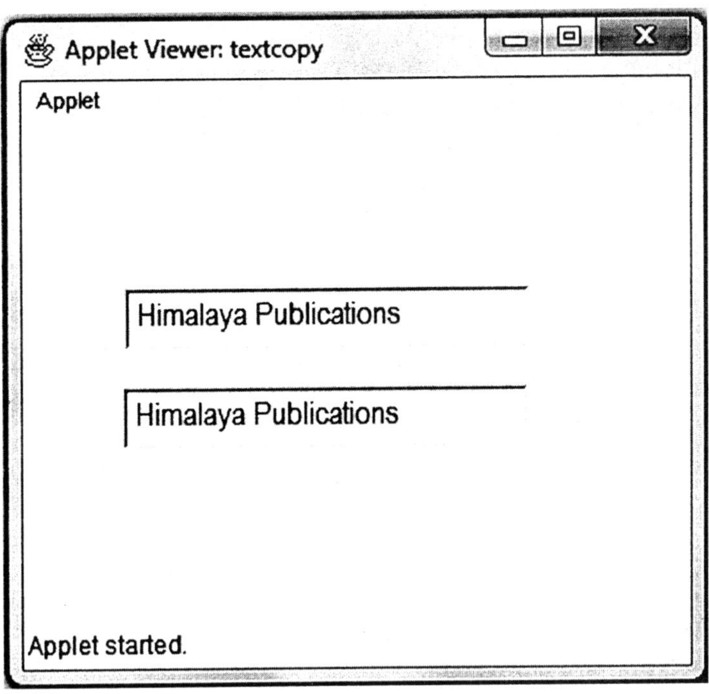


### 7.7.3 Demonstrating event on Checkbox using ItemListener

Here is a program that performs event on check or uncheck operation of three checkboxes and updates the label accordingly.

```
import java.awt.*;
import java.applet.*;
import java.awt.event.*;

/*
<applet code="checkbox_event" width="400" height="400">
</applet>
*/

public class checkbox_event extends Applet implements ItemListener
{
        Label lb1,lb2,lb3;
        Checkbox ch1,ch2,ch3;
        public void start()
```

```
        {
                setLayout(null);
                ch1 = new Checkbox("Option 1");
                ch2 = new Checkbox("Option 2");
                ch3 = new Checkbox("Option 3");
                lb1 = new Label("Option 1 is : false");
                lb2 = new Label("Option 2 is : false");
                lb3 = new Label("Option 3 is : false");
                add(ch1);add(ch2);add(ch3);
                add(lb1);add(lb2);add(lb3);
                ch1.setBounds(50,50,100,30);
                ch2.setBounds(160,50,100,30);
                ch3.setBounds(270,50,100,30);
                lb1.setBounds(150,100,100,30);
                lb2.setBounds(150,130,100,30);
                lb3.setBounds(150,160,100,30);
                ch1.addItemListener(this);
                ch2.addItemListener(this);
                ch3.addItemListener(this);
        }

        public void itemStateChanged(ItemEvent ie)
        {
                lb1.setText("Option 1 is : " + ch1.getState());
                lb2.setText("Option 2 is : " + ch2.getState());
                lb3.setText("Option 3 is : " + ch3.getState());
        }
}
```

Three Checkboxes are registered for ItemEvent and hence on each change of state of each checkboxes the method itemStateChanged( ) gets invoked and we update the labels according to state of checkbox. Following is the output of above program.

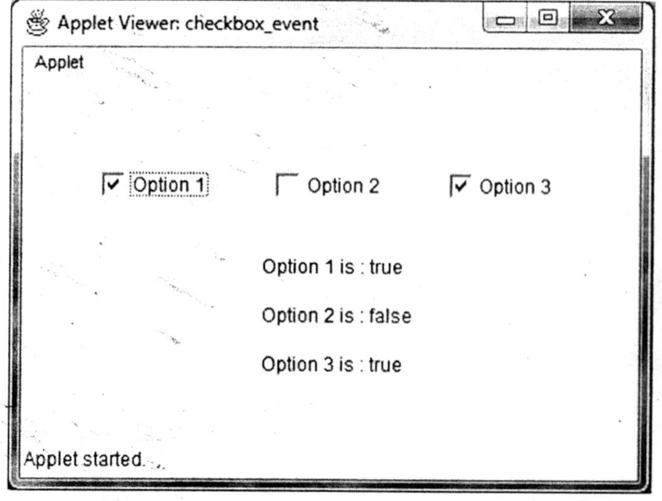


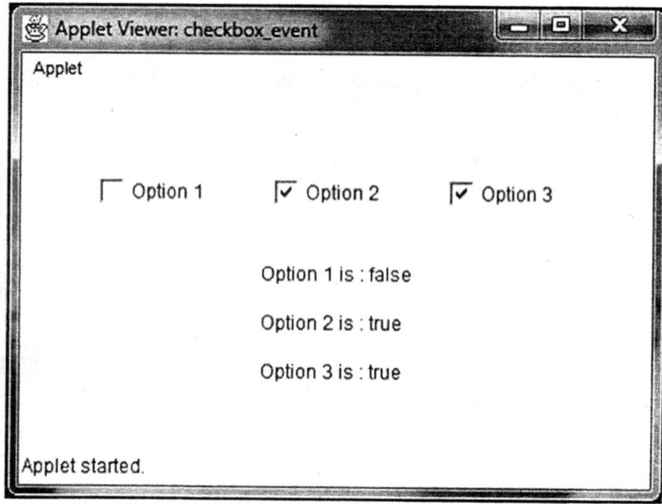

### 7.7.4 Demonstrating event on List using ItemListener

Here is a program performing event on List when its selection is changed.

```
import java.awt.*;
import java.awt.event.*;
import java.applet.*;

/*
<applet code="ListDemo" width=300 height=180>
</applet>
*/

public class ListDemo extends Applet implements ItemListener
{
        List os, browser;
        Label lb1,lb2;
        public void start()
        {
                setLayout(null);
                os = new List(4, false);
                browser = new List(4, false);
                lb1 = new Label("Operating System is : ");
                lb2 = new Label("Browse is : ");
                // add items to os list
                os.add("Windows 98/XP");
                os.add("Windows NT/2000");
                os.add("Solaris");
                os.add("MacOS");
                os.select(0);

                // add items to browser list
                browser.add("Netscape 3.x");
                browser.add("Netscape 4.x");
                browser.add("Netscape 5.x");
                browser.add("Netscape 7.x");
                browser.add("Internet Explorer 4.0");
                browser.add("Internet Explorer 5.0");
                browser.add("Internet Explorer 7.0");
                browser.add("Lynx 2.4");
                browser.select(0);

                // add lists to window
                add(os);
                add(browser);
                add(lb1);
                add(lb2);

                // register to receive action events
                os.addItemListener(this);
                browser.addItemListener(this);
```

```
            os.setBounds(20,20,150,100);
            browser.setBounds(190,20,150,100);
            lb1.setBounds(50,150,200,30);
            lb2.setBounds(50,190,200,30);
    }

    public void itemStateChanged(ItemEvent ie)
    {
            lb1.setText("Operating System is : " + os.getSelectedItem());
            lb2.setText("Browser is : " + browser.getSelectedItem());
    }
}
```

Above program will update the label when selection of List is changed. Both the lists are registered for ItemEvent and when selection state is changed the listener invokes the itemStateChanged( ) method to perform event. Following is the output of above program.

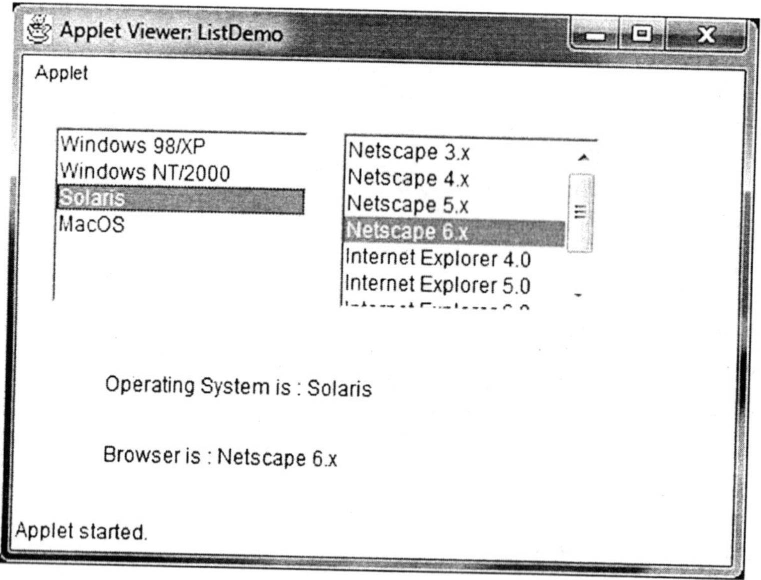


### 7.7.5 Demonstrating event on JButton using ActionListener

Let's see a program that displays the country name when its related flag JButton is clicked.

```
import java.awt.*;
import java.awt.event.*;
import javax.swing.*;

/*
<applet code="JButtonEvent" width=250 height=300>
</applet>
*/

public class JButtonEvent extends JApplet implements ActionListener
{
        JTextField jtf;
        public void start( )
```

```
	{
		Container contentPane = getContentPane();
		contentPane.setLayout(new FlowLayout());
		ImageIcon france = new ImageIcon("france.gif");
		JButton jb = new JButton(france);
		jb.setActionCommand("France");
		jb.addActionListener(this);
		contentPane.add(jb);
		ImageIcon germany = new ImageIcon("germany.gif");
		jb = new JButton(germany);
		jb.setActionCommand("Germany");
		jb.addActionListener(this);
		contentPane.add(jb);
		ImageIcon india = new ImageIcon("india.gif");
		jb = new JButton(india);
		jb.setActionCommand("India");
		jb.addActionListener(this);
		contentPane.add(jb);
		ImageIcon japan = new ImageIcon("japan.gif");
		jb = new JButton(japan);
		jb.setActionCommand("Japan");
		jb.addActionListener(this);
		contentPane.add(jb);
		jtf = new JTextField(15);
		contentPane.add(jtf);
	}

	public void actionPerformed(ActionEvent ae)
	{
		jtf.setText(ae.getActionCommand( ));
	}
}
```

Above program contains four JButtons, each containing country flag as ImageIcons. When the JButton is clicked, it displays country name of selected flag into the JTextField. Output of above program will be as follows.

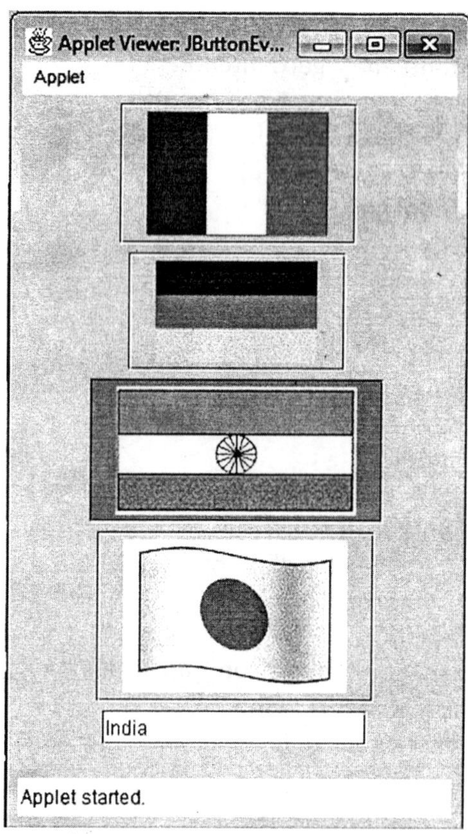


### 7.7.6 Demonstrating event on MenuItems using ActionListener

Let's see a program that adds a series of nested menus to a pop-up window. The item selected is displayed in the window. The state of the two check box menu items is also displayed.

```
import java.awt.*;
import java.awt.event.*;
import java.applet.*;


/*
<applet code="MenuDemo" width=250 height=250>
</applet>
*/

class MenuFrame extends Frame
{
        String msg = "";
        CheckboxMenuItem debug, test;
        MenuFrame(String title)
        {
                super(title);
                MenuBar mbar = new MenuBar();
                setMenuBar(mbar);
                Menu file = new Menu("File");
                MenuItem item1,item2,item3,item4,item5;
                file.add(item1 = new MenuItem("New..."));
                file.add(item2 = new MenuItem("Open..."));
```

```
            file.add(item3 = new MenuItem("Close"));
            file.add(item4 = new MenuItem("-")); // creates separator
            file.add(item5 = new MenuItem("Quit..."));
            mbar.add(file);
            Menu edit = new Menu("Edit");
            MenuItem item6, item7, item8, item9;
            edit.add(item6 = new MenuItem("Cut"));
            edit.add(item7 = new MenuItem("Copy"));
            edit.add(item8 = new MenuItem("Paste"));
            edit.add(item9 = new MenuItem("-"));
            Menu sub = new Menu("Special");
            MenuItem item10, item11, item12;
            sub.add(item10 = new MenuItem("First"));
            sub.add(item11 = new MenuItem("Second"));
            sub.add(item12 = new MenuItem("Third"));
            edit.add(sub);
            debug = new CheckboxMenuItem("Debug");
            edit.add(debug);
            test = new CheckboxMenuItem("Testing");
            edit.add(test);
            mbar.add(edit);
            MyMenuHandler handler = new MyMenuHandler(this);
            item1.addActionListener(handler);
            item2.addActionListener(handler);
            item3.addActionListener(handler);
            item4.addActionListener(handler);
            item5.addActionListener(handler);
            item7.addActionListener(handler);
            item7.addActionListener(handler);
            item8.addActionListener(handler);
            item9.addActionListener(handler);
            item10.addActionListener(handler);
            item11.addActionListener(handler);
            item12.addActionListener(handler);
            debug.addItemListener(handler);
            test.addItemListener(handler);
            addWindowListener(adapter);
      }
      public void paint(Graphics g)
      {
            g.drawString(msg, 10, 200);
            if(debug.getState())
            g.drawString("Debug is on.", 10, 220);
            else
            g.drawString("Debug is off.", 10, 220);
            if(test.getState())
            g.drawString("Testing is on.", 10, 240);
            else
            g.drawString("Testing is off.", 10, 240);
      }
}
```

```
class MyWindowAdapter extends WindowAdapter
{
	MenuFrame menuFrame;
	public MyWindowAdapter(MenuFrame menuFrame)
	{
		this.menuFrame = menuFrame;
	}
	public void windowClosing(WindowEvent we)
	{
		menuFrame.setVisible(false);
	}
}

class MyMenuHandler implements ActionListener, ItemListener
{
	MenuFrame menuFrame;
	public MyMenuHandler(MenuFrame menuFrame)
	{
		this.menuFrame = menuFrame;
	}
	public void actionPerformed(ActionEvent ae)
	{
		String msg = "You selected ";
		String arg = (String)ae.getActionCommand( );
		if(arg.equals("New..."))
		msg += "New.";
		else if(arg.equals("Open..."))
		msg += "Open.";
		else if(arg.equals("Close"))
		msg += "Close.";
		else if(arg.equals("Quit..."))
		msg += "Quit.";
		else if(arg.equals("Edit"))
		msg += "Edit.";
		else if(arg.equals("Cut"))
		msg += "Cut.";
		else if(arg.equals("Copy"))
		msg += "Copy.";
		else if(arg.equals("Paste"))
		msg += "Paste.";
		else if(arg.equals("First"))
		msg += "First.";
		else if(arg.equals("Second"))
		msg += "Second.";
		else if(arg.equals("Third"))
		msg += "Third.";
		else if(arg.equals("Debug"))
		msg += "Debug.";
		else if(arg.equals("Testing"))
		msg += "Testing.";
		menuFrame.msg = msg;
		menuFrame.repaint();
```

```
        }
        public void itemStateChanged(ItemEvent ie)
        {
                menuFrame.repaint( );
        }
}

public class MenuDemo extends Applet
{
        Frame f;
        public void init( )
        {
                f = new MenuFrame("Menu Demo");
                int width = Integer.parseInt(getParameter("width"));
                int height = Integer.parseInt(getParameter("height"));
                setSize(new Dimension(width, height));
                f.setSize(width, height);
                f.setVisible(true);
        }
        public void start( )
        {
                f.setVisible(true);
        }
        public void stop( )
        {
                f.setVisible(false);
        }
}
```

Output of above program will be shown through following screen-shots.

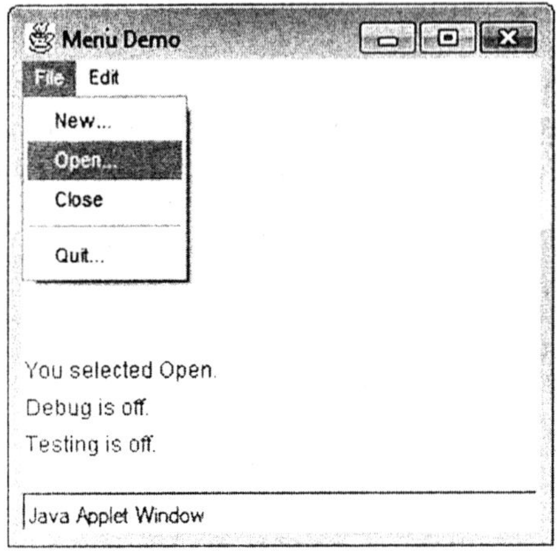


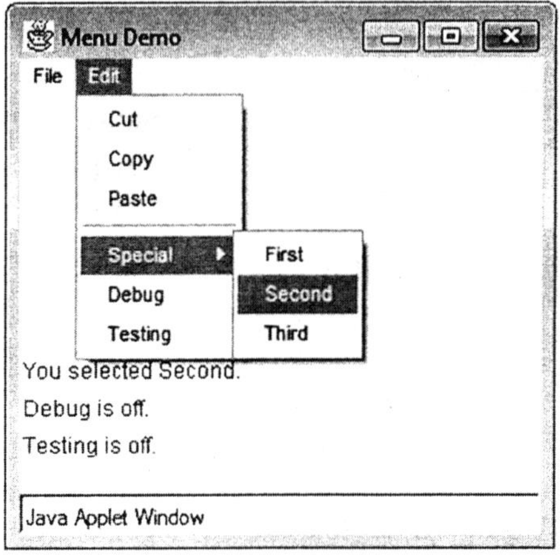


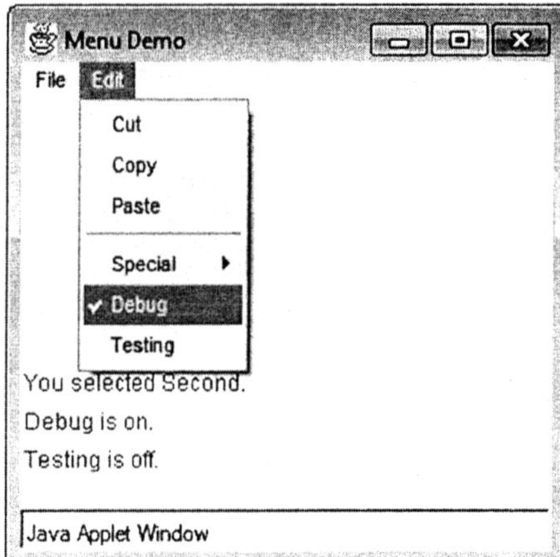


* * * * *

# Chapter 8

# JDBC ODBC connectivity

Enterprise applications that are created using the Java EE technology need to interact with databases to store application-specific information. In current world it is very hard to find a web application or enterprise application that does not have some sort of database connectivity. For example, **search engines** use databases to store information about the web pages and **job portals** use databases to store information about the candidates and employers who access the websites to search and advertise jobs on the internet. Interacting with databases requires database connectivity, which can be achieved by using the Open Database Connectivity (ODBC) driver. This driver is used with Java Database Connectivity (JDBC) to interact with various types of databases, such as *Oracle, MS Access, My SQL* and *SQL Server*. JDBC is an API which is used in Java programming to interact with databases. JDBC works with different database drivers to connect to different databases.

In this chapter we will focus on JDBC, which is used to provide database connectivity to enterprise applications. In this chapter, we begin with Components of JDBC, types of JDBC drivers, JDBC architecture and then some examples of JDBC connectivity.

## 8.1 Java as database front end

We are already familiar with the concept of **front end** and **back end** of an application. The front end of the application is the GUI part of the application used to interact with the user. Generally the programming languages such as VB, VB.net, Java, ASP.net, PHP, etc provide the facility (APIs) to develop front end of the application. The back end of the application is the part that does the work, but the user is unaware of it. Generally databases are used as back end of the application.

We can also be agree on, *"The front-end is a kind of interface between the user and the back-end."* As mentioned above, Java provides class libraries (APIs) to develop designing part / GUI part / presentation part of the application. As studied in previous chapters **Applet & GUI Programming** and **Swings** we have discussed all the possible points on designing an application using AWT and Swing classes.

Obviously, Java entrenched itself on the server side where it has clear advantages over any other existing technology. There are many points which we can note down that proves the Java as the best option for developing front end of any application.

- HTML client with JSP / Servlets
- Swing based GUI client
- Swing and its deployment models
- Plug-in provided by Java (Such as JDBC-ODBC, JavaMail, Services, Hibernating, etc.)
- Java web start
- Deployment of Java swing as pure HTML contents
- Emerging XML / XSLT client

Finally, each front-end technology has its benefits and disadvantages. But when it comes to the interface to your Java applications, none of them is superior to Java in all aspects. For each specific application, you must perform an evaluation of these technologies with analysis of requirements and user expectations.

## 8.2 What is JDBC?

JDBC is a specification from Sun Microsystems that provides a standard abstraction (API / Protocol) for Java application to communicate with different databases. It is used in the application / programs which requires connection and access to certain databases and spreadsheets.

JDBC is the API that can access any kind of tabular data, especially data stored in a **Relational Database**. JDBC works with Java on a variety of platforms, such as Windows, Mac OS, and the various versions of UNIX. The JDBC API allows Java programs to execute SQL statements and retrieve results. The classes and interfaces of JDBC allow a Java application to send requests made by users to the specified DBMS. The following are the characteristics of JDBC.

- Supports a wide level of portability.
- Provides Java interfaces that are compatible with Java applications. These providers are also responsible for providing the driver services.
- Provides higher level APIs for application programmers. The JDBC API specification is used as an interface for the application and DBMS.
- Provides support for ODBC using JDBC-ODBC Bridge.
- Provides support for using SQL statements. These statements are responsible for the entire communication with the database.

## 8.3 Components of JDBC

The JDBC has four main components through which it communicates with a database. These components are discussed here in brief.

1. **The JDBC API** - The JDBC API provides programmatic access to relational data from the Java programming language. Using the JDBC API, applications can execute SQL statements, retrieve results, and propagate changes back to an underlying data source. The JDBC API can also interact with multiple data sources in a distributed, heterogeneous environment.
   The JDBC API is part of the Java platform, which includes the *Java Standard Edition* (Java SE) and the *Java Enterprise Edition* (Java EE). The JDBC 4.0 API is divided into two packages: *java.sql* and *javax.sql*. Both packages are included in the Java SE and Java EE platforms.
2. **The JDBC DriverManager** - The JDBC DriverManager class defines objects which can connect Java applications to a JDBC driver. DriverManager has traditionally been the backbone of the JDBC architecture. It is quite small and simple.
   The Standard Extension packages *javax.naming* and *javax.sql* let you use a *DataSource* object registered with a *Java Naming and Directory Interface* (JNDI) naming service to establish a connection with a data source. You can use either connecting mechanism, but using a DataSource object is recommended whenever possible.
3. **The JDBC test suit** - The JDBC driver test suite helps you to determine that JDBC drivers will run your program. These tests are not comprehensive or exhaustive, but they do exercise many of the important features in the JDBC API.
4. **The JDBC – ODBC bridge** - The Java Software bridge provides JDBC access via ODBC drivers. Note that you need to load ODBC binary code onto each client machine that uses this driver. As a result, the ODBC driver is most appropriate on a corporate network where client installations are not a major problem, or for the application server code written in Java in a **three-tier architecture**.

This current session uses the first two of these four components to connect to a database and then build a java program that uses SQL commands to communicate with a test Relational Database. The last two components are used in specialized environments to test web applications, or to communicate with ODBC-aware DBMSs.

## 8.4 Types of JDBC drivers

There are four types of JDBC drivers which are listed in here and described subsequently.

- Type 1 Driver : JDBC-ODBC Bridge driver
- Type 2 Driver : Native API / partly Java driver
- Type 3 Driver : All Java / Net-protocol driver
- Type 4 Driver : Native protocol / all - Java driver

**Type I : JDBC ODBC Bridge driver**

The Type 1 driver translates all JDBC calls into ODBC calls and sends them to the ODBC driver. ODBC is a generic API. The JDBC-ODBC Bridge driver is recommended only for experimental use or when no other alternative is available. This driver also helps programmers to use JDBC and develop Java applications to communicate with existing data sources. This driver is included in the Java2 SDK within the *sun.jdbc.odbc* package. This driver converts the JDBC calls into ODBC calls and redirects the request to the ODBC driver. The architecture of the type I driver is shown here.

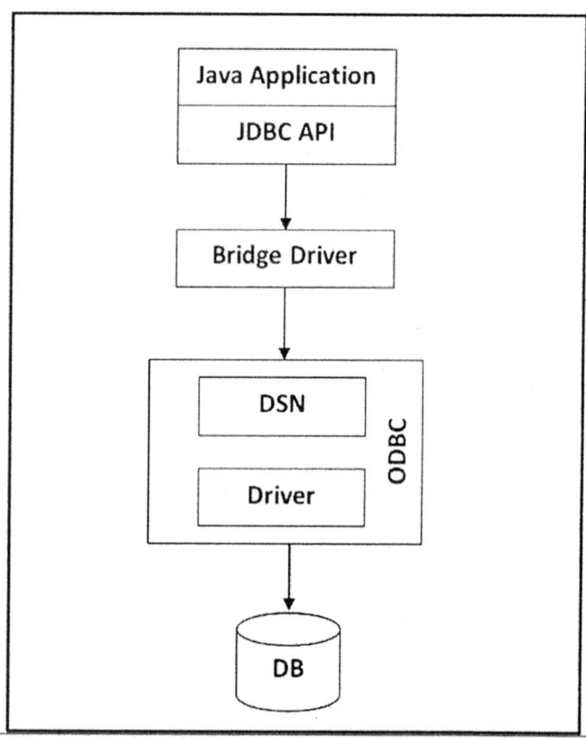


**Advantages**

- Represents a single driver implementation to interact with different data stores.
- Allows us to communicate with all the databases supported by the ODBC driver.
- Represents a vendor independent driver.

**Disadvantages**

- Since the Bridge driver is not written fully in Java, Type 1 drivers are not portable.
- A performance issue is seen as a JDBC call goes through the bridge to the ODBC driver, then to the database, and this applies even in the reverse process. They are the slowest of all driver types.
- The client system requires the ODBC Installation to use the driver.
- Not good for the Web.

**Type II : Native API / partly Java driver**

The distinctive characteristics of Type II JDBC drivers are that it converts JDBC calls into database-specific calls i.e. this driver is specific to a particular database. For example: Oracle will have oracle native API. Some distinctive characteristic of type II JDBC drivers are shown below.

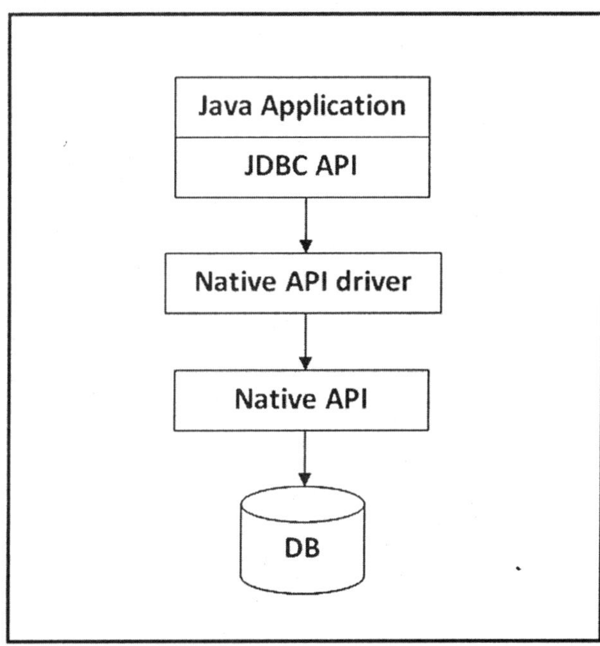


As shown in above diagram, the Java application that needs to communicate with the database is programmed using JDBC API. These JDBC calls are converted into database specific native calls in the client machine and the request is then dispatched to the database specific native libraries.

**Advantages**

- Helps to access the data faster as compare to type I drivers.
- Contains additional features provided by the specific database vendor, which are also supported by the JDBC specification.

**Disadvantages**

- Native API must be installed in the Client System and hence type 2 drivers cannot be used for the Internet.
- Like Type 1 drivers, it's not written in Java Language which forms a portability issue.
- If we change the Database we have to change the native api as it is specific to a database
- Mostly obsolete now
- Usually not thread safe.

**Type III : All Java / Net-protocol driver**

Type 3 database requests are passed through the network to the middle-tier server. This driver translates the JDBC calls into database server independent and middleware-server-specific calls. With the help of the middleware server, the translated JDBC calls are further translated into database server specific calls.

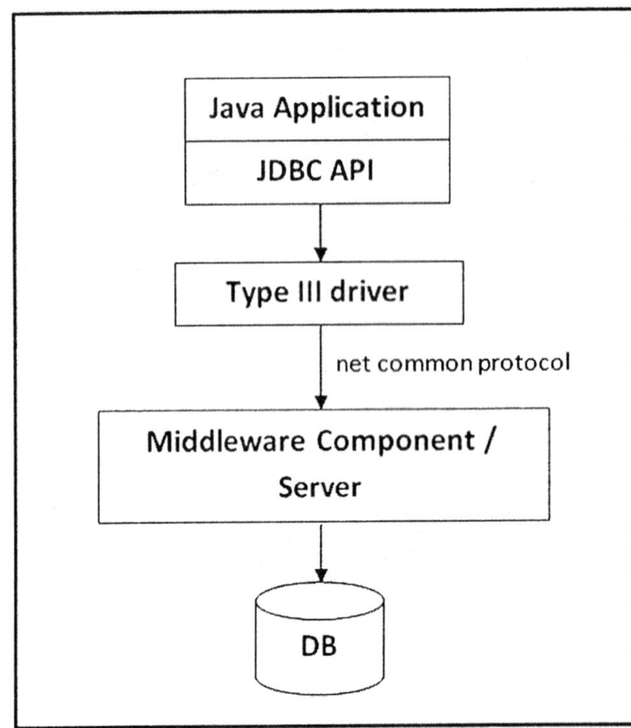


As shown in above diagram, JDBC Type-III drivers listens for JDBC calls from the Java application and translates them into middleware server specific calls. After that, the driver communicates with the middleware server over a socket. The middleware server converts these calls into database specific calls. These types of drivers are also known as *net-protocol drivers*.

**Advantages**

- This driver is server-based, so there is no need for any vendor database library to be present on client machines.
- This driver is fully written in Java and hence Portable. It is suitable for the web.
- There are many opportunities to optimize portability, performance, and scalability.
- The net protocol can be designed to make the client JDBC driver very small and fast to load.
- The type 3 driver typically provides support for features such as caching (connections, query results, and so on), load balancing, and advanced system administration such as logging and auditing.
- This driver is very flexible allows access to multiple databases using one driver.
- They are the most efficient amongst all driver types.

**Disadvantages**

- It requires another server application to install and maintain. Traversing the recordset may take longer, since the data comes through the backend server.

**Type IV Driver : Native protocol / all - Java driver**

The Type 4 uses java networking libraries to communicate directly with the database server. Following diagram shows the characteristics of type IV driver.

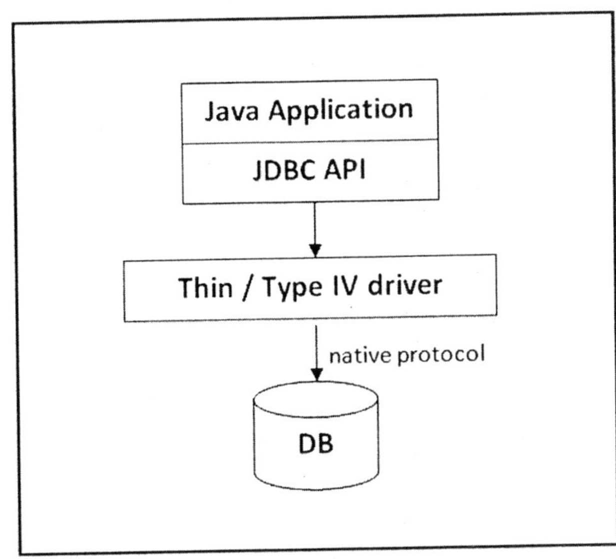


As shown here in diagram, the Type-IV drivers prepares a DBMS specific network message through native protocol and then communicates with database server over a socket. This type of driver is light-weight and generally known as a thin driver. The Type-IV driver uses database specific proprietary protocols for communication. Generally, this type of driver is implemented by DBMS vendors, since the protocols used are proprietary.

**Advantages**

- The major benefit of using a Type-IV JDBC drivers are that they are completely written in Java to achieve platform independence and eliminate deployment administration issues. It is most suitable for the web.
- Number of translation layers is very less i.e. Type -IV JDBC drivers don't have to translate database requests to ODBC or a native connectivity interface or to pass the request on to another server, performance is typically quite good.
- You don't need to install special software on the client or server. Further, these drivers can be downloaded dynamically.

**Disadvantages**

- With type 4 drivers, the user needs a different driver for each database.

## 8.5 JDBC architecture

A JDBC driver is required to process the SQL requests and generates results. JDBC API provides classes and interfaces to handle database specific calls from users. Some of the important classes and interfaces are listed here.

- DriverManager
- Driver
- Connection
- Statement
- PreparedStatement
- CallableStatement
- Class
- ResultSet
- DatabaseMetaData
- ResultSetMetaData

- SqlData
- Blob
- Clob

The DriverManager class in the JDBC API plays an important role in the JDBC architecture. It uses some database specific drivers to effectively connect enterprise applications to databases. Following diagram shows the simple JDBC architecture.

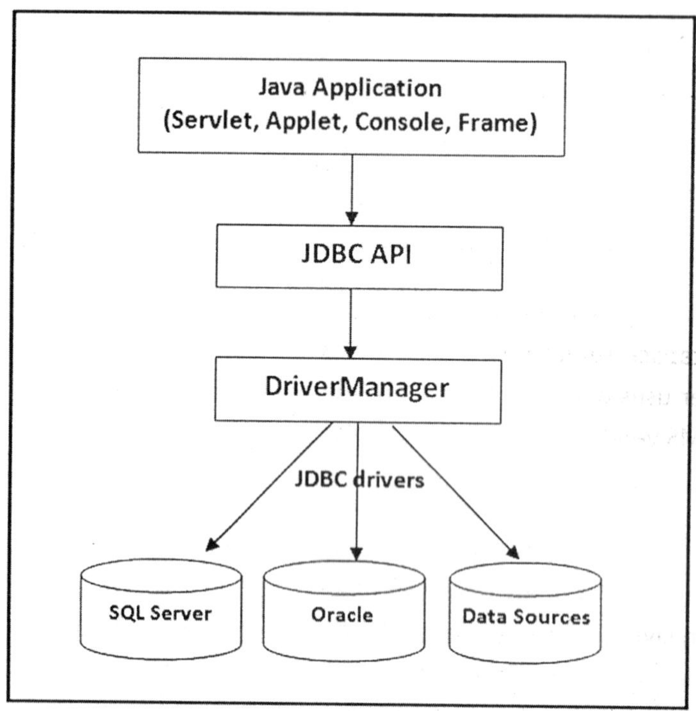


As shown in above diagram, the Java application communicates with a databases using JDBC API. The JDBC driver supporting data sources such as Oracle and SQL, has to be added in the Java application for JDBC support, which can be done dynamically plugging of the JDBC drivers ensures that the Java application is vendor independent. In other words, if you want to communicate with any data source through JDBC, you need a JDBC driver that intelligently communicates with the respective data sources. Currently, there are more than 220 JDBC drivers available in the market, which are designed to communicate with different data sources.

## 8.6 JDBC APIs

The JDBC API is mainly divided into two packages.

- *java.sql*
- *javax.sql*

Following table shows the classes and interfaces available under these packages.

### *java.sql* package

The *java.sql* package is also known as the JDBC core API. This package includes the classes and interfaces to perform JDBC core operations, such as creating and executing SQL queries. The *java.sql* package consists of the interfaces and classes that need to be implemented in an application to access a database. The developer uses these operations to access the database in an application. The classes and interfaces of the *java.sql* package are listed and briefly described here.

*java.sql classes*

| | |
|---|---|
| Array | The mapping in the Java programming language for the SQL type ARRAY. |
| Blob | The representation (mapping) in the Java programming language of an SQL BLOB value. |
| CallableStatement | The interface used to execute SQL stored procedures. |
| Clob | The mapping in the Java programming language for the SQL CLOB type. |
| Connection | A connection (session) with a specific database. |
| DatabaseMetaData | Comprehensive information about the database as a whole. |
| Driver | The interface that every driver class must implement. |
| NClob | The mapping in the Java programming language for the SQL NCLOB type. |
| ParameterMetaData | An object that can be used to get information about the types and properties for each parameter marker in a PreparedStatement object. |
| PreparedStatement | An object that represents a precompiled SQL statement. |
| Ref | The mapping in the Java programming language of an SQL REF value, which is a reference to an SQL structured type value in the database. |
| ResultSet | A table of data representing a database result set, which is usually generated by executing a statement that queries the database. |
| ResultSetMetaData | An object that can be used to get information about the types and properties of the columns in a ResultSet object. |
| RowId | The representation (mapping) in the Java programming language of an SQL ROWID value. |
| Savepoint | The representation of a savepoint, which is a point within the current transaction that can be referenced from the Connection.rollback method. |
| SQLData | The interface used for the custom mapping of an SQL user-defined type (UDT) to a class in the Java programming language. |
| SQLInput | An input stream that contains a stream of values representing an instance of an SQL structured type or an SQL distinct type. |
| SQLOutput | The output stream for writing the attributes of a user-defined type back to the database. |
| SQLXML | The mapping in the JavaTM programming language for the SQL XML type. |
| Statement | The object used for executing a static SQL statement and returning the results it produces. |
| Struct | The standard mapping in the Java programming language for an SQL structured type. |
| Wrapper | Interface for JDBC classes which provide the ability to retrieve the delegate instance when the instance in question is in fact a proxy class. |

*java.sql interfaces*

| | |
|---|---|
| Date | A thin wrapper around a millisecond value that allows JDBC to identify this as an SQL DATE value. |
| DriverManager | The basic service for managing a set of JDBC drivers. |
| DriverPropertyInfo | Driver properties for making a connection. |
| SQLPermission | The permission for which the SecurityManager will check when code that is running in an applet, or an application with a SecurityManager enabled, calls the DriverManager.setLogWriter method, DriverManager.setLogStream (deprecated) method, SyncFactory.setJNDIContext method, SyncFactory.setLogger method, Connection.setNetworktimeout method, or the Connection.abort method. |

| | |
|---|---|
| Time | A thin wrapper around the java.util.Date class that allows the JDBC API to identify this as an SQL TIME value. |
| Timestamp | A thin wrapper around java.util.Date that allows the JDBC API to identify this as an SQL TIMESTAMP value. |
| Types | The class that defines the constants that are used to identify generic SQL types, called JDBC types. |

## javax.sql package

The *javax.sql* package is also called as the JDBC extension API and provides classes and interfaces to access server side data sources and process Java programs. The JDBC extension package supplements the *javax.sql* package and provides following classes and interfaces.

*javax.sql classes*

| | |
|---|---|
| CommonDataSource | Interface that defines the methods which are common between DataSource, XADataSource and ConnectionPoolDataSource. |
| ConnectionEventListener | An object that registers to be notified of events generated by a PooledConnection object. |
| ConnectionPoolDataSource | A factory for PooledConnection objects. |
| DataSource | A factory for connections to the physical data source that this DataSource object represents. |
| PooledConnection | An object that provides hooks for connection pool management. |
| RowSet | The interface that adds support to the JDBC API for the JavaBeans component model. |
| RowSetInternal | The interface that a RowSet object implements in order to present itself to a RowSetReader or RowSetWriter object. |
| RowSetListener | An interface that must be implemented by a component that wants to be notified when a significant event happens in the life of a RowSet object. |
| RowSetMetaData | An object that contains information about the columns in a RowSet object. |
| RowSetReader | The facility that a disconnected RowSet object calls on to populate itself with rows of data. |
| RowSetWriter | An object that implements the RowSetWriter interface, called a *writer*. |
| StatementEventListener | An object that registers to be notified of events that occur on PreparedStatements that are in the Statement pool. |
| XAConnection | An object that provides support for distributed transactions. |
| XADataSource | A factory for XAConnection objects that is used internally. |

*javax.sql interfaces*

| | |
|---|---|
| ConnectionEvent | An Event object that provides information about the source of a connection-related event. |
| RowSetEvent | An Event object generated when an event occurs to a RowSet object. |
| StatementEvent | A StatementEvent is sent to all StatementEventListeners which were registered with a PooledConnection. |

## 8.7 Exploring major classes and interfaces of JDBC

In above section we have already gone through classes and interfaces of *java.sql* and *javax.sql* packages. Among these, some striking classes and interfaces plays an important role in JDBC implementation in a Java application. These classes and interfaces are explained in this section. These classes and interfaces allow you to load a driver, create a connection and fire the query.

- **Class class**

This class actually has multipurpose applications but in this section we will discuss its application in JDBC. This class is used to load JDBC driver for connecting databases. **Class** has no public constructor. Instead **Class** objects are constructed automatically by the Java Virtual Machine as classes are loaded and by calls to the **defineClass( )**method in the class loader. This class is defined as:

*public final class Class<T> extends Object implements Serializable, GenericDeclaration, Type, AnnotatedElement*

Here, T - the type of the class modeled by this **Class** object. For example, the type of *String.class* is *Class<String>*. Use *Class<?>* if the class being modeled is *unknown*.

Instances of the class **Class** represent classes and interfaces in a running Java application. An *enum* is a kind of class and an annotation is a kind of interface. Every array also belongs to a class that is reflected as a **Class** object that is shared by all arrays with the same element type and number of dimensions. The primitive Java types (*boolean, byte, char, short, int, long, float, and double*), and the keyword *void* are also represented as **Class** objects.

This class has a mass of methods, but we are listing only few of them.

| **Method** | **Description** |
|---|---|
| Boolean desiredAssertionStatus( ) | Returns the assertion status that would be assigned to this class if it were to be initialized at the time this method is invoked. |
| static Class<?> forName (String className) | Returns the **Class** object associated with the class or interface with the given string name. |
| static Class<?> forName (String name, boolean initialize, ClassLoader loader) | Returns the Class object associated with the class or interface with the given string name, using the given class loader. |
| String getCanonicalName( ) | Returns the canonical name of the underlying class as defined by the Java Language Specification. |
| ClassLoader getComponentType( ) | Returns the Class representing the component type of an array. |
| Field getDeclaredField(String name) | Returns a Field object that reflects the specified declared field of the class or interface represented by this Class object. |
| Field[]getDeclaredFields( ) | Returns an array of Field objects reflecting all the fields declared by the class or interface represented by this Class object. |
| Method getDeclaredMethod (String name) | Returns a Method object that reflects the specified declared method of the class or interface represented by this Class object. |
| Method[]getDeclaredMethods( ) | Returns an array of Method objects reflecting all the methods declared by the class or interface represented by this Class object. |
| int getModifiers( ) | Returns the Java language modifiers for this class or interface, encoded in an integer. |
| String getName( ) | Returns the name of the entity (class, interface, array class, primitive type, or void) represented by this Class object, as a String. |
| Package getPackage( ) | Gets the package for this class. |
| URL getResource(String name) | Finds a resource with a given name. |
| String getSimpleName( ) | Returns the simple name of the underlying class as given in the source code. |
| boolean isArray( ) | Determines if this Class object represents an array class. |
| boolean isEnum( ) | Returns true if and only if this class was declared as an enum in the source code. |
| Boolean isPrimitive( ) | Determines if the specified Class object represents a primitive type. |
| String toString( ) | Converts the object to a string. |

Most widely we use its static *forName(String classname)* method to load the JDBC drivers.

- **DriverManager class**

As part of its initialization, the *DriverManager* class will attempt to load the driver classes referenced in the *jdbc.drivers* system property. This allows a user to customize the JDBC Drivers used by their applications. This class is defined as:

```
public class DriverManager extends Object
```

The DriverManager provides a basic service for managing a set of JDBC drivers. As part of its initialization, the DriverManager class will attempt to load the driver classes referenced in the *"jdbc.drivers"* system property. This allows a user to customize the JDBC Drivers used by their applications.

For example in your ~/.hotjava/properties file you might specify:

*"jdbc.drivers=foo.bah.Driver:wombat.sql.Driver:bad.taste.yourDriver"*

A program can also explicitly load JDBC drivers at any time. For example, the my.sql.Driver is loaded with the following statement:

*Class.forName("my.sql.Driver");*

Following are some of the important methods of this class.

| Method | Description |
|---|---|
| static void deregisterDriver (Driver driver) | Drops a driver from the DriverManager's list. |
| static connection getConnection (String url) | Attempts to establish a connection to the given database URL. |
| static connection getConnection (String url, Properties info) | Attempts to establish a connection to the given database URL. |
| static connection getConnection (String url, String user, String password) | Attempts to establish a connection to the given database URL. |
| static Driver getDriver(String url) | Attempts to locate a driver that understands the given URL. |
| static int getLoginTimeout( ) | Gets the maximum time in seconds that a driver can wait when attempting to log in to a database. |
| static PrintWriter getLogWriter( ) | Retrieves the log writer. |
| static void println(String message) | Prints a message to the current JDBC log stream. |
| static void registerDriver (Driver driver) | Registers the given user defined driver with the DriverManager. |
| static void setLoginTimeout (int seconds) | Sets the maximum time in seconds that a driver will wait while attempting to connect to a database. |
| static void setLogWriter (PrintWriter out) | Sets the logging/tracing *PrintWriter* object that is used by the DriverManager and all drivers. |

When **getConnection( )** is called the DriverManager will attempt to locate a suitable driver from amongst those loaded at initialization and those loaded explicitly using the same classloader as the current applet or application.

- **Connection interface**

A Connection is the session between java application and database. SQL statements are executed and results are returned within the context of a connection. The Connection interface is a factory of Statement, PreparedStatement, and DatabaseMetaData. i.e. the object of Connection can be used to obtain object of Statement, PreparedStatement, DatabaseMetaData, CallableStatement. This interface is defined as:

```
public interface Connection extends Wrapper, AutoCloseable
```

The connection can be established with the database by two ways. One is by using *Data Sources* and second is by manually providing *database driver* and *database name*. (Section 8.8 shows how to create Data Sources) Refer following statements.

```
//providing data source name:
Connection con = DriverManager.getConnection("jdbc:odbc:temp");
```

```
// providing database driver and database name
Connection con =
DriverManager.getConnection("jdbc:odbc:Driver={Microsoft Access Driver (*.mdb)}; database=D:/abcd.mdb");
```

In last section of this chapter some important JDBC examples are given. In all those examples, I have used data source name. But instead you can use second method and provide driver - database name manually.

Following are some of the commonly used methods of Connection interface.

| Method | Description |
|---|---|
| void abort(Executor executor) | Terminates an open connection. |
| void clearWarnings( ) | Clears all warnings reported for this Connection object. |
| void close( ) | Releases this Connection object's database and JDBC resources immediately *instead of waiting for them to be automatically released.* |
| void commit( ) | Makes all changes made since the previous commit/rollback permanent and releases any database locks currently held by this Connection object. |
| Blob createBlob( ) | Constructs an object that implements the Blob interface. |
| Clob createClob( ) | Constructs an object that implements the Clob interface. |
| NClob createNClob( ) | Constructs an object that implements the NClob interface. |
| SQLXML createSQLXML( ) | Constructs an object that implements the SQLXML interface. |
| Statement createStatement( ) | Creates a Statement object for sending SQL statements to the database. |
| Statement createStatement (int resultSetType, int resultSetConcurrency) | Creates a Statement object that will generate ResultSet objects with the given type and concurrency. |
| String getCatalog( ) | Retrieves this Connection object's current catalog name. |
| Properties getClientInfo( ) | Returns a list containing the name and current value of each client info property supported by the driver. |
| String getClientInfo(String name) | Returns the value of the client info property specified by client's name. |
| DatabaseMetaData getMetaData( ) | Retrieves a DatabaseMetaData object that contains metadata about the database to which this Connection object represents a connection. |
| boolean isClosed( ) | Retrieves whether this Connection object has been closed. |
| boolean isReadOnly( ) | Retrieves whether this Connection object is in read-only mode. |
| String nativeSQL(String sql) | Converts the given SQL statement into the system's native SQL grammar. |
| CallableStatement prepareCall(String sql) | Creates a CallableStatement object for calling database stored procedures. |
| CallableStatement prepareCall (String sql, int resultSetType, int resultSetConcurrency) | Creates a CallableStatement object that will generate ResultSet objects with the given type and concurrency. |
| PreparedStatement | Creates a PreparedStatement object for sending parameterized SQL |

| | |
|---|---|
| prepareStatement(String sql) | statements to the database. |
| PreparedStatement prepareStatement(String sql, int autoGeneratedKeys) | Creates a default PreparedStatement object that has the capability to retrieve auto-generated keys. |
| PreparedStatement prepareStatement(String sql, int resultSetType, int resultSetConcurrency) | Creates a PreparedStatement object that will generate ResultSet objects with the given type and concurrency. |
| PreparedStatement prepareStatement(String sql, String[] columnNames) | Creates a default PreparedStatement object capable of returning the auto-generated keys designated by the given array. |
| void releaseSavepoint (Savepoint savepoint) | Removes the specified Savepoint and subsequent Savepoint objects from the current transaction. |
| void setReadOnly (boolean readOnly) | Puts this connection in read-only mode as a hint to the driver to enable database optimizations. |
| SavePoint setSavepoint( ) | Creates an unnamed savepoint in the current transaction and returns the new Savepoint object that represents it. |
| SavePoint setSavepoint (String name) | Creates a savepoint with the given name in the current transaction and returns the new Savepoint object that represents it. |

Remember that, by default, connection commits the changes after executing queries.

- **Statement interface**

Once a connection is obtained we can interact with the database. The object of this interface is used for executing a static SQL or PL/SQL statement and returning the results it produces.

This interface is defined as:

```
public interface Statement extends Wrapper, AutoCloseable
```

The statement converts a static SQL or PL/SQL statements into an executable query and affects to database. Following example statements shows how to obtain a statement object from Connection.

```
Statement stmt = con.createStatement( );
```

Following are some of the important methods of Statement interface.

| Method | Description |
|---|---|
| void addBatch(String sql) | Adds the given SQL command to the current list of commmands for this Statement object. |
| void cancel( ) | Cancels this Statement object if both the DBMS and driver support aborting an SQL statement. |
| void clearBatch( ) | Empties this Statement object's current list of SQL commands. |
| void close( ) | Releases this Statement object's database and JDBC resources immediately instead of waiting for this to happen when it is automatically closed. |
| void closeOnCompletion( ) | Specifies that this Statement will be closed when all its dependent ResultSets are closed. |
| boolean execute(String sql) | Executes the given SQL statement, which may return multiple results. |
| boolean execute(String sql, int autoGeneratedKeys) | Executes the given SQL statement, which may return multiple results, and signals the driver that any auto-generated keys should be made available for retrieval. |

| | |
|---|---|
| int[ ] executeBatch( ) | Submits a batch of commands to the database for execution and if all commands execute successfully, returns an array of update counts. |
| ResultSet executeQuery (String sql) | Executes the given SQL statement, which returns a single ResultSet object. |
| int executeUpdate(String sql) | Executes the given SQL statement, which may be an INSERT, UPDATE, or DELETE statement or an SQL statement that returns nothing, such as an SQL DDL statement. |
| int executeUpdate(String sql, int autoGeneratedKeys) | Executes the given SQL statement and signals the driver with the given flag about whether the auto-generated keys produced by this Statement object should be made available for retrieval. |
| int executeUpdate(String sql, String[] columnNames) | Executes the given SQL statement and signals the driver that the auto-generated keys indicated in the given array should be made available for retrieval. |
| Connection getConnection( ) | Retrieves the Connection object that produced this Statement object. |
| ResultSet getGeneratedKeys( ) | Retrieves any auto-generated keys created as a result of executing this Statement object. |
| int getMaxRows( ) | Retrieves the maximum number of rows that a ResultSet object produced by this Statement object can contain. |
| boolean getMoreResults( ) | Moves to this Statement object's next result, returns true if it is a ResultSet object, and implicitly closes any current ResultSet object(s) obtained with the method getResultSet( ). |
| ResultSet getResultSet( ) | Retrieves the current result as a ResultSet object. |
| boolean isClosed( ) | Retrieves whether this Statement object has been closed. |
| boolean isPoolable( ) | Returns a value indicating whether the Statement is poolable or not. |
| void setMaxRows(int max) | Sets the limit for the maximum number of rows that any ResultSet object generated by this Statement object can contain to the given number. |
| void setPoolable (boolean poolable) | Requests that a Statement be pooled or not pooled. |
| void setQueryTimeout (int seconds) | Sets the number of seconds the driver will wait for a Statement object to execute to the given number of seconds. |

This interface generates a multilevel structure where PreparedStatement is directly derived from Statement interface. This will be studied further in next interface.

- **PreparedStatement interface**

This interface is use when you plan to use one SQL statements many times. The PreparedStatement interface accepts input parameters at runtime. This interface is derived from Statement interface. Refer following definition.

```
public interface PreparedStatement extends Statement
```

The prepareStatement( ) of Connection interface, prepares this precompiled SQL statement and returns it as PreparedStatement object. We can use this object multiple times. For example,

```
PreparedStatement stmt = con.prepareStatement ("UPDATE EMPLOYEES SET SALARY = ? WHERE ID = ?");
```

Following table shows some of the frequently used methods of PreparedStatement interface.

| Method | Description |
|---|---|
| void addBatch( ) | Adds a set of parameters to this PreparedStatement object's batch of commands. |
| void clearParameters( ) | Clears the current parameter values immediately. |
| boolean execute( ) | Executes the SQL statement in this PreparedStatement object, which may be any kind of SQL statement. |

| | |
|---|---|
| ResultSet executeQuery( ) | Executes the SQL query in this PreparedStatement object and returns the ResultSet object generated by the query. |
| int executeUpdate( ) | Executes the SQL statement in this PreparedStatement object, which must be an SQL Data Manipulation Language (DML) statement, such as INSERT, UPDATE or DELETE; or an SQL statement that returns nothing, such as a DDL statement. |
| ResultSetMetaData getMetaData( ) | Retrieves a ResultSetMetaData object that contains information about the columns of the ResultSet object that will be returned when this Prepared-Statement object is executed. |
| ParameterMetaData getParameterMetaData( ) | Retrieves the number, types and properties of this PreparedStatement object's parameters. |
| void setArray (int parameterIndex, Array x) | Sets the designated parameter to the given java.sql.Array object. |
| void setBlob (int parameterIndex, Blob x) | Sets the designated parameter to the given java.sql.Blob object. |
| void setBlob(int parameterIndex, InputStream inputStream, long length) | Sets the designated parameter to a InputStream object. |
| void setBoolean (int parameterIndex, boolean x) | Sets the designated parameter to the given Java boolean value. |
| void setByte(int parameterIndex, byte x) | Sets the designated parameter to the given Java byte value. |
| void setBytes(int parameterIndex, byte[ ] x) | Sets the designated parameter to the given Java array of bytes. |
| void setCharacterStream(int parameterIndex, Reader reader) | Sets the designated parameter to the given Reader object. |
| void setCharacterStream (int parameterIndex, Reader reader, int length) | Sets the designated parameter to the given Reader object, which is the given number of characters long. |
| void setClob(int parameterIndex, Clob x) | Sets the designated parameter to the given java.sql.Clob object. |
| void setClob(int parameterIndex, Reader reader, long length) | Sets the designated parameter to a Reader object. |
| void setDate(int parameterIndex, Date x, Calendar cal) | Sets the designated parameter to the given java.sql.Date value, using the given Calendar object. |
| void setDouble(int parameterIndex, double x) | Sets the designated parameter to the given Java double value. |
| void setFloat(int parameterIndex, float x) | Sets the designated parameter to the given Java float value. |
| void setInt(int parameterIndex, int x) | Sets the designated parameter to the given Java int value. |
| void setLong(int parameterIndex, long x) | Sets the designated parameter to the given Java long value. |
| void setObject(int parameterIndex, Object x) | Sets the value of the designated parameter using the given object. |
| void setShort(int parameterIndex, short x) | Sets the designated parameter to the given Java short value. |
| void setString(int parameterIndex, String x) | Sets the designated parameter to the given Java String value. |
| void setURL(int parameterIndex, URL x) | Sets the designated parameter to the given java.net.URL value. |
| void setTime(int parameterIndex, | Sets the designated parameter to the given java.sql.Time value. |

| Time x) | |
|---|---|
| void setNClob(int parameterIndex, Reader reader) | Sets the designated parameter to a Reader object. |
| void setNull(int parameterIndex, int sqlType) | Sets the designated parameter to SQL NULL. |

- **CallableStatement interface**

This interface used to execute SQL stored procedures. The JDBC API provides a stored procedure SQL escape syntax that allows stored procedures to be called in a standard way for all RDBMSs. Refer following syntax:

```
{ ? = call <procedure-name> [ (<arg1>,<arg2> , ... ) ] }
{ call <procedure-name> [ (<arg1>,<arg2> , ... ) ] }
```

This syntax has one form that includes a result parameter and one that does not. If used, the result parameter must be registered as an OUT parameter. The other parameters can be used for input, output or both. Parameters are referred to sequentially, by number, with the first parameter being 1.

IN parameter values are set using the set methods inherited from PreparedStatement. The type of all OUT parameters must be registered prior to executing the stored procedure; their values are retrieved after execution via the get methods provided here.

A CallableStatement can return one ResultSet object or multiple ResultSet objects. Multiple ResultSet objects are handled using operations inherited from Statement.

For maximum portability, a call's ResultSet objects and update counts should be processed prior to getting the values of output parameters. Following table shows some commonly used methods of CallableStatement interface.

| Method | Description |
|---|---|
| Array getArray (int parameterIndex) | Retrieves the value of the designated JDBC ARRAY parameter as an Array object in the Java programming language. |
| Array getArray (String parameterName) | Retrieves the value of a JDBC ARRAY parameter as an Array object in the Java programming language. |
| BigDecimal getBigDecimal (int parameterIndex) | Retrieves the value of the designated JDBC NUMERIC parameter as a *java.math.BigDecimal* object with as many digits to the right of the decimal point as the value contains. |
| Blob getBlob (int parameterIndex) | Retrieves the value of the designated JDBC BLOB parameter as a Blob object in the Java programming language. |
| Blob getBlob (String parameterName) | Retrieves the value of a JDBC BLOB parameter as a Blob object in the Java programming language. |
| Boolean getBoolean (int parameterIndex) | Retrieves the value of the designated JDBC `BIT` or `BOOLEAN` parameter as a `boolean` in the Java programming language. |
| boolean getBoolean (String parameterName) | Retrieves the value of a JDBC BIT or BOOLEAN parameter as a boolean in the Java programming language. |
| byte getByte (int parameterIndex) | Retrieves the value of the designated JDBC TINYINT parameter as a byte in the Java programming language. |
| byte getByte (String parameterName) | Retrieves the value of a JDBC TINYINT parameter as a byte in the Java programming language. |
| Clob getClob (int parameterIndex) | Retrieves the value of the designated JDBC CLOB parameter as a java.sql.Clob object in the Java programming language. |
| double getDouble (int parameterIndex) | Retrieves the value of the designated JDBC DOUBLE parameter as a double in the Java programming language. |
| double getDouble (String parameterName) | Retrieves the value of a JDBC DOUBLE parameter as a double in the Java programming language. |
| float getFloat | Retrieves the value of the designated JDBC FLOAT parameter as a float in the Java |

| | |
|---|---|
| (int parameterIndex) | programming language. |
| float getFloat (String parameterName) | Retrieves the value of a JDBC FLOAT parameter as a float in the Java programming language. |
| int getInt (int parameterIndex) | Retrieves the value of the designated JDBC INTEGER parameter as an int in the Java programming language. |
| int getInt (String parameterName) | Retrieves the value of a JDBC INTEGER parameter as an int in the Java programming language. |
| long getLong (int parameterIndex) | Retrieves the value of the designated JDBC BIGINT parameter as a long in the Java programming language. |
| long getLong (String parameterName | Retrieves the value of a JDBC BIGINT parameter as a long in the Java programming language. |
| Ref getRef (int parameterIndex) | Retrieves the value of the designated JDBC REF(<structured-type>) parameter as a Ref object in the Java programming language. |
| Ref getRef (String parameterName) | Retrieves the value of a JDBC REF(<structured-type>) parameter as a Ref object in the Java programming language. |

- **ResultSet class**

In case of a query returns dataset of selected records, a *ResultSet* object maintains a cursor pointing to its current row of data. This method is defined as:

```
public interface ResultSet extends Wrapper, AutoCloseable
```

Initially the cursor is positioned before the first row. The next method moves the cursor to the next row, and because it returns false when there are no more rows in the ResultSet object, it can be used in a while loop to iterate through the result set. For example,

```
ResultSet rs = stmt.executeQuery("Select * from emp");
```

A default ResultSet object is not updatable and has a cursor that moves forward only. Thus, you can iterate through it only once and only from the first row to the last row. It is possible to produce ResultSet objects that are scrollable and/or updatable. Following table shows some commonly used methods of ResultSet interface.

| Method | Description |
|---|---|
| boolean absolute(int row) | Moves the cursor to the given row number in this ResultSet object. |
| void afterLast( ) | Moves the cursor to the end of this ResultSet object, just after the last row. |
| void beforeFirst( ) | Moves the cursor to the front of this ResultSet object, just before the first row. |
| void cancelRowUpdates( ) | Cancels the updates made to the current row in this ResultSet object. |
| void close( ) | Releases this ResultSet object's database and JDBC resources immediately instead of waiting for this to happen when it is automatically closed. |
| void deleteRow( ) | Deletes the current row from this ResultSet object and from the underlying database. |
| int findColumn (String columnLabel) | Maps the given ResultSet column label to its ResultSet column index. |
| boolean first( ) | Moves the cursor to the first row in this ResultSet object. |
| Array getArray(int columnIndex) | Retrieves the value of the designated column in the current row of this ResultSet object as an Array object in the Java programming language. |
| Array getArray (String columnLabel) | Retrieves the value of the designated column in the current row of this ResultSet object as an Array object in the Java programming language. |
| boolean getBoolean (int columnIndex) | Retrieves the value of the designated column in the current row of this `ResultSet` object as a `boolean` in the Java programming language. |

| | |
|---|---|
| boolean getBoolean (String columnLabel) | Retrieves the value of the designated column in the current row of this ResultSet object as a boolean in the Java programming language. |
| byte getByte(int columnIndex) | Retrieves the value of the designated column in the current row of this ResultSet object as a byte in the Java programming language. |
| byte getByte (String columnLabel) | Retrieves the value of the designated column in the current row of this ResultSet object as a byte in the Java programming language. |
| byte[ ] getBytes (int columnIndex) | Retrieves the value of the designated column in the current row of this ResultSet object as a byte array in the Java programming language |
| byte[ ] getBytes (String columnLabel) | Retrieves the value of the designated column in the current row of this ResultSet object as a byte array in the Java programming language. |
| double getDouble(int columnIndex) | Retrieves the value of the designated column in the current row of this ResultSet object as a double in the Java programming language. |
| double getDouble (String columnLabe) | Retrieves the value of the designated column in the current row of this ResultSet object as a double in the Java programming language. |
| float getFloat(int columnIndex) | Retrieves the value of the designated column in the current row of this ResultSet object as a float in the Java programming language. |
| float getFloat(String columnLabel) | Retrieves the value of the designated column in the current row of this ResultSet object as a float in the Java programming language. |
| int getInt(int columnIndex) | Retrieves the value of the designated column in the current row of this ResultSet object as an int in the Java programming language. |
| int getInt(String columnLabel) | Retrieves the value of the designated column in the current row of this ResultSet object as an int in the Java programming language. |
| long getLong(int columnIndex) | Retrieves the value of the designated column in the current row of this ResultSet object as a long in the Java programming language. |
| long getLong(String columnLabel) | Retrieves the value of the designated column in the current row of this ResultSet object as a long in the Java programming language. |
| int getRow( ) | Retrieves the current row number. |
| String getString(int columnIndex) | Retrieves the value of the designated column in the current row of this ResultSet object as a String in the Java programming language. |
| String getString (String columnLabel) | Retrieves the value of the designated column in the current row of this ResultSet object as a String in the Java programming language. |
| boolean isClosed( ) | Retrieves whether this ResultSet object has been closed. |
| boolean last( ) | Moves the cursor to the last row in this ResultSet object. |
| boolean next( ) | Moves the cursor froward one row from its current position. |
| boolean previous( ) | Moves the cursor to the previous row in this ResultSet object. |

## 8.8 Creating Data Sources

A DSN (also called as ODBC DSN) is the intermediate between Java application and a database. When you are creating a database table fingerprint or setting up database discovery, you are prompted for DSN name. This is an ODBC term that refers to the name of the database to which you're connecting. You can create a DSN for your data source as follows:

Step 1 : Open **Control Panel → Administrative Tools → Data Sources (ODBC)**. Following "ODBC Data Source Administrator" window will appear.

ODBC Data Source Administrator

User DSN | System DSN | File DSN | Drivers | Tracing | Connection Pooling | About

User Data Sources:

| Name | Driver |
|---|---|
| dBASE Files | Microsoft Access dBASE Driver (*.dbf, *.ndx |
| Excel Files | Microsoft Excel Driver (*.xls, *.xlsx, *.xlsm, *.x |
| MS Access Database | Microsoft Access Driver (*.mdb, *.accdb) |
| temp | Microsoft Access Driver (*.mdb, *.accdb) |

Add... Remove Configure...

An ODBC User data source stores information about how to connect to the indicated data provider. A User data source is only visible to you, and can only be used on the current machine.

OK Cancel Apply Help

Step 2 : Click on "Add" button to add new DSN. Following "Create New Data Source" window will appear.

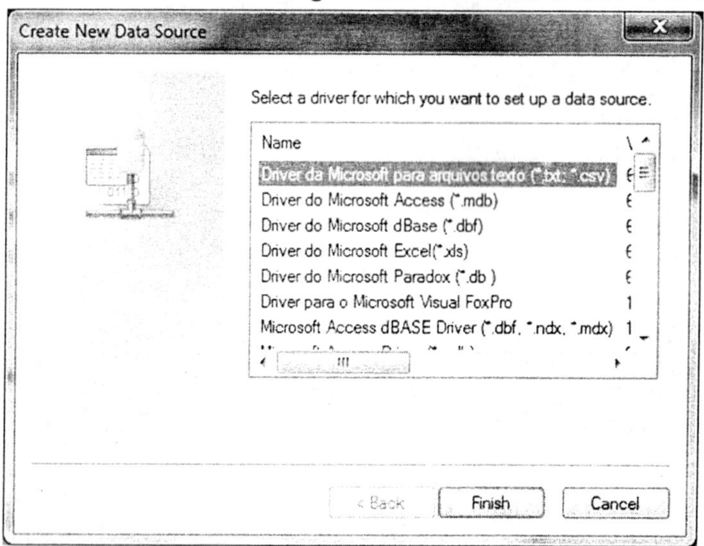


Step 3 : This window contains a list of available ODBC drivers. Select required driver according to your database and click on "Finish". For example, I am selecting "Microsoft Access Driver (*.mdb , *.accdb) "

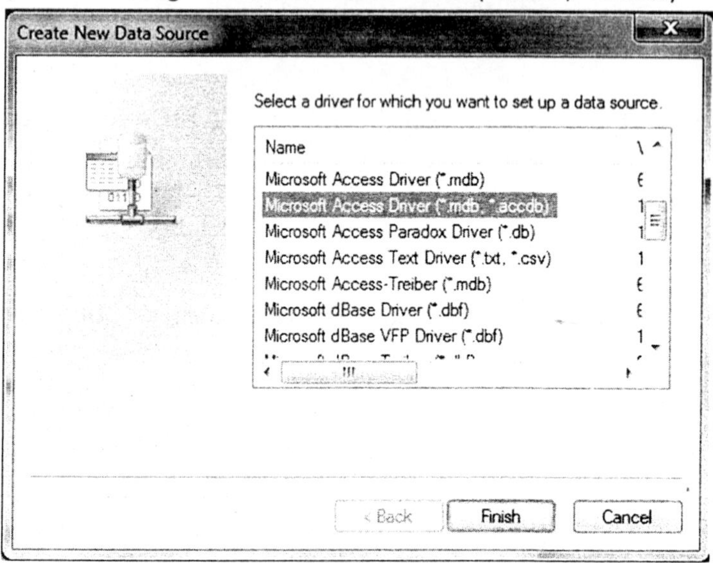

Step 4 : You will get a new "ODBC Microsoft Access Setup" window. Enter Data Source Name, Description and click on "Select" to select database file from local machine.

Step 5 : You will get a new "Select Database" window to select database from local machine. Select required database and click "OK".

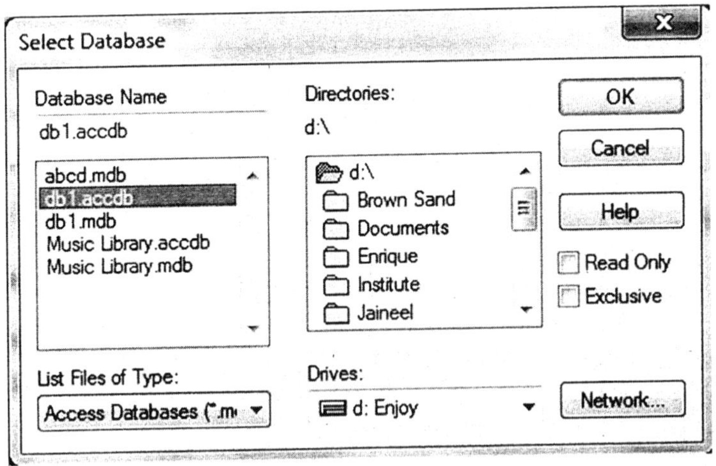


Step 6 : After performing above steps, you will get a user DSN gets created as "new_dsn" name.

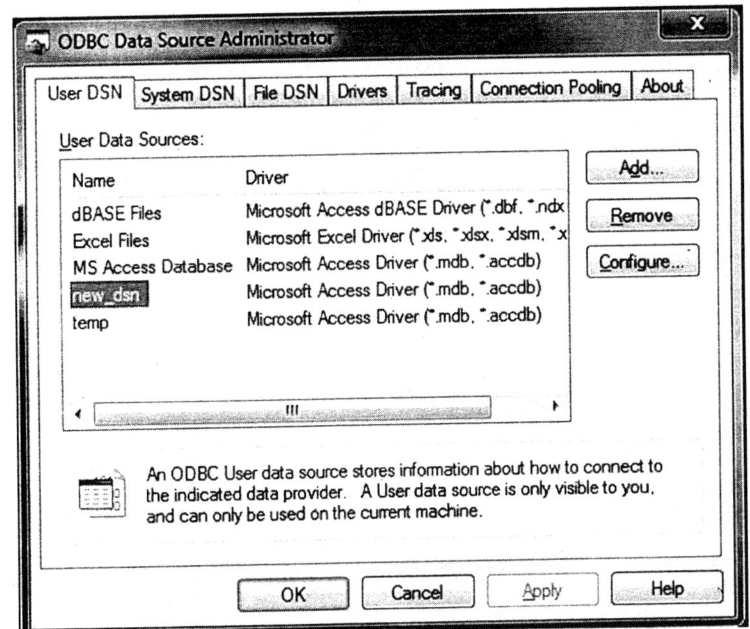

As now a new DSN is created, we you can directly use it in JDBC – ODBC connectivity statements.

You can change / modify the DSN settings and configurations by clicking on "Configure" and you can remove the user DSN by clicking on "Remove" button.

## 8.9 Closing the database connection

After working on an open connection it is always important to close it. The connection interface provides close( ) method, used to close a connection. (Refer above table showing methods of *Connection interface*.)

For example, if *con* is the connection object then to close that connection use:

*con.close( )*

> Note : As java is an auto-destructive programming language, it automatically close the connection when the destructor of processing method executes.

## 8.10 Examples on database connectivity

**Example 1 : Prepare a GUI to accept Employee ID, name and city. Accept the details from the user and insert these details into the employee database in a button click.**

```
import java.awt.*;
import java.awt.event.*;
import java.sql.*;

class jdbc_insert extends Frame implements ActionListener
{
        TextField tf1,tf2,tf3;
        Label lb;
        public jdbc_insert( )
        {
                setLayout(null);
                tf1 = new TextField( );
                tf2 = new TextField( );
                tf3 = new TextField( );
                Label l1 = new Label("Enter Employee ID :");
                Label l2 = new Label("Enter Employee Name :");
                Label l3 = new Label("Enter City :");
                lb = new Label( );
                Button bt = new Button("Submit");
                add(l1);add(l2);add(l3);
                add(tf1);add(tf2);add(tf3);add(bt);add(lb);
                tf1.setBounds(80,50,200,30);
                tf2.setBounds(80,100,200,30);
                tf3.setBounds(80,150,200,30);
                bt.setBounds(150,200,80,30);
                lb.setBounds(100,180,150,30);
                lb.setForeground(Color.red);
                bt.addActionListener(this);
        }

        public void actionPerformed(ActionEvent ae)
```

```
	{
		Connection con;
		Statement stmt;
		String s1,s2,s3;
		s1 = tf1.getText( );
		s2 = tf2.getText( );
		s3 = tf3.getText( );
		try
		{
			// loading JDBC driver
			Class.forName("sun.jdbc.odbc.JdbcOdbcDriver");

			// obtaining connection to DNS temp
			con = DriverManager.getConnection("jdbc:odbc:temp");

			// preparing statement object to fire query on created connection
			stmt = con.createStatement( );

			// concatenating and firing insert query
			stmt.executeUpdate("insert into emp values('" + s1 +"','" + s2 + "','" + s3 + "')");

			// closing connection
			con.close();

			// display message for confirmation
			lb.setText("Success...!");
		}
		catch(Exception e)
		{
			lb.setText("Failed...!");
		}
	}

	public static void main(String ar[ ])
	{
		jdbc_insert j1 = new jdbc_insert( );
		j1.setSize(500,500);
		j1.setTitle("Inserting employee Details");
		j1.setVisible(true);
	}
}
```

In above program, *jdbc:odbc:temp* specifies that temp is a DSN name prepared by ODBC data source and *emp* is the table name. (Refer section 8.8 creating connection). After successful compilation and execution of frame, we get following output.

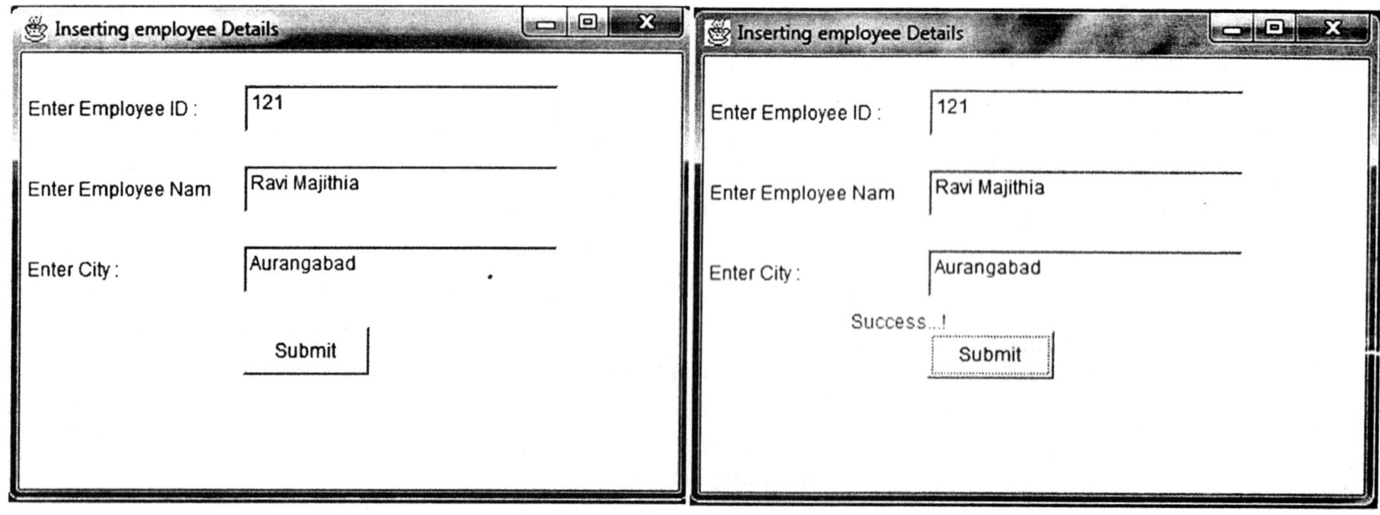


**Example 2 : Lets reverse above program, where we enter Employee ID and retrieve Name and City of that employee.**

```
import java.awt.*;
import java.awt.event.*;
import java.sql.*;

class jdbc_retrieve extends Frame implements ActionListener
{
        TextField tf1,tf2,tf3;
        Label lb;
        public jdbc_retrieve( )
        {
                setLayout(null);
                tf1 = new TextField();
                tf2 = new TextField();
                tf3 = new TextField();
                Label l1 = new Label("Enter Employee ID :");
                Label l2 = new Label("Enter Employee Name :");
                Label l3 = new Label("Enter City :");
                lb = new Label( );
                Button bt = new Button("Retrieve");
                add(l1);add(l2);add(l3);
                add(tf1);add(tf2);add(tf3);add(bt);add(lb);

                // making textboxes as read-only
                tf2.setEditable(false);
                tf3.setEditable(false);
                tf1.setBounds(150,50,200,30);
                tf2.setBounds(150,100,200,30);
                tf3.setBounds(150,150,200,30);
                l1.setBounds(10,50,140,30);
                l2.setBounds(10,100,140,30);
                l3.setBounds(10,150,140,30);
                bt.setBounds(150,200,80,30);
                lb.setBounds(100,180,150,30);
                lb.setForeground(Color.red);
```

```
            bt.addActionListener(this);
    }

    public void actionPerformed(ActionEvent ae)
    {
            Connection con;
            Statement stmt;

            // preparing select query
            String s1 = "select ename,city from emp where e_id = ' " + tf1.getText( ) + " ' ";
            try
            {
                    // loading driver
                    Class.forName("sun.jdbc.odbc.JdbcOdbcDriver");
                    // obtaining connection using DSN
                    con = DriverManager.getConnection("jdbc:odbc:temp");

                    // creating statement to fire query
                    stmt = con.createStatement();

                    // firing select query
                    ResultSet rs = stmt.executeQuery(s1);

                    //  filling textboxes
                    while(rs.next( ))
                    {
                            tf2.setText(rs.getString("ename"));
                            tf3.setText(rs.getString("city"));
                    }

                    //closing connection
                    con.close( );
                    lb.setText("Success...!");
            }
            catch(Exception e)
            {
                    lb.setText("Failed...!");
            }
    }

    public static void main(String ar[ ])
    {
            jdbc_retrieve j1 = new jdbc_retrieve( );
            j1.setSize(500,500);
            j1.setTitle("Retrieving employee Details");
            j1.setVisible(true);
    }
}
```

Above program retrieves the Employee name and City name by referring Employee_ID. Here, executeQuery( ) method is used because we are using *select query*. The returned result is retrieved in ResultSet and filled into textboxes.

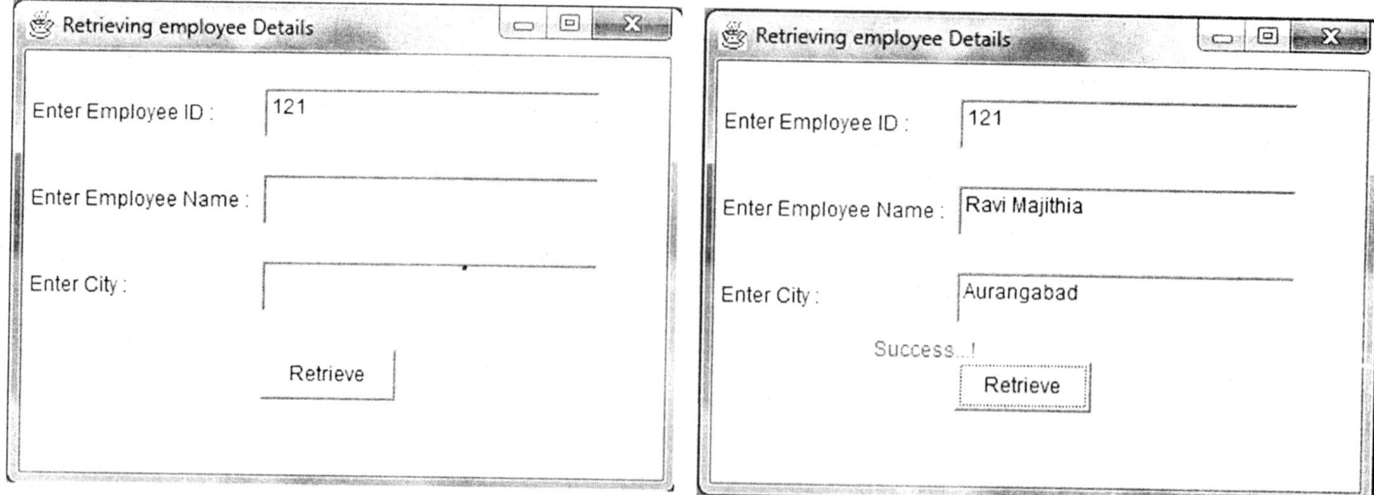


**Example 3 : Lets study a program to fill Country names into a Listbox from a database.**

```
import java.awt.*;
import java.awt.event.*;
import java.sql.*;
import javax.swing.*;

public class fill_combo extends JFrame implements ItemListener
{
        public JTextField tf;
        JComboBox combo;
        public fill_combo()
        {
                Container ct = getContentPane();
                ct.setLayout(null);
                JLabel lb = new JLabel("Select Country");
                JLabel lbl = new JLabel("You Select");
                combo = new JComboBox();
                tf = new JTextField();
                ct.add(tf);
                ct.add(combo);
                ct.add(lb);
                ct.add(lbl);
                lb.setBounds(10,50,100,30);
                lbl.setBounds(10,120,100,30);
                tf.setBounds(110,120,100,30);
                combo.setBounds(110,50,150,30);
                Connection con;
                Statement stmt;
                String s1;
                s1 = "select c_list from countries";
                try
                {
                        Class.forName("sun.jdbc.odbc.JdbcOdbcDriver");
                        con = DriverManager.getConnection("jdbc:odbc:temp");
                        stmt = con.createStatement();
                        ResultSet rs = stmt.executeQuery(s1);
                        while(rs.next())
```

```
                {
                combo.addItem(rs.getString("c_list"));
                }
                con.close();
            }
            catch(Exception e)
            { }
            combo.addItemListener(this);
    }

    // handling event on selection changed in combobox
    public void itemStateChanged(ItemEvent ie)
    {
            String s = (String)combo.getSelectedItem();
            tf.setText(s);
    }

    public static void main(String ar[])
    {
            fill_combo j1 = new fill_combo();
            j1.setSize(300,300);
            j1.setTitle("Filling countries");
            j1.setVisible(true);
    }
}
```

Above program fills a JComboBox with Country list from database and following JTextBox shows the selected country. Refer following screenshots.

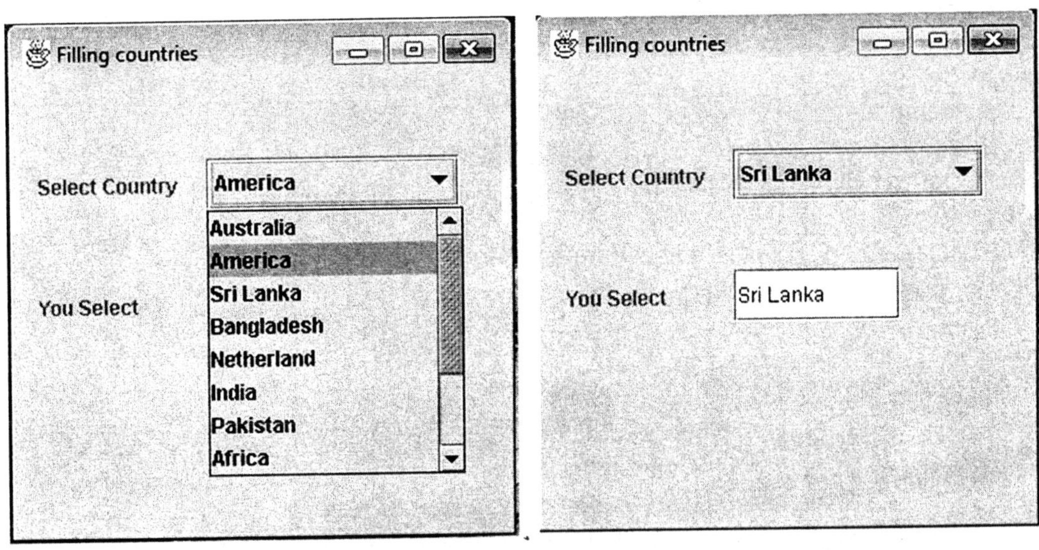


**Example 4 : Retrieving Employee details from database and display it in console application.**

```
import java.sql.*;
class jdbcdemo2
{
        public static void main(String ar[])
        {
```

```
            Connection con;
            Statement stmt;
            String s1,s2,s3;
            try
            {
                Class.forName("sun.jdbc.odbc.JdbcOdbcDriver");
                con = DriverManager.getConnection("jdbc:odbc:temp");
                stmt = con.createStatement();
                ResultSet rs = stmt.executeQuery("Select * from emp");
                System.out.println("\n\nE_id\tEmp Name\tCity");
                while(rs.next())
                {
                    s1=rs.getString("e_id");
                    s2=rs.getString("ename");
                    s3=rs.getString("city");
                    System.out.println(s1 + "\t" + s2 + "\t" +s3);
                }
                stmt.close();
            }
            catch (Exception e)
            {
                System.err.println("Got an exception! ");
                System.err.println(e.getMessage());
            }
        }
    }
```

**Example 5 : Accepting employee details from the user and inserting into the database.**

```
    import java.sql.*;
    import java.io.*;
    class jdbcinsertdemo
    {
        public static void main(String ar[ ])
        {
            DataInputStream dis = new DataInputStream(System.in);
            try
            {
                Connection con;

                // preparing query containing ? for user input
                String q ="insert into emp(e_id,ename,city) values(?,?,?)";
                String s1,s2,s3;
                System.out.println("Enter Employee ID : ");
                s1 = dis.readLine( );
                System.out.println("Enter Employee Name : ");
                s2 = dis.readLine( );
                System.out.println("Enter City : ");
                s3 = dis.readLine( );
                Class.forName("sun.jdbc.odbc.JdbcOdbcDriver");
                con = DriverManager.getConnection("jdbc:odbc:temp");
```

```
                // using PreparedStatement interface
                PreparedStatement ps = con.prepareStatement(q);

                // providing column-wise input to replace ? in query
                ps.setString(1,s1);
                ps.setString(2,s2);
                ps.setString(3,s3);

                // firing query
                ps.executeUpdate( );
                System.out.println("Successful..!");
            }
            catch (Exception e)
            {
                System.err.println("Got an exception! ");
                System.err.println(e.getMessage());
            }
        }
    }
```

Output of above program will be :

```
C:\Windows\system32\cmd.exe

C:\jdk1.3\bin>javac jdbcinsertdemo.java
Note: jdbcinsertdemo.java uses or overrides a deprecated API.
Note: Recompile with -deprecation for details.

C:\jdk1.3\bin>java jdbcinsertdemo
Enter Employee ID :
123
Enter Employee Name :
Kaushik Deoda
Enter City :
Pune
Successful..!

C:\jdk1.3\bin>_
```

*****

# Chapter 9
# Networking & Socket Programming

In previous chapters, we have developed small applets and frames and by adding some more concepts to it, such as database connectivity, servlet, Beans, etc; we can prepare basic internet applications very easily.

We know that, internet is the most extensively used technology in the globe. No discussion of internet would be complete without a brief introduction of networking concepts.

In this chapter we will explore the basic classes of *java.net* package and socket programming, which provides great support for networking. This chapter will study about sockets, proxy servers, Internet addressing, *URLConnection* class and TCP/IP socket classes, Datagram, and communication protocols.

## 9.1 Network basics

In 1984, a new version of UNIX was released, known as 4.2BSD (commonly known as *Berkeley* UNIX), with many new features such as virtual memory, full screen display, fast file system, reliable signals and processing, interprocess communication and, most importantly, **networking**.

This new UNIX project was designed and implemented by a team headed by *Bill Joy* (one of the inventor of Java). The networking support was first found in this UNIX and given many TCP/IP standards for communication over the internet. The vital apparatus of internet, such as sockets, interprocess communication and internet addressing, are derived from 4.2BSD UNIX.

Java has provided very little but effective concepts of networking that makes it more appropriate for writing networked programs, as compare to famous C++ and FORTRAN. All the network related classes are defined inside *java.net* package.

Following are the overview of networking standards and important components that should be understood before talking about Java's network related classes.

### 9.1.1 Socket overview

The computer machines communicate over the network by plugging-in itself into a socket. The network socket is a lot like electrical socket, where we plug-in an electronic device and use electricity/electrons to make the device work. Same idea is applied to network socket. Here the electrical socket is replaced by network socket, the electronic device is replaced by the computer machines, and the electricity/electrons are replaced by TCP/IP packets.

The working of network sockets requires IP and TCP or UDP protocols, anything that follows the standards of these protocols, can plug-in to socket and communicate over the network.

The **Internet Protocol (IP)** is a low level routing protocol that breaks data into small pieces (called packets) and sends it to specific address over a network. The **Transmission Control Protocol (TCP)** is a higher level protocol that manages to align together these packets and sorting-retransmitting them as necessary. The **User Datagram Protocol (UDP)** is an alternate to TCP and can be used directly to support fast, connectionless, unreliable transport of packets. The last section of this chapter describes the difference between TCP and UDP protocols.

### 9.1.2 Client/Server

The most common term that you hear in any networked application is client/server. According to computer network, a **server** is anything that has some resources to be share and a **client** is anything that simply wants to gain access to particular resource(s) of server.

The communication between client and server is done over the network through protocols. Network clients make requests to a server by sending messages, and servers respond to their clients by acting on each request and returning results back to them. One server generally supports numerous clients, and multiple servers can be networked together in a pool to handle the increased processing load as the number of clients grows.

According to Berkeley socket, there are two types of sockets. The *server socket* that allows a single computer to serve different types of information to different clients at once and the *client socket* that connects to server socket and requests.

The Berkeley socket has also introduced another term, called as *port*. The port is special type of numbered socket to which client connects. A server is allowed to accept multiple clients' connections; connected to the same port number, although each session is uniquely maintained by TCP/UDP connection. To manage multiple client connections, a server process must be multithreaded or have some sort of real-time system to work on input output.

### 9.1.3 Reserved sockets

In above section, we have discussed about sockets and ports. We came to know that, port is special type of numbered socket to which client connects. Once a client connects to a server port, the higher level protocol ensures on which protocol we are connected. TCP/IP has reserved some socket ports for precised protocols, called as reserved sockets. There are around 1024 reserved ports. Following list shows some well-known reserved sockets with port numbers.

- 20 and 21 (File Transfer Protocol, FTP)
- 22 (Secure Shell, SSH)
- 23 (Telnet)
- 25 (Simple Mail Transfer Protocol, SMTP)
- 53 (Domain Name System, DNS)
- 69 (Trivial File Transfer Protocol, TFTP)
- 79 (finger)
- 80 (Hypertext Transfer Protocol, HTTP)
- 110 (Post Office Protocol v3, POP3)
- 119 (Network News Protocol, NNTP)
- 161 and 162 (Simple Network Management Protocol, SNMP)
- 443 (Secure Sockets Layer over HTTP, HTTPS)

### 9.1.4 Proxy servers

There is a common situation that in most institutes' computer laboratories the clients/students has certain restriction on accessing particular website(s). In other words, some website(s) are blocked for clients/students. In this case a client would connect to a proxy server, and proxy server will communicate with server for the client. *The proxy server is the virtual server that speaks the client side of a protocol to another server.* Along with this, a proxy server has many additional abilities, such as:

- Filter certain requests or cache the results of those requests for future use.
- Set upload and download limit.
- Fetch the contents of a web server's popular pages once and save it to provide faster access to clients.
- Shows the graphical analysis (a graph) of uploaded and downloaded data packets.

### 9.1.5 Internet addressing

An internet address is a number that uniquely identifies each computer on the internet. There are two internet addressing schemes available currently. One is consisting 32-bit values, called IPv4 and second consisting 128-bit values, called IPv6.

Obviously the IPv6 is advantageous than IPv4. One say, IPv6 supports larger address space than IPv4. In current internet world IPv4 is most widely used scheme but soon IPv6 will grab the market very soon.

Because of rising in use of IPv6, the Java has also provided support for that in JDK 1.4. In current situation, we can say that almost all the environments are supporting IPv6. In many following examples, we have used IPv4.

The IPv4 is a 32-bit addressing system and is a sequence of four numbers/bytes between 0 to 255 and separated by dots(.). This numbering makes it easier to remember. Refer the output of examples given in section 9.6.1 and 9.6.2 showing the IPv4 internet addressing. Don't misguide yourself by saying this numbers are randomly assigned. It is a special type of hierarchy specifying the class, called as *network classes*. There are five network classes lettered A, B, C, D and E. According to the internet addressing standards first byte specifies the network class and the last byte actually identifies the individual computer on the network. Following are the basic characteristics of these network classes.

**Characteristics of class A networks:**

- Class A addresses range from 0.0.0.0 to 127.255.255.255.
- The leftmost bit in a class A network is always 0.
- The first 8 bits (first byte) define the *netid.*
- The remaining 24 bits define the *hostid.*

**Characteristics of class B networks:**

- Class B network addresses range from 129.0.0.0 to 191.255.255.255.
- The first 2 bits in a class B address are always 10 (128).
- In a class B network, the *netid* is determined by the first 16 bits (first 2 bytes).
- The *hostid* is determined by the last 16 bits (last 2 bytes).
- There are 2 (65,536) possible IP addresses for each class B network.
- The *netids* 172.16.0.0 to 173.31.0.0 are reserved for special use. This makes the actual maximum number of class B *netids* 2 minus 2, or 65,534.

**Characteristics of class C networks:**

- Class C network addresses range from 192.0.0.0 to 223.255.255.255.
- Class C networks use the first 24 bits to determine the *netid.*
- The three leftmost bits in a class C network are always 110 (192).
- The next 21 bits are used to define network.
- There are 2, or 2,097,152, possible class C networks.
- In class C networks, 8 bits are used to define the *hostid.* Because an address with all bits set to 1 or all bits set to 0 is not allowed, the maximum number of *hostids* on a class C network is 2 minus 2, or 254 hostids.

**Characteristics of class D networks:**

- Class D network addresses range from 224.0.0.0 to 239.255.255.255
- In class D addresses, the first 4 bits are always 1110 (224).
- The remaining 28 bits are used to define multicast addresses.
- There is no *netid* or *hostid* in a class D address.
- The whole address is used for multicasting.

**Characteristics of class E networks:**

- Class E network addresses range from 239.0.0.0 to 255.255.255.255
- Class E addresses are reserved for special use on the Internet.
- There is no *netid* or *hostid* in class E address.

### 9.1.6 Domain Naming Service (DNS)

Domain Name Service is an internet service that translates domain names into IP addresses. Just because domain names are alphabetic, they're easier to remember. But the internet is based on IP addresses. Hence, the DNS is required to translate that name into the corresponding IP address. For example, the domain name *"jws.himpub.com"* gets translate to *163.143.161.170*

**Note: The DNS system has its own network. If one DNS server doesn't know how to translate a particular domain name into IP address, it asks another DNS server, and so on, until the correct IP address is returned.**

### 9.1.7 Sockets and Socket-based communication

Sockets provide an interface for programming networks at the transport layer. Network communication using Sockets is very much similar to performing file I/O. In fact, socket handle is treated like file handle.

The streams used in file I/O operation are also applicable to socket-based I/O. Socket-based communication is independent of a programming language used for implementing it. That means, a socket program written in Java language can communicate to a program written in non-Java (say C or C++) socket program.

A server (program) runs on a specific computer and has a socket that is bound to a specific port. The server listens to the socket for a client to make a connection request (see Fig. A). If everything goes well, the server accepts the connection (see Fig. B). Upon acceptance, the server gets a new socket bound to a different port. It needs a new socket (consequently a different port number) so that it can continue to listen to the original socket for connection requests while serving the connected client.

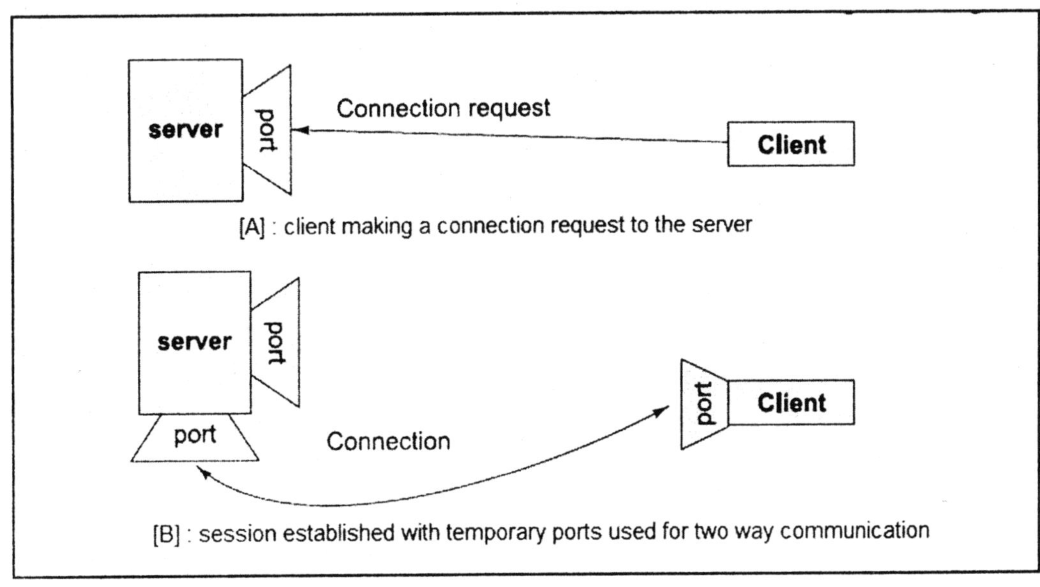

## 9.2 Java & the net

After discussing fundamental concepts about networking, let's now discuss how Java provides support for preparing networked applications.

The java.net package provides a huge library of classes and interfaces that are used for creating networked applications. Refer following list.

**Classes included in java.net**

| | | |
|---|---|---|
| Authenticator | InetSocketAddress | SocketImpl |
| ContentHandler | JarURLConnection | SocketPermission |
| DatagramPacket | MulticastSocket | URI |
| DatagramSocket | NetPermission | URL |
| DatagramSocketImpl | NetworkInterface | URLClassLoader |
| HttpURLConnection | PasswordAuthentication | URLConnection |
| InetAddress | ServerSocket | URLDecoder |
| Inet4Address | Socket | URLEncoder |
| Inet6Address | SocketAddress | URLStreamHandler |

**Interfaces included in java.net**

| | | |
|---|---|---|
| ContentHandlerFactory | SocketImplFactory | URLStreamHandlerFactory |
| FileNameMap | SocketOptions | DatagramSocketImplFactory |

**Exception classes included in java.net**

| | | |
|---|---|---|
| BindException | ConnectException | MalformedURLException |
| NoRouteToHostException | ProtocolException | SocketException |
| UnknownHostException | UnknownServiceException | |

Among these classes and interfaces, many are added by Java 2 (JDK 1.4) to provide support for IPv6 and for new IO streams.

## 9.3 InetAddress

The InetAddress class deals with internet address by encapsulating IP address and the domain name. An object of this class stores internet addresses by referencing a domain name or IP address (using its methods). We know that to do any task over the internet; such as making a voice/video call, sending mail, online purchase or connecting with other machines over the internet, the internet addresses are fundamental.

This class provides a facility to interact with other machines even by using the host name, instead of using IP address. The use of host name is far more convenient and understandable then using complex IP addresses.

AS discussed above, there are two possible types of internet addressing, IPv4 and IPv6, fortunately this class supports both (IPv6 is supported from JDK 1.4 onwards).

This library class has a few factory methods (static methods) and a few instance methods (non-static methods). Following section will explain a few of them.

Remember that, the InetAddress class has no visible constructor. Therefore to create an instance of this class we have to use one of its instance methods. The objects created by using instance methods are used to invoke factory methods, which return required entities.

### 9.3.1 Factory methods

The factory methods are actually static methods defined in InetAddress class. These methods return an instance of InetAddress class, as internet address, which is used to instantiate InetAddress objects. Following list shows the commonly used factory methods.

*static InetAddress getLocalHost( ) throws UnknownHostException*

*static InetAddress getByName(String host_name) throws UnknownHostException*

*static InetAddress getAllByName(String host_name) throws UnknownHostException*

*static InetAddress getByAddress(String IP_address) throws UnknownHostException*

The **getLocalHost( )** method returns the internet address of the local host. The **getByName( )** method returns an internet address of the *host_name* passed to it. The **getAllByName( )** method returns an array of internet addresses that represent all of the addresses that a particular *host_name* resolves to. The **getByAddress( )** method returns the internet address concerned with the specified *IP_ address*.

Note that all these methods throws *UnknownHostException* therefore the method that invokes this factory methods must handle *UnknownHostException*.

Refer following example, that displays the purpose of factory methods.

```
import java.net.*;
	class InetAddressDemo
	{
		public static void main(String ar[ ]) throws UnknownHostException
		{
			InetAddress addr1 = InetAddress.getLocalHost( );
			System.out.println(addr1);
			InetAddress addr2 = InetAddress.getByName("ptu.ac.in");
			System.out.println(addr2);
			InetAddress addr3[ ] = InetAddress.getAllByName("www.google.com");
			for (int i=0; i<addr3.length; i++)
			System.out.println(addr3[i]);
		}
	}
```

The output of above program will be:

```
C:\Windows\system32\cmd.exe

C:\jdk1.3\bin>javac InetAddressDemo.java

C:\jdk1.3\bin>java InetAddressDemo
Majithia-PC/192.168.43.236
ptu.ac.in/115.124.107.43
www.google.com/74.125.236.148
www.google.com/74.125.236.146
www.google.com/74.125.236.147
www.google.com/74.125.236.145
www.google.com/74.125.236.144

C:\jdk1.3\bin>_
```

### 9.3.2 Instance methods

The instance methods are non-static methods of InetAddress class that returns different entities based on invoking object. Following are the commonly used instance methods.

*boolean equals(Object another_obj)*
*byte[ ] getAddress( )*
*String getHostAddress( )*
*String getHostName( )*
*boolean isMulticastAddress( )*
*String toString( )*

The **equals( )** returns *true* if invoking object has the same Internet address as *another_obj* otherwise returns *false*. The **getAddress( )** returns a byte array that represents the object's Internet address in network byte order. The **getHostAddress( )** returns a string that represents the host address associated with the invoking InetAddress object. The **getHostName( )** a string that represents the host name associated with the invoking InetAddress object. The **isMulticastAddress( )** returns *true* if invoking Internet address is a multicast address, otherwise *false*. The **toString( )** returns the encapsulated string containing the host name and IP address.

Following program demonstrates the use of instance methods of InetAddress class.

```
import java.net.*;
class InstanceMethodsDemo
{
        public static void main(String ar[ ]) throws Exception
        {
                InetAddress addr1 = InetAddress.getByName("ptu.ac.in");
                InetAddress addr2 = InetAddress.getByName("jws.himpub.com");
                System.out.println("\nIs " + addr1 + " equals " + addr2 + " ? : " + addr1.equals(addr2));
                System.out.println("\nHost Address of " + addr1 + " is : " + addr1.getHostAddress( ));
                System.out.println("\nHost Name of " + addr1 + " is : " + addr1.getHostName( ));
                System.out.println("\nIs " + addr1 + " a Multicast Address? : " + addr1.isMulticastAddress( ));
                System.out.println("\nConversion of " + addr1 + " to string is : " + addr1.toString( ));
        }
}
```

Output of above program will be:

```
C:\Windows\system32\cmd.exe

C:\jdk1.3\bin>javac InstanceMethodsDemo.java
C:\jdk1.3\bin>java InstanceMethodsDemo
Is ptu.ac.in/115.124.107.43 equals jws.himpub.com/168.143.161.170 ? : false
Host Address of ptu.ac.in/115.124.107.43 is : 115.124.107.43
Host Name of ptu.ac.in/115.124.107.43 is : ptu.ac.in
Is ptu.ac.in/115.124.107.43 a Multicast Address? : false
Conversion of ptu.ac.in/115.124.107.43 to string is : ptu.ac.in/115.124.107.43
C:\jdk1.3\bin>_
```

## 9.4 Inet4Address and Inet6Address

Both the classes *Inet4Address* and *Inet6Address* are the final classes and derived from *InetAddress* class. These classes represent an internet protocol address. Let's discuss about these classes.

### 9.4.1 java.net.Inet4Address

This class represents an Internet Protocol version 4 (IPv4) address, defined by IP version 4 addressing architecture. *Inet4Address* provides to get *InetAddress* by host-name or by host-address. InetAddress can provide canonical name, host address etc. Inet4Address provides IPv4 i.e. Internet protocol version 4 address. This class is defined as:

*public final class Inet6Address extends InetAddress*

This class has no visible constructors. Textual representation of IPv4 address used as input to methods takes one of the following forms:

1) x. x. x. x
2) x. x. x
3) x. x
4) x

Let's discuss these four input methods.

1) When four part address is specified, each is interpreted as a byte of data and assigned, from left to right, to the four bytes of an IPv4 address.
2) When a three part address is specified, the last part is interpreted as a 16-bit quantity and placed in the right most two bytes of the network address. This makes the three part address format convenient for specifying Class B network addresses as 129.*net.host*.
3) When a two part address is supplied, the last part is interpreted as a 24-bit quantity and placed in the right most three bytes of the network address. This makes the two part address format convenient for specifying Class A network addresses as *net.host*.
4) When only one part is given, the value is stored directly in the network address without any byte rearrangement.

**Note: For methods that return a textual representation as output value, the first form, i.e. a dotted-quad string, is used.**

Following is the list of methods of *Inet4Address* class.

| Method | Description |
|---|---|
| boolean isMulticastAddress( ) | Utility routine to check if the InetAddress is an IP multicast address. |
| boolean isSiteLocalAddress( ) | Utility routine to check if the InetAddress is a site local address. |
| boolean equals(Object obj) | Compares this object against the specified object. |
| byte[ ] getAddress( ) | Returns the raw IP address of this InetAddress object. |
| String getHostAddress( ) | Returns the IP address string in textual presentation form. |
| int hashCode( ) | Returns a hashcode for this IP address. |
| boolean isAnyLocalAddress( ) | Utility routine to check if the InetAddress in a wildcard address. |
| boolean isLinkLocalAddress( ) | Utility routine to check if the InetAddress is an link local address. |
| boolean isLoopbackAddress( ) | Utility routine to check if the InetAddress is a loopback address. |
| boolean isMCGlobal( ) | Utility routine to check if the multicast address has global scope. |
| boolean isMCLinkLocal( ) | Utility routine to check if the multicast address has link scope. |
| boolean isMCNodeLocal( ) | Utility routine to check if the multicast address has node scope. |
| boolean isMCOrgLocal( ) | Utility routine to check if the multicast address has organization scope. |
| boolean isMCSiteLocal( ) | Utility routine to check if the multicast address has site scope. |

Following is the program to demonstrate Inet4Address class.

```
import java.net.Inet4Address;
import java.net.InetAddress;
import java.net.UnknownHostException;

public class Inet4AddressTest
{
        static void main(String ar[ ]) throws UnknownHostException
        {
                String host = "www.gujaratuniversity.org.in";
                InetAddress[ ] inAdd = Inet4Address.getAllByName(host);
                for(InetAddress ia:inAdd)
                {
                        System.out.println(ia.getCanonicalHostName( ));
                        System.out.println(ia.getCanonicalHostName( ));
                }
                InetAddress ina=Inet4Address.getLocalHost( );
                System.out.println(ina.getCanonicalHostName( ));
                System.out.println(ina.getHostAddress( ));
        }
}
```

### 9.4.2 java.net.Inet6Address

This class represents an Internet Protocol version 6 (IPv6) address, defined by IP Version 6 Addressing Architecture. Inet6Address provides to get InetAddress by host name or by host address. InetAddress can provide canonical name, host address etc. Inet6Address provides IPv6 ie Internet protocol version 6 address. This class is defined as:

*public final class Inet6Address extends InetAddress*

This class has no visible constructors. Textual representation of IPv6 address used as input to methods takes one of the following forms:

1) y : y : y : y : y : y : y : y
2) z :: y : y : y : y
3) :: y : x . x . x . x

Let's discuss these four input methods.

1) The preferred form is y : y : y : y: y : y : y : y , where the y's are the hexadecimal values of the eight 16-bit pieces of the address. This is the full form. For example,

   *1080:0:0:0:8:800:200C:417A*

2) Due to some methods of allocating certain styles of IPv6 addresses, it will be common for addresses to contain long strings of zero bits. In order to make writing addresses containing zero bits easier, a special syntax is available to compress the zeros. The use of "::" indicates multiple groups of 16-bits of zeros. The "::" can only appear once in an address. The "::" can also be used to compress the leading and/or trailing zeros in an address. For example,

   *1080::8:800:200C:417A*

3) An alternative form that is sometimes more convenient when dealing with a mixed environment of IPv4 and IPv6 nodes is x:x:x:x:x:x:y.y.y.y, where the 'x's are the hexadecimal values of the six high-order 16-bit pieces of the address, and the y's are the decimal values of the four low-order 8-bit pieces of the standard IPv4 representation address, for example,

   ::FFFF:129.144.52.38

   ::129.144.52.3

Following is the list of methods of *Inet4Address* class.

| Method | Description |
|---|---|
| boolean isMulticastAddress( ) | Utility routine to check if the InetAddress is an IP multicast address. |
| boolean isSiteLocalAddress( ) | Utility routine to check if the InetAddress is a site local address. |
| Boolean equals(Object obj) | Compares this object against the specified object. |
| byte[ ] getAddress( ) | Returns the raw IP address of this InetAddress object. |
| static Inet6Address getByAddress(String host, byte[ ] addr, int scope_id) | Create an Inet6Address in the exact manner of InetAddress's getByAddress( ) method except that the IPv6 *scope_id* is set to the given numeric value. |
| static Inet6Address getByAddress(String host, byte[] addr, NetworkInterface nif) | Create an Inet6Address in the exact manner of InetAddress's getByAddress( ) except that the IPv6 *scope_id* is set to the value corresponding to the given interface for the address type specified in *addr*. |
| String getHostAddress( ) | Returns the IP address string in textual presentation. |
| NetworkInterface getScopedInterface( ) | Returns the scoped interface, if this instance was created with with a scoped interface. |
| int getScopeId( ) | Returns the numeric scopeId, if this instance is associated with an interface. |
| int hashCode( ) | Returns a hashcode for this IP address. |
| boolean isAnyLocalAddress( ) | Utility routine to check if the InetAddress in a wildcard address. |
| boolean isIPv4CompatibleAddress( ) | Utility routine to check if the InetAddress is an IPv4 compatible IPv6 address. |
| boolean isLinkLocalAddress( ) | Utility routine to check if the InetAddress is an link local address. |
| boolean isLoopbackAddress( ) | Utility routine to check if the InetAddress is a loopback address. |
| boolean isMCGlobal( ) | Utility routine to check if the multicast address has global scope. |
| boolean isMCLinkLocal( ) | Utility routine to check if the multicast address has link scope. |
| boolean isMCNodeLocal( ) | Utility routine to check if the multicast address has node scope. |
| boolean isMCOrgLocal( ) | Utility routine to check if the multicast address has organization scope. |
| boolean isMCSiteLocal( ) | Utility routine to check if the multicast address has site scope. |

Following is the program to demonstrate Inet6Address class.

```
import java.net.Inet6Address;
import java.net.InetAddress;
import java.net.UnknownHostException;

public class Inet6AddressTest
{
        public static void main(String ar[ ]) throws UnknownHostException
        {
                String host = "www.nagpuruniversity.org";
                InetAddress[] inAdd = Inet6Address.getAllByName(host);
                for(InetAddress ia:inAdd)
                {
                        System.out.println(ia.getCanonicalHostName());
                        System.out.println(ia.getCanonicalHostName());
                }
                InetAddress ina=Inet6Address.getLocalHost( );
                System.out.println(ina.getCanonicalHostName( ));
                System.out.println(ina.getHostAddress( ));
        }
}
```

## 9.5 URL

Class URL represents a Uniform Resource Locator, a pointer to a "resource" on the World Wide Web. A resource can be something as simple as a file or a directory, or it can be a reference to a more complicated object, such as a query to a database or to a search engine.

*public final class URL extends Object implements Serializable*

A URL can optionally specify a "port", which is the port number to which the TCP connection is made on the remote host machine. If the port is not specified, the default port for the protocol is used instead. For example, the default port for http is 80.

There can be different forms of writing URL. Such as:

*http://www.nagpuruniversity.org/links/Departments.htm*
*http://www.gujaratuniversity.org.in/*
*http://puchd.ac.in/*

Following is the list of constructors of URL class.

*URL(String spec)*
*URL(String protocol, String host, int port, String file)*
*URL(String protocol, String host, int port, String file, URLStreamHandler handler)*
*URL(String protocol, String host, String file)*
*URL(URL context, String spec)*
*URL(URL context, String spec, URLStreamHandler handler)*

The first form creates a URL object from the String representation. Second form creates a URL object from the specified protocol, host, port number, and file. Third form creates a URL object from the specified protocol, host, port number, file, and handler. Fourth form creates a URL from the specified protocol name, host name, and file name. Fifth form creates a URL by parsing the given spec within a specified context. Sixth form creates a URL by parsing the given spec with the specified handler within a specified context.

Following table shows the methods of java.net.URL class.

| Method | Description |
|---|---|
| boolean equals(Object obj) | Compares this URL for equality with another object. |
| String getAuthority( ) | Gets the authority part of this URL. |
| Object getContent( ) | Gets the contents of this URL. |
| Object getContent(Class classes[ ]) | Gets the contents of this URL. |
| int getDefaultPort( ) | Gets the default port number of the protocol associated with this URL. |
| String getFile( ) | Gets the file name of this URL. |
| String getHost( ) | Gets the host name of this URL, if applicable. |
| String getPath( ) | Gets the path part of this URL. |
| int getPort( ) | Gets the port number of this URL. |
| String getProtocol( ) | Gets the protocol name of this URL. |
| String getQuery( ) | Gets the query part of this URL. |
| String getRef( ) | Gets the anchor (also known as the "reference") of this URL. |
| String getUserInfo( ) | Gets the userInfo part of this URL. |
| int hashCode( ) | Creates an integer suitable for hash table indexing. |
| URLConnection openConnection( ) | Returns a URLConnection instance that represents a connection to the remote object referred to by the URL. |
| URLConnection openConnection(Proxy proxy) | Same as openConnection( ), except that the connection will be made through the specified proxy; Protocol handlers that do not support proxing will ignore the proxy parameter and make a normal connection. |
| InputStream openStream( ) | Opens a connection to this URL and returns an InputStream for reading from that connection. |
| boolean sameFile(URL other) | Compares two URLs, excluding the fragment component. |
| void set(String protocol, String host, int port, String file, String ref) | Sets the fields of the URL. |
| String toExternalForm() | Constructs a string representation of this URL. |
| URI toURI() | Returns a URI equivalent to this URL. |
| String toString() | Constructs a string representation of this URL. |

Following program demonstrates the use of URL class and its some methods.

```
import java.io.*;
import java.net.*;

class URLDemo
{
        public static void main (String ar[ ]) throws IOException
        {
                String st = "http://admissions.puchd.ac.in/"
                if (st.length != 1)
                {
                        System.err.println ("usage: java URLDemo url");
                        return;
                }
```

```
            URL url = new URL (st);
            System.out.println ("Authority = " + url.getAuthority());
            System.out.println ("File = " +url.getFile());
            System.out.println ("Host = " +url.getHost());
            System.out.println ("Path = " +url.getPath());
            System.out.println ("Port = " +url.getPort());
            System.out.println ("Protocol = " +url.getProtocol());
            System.out.println ("Query = " +url.getQuery());
            System.out.println ("Ref = " +url.getRef());
            System.out.println ("User Info = " +url.getUserInfo());
            System.out.print ('\n');
            InputStream is = url.openStream();
            int ch;
            while ((ch = is.read ( )) != -1)
            System.out.print ((char) ch);
            is.close ( );
        }
    }
```

See following output where *http://admissions.puchd.ac.in/* is provided as input URL.

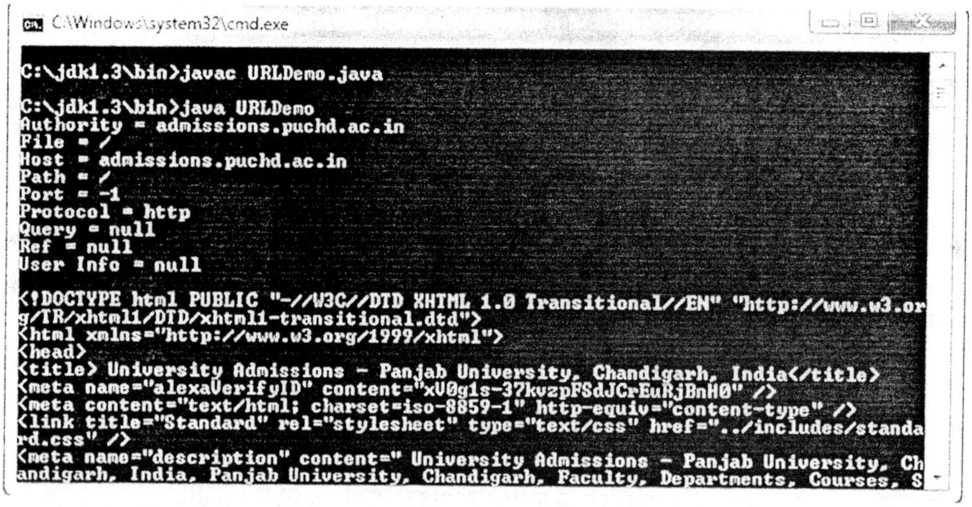

```
C:\Windows\system32\cmd.exe

C:\jdk1.3\bin>javac URLDemo.java

C:\jdk1.3\bin>java URLDemo
Authority = admissions.puchd.ac.in
File = /
Host = admissions.puchd.ac.in
Path = /
Port = -1
Protocol = http
Query = null
Ref = null
User Info = null

<!DOCTYPE html PUBLIC "-//W3C//DTD XHTML 1.0 Transitional//EN" "http://www.w3.or
g/TR/xhtml1/DTD/xhtml1-transitional.dtd">
<html xmlns="http://www.w3.org/1999/xhtml">
<head>
<title> University Admissions - Panjab University, Chandigarh, India</title>
<meta name="alexaVerifyID" content="xV0g1s-37kvzpFSdJCrEuRjBnH0" />
<meta content="text/html; charset=iso-8859-1" http-equiv="content-type" />
<link title="Standard" rel="stylesheet" type="text/css" href="../includes/standa
rd.css" />
<meta name="description" content=" University Admissions - Panjab University, Ch
andigarh, India, Panjab University, Chandigarh, Faculty, Departments, Courses, S
```

At the end, this program shows the resource data as a byte sequence, and this is because of openStream( ) method.

## 9.6 URI

The Network API makes it possible to work with URIs at the source code level, by providing the class URI. URI's constructors create URI. Many people did not get the difference between URL and URI. But remember, *every URL is a URI, abstractly speaking, but not every URI is a URL.*

Actually, *A Uniform Resource Identifier (URI) is a compact sequence of characters that identifies an abstract or physical resource*. And A URI can be further classified as a locator, a name, or both. *The "Uniform Resource Locator" (URL) refers to the subset of URIs that, in addition to identifying a resource, provide a means of locating the resource by describing its primary access mechanism (e.g., its network "location")*. The conceptual distinction between URIs and URLs is reflected as follows.

**An instance of URI class** represents a URI reference in the syntactic sense defined by RFC 2396. A URI may be either absolute or relative. A URI string is parsed according to the generic syntax without regard to the scheme, if any, that it specifies. No lookup of the host, if any, is performed, and no scheme-dependent stream handler is constructed.

Equality, hashing, and comparison are defined strictly in terms of the character content of the instance. In other words, a URI instance is little more than a structured string that supports the syntactic, scheme-independent operations of comparison, normalization, resolution, and relativization.

**An instance of the URL class**, by contrast, represents the syntactic components of a URL together with some of the information required to access the resource that it describes. A URL must be absolute, that is, it must always specify a scheme. A URL string is parsed according to its scheme. A stream handler is always established for a URL, and in fact it is impossible to create a URL instance for a scheme for which no handler is available. Equality and hashing depend upon both the scheme and the Internet address of the host, if any; comparison is not defined. In other words, a URL is a structured string that supports the syntactic operation of resolution as well as the network I/O operations of looking up the host and opening a connection to the specified resource.

Following are the different overloaded constructors of URI class.

*URI(String str)*
*URI(String scheme, String ssp, String fragment)*
*URI(String scheme, String userInfo, String host, int port, String path, String query, String fragment)*
*URI(String scheme, String host, String path, String fragment)*
*URI(String scheme, String authority, String path, String query, String fragment)*

The first form constructs a URI by parsing the given string. The second form constructs a URI from the given components. The third form constructs a hierarchical URI from the given components. Fourth form constructs a hierarchical URI from the given components. Fifth form constructs a hierarchical URI from the given components.

Following table shows the methods of java.net.URI class.

| Method | Description |
|---|---|
| int compareTo(URI that) | Compares this URI to another object, which must be a URI. |
| static URI create(String str) | Creates a URI by parsing the given string. |
| boolean equals(Object ob) | Tests this URI for equality with another object. |
| String getAuthority() | Returns the decoded authority component of this URI. |
| String getFragment() | Returns the decoded fragment component of this URI. |
| String getHost() | Returns the host component of this URI. |
| String getPath() | Returns the decoded path component of this URI. |
| int getPort() | Returns the port number of this URI. |
| String getQuery() | Returns the decoded query component of this URI. |
| String getRawAuthority() | Returns the raw authority component of this URI. |
| String getRawFragment() | Returns the raw fragment component of this URI. |
| String getRawPath() | Returns the raw path component of this URI. |
| String getRawQuery() | Returns the raw query component of this URI. |
| String getRawSchemeSpecificPart() | Returns the raw scheme-specific part of this URI. |
| String getRawUserInfo() | Returns the raw user-information component of this URI. |
| String getScheme() | Returns the scheme component of this URI. |
| String getSchemeSpecificPart() | Returns the decoded scheme-specific part of this URI. |
| String getUserInfo() | Returns the decoded user-information component of this URI. |
| int hashCode() | Returns a hash-code value for this URI. |
| boolean isAbsolute() | Tells whether or not this URI is absolute. |
| boolean isOpaque() | Tells whether or not this URI is opaque. |
| URI normalize() | Normalizes this URI's path. |
| URI parseServerAuthority() | Attempts to parse this URI's authority component, if defined, into user-information, host, and port components. |

| | |
|---|---|
| URI relativize(URI uri) | Relativizes the given URI against this URI. |
| URI resolve(String str) | Constructs a new URI by parsing the given string and then resolving it against this URI. |
| URI resolve(URI uri) | Resolves the given URI against this URI. |
| String toASCIIString() | Returns the content of this URI as a US-ASCII string. |
| String toString() | Returns the content of this URI as a string. |
| URL toURL() | Constructs a URL from this URI. |

Following program demonstrates the use of URL class and its some methods.

```
import java.net.*;

class URIDemo
{
        public static void main (String ar[ ]) throws Exception
        {
                String st = "http://admissions.puchd.ac.in/";
                if (st.length() != 1)
                {
                        System.err.println ("usage: java URIDemo uri");
                        return;
                }
                URI uri = new URI(st);
                System.out.println ("Authority = " + uri.getAuthority ( ));
                System.out.println ("Fragment = " + uri.getFragment ( ));
                System.out.println ("Host = " + uri.getHost ( ));
                System.out.println ("Path = " + uri.getPath ( ));
                System.out.println ("Port = " + uri.getPort ( ));
                System.out.println ("Query = " + uri.getQuery ( ));
                System.out.println ("Scheme = " + uri.getScheme ( ));
                System.out.println ("Scheme-specific part = " + uri.getSchemeSpecificPart ( ));
                System.out.println ("User Info = " + uri.getUserInfo ( ));
                System.out.println ("URI is absolute: " + uri.isAbsolute ( ));
                System.out.println ("URI is opaque: " + uri.isOpaque ( ));
        }
}
```

Execute above program and check the result.

## 9.7 URLConnection

Once a client makes connection to the remote server, the role of *URLConnection* class starts. The instance of *URLConnection* class examines the properties of the remote object prior to transporting it locally. This class is an abstract class and it is defined as:

*public abstract class URLConnection extends Object*

This class has only one constructor and it is defined as:

*protected URLConnection(URL url)*

This constructor, constructs a URL connection to the specified URL. Along with this constructor, the *URLConnection* class contains many methods that allow communicating with the URL over the network. Two of the commonly used methods are openConnection( ) and connect( ). The **openConnection( )** method is used to create connection object on a URL. The **connect( )** method is used to make connection to the remote object.

Creating a connection to a URL is multi step process. The steps included are:

```
//step 1: connection object is created by invoking the openConnection( ) method on a URL.
        URL url = new URL("puchd.ac.in/");
        URLConnection conn = url.openConnection( );

//step 2: setup parameters and general request properties are manipulated.
        DataInputStream dis = new DataInputStream(conn.getInputStream( ));

//step 3: actual connection to the remote object is made, using the connect( ) method.
        conn.connect( );

//step 4: access the header fields and the contents of the remote object using any iterative statement.
        while ((String inputLine = dis.readLine( )) != null)
        {
            System.out.println(inputLine);
        }

//step 5: close the of input / output stream connection.
        dis.close( );
```

Following table shows the methods of java.net.URLConnection class.

| Method | Description |
|---|---|
| void addRequestProperty(String key, String value) | Adds a general request property specified by a key-value pair. |
| abstract void connect() | Opens a communications link to the resource referenced by this URL, if such a connection has not already been established. |
| boolean getAllowUserInteraction() | Returns the value of the allowUserInteraction field for this object. |
| int getConnectTimeout() | Returns setting for connect timeout. |
| Object getContent() | Retrieves the contents of this URL connection. |
| Object getContent(Class[] classes) | Retrieves the contents of this URL connection. |
| String getContentEncoding() | Returns the value of the content-encoding header field. |
| int getContentLength() | Returns the value of the content-length header field. |
| long getContentLengthLong() | Returns the value of the content-length header field as a long. |
| String getContentType() | Returns the value of the content-type header field. |
| long getDate() | Returns the value of the date header field. |
| static boolean getDefaultAllowUserInteraction() | Returns the default value of the allowUserInteraction field. |
| boolean getDefaultUseCaches() | Returns the default value of a URLConnection's useCaches flag. |
| boolean getDoInput() | Returns the value of this URLConnection's doInput flag. |
| boolean getDoOutput() | Returns the value of this URLConnection's doOutput flag. |
| long getExpiration() | Returns the value of the expires header field. |
| static FileNameMap getFileNameMap() | Loads filename map (a mimetable) from a data file. |
| String getHeaderField(int n) | Returns the value for the nth header field. |
| String getHeaderField(String name) | Returns the value of the named header field. |
| long getHeaderFieldDate(String name, long Default) | Returns the value of the named field parsed as date. |

| int getHeaderFieldInt(String name, int Default) | Returns the value of the named field parsed as a number. |
|---|---|
| String getHeaderFieldKey(int n) | Returns the key for the nth header field. |
| long getHeaderFieldLong(String name, long Default) | Returns the value of the named field parsed as a number. |
| Map<String,List<String>> getHeaderFields() | Returns an unmodifiable Map of the header fields. |
| long getIfModifiedSince() | Returns the value of this object's ifModifiedSince field. |
| InputStream getInputStream() | Returns an input stream that reads from this open connection. |
| long getLastModified() | Returns the value of the last-modified header field. |
| OutputStream getOutputStream() | Returns an output stream that writes to this connection. |
| Permission getPermission() | Returns a permission object representing the permission necessary to make the connection represented by this object. |
| int getReadTimeout() | Returns setting for read timeout. |
| Map<String,List<String>> getRequestProperties() | Returns an unmodifiable Map of general request properties for this connection. |
| String getRequestProperty(String key) | Returns the value of the named general request property for this connection. |
| URL getURL() | Returns the value of this URLConnection's URL field. |
| boolean getUseCaches() | Returns the value of this URLConnection's useCaches field. |
| static String guessContentTypeFromName(String fname) | Tries to determine the content type of an object, based on the specified "file" component of a URL. |
| static String guessContentTypeFromStream(InputStream is) | Tries to determine the type of an input stream based on the characters at the beginning of the input stream. |
| void setAllowUserInteraction(boolean allowuserinteraction) | Set the value of the allowUserInteraction field of this URLConnection. |
| void setConnectTimeout(int timeout) | Sets a specified timeout value, in milliseconds, to be used when opening a communications link to the resource referenced by this URLConnection. |
| static void setContentHandlerFactory (ContentHandlerFactory fac) | Sets the ContentHandlerFactory of an application. |
| void setDoInput(boolean doinput) | Sets the value of the doInput field for this URLConnection to the specified value. |
| void setDoOutput(boolean dooutput) | Sets the value of the doOutput field for this URLConnection to the specified value. |
| static void setFileNameMap(FileNameMap map) | Sets the FileNameMap. |
| void setIfModifiedSince(long ifmodifiedsince) | Sets the value of the ifModifiedSince field of this URLConnection to the specified value. |
| void setReadTimeout(int timeout) | Sets the read timeout to a specified timeout, in milliseconds. |
| void setRequestProperty(String key, String value) | Sets the general request property. |
| void setUseCaches(boolean usecaches) | Sets the value of the useCaches field of this URLConnection to the specified value. |
| String toString() | Returns a String representation of this URL connection. |

**Note: The methods included in *URLConnection* class throws *MalformedURLException* and *IOException*.**

## 9.8 HttpURLConnection

The HttpURLConnection instance is a URLConnection with support for HTTP-specific features. This method is defined as:

*public abstract class HttpURLConnection extends URLConnection*

Each HttpURLConnection instance is used to make a single request but the underlying network connection to the HTTP server may be transparently shared by other instances. Calling the *close( )* methods on the InputStream or OutputStream of an *HttpURLConnection* after a request may free network resources associated with this instance but has no effect on any shared persistent connection. Calling the *disconnect( )* method may close the underlying socket if a persistent connection is otherwise idle at that time.

This class has following single constructor.

*protected HttpURLConnection(URL url)*

This constructor, constructor for the HttpURLConnection. Following table shows the methods of HttpURLConnection class.

| Method | Description |
|---|---|
| abstract void disconnect( ) | Indicates that other requests to the server are unlikely in the near future. |
| InputStream getErrorStream( ) | Returns the error stream if the connection failed but the server sent useful data nonetheless. |
| static boolean getFollowRedirects( ) | Returns a boolean indicating whether or not HTTP redirects (3xx) should be automatically followed. |
| String getHeaderField(int n) | Returns the value for the nth header field. |
| long getHeaderFieldDate(String name, long Default) | Returns the value of the named field parsed as date. |
| String getHeaderFieldKey(int n) | Returns the key for the nth header field. |
| Permission getPermission( ) | Returns a SocketPermission object representing the permission necessary to connect to the destination host and port. |
| String getRequestMethod( ) | Get the request method. |
| int getResponseCode( ) | Gets the status code from an HTTP response message. |
| String getResponseMessage( ) | Gets the HTTP response message, if any, returned along with the response code from a server. |
| void setChunkedStreamingMode(int chunklen) | This method is used to enable streaming of a HTTP request body without internal buffering, when the content length is not known in advance. |
| void setFixedLengthStreamingMode(int contentLength) | This method is used to enable streaming of a HTTP request body without internal buffering, when the content length is known in advance. |
| void setFixedLengthStreamingMode (long contentLength) | This method is used to enable streaming of a HTTP request body without internal buffering, when the content length is known in advance. |
| static void setFollowRedirects (boolean set) | Sets whether HTTP redirects (requests with response code 3xx) should be automatically followed by this class. |
| void setInstanceFollowRedirects (boolean followRedirects) | Sets whether HTTP redirects (requests with response code 3xx) should be automatically followed by this HttpURLConnection instance. |
| void setRequestMethod(String method) | Set the method for the URL request, one of: GET POST HEAD OPTIONS PUT DELETE TRACE are legal, subject to protocol restrictions. |
| abstract boolean usingProxy( ) | Indicates if the connection is going through a proxy. |

Following program demonstrates the use of HttpURLConnection class.

```
import java.net.HttpURLConnection;
import java.net.URL;
import java.net.MalformedURLException;
import java.io.IOException;
import java.io.*;
public class HttpURLConnectionDemo
```

```
{
        public static void main(String ar[ ])
        {
                HttpURLConnection urlConn = null;
                BufferedReader in;
                try
                {
                        System.out.println("Starting LecNotify");
                        URL url = new URL("www.myurl.com");
                        urlConn = (HttpURLConnection)url.openConnection();
                        urlConn.setRequestMethod("GET");
                        urlConn.setDoInput (true);
                        urlConn.setDoOutput (true);
                        urlConn.setRequestProperty ("Content-Type","application/x-www-form-urlencoded");
                        in = new BufferedReader(new InputStreamReader(urlConn.getInputStream()));
                        System.out.println("Done");
                }
                catch(MalformedURLException e)
                { }
                catch(IOException e)
                { }
                catch(Exception e)
                {
                        System.out.println(e.getMessage( ));
                        System.out.println(e.getStackTrace( ));
                }
        }
}
```

Following is another program showing the redirection of pages using this class.

```
import java.io.BufferedReader;
import java.io.InputStreamReader;
import java.net.HttpURLConnection;
import java.net.URL;

public class HttpRedirectExample
{
        public static void main(String ar[ ])
        {
        try
        {
                String url = "http://www.twitter.com";
                URL obj = new URL(url);
                HttpURLConnection conn = (HttpURLConnection) obj.openConnection();
                conn.setReadTimeout(5000);
                conn.addRequestProperty("Accept-Language", "en-US,en;q=0.8");
                conn.addRequestProperty("User-Agent", "Mozilla");
                conn.addRequestProperty("Referer", "google.com");
                System.out.println("Request URL ... " + url);
                boolean redirect = false;
                int status = conn.getResponseCode();
```

```
                if (status != HttpURLConnection.HTTP_OK)
                {
                        if (status == HttpURLConnection.HTTP_MOVED_TEMP|| status ==
                HttpURLConnection.HTTP_MOVED_PERM || status == HttpURLConnection.HTTP_SEE_OTHER)
                {
                        redirect = true;
                }
                }
                System.out.println("Response Code ... " + status);
                if (redirect)
                {
                        // get redirect url from "location" header field
                        String newUrl = conn.getHeaderField("Location");

                        // get the cookie if need, for login
                        String cookies = conn.getHeaderField("Set-Cookie");

                        // open the new connnection again
                        conn = (HttpURLConnection) new URL(newUrl).openConnection();
                        conn.setRequestProperty("Cookie", cookies);
                        conn.addRequestProperty("Accept-Language", "en-US,en;q=0.8");
                        conn.addRequestProperty("User-Agent", "Mozilla");
                        conn.addRequestProperty("Referer", "google.com");
                        System.out.println("Redirect to URL : " + newUrl);
                }
                BufferedReader in = new BufferedReader(new InputStreamReader(conn.getInputStream()));
                String inputLine;
                StringBuffer html = new StringBuffer();
                while ((inputLine = in.readLine()) != null)
                {
                        html.append(inputLine);
                }
                in.close( );
                System.out.println("URL Content... \n" + html.toString());
                System.out.println("Done");
        }
        catch (Exception e)
        {
                e.printStackTrace( );
        }
        }
}
```

Output of above program will be:

```
Request URL ... http://www.twitter.com
Response Code ... 301
Redirect to URL : https://twitter.com/
URL Content...
<!DOCTYPE html><!--[if IE 8]><html class= // twitter.com url content...
```

**Note: we can remove the last placed while loop that reads the contents of a web page.**

## 9.9 TCP/IP socket classes

As discussed in above sections, TCP/IP sockets are used in writing networked programs that executes across multiple computers over the network. The java.net package provides collection of classes and interfaces that provides low level communication support between computers.

The most widely used classes for socket programming are:

*java.net.Socket*
*java.net.ServerSocket*

Let's study about them, in brief, one by one.

### 9.9.1 Socket class

This class represents the socket that both the client and server use to communicate with each other (Generally, preferred for defining client objects). This class is defined as:

*public class Socket extends Object implements Closeable*

The following list shows the overloaded constructors of Socket class.

*Socket( )*
*Socket(InetAddress address, int port)*
*Socket(InetAddress address, int port, InetAddress localAddr, int localPort)*
*Socket(Proxy proxy)*
*Socket(SocketImpl impl)*
*Socket(String host, int port)*
*Socket(String host, int port, InetAddress local*Addr, int localPort)

The first constructor creates an unconnected socket. Later, the *connect*( ) method is used to connect this socket to specific server. The second constructor creates a socket and connects it to the specified port number at specified internet address. Third constructor creates a socket and connects it to the specified remote address on the specified remote port. Fourth constructor creates an unconnected socket but work for specified type of proxy. Fifth constructor creates an unconnected Socket with a user-specified *SocketImpl*. Sixth constructor creates a stream socket and connects it to the specified port number on the named host. Seventh constructor creates a socket and connects it to the specified remote host on the specified remote port.

Following table shows the methods of Socket class.

| Method | Description |
|---|---|
| void bind(SocketAddress bindpoint) | Binds the socket to a local address. |
| void close() | Closes this socket. |
| void connect(SocketAddress endpoint) | Connects this socket to the server. |
| void connect(SocketAddress endpoint, int timeout) | Connects this socket to the server with a specified timeout value. |
| SocketChannel getChannel() | Returns the unique SocketChannel object associated with this socket, if any. |
| InetAddress getInetAddress() | Returns the address to which the socket is connected. |
| InputStream getInputStream() | Returns an input stream for this socket. |
| InetAddress getLocalAddress() | Gets the local address to which the socket is bound. |
| int getLocalPort() | Returns the local port number to which this socket is bound. |
| SocketAddress getLocalSocketAddress() | Returns the address of the endpoint this socket is bound to, or null if it is not bound yet. |

| | |
|---|---|
| OutputStream getOutputStream() | Returns an output stream for this socket. |
| int getPort() | Returns the remote port number to which this socket is connected. |
| SocketAddress getRemoteSocketAddress() | Returns the address of the endpoint this socket is connected to, or null if it is unconnected. |
| int getTrafficClass() | Gets traffic class or type-of-service in the IP header for packets sent from this Socket |
| boolean isBound() | Returns the binding state of the socket. |
| boolean isClosed() | Returns the closed state of the socket. |
| boolean isConnected() | Returns the connection state of the socket. |
| boolean isInputShutdown() | Returns whether the read-half of the socket connection is closed. |
| boolean isOutputShutdown() | Returns whether the write-half of the socket connection is closed. |
| void sendUrgentData(int data) | Send one byte of urgent data on the socket. |
| void setPerformancePreferences(int connectionTime, int latency, int bandwidth) | Sets performance preferences for this socket. |
| static void setSocketImplFactory(SocketImplFactory fac) | Sets the client socket implementation factory for the application. |
| void setTrafficClass(int tc) | Sets traffic class or type-of-service octet in the IP header for packets sent from this Socket. |
| void shutdownInput() | Places the input stream for this socket at "end of stream". |
| void shutdownOutput() | Disables the output stream for this socket. |
| String toString() | Converts this socket to a String. |

After discussing on methods of Socket class, let's discuss the steps involved in creating a client application.

```
//step 1: Create a Socket Object
        Socket client = new Socket(server, port_id);

//step 2: Create I/O streams for communicating with the server
        is = new DataInputStream(client.getInputStream());
        os = new DataOutputStream(client.getOutputStream());

//step 3: Perform I/O or communication with the server
        Receive data from the server: String line = is.readLine();
        Send data to the server: os.writeBytes("Hello\n");

//step 4: Close the socket when done
        client.close( );
```

Following program demonstrates the use of Socket class and it creates a client program that connects to a server by using a socket and sends a greeting and then waits for response. Provide server name and port number as command line argument, to which this client program has to connect.

```
import java.net.*;
import java.io.*;

public class GreetingClient
{
        public static void main(String ar[ ])
        {
                String serverName = args[0];
                int port = Integer.parseInt(args[1]);
```

```
                try
                {
                        System.out.println("Connecting to " + serverName + " on port " + port);
                        Socket client = new Socket(serverName, port);
                        System.out.println("Just connected to " + client.getRemoteSocketAddress());
                        OutputStream outToServer = client.getOutputStream();
                        DataOutputStream out = new DataOutputStream(outToServer);
                        out.writeUTF("Hello from " + client.getLocalSocketAddress());
                        InputStream inFromServer = client.getInputStream();
                        DataInputStream in = new DataInputStream(inFromServer);
                        System.out.println("Server says " + in.readUTF());
                        client.close( );
                }
                catch(IOException e)
                {
                        e.printStackTrace();
                }
        }
}
```

### 9.9.2 ServerSocket class

This class is used by server applications to obtain a port and listen for client requests. This class is defined as:

*public class ServerSocket extends Object implements Closeable*

The noticeable point about *ServerSocket* class is it's *accept( )* method. This method Listens for a connection request to be made to this socket and accepts it. Following list shows the overloaded constructors of *ServerSocket* class.

*ServerSocket( )*
*ServerSocket(int port)*
*ServerSocket(int port, int backlog)*
*ServerSocket(int port, int backlog, InetAddress bindAddr)*

The first constructor creates an unbound server socket. Later, to which client binds using *accept( )* method. The second constructor creates a server socket, bound to the specified port. Third constructor creates a server socket and binds it to the specified local port number, with the specified backlog. Fourth constructor creates a server with the specified port, listen backlog, and local IP address to bind to.

Following table shows the methods of ServerSocket class.

| Method | Description |
|---|---|
| Socket accept() | Listens for a connection to be made to this socket and accepts it. |
| void bind(SocketAddress endpoint) | Binds the ServerSocket to a specific address (IP address and port number). |
| void bind(SocketAddress endpoint, int backlog) | Binds the ServerSocket to a specific address (IP address and port number). |
| void close() | Closes this socket. |
| ServerSocketChannel getChannel() | Returns the unique ServerSocketChannel object associated with this socket, if any. |
| InetAddress getInetAddress() | Returns the local address of this server socket. |
| int getLocalPort() | Returns the port number on which this socket is listening. |
| SocketAddress getLocalSocketAddress() | Returns the address of the endpoint this socket is bound to, or null if it is |

| | |
|---|---|
| | not bound yet. |
| protected void implAccept(Socket s) | Subclasses of ServerSocket use this method to override accept() to return their own subclass of socket. |
| boolean isBound() | Returns the binding state of the ServerSocket. |
| boolean isClosed() | Returns the closed state of the ServerSocket. |
| void setPerformancePreferences(int connectionTime, int latency, int bandwidth) | Sets performance preferences for this ServerSocket. |
| static void setSocketFactory(SocketImplFactory fac) | Sets the server socket implementation factory for the application. |
| String toString() | Returns the implementation address and implementation port of this socket as a String. |

After studying methods, lets discuss the steps to create a simple server program in Java.

```
//step 1: Open the Server Socket:
        ServerSocket server = new ServerSocket( PORT );

//step 2: Wait for the Client Request
        Socket client = server.accept( );

//step 3: Create I/O streams for communicating to the client
        DataInputStream is = new DataInputStream(client.getInputStream());
        DataOutputStream os = new DataOutputStream(client.getOutputStream());

//step 4: Perform communication with client
        Receive from client: String line = is.readLine( );
        Send to client: os.writeBytes("Hello\n");

//step 5: Close socket
        client.close( );
```

The following *GreetingServer* program is an example of a server application that uses the Socket class to listen for clients on a port number specified by a command-line argument:

```
import java.net.*;
import java.io.*;

public class GreetingServer extends Thread
{
        private ServerSocket serverSocket;
        public GreetingServer(int port) throws IOException
        {
                serverSocket = new ServerSocket(port);
                serverSocket.setSoTimeout(10000);
        }
        public void run()
        {
                while(true)
                {
                        try
```

```
                {
                        System.out.println("Waiting for client on port " +
                        serverSocket.getLocalPort() + "...");
                        Socket server = serverSocket.accept();
                        System.out.println("Just connected to " + server.getRemoteSocketAddress());
                        DataInputStream in = new DataInputStream(server.getInputStream());
                        System.out.println(in.readUTF());
                        DataOutputStream out = new DataOutputStream(server.getOutputStream());
                        out.writeUTF("Thnk you for connecting to " + server.getLocalSocketAddress() +
                        "\nGoodbye!");
                        server.close( );
                }
                catch(SocketTimeoutException s)
                {
                        System.out.println("Socket timed out!");
                        break;
                }
                catch(IOException e)
                {
                        e.printStackTrace();
                        break;
                }
            }
        }
        public static void main(String ar[ ])
        {
            int port = Integer.parseInt(args[0]);
            try
            {
                Thread t = new GreetingServer(port);
                t.start( );
            }
            catch(IOException e)
            {
                e.printStackTrace( );
            }
        }
}
```

Compile client and server and then start server as follows:

**server program**

*java GreetingServer 6066*
*Waiting for client on port 6066*

**client program**

*java GreetingClient localhost 6066*
*Connecting to localhost on port 6066*
*Just connected to localhost/127.0.0.1:6066*
*Server says Thank you for connecting to /127.0.0.1:6066*
*Goodbye!*

## 9.10 Secure communication

One of the persistent fears of consumers buying goods over the Internet is that some hacker will steal our credit card number and misuse it. In reality, it's very much similar to that a billing guy at a department store will read our credit card number from a store receipt and misuse it. In fact, as of mid-2004, the major online thefts of credit card numbers have been accomplished by stealing the information from poorly secured databases and file-systems after the information has been safely transmitted across the Internet. However, to make Internet connections more fundamentally secure, sockets can be encrypted. This allows transactions to be confidential, authenticated, and accurate.

However, encryption is a complex subject. To perform it properly, detailed understanding not only of the mathematical algorithms (used to encrypt data) but also of the protocols used to exchange keys and encrypted data are required.

As a result, writing encryption software is a task best done by experts. And the beginners with only a bit of understanding of the underlying protocols and algorithms can secure their communications with software designed by experts.

As a result, writing encryption software is the task left for the expert developers and beginners can secure their communication with these softwares, designed by experts. There are two possible types of encryptions: *symmetric encryption* (also called as secret key) and *asymmetric encryption* (also called as secret key).

In *secret key* (or symmetric) encryption, the same key is used for both encrypting and decrypting the data. Both the sender and the receiver have to possess the single key. For example, say Neha wants to send Ajay a secret message. She first sends Ajay the key they'll use to exchange the secret. But the key can't be encrypted because Ajay doesn't have the key yet, so Neha has to send the key unencrypted. Now suppose, Deepak is spying on the connection between Neha and Ajay. He will get the key at the same time that Ajay does. From that point forward, he can read anything Neha and Ajay say to each other using that key.

In *public key* (or asymmetric) encryption, different keys are used to encrypt and decrypt the data. One of the key is, the public key, used to encrypt the data. This key can be given to anyone. A different key, called the *private key*, is used to decrypt the data. This must be kept secret but needs to be possessed by only one of the correspondents. If Neha wants to send a message to Ajay, she asks Ajay for his public key. Ajay sends it to her over an unencrypted connection. Neha uses Ajay's public key to encrypt her message and sends it to him. If Deepak is spying when Ajay sends Neha his key, Deepak also gets Ajay's public key. However, this doesn't allow Deepak to decrypt the message Neha sends Ajay, since decryption requires Ajay's private key. The message is safe even if the public key is detected in transit.

Another way of using asymmetric encryption can be for authentication and message integrity checking. For this use, Neha would encrypt a message with her private key before sending it. When Ajay received it, he'd decrypt it with Neha's public key. If the decryption succeeded, Ajay would know that the message came from Neha. After all, no one else could have produced a message that would decrypt properly with her public key. Ajay would also know that the message wasn't changed in the route, either by Deepak or by any buggy software, since any such change would have twist up the decryption. With a little more effort, Neha can double-encrypt the message, once with her private key, once with Ajay's public key, thus getting all three benefits of privacy, authentication, and integrity.

In practice, public key (asymmetric) encryption is much more CPU dependent and much slower than secret (symmetric) key encryption. Therefore, instead of encrypting the entire transmission with Ajay's public key, Neha encrypts a traditional secret key and sends it to Ajay. Ajay decrypts it with his private key. Now Neha and Ajay both know the secret key, but Deepak doesn't. Therefore, Ajay and Neha can now use faster secret-key encryption to communicate privately without Deepak listening in.

As this example indicates, the theory and practical experience of encryption – decryption and authentication, both algorithms and protocols, is a challenging field that filled everyone with surprises.

Luckily, to use cryptography In Java networked programs; we don't have to be a encryption – decryption expert. *Java Secure Sockets Extension* (JSSE) helps in all the way to create sockets and server sockets that automatically handle the encryption necessary for secured communication. All we have to do is to use the protocols and classes that are mentioned in above sections and left remaining for Java. The Java Secure Socket Extension is divided into four packages:

- *javax.net.ssl*
  contains the abstract classes that define Java's API for secure network communication.
- *javax.net*
  contains the abstract socket factory classes used instead of constructors to create secure sockets.
- *javax.security.cert*
  contains a minimal set of classes for handling public key certificates that's needed for SSL in Java 1.1. (In Java 1.2 and later, the java.security.cert package should be used instead.)
- *com.sun.net.ssl*
  contains the concrete classes that implement the encryption algorithms and protocols in Sun's reference implementation of the JSSE.

### 9.10.1 Creating secure client socket using SSLSocketFactory

To create a secure client socket, rather than constructing a *java.net.Socket* (for client) object, you should create *javax.net.ssl.SSLSocketFactory* object. This SSLSocketFactory is an abstract class and it is defined as:

*public abstract class SSLSocketFactory extends SocketFactory*

As this class is an abstract class, we cannot instantiate it directly. To do this task we use its **createSocket( )** method. Following is the overloaded versions of createSocket( ) method, use to build an SSLSocket.

*public abstract Socket createSocket(String host, int port) throws IOException, UnknownHostException*

*public abstract Socket createSocket(InetAddress host, int port) throws IOException*

*public abstract Socket createSocket(String host, int port, InetAddress interface, int localPort) throws IOException, UnknownHostException*

*public abstract Socket createSocket(InetAddress host, int port, InetAddress interface, int localPort) throws IOException, UnknownHostException*

*public abstract Socket createSocket(Socket proxy, String host, int port, boolean autoClose) throws IOException*

The first two signatures create and return a socket that's connected to the specified host and port. The third and fourth signatures connect and return a socket that's connected to the specified host and port from the specified local network interface and port. The last signature connects and returns a socket that's connected to specified proxy server and to the specified host and port. it's *autoClose* argument determines whether the underlying proxy socket should be closed when this socket is closed.

**Note: All these signatures will return the socket that will be the instance of *javax.net.ssl.SSLSocket* which is a sub class of *java.net.Socket*.**

Once the secure socket has been created, we use it just like any other socket, through its **getInputStream( ), getOutputStream( ),** and other methods.

Refer following code block that encrypts the person's data before sending it with a purchase order. This code uses secure socket of *SSLSocketFactory.*

```
try
{
    // This statement is only needed if you didn't add
    security.provider.3=com.sun.net.ssl.internal.ssl.Provider // this is needed only if we didn't add to our
    java.security file
    Security.addProvider(new com.sun.net.ssl.internal.ssl.Provider( ));
    SSLSocketFactory factory  = (SSLSocketFactory) SSLSocketFactory.getDefault( );
    SSLSocket socket = factory.createSocket("www.msbte.org", 7000);
    String[] supported = socket.getSupportedCipherSuites( );    // enabling all the suits
    socket.setEnabledCipherSuites(supported);
    Writer out = new OutputStreamWriter(socket.getOutputStream( ), "ASCII");
    out.write("Name: Rakesh Jain\r\n");
    out.write("Product-ID: 67X-89\r\n");
    out.write("Address: Toy World, Osmanpura, Aurangabad 431005\r\n");
    out.write("Card number: 4000-1234-5678-9012\r\n");
    out.write("Expires: 08/15\r\n");
    out.flush( );
    out.close( );
    socket.close( );
}
catch (IOException ex)
{
    ex.printStackTrace( );
}
```

Note the only first three statements that are different from what we have used in previous socket sections and the rest of the code just uses the normal methods of the Socket, OutputStream, and Writer classes.

### 9.10.2 Creating secure server socket Using SSLServerSocketFactory

Securing client socket is the only half of the operation. Another half is to secure the server socket. These are instances of the javax.net.SSLServerSocket class:

*public abstract class SSLServerSocket extends ServerSocket*

Like SSLSocket, all the constructors in this class are protected. Like SSLSocket, instances of SSLServerSocket are created by an abstract factory class, javax.net.*SSLServerSocketFactory*:

*public abstract class SSLServerSocketFactory extends ServerSocketFactory*

Like *SSLSocketFactory*, *SSLServerSocketFactory* has three overloaded create*ServerSocket( )* methods that return instances of *SSLServerSocket*. Following are the different versions of createServerSocket( ) method.

*public abstract ServerSocket createServerSocket(int port) throws IOException*

*public abstract ServerSocket createServerSocket(int port, int queueLength) throws IOException*

*public abstract ServerSocket createServerSocket(int port, int queueLength, InetAddress interface) throws IOException*

An instance of *SSLServerSocketFactory* can also be returned by a static *SSLServerSocketFactory.getDefault( )* method. It is defined as:

*public static ServerSocketFactory getDefault( )*

Following is the example, that is using getDefault( ) method to create an instance of *SSLServerSocketFactory* and creates a server socket with port 5432.,

```
import java.io.PrintStream;
import java.net.ServerSocket;
import java.net.Socket;
import javax.net.ssl.SSLServerSocketFactory;

public class MainClass
{
        public static void main(String args[]) throws Exception
        {
                SSLServerSocketFactory ssf = (SSLServerSocketFactory) SSLServerSocketFactory.getDefault( );
                ServerSocket ss = ssf.createServerSocket(5432);
                while(true)
                {
                        Socket s = ss.accept( );
                        PrintStream out = new PrintStream(s.getOutputStream());
                        out.println("This is server socket example");
                        out.close( );
                        s.close( );
                }
        }
}
```

## 9.11 UDP protocol

UDP (User Datagram Protocol) is a simple OSI transport layer protocol for client/server network applications based on Internet Protocol (IP). UDP is the main alternative to TCP and one of the oldest network protocols in existence, introduced in 1980.

UDP works a bit differently from TCP. When we send data via TCP we first create a connection. Once the TCP connection is established TCP guarantees that our data arrives at the other end, or it will tell we that an error occurred.

With UDP we just send packets of data (datagram) to some IP address on the network. We have no guarantee that the data will arrive. We also have no guarantee about the order which UDP packets arrive in at the receiver. This means that UDP has less protocol overhead (no stream integrity checking) than TCP.

UDP is appropriate for data transfers where it doesn't matter if a packet is lost in transition. For instance, imagine a transfer of a live TV-signal over the internet. We want the signal to arrive at the clients as close to live as possible. Therefore, if a frame or two are lost, we don't really care. We don't want the live broadcast to be delayed just to make sure all frames are shown at the client. We'd rather skip the missed frames, and move directly to the newest frames at all times.

This could also be the case with a surveillance camera broadcasting over the internet. Who cares what happened in the past, when we are trying to monitor the present. We don't want to end up being 30 seconds behind reality, just because we want to show all frames to the person monitoring the camera. It is a bit different with the storage of the camera recordings. We may not want to lose a single frame when recording the images from the camera to disk. We may rather want a little delay, than not have those frames to go back and examine, if something important occurs.

The java.net package provides a few simple but effective classes that are used to send packets of data (datagram) to some IP address on the network, preferably using UDP. They are:

- *java.net.DatagramPacket*
- *java.net.DatagramSocket*

Following section, describes the application of these three classes in detail.

## 9.12 Datagram, DatagramPacket and DatagramSocket

Let's discuss these important concepts in detail.

### 9.12.1 Datagram

UDP network traffic is organized in the form of datagrams. A datagram comprises one message unit. The first eight (8) bytes of a datagram contain header information and the remaining bytes contain message data.

A UDP datagram header consists of four (4) fields of two bytes each:

- source port number
- destination port number
- datagram size
- checksum

**UDP source/destination port numbers** allow different applications to maintain their own channels for data similar to TCP. UDP port headers are two bytes long; therefore, valid UDP port numbers range from 0 to 65535.

**UDP datagram size** is a count of the total number of bytes contained in header and data sections. As the header length is a fixed size, this field effectively tracks the length of the variable-sized data portion (sometimes called payload). The size of datagrams varies depending on the operating environment but has a maximum of 65535 bytes.

**UDP checksums** protect message data from tampering. The checksum value represents an encoding of the datagram data calculated first by the sender and later by the receiver. Should an individual datagram be tampered with or get corrupted during transmission, the UDP protocol detects a checksum calculation mismatch. In UDP, checksumming is optional as opposed to TCP where checksums are mandatory.

### 9.12.2 DatagramPacket

This *java.net.DatagramPacket* is the final class, responsible for connectionless packet (Datagram) delivery service. This class is defined as:

*public final class DatagramPacket extends Object*

Each data packet is routed from one machine to another, based only on information contained within that packet. Multiple packets sent from one machine to another might be routed differently, and might arrive in any order. Packet delivery is not guaranteed.

Following is the list of DatagramPacket constructors.

*DatagramPacket(byte[] buf, int len)*
*DatagramPacket(byte[] buf, int len, InetAddress address, int port)*
*DatagramPacket(byte[] buf, int offset, int len)*
*DatagramPacket(byte[] buf, int offset, int len, InetAddress address, int port)*
*DatagramPacket(byte[] buf, int offset, int len, SocketAddress address)*
*DatagramPacket(byte[] buf, int len, SocketAddress address)*

The **first** constructor constructs a DatagramPacket for receiving packets of length *len*. **Second** constructor constructs a datagram packet for sending packets of length *len* to the specified port number on the specified host. **Third** constructor constructs a DatagramPacket for receiving packets of length *len*, specifying an offset into the buffer. **Fourth** constructor constructs a datagram packet for sending packets of length *len* with offset to the specified port number on the specified host. **Fifth** constructor constructs a datagram packet for sending packets of length *len* with offset to the specified port number on the specified host. **Sixth** constructor constructs a datagram packet for sending packets of length *len* to the specified port number on the specified host.

A datagram socket is the sending or receiving point for a packet delivery service. Each packet sent or received on a datagram socket is individually addressed and routed. Multiple packets sent from one machine to another may be routed differently, and may arrive in any order.

Following table shows the methods related to *java.net.DatagramPacket* class.

| Method | Description |
|---|---|
| InetAddress getAddress() | Returns the IP address of the machine to which this datagram is being sent or from which the datagram was received. |
| byte[] getData() | Returns the data buffer. |
| int getLength() | Returns the length of the data to be sent or the length of the data received. |
| int getOffset() | Returns the offset of the data to be sent or the offset of the data received. |
| int getPort() | Returns the port number on the remote host to which this datagram is being sent or from which the datagram was received. |
| SocketAddress getSocketAddress() | Gets the SocketAddress (usually IP address + port number) of the remote host that this packet is being sent to or is coming from. |
| void setAddress(InetAddress iaddr) | Sets the IP address of the machine to which this datagram is being sent. |
| void setData(byte[ ] buf) | Set the data buffer for this packet. |
| void setData (byte[ ] buf, int offset, int length) | Set the data buffer for this packet. |
| void setLength(int length) | Set the length for this packet. |
| void setPort(int port) | Sets the port number on the remote host to which this datagram is being sent. |
| void setSocketAddress(SocketAddress address) | Sets the SocketAddress of the remote host to which this datagram is being sent. |

### 9.12.3 DatagramSocket

The *java.net.DatagramSocket* class represents a connection-less socket for sending and receiving datagram packets. Datagram is basically information but there is no guarantee of its content, arrival or arrival time. This class is defined as:

*public class DatagramSocket extends Object implements Closeable*

This class represents a socket for sending and receiving datagram packets.

A datagram socket is the sending or receiving point for a packet delivery service. Each packet sent or received on a datagram socket is individually addressed and routed. Multiple packets sent from one machine to another may be routed differently, and may arrive in any order.

Following is the list of constructors of this class.

*DatagramSocket( )*
*protected DatagramSocket(DatagramSocketImpl impl)*
*protected DatagramSocket(int port)*
*protected DatagramSocket(int port, InetAddress laddr)*
*protected DatagramSocket(SocketAddress bindaddr)*

The **first** constructor constructs a datagram socket and binds it to any available port on the local host machine. **Second** constructor creates an unbound datagram socket with the specified *DatagramSocketImpl*. **Third** constructor constructs a datagram socket and binds it to the specified port on the local host machine. **Fourth** constructor creates a datagram socket, bound to the specified local address. **Fifth** constructor creates a datagram socket, bound to the specified local socket address.

Following is the table, showing methods of this class.

| Method | Description |
|---|---|
| void bind(SocketAddress addr) | Binds this DatagramSocket to a specific address & port. |
| void close() | Closes this datagram socket. |
| void connect(InetAddress address, int port) | Connects the socket to a remote address for this socket. |
| void connect(SocketAddress addr) | Connects this socket to a remote socket address (IP address + port number). |
| void disconnect() | Disconnects the socket. |
| DatagramChannel getChannel() | Returns the unique DatagramChannel object associated with this datagram socket, if any. |
| InetAddress getInetAddress() | Returns the address to which this socket is connected. |
| InetAddress getLocalAddress() | Gets the local address to which the socket is bound. |
| int getLocalPort() | Returns the port number on the local host to which this socket is bound. |
| SocketAddress getLocalSocketAddress() | Returns the address of the endpoint this socket is bound to. |
| int getPort() | Returns the port number to which this socket is connected. |
| SocketAddress getRemoteSocketAddress() | Returns the address of the endpoint this socket is connected to, or null if it is unconnected. |
| int getTrafficClass() | Gets traffic class or type-of-service in the IP datagram header for packets sent from this DatagramSocket. |
| boolean isBound() | Returns the binding state of the socket. |
| boolean isClosed() | Returns whether the socket is closed or not. |
| boolean isConnected() | Returns the connection state of the socket. |
| void receive(DatagramPacket p) | Receives a datagram packet from this socket. |
| void send(DatagramPacket p) | Sends a datagram packet from this socket. |
| static void setDatagramSocketImplFactory (DatagramSocketImplFactory fac) | Sets the datagram socket implementation factory for the application. |
| void setTrafficClass(int tc) | Sets traffic class or type-of-service octet in the IP datagram header for datagrams sent from this DatagramSocket. |

## 9.13 Sending and receiving Data packets using DatagramSocket and DatagramPacket

The DatagramSocket and DatagramPacket classes are used for connection-less socket programming. Let's discuss the steps and procedures to send and receive Data packets using DatagramSocket and DatagramPacket with an example.

### 9.13.1 Sending Data via a DatagramSocket

To send data via Java's DatagramSocket you must first create a *DatagramPacket*. Here is how that is done:

```
byte[] buffer = new byte[65508];
InetAddress address = InetAddress.getByName("ptu.ac.in ");
DatagramPacket packet = new DatagramPacket(buffer, buffer.length, address, 9000);
```

The byte buffer (the byte array) is the data that is to be sent in the UDP datagram. The length of the above buffer, 65508 bytes, is the maximum amount of data you can send in a single UDP packet.

The length given to the *DatagramPacket* constructor is the length of the data in the buffer to send. All data in the buffer after that amount of data is ignored.

The *InetAddress* instance contains the address of the node (e.g. server) to send the UDP packet to. The *InetAddress* class represents an IP address (Internet Address). The *getByName( )* method returns an *InetAddress* instance with the IP address matching the given host name.

The port parameter is the UDP port the server to receive the data is listening on. UDP and TCP ports are not the same. A computer can have different processes listening on e.g. port 80 in UDP and in TCP at the same time.

To send the DatagramPacket you must create a DatagramSocket targeted at sending data. Here is how that is done:

```
DatagramSocket datagramSocket = new DatagramSocket();
```

To send data you call the send() method, like this:

```
datagramSocket.send(packet);
```

Here is a full example:

```
import java.net.*;
public class DataSender
{
        public static void main(String ar[ ]) throws Exception
        {
                DatagramSocket ds = new DatagramSocket( );
                String str = "Welcome java";
                InetAddress ip = InetAddress.getByName("127.0.0.1");
                DatagramPacket dp = new DatagramPacket(str.getBytes(), str.length(), ip, 3000);
                ds.send(dp);
                ds.close();
        }
}
```

### 9.13.2 Receiving Data via a DatagramSocket

Receiving data via a DatagramSocket is done by first creating a DatagramPacket and then receiving data into it via the DatagramSocket's receive() method. Here is an example:

```
import java.net.*;
public class DataReceiver
{
        public static void main(String[] args) throws Exception
        {
                DatagramSocket ds = new DatagramSocket(3000);
                byte[] buf = new byte[1024];
                DatagramPacket dp = new DatagramPacket(buf, 1024);
                ds.receive(dp);
                String str = new String(dp.getData( ), 0, dp.getLength());
                System.out.println(str);
                ds.close( );
        }
}
```

Notice how the *DatagramSocket* is instantiated with the parameter value 80 passed to its constructor. This parameter is the UDP port the DatagramSocket is to receive UDP packets on. As mentioned earlier, TCP and UDP ports are not the same, and thus do not overlap. You can have two different processes listening on both TCP and UDP port 80, without any conflict.

Second, a *byte buffer* and a *DatagramPacket* is created. Notice how the *DatagramPacket* has no information about the node to send data to, as it does when creating a *DatagramPacket* for sending data. This is because we are going to use the DatagramPacket for receiving data, not sending it. Thus no destination address is needed.

Finally, the *DatagramSocket's receive( )* method is called. The data received is located in the *DatagramPacket's* byte buffer. This buffer can be obtained by calling:

```
byte[ ] buffer = packet.getData( );
```

## 9.14 Multicast socket

Multicast is a special feature of UDP protocol that enable programmer to send message to a group of receivers on a specific multicast IP address and port. Multicast has advantage in this scenario. Refer following:

Let us say I want to send "Hello" message to 100 computers on my network. Perhaps, my first solution is to send the "Hello" message to each of them via UDP or TCP.

There are 3 generic problems in this:

- Consume a lot of processing power on sender as it needs to send to every receiver
- Bandwidth flooding
- The arrival time is not the same for every receiver

Seeing this problem, we intend to use our second solution by employing Multicast. Multicast runs over UDP protocol. The multicasting has following characteristics.

- Multicast is using UDP under the hood. So sending and receiving data are much the same as UDP
- The big noticeable from UDP
    - Sender should address packages to an IP number in the range between 224.0.0.1 and 239.255.255.254.
    - Receivers must join multicast group to receive packet

- Several multicast sockets can be bound simultaneously to the same port (Contrary to UDP and TCP)
- Multicast is viable for video conference, service discovery application, etc.

Java provides *java.net.MulticastSocket* class, used for sending and receiving IP multicast. Following are the two overloaded constructors of this class.

*MulticastSocket()*
*MulticastSocket(int)*

The **first** constructor creates a multicast socket and **second** constructor creates a multicast socket and binds it to a specific port.

Following table shows the methods of MulticastSocket class.

| Method | Description |
|---|---|
| InetAddress getInterface( ) throws IOException | Retrieve the address of the network interface used for multicast packets. |
| void joinGroup(InetAddress) throws IOException | Joins a multicast group. |
| void leaveGroup(InetAddress) throws IOException | Leave a multicast group. |
| synchronized void send(DatagramPacket, byte) throws IOException | Sends a datagram packet to the destination |
| void setInterface(InetAddress) throws IOException | Set the outgoing network interface for multicast packets on this socket, to other than the system default. |

Below is to send multicast message with indexing to multicast IP (224.2.2.3) and port 8889. If the clients wish to receive multicast message, it must join the group with multicast ip (224.2.2.3) and port 8889.

Program to send multicast message:

```
import java.io.*;
import java.net.*;

public class MulticastSender
{
        public static void main(String ar[ ])
        {
                DatagramSocket socket = null;
                DatagramPacket outPacket = null;
                byte[ ] outBuf;
                final int PORT = 8888;
                try
                {
                        socket = new DatagramSocket( );
                        long counter = 0;
                        String msg;
                        while (true)
                        {
                                msg = "This is multicast! " + counter;
                                counter++;
                                outBuf = msg.getBytes( );

                                //Send to multicast IP address and port
                                InetAddress address = InetAddress.getByName("224.2.2.3");
                                outPacket = new DatagramPacket(outBuf, outBuf.length, address, PORT);
```

```
                    socket.send(outPacket);
                    System.out.println("Server sends : " + msg);
                    try
                    {
                        Thread.sleep(500);
                    }
                catch (InterruptedException ie)
                { }
                }
            }
            catch (IOException ioe)
            {
                System.out.println(ioe);
            }
        }
    }
```

Program to receive multicast message:

```
import java.io.*;
import java.net.*;

public class MulticastReceiver
{
    public static void main(String ar[ ])
    {
        MulticastSocket socket = null;
        DatagramPacket inPacket = null;
        byte[ ] inBuf = new byte[256];
        try
        {
            //Prepare to join multicast group
            socket = new MulticastSocket(8888);
            InetAddress address = InetAddress.getByName("224.2.2.3");
            socket.joinGroup(address);
            while (true)
            {
                inPacket = new DatagramPacket(inBuf, inBuf.length);
                socket.receive(inPacket);
                String msg = new String(inBuf, 0, inPacket.getLength( ));
                System.out.println("From " + inPacket.getAddress() + " Msg : " + msg);
            }
        }
        catch (IOException ioe)
        {
            System.out.println(ioe);
        }
    }
}
```

**Note: Currently applets are not allowed to use multicast sockets.**

## 9.15 Difference between TCP and UDP

| TCP | UDP |
|---|---|
| TCP is a connection-oriented protocol. | UDP is a connectionless protocol. |
| TCP header size is 20 bytes. | UDP Header size is 8 bytes. |
| TCP does error checking. | UDP does error checking, but no recovery options. |
| The speed for TCP is slower than UDP. | The speed of UDP is faster than TCP. |
| TCP guarantee the data transferred remains intact and arrives in the same order in which it was sent. | UDP does not guarantee that the messages or packets sent would reach at all. |
| TCP rearranges data packets in the order specified. | UDP has no inherent order as all packets are independent of each other. If ordering is required, it has to be managed by the application layer. |
| TCP is suited for applications that require high reliability, and transmission time is relatively less critical. | UDP is suitable for applications that need fast, efficient transmission, such as games and many for servers that answer small queries from huge numbers of clients. |
| HTTP, HTTPs, FTP, SMTP, Telnet are examples of TCP protocol. | DNS, DHCP, TFTP, SNMP, RIP, VOIP are examples of UDP protocol. |

* * * * *

# Part IV
# Server Side Development using Java EE

---

- Servlet
- Cookies
- Session
- JSP
- Struts
- Enterprise JavaBeans
- Hibernating
- Client Server Technology & Web Services
- Java Server Faces
- Java RMI

# Chapter 10

# Servlets

Servlets are pieces of Java source code that add functionality to a web server in a manner similar to the way applets add functionality to a browser. Servlets are designed to support a request/response computing model that is commonly used in web servers. In a request/response model, a client sends a request message to a server and the server responds by sending back a reply message.

From the **Java Servlet Development Kit (JSDK)**, we use the Java Servlet API to create servlets for responding to requests from clients. These servlets can do many tasks, like processing HTML forms or manage middle-tier processing to connect to existing data sources, connecting through a corporate firewall and many more. In addition, servlets can maintain services, like database sessions, between requests to manage resources better than Common Gateway Interface (CGI) technologies.

The Java Servlet API is based on several Java interfaces that are provided in *standardJava Extension (javax) packages*. The servlet API consists of two packages, *javax.servlet*and*javax.servlet.http*. The topic of servlets is quite large, and it is beyond the scope of this chapter to cover it all. Instead, we will focus on the core concepts, interfaces, and classes, and develop several examples.

## 10.1 Why servlet?

While this sounds like every other dynamic content technology (such CGI, ISAPI, ASP, PHP, and the like), servlets have some major advantages. One of them is,*servlets are persistent between invocations*, which dramatically improve performance comparative to CGI-style programs. *Servlets are also 100% portable* across operating systems and servers, unlike any of the alternatives. Finally, servlets have access to all the APIs of the Java platform, so, for example, it is easy to create a servlet that interacts with a database, using the JDBC API.

## 10.2 What is servlet container?

Like other Java technology-based components, servlets are platform-independent Java classes that are compiled to platform-neutral byte code that can be loaded dynamically into and run by a Java technology-enabled Web server. Containers, sometimes called servlet engines, are Web server extensions that provide servlet functionality. Servlets interact with Web clients via a request/response paradigm implemented by the servlet container.

We need a servlet container to run servlets. A servlet container uses a Java Virtual Machine to run servlet code as requested by a web server. The servlet container is also responsible for managing other aspects of the servlet lifecycle; such as, user sessions, class loading, servlet contexts, servlet configuration information, servlet persistence, and temporary storage. Along with that, the servlet container is a part of a Web server or application server that provides the network services over which requests and responses are sent, decodes MIME-based requests, and formats MIME-based responses.

Most interestingly, all servlet containers must support HTTP (and HTTPS) as a protocol for requests and responses. The container may have a caching mechanism and it may modify requests of the clients before delivering them to the servlet, and may modify responses produced by servlets before sending them to the clients, or may respond to client's requests without delivering them to the servlet.

A servlet container may place security restrictions on the environment in which a servlet executes. For example, high-end application servers may limit the creation of a *Thread* object to insure that other components of the container are not negatively impacted.

## 10.3 Understanding Web server and Application server

Application server and web server in Java both are used to host Java web application. Though both application server and web server are generic terms, difference between application server and web server is a famous Java EE theme. On Java J2EE perspective main difference between web server and application server is support of EJB. In order to run EJB or host enterprise Java application (.ear) file we need an application server like JBoss, WebLogic, WebSphere or Glassfish, while we can still run your servlet and JSP or java web application (.war) file inside any web server like Tomcat or Jetty.

Following are some of the key differences in features of Web Server and Application Server:

- Web Server is designed to serve HTTP Content. Application Server can also serve HTTP Content but is not limited to just HTTP. It can be provided other protocol support such as RMI/RPC
- Web Server is mostly designed to serve static content, though most Web Servers have plug-ins to support scripting languages like Perl, PHP, ASP, JSP etc. through which these servers can generate dynamic HTTP content.
- Most of the Application servers have Web Server as integral part of them; that means Application Server can do whatever Web Server is capable of. Additionally Application Server has components and features to support Application level services such as Connection Pooling, Object Pooling, Transaction Support, Messaging services etc.
- As Web servers are well suited for static content and Application servers for dynamic content, most of the production environments have web server acting as reverse proxy to app server. That means while servicing a page request, static contents (such as images/Static HTML) are served by web server that interprets the request. Using some kind of filtering technique (mostly extension of requested resource) web server identifies dynamic content request and transparently forwards to app server
- Example of such configuration is Apache Tomcat HTTP Server and Oracle WebLogic Server. Apache Tomcat HTTP Server is Web Server and Oracle WebLogic is Application Server.
- In some cases the servers are tightly integrated such as IIS and .NET Runtime. IIS is web server. When equipped with .NET runtime environment, IIS is capable of providing application services.

## 10.4 Servlet: a better replacement of CGI technology

We know that there are two types of web pages, *static web page* and *dynamic web page*. Let's have a basic understanding of how web browsers and servers cooperate to provide content to a user.

*Consider a request for a static web page*, a user enters URL into the web browser and browser generates an HTTP request to appropriate web server. The web server directs this request to a specific file. This file is returned in an HTTP response to the browser. The HTTP header in the response indicates the type of the content using Multipurpose Internet Mail Extension (MIME). For example, MIME type of an ordinary ASCII text is text/plain and MIME type of an HTML source code is text/html.

*Now, consider a request for a dynamic web page*, assume a person is having the business of music library. He has a database, on local billing computer, containing items for sale, price, available quantity, stock and many more. He wants to start a web site and want this database information to be public via web pages. The contents of those web pages must be dynamically generated to display the latest availability information to the customers who view his web site.

In early days of the web, a server could dynamically generate a web page by creating different processes to open connections to one or more databases in order to obtain the necessary information. This communication with database is done via an interface known as the Common Gateway Interface (CGI). CGI allowed the separate process to read data from the HTTP request and write data to the HTTP response. A variety of different languages were used to build CGI programs, includes C, C++ and Perl.

This CGI suffered serious performance related problems. Such as:

- Expensive in terms of processor and memory.
- Expensive to open and close database connections.
- Not platform independent.
- Experienced programmers are needed to work with CGI.

Because of these problems, many new technologies were introduced and Servlet is one of them. As compare to CGI the servlets provides many benefits, such as:

- Comparatively better performance.
- Executes within the addressed space of a web server.
- No separate processes are required to handle different client requests and connecting to database.
- Are platform independent.
- Java security manager on the server protects the resources on a server machine.
- Can communicate with Applets, different databases and other remote resources via RMI (chapter 18) and Socket programming (chapter 8).

## 10.5 What is new in Servlet 3.1?

Servlet 3.0 was released as part of Java EE 6 and made huge changes focused at ease-of-use. The idea was to influence the latest language features such as annotations and generics and modernize how Servlets can be written. The web.xml was made as optional as possible. The Servlet 3.1, scheduled to be part of Java EE 7, is an incremental release focusing on couple of key features and some clarifications in the specification.

The main features of Servlet 3.1 are explained below:

- **Non-blocking I/O** - Servlet 3.0 allowed asynchronous request processing but only traditional I/O was permitted. This can restrict scalability of your applications. In Servlet 3.1, Non-blocking I/O allows to build scalable applications.
- **HTTP protocol upgrade mechanism** – The Servlet 3.1 allows to transition from HTTP 1.1 to some other, incompatible protocol. The capabilities and nature of the application-layer communication after the protocol change is entirely dependent upon the new protocol chosen. After an upgrade is negotiated between the client and the server, the subsequent requests use the new chosen protocol for message exchanges. A typical example is, WebSocket protocol is upgraded from HTTP.
- Applied run-as security roles to **init( )** and **destroy( )** methods.
- Session fixation by adding ***HttpServletRequest.changeSessionId( )*** *method* and a new interface ***HttpSessionIdListener***.
- **ServletResponse.setCharacterEncoding( )** method is added, which sets the character encoding (MIME charset) of the response being sent to the client, for example, to UTF-8.
- Relative protocol URL can be specified in **HttpServletResponse.sendRedirect( )** method. This will allow a URL to be specified without a scheme. That means instead of specifying "*http://anotherhost.com/example/page2.jsp*" as a redirect address, "*//anotherhost.com/example/page2.jsp*" can be specified. In this case the scheme of the corresponding request will be used.

- Along with **ServletResponse.reset( )** method, **getServletOutputStream( )** or **getWriter( )** methods are added that clears any data that exists in the buffer as well as the status code, headers.
- More appropriate working in **HttpServletRequest.getPart( )** and **HttpServletRequest.getParts( )** without multipart configuration.

## 10.6 Servlet and the 3-tier application architecture

Using Java Servlets help the user to opt to opt for 3-tier applications. Many organization and establishments also require to use multi-tier applications. Most clients and single server models give way to one application, which includes many servers, where servers exchange the data between each other. Following diagram shows how Servlets can be used to connect the 2nd tier of application to the 1st tier. A variety of client technologies may be used to connect to other tiers.

The 1st tier of an application could use any number of Java enabled browsers, including the one running on *Network Computers* as well as the ones built on more traditional platforms such as personal computers or workstations. Here, all user interface tasks would be handled by Java applets; while simpler tasks could be handled by using standard HTML forms.

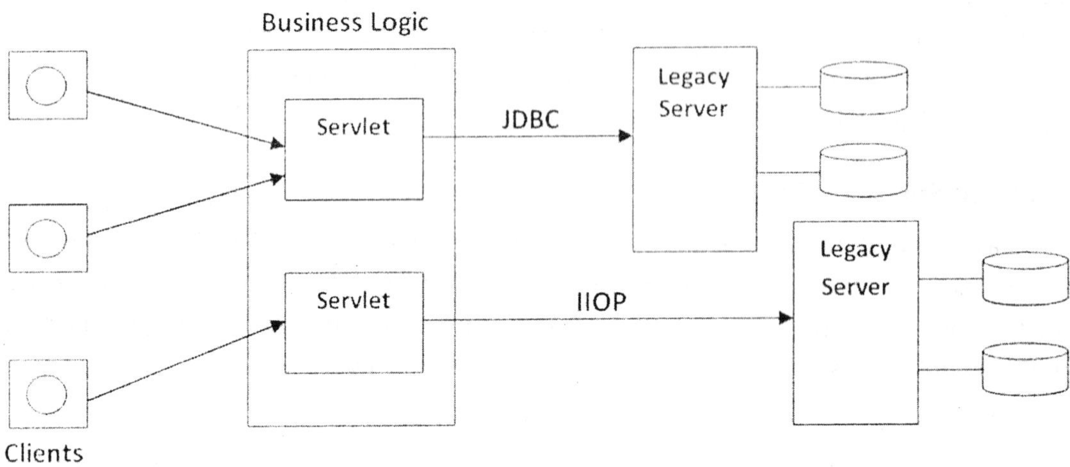


The 2nd tier of an application would consist of Web servers (consisting Servlets), which encapsulate the particular business rules and logic of the application. Such rules could include application-specific access controls for sensitive corporate data.

The 3rd tier of application consists of data repositories. Using relational database interfaces such as JDBC or hibernate or any other interfaces supported by legacy servers.

## 10.7 The life cycle of a Servlet

When a client makes a request involving a servlet, the server loads and executes the appropriate Java classes. Those classes generate content, and the server sends the content back to the client. In most cases, the client is a web browser; the server is a web server, and the servlet returns standard HTML. From the web browser's perspective, this isn't any different from requesting a page generated by a CGI script, or, indeed, standard HTML. Instead of shutting down at the end of each request, the servlet can remain loaded, ready to handle subsequent requests.

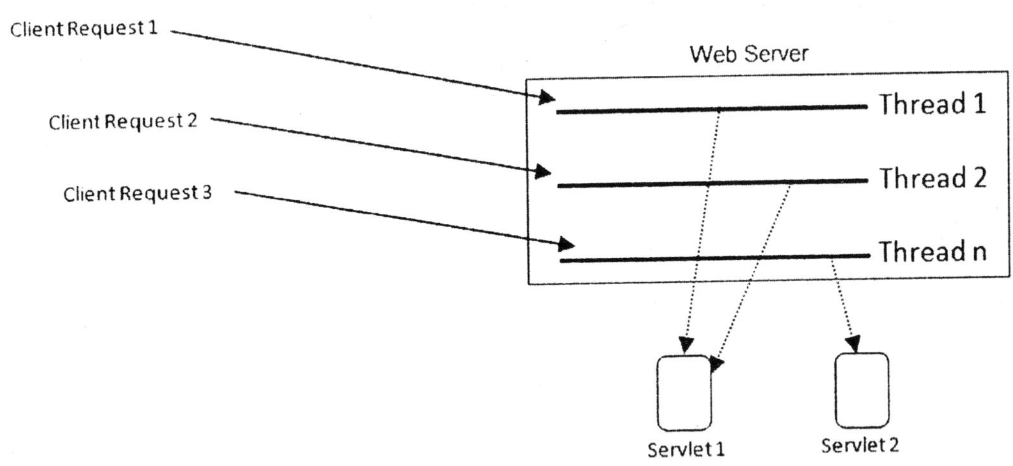


Three methods are central to the life cycle of a servlet. These are init( ), service( ), and destroy( ). They are implemented by every servlet and are invoked at specific times by the server. Let's consider a standard situation and understand when these methods are called.

**First**, assume that a user enters a Uniform Resource Locator (URL) to a web browser. The browser then generates an HTTP request for this URL. This request is then sent to the appropriate server.

**Second**, this HTTP request is received by the web server. The server maps this request to a particular servlet. The servlet is dynamically retrieved and loaded into the address space of the server.

**Third**, the server invokes the **init( )** method of the servlet. This method is invoked only when the servlet is first loaded into memory. It is possible to pass initialization parameters to the servlet so it may configure itself (instance of *ServletConfig* interface is used for this purpose).

**Fourth**, the server invokes the **service( )** method of the servlet. This method is called to process the HTTP request. It is possible for the servlet to read data that has been provided in the client's HTTP request. This method will generate the HTTP response for the client.

The servlet remains in the server's address space and remains available to process on any other HTTP requests of client. The service( ) method is called to respond to each client request.

Finally, when servlet feels that the server is no longer useful, the server unloads it from the server's address space and executes **destroy( )** method. This execution of destroy( ) method is to release the resources that were allocated to servlet. Important data may be saved to a permanent storage (Such as database or file). Remember that, this unloading decision belongs to the server.

## 10.8 Creating a servlet using NetBeans IDE

To create a servlet using NetBeans IDE refer the **section 4.8**. However, it is also possible to define it manually in a standard text editor. This is done by manually defining a servlet class by extending *GenericServlet* or *HttpServlet* to it. The *HttpServlet* class is derived class of *GenericServlet* class, that includes special methods for handling HTTP specific requests and responses. GenericServlet provides three standard methods init( ), service( ) and destroy( ). Whereas, HttpServlet provides doGet( ), doPost( ), doPut( ) and many more methods to handle particular types of HTTP requests. These *HttpServlet* methods GET, POST, PUT and other methods are called by the default implementation of the service( ) method, which figures out what kind of request is being made and then invokes the appropriate method. Following section shows the default Servlet skeleton when *HttpServlet* class is extended.

## 10.9 NetBeans IDE default Servlet skeleton

When a Servlet is created using NetBeans IDE, it shows the following default skeleton. We can modify this skeleton by adding required statements and user defined methods.

```
package Servlet2;

import java.io.IOException;
import java.io.PrintWriter;
import javax.servlet.ServletException;
import javax.servlet.ServletRequest;
import javax.servlet.ServletResponse;
import javax.servlet.http.HttpServlet;
import javax.servlet.http.HttpServletRequest;
import javax.servlet.http.HttpServletResponse;

/*
 * @author Majithia
 */

public class NewServletDemo extends HttpServlet {

  protected void processRequest(HttpServletRequest request, HttpServletResponse response)
        throws ServletException, IOException {
    response.setContentType("text/html;charset=UTF-8");
    PrintWriter out = response.getWriter();
    try {
      /* TODO output your page here. You may use following sample code. */
      out.println("<!DOCTYPE html>");
      out.println("<html>");
      out.println("<head>");
      out.println("<title>Servlet NewServlet</title>");
      out.println("</head>");
      out.println("<body>");
      out.println("<h1>Servlet NewServlet at " + request.getContextPath() + "</h1>");
      out.println("</body>");
      out.println("</html>");
    } finally {
      out.close( );
    }
  }

  @Override
  protected void doGet(HttpServletRequest request, HttpServletResponse response)
        throws ServletException, IOException {
    processRequest(request, response);
  }

  @Override
  protected void doPost(HttpServletRequest request, HttpServletResponse response)
        throws ServletException, IOException {
    processRequest(request, response);
  }
```

```
    @Override
    protected void doPut(HttpServletRequest req, HttpServletResponse resp) throws ServletException,
IOException {
        // todo code here
    }

    @Override
    protected void doDelete(HttpServletRequest req, HttpServletResponse resp) throws ServletException,
IOException {
        // todo code here
    }

    @Override
    protected void doOptions(HttpServletRequest req, HttpServletResponse resp) throws ServletException,
IOException {
        // todo code here
    }

    @Override
    public String getServletInfo() {
        return "Short description";
    }
}
```

## 10.10 The servlet API

The servlet API contains two important java packages. They are:

**javax.servlet**

The *javax.servlet* package contains a number of classes and interfaces that describe and define the contracts between a servlet class and the runtime environment provided for an instance of such a class by a conforming servlet container.

**javax.servlet.http**

The *javax.servlet.http* package contains a number of classes and interfaces that describe and define the contracts between a servlet class running under the HTTP protocol and the runtime environment provided for an instance of such a class by a conforming servlet container.

Following sections explains both these packages in depth with list of all the interfaces, classes and exceptions included in them.

## 10.11 The javax.servlet package

The *javax.servlet* package contains a number of classes and interfaces that describe and define the contracts between a servlet class and the runtime environment provided for an instance of such a class by a conforming servlet container. Following tables enlists the interfaces, classes and exceptions included in *javax.servlet* package.

**Interfaces included in javax.servlet**

| Interface | Description |
|---|---|
| Filter | A filter is an object that performs filtering tasks on either the request to a resource or on the response from a resource, or both. |
| FilterChain | A FilterChain is an object provided by the servlet container to the developer giving a view into the invocation chain of a filtered request for a resource. |
| FilterConfig | A filter configuration object used by a servlet container to pass information to a |

| | |
|---|---|
| | filter during initialization. |
| RequestDispatcher | Defines an object that receives requests from the client and sends them to any resource (such as a servlet, HTML file, or JSP file) on the server. |
| Servlet | Defines methods that all servlets must implement. |
| ServletConfig | A servlet configuration object used by a servlet container to pass information to a servlet during initialization. |
| ServletContext | Defines a set of methods that a servlet uses to communicate with its servlet container, for example, to get the MIME type of a file, dispatch requests, or write to a log file. |
| ServletContextAttributeListener | Implementations of this interface receive notifications of changes to the attribute list on the servlet context of a web application. |
| ServletContextListener | Implementations of this interface receive notifications about changes to the servlet context of the web application they are part of. |
| ServletRequest | Defines an object to provide client request information to a servlet. |
| ServletRequestAttributeListener | A ServletRequestAttributeListener can be implemented by the developer interested in being notified of request attribute changes. |
| ServletRequestListener | A ServletRequestListener can be implemented by the developer interested in being notified of requests coming in and out of scope in a web component. |
| ServletResponse | Defines an object to assist a servlet in sending a response to the client. |

<u>Classes included in javax.servlet</u>

| Class | Description |
|---|---|
| GenericServlet | Defines a generic, protocol-independent servlet. |
| ServletContextAttributeEvent | This is the event class for notifications about changes to the attributes of the servlet context of a web application. |
| ServletContextEvent | This is the event class for notifications about changes to the servlet context of a web application. |
| ServletInputStream | Provides an input stream for reading binary data from a client request, including an efficient readLine method for reading data one line at a time. |
| ServletOutputStream | Provides an output stream for sending binary data to the client. |
| ServletRequestAttributeEvent | This is the event class for notifications of changes to the attributes of the servlet request in an application. |
| ServletRequestEvent | Events of this kind indicate lifecycle events for a ServletRequest. |
| ServletRequestWrapper | Provides a convenient implementation of the ServletRequest interface that can be subclassed by developers wishing to adapt the request to a Servlet. |
| ServletResponseWrapper | Provides a convenient implementation of the ServletResponse interface that can be subclassed by developers wishing to adapt the response from a Servlet. |

**<u>Exceptions in javax.servlet</u>**

| Exception | Description |
|---|---|
| ServletException | Defines a general exception a servlet can throw when it encounters difficulty. |
| UnavailableException | Defines an exception that a servlet or filter throws to indicate that it is permanently or temporarily unavailable. |

Explaining each of these interfaces and classes will go beyond the scope of this chapter. Hence following are brief explanation on some commonly used interfaces and classes.

- ***<u>Servlet interface</u>***

All servlets must implement the Servlet interface. It declares the init( ), service( ), and destroy( ) methods that are called by the server during the life cycle of a servlet. A method is also provided that allows a servlet to obtain any initialization parameters. This interface is defined as:

*public interface Servlet*

In addition with these servlet life cycle methods, this interface also contains two more methods. Following table shows the methods included in this interface.

| Method | Description |
|---|---|
| void destroy( ) | Called by the servlet container to indicate to a servlet that the servlet is being taken out of service. |
| ServletConfig getServletConfig( ) | Returns a *ServletConfig* object, which contains initialization and startup parameters for invoking servlet. |
| String getServletInfo( ) | Returns information about the servlet, such as author, version, and copyright. |
| void init(ServletConfig *config*) | Called by the servlet container to indicate to a servlet that the servlet is being placed into service. Throws *ServletException*. |
| void service(ServletRequest *req*, ServletResponse *res*) | Called by the servlet container to allow the servlet to respond to a request. Throws *ServletException* and *IOException*. |

- ***ServletContext interface***

The ServletContext interface enables servlets to obtain information about their environment and also to communicate with its servlet container. This interface is defined as:

*public interface ServletContext*

Several of its methods are summarized in following table.

| Method | Description |
|---|---|
| Object getAttribute(String *name*) | Returns the servlet container attribute with the given *name*, or null if there is no attribute by that name. |
| Enumeration getAttributeNames( ) | Returns an *enumeration* containing the attribute names available within this servlet context. |
| String getInitParameter(String *name*) | Returns a String containing the value of the named context-wide initialization parameter, or null if the parameter does not exist. |
| String getMimeType(String *file*) | Returns the MIME type of the specified file or null if the MIME type is not known. |
| RequestDispatcher getRequestDispatcher(String *path*) | Returns a *RequestDispatcher* object that acts as a wrapper for the resource located at the given *path*. |
| String getServerInfo( ) | Returns the name and version of the servlet container on which the servlet is running. |
| Servlet getServlet(String *name*) | Retrieves a servlet from a ServletContext. So that, servlets can share information using the ServletContext class and can perform shared business logic by invoking methods on common non-servlet classes. |
| void log(String *mesg*) | Writes the specified message to a servlet log file, usually an event log. |
| void log(String *message*, Throwable *throwable*) | Writes an explanatory message and a stack trace for a given *Throwable* exception to the servlet log file. |
| void removeAttribute(String *attr_name*) | Removes the attribute with the given *attr_name* from the servlet context. |
| void setAttribute(String *attr_name*, Object *attr_value*) | Binds specified *attr_value* as attribute value with specified attribute name *attr_name* servlet context. |

- ***ServletConfig interface***

The ServletConfig interface allows a servlet to obtain configuration data when it is loaded. This interface is defined as:

*public interface ServletConfig*

Following table shows the methods included in this interface.

| Methods | Description |
|---|---|
| String getInitParameter(String *name*) | Returns a String containing the value of the named initialization parameter, or null if the parameter does not exist. |
| Enumeration getInitParameterNames( ) | Returns the names of the servlet's initialization parameters as an Enumeration of String objects, or an empty Enumeration if the servlet has no initialization parameters. |
| ServletContext getServletContext( ) | Returns a reference to the ServletContext in which the caller is executing. |
| String getServletName( ) | Returns the name of this servlet instance. |

- ***ServletRequest interface***

This interface defines an object to provide client request information to a servlet. The servlet container creates a ServletRequest object and passes it as an argument to the servlet's service method. This interface is defined as:

*public interface ServletRequest*

A ServletRequest object provides data including parameter name and values, attributes, and an input stream. Interfaces that extend ServletRequest can provide additional protocol-specific data. Following table shows several commonly used methods included in this interface.

| Method | Description |
|---|---|
| Object getAttribute(String *name*) | Returns the value of the named attribute as an *Object*, or null if no attribute of the given name exists. |
| int getContentLength( ) | Returns the length, in bytes, of the request body and made available by the input stream, or -1 if the length is not known. |
| String getContentType( ) | Returns the MIME type of the body of the request, or null if the type is not known. |
| ServletInputStream getInputStream( ) | Retrieves the body of the request as binary data using a *ServletInputStream*. |
| Locale getLocale( ) | Returns the preferred Locale that the client will accept content in, based on the Accept-Language header. |
| int getLocalPort( ) | Returns the IP port number of the interface on which the request was received. |
| String getParameter(String *name*) | Returns the value of a request parameter as a String, or null if the parameter does not exist. |
| String getProtocol( ) | Returns the name and version of the protocol. |
| BufferedReader getReader( ) | Retrieves the body of the request as character data using a *BufferedReader*. |
| String getRemoteAddr( ) | Returns the IP address of the client or last proxy that sent the request. |
| String getRemoteHost( ) | Returns the fully qualified name of the client or the last proxy that sent the request. |
| int getRemotePort( ) | Returns the IP source port of the client or last proxy that sent the request. |
| RequestDispatcher getRequestDispatcher(String *path*) | Returns a *RequestDispatcher* object that acts as a wrapper for the resource located at the given path. |
| String getServerName( ) | Returns the host name of the server to which the request was sent. |

| | |
|---|---|
| int getServerPort( ) | Returns the port number to which the request was sent. |
| ServletContext getServletContext( ) | Gets the servlet context to which this *ServletRequest* was last dispatched. |
| boolean isSecure( ) | Returns a boolean indicating whether this request was made using a secure channel, such as HTTPS. |
| void setCharacterEncoding(String *env*) | Overrides the name of the character encoding used in the body of this request. |
| void removeAttribute(String *attr_name*) | Removes the attribute with the given *attr_name* from the servlet context. |
| void setAttribute(String *attr_name*, Object *attr_value*) | Binds specified *attr_value* as attribute value with specified attribute name *attr_name* servlet context. |

- ***ServletResponse interface***

The ServletResponse interface enables a servlet to formulate a response for a client. The servlet container creates a *ServletResponse* object and passes it as an argument to the servlet's service method. This interface is defined as:

*public interface ServletResponse*

Following table shows the methods included in this interface.

| Method | Description |
|---|---|
| void flushBuffer( ) | Forces any content in the buffer to be written to the client. |
| int getBufferSize( ) | Returns the actual buffer size used for the response. |
| String getCharacterEncoding( ) | Returns the name of the character encoding used for the body sent in this response. |
| String getContentType( ) | Returns the content type used for the MIME body sent in this response. |
| Locale getLocale( ) | Returns the locale specified for invoking response. |
| ServletOutputStream getOutputStream( ) | Returns a *ServletOutputStream* suitable for writing binary data in the response. |
| PrintWriter getWriter( ) | Returns a *PrintWriter* object that can send character text to the client. |
| boolean isCommitted( ) | Returns a boolean indicating if the response has been committed. |
| void reset( ) | Clears any data that exists in the buffer as well as the status code and headers. |
| void resetBuffer( ) | Clears the content of the underlying buffer in the response without clearing headers or status code. |
| void setBufferSize(int *size*) | Sets the preferred buffer *size* for the body of the response. |
| void setCharacterEncoding(String *charset*) | Sets the character encoding of the response being sent to the client. |
| void setContentLength(int *len*) | Sets the length of the content body in the response In HTTP servlets. |
| void setContentType(String *type*) | Sets the content type of the response being sent to the client. |
| void setLocale(Locale *loc*) | Sets the locale of the response. |

- ***GenericServlet class***

The abstract GenericServlet class provides implementations of the basic life cycle methods for a servlet. This class is defined as:

*public abstract class GenericServlet extends Object implements Servlet, ServletConfig, Serializable*

GenericServlet makes writing servlets easier. It provides simple versions of the lifecycle methods init( ) and destroy( ) and of the methods in the *ServletConfig* interface. Following table contains methods included in this class. Note that, this class contains *service( )* as abstract method.

| Method | Description |
|---|---|
| void destroy( ) | Called by the servlet container to indicate to a servlet that the servlet is being taken out of service. |
| String getInitParameter(String *name*) | Returns a String containing the value of the named initialization parameter, or null if the parameter does not exist. |
| Enumeration getInitParameterNames( ) | Returns the names of the servlet's initialization parameters as an *Enumeration* of String objects, or an empty *Enumeration* if the servlet has no initialization parameters. |
| ServletConfig getServletConfig( ) | Returns this servlet's *ServletConfig* object. |
| ServletContext getServletContext( ) | Returns a reference to the *ServletContext* in which this servlet is running. |
| String getServletInfo( ) | Returns information about the servlet, such as author, version, and copyright. |
| String getServletName( ) | Returns the name of this servlet instance. |
| void init( ) | A convenience method which can be overridden so that there's no need to call *super.init(config).* |
| void init(ServletConfig *config*) | Called by the servlet container to indicate to a servlet that the servlet is being placed into service. |
| void log(String *msg*) | Writes the specified message to a servlet log file, pretended by the servlet's name. |
| void log(String *message*, Throwable *t*) | Writes an explanatory message and a stack trace for a given *Throwable* exception to the servlet log file, pretended by the servlet's name. |
| abstract void service(ServletRequest *req*, ServletResponse *res*) | Called by the servlet container to allow the servlet to respond to a request. |

- ***ServletInputStream class***

It is implemented by the servlet container and provides an input stream that a servlet developer can use to read the data from a client request. Following is the signature of this class.

*public abstract class ServletInputStream extends java.io.InputStream*

It defines the default constructor. In addition, a method is provided to read bytes from the stream. It is shown here:

*int readLine(byte[ ] buffer, int offset, int size) thows IOException*

Here, buffer is the array into which size bytes are placed starting at offset. The method returns the actual number of bytes read or –1 if an end-of-stream condition is encountered.

- ***ServletOutputStream class***

It is implemented by the servlet container and provides an output stream that a servlet developer can use to write data to a client response.

*public abstract class ServletOutputStream extends java.io.OutputStream*

A default constructor is defined for this class. It also defines the overloaded print( ) and println( ) methods, which outputs data to the stream.

This class contains abstract java.io.OutputStream.write(int) method.

## 10.12 The javax.servlet.http package

The javax.servlet.http package contains a number of classes and interfaces that describe and define the contracts between a servlet class running under the HTTP protocol and the runtime environment provided for an instance of such a class by a conforming servlet container. Following tables enlists the interfaces, classes and exceptions included in *javax.servlet.http* package.

Interface included in javax.servlet.http

| Interfaces | Description |
| --- | --- |
| HttpServletRequest | Extends the ServletRequest interface to provide request information for HTTP servlets. |
| HttpServletResponse | Extends the ServletResponse interface to provide HTTP-specific functionality in sending a response. |
| HttpSession | Provides a way to identify a user across more than one page request or visit to a Web site and to store information about that user. |
| HttpSessionActivationListener | Objects that are bound to a session may listen to container events notifying them that sessions will be passivated and that session will be activated. |
| HttpSessionAttributeListener | This listener interface can be implemented in order to get notifications of changes to the attribute lists of sessions within this web application. |
| HttpSessionBindingListener | Causes an object to be notified when it is bound to or unbound from a session. |
| HttpSessionListener | Implementations of this interface are notified of changes to the list of active sessions in a web application. |

Classes included in javax.servlet.http

| Classes | Description |
| --- | --- |
| Cookie | Creates a cookie, a small amount of information sent by a servlet to a Web browser, saved by the browser, and later sent back to the server. |
| HttpServlet | Provides an abstract class to be subclassed to create an HTTP servlet suitable for a Web site. |
| HttpServletRequestWrapper | Provides a convenient implementation of the HttpServletRequest interface that can be subclassed by developers wishing to adapt the request to a Servlet. |
| HttpServletResponseWrapper | Provides a convenient implementation of the HttpServletResponse interface that can be subclassed by developers wishing to adapt the response from a Servlet. |
| HttpSessionBindingEvent | Events of this type are either sent to an object that implements HttpSessionBindingListener when it is bound or unbound from a session, or to a HttpSessionAttributeListener that has been configured in the deployment descriptor when any attribute is bound, unbound or replaced in a session. |
| HttpSessionEvent | This is the class representing event notifications for changes to sessions within a web application. |

Explaining each of these interfaces and classes will go beyond the scope of this chapter. Hence following are brief explanation on some commonly used interfaces and classes.

- ***HttpServletRequest interface***

The HttpServletRequest interface enables an HTTP servlet to obtain information about a client request. This interface is defined as:

*public interface HttpServletRequest extends ServletRequest*

This interface extends the *ServletRequest* interface to provide request information for servlets. Following table shows commonly used methods of this interface.

| Method | Description |
| --- | --- |
| String getAuthType( ) | Returns the name of the authentication scheme used to protect the servlet. |
| String getContextPath( ) | Returns the portion of the request URI that indicates the context of the request. |

| | |
|---|---|
| Cookie[ ] getCookies( ) | Returns an array containing all of the Cookie objects the client sent with this request. |
| long getDateHeader(String *name*) | Returns the value of the specified request header as a long value that represents a Date object. |
| String getHeader(String *name*) | Returns the value of the specified request header as a String. |
| Enumeration<*String*> getHeaderNames( ) | Returns an enumeration of all the header names this request contains. |
| int getIntHeader(String *name*) | Returns the value of the specified request header as an int. |
| String getMethod( ) | Returns the name of the HTTP method with which this request was made, for example, GET, POST, or PUT. |
| String getPathInfo( ) | Returns any extra path information associated with the URL the client sent when it made this request. |
| String getPathTranslated( ) | Returns any extra path information after the servlet name but before the query string, and translates it to a real path. |
| String getQueryString( ) | Returns the query string that is contained in the request URL after the path. |
| String getRemoteUser( ) | Returns the login of the user making this request, if the user has been authenticated, or null if the user has not been authenticated. |
| String getRequestedSessionId( ) | Returns the session ID specified by the client. |
| String getRequestURI( ) | Returns the part of this request's URL from the protocol name up to the query string in the first line of the HTTP request. |
| StringBuffer getRequestURL( ) | Reconstructs the URL the client used to make the request. |
| String getServletPath( ) | Returns the part of this request's URL that calls the servlet. |
| HttpSession getSession( ) | Returns the current session associated with this request, or if the request does not have a session, creates one. |
| HttpSession getSession(boolean *create*) | Returns the current HttpSession associated with this request or, if there is no current session and create is true, returns a new session. |
| boolean isRequestedSessionIdFromCookie( ) | Checks whether the requested session ID came in as a cookie. |
| boolean isRequestedSessionIdFromURL( ) | Checks whether the requested session ID came in as part of the request URL. |
| boolean isRequestedSessionIdValid( ) | Checks whether the requested session ID is still valid. |
| void login(String *username*, String *password*) | Validate the provided username and password in the password validation realm used by the web container login mechanism configured for the ServletContext. |
| void logout( ) | Establish null as the value returned when getUserPrincipal, getRemoteUser, and getAuthType is called on the request. |

- ***<u>HttpServletResponse interface</u>***

The HttpServletResponse interface enables a servlet to formulate an HTTP response to a client. This interface is defined as:

*public interface HttpServletResponse extends ServletResponse*

This interface extends the *ServletResponse* interface to provide HTTP-specific functionality in sending a response. For example, it has methods to access HTTP headers and cookies. Following table contains the commonly used methods of this interface.

| Method | Description |
|---|---|
| void addCookie(Cookie *cookie*) | Adds the specified cookie to the response. |
| void addDateHeader(String *name*, long *date*) | Adds a response header with the given name and date-value. |
| void addHeader(String *name*, String *value*) | Adds a response header with the given name and value. |

| | |
|---|---|
| void addIntHeader(String *name*, int *value*) | Adds a response header with the given name and integer value. |
| boolean containsHeader(String *name*) | Returns a boolean indicating whether the named response header has already been set. |
| String encodeRedirectURL(String *url*) | Encodes the specified URL for use in the sendRedirect method or, if encoding is not needed, returns the URL unchanged. |
| String encodeURL(String *url*) | Encodes the specified URL by including the session ID in it, or, if encoding is not needed, returns the URL unchanged. |
| void sendError(int *sc*) | Sends an error response to the client using the specified status code and clearing the buffer. |
| void sendError(int *sc*, String *mesg*) | Sends an error response to the client using the specified status. |
| void sendRedirect(String location) | Sends a temporary redirect response to the client using the specified redirect location URL. |
| void setDateHeader(String name, long date) | Sets a response header with the given name and date-value. |
| void setHeader(String *name*, String *value*) | Sets a response header with the given name and value. |
| void setIntHeader(String *name*, int *value*) | Sets a response header with the given name and integer value. |
| void setStatus(int *sc*) | Sets the status code for this response. |

- ***HttpSession interface***

The HttpSession interface enables a servlet to read and write the state information that is associated with an HTTP session. This interface is defined as:

*public interface HttpSession*

The session provides a way to identify a user across more than one page request or visit to a Web site and to store information about that user. (Upcoming chapter 11 explains the Session in detail.) Several of its methods are summarized in following table.

| Method | Description |
|---|---|
| Object getAttribute(String name) | Returns the object bound with the specified name in this session, or null if no object is bound under the name. |
| Enumeration<String> getAttributeNames( ) | Returns an Enumeration of String objects containing the names of all the objects bound to this session. |
| long getCreationTime( ) | Returns the time when this session was created, measured in milliseconds since midnight January 1, 1970 GMT. |
| String getId( ) | Returns a string containing the unique identifier assigned to this session. |
| long getLastAccessedTime( ) | Returns the last time the client sent a request associated with this session, as the number of milliseconds since midnight January 1, 1970 GMT, and marked by the time the container received the request. |
| int getMaxInactiveInterval( ) | Returns the maximum time interval, in seconds, that the servlet container will keep this session open between client accesses. |
| void invalidate( ) | Invalidates this session then unbinds any objects bound to it. |
| boolean isNew( ) | Returns true if the client does not yet know about the session or if the client chooses not to join the session. |
| void removeAttribute(String name) | Removes specified attribute. |
| void setAttribute(String name, Object value) | Binds an object to this session, using the name specified. |
| void setMaxInactiveInterval(int interval) | Specifies the time, in seconds, between client requests before the servlet container will invalidate this session. |

All of these methods throw an IllegalStateException if the session has already been invalidated.

- ***HttpSessionBindingListener interface***

The HttpSessionBindingListener interface is implemented by objects that need to be noti�ed when they are bound to or unbound from an HTTP session. The signature of this interface i:

*public interface HttpSessionBindingListener extends EventListener*

This interface extends *EventListener* interface, which comes under *java.util* package. This interface causes an object to be notified when it is bound to or unbound from a session. The object is notified by an *HttpSessionBindingEvent* object. This may be as a result of a servlet programmer explicitly unbinding an attribute from a session, due to a session being invalidated, or due to session timing out. This interface has only two methods that are invoked when an object is bound or unbound.

| Method | Description |
|---|---|
| void valueBound(HttpSessionBindingEvent event) | Notifies the object that it is being bound to a session and identifies the session. |
| void valueUnbound(HttpSessionBindingEvent event) | Notifies the object that it is being unbound from a session and identifies the session. |

- ***Cookie class***

Instance of this class creates a cookie, a small amount of information sent by a servlet to a Web browser, saved by the browser, and later sent back to the server. A cookie's value can uniquely identify a client, so cookies are commonly used for session management. This class is defined as:

*public class Cookie extends Object implements Cloneable*

A cookie has a name, a single value, and optional attributes such as a comment, path and domain qualifiers, a maximum age, and a version number. Some Web browsers have bugs in how they handle the optional attributes, so use them sparingly to improve the interoperability of your servlets. (Upcoming chapter 10 explains more on cookies.) Following table describes the commonly used methods of Cookie class.

| Method | Description |
|---|---|
| Object clone( ) | Overrides the standard java.lang.Object.clone method to return a copy of this cookie. |
| String getComment( ) | Returns the comment describing the purpose of this cookie, or null if the cookie has no comment. |
| String getDomain( ) | Returns the domain name set for this cookie. |
| int getMaxAge( ) | Returns the maximum age of the cookie, specified in seconds, By default, -1 indicating the cookie will persist until browser shutdown. |
| String getName( ) | Returns the name of the cookie. |
| String getPath( ) | Returns the path on the server to which the browser returns this cookie. |
| boolean getSecure( ) | Returns true if the browser is sending cookies only over a secure protocol, or false if the browser can send cookies using any protocol. |
| String getValue( ) | Returns the value of the cookie. |
| int getVersion( ) | Returns the version of the protocol this cookie complies with. |
| void setComment(String *purpose*) | Specifies a comment that describes a cookie's purpose. |
| void setDomain(String *pattern*) | Specifies the domain within which this cookie should be presented. |
| void setMaxAge(int *expiry*) | Sets the maximum age of the cookie in seconds. |
| void setPath(String *uri*) | Specifies a path for the cookie to which the client should return the cookie. |
| void setSecure(boolean *flag*) | Indicates to the browser whether the cookie should only be sent using a secure protocol, such as HTTPS or SSL. |
| void setValue(String *newValue*) | Assigns a new value to a cookie after the cookie is created. |
| void setVersion(int *v*) | Sets the version of the cookie protocol this cookie complies with. |

- ***HttpServlet class***

The HttpServlet class is commonly used when developing servlets that receive and process HTTP requests. This class is defined as:

*public abstract class HttpServlet extends GenericServlet implements Serializable*

A subclass of HttpServlet must override at least one method, usually one of these:

- doGet( ), if the servlet supports HTTP GET requests
- doPost( ), for HTTP POST requests
- doPut( ), for HTTP PUT requests
- doDelete( ), for HTTP DELETE requests
- init( ) and destroy( ), to manage resources that are held for the life of the servlet
- getServletInfo( ), which the servlet uses to provide information about itself

There's almost no reason to override the service( ) method. service( ) method handles standard HTTP requests by dispatching them to the handler methods for each HTTP request type. Similarly there is no reason to override the doOptions( ) and doTrace( ) methods. Following table shows the methods included in this class.

| Method | Description |
|---|---|
| protected void doDelete(HttpServletRequest req, HttpServletResponse resp) | Called by the server to allow a servlet to handle a DELETE request. |
| protected void doGet(HttpServletRequest req, HttpServletResponse resp) | Called by the server to allow a servlet to handle a GET request. |
| protected void doHead(HttpServletRequest req, HttpServletResponse resp) | Receives an HTTP HEAD request from the protected service method and handles the request. |
| protected void doOptions(HttpServletRequest req, HttpServletResponse resp) | Called by the server to allow a servlet to handle a OPTIONS request. |
| protected void doPost(HttpServletRequest req, HttpServletResponse resp) | Called by the server to allow a servlet to handle a POST request. |
| protected void doPut(HttpServletRequest req, HttpServletResponse resp) | Called by the server to allow a servlet to handle a PUT request. |
| protected void doTrace(HttpServletRequest req, HttpServletResponse resp) | Called by the server to allow a servlet to handle a TRACE request. |
| protected long getLastModified(HttpServletRequest req) | Returns the time the HttpServletRequest object was last modified, in milliseconds since midnight January 1, 1970 GMT. |
| protected void service(HttpServletRequest req, HttpServletResponse resp) | Receives standard HTTP requests from the public service method and dispatches them to the doXXX methods defined in this class. |
| void service(ServletRequest req, ServletResponse res) | Dispatches client requests to the protected service method. |

- ***HttpSessionEvent class***

The *HttpSessionEvent* class encapsulates session events. It extends *EventObject* and is generated when a change occurs to the session. The signature of this class is:

*public class HttpSessionEvent extends java.util.EventObject*

The *EventObject* class belongs to *java.util* package. This class provides one constructor. It is:

*HttpSessionEvent(HttpSession source)*

This constructor constructs a session event from the given source. This class has only one method. It is:

*HttpSession getSession( )*

This method return the session that is changed.

- ***HttpSessionBindingEvent class***

The HttpSessionBindingEvent class extends HttpSessionEvent. It is generated when a listener is bound or unbound in an HttpSession object. It is also generated when an attribute is bound or unbound. Following are the constructors of this class.

*HttpSessionBindingEvent(HttpSession session, String name)*
*HttpSessionBindingEvent(HttpSession session, String name, Object val)*

Here, session is the source of the event, and *name* is the name associated with the object that is being bound or unbound. If an attribute is being bound or unbound, its value is passed in *val*. Following table shows the methods included in this class.

| Method | Description |
|---|---|
| String getName( ) | Returns the name with which the attribute is bound to or unbound from the session. |
| HttpSession getSession( ) | Return the session that changed. |
| Object getValue( ) | Returns the value of the attribute that has been added, removed or replaced. |

## 10.13 Servlet template

After understanding all servlet basics and its interfaces and classes we can now move further to discuss about servlet programs and how a servlet handles parameters.

A browser generates this request when the user enters a URL on the address line, follows a link from a Web page, or submits an HTML form that either does not specify a method or specifies METHOD = "GET" method. Servlets can also easily handle POST requests, which are generated when someone submits an HTML form that specifies METHOD="POST". This will be more clear when we will discuss about JSP combination with a Servlet.

Following block shows a servlet's template that extends *HttpServlet*.

```
import java.io.*;
import javax.servlet.*;
import javax.servlet.http.*;
public class ServletTemplate extends HttpServlet
{
        public void doGet(HttpServletRequest request, HttpServletResponse response)
        throws ServletException, IOException
        {
                // Use "request" to read incoming HTTP headers
                // (e.g., cookies) and query data from HTML forms.

                // Use "response" to specify the HTTP response status
                // code and headers (e.g., the content type, cookies).

                PrintWriter out = response.getWriter( );
                // Use "out" to send content to browser.
        }
}
```

Servlets typically extend *HttpServlet* and override **doGet( )** or **doPost( )** method, depending on whether the data is being sent by GET or by POST. If a servlet is made to take the same action for both GET and POST requests, simply have **doGet( )** calls to **doPost( )**, or vice versa.

Both **doGet( )** and **doPost( )** methods take two arguments: an *HttpServletRequest* and an *HttpServletResponse*. The *HttpServletRequest* gets at all of the requesting data; the class has methods by which we can find out about information such as form (query) data, HTTP request headers, and the client's hostname. The *HttpServletResponse* allow to specify outgoing information such as HTTP status codes and response headers (such as, Content-Type, Set-Cookie, etc.). Most importantly, *HttpServletResponse* allows obtaining a *PrintWriter* that we use to send document content back to the client. For simple servlets, most of the effort is spent in **println( )** statements that generate the desired page. Form data, HTTP request headers, HTTP responses, and cookies are all discussed in next chapters.

Since **doGet( )** and **doPost( )** throw two exceptions *ServletException* and *IOException*, we must need to include them in the method definitions. Finally, we must import *java.io* (for *PrintWriter*, etc.), *javax.servlet* (for *HttpServlet*, etc.), and *javax.servlet.http* (for *HttpServletRequest* and *HttpServletResponse*).

```
import java.io.*;
import javax.servlet.*;
import javax.servlet.http.*;
public class HelloWorld extends HttpServlet
{
        public void doGet(HttpServletRequest request, HttpServletResponse response)
        throws ServletException, IOException
        {
                PrintWriter out = response.getWriter( );
                out.println("Hello World");
        }
}
```

Finally, invoke your servlet. This last step involves using either the default URL of *http://host/servlet/ServletName* or a custom URL defined in the web.xml file

## 10.14 Servlet Development options

To create servlets, we need access to a servlet container/server. Two popular ones are Glassfish and Tomcat. Glassfish is from Oracle and is provided by the Java EE SDK. It is supported by NetBeans. Tomcat is an open-source product maintained by the Apache Software Foundation. It can also be used by NetBeans. Both Tomcat and Glassfish can also be used with other IDEs, such as Eclipse. The examples and descriptions in this chapter use Tomcat for reasons that will soon be apparent.

The IDEs, such as NetBeans and Eclipse, are very useful and can streamline the creation of servlets. From the beginning of this book we have focused on using NetBeans IDE. Similarly here also we will continue our discussion with NetBeans IDE only. To work with NetBeans IDE for developing servlet, steps are provided in section 3.6. You can go through those steps and develop a Servlet.

For almost all development Furthermore, many developers will be using the command-line tools rather than an IDE. For more details about servlets, the instructions given here and elsewhere in this chapter assume that only the command-line tools are employed. Thus, they will work for nearly any reader.

Many developers also prefer the command-line tools rather than an IDE. Hence here we will try something different by using command-line tools for configuring and developing a servlet.

In this chapter we will be using Tomcat server, because it makes it relatively easy to run the example servlets using only command-line tools and a text editor. It is also widely available in various programming environments. Furthermore, since only command-line tools are used, no need to use any IDEs to experiment with servlets. Understand, however, that even if you are developing in an environment that uses Glassfish, the concepts presented here still apply. It is just that the mechanics of preparing a servlet for testing will be slightly different.

Tomcat contains the class libraries, documentation, and run time support that you will need to create and test servlets.

The examples and explanations in this section assumes a 64-bit Windows environment and 64-bit version of Tomcat 7.0.4 was unpacked from the root directly, to the default location:

*C:\apache-tomcat-7.0.4-windows-x64\apache-tomcat-7.0.4*

If you unpack your Tomcat in a different location or use a different version, you will need to make appropriate changes to the examples. You may need to set the environmental variable **JAVA_HOME** to the top-level directory in which the Java Development Kit is installed.

Once installed, start Tomcat by selecting **startup.bat** from the bin directly under the apache tomcat directory. To stop Tomcat, execute **shutdown.bat**, is also available in the bin directory.

The classes and interfaces needed to build servlets are contained in **servlet-api.jar**, which is in the following directory:

*C:\apache-tomcat-7.0.4-windows-x64\apache-tomcat-7.0.4\lib*

To make **servlet-api.jar** accessible, update your CLASSPATH environment variable so that it includes

*C:\apache-tomcat-7.0.4-windows-x64\apache-tomcat-7.0.4\lib\servlet-api.jar*

Alternatively, you can specify this file when you compile the servlets. For example, the following command compiles above **HelloWorld** example:

*javac HelloWorld.java -classpath "C:\apache-tomcat-7.0.4-windowsx64\ apache-tomcat-7.0.4\lib\servlet-api.jar"*

Once you have compiled a servlet, you must enable Tomcat to find it. For our purposes, this means putting it into a directory under Tomcat's **webapps** directory and entering its name into a web.xml file. Here is the procedure that you will follow.

First, copy the servlet's class file into the following directory:

*C:\apache-tomcat-7.0.4-windows-x64\apache-tomcat-7.0.4\webapps\examples\WEB-INF\classes*

Next, add the servlet's name and mapping to the **web.xml** file in the following directory:

*C:\apache-tomcat-7.0.4-windows-x64\apache-tomcat-7.0.4\webapps\examples\WEB-INF*

For the first example, called **HelloWorld**, we need to add the following lines in the section that defines the servlets:

```
<servlet>
<servlet-name>HelloWorld</servlet-name>
<servlet-class>HelloWorld</servlet-class>
</servlet>
```

Next, add the following lines to the section that defines the servlet mappings:

```
<servlet-mapping>
<servlet-name>HelloWorld</servlet-name>
<url-pattern>/servlet/HelloWorld</url-pattern>
</servlet-mapping>
```

Follow this same general procedure for all of the examples.

## 10.15 Building a test servlet

To become familiar with the key servlet concepts, we consider above **HelloWorld** servlet is build. Now following are the basic steps that helps to deploy and executing a servlet.

1. Create and compile the servlet source code. Then, copy the servlet's class file to the proper directory, and add the servlet's name and mappings to the web.xml file.

2. Start Tomcat.

3. Start a web browser and request the servlet by entering following URL.

*http://localhost:8080/examples/servlets/servlet/HelloWorld*

Alternatively, following URL will also work.

*http://127.0.0.1:8080/examples/servlets/servlet/HelloWorld*

## 10.16 Reading servlet parameter

If you did enough practice on servlets, you must come across a situation where you need to pass some information from your web browser to the web server or to backend of your application. The browser uses two methods to pass any information to web server. These methods are GET and POST methods.

### GET method

The GET method sends the encoded user information appended to the page request. The page and the encoded information are separated by '?'. See following URL.

*http://www.test.com/hello?key1=value1&key2=value2*

The GET method is the default method to pass information from browser to web server and it produces a long string that appears in your browser's address-bar. Never use the GET method if password or other sensitive information to pass to the server. The GET method has size limitation of only 1024 characters.

This information is passed using QUERY_STRING header and will be accessible through QUERY_STRING environment variable and Servlet handles this type of requests using **doGet( )** method.

### POST method

A generally more reliable method of passing information to a backend program is the POST method. This packages the information in exactly the same way as GET methods, but instead of sending it as a text string after '?' in the URL, it sends it as a separate message. This message comes to the backend program in the form of the standard input which we can parse and use for your processing. Servlet handles this type of requests using **doPost( )** method.

### Reading data using servlet

Servlets handles form data parsing automatically using the following methods depending on the situation.

- **getParameter( ):** we call this method to get the value of a form parameter.
- **getParameterValues( ):** we call this method if the parameter appears more than once and returns multiple values. For example, a checkbox.
- **getParameterNames( ):** We call this method if we want a complete list of all parameters in the current request.

## GET method example using getParameter( ) method

Here is a simple URL that passes two values to HelloForm program using GET method.

*http://localhost:8080/HelloForm?first_name=James&last_name=Gosling*

Following is **HelloForm.java** servlet program to handle input given by web browser. We are going to use getParameter( ) method which makes it very easy to access passed information. Remember, in above URL '?' is used which shows that the parameters are passed using GET method.

```
import java.io.*;
import javax.servlet.*;
import javax.servlet.http.*;
// Extend HttpServlet class
public class HelloForm extends HttpServlet
{
        public void doGet(HttpServletRequest request, HttpServletResponse response)
        throws ServletException,IOException
        {
                // Set response content type
                response.setContentType("text/html");
                PrintWriterout= response.getWriter( );
                String title ="Using GET Method to Read Form Data";
                String docType = "<!doctype html public \"-//w3c//dtd html 4.0 "+ "transitional//en\">\n";
                out.println(docType + "<html>\n"+ "<head><title>"+ title +"</title></head>\n"+
                "<h1 align=\"center\">"+ title +"</h1>\n"+ "<ul>\n"+ " <li><b>First Name</b>: "
                + request.getParameter("first_name")+"\n"+ " <li><b>Last Name</b>: " +
                request.getParameter("last_name")+"\n"+ "</ul>\n"+ "</body></html>");
        }
}
```

Assuming the environment is setup properly, compile HelloForm.java as:

```
javac HelloForm.java
```

After successful compilation above program will produce **HelloForm.class** file. Next we will have to copy this class file in:

*<Tomcat-installation-directory>/webapps/ROOT/WEB-INF/classes*

Now, create following entries in **web.xml** file located in

```
<servlet>
<servlet-name>HelloForm</servlet-name>
<servlet-class>HelloForm</servlet-class>
</servlet>
<servlet-mapping>
<servlet-name>HelloForm</servlet-name>
<url-pattern>/HelloForm</url-pattern>
</servlet-mapping>
```

Now type

*http://localhost:8080/HelloForm?first_name=James&last_name=Gosling*

In web browser's address-bar and make sure the tomcat server is already started, before firing above command in the browser. This would generate following result:

## Using GET Method to Read Form Data

**First Name**: James
**Last Name**: Gosling

We can also produce the same example by creating an HTML form and a submit button. Above **HelloForm** servlet will be kept as it is. See following HTML FORM.

```
<html>
<body>
<form action="HelloForm" method="GET">
First Name: <input type="text" name="first_name">
<br/>
Last Name: <input type="text" name="last_name"/>
<input type="submit" value="Submit"/>
</form>
</body>
</html>
```

Call this file Hello.html and put it in Tomcat's ROOT directory. This time type:

*http://localhost:8080/Hello.html*

in your web browser's address-bar and you will get following output. Input First Name, Last Name and click submit button.

**POST method example using FORM**

We can also create a common servlet program that can handle both GET and POST methods. Logically, add following method in above HelloForm.java servlet.

```
public void doPost(HttpServletRequest request, HttpServletResponse response)
throws ServletException, IOException
{
        doGet(request, response);
}
```

Now, compile and deploy the modified servlet and also modify **Hello.html** as follows.

```
<html>
<body>
<form action="HelloForm"method="POST">
First Name: <input type="text" name="first_name">
<br/>
Last Name: <input type="text" name="last_name"/>
<input type="submit" value="Submit"/>
</form>
```

```
</body>
</html>
```

Above Hello.html will produce two textboxes for entering First Name, Last Name and a **Submit** button.

| First Name: | |
|---|---|
| Last Name: | Submit |

Based on input we provide, it will generate the same result as above example.

## 10.17 Servlet Filters

Servlet Filters are Java classes that can be used in Servlet Programming for the following purposes:

- To intercept requests from a client before they access a resource at back end.
- To manipulate responses from server before they are sent back to the client.

There are various types of filters suggested by the specifications:

- Authentication Filters
- Data compression Filters
- Encryption Filters
- Filters that trigger resource access events
- Image Conversion Filters
- Logging and Auditing Filters
- MIME-TYPE Chain Filters
- Tokenizing Filters
- XSL/T Filters That Transform XML Content

Filters are deployed in the deployment descriptor file web.xml and then map to either servlet names or URL patterns in your application's deployment descriptor.

When the web container starts up your web application, it creates an instance of each filter that you have declared in the deployment descriptor. The filters execute in the order that they are declared in the deployment descriptor.

**Servlet Filter Methods**

A filter is simply a Java class that implements the *javax.servlet.Filter* interface. The *javax.servlet.Filter* interface defines three methods:

| Method | Description |
|---|---|
| public void doFilter (ServletRequest *req*, ServletResponse *res*, FilterChain *fchain*) | This method is called by the container each time a request/response pair is passed through the chain due to a client request for a resource at the end of the chain. |
| public void init(FilterConfig *fconfig*) | This method is called by the web container to indicate to a filter that it is being placed into service. |
| public void destroy( ) | This method is called by the web container to indicate to a filter that it is being taken out of service. |

## Servlet Filter Example

Following is the Servlet Filter Example that would print the clients IP address and current date time. This example would give a basic understanding of Servlet Filter, but we can write more sophisticated filter applications using the same concept:

```
import java.io.*;
import javax.servlet.*;
import javax.servlet.http.*;
import java.util.*;

// Implements Filter class
public class LogFilter implements Filter
{
        publicvoid init(FilterConfig config) throwsServletException
        {
                // Get init parameter
                String testParam = config.getInitParameter("test-param");

                //Print the init parameter
                System.out.println("Test Param: "+ testParam);
        }

        publicvoid doFilter(ServletRequest request, ServletResponse response, FilterChain chain)
        throws java.io.IOException,ServletException
        {
                // Get the IP address of client machine.
                String ipAddress = request.getRemoteAddr( );

                // Log the IP address and current timestamp.
                System.out.println("IP "+ ipAddress +", Time " +newDate( ).toString( ));

                // Pass request back down the filter chain
                chain.doFilter(request,response);
        }

        publicvoid destroy( )
        {
                /* Called before the Filter instance is removed
                from service by the web container*/
        }
}
```

Compile **LogFilter.java** in usual way and put this class file in

*<Tomcat-installation-directory>/webapps/ROOT/WEB-INF/classes*

## Servlet Filter mapping in web.xml

Filters are defined and then mapped to a URL or Servlet, in much the same way as Servlet is defined and then mapped to a URL pattern. Create the following entry for filter tag in the deployment descriptor file **web.xml**

```
<filter>
<filter-name>LogFilter</filter-name>
<filter-class>LogFilter</filter-class>
<init-param>
<param-name>test-param</param-name>
<param-value>Initialization Paramter</param-value>
</init-param>
</filter>
<filter-mapping>
<filter-name>LogFilter</filter-name>
<url-pattern>/*</url-pattern>
</filter-mapping>
```

The above filter would apply to all the servlets because we specified **/*** in our configuration. We can specify a particular servlet path if we want to apply filter on few servlets only.

Now try to call any servlet in usual way and you would see generated log in your web server log. We can also apply **Log4J logger** to log above log in a separate file.

**Applying multiple Filters**

A web application may define several different filters with a specific purpose. Consider we need define two filters *AuthenFilter* and *LogFilter*. Rest of the process would remain as explained above except we need to create a different mapping as mentioned below:

```
<filter>
<filter-name>LogFilter</filter-name>
<filter-class>LogFilter</filter-class>
<init-param>
<param-name>test-param</param-name>
<param-value>Initialization Paramter</param-value>
</init-param>
</filter>
<filter>
<filter-name>AuthenFilter</filter-name>
<filter-class>AuthenFilter</filter-class>
<init-param>
<param-name>test-param</param-name>
<param-value>Initialization Paramter</param-value>
</init-param>
</filter>
<filter-mapping>
<filter-name>LogFilter</filter-name>
<url-pattern>/*</url-pattern>
</filter-mapping>
<filter-mapping>
<filter-name>AuthenFilter</filter-name>
<url-pattern>/*</url-pattern>
</filter-mapping>
```

**Filters application order**

The order of filter-mapping elements in web.xml determines the order in which the web container applies the filter to the servlet. To reverse the order of the filter, we just need to reverse the filter-mapping elements in the **web.xml** file. For example, above example would apply *LogFilter* first and then it would apply *AuthenFilter* to any servlet but the following example would reverse the order:

```
<filter-mapping>
<filter-name>AuthenFilter</filter-name>
<url-pattern>/*</url-pattern>
</filter-mapping>
<filter-mapping>
<filter-name>LogFilter</filter-name>
<url-pattern>/*</url-pattern>
</filter-mapping>
```

## 10.18 A simple example: passing checkbox data to a servlet

Following is the servlet program that accepts the checked or unchecked status from an HTML FORM and displays the status as result.

Here is the HTML FORM, called **Checkbox.html** having three checkboxes.

```
<html>
<body>
<formaction="CheckBox"method="POST"target="_blank">
<inputtype="checkbox"name="maths"checked="checked"/> Maths
<inputtype="checkbox"name="physics"/> Physics
<inputtype="checkbox"name="chemistry"checked="checked"/>
Chemistry
<inputtype="submit"value="Select Subject"/>
</form>
</body>
</html>
```

When you run this html file, you will get following result.

☑ Maths ☐ Physics ☑ Chemistry [Select Subject]

Following is the Checkbox.java program; a servlet that displays the status of checkboxes.

```
import java.io.*;
import javax.servlet.*;
import javax.servlet.http.*;

public class Checkbox extends HttpServlet
{
	public void doGet(HttpServletRequest request, HttpServletResponse response)
	throws ServletException, IOException
	{
		response.setContentType("text/html");
```

```
            PrintWriterout= response.getWriter( );
            String title ="Reading Checkbox Data";
            String docType = "<!doctype html public \"-//w3c//dtd html 4.0 "+ "transitional//en\">\n";
            out.println(docType + "<html>\n"+ "<head><title>"+ title +"</title></head>\n"+
            "<h1 align=\"center\">"+ title +"</h1>\n"+
            "<ul>\n"+ " <li><b>Maths Flag : </b> " + request.getParameter("maths")+"\n"+
            " <li><b>Physics Flag: </b> " + request.getParameter("physics")+"\n"+
            " <li><b>Chemistry Flag: </b>" + request.getParameter("chemistry")+"\n"+
            "</ul>\n" + "</body></html>");
      }

      publicvoid doPost(HttpServletRequest request, HttpServletResponse response)
      throws ServletException, IOException
      {
            doGet(request, response);
      }
}
```

After successful compilation and setting all execution environments, this program will show following output.

## Reading Checkbox Data

**Maths Flag:** on
**Physics Flag:** null
**Chemistry Flag:** on

*****

# Chapter 11

# Cookies

In previous chapter we get some essential information about servlet and working of servlet. We know that web applications are typically a series of Hypertext Transfer Protocol (HTTP) requests and responses. As HTTP is a stateless protocol, information is not automatically saved between HTTP requests. Web applications use cookies to store state information on the client. Cookies can be used to store information about the user, the user's shopping cart, and so on.

HTTP does not maintain a persistent connection. Each request made by a web browser is made using a new connection. Hence this protocol does not maintain state across HTTP requests.

Usually, a web browser generates a request. This request is forwarded to the web server through the internet. The web server immediately responds to this request and then forgets about the browser and its request due to lake of constant connection. This causes a problem for website attempting to do business on the internet.

This problem arises when a user wish to make multiple purchases from a website. The web server forgets the browser once and continuity in client's navigations will not be maintained. Hence, web server will find it impossible to create a single bill for multiple purchases made through different requests by a client.

## 11.1 What are cookies?

Cookies are text files stored on the client computer by web server and they are kept for various information tracking purpose. Java Servlets transparently supports HTTP cookies.

There are three steps involved in identifying returning users:

- Server script sends a set of cookies to the browser. For example name, age, or identification number etc.
- Browser stores this information on local machine for future use.
- When next time browser sends any request to web server then it sends those cookies information to the server and server uses that information to identify the user.

This chapter will teach you how to set or reset cookies, how to access them and how to delete them.

A cookie generally contains a name and a value. But in fact, a cookie contains total 6 parameters.

- The name of cookie
- The value of cookie
- The expiration date of cookie
- The path the cookie is valid for
- The domain the cookie is valid for
- The need for a secure connection to exists to use the cookie

Two of these parameters are mandatory [i.e. cookie name and its value]. All these information are stored as a text file, in a special sub-directory on the hard disk of the computer from which the request is sent.

## 11.2 How cookie works?

Whenever, the browser makes any attempt to contact the web server, the browser executables has built-in instructions to first scan this special sub-directory on the hard disk of the computer on which the browser is running.

If any cookies related to same web server, are identified then the browser automatically sends the cookie(s) back to the web server with every request information.

Once the web server receives cookie information, a servlet program will run, that will process the cookie information returned by the browser. This will force the web server to immediately recognize that it has received another request from the same browser. This thus overcomes the problem of maintaining continuity of request and maintains the constant state between the browser and the web server. This gives the empowerment to request and response paradigm of the internet.

## 11.3 Types of cookies

There are two types of cookies

**Session / Transient cookies**

Session or transient cookies are those cookies that are stored in computer's memory only during a user's browsing session and are automatically deleted from the user's computer when the browser is closed.

These cookies usually store a session ID that is not permanently bound to the user, allowing the user to move from page to page without having login repeatedly. They are widely used by commercial websites (Such as to add items to shopping cart)

Session cookies are never written on the hard drive and they do not collect any information from the user's computer. Session cookies expire at the end of the user's browsing session. They also become no longer accessible after the session has been inactive for a specified length of time.

Without cookies, websites and their servers have no memory. A cookie, like a key, enables swift passage from one place to the next. Without a cookie every time you open a new web page the server where that page is stored will treat you like a completely new visitor.

Websites typically use session cookies to ensure that you are recognised when you move from page to page within one site and that any information you have entered is remembered. For example, if an e-commerce site did not use session cookies then items placed in a shopping basket would disappear by the time you reach the checkout. You can choose to accept session cookies by changing the settings in your browser.

**Permanent / Persistent cookies**

Permanent or Persistent cookies are those cookies that are stored on user's computer and will not be deleted when browser is closed. Permanent cookies can retain user preferences for a particular website, allowing those preferences to be used in all future browsing sessions.

Permanent cookies can be used to identify individual users, so that the website can analyze the user's surfing behavior within the website. Cookies can also be used to provide site information such as the number of visitors, the average time spent on a particular page and generally the performance of the website. They are usually configured to keep track of users for a prolonged period of time.

Persistent cookies help websites remember your information and settings when you visit them in the future. This result in faster and more convenient access since, for example, you don't have to login again.

Besides authentication, other website features made possible by persistent cookies include: language selection, theme selection, menu preferences, internal site bookmarks or favorites, among many others. On your first visit, the website is presented in default mode. During your visit, you select your preferences and these preferences are remembered, through the use of the persistent cookie, the next time you visit the site.

For example, a website may offer its contents in different languages. On your first visit, you may choose to have the content delivered in French and the site may record that preference in a persistent cookie set on your browser. When you revisit that site it will use the cookie to ensure that the content is delivered in French. (We can experience this in google.com)

## 11.4 Uses of cookies

We primarily use cookies for web analysis and optimization of the user experience on the website. Cookies are set in order to detect discrepancies on the site, such as broken links and accessibility errors, and to analyze how users use the site.

Cookies are small text files, which enhance the user experience on a web site by allowing the system to recognize returning visitors, etc. Cookies are sent back and forth between your browser and a web server and contain information about:

- user preferences
- contents of cart
- if a user is logged in
- how the website is being used

A cookie is a passive file and cannot spread computer viruses or other malicious programs. Often cookies help analyze how the website is used, and the web editor can improve the user experience. In several cases, cookies may be necessary to provide a service. Cookies are mostly erased automatically from the browser when it is closed (so-called session cookies). Cookies can also be set with an expiration time so that data exists for a shorter or longer period (persistent cookies). Persistent cookies are usually stored on the hard disk. Moreover distinction is usually drawn between first-party cookies and third party cookies. First-party cookies are set by the page the user is visiting. Third-party cookies are set by a third party that has elements embedded on the page the user visits. Third-party cookies are set among other by web analytics programs. Following three explains some of the most basic uses of cookies.

**Web analytics cookie**

This cookie is made to find discrepancies so we can improve the user experience on our website, and contains a randomly generated ID that is used to recognize your browser when you read a page. The cookie contains no personal information and is used only for web analysis. The cookie is set to expire 1000 days after your last visit and is a persistent cookie.

**Cookie from Google Analytics**

We use Google Analytics to analyze how users use the website. The information the cookie collects about your use (traffic data, including your IP address) is transmitted to and stored on Google servers in the U.S.; Google uses this information to evaluate your use of the website, compiling reports on website activity and providing other services relating to website activity and internet usage. Google may also transfer this information to third parties if required by law or if third parties process the information on Google's behalf. Google will not associate your IP address with any other data and information held by Google.

**To reject the use of cookies**

You may refuse to use cookies on your computer by selecting the appropriate settings in your browser. Be aware that without cookies you may not be able to use all site features. Because a cookie is stored on your computer, it is always possible for you to view, modify or delete it. We hope you will allow the cookies we set, as they help us improve our website. If you do not want cookies, most new browsers let you select advanced cookie settings under Internet options and add this domain to the list of websites you want to block cookies from. You also have the possibility to delete individual cookies or cookies that your browser has saved. If you set your browser to refuse cookies, please be aware that functionality at different websites may not be working. If you do not want your visit to be recorded by Google Analytics, you can take advantage of Google's Opt-Out Browser Add-on. Be aware that your visits to other sites that use Google Analytics not will be registered, if you install this browser plug-in.

## 11.5 Creating cookies using servlet

The Servlet API provides **javax.servlet.http.Cookie** class that makes working with cookies very easy. New cookie instances can be created by using this class. The HTTP header details of the cookies are handled by the Servlet API.

To create a cookie, constructor of cookie class is used. This constructor is defined as:

*Cookie(String name, String value)*

As discussed earlier, a cookie requires name and value. In addition to that a cookie can have other parameters also. (Refer section 11.1). For example:

```
Cookie  ck = new Cookie("mycookie", "firstcookie");
```

The cookie class also has some member functions. Following are some of the methods to set/get values to/from attributes for invoking cookie object.

| Method | Signature | Description |
|---|---|---|
| setVersion( ) | void setVersion(String protocol) | Sets the version of the cookie protocol the cookie compiles with. |
| getVersion( ) | String getVersion( ) | Returns the version of the cookie protocol using which cookie is compiled. |
| setDomain( ) | void setDomain(String domain_name) | Specifies the domain restriction pattern. This cookie will be accessible only to those servers, which are specified in the domain pattern. |
| getDomain( ) | String getDomain( ) | Returns the domain name for which the cookie is set as accessible. |
| setPath( ) | void setPath(String URI/path) | Specifies the path for the cookie, which is the subset of URIs to which cookie is sent. By default, cookies are sent to the page that set the cookie and to all the pages in that directory or sub directory. |
| getPath( ) | String getPath( ) | Returns the specified path or URI to which the browser returns the cookie. |
| setMaxAge( ) | void setMaxAge(int seconds) | Specifies the life time of the cookie in terms of numbers of seconds. When this time elapsed, the cookie expires automatically. A **zero (0)** as value indicates the web browser to delete the cookie immediately and **negative** value indicates to delete when the web browser is closed. |
| getMaxAge( ) | int getMaxAge( ) | Returns the maximum age of the cookie in seconds. |
| setSecure( ) | void setSecure(boolean value) | Specifies the browser whether the cookie should be sent over a secure channel such as **HTTPS** or **SSL**. The default value is false. |

| | | |
|---|---|---|
| getSecure( ) | boolean getSecure( ) | Returns true or false as the value depending on the protocol used by the web browser. Returns true if web browser has used HTTPS or SSL and returns false for other standard protocols. |
| setComment( ) | void setComment( ) | Sets a value as the comment of the cookie. A comment describes the purpose of creating this cookie. |
| getComment( ) | String getComment( ) | Returns the a string containing comment, describing the purpose of creating this cookie. Returns **null** if no comment is set. |
| setValue( ) | String setValue( ) | Assigns or updates new value to the existing cookie. A new value can be anything the server chooses to send and usually does not make any sense to the web browser. |
| getValue( ) | String getValue( ) | Returns a string containing the value of the cookie. |
| getName( ) | String getName( ) | Returns the string containing the name of the cookie. Remember, the name of cookie cannot be changed after creation of that cookie. |
| setHttpOnly( ) | void setHttpOnly(boolean *value*) | Mark or unmark the cookie as HttpOnly. If the cookie is set as HttpOnly then client-side scripting cannot modify any attribute of cookie. |
| IsHttpOnly( ) | boolean isHttplOnly( ) | Returns true or false based on the value set for HttpOnly. |

## 11.6 Sending cookie to the client

A cookie is created by using constructor of cookie class, containing cookie name and a value. For example:

Cookie ck = new Cookie("mycookie", "firstcookie");

The Servlet wish to set cookies, must add their cookie to the response and send it to the client's browser. To add a cookie to client's browser use addCookie( ) method provided by **HttpServletResponse.** This method is defined as:

void addCookie(Cookie *obj*)

The specified cookie will be sent to client's browser as response. For example, above cookie **ck** can be added as:

*response.addCookie(ck);*

Where, *response* is the object of **HttpServletResponse**. More cookies can be added with subsequent calls to the addCookie( ). The cookies are sent using HTTP headers, therefore it is necessary to add them to the response object before sending any content.

**Note: However, the number of cookies per domain name varies from browser to browser. Usually, browsers are only allowed to accept 20 cookies from each web server, 300 cookies total and each cookie of 4 KB maximum.**

The following program create a cookie named **firstcookie** and sends to the client. Create a servlet named as **firstcookieservlet.java** and type following code in it.

```
import java.io.IOException;
import java.io.PrintWriter;
import javax.servlet.ServletException;
import javax.servlet.annotation.WebServlet;
import javax.servlet.http.Cookie;
import javax.servlet.http.HttpServlet;
import javax.servlet.http.HttpServletRequest;
import javax.servlet.http.HttpServletResponse;

@WebServlet(name = "FirstCookieServlet", urlPatterns = {"/FirstCookieServlet"})
public class FirstCookieServlet extends HttpServlet
{
  protected void processRequest(HttpServletRequest request, HttpServletResponse response)
      throws ServletException, IOException
  {
    response.setContentType("text/html;charset=UTF-8");
    PrintWriter out = response.getWriter( );
    Cookie firstcookie = new Cookie("mycookie","myvalue");
    firstcookie.setMaxAge(3600);
    response.addCookie(firstcookie);
    try
    {
      out.println("<html><head><title>creating first cookie using servlet</title><head>");
      out.println("<body>");
      out.println("<b>Cookie is created on client machine</b>");
      out.println("</br></br><b>Cookie name is : " + firstcookie.getName( ) + "</b>");
      out.println("</br></br><b>Cookie value is : " + firstcookie.getValue( ) + "</b>");
      out.println("</body></html>");
    }
    finally
    {
      out.close( );
    }
  }
}
```

## 11.7 Retrieving cookie

Cookies are always returned as fields added to the HTTP request headers. To retrieve specific cookie, the **getCookies( )** method of **HttpServletRequest**. The getCookies( ) method returns an array of cookie object. This array can then be searched for specific cookie. This method is defined as:

*Cookie[ ] getCookies( )*

**Note: A single cookie cannot be retrieved, we need to retrieve all the available cookies of current session and search for specific cookie.**

Following servlet demonstrates Retrieval of all the session cookies when at the expiration of session.

First of all, create an **index.jsp** page containing two textboxes to retrieve cookie name and cookie value as follows.

```
<%@page contentType="text/html" pageEncoding="UTF-8"%>
<!DOCTYPE html>
<html>
  <head>
    <meta http-equiv="Content-Type" content="text/html; charset=UTF-8">
    <title>JSP Page</title>
  </head>
  <body>
    <h1>Cookie demonstration</h1>
    <form method="post" action="RetrieveCookieServlet">
        <label for="name">Enter Cookie name : </label>
      <input type="text" id="txtname"/>
      <br><br><label for="name">Enter Cookie value : </label>
      <input type="text" id="txtvalue"/>
      <br><br><input type="submit" value="Create"/>
  </form>
   </body>
</html>
```

above index.jsp creates a following GUI. Enter the cookie name and cookie value in the data entry fields as shown in diagram. Click "Create" button to create that cookie.

Now create RetrieveCookieServlet.java and update it with following code.

```
import java.io.IOException;
import java.io.PrintWriter;
import javax.servlet.ServletException;
import javax.servlet.annotation.WebServlet;
import javax.servlet.http.Cookie;
import javax.servlet.http.HttpServlet;
import javax.servlet.http.HttpServletRequest;
import javax.servlet.http.HttpServletResponse;
import javax.servlet.http.HttpSession;

@WebServlet(name = "RetrieveCookieServlet", urlPatterns = {"/RetrieveCookieServlet"})
public class RetrieveCookieServlet extends HttpServlet
{
  public int count=0;
  protected void processRequest(HttpServletRequest request, HttpServletResponse response)
        throws ServletException, IOException
  {
    response.setContentType("text/html;charset=UTF-8");
    PrintWriter out = response.getWriter();
    HttpSession ses1 = request.getSession(true);
    String n = request.getParameter("txtname");
    String v = request.getParameter("txtvalue");
    Cookie firstcookie = new Cookie(n,v);
    response.addCookie(firstcookie);
```

```
        count++;
        if(count % 5 == 0)
        {
          out.println("<h3>Cookie Name\tCookie Value</h3>");
            Cookie retrieve[ ] = request.getCookies( );
            for(int i=0;i<retrieve.length;i++)
            {
            out.println(retrieve[i].getName( ) + "\t" + retrieve[i].getValue( ));
            }
            out.println("<h3>Session ID is : " + ses1.getId() + "</h3>");
            ses1.invalidate( );
        }
          out.close();
          response.sendRedirect("index.jsp");
        }
    }
```

Above servlet creates a new session on each 5 cookies created. At the end it shows all 5 created cookies with cookie name and cookie value. At the end it invalidates the session. Following screenshot demonstrates the output.

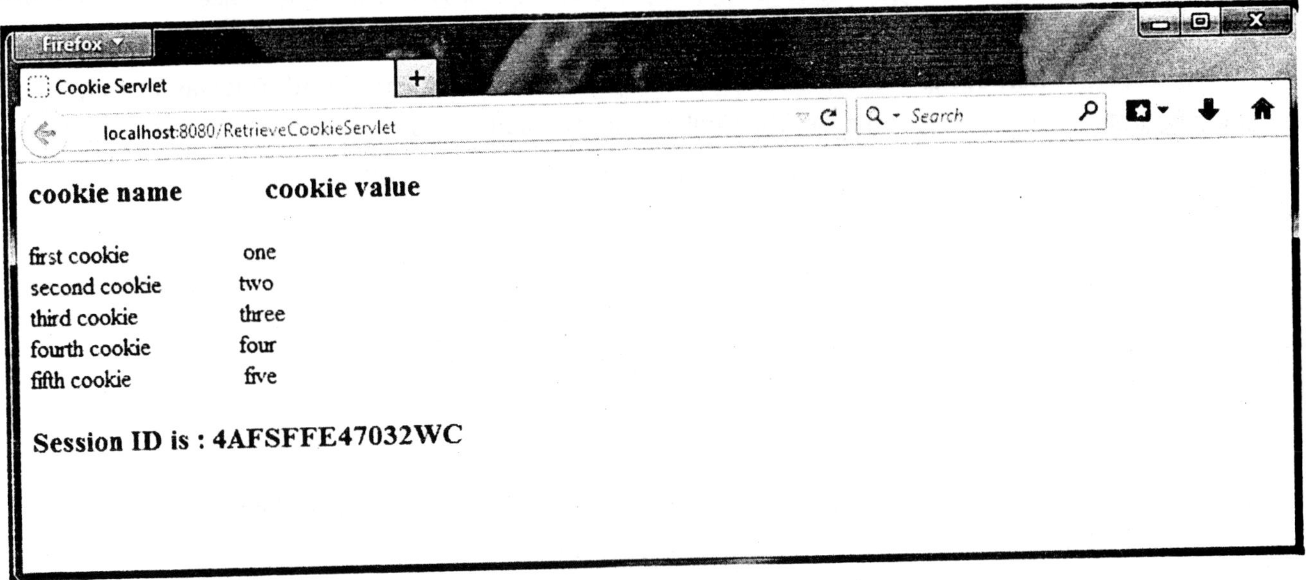


## 11.8 Expiration of cookie

Depending on the purpose of the cookie and the data it holds, it is essential to make a decision whether to keep the cookie alive or just expire it. Since anyone using the browser will have the cookie sent on their behalf, it may appear to be the same user when in reality it is not. This generally happens during surfing in internet cafes, school or college computer labs.

If the cookie holds user identification that allows the access of sensitive data or allows modifying (for e.g. web based email service) then such cookies should expire after a small period of time. If the cookie holds the simple information (for e.g. user's preferences, communication languages) then such cookies will not be harmful if they remain on client's system.

## 11.9 Destroying cookie

In above section, we discussed the need of expiring the cookies. Now, to destroy a cookie the following two steps need to be performed.

- Set the cookie's value to **null**
- set the maximum age of cookie to **zero**

The reason that both the above actions needs to be carried out, is that by simply setting the expiration to zero will not change its value until the web browser is closed. Refer following statements.

To understand how to delete a cookie, create a new cookie instance having the same name as the cookie that needs to be deleted and set its maximum age to zero [0]. Add this cookie to the response object and the matching cookie on the client will be deleted. Refer following code.

```
Cookie ck = new Cookie("mycookie", " ");   ← setting value as null
ck.setMaxAge(0);   ← setting max age to zero
response.addCookie(ck);
```

This will set the cookie named as **ck** to null and makes its max age to zero. This informs the web browser that the cookie existed in the past and consequenly triggers the cookie removal mechanism in a browser.

## 11.10 HTTPOnly cookie

One of the more popular targets for cross-site scripting [XSS] attacks is the session/transient cookie. This cookie can be enabled an attacker to impersonate the user, get access to personal information or even the bank account details.

Originally in **Microsoft's Internet Explorer 6** the concept of HttpOnly cookie was introduced. This was logically implemented by setting flag in cookie response. The similar concept is added by Java also in **servlet 3.0**.

Java provides a method setHttpOnly( ) to set a cookie as HttpOnly. This method is defined as:

void setHttpOnly(boolean *httponly*)

When this is method is invoked for a cookie object as its boolean value is set to **true** then web browser forbids any access to it from client side scripting code. Hence, any scripting code will not be able to read or modify the information parameters stored in cookie. Default value of this method will be **false**. For example,

```
Cookie ck = new Cookie("mycookie", "firstcookie");
ck.setHttpOnly(true);
```

We can also determine whether a cookie is set to httponly or not by invoking isHttpOnly( ). This method is defined as:

boolean isHttpOnly( )

This method returns **true** if the cookie is set to httponly otherwise returns **false**. For example,

```
boolean res = ck.isHttpOnly( );
```

Returns **true**, w.r.to above created cookie object '**ck**'.

*****

# Chapter 12

# Sessions

In previous chapter we get some essential information about servlet and working of servlet. And we get the working of web applications through **HttpServletRequest** and **HttpServletResponse** objects. We know that web applications are typically a series of hyperlinks, arranged in a specific manner to produce meaningful results. The procedure of requesting and responding are done from client and server, respectively. The HTTP protocol is the foundation of this communication between client and server.

The HTTP protocol is a **stateless** protocol and hence there are numbers of problems that arises from this fact, because even if a user sends a sequence of requests from the same browser, the server is not able to tell that those are from the same user. This makes applications like **shopping carts** very problematic: when you add an entry to your cart, how does the server know what you have added earlier? When you move from the page where you specify what you want to buy to the page that takes your credit card number and shipping address, how does the server know what is in your cart?

Servlets provide an outstanding technical solution: the `HttpSession` API. This is a high-level interface that allows the server to "remember" a set of information relevant to a particular user's on-going transaction, so that it can retrieve this information to handle any future requests from the same user.

Because of HTTP's stateless nature, a visitor who navigates through a website cannot be tracked. Every request from the visitor's web browser is treated as a new request from the new client, though it is sent from same visitor and web browser.

This stateless nature also has some advantages that strengthen the use of HTTP protocol for developers. Such as:

- Keeps the protocol simple and straightforward.
- Consumes fewer resources on the web server.
- Can support simultaneous visitors, as it is not required to maintain client credentials and connections.

Whenever, we need to remember some information about what the user does, we start a new HttpSession and attach (or store) the information to this session. Then behind the scene, the **Tomcat server** will assign a unique "session ID" to the session and send this id to the browser, asking the browser to send back the id in any future requests. This way, the Tomcat server will be able to trace the requests coming from the same user, and let you retrieve whatever has been stored to handle the user's requests.

## 12.1 What are sessions?

Sessions are great for storing temporary data about the visitors. Sessions are used when the website does not want this data to be accessible external to the web server. The sessions and cookies share a relationship between them and serve for the purpose of maintaining continuity of visitor's navigations.

The servlet container uses **HttpSession** interface to create a session between an HTTP client and an HTTP server. The session persists for a specified time period, across more than one connection or page request from the user. A session usually corresponds to one user, who may visit a site many times. The server can maintain a session in many ways such as using cookies or rewriting URLs.

This interface allows a servlet to:

- View and manipulate information about a session, such as the session identifier, creation time, and last accessed time
- Bind objects to sessions, allowing user information to persist across multiple user connections

## 12.2 Life cycle of HTTP session

The following steps explains life cycle of HttpSesion.

- A visitor makes a request for a resource, using a web browser, to web server.
- The web server delivers the authentication module that result in the visitor's web browser. (such as, displaying a login page)
- The visitor enters valid username and password, which is then returned to the web server.
- The web server returns a valid SESSION ID that allows this visitor to be uniquely identified. (**This starts a new session**)
- Now, the visitor's web browser can send any number of requests to the web server. These all requests are verified using the SESSION ID and hence, the visitor's navigations through the website get continuity.
- At last, the **session expires** on logging off or explicitly closing the web browser (even without logging off).

Remember, there are three **characteristics of session management**.

- Session state must be stored
- Carry an identifier that uniquely identifies session (i.e. SESSION ID)
- Session must have a timeout.

## 12.3 Creating session

Every client side java application provides a public **interface HttpSession** associated with **javax.servlet.http** package. The servlet container uses this interface to create a session between an HTTP client and an HTTP server. The session persists for a specified time period, across more than one connection or page request from the user. A session usually corresponds to one user, who may visit a site many times. The server can maintain a session in many ways such as using cookies or rewriting URLs.

This interface allows servlet to:

- View and manipulate information about a session, such as the session identifier, creation time, and last accessed time
- Bind objects to sessions, allowing user information to persist across multiple user connections

As discussed, HttpSession is an interface hence it **do not have any visible constructor** to create its object. We need to call **getSession( )** method of **HttpServletRequest** class to obtain client's current HTTP session. This method is defined as:

*public HttpSession getSession(boolean create_new)*

This method returns current HTTP session controls to specified HttpSession object. The boolean value specifies whether to create a new session or not. If **false** is specified then no session will be created in case there is no sessions existed on client and **true** specifies to create a new session in case there is no session existed on client. For example,

*HttpSession mysession = request.getSession(true);*

The following program demonstrates creation of session. This also detects whether the user has visited this page first time or has visited earlier also.

```
package Servlet;

import java.io.IOException;
import java.io.PrintWriter;
import javax.servlet.ServletException;
import javax.servlet.http.HttpServlet;
import javax.servlet.http.HttpServletRequest;
import javax.servlet.http.HttpServletResponse;
import javax.servlet.http.HttpSession;

public class CalcVisits extends HttpServlet
{
   private int count=1;
   @Override
   protected void doGet(HttpServletRequest request, HttpServletResponse response)
        throws ServletException, IOException
   {
      PrintWriter pw = response.getWriter();
      response.setContentType("text/html;charset=UTF-8");
      HttpSession ses1 = request.getSession(true);
      if(ses1.isNew())
      {
         pw.println("This is the first time you are visiting this page");
      }
      else
      {
         pw.println("Welcome back to this page");
         synchronized(this)
         {
            pw.println("You have visited this page " + (++count) + "time(s)");
         }
      }
   }
}
```

In above program **ses1** is the HttpSession object obtained by getSession( ) method. The isNew( ) method returns **true** if the session is newly created and for an existing session it returns **false**. The page will display messages along with visit count according to the correctness of condition.

We need to modify the index.jsp page as follows:

```
<%@page contentType="text/html" pageEncoding="UTF-8"%>
<!DOCTYPE html>
<html>
  <head>
    <meta http-equiv="Refresh" content="0; URL="CalcVisits">
  </head>
  <body>     </body>
</html>
```

Compile, build and run above servlet. You will get following output:

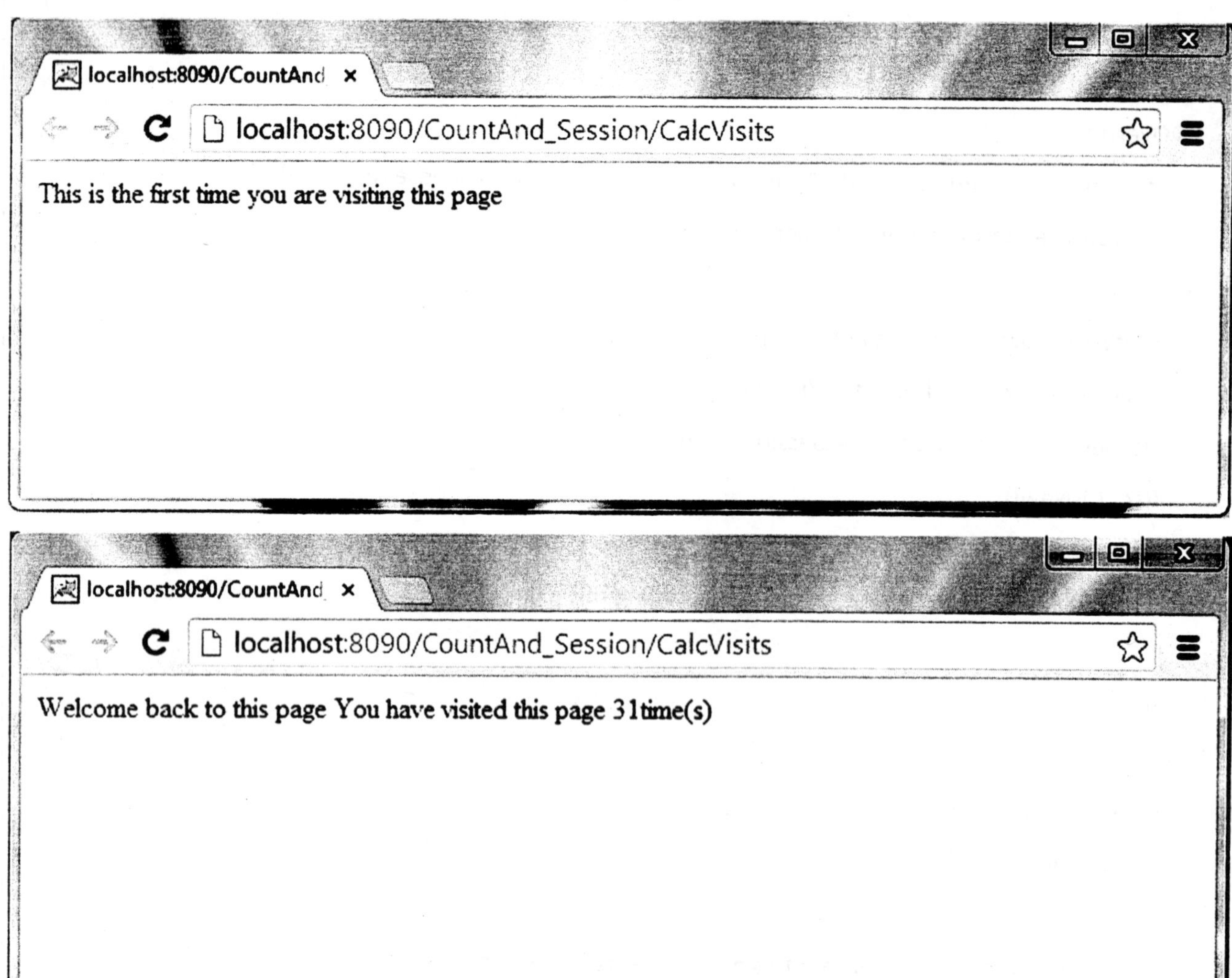


## 12.4 Destroying session

It is necessary to destroy a session when the visitor logout to block the access of visitor's resources. This is simply done by calling **invalidate( )** method of HttpSession object. For example, *ses1.invalidate( );*

Following program demonstrates invalidation of a session on each fifth visit.

```
import java.io.IOException;
import java.io.PrintWriter;
import javax.servlet.ServletException;
import javax.servlet.http.HttpServlet;
import javax.servlet.http.HttpServletRequest;
import javax.servlet.http.HttpServletResponse;
import javax.servlet.http.HttpSession;

public class DestroySessionServlet extends HttpServlet
{
   private int count=0;
   @Override
   protected void doGet(HttpServletRequest request, HttpServletResponse response)
        throws ServletException, IOException
   {
     PrintWriter pw = response.getWriter();
     response.setContentType("text/html; charset=UTF-8");
     synchronized(this)
     {
         HttpSession ses1 = request.getSession(true);
         if(ses1.isNew())
         {
                  pw.println("<html><body>");
                  pw.println("<h1>Sesson ID is :" + ses1.getId() + "</h1>");
                  pw.println("</br></br>You visited this page  " + (++count) + "  time(s)");
                  pw.println("</body></html>");
         }
         else
         {
                  pw.println("<html><body>");
                  pw.println("<h1>Sesson ID is :" + ses1.getId() + "</h1>");
                  pw.println("</br></br>You visited this page  " + (++count) + "  time(s)");
                   pw.println("</body></html>");
                  if(count%5==0)
                  {
                           ses1.invalidate( );
                  }
         }
     }  // end of synchronized
   }     //end of doGet( )
  }      //end of class
```

Compile, build and run above servlet. We will get following output.

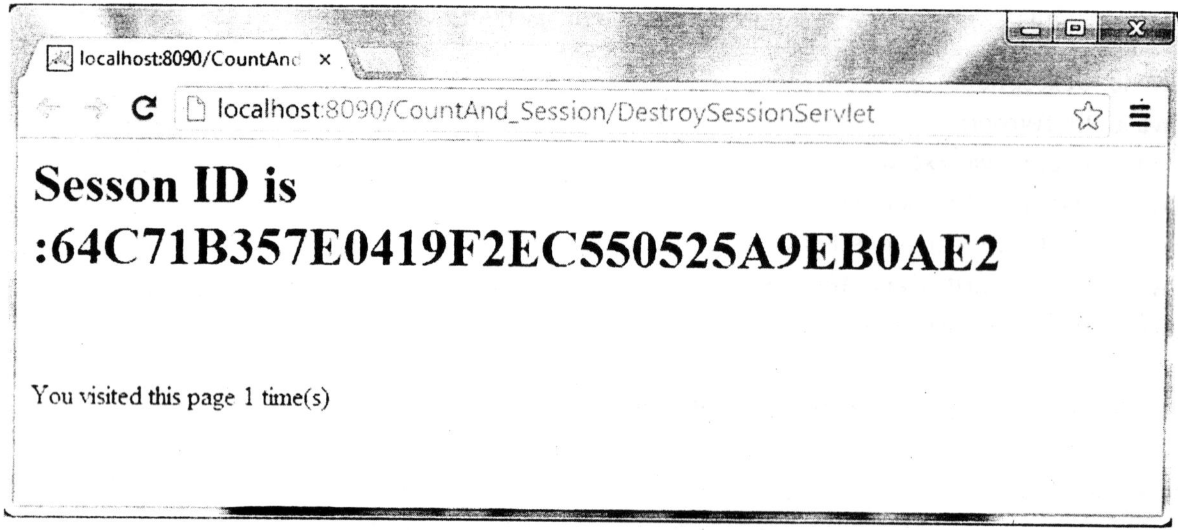

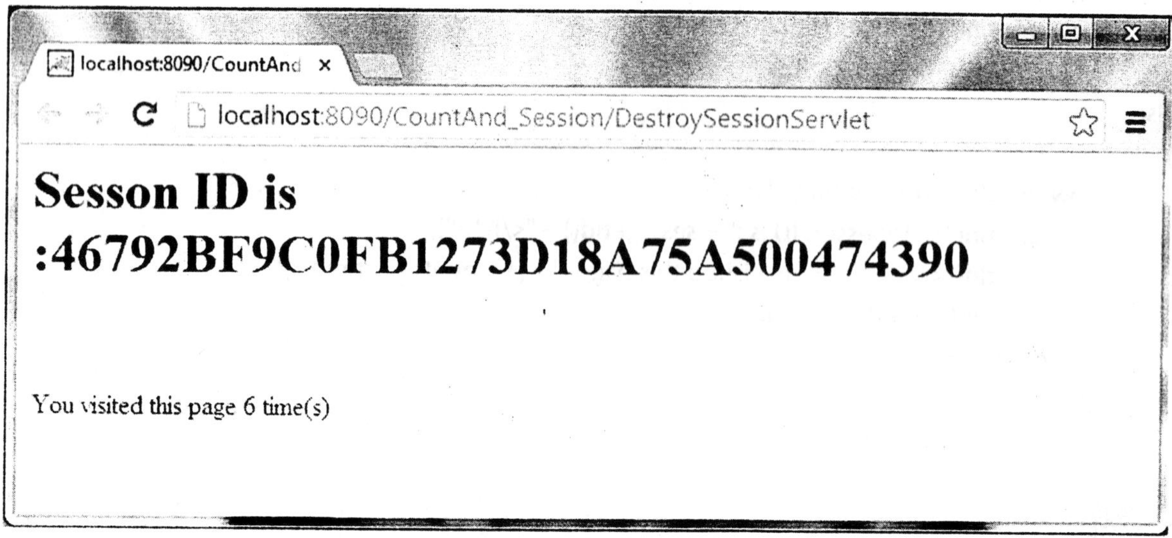


Note that, for five visits the same session and Session ID remains and for next five visits the previous session expires and new session with new session ID starts.

## 12.5 Managing session's lifetime

The HttpSession object lives on the web server and therefore, they are automatically associated with the request, which is sent by the client through cookies or URL rewriting. HttpSession object has a built-in data structure that allows storing any number of keys and associated values. There are some methods which are used to manage a session's lifetime and for storing and retrieving data.

- **getAttribute( )**

Returns the attribute bound to a specified name in current session. Returns **null** if no object is found bounded to the name. This method is define as:

*Object getAttribute(String control_name)*

For example,

*String fname = (String) mysession.getAttribute("txtfirstname");*

- **getAttributeNames( )**

Returns an *Enumeration* of String objects containing the names of all the objects bound to this session. This method is defined as :

*Enumeration getAttributeNames( )*

For example,

*Enumeration en = mysession.getAttributeNames( )*

- **getCreationTime( )**

Returns the time when this session was created, measured in milliseconds since midnight January 1, 1970 GMT. This method is defined as :

*long getCreationTime( )*

For example,

*Date cr_date = (Date)mysession.getCreationTime( )*

Here, returned **long** value is casted into **Date** object to get the date related retuned long milliseconds.

- **getId( )**

Returns a string containing the unique identifier assigned to this session. The identifier is assigned by the servlet container and is implementation dependent. This method is defined as :

*String getId( )*

For example,

*String ses_id = mysession.getId( );*

- **getLastAccessedTime( )**

Returns the last time the client sent a request associated with this session, as the number of milliseconds since midnight January 1, 1970 GMT, and marked by the time the container received the request. This method is defined as:

*long getLastAccessedTime( )*

For example,

*Date last_acc_date = (Date)mysession.getLastAccessedTime( );*

Type casting to Date is again required here to cast returned long milliseconds into related date.

- **getSevletContext( )**

Returns the ServletContext to which this session belongs. This method is defined as :

*ServletContext getServletContext( )*

For example,

ServletContext sc = mysession.getSevletContext( );

- **seMaxInactiveInterval( )**

Specifies the time, in seconds, between client requests before the servlet container will invalidate this session. A negative time indicates the session should never timeout. This method is defined as :

*void setMaxInactiveInterval(int interval_time)*

For example,

*mysession.setMaxInactiveInterval(10000);*

- **getMaxInactiveInterval( )**

Returns the maximum time interval, in seconds, that the servlet container will keep this session open between client accesses. After this interval, the servlet container will invalidate the session. The maximum time interval can be set with the `setMaxInactiveInterval` method. A negative time indicates the session should never timeout. This method is defined as :

*int getMaxInactiveInterval( )*

For example,

*int max_intvl = mysession.getMaxInactiveInterval( );*

- **getValue( )**

Returns the value of specified name in current session. This method is updated and replace by *getAttribute( )*. This method is defined as :

*Object getValue(String name)*

For example,

*String val = (String)mysession.getValue("txtfirstname");*

- **setAttribute( )**

Binds an object to this session, using the name specified. If an object of the same name is already bound to the session, the object is replaced. If the value passed in is null, this has the same effect as calling removeAttribute( ). This method is defined as :

*void setAttribute(String name, Object value)*

For example,

*mysession.setAttribute("fname","txtfirstname");*

After this statement, if we use *fname* in a statement then It ultimately refers *txtfirstname*.

- **removeAttribute( )**

Removes the object bound with the specified name from this session. If the session does not have an object bound with the specified name, this method does nothing.

After this method executes, and if the object implements HttpSessionBindingListener, the container calls HttpSessionBindingListener.valueUnbound. The container then notifies any HttpSessionAttributeListeners in the web application. This method is defined as :

*void removeAttribute(String name)*

For example,

*mysession.removeAttribute("fname");*

This will remove the object *fname* bounded with any session object.

- **invalidate( )**

Invalidates any session and unbinds any objects connected to it. This method is defined as :

*void invalidate( )*

For example

*mysession.invalidate( );*

- **isNew( )**

Returns true if session is newly created but the client has yet not joined. Returns false is session already exists and client is already joined. This method is defined as :

*boolean isNew( )*

For example,

*boolean result = mysession.isNew( );*

**Note: Most of the above methods throws IllegalStateException if that method is called on an already invalidated session.**

## 12.6 Session tracking methods

Session tracking is one of the important roles played by java servlet. HTTP is a "stateless" protocol: each time a client retrieves a Web page, the client opens a separate connection to the Web server and the server does not automatically maintain contextual information about the client. Even with servers that support persistent (keep-alive) HTTP connections and keep sockets open for multiple client requests that occur in rapid succession, there is no built-in support for maintaining contextual information. This lack of context causes a number of difficulties. For example, then clients at an online store add an item to their shopping carts, how does the server know what's already in the carts? Similarly, when clients decide to proceed to checkout, how can the server determine which previously created shopping carts are theirs? These questions seem very simple, yet, because of the inadequacies of HTTP, answering them is surprisingly complicated.

There are three typical solutions to this problem: **cookies**, **URL rewriting**, **hidden form fields and using SSL**. The following subs sections quickly summarize what would be required if you had to implement session tracking yourself (without using the built-in session-tracking API) for each of the three ways.

- **Cookies**

Cookies preset a convenient way of store state information on a visitor's hard disk. A cookie is a web-server generated container that can automatically store small amount of state information on the visitor's hard disk, through a request to the visitor's browser.

When the cookies are generated with such informations, each time when visitor's browser communicates with the web server, that has sets the cookie, it automatically returns the contents of cookie back to the web server in its request along with other requesting data.

Hence, cookies provide a simple method of maintaining state and session information between a visitor's browser and web server with minimum efforts. Using cookies in this manner is an excellent solution and is the most widely used approach for session handling. Still, it is nice that servlets have a higher-level API that handles all this plus the following tedious tasks:

- Extracting the cookie that stores the session identifier from the other cookies (there may be many cookies, after all).
- Determining when idle sessions have expired, and reclaiming them.
- Associating the hash tables with each request.
- Generating the unique session identifiers

This may not be an effective way because many time web browser does not support a cookie, so I would not recommend to use this procedure to maintain the sessions.

- **URL rewriting**

  With URL rewriting approach, the client appends some additional data at the end of each URL, which logically identifies the session for web server. In other words, URL rewriting stores session details as part of the URL itself.

  For example, consider the following link of a web page:

  *<a href = "bookshop/logincheck.html">*

  This can be rewritten with session id as:

  *<a href = "bookshop/logincheck.html;sessionid=KSJDFW902921ISDSA">*

  When the user clicks the link, the modified URL is sent to the server as part of the client's request. The web container identifies ***KSJDFW902921ISDSA*** as session id and saves it for obtaining the proper HttpSession object for this client.

  URL rewriting is **a better way** to maintain sessions and works for the browsers when they don't support cookies but here drawback is that you would have generate every URL dynamically to assign a session ID though page is simple static HTML page.

- **Hidden Form Fields**

  In commercial applications occasionally it is necessary to return to the web server some client information, which is bounded specifically to the application running in the client's browser. For example, which command button is clicked by the visitor? This is normally done by using hidden fields on the form. A hidden field is a simple textbox which is invisible to the visitor and which can never be modified by the visitor. The value of hidden field is filled with the name of button which is clicked. When the page is submitted, the visitor's browser returns the hidden field's value and name back to the web server with all other information. The same procedure can be used to store SESSION ID and web server can get the session id from it. The hidden fields can be created as:

  *<input type = "hidden" name = "hid_field1" value = " ">*

  When data is submitted to web server, the servlet can run the following statement and get the value of hidden field.

```
public void doPost(HttpServletRequest request, HttpServletResponse response) throws .......
{
        String val = request.getParameter("hid_field1");
        ......
        ......
}
```

- **Using SSL [Secure Socket Layer]**

  *The SSL was introduced by Netscape in Netscape Navigator version 1.* The SSL is a protocol that sits between application level protocol [HTTP] and the low level transport protocol [TCP/IP]. It handles the details of the security management using public key cryptography to encrypt all client-server communication.

  The Secure Sockets Layer (SSL) protocol uses a combination of public-key and symmetric-key encryption. Symmetric-key encryption is much faster than public-key encryption; however, public-key encryption provides better authentication techniques. An SSL session always begins with an exchange of messages called the SSL handshake. The handshake allows the server to authenticate itself to the client by using public-key techniques, and then allows the client and the server to cooperate in the creation of symmetric keys used for rapid encryption, decryption, and tamper detection during the session that follows. Optionally, the handshake also allows the client to authenticate itself to the server.

  The steps involved in the working of SSL are as follows (note that the following steps assume the use of the cipher suites)

1. The client sends the server the client's SSL version number, cipher settings, session-specific data, and other information that the server needs to communicate with the client using SSL.
2. The server sends the client the server's SSL version number, cipher settings, session-specific data, and other information that the client needs to communicate with the server over SSL. The server also sends its own certificate, and if the client is requesting a server resource that requires client authentication, the server requests the client's certificate.
3. The client uses the information sent by the server to authenticate the server. If the server cannot be authenticated, the user is warned of the problem and informed that an encrypted and authenticated connection cannot be established. If the server can be successfully authenticated, the client proceeds to step 4.
4. Using all data generated in the handshake thus far, the client (with the cooperation of the server, depending on the cipher being used) creates the pre-master secret for the session, encrypts it with the server's public key (obtained from the server's certificate, sent in step 2), and then sends the encrypted pre-master secret to the server.
5. If the server has requested client authentication (an optional step), the client also signs another piece of data that is unique to this handshake and known by both the client and server. In this case, the client sends both the signed data and the client's own certificate to the server along with the encrypted pre-master secret.
6. If the server has requested client authentication, the server attempts to authenticate the client. If the client cannot be authenticated, the session ends. If the client can be successfully authenticated, the server uses its private key to decrypt the pre-master secret, and then performs a series of steps (which the client also performs, starting from the same pre-master secret) to generate the master secret.
7. Both the client and the server use the master secret to generate the session keys, which are symmetric keys used to encrypt and decrypt information exchanged during the SSL session and to verify its integrity (that is, to detect any changes in the data between the time it was sent and the time it is received over the SSL connection).
8. The client sends a message to the server informing it that future messages from the client will be encrypted with the session key. It then sends a separate (encrypted) message indicating that the client portion of the handshake is finished.

9. The server sends a message to the client informing it that future messages from the server will be encrypted with the session key. It then sends a separate (encrypted) message indicating that the server portion of the handshake is finished.

10. The working of SSL is now complete and the session begins. The client and the server use the session keys to encrypt and decrypt the data they send to each other and to validate its integrity.

11. This is the normal operation condition of the secure channel. At any time, due to internal or external stimulus (either automation or user intervention), either side may renegotiate the connection, in which case, the process repeats itself.

In SSL, sessions are used to describe an ongoing relationship between two entities. Each SSL connection involves one session at a time, but that session may be used on many connections between those entities, simultaneously or sequentially. The session used on a connection may also be replaced by a different session. Sessions are created, or rejoined, as part of the SSL handshaking protocol. Sessions may be invalidated due to policies affecting security or resource usage, or by an application explicitly calling `invalidate`. Session management policies are typically used to tune performance.

*****

# Chapter 13
# Java Server Pages (JSP)

Since modern enterprise applications are moving from two-tier to three-tier and n-tier application architecture. Hence, a new way of separating the presentation (GUI) logic from the business logic is required that helps directly to embed Java code in static HTML pages. JSP provides solution for such situation where the presentation logic is provided by HTML tags and the business logic for dynamic content is handled by JSP.

This chapter begins by providing an introduction to JSP technology, and then we learn about new features of JSP that separates JSP from servlet. Apart from that, we will study the different architectures of JSP pages along with life cycle of a JSP page and also explore the various JSP basic tags, implicit objects and action tags.

## 13.1 What is JSP?

JSP stands for Java Server Pages, which is a Java based technology developed by SUN Microsystems to simplify the development of dynamic pages. JSP is a server side technology and JSP pages are processed on a web server in the *JSP servlet engine*. JSP serves as an advancement of the Java servlet technology.

Before the arrival of JSP pages, Servlets were used by Java programmers to provide dynamic content to clients. In case of servlets, both the processing of requests and the generation of responses were handled by a single servlet class. Servlets usually contain HTML code embedded in Java code. Therefore, programmers who created servlets needed a thorough knowledge of Java programming and basic knowledge about HTML programming. In addition, servlets do not separate the presentation (GUI) logic from the business logic in the application.

JSP greatly simplifies the process of creating dynamic web pages. There is a clear separation between the presentation logic (provided by HTML tags) and business logic (provided by embedded Java code). This separation allows you to divide the tasks between the designers and programmers having different skills. This means that, in case of JSP, designers can code for dynamic contents to implement the business logic. As far as their execution is concerned, JSP pages provide all the benefits of servlets. Apart from this, JSP pages are easier to write than servlets. *JSP pages are translated into a servlet during compilation* and the response is sent to a client by generating dynamic content in the form of the servlet.

Various versions of JSP have been released since the development of JSP technology. JSP 2.1 is the latest release. On each new release, several new features are added to simplify the development. Here is a small list of new features of JSP 2.1.

- includes Java Standard Tag Library (JSTL)
- includes Java Server Faces (JSF)
- new EL syntax is included
- advanced use of annotations to configure and include resources and environment data
- removed writing entries in Deployment Descriptor files (DD)
- introduces the concept of qualified functions
- includes support for literal expressions and enumerations in EL
- includes support for Property Resolver Application Programming Interface (PR – API)
- JavaBean methods are now being referenced by using EL and invoked by using the Method Binding APIs.

## 13.2 Why to use JSP?

Till now we have discussed dozens of advantages of JSP technology. Then also still there are some impressive points that can even more amaze you to work will JSP. They are:

- Nobody can borrow the code
- Faster loading of Pages
- No browser compatibility issues
- Easy compilation
- JSP elements in HTML / XML tags

## 13.3 Advantages of JSP over Servlet

JSP provides many advantages of Java servlet. It provides a better server side scripting support as compare to Java servlet. Java programmers can create servlets easily, but handling Java code is always a difficult job for web page designers. As discussed earlier, a JSP page has HTML code, and some Java code can be embedded with the HTML code. You can use the Java code to add dynamic contents to the page. The Java code is embedded by using different JSP constructors.

Here are some reasons that justify, why to prefer JSP over Servlet.

- Allows you to place static code and components symmetrically in a web page. These static web pages are designed by web designers by using HTML code. Designing static web pages by using servlets requires a good knowledge of Java, but web designers may not be comfortable with Java programming constructs. In addition, while using servlets, you have to enclose HTML code in the **PrintWriter's** *println( )* method, which disables all IDE support for generating HTML content. Therefore, using JSP is always easier than using servlet for the same HTML output.
- Facilitates automatic recompilation of a JSP page by a web container for any update in the code; whereas, you need to recompile your servlet for every single change in the source code.
- Allows you to access a JSP page directly as a simple HTML page; whereas, servlets cannot be accessed directly and have to be first mapped in the *web.xml* file
- Allows you to create a JSP page by using a simple HTML template and the JSP page is automatically handled by the JSP container. However, in servlets you need to provide the Java code to generate dynamic HTML pages.

All these advantages makes it a very popular technology to use in the presentation (GUI) logic of any web application.

## 13.4 Architecture of JSP page

According to JSP specifications, there are two approaches to build web applications using JSP. These approaches are known as JSP Model-I and JSP Model-II architecture.

- **JSP Model-I architecture**

In JSP Model-I architecture, a web browser directly accesses JSP pages of a web container. These JSP pages interact with JavaBean in an application. When a client sends a request from a JSP page, the response is sent back to the client depending on which hyperlinks are selected or which request parameters are invoked by the client request.

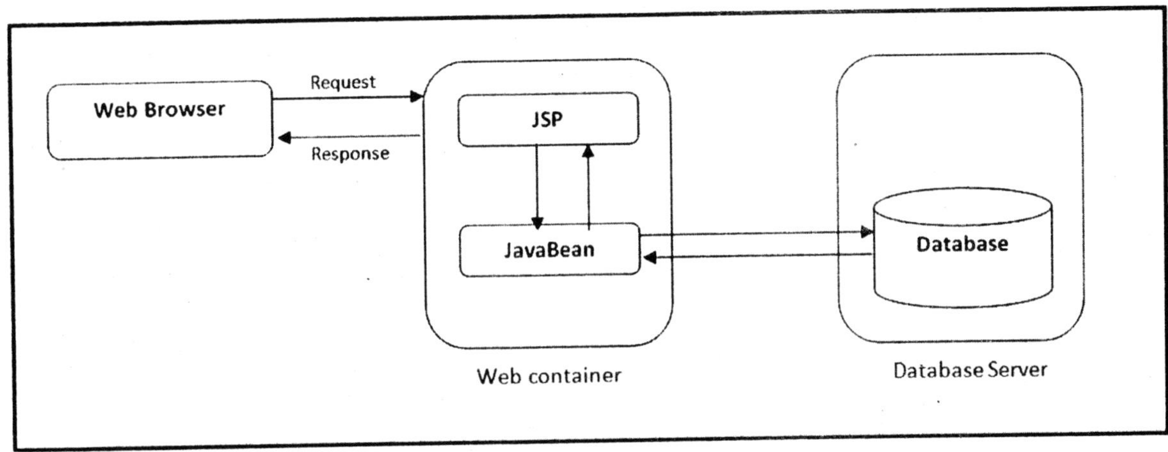


If the generated response requires accessing a database, the JSP page uses a JavaBean, which retrieves the required data from the database. Above figure shows the architecture of JSP Model-I.

- **JSP Model-II architecture**

In the JSP Mode-II architecture, servlets are used by a web browser to communicate with a JSP page. The servlets are positioned between the web browser and the JSP pages, and they act as a controller to dispatch requests to the next requested JSP page based on the requested *URL and input parameters*. The servlet also creates JavaBean instances, if they are required by the JSP page to store data. The controller servlet then decides which JSP page to forward to as a response, based on the client request.

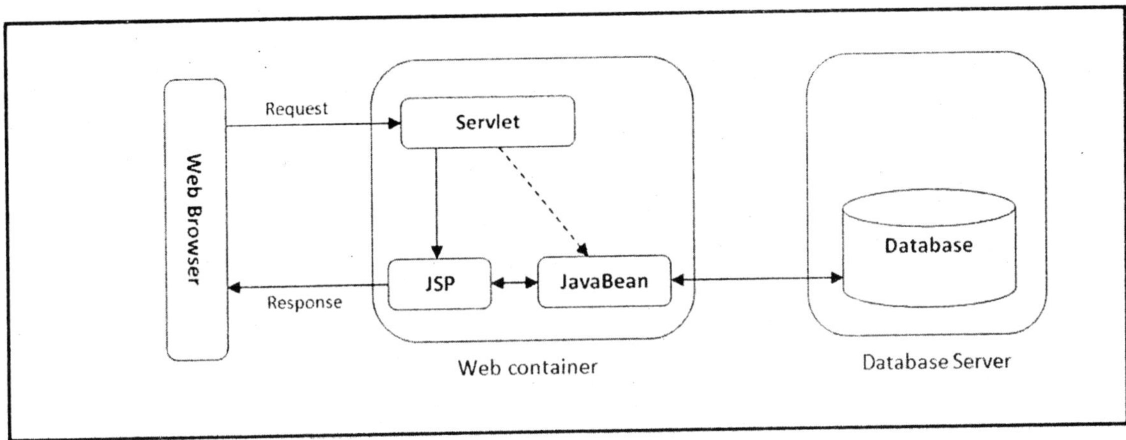


A JavaBean invokes the database server if data is needed from database. Above figure shows the architecture of JSP Model-II.

## 13.5 Life Cycle of a JSP page

A JSP page also follows a specific stage by stage process that creates its life cycle. The life cycle of a JSP page is divided into five stages.

- page translation stage
- compilation stage
- loading & initializing stage
- request handling stage
- destroying stage

Let's now discuss each stage of the JSP life cycle one by one.

- **page translation stage**

During the translation phase each type of data in a JSP page is treated differently. Static data is transformed into code that will emit the data into the response stream i.e. a web container converts the JSP document into an equivalent Java code (i.e. into servlet).

In page translation stage, the web container performs following operations:

- locates the requested JSP page
- validates the syntactic correctness of the JSP page
- interprets the standard JSP directives, actions and custom actions used in the JSP page
- writes the source code of the equivalent servlet for the JSP page

After the page has been translated into a servlet, all the requests for that JSP pages are served by its corresponding servlet class. This servlet class works similar to any other simple servlet. The translation of JSP is done automatically by the web server. JSP page translation occurs only when necessary, i.e., at some point before the page has to serve its first request. This process is also performed when the JSP source code is updated and the page is deployed. A web container can decide when the translation should occur.

If there is any error in the translation of the page, the container raises the 500 (internal server error) exception and if a change occurs in JSP page, all the stages of the JSP life cycle are executed again.

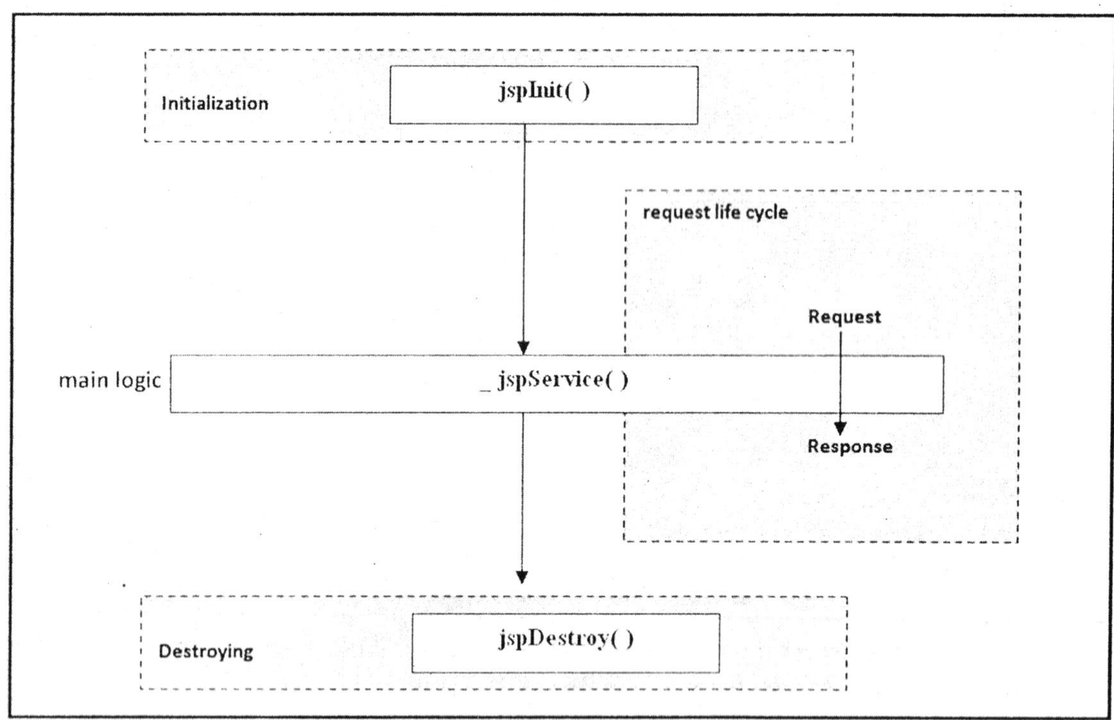


- **compilation stage**

The page translation stage is followed by the compilation stage of the JSP life cycle. In compilation stage, the Java source code for the corresponding servlet is compiled by the JSP container. The container converts the source code into Java bytecode. After the class file is generated, the container decides to either discard the code or retain it for debugging. Generally, most containers discard the generated Java source code by default. After the compilation stage, the servlet is ready to be loaded and initialized.

- **loading and initializing stage**

During the loading and initializing stage of JSP page, the JSP container loads and instantiates the servlet that has been generated and compiled. The JSP container performs the following operations during this stage.

- Loading : loads the servlet generated during the translation and compilation stages. The loading process is terminated if the web container fails to load the servlet class.

- Instantiation : Creates an instance of the servlet class. To create a new instance of the generated servlet, the JSP container uses the no-argument constructor.
- Initialization : Initializes the instantiated object after successful instantiation of JSP equivalent servlet object. In the case of a JSP equivalent servlet, the container invokes the *jspInit( )* method to initialize.

If the loading and initializing stage is performed successfully, the web container activates the servlet object and makes it available and ready for handling client request.

- **request handling stage**

During the request handling stage of the JSP life cycle, only those objects of a JSP equivalent sevlet that are initialized successfully are used by the web container to handle client requests. The container performs the following operations in the request handling stage.

- Creates the *ServletRequest* and *ServletResponse* objects according to the protocols used by client.
- Passes the request and response created in the preceding step to the servlet object to invoke the *service( )* method. In the case of a JSP equivalent servlet, the container invokes the *_jspService( )* method.

- **destroying stage**

If a servlet container decides to destroy a servlet instance of JSP page, the container needs to end the services provided by the instance. The servlet container performs the following operations to destroy the servlet instance:

- Allows all the currently running threads in the *service( )* method to complete their operations. Meanwhile, the servlet container makes the servlet instances unavailabale for new coming requests.
- Allows the servlet container to invoke the *destroy( )* method on the servlet instances. The *destroy( )* method leads to the execution of *_jspDestroy( )* method.

## 13.6 Components of JSP Page

A JSP page is very much similar to an HTML or XML page. Every JSP page holds text marked with a variety of tags. A standard JSP page is not a valid XML page; however there are some separate JSP tags which are allowed to be used within an XML Document.

The JSP tags are not processed by the client browser, but instead they are processed by the web server. This allows the contents of a page to be changed dynamically. The use of JSP tags depends on the programmer's choice. While creating a JSP page a programmer is asked for type of syntax as options. If the programmer chooses **JSP File (Standard Syntax)** then programmer needs to use the standard syntactical tags and if the programmer chooses **JSP Document (XML Syntax)** then programmer needs to use the XML tags only.

Following are some important components of a JSP page.

### 13.6.1 Comments

Specifically talking about JSP, then there is only one type of JSP comment tag available by JSP specifications i.e.

```
<% - - comment here - - %>
```

This JSP comment tag tells the JSP container to ignore the comment part from compilation. That is, the commented part of source code is not considered for the content parsed for 'response'. For example:

```
<% - - This JSP comment part will not be included in the response object - - %>
```

**Note:**

- **<!-- comment --> is not a JSP comment. This is HTML comment (but you can use it). The JSP container treats this HTML comment tag as equal as any other HTML tags.**
- **// and /* comment */ used inside the <% %> scriplet tag is also not a JSP comment (but you can use it). This is just a java comment and JSP container doesn't reserve any special treatment for this comments usage.**

### 13.6.2 JSP document

While creating a JSP page a programmer is asked for type of syntax as options. (See following screenshot)

1. JSP File (Standard Syntax)
2. JSP Document (XML Syntax)

If the programmer chooses **JSP File (Standard Syntax)** then programmer needs to use the standard JSP syntactical tags.

If the programmer chooses **JSP Document (XML Syntax)** then programmer needs to use the XML tags only.

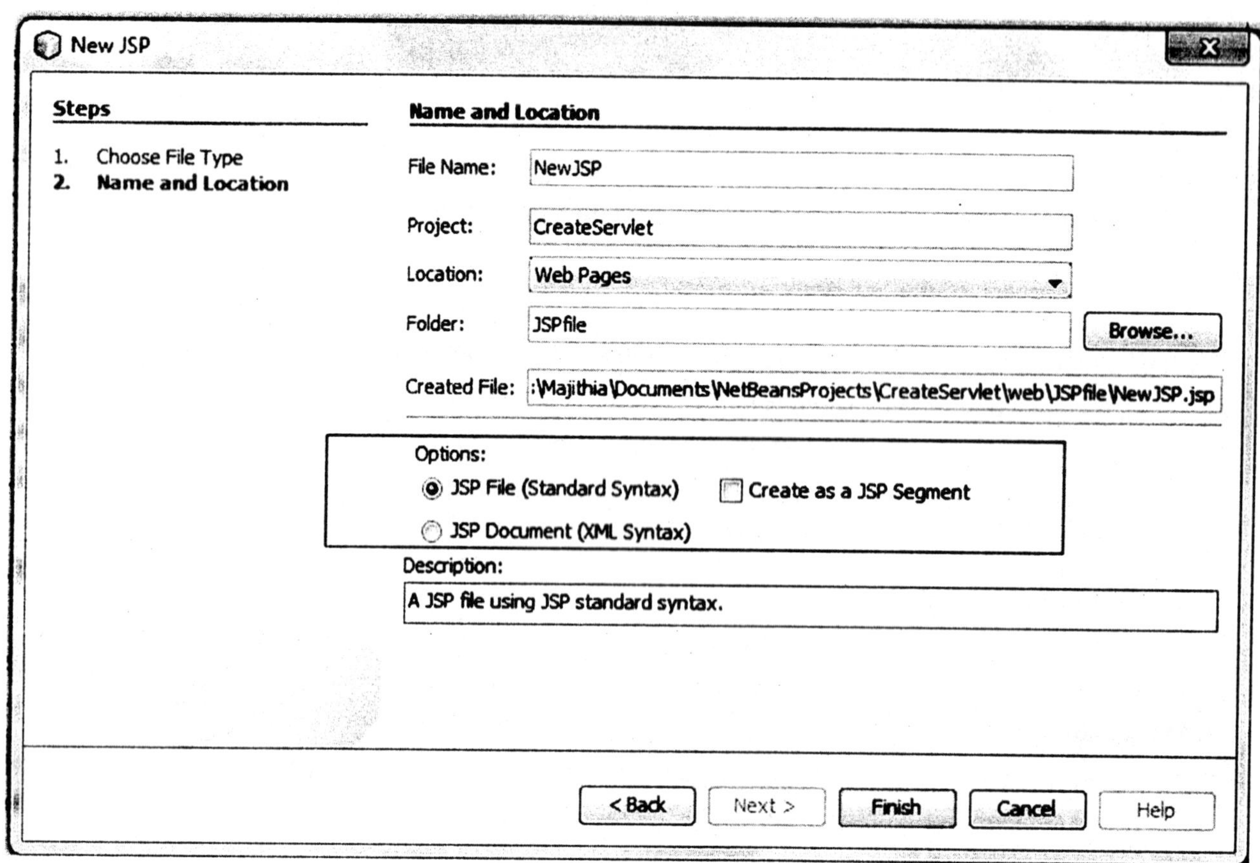


### 13.6.3 JSP Basic Tags

Java scripting tags, also called JSP scripting elements, allow you to add Java coding statements into a JSP page. The Java code incorporated by using scripting elements is translated and generated by the JSP translator while translating the page into a servlet. In most cases, Java is the scripting language used to build a JSP page. However, other supported languages can also be used, depending on the language supported by a web container. Let's now learn about the scripting elements and their use of elements.

The JSP scripting tags are categorized into following three types.

- **The scriplet tag**

The scriplet tag allow you to write the script code to implement the _jspService( ) method functionality. The JSP translator translates the statements of this tag into the _jspService( ) method.

You can include multiple scriplet tags in a single JSP page. The following code block shows the syntax of using scriplet tag.

standard JSP syntax

```
<%
        script code here, allows multiple statements also
%>
```

XML based syntax

```
<jsp:scriptlet>
        script code here, allows multiple statements also
</jsp:scriptlet>
```

Lets now look at one example that shows the use of this tag.

standard JSP syntax

```
<html>
<body>
<%
        for(int i=1;i<=5;i++)
        {
                out.println(i);
        }
%>
</body>
</html>
```

XML based syntax

```
<html>
<body>
<jsp:scriptlet>
        for(int i=1 ; i<=5 ; i++)
        {
                out.println(i);
        }
</jsp:scriptlet>
</body>
</html>
```

See the following code block that will show equivalent servlet code of above JSP code.

```
public void _jspService(HttpServletRequest request, HttpServletResponse response)
throws ServletException,IOException
{
        out.println("<html><body>");
        for( int i = 1 ; i<=5 ; i++)
        {
                out.println(i);
        }
        out.println("</body></html>");
}
```

- **The declarative tag**

The declarative tag allows you to write the script code you need to provide in the generated servlet class, outside the _jspService( ) method. This tag allows you to declare other objects, methods and data members. The code written in this tag will not be added into the _jspService( ) method.

The following code block shows the syntax of using declaration tag.

standard JSP syntax

```
<% !
        script code here, allows multiple statements also
%>
```

XML based syntax

```
<jsp:declaration>
        script code here, allows multiple statements also
</jsp:declaration>
```

Let's now look at one example that shows the use of declaration tag.

```
<% !
        int a,b,c;
        int add(int x  , int y)
        {
                return(x+y);
        }
%>
<% a=4; %>
<%b=6; %>
<% c = add(a,b); %>
<% out.println("Sum is " + c); %>
```

The code written in declaration tag:

```
int a,b,c;                      will be the data members of the servlet class, after translation
int add(int x , int y)  }
{                       }
        return(x+y);    }       will define a member function in the same servlet class, after translation
}                       }
```

See the following code block that will show equivalent servlet code of above JSP code.

```
class demo_jsp extends HttpServlet
{
        int a,b,c;
        int add(int x,int y)
        {
                return(x+y);
        }
```

```
        public void _jspService(HttpServletRequest request, HttpServletResponse response)
        throws ServletException,IOException
        {
                a=4;
                b=6;
                c=add(a,b);
                out.println("<html><body>");
                out.println("Sum is " + c);
                out.println("</body></html>");
        }
}
```

- **The expression tag**

An expression tag allows you to write Java expression, which is then resolved and resulting value is displayed. The expression tag puts the expression in out.print( ) method, during the translation.

An expression tag also provide a simple and convenient way to accept script variables. The following code block shows the syntax of using expression tag.

standard JSP syntax

```
<% =
        script code here, allows multiple statements also
%>
```

XML based syntax

```
<jsp:expression>
        script code here, allows multiple statements also
</jsp:expression>
```

Let's now look at one example to use the expression tag.

```
<% ! int count; %>
<html>
<body>
<% count ++; %>
        This page is requested by <% = count %> number of users till now.
</body>
</html>
```

The part above in bold, shows the use of expression tag to grab the value of a variable during a statement. Each time when a new user accesses the JSP page on the browser, the value of *count* variable is incremented by one and displays the same.

**Note: Notice that the expression tag has not used semi-colon (;) at the end, because it is place inside a messaging statement.**

Following program uses the all these three tags.

```
<%--
   Document   : index
   Created on : Apr 13, 2014, 8:12:21 PM
   Author     : Majithia
--%>

<%@page import="java.util.*" language="java" contentType="text/html" pageEncoding="UTF-8"%>
<!DOCTYPE html>
<html>
   <body>
   <center> <h1> Showing use of JSP scripting tags</h1></center>
   <%!
      int count,a,b,c;
      int add(int x,int y)
      {
         return(x+y);
      }
   %>
   <%
      a=4;
      b=6;
      count++;
      for(int i=1;i<=5;i++)
      {
         out.println("</br>Value of i is :<b> " + i + "</b>");
      }
      c=add(a,b);
      out.println("</br></br>The sum returned by add() method is : <b>" + c + "</b></br>");
  %>
   <br>This page is requested<b> <%=count%> </b>times on date <b><%=new Date()%> </b>
  </body>
</html>
```

Compile and run above JSP file and you will see following output.

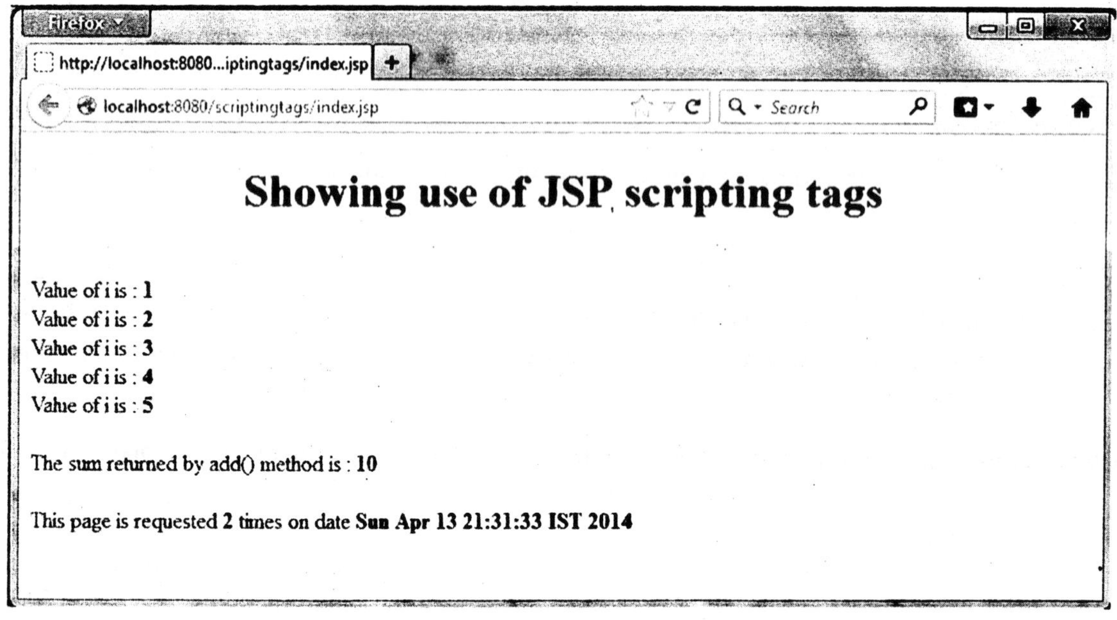

### 13.6.4 JSP Directive Tags

The directive tags provide directions that are used by the JSP translator during the translation stage of the JSP life cycle. These tags are used to set global values, such as class declarations, methods to be implemented, additional files to included, importing APIs, output content type, etc. In following section various types of directive tags are discussed.

- ***page* directive**

The *page* directive holds the instructions that are used by a JSP translator during the translation stage of the JSP life cycle. These instructions affect different properties associated with the whole JSP page. The *page* directive can be used multiple times in a single page and you write it at any part of the page, it automatically affects entire page. But it is a good programming skill that you write it at the top of the page only. Following is the syntax of *page* directive.

<u>Standard JSP syntax</u>

```
<%@page attribute %>
```

<u>XML based syntax</u>

```
<jsp:directive.page attributes />
```

See following screenshot, showing all attributes of *page* directive.

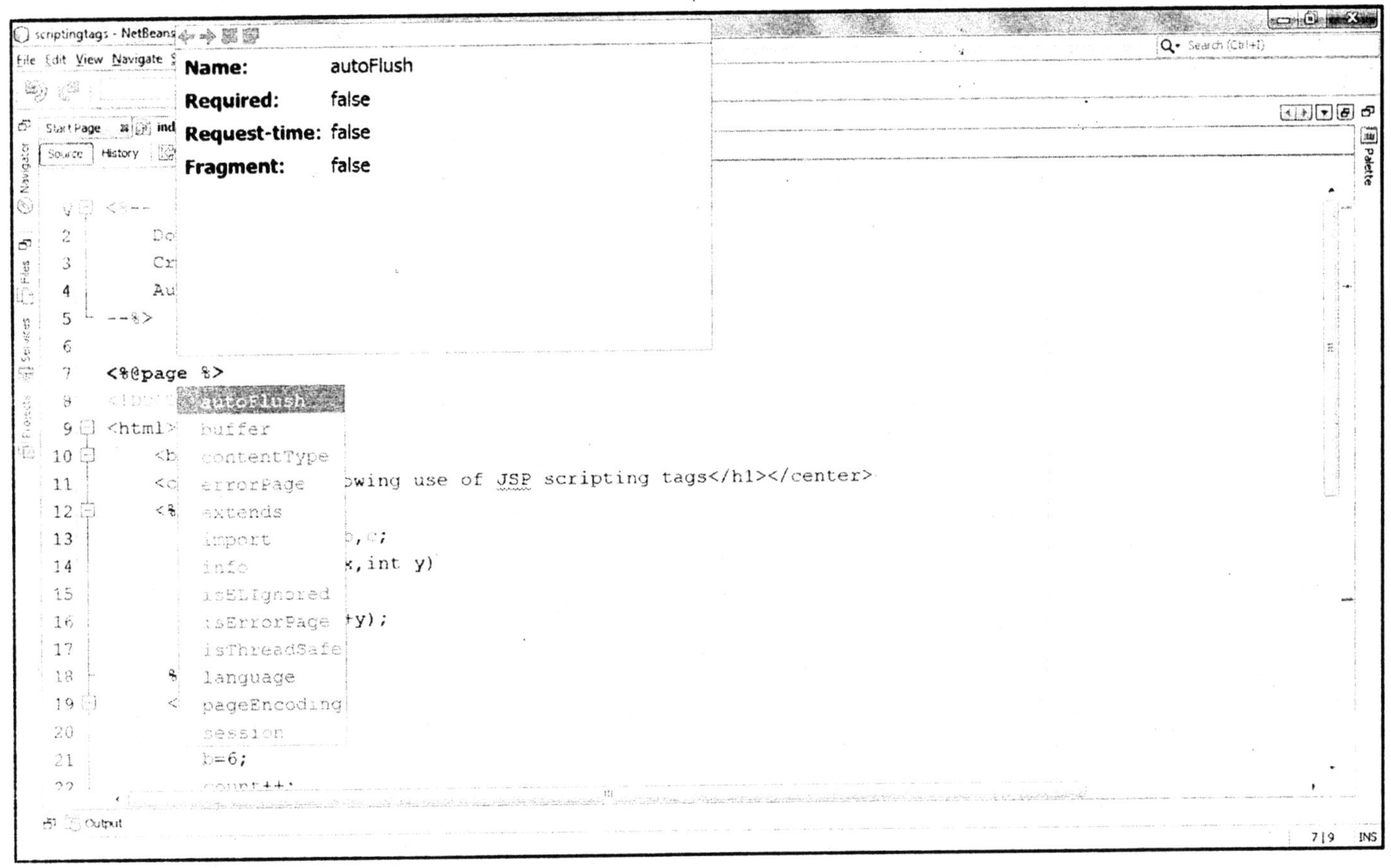

You can see that there are total 13 attributes available in the *page* directive tag. Following table explains them in brief.

| Attribute | Description |
|---|---|
| autoFlush | Specifies whether or not to automatically flush the output when the buffer is full. If it is set to *true* then it automatically flushes the buffer as soon as buffer gets full. If it is set to *false* then an exception is generated when the buffer overflows. Its default value is *true*. |
| buffer | Allow to set the buffer size. Its possible values are *none, 8kb, 16kb, 32kb* and *64kb*. Its default value is *8kb*. |
| contentType | Specifies the response type and sometimes optionally character encoding. Its default value is *html/text* |
| errorPage | Redirects to specified page, when error or exception occurs in current page. |
| extends | Takes a complete qualified class name of the class that is extended by the equivalent servlet class translated by the translator. |
| import | Use to import Java's built-in and user defined APIs to current JSP page. Multiple APIs are separated by comma. |
| info | A string applied to this attribute will be considered as information of current JSP page and will be returned when getServletInfo( ) is invoked. |
| isELIgnored | Takes *true* or *false* as value to justify whether EL expressions should be ignored for current JSP page or not. |
| isErrorPage | Takes *true* or *false* as value to justify whether the current JSP page is considered as an error page or not. If it is set to *true*, then you can redirect to this page when an error or exception occurs in other JSP page. (read above *errorPage* attribute) |
| isThreadSafe | Takes true or false as value to specify whether current page is thread-safe or not. In other words, it specifies whether the instance of the equivalent servlet class of the JSP page will be capable of handling simultaneous requests or not. |
| language | Accepts the language name which is to be used as scripting language. Its default value is *Java.* |
| pageEncoding | Specifies the encoding type of current JSP page. Some examples of page encoding are *UTF-8* and *ISO-8859-1* |
| session | Takes *true* or *false* to specify whether a session is required or not. Its default value is *true*. |

Following is the syntactical structure of page directive.

```
<%@page autoFlush="true" buffer="32kb" contentType="html/text" errorPage="page_name.jsp/java"
extends="class_name" import="java.io.*, java.util.*" info="a string to provide this JSP page information"
isELIgnored="true" isErrorPage="false" isThreadSafe="true" language="Java" pageEncoding="UTF-8" session="true"
%>
```

- **include directive**

The include directive is used to combine the contents of two or more files during the translation of the JSP life cycle. This directive appends the code of included file to the current JSP page, without any modification. The include can be static or dynamic.

This is same as we use "*RequestDispatcher*" interface in servlet. Following is the syntax of *page* directive.

Standard JSP syntax

```
<%@include attribute %>
```

XML based syntax

```
<jsp:directive.include attribute />
```

See following screenshot, showing all attribute of *include* directive.

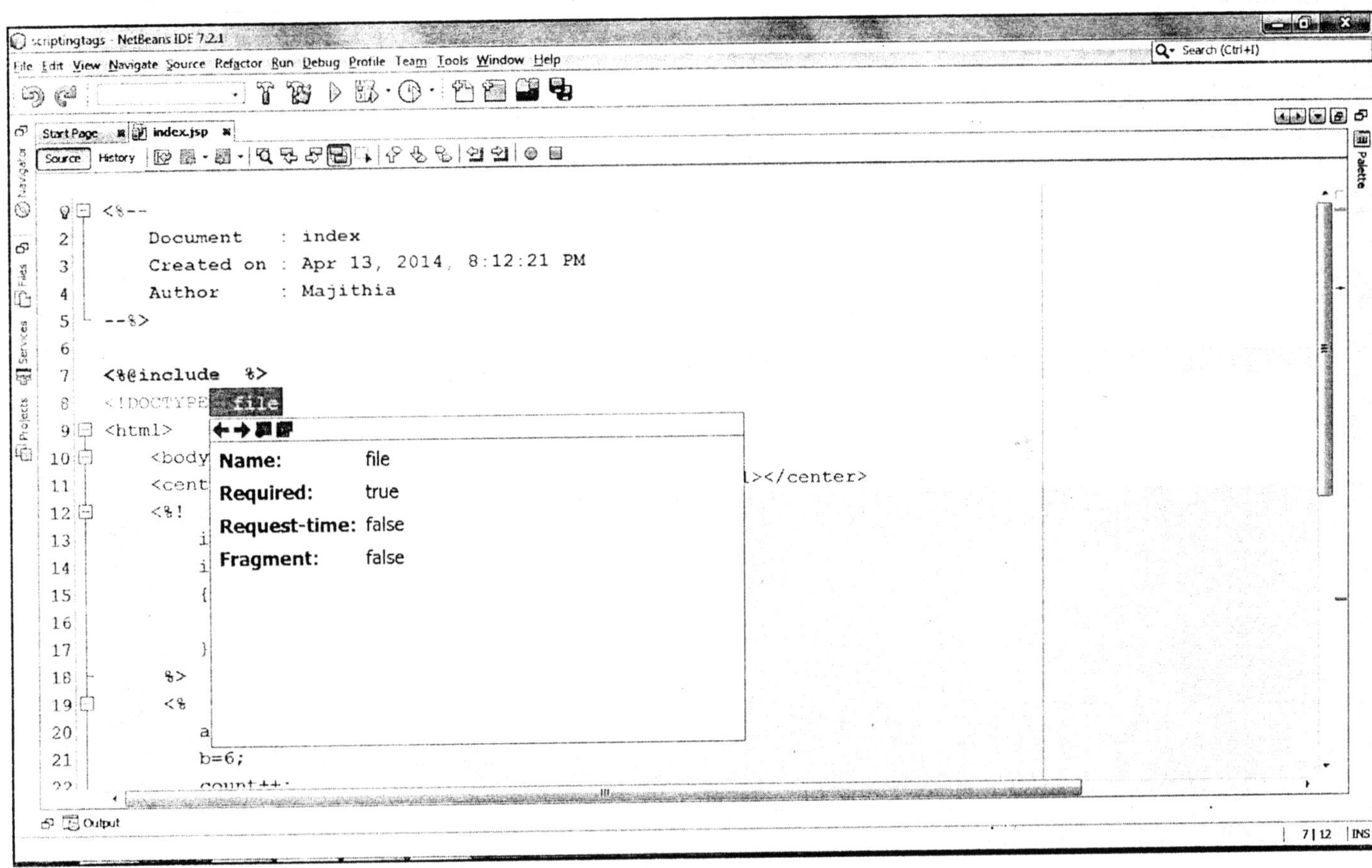


We can see that, this tag has only one attribute and it is *file.* This tag is used to specify the file name which is needed to be included. This file can be a JSP file or a Java file or an HTML file. For example,

```
<%@include file= "/Text.jsp" %>

<%@include file= "/one.html" %>
```

Note that if any changes are made to the included page, the behavior of the *include* directive tag with respect to the compilation of the page depends on a web container. This means some depending on web containers, some will recognize and apply changes while others do not.

- **taglib directive**

The *taglib* directive declares that your JSP page uses a set of custom tag, identifies the location of the library, and provides a means for identifying the custom tags in your JSP page. The following code block shows the syntax of *taglib* directive.

Standard JSP syntax

```
<%@taglib attributes %>
```

XML based syntax

```
<jsp:directive.taglib attributes />
```

See following screenshot, showing all attribute of *taglib* directive.

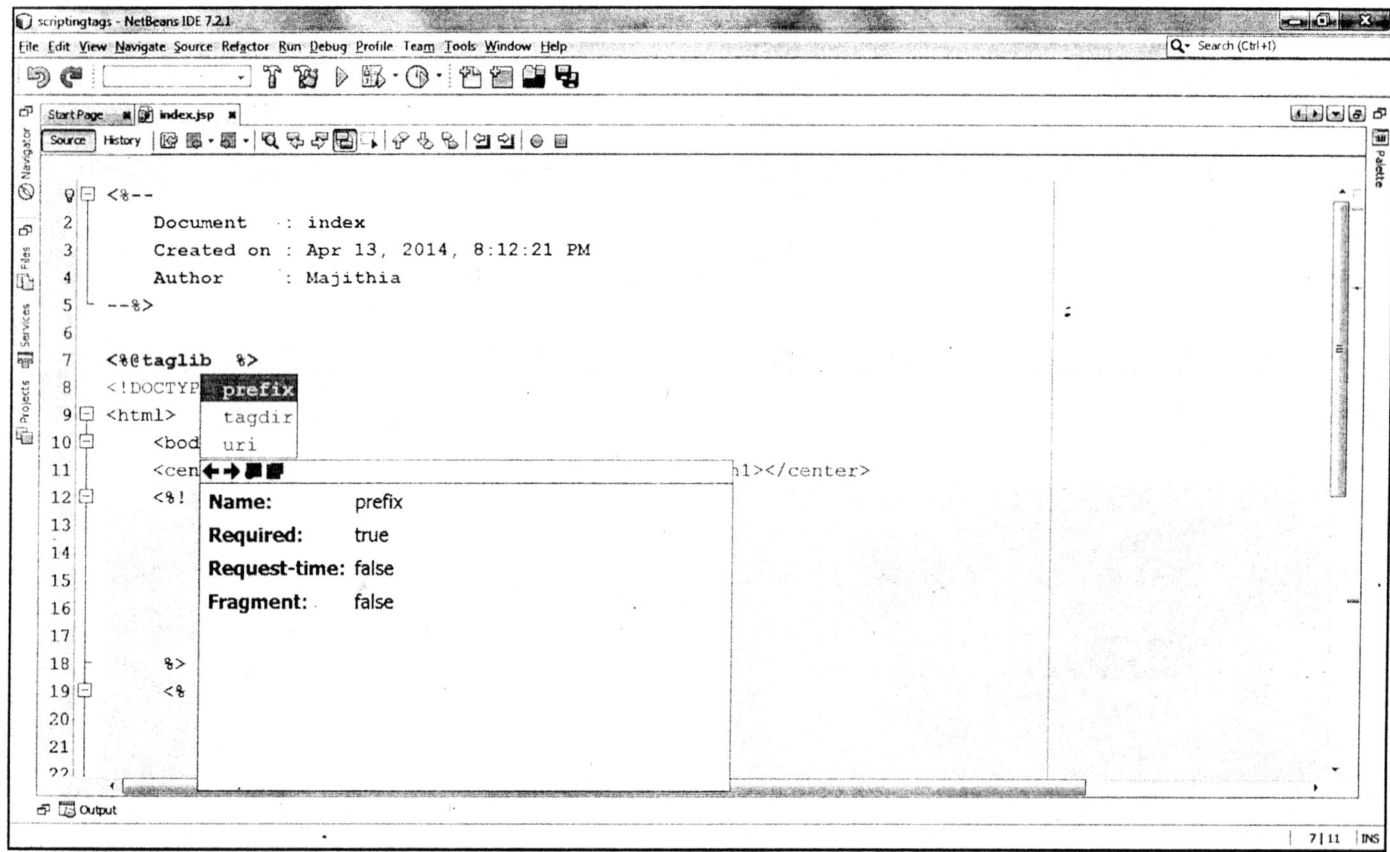

As we can see, this tag has three attributes.

| Attribute | Description |
|---|---|
| uri | Resolves to a location the container understands. |
| prefix | Informs a container what bits of markup are custom actions. |
| tagdir | specifies the directory name where the custom tags are stored. |

Generally every programmer specifies uri and prefix attributes only. See following example,

```
<%@taglib uri= "http://www.example.com/custlib" prefix= "mytag" %>
<html>
<body>
<mytag:hello />
</body>
</html>
```

Here, we would be able to call another piece of code using <mytag:hello>.

### 13.6.5 JSP Implicit Objects

JSP implicit objects are the predefined objects that are accessible to all JSP pages. JSP implicit objects are used to make a JSP page as dynamic page. These objects are called as implicit objects because programmers need not to instantiate these objects. JSP implicit objects are automatically instantiated by the JSP container.

These implicit objects help the programmers in many ways, such as:

- To access the services and resource provided by JSP container.
- Helps to generate dynamic contents of web pages.
- Need not to import and declare objects explicitly, which saves developer's time.
- Helps in handling HTML parameters, sending requests and receiving responses to/from a web component.

When a JSP page is translated, following table shows the nine objects that are initialized by the JSP servlet engine in _*jspService( )* method.

| **Implicit Objects** | **Description** |
|---|---|
| request | The *request* object is passed as a parameter to the _jspService( ) method when a client request is made. This request object is of *javax.servlet.http.HttpServletRequest* class. We can use it in the same way as we use it in servlet classes. |
| response | The *response* object is used to carry response of a client request after the _jspService( ) method is executed. This object is of *javax.servlet.http.HttpServletResponse* class. |
| out | The out object provides access to the output stream of a servlet. This object is of *javax.servlet.jsp.JspWriter* class. This object can be directly used in JSP scriplet to display text data on browser. |
| page | The *page* object refers to a servlet of the JSP page processing a current request. It also works as an instance of the generated servlet in a JSP page. This object is of *java.lang.Object* class. This object is rarely used in JSP page. |
| pageContext | The *pageContenxt* object represents the context of the current JSP page. It provides a single API to manage different scoped attributes. This object is of *javax.servlet.jsp.PageContext* type. |
| application | The *application* object refers to the entire environment of a web application to which a JSP page belongs. This object is of *javax.servlet.ServletContext* type. |
| session | The *session* object helps to access session data and is of the *javax.servlet.http.HttpSession* type. It automatically gets declared if *session* attribute of *page directive* is set to *true*. |
| config | The config object specifies the configuration of the parameters passed to a JSP page. This object is of *javax.servlet.ServletConfig* type. |
| exception | This object is available for exception handling. This object is of *java.lang.Throwable* type. This object will be available to the JSP page if the *isErrorPage* attribute of *page directive* is set to *true*. |

## 13.7 Working with Action Tags in JSP

Actions tags were added in JSP 1.1 and then on each new version, additional tags were added. Action tags allow Java programmers to include some basic actions, such as inserting resources of other page, forwarding and including request to another page, creating or locating JavaBean instances, setting and retrieving JavaBean properties in a JSP page, etc. Let's now discuss these action tags in brief.

Action tags are specific to a JSP page. While translating a JSP page, if any action tag is encountered by JSP container, then it generates a Java code corresponding to the task performed by that action tag. Following are some important action tags of JSP page.

- <jsp:include>
- <jsp:forward>
- <jsp:param>
- <jsp:useBean>
- <jsp:setProperty>
- <jsp:getProperty>
- <jsp:plugin>
- <jsp:params>
- <jsp:fallback>
- <jsp:attribute>
- <jsp:body>
- <jsp:element>
- <jsp:text>

**The <jsp:include> tag**

The <jsp:include> action tag allows to include static or dynamic resources, such as an HTML or a JSP page in the current JSP page. If the resource to be included is an HTML file then, its contents are directly included in current JSP page. If the resource to be included is another JSP page or Java program then, that page processes on request and generates output. This generated output is included in requesting JSP page. Following screenshot shows the attribute list of <jsp:include> action tag.

**The flush attribute** takes either true or false value, to indicate whether the buffer needs to be flushed or not before including the specified resource page.

**The page attribute** takes a relative URL, which specifies the location of the resource to be included in the JSP page. The relative URL can be specified directly or as an expression within a page attribute.

The syntax to use this tag is:

```
<jsp:include attributes>

</jsp:include>
```

For example:

```
<jsp:include page= "test.jsp" flush="true">

</jsp:include>
```

**The <jsp:forward> tag**

The <js[:forward> action tag forwards a JSP request to another resource, which can be either static or dynamic. If the request is forwarded to a dynamic resource, then a *<jsp:param>* tag is used to pass the dynamic parameters to that page. This tag has only one attribute i.e. *page*. Following screenshot shows the attribute list of <jsp:forward> action tag.

```
<jsp:forward
            page
```

**The page attribute** takes a relative URL to specify the page to which the current request is to be forwarded.

The syntax to use this tag is:

```
<jsp:forward attributes>

</jsp:forward>
```

For example:

```
<jsp:forward page= "/Header.html">

</jsp:forward>
```

or you can also use expression tag as follows.

```
<jsp:forward page= "<%=mypath%>">

</jsp:forward>
```

**The <jsp:param> tag**

The <jsp:param> action tag allows Java programmers to pass a name and value of a parameter to a dynamic resource, while including it in a JSP page or forwarding a request from a JSP page to another JSP page. This tag can also be used to pass parameters to an applet configured in the JSP page by using the *<jsp:plugin>* tag. The following screenshot shows the attribute list of <jsp:param> tag.

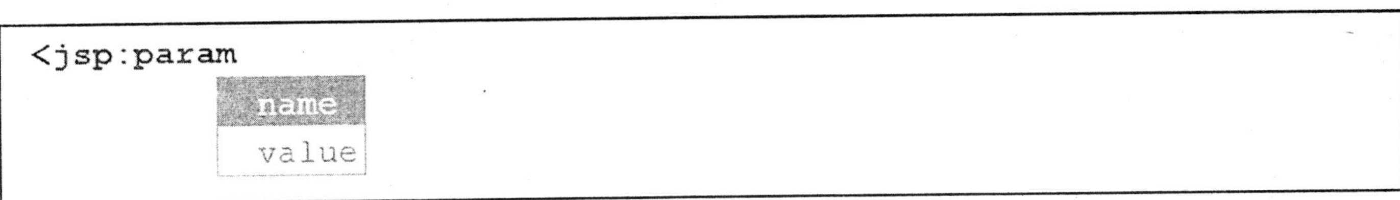

**The name attribute** specifies the name of the parameter. This name should be unique and case sensitive string parameter.

**The value attribute** specifies the value of the parameter. It takes a case sensitive string as value of parameter.

The syntax to use this tag is:

```
<jsp:param attributes>
</jsp:param>
```

For example:

```
<jsp:param name= "uname" value= "user1"/>
<jsp:param name= "user_type" value= "admin" />
```

**The <jsp:useBean> tag**

The <jsp:useBean> action tag is used to instantiate a JavaBean or locate an existing JavaBean instance, and assign it to a variable name or id. The following screenshot shows the attribute list of <jsp:useBean> tag.

```
<jsp:useBean
            beanName
            class
            id
            scope
            type
```

**The beanName attribute** takes a qualified class name or an expression of a JavaBean. A JSP container uses the *instantiate* method to instantiate the JavaBean.

**The class attribute** takes a qualified class name to create a JavaBean instance if the JavaBean instance is not found in the given scope. The class specified by the class name assigned to the class attribute should not be an abstract class and should have a no-argument constructor.

**The id attribute** represents the name assigned to a JavaBean, which is later used as variable to access the JavaBean. This attribute is used to locate an existing JavaBean instance in the appropriate scope specified in the <jsp:useBean> tag.

**The scope attribute** represents the scope in which a JavaBean instance has to be located or created. The value of scope for the JavaBean instance can be *page*, *request*, *session* and *application*.

**The type attribute** takes a qualified class or interface name, which can be the class name given in the *class* or *beanName* attribute. This attribute is also used with or without class or beanName.

The syntax to use this tag is:

```
<jsp:useBean attributes>
</jsp:useBean>
```

For example:

```
<jsp:useBean beanName= "bean_name" class= "bean_class_name" id= "bean_id" scope= "page"
 type= "bean_type">
</jsp:useBean>
```

**The <jsp:setProperty> tag**

The <jsp:setProperty> action tag sets the value of a property by using the *setter* methods of JavaBean. Before using this tag, the JavaBean must be instantiated. In addition, the name attribute of the JavaBean must be the same as the reference variable name of the JavaBean instance. Following screenshot shows the list of the <jps:setPropery> tag.

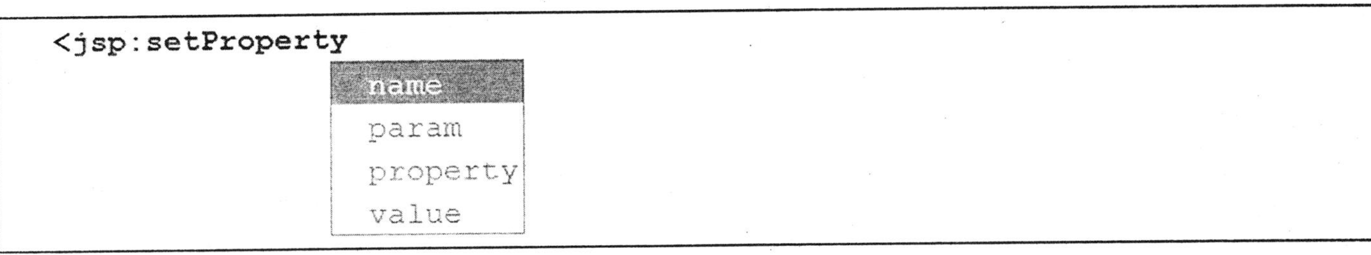


**The name attribute** takes the name of an existing JavaBean as a reference variable to invoke the *setter* method. The value of this attribute must match the value of id attribute of *<jsp:useBean>* tag to set the properties of a bean.

**The param attribute** specifies the request parameter name whose value is to be assigned to a JavaBean property. While setting JavaBean properties from request parameter, it is not always necessary for the JavaBean to have the same property name as the request parameters.

**The property attribute** takes the name of the property to be set, and specifies the setter method to be invoked. This attribute is used in two different ways. One is to use an asterisk (*) with the value of the *property* attribute. Second is to use specific name with full path.

**The value attribute** takes the value that has to be set to specified JavaBean property. This attribute accepts the value as the *String* type or as an expression that is evaluated runtime.

The syntax to use this tag is:

```
<jsp:setProperty attributes>
</jsp:setProperty>
```

For example:

```
<jsp:setProperty name= "abcbean" property= "property name or * " value= "property
value as string" param= "uname">
</jsp:setProperty>
```

**The <jsp:getProperty> tag**

The<jsp:getProperty> action tag retrieves the value of a property by using the *getter* method of JavaBean and writes the value to the current JspWriter. Following screenshot shows the list of attributes of <jsp:getProperty> tag.

```
<jsp:getProperty
                  name
                  property
```

**The name attribute** takes the reference variable name on which you want to invoke the getter method. If a JavaBean is instantiated by using the *<jsp:useBean>* tag, the value assigned to the name attribute should match the id attribute value of the *<jsp:useBean>* tag. This means that. the *<jsp:useBean>* tag must appear before the *<jsp:setProperty>* tag.

**The property attribute** takes the value of a JavaBean property and invokes the getter method of the property. This attribute takes the name of the property as an argument.

The syntax to use this tag is:

```
<jsp:getProperty attributes>
</jsp:getProperty>
```

For example:

```
<jsp:getProperty name="mybeab" property= "uname">
</jsp:getProperty>
```

**The <jsp:plugin> tag**

The <jsp:plugin> action tag provides support for including a Java applet or JavaBean in a client web browser, by using a built-in or downloaded java plug-in. In the request handling stage of the JSP life cycle, the *<jsp:plugin>* tag is substituted by either the *<object>* or *<embed>* tag, depending on the browser version. Following screenshot shows the attribute list of <jsp:plugin> tag.

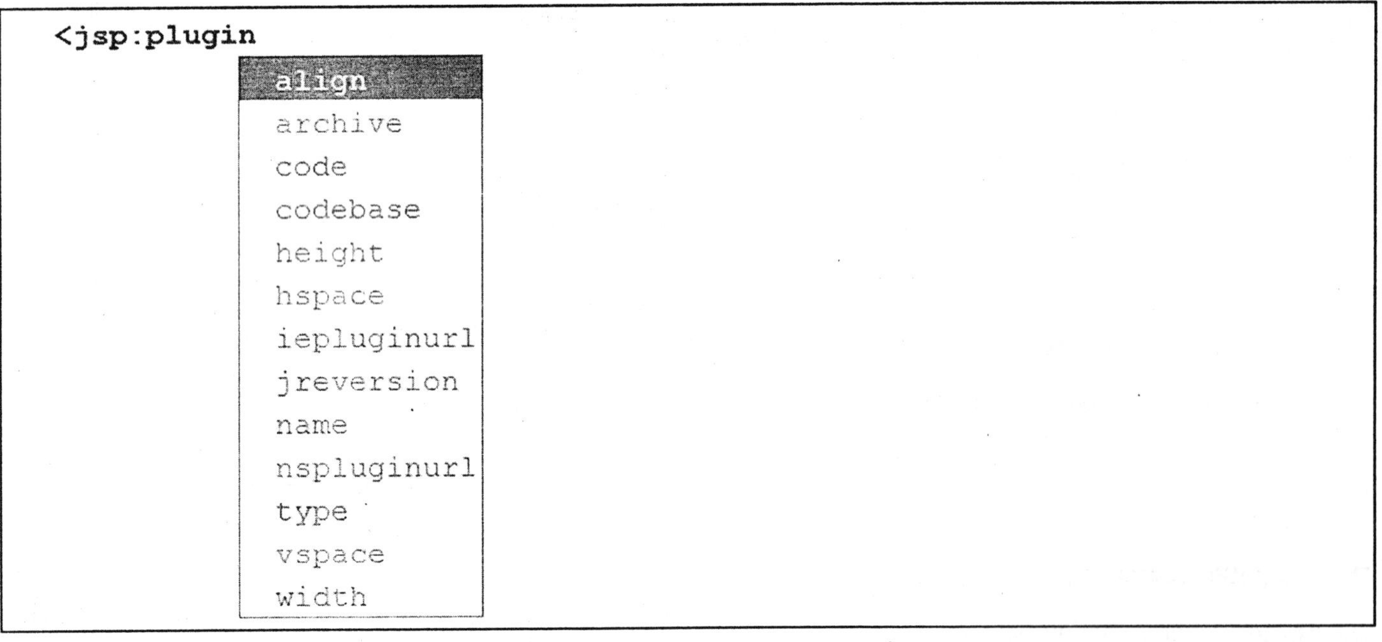


**The align attrib**ute specifies the position of an applet. The values the align tag can take are *bottom, top, middle, left* or *right*. The default value is bottom.

**The achieve attribute** specifies a comma separated list representing pathnames. A pathname is used to locate archive files, which are preloaded with a class loader that is present in the directory named codebase. Archive files distinctively improves the performance of an applet and are loaded securely over a network.

**The code attribute** takes the qualified class name of the object that has to be presented.

**The codebase attribute** takes the base URL where the specified class can be located. This is an optional attribute.

**The height attribute** specifies the initial height in pixels for the image shown by an applet or a JavaBean.

**The hspace attribute** specifies the amount of horizontal space in pixels that should be assigned to the left and right side an applet or a JavaBean displayed by the browser.

**The iepluginurl attribute** specifies the URL from which a client can download the JRE plug-in as required for the internet explorer. The value of this attribute can be a complete URL, protocol name, port number or a domain name.

**The jreversion attribute** specifies the version of Java Runtime Environment (JRE) as required by the corresponding applet or JavaBean.

**The type attribute** specifies the type of object that needs to be presented to the browser. The object can be an applet or a JavaBean.

**The vspace attribute** specifies the amount of vertical space in pixels that should be assigned to the bottom and top of an applet or a JavaBean displayed by the browser.

**The width attribute** specifies the initial width in pixels for the image shown by an applet or a JavaBean.

The syntax to use this tag is:

```
<jsp:plugin attributes>
</jsp:plugin>
```

**The <jsp:params> tag**

The <jsp:params> action tag sends the parameters that you want to pass to an applet or a JavaBean. The following screenshot shows that this tag has no attributes. The <jsp:param> tags are included in this tag.

```
<jsp:params
        No suggestions
```

Following code block shows the syntax to use <jsp:params> tag.

```
<jsp:params>
        one or more <jsp:param> tags
</jsp:params>
```

**The <jsp:fallback> tag**

The <jsp:fallback> action tag allows you to specify a text message that is displayed if the required plug-in cannot run. This action tag must be used as a child tag with the <jsp:plugin> tag. If the plug-in runs and the applet or JavaBean cannot run, the plug-in generally displays a popup window clarifying the error to the user. Following screenshot shows that this tag has no attributes.

```
<jsp:fallback
                No suggestions
```

The following code block shows the syntax to use <jsp:fallback> tag.

```
<jsp:fallback>

        text message that has to be displayed if plug-in cannot be started

</jsp:fallback>
```

**The <jsp:attribute> tag**

The<jsp:attribute> action tag is used to specify the value of a standard or custom action attribute. For example, you can use the <jsp:attribute> tag to set the attributes of the <jsp:setProperty> tag. The following screenshot shows the list of attributes of <jsp:attribute> tag.

```
<jsp:attribute
```

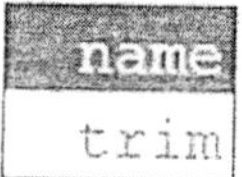


**The name attribute** takes *true* or *false*, indicating whether the whitespace coming at the beginning and the end of the <jsp:attribute> tag should be discarded or not. By default this value is *true*.

**The trim attribute** specifies the attribute name that you want to set.

The following code block shows the syntax to use <jsp:fallback> tag.

```
<jsp:attribute attributes>

</jsp:attribute>
```

For example,

```
<jsp:attribute name= "mybean" trim= "true">

</jsp:attribute>
```

**The <jsp:body> tag**

The <jsp:body> action tag is used to specify the content of a standard or custom action tag. Generally, the body content of a standard or custom action invocation is implicitly defined as the body of that tag. However, if one or more <jsp:attribute> tag appears in the body of the tag, the body of a standard of custom action can be defined explicitly by using <jsp:body> tag. The following screenshot shows that this tag has no attributes.

```
<jsp:body
        No suggestions
```

The following code block shows the use of <jsp:body> tag.

```
<jsp:body>

        <jsp:setProperty name= "myBean" property= "*" />

<jsp:body>
```

**The <jsp:element> tag**

The <jsp:element> action tag is used to dynamically define the value of the tag of an XML element. This action tag allows you to create an XML tag with a given name. The content of the <jsp:element> tag is a template for the attributes and child nodes of the XML tag you want to create. The following screenshot shows that there is only one attribute of <jsp:element> tag.

```
<jsp:element
            name
```

The name attribute specifies the name of the XML element it has to create. The *<jsp:element>* tag can be an empty tag or can contain one *<jdp:body>* or multiple *<jsp:attribute>* tags with one or more *<jsp:body>* tags.

The following code block shows the use of <jsp:element> tag.

```
<jsp:element name= "mytag">
        <jsp:attribute name= "myattr"> MyValue </jsp:attribute>
</jsp:element>
```

**The <jsp:text> tag**

The <jsp:text> action tag is used to enclose template data in an XML tag. This tag can be used in a JSP page or tag file. The content of a <jsp:text> tag is passed to the implicit object *"out"*. The following screenshot shows that this tag has no attributes.

```
<jsp:text
        No suggestions
```

This tag will appear at any place where template data appears. The following code block shows the syntax to use <jsp:text> tag.

```
<jsp:text>
        template data
</jsp:text>
```

## 13.8 EL in JSP

This section introduces the **Expression Language** (also referred to as the EL), which provides an important mechanism for enabling the presentation layer (web pages) to communicate with the application logic (managed beans). The EL is used by both **Java Server Faces** (JSF) and **Java Server Pages** (JSP) technologies.

To activate or deactivate use of EL expressions in a JSP page, set

```
<%@ page isELIgnored ="true|false" %>
```

The valid values of this attribute are *true* and *false*. If it is *true*, EL expressions are ignored when they appear in static text or tag attributes. If it is *false*, EL expressions are evaluated by the container.

### 13.8.1 Use of EL expressions

EL expressions can be used:

- In static text
- In any standard or custom tag attribute that can accept an expression

The value of an expression in static text is computed and inserted into the current output. If the static text appears in a tag body, note that an expression will not be evaluated if the body is declared to be tagdependent (see body-content Attribute).

There are three ways to set a tag attribute value:

- With a single expression construct:

```
<some:tag value="${expr}"/>
```

The expression is evaluated and the result is coerced to the attribute's expected type.

- With one or more expressions separated or surrounded by text:

```
<some:tag value="some${expr}${expr}text${expr}"/>
```

The expressions are evaluated from left to right. Each expression is coerced to a String and then concatenated with any intervening text. The resulting String is then coerced to the attribute's expected type.

- With text only:

```
<some:tag value="sometext"/>
```

In this case, the attribute's String value is coerced to the attribute's expected type.

Expressions used to set attribute values are evaluated in the context of an expected type. If the result of the expression evaluation does not match the expected type exactly, a type conversion will be performed. For example, the expression ${1.2E4} provided as the value of an attribute of type float will result in the following conversion:

```
Float.valueOf("1.2E4").floatValue( )
```

### 13.8.2 Literal Expressions

A literal expression evaluates to the text of the expression, which is of type String. It does not use the ${} or #{} delimiters.

If you have a literal expression that includes the reserved ${} or #{} syntax, you need to escape these characters as follows.

- By creating a composite expression as shown here:

```
${'${'}exprA}
#{'#{'}exprB}
```

The resulting values would then be the strings ${exprA} and #{exprB}.

- The escape characters \$ and \# can be used to escape what would otherwise be treated as an eval-expression:

```
\${exprA}
\#{exprB}
```

The resulting values would again be the strings ${exprA} and #{exprB}.

When a literal expression is evaluated, it can be converted to another type. Following shows examples of various literal expressions and their expected types and resulting values.

| Expression | Expected Type | Result |
|---|---|---|
| Hi | String | Hi |
| true | boolean | Boolean.TRUE |
| 42 | int | 42 |

Literal expressions can be evaluated immediately or deferred and can be either value or method expressions. At what point a literal expression is evaluated depends on where it is being used. If the tag attribute that uses the literal expression is defined as accepting a deferred value expression, then the literal expression references a value and is evaluated at a point in the life cycle that is determined by where the expression is being used and to what it is referring.

In the case of a method expression, the method that is referenced is invoked and returns the specified *String* literal. The *commandButton* tag of the Guess Number application uses a literal method expression as a logical outcome to tell the Java Server Faces navigation system which page to display next.

### 13.8.3 Resolving Expressions

The unified EL introduces a new, pluggable API for resolving expressions. The main pieces of this API are:

- The *ValueExpression* class, which defines a value expression
- The *MethodExpression* class, which defines a method expression
- An *ELResolver* class that defines a mechanism for resolving expressions
- A set of *ELResolver* implementations, in which each implementation is responsible for resolving expressions that reference a particular type of object or property
- An *ELContext* object that saves statè relating to EL resolution, holds references to EL resolvers, and contains context objects (such as JspContext) needed by the underlying technology to resolve expressions

Most application developers will not need to use these classes directly unless they plan to write their own custom EL resolvers. Those writing Java Server Faces custom components will definitely need to use *ValueExpression* and *MethodExpression*. This section details how expressions are resolved for the benefit of these developers. It does not explain how to create a custom resolver.

### 13.8.4 Process of Expression Evaluation

When a value expression that is included in a page is parsed during an initial request for the page, a *ValueExpression* object is created to represent the expression. Then, the *ValueExpression* object's *getValue( )* method is invoked. This method will in turn invoke the *getValue( )* method of the appropriate resolver. A similar process occurs during a postback when *setValue( )* is called if the expression is an lvalue expression.

In the case of a method expression, a BeanELResolver is used to find the object that implements the method to be invoked or queried. Similarly to the process for evaluating value expressions, when a method expression is encountered, a *MethodExpression* object is created. Subsequently, either the *invoke( )* or *getMethodInfo( )* method of the *MethodExpression* object is called. This method in turn invokes the *BeanELResolver* object's getValue( ) method. The *getMethodInfo* is mostly for use by tools.

After a resolver completes resolution of an expression, it sets the *propertyResolved* flag of the *ELContext* to *true* so that no more resolvers are consulted.

### 13.8.5 The EL Resolver

At the center of the EL machinery is the extensible *ELResolver* class. A class that implements *ELResolver* defines how to resolve expressions referring to a particular type of object or property. In terms of the following expression, a *BeanELResolver* instance is called the first time to find the base object, employee, which is a JavaBeans component. Once the resolver finds the object, it is called again to resolve the property, *lName* of the employee object.

```
${employee.lName}
```

The unified EL includes a set of standard resolver implementations. Following table lists these standard resolvers and includes example expressions that they can resolve.

| Resolver | Example Expression | Description |
|---|---|---|
| ArrayELResolver | *${myArray[1]}* | Returns the value at index 1 in the array called *myArray* |
| BeanELResolver | *${employee.lName}* | Returns the value of the *lName* property of the employee bean |
| ListELResolver | *${myList[5]}* | Returns the value at index 5 of *myList* list |
| MapELResolver | *${myMap.someKey}* | Returns the value stored at the key, *someKey*, in the Map, *myMap* |
| ResourceBundleELResolver | *${myRB.myKey}* | Returns the message at *myKey* in the resource bundle called *myRB* |

Depending on the technology using the unified EL, other resolvers might be available. In addition, application developers can add their own implementations of *ELResolver* to support resolution of expressions not already supported by the unified EL by registering them with an application.

All of the standard and custom resolvers available to a particular application are collected in a chain in a particular order. This chain of resolvers is represented by a *CompositeELResolver* instance. When an expression is encountered, the *CompositeELResolver* instance iterates over the list of resolvers and consults each resolver until it finds one that can handle the expression.

If an application is using JSP technology, the chain of resolvers includes the *ImplicitObjectELResolver* and the *ScopedAttributeELResolver*.

### 13.8.6 Operators in EL

In addition to the . and [] operators discussed in Value and Method Expressions, the JSP expression language provides the following operators, which can be used in rvalue expressions only:

- **Arithmetic:** +, - (binary), *, / and *div*, % and *mod*, - (unary)
- **Logical:** *and*, &&, *or*, *||*, *not*, *!*
- **Relational:** *==*, *eq*, *!=*, *ne*, *<*, *lt*, *>*, *gt*, *<=*, *ge*, *>=*, *le*. Comparisons can be made against other values, or against boolean, string, integer, or floating point literals.
- **Empty:** The *empty* operator is a prefix operation that can be used to determine whether a value is null or empty. (See following table)
- **Conditional:** The operators *?* and *:* are conditional operators.

*empty* values for different datatypes are shown in following table.

| Data Type | Empty Value |
|---|---|
| String | " " |
| Identifier | Null |
| Array | No elements |
| Map | No elements |
| List | No elements |

**13.8.7 Reserve Words**

The following words are reserved for the JSP expression language and should not be used as identifiers.

| and | or | not | eq |
|---|---|---|---|
| ne | lt | gt | le |
| ge | true | false | null |
| instanceof | empty | div | mod |

Note that many of these words are not in the Java language now, but they may be in the future, so you should avoid using them.

**13.8.8 Example Expressions**

Following table contains example EL expressions and the result of evaluating them.

| EL Expression | Result |
|---|---|
| *${1 > (4/2)}* | false |
| *${4.0 >= 3}* | true |
| *${100.0 == 100}* | true |
| *${(10*10) ne 100}* | flase |
| *${'a' < 'b'}* | true |
| *${'hip' gt 'hit'}* | false |
| *${4 > 3}* | true |
| *${1.2E4 + 1.4}* | 12001.4 |
| *${3 div 4}* | 0.75 |
| *${10 mod 4}* | 2 |
| *${!empty param.Add}* | false if the request parameter named Add is null or an empty string |
| *${pageContext.request.contextPath}* | The context path |

| | |
|---|---|
| *${sessionScope.cart.numberOfItems}* | The value of the *numberofItems* property of the session scoped attribute named *cart*. |
| *${param['mycom.productId']}* | The value of the request parameter named *mycom.productId.* |
| *${header["host"]}* | The host |
| *${departments[deptName]}* | The value of the entry named *deptName* in the *departments* map. |
| *${requestScope['javax.servlet.forward.servlet_path']}* | The value of the request scoped attribute name *javax.servlet.forward.servlet_path* |
| *#{customer.lName}* | Gets the value of the property *lName* from the *customer* bean during an initial request. Sets the value of *lName* during a postback. |
| *#{customer.calcTotal}* | The returned value of the method *calcTotal* of the *customer* bean |

Following program shows the use of EL operators in JSP.

```
<%--
  Document  : index
  Created on : Apr 17, 2014, 2:24:48 PM
  Author    : Majithia
--%>

<%@page contentType="text/html" pageEncoding="UTF-8" isELIgnored="false"%>
<!DOCTYPE html>
<html>
    <head>
     <title>Demonstrating EL Operators</title>
   </head>
   <body>
     <h2>Using EL operators</h2></br>
     <h3>Arithmetic expressions</h3></br>
     <b>Your CGPA score is ${1 + 2 * 4 - 6 / 2}.</b></br>
     <b>Today temperature in Ahmedabad is ${-4-8} degree celcius.</b></br>
```

```
        <b>Is 3/4 equals to 0.75? ${(3/4==0.75)?"Yes":"No"}</b></br>
        <b>Mathematical Constant PI has value ${22/7}</b></br>
        <b>GDP of India is ${20 div 2}</b></br>
        <b>I have ${2003 mod 8} cell phones.</b></br>
        <b>I have ${2003 % 8} cell phones.</b></br>

        <h3>Logical operators</h3>
        <b>This Logical EL expression \${(1&lt;2) && (4&lt;3)} is : ${(1<2) && (4<3)}</b></br>
        <b>This Logical EL expression \${(1&lt;2) || (4&lt;3)} is : ${(1<2) || (4<3)}</b></br>
        <b>This Logical EL expression \${!(1&lt;2)} is : ${!(1<2)}</b></br>

        <h3>Comparison Operator</h3>
        <b>Is 4>3? : ${4>3}</b></br>
        <b>Is 4>=3? : ${4 ge 3}</b></br>
        <b>Is 4==4? : ${4==4}</b></br>

        <h3>Empty operators</h3>
        <b>empty "" : ${empty ""}</b></br>
        <b>empty "string" : ${empty "string"}</b><br/>
        <b>empty null : ${empty null}</b>
    </body>
</html>
```

Output of above program will be:

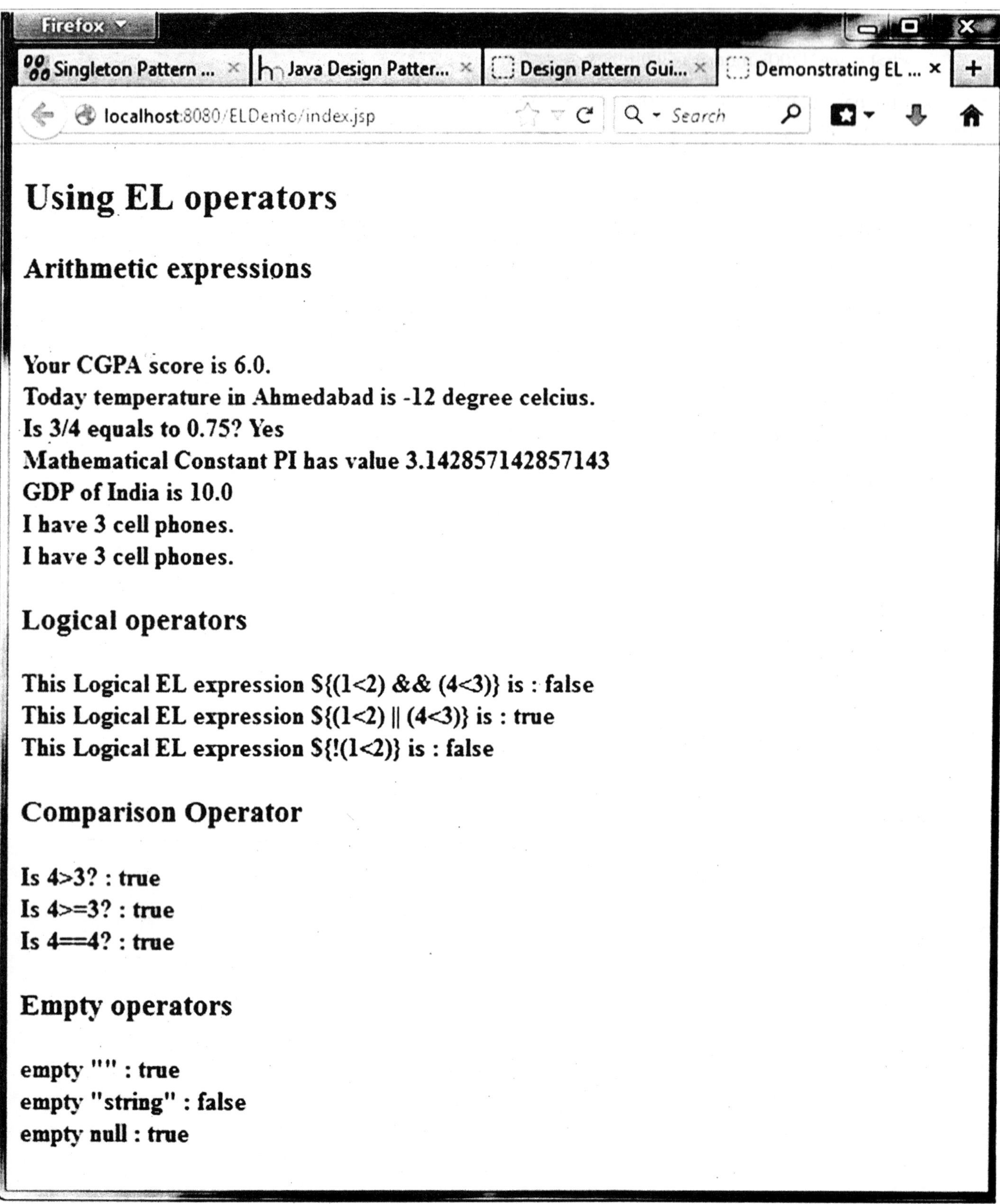

## 13.9 Java Standard Tag Library (JSTL)

The JavaServer Pages Standard Tag Library (JSTL) is a collection of useful JSP tags which encapsulates core functionality common to many JSP applications.

JSTL has support for common, structural tasks such as iteration and conditionals, tags for manipulating XML documents, internationalization tags, and SQL tags. It also provides a framework for integrating existing custom tags with JSTL tags.

The JSTL tags can be classified, according to their functions, into following JSTL tag library groups that can be used when creating a JSP page:

- Core Tags
- Formatting tags
- SQL tags
- XML tags
- JSTL Functions

If you are using Apache Tomcat container then follow the following two simple steps:

- Download the binary distribution from Apache Standard Taglib and unpack the compressed file.
- To use the Standard Taglib from its Jakarta Taglibs distribution, simply copy the JAR files in the distribution's 'lib' directory to your application's webapps\ROOT\WEB-INF\lib directory.

To use any of the libraries, you must include a <taglib> directive at the top of each JSP that uses the library.

- **Core Tags**

The core group of tags is the most frequently used JSTL tags. Following is the syntax to include JSTL *core library* in your JSP:

```
<%@ taglib prefix="c" uri="http://java.sun.com/jsp/jstl/core" %>
```

There are following Core JSTL Tags.

| Tag | Description |
|---|---|
| <c:out > | Like <%= ... >, but for expressions. |
| <c:set > | Sets the result of an expression evaluation in a 'scope' |
| <c:remove > | Removes a scoped variable (from a particular scope, if specified). |
| <c:catch> | Catches any Throwable that occurs in its body and optionally exposes it. |
| <c:if> | Simple conditional tag which evalutes its body if the supplied condition is true. |
| <c:choose> | Simple conditional tag that establishes a context for mutually exclusive conditional operations, marked by <when> and <otherwise> |
| <c:when> | Subtag of <choose> that includes its body if its condition evalutes to 'true'. |
| <c:otherwise > | Subtag of <choose> that follows <when> tags and runs only if all of the prior conditions evaluated to 'false'. |

| | |
|---|---|
| <c:import> | Retrieves an absolute or relative URL and exposes its contents to either the page, a String in 'var', or a Reader in 'varReader'. |
| <c:forEach > | The basic iteration tag, accepting many different collection types and supporting subsetting and other functionality . |
| <c:forTokens> | Iterates over tokens, separated by the supplied delimeters. |
| <c:param> | Adds a parameter to a containing 'import' tag's URL. |
| <c:redirect > | Redirects to a new URL. |
| <c:url> | Creates a URL with optional query parameters |

- **Formatting Tags**

The JSTL formatting tags are used to format and display text, the date, the time, and numbers for internationalized Web sites. Following is the syntax to include JSTL *formatting library* in your JSP:

```
<%@ taglib prefix="fmt" uri="http://java.sun.com/jsp/jstl/fmt" %>
```

Following is the list of Formatting JSTL Tags:

| Tag | Description |
|---|---|
| <fmt:formatNumber> | To render numerical value with specific precision or format. |
| <fmt:parseNumber> | Parses the string representation of a number, currency, or percentage. |
| <fmt:formatDate> | Formats a date and/or time using the supplied styles and pattern |
| <fmt:parseDate> | Parses the string representation of a date and/or time |
| <fmt:bundle> | Loads a resource bundle to be used by its tag body. |
| <fmt:setLocale> | Stores the given locale in the locale configuration variable. |
| <fmt:setBundle> | Loads a resource bundle and stores it in the named scoped variable or the bundle configuration variable. |
| <fmt:timeZone> | Specifies the time zone for any time formatting or parsing actions nested in its body. |
| <fmt:setTimeZone> | Stores the given time zone in the time zone configuration variable |
| <fmt:message> | To display an internationalized message. |
| <fmt:requestEncoding> | Sets the request character encoding |

- **SQL Tags**

The JSTL SQL tag library provides tags for interacting with relational databases (RDBMSs) such as Oracle, mySQL, or Microsoft SQL Server. Following is the syntax to include JSTL *SQL library* in your JSP:

```
<%@ taglib prefix="sql" uri="http://java.sun.com/jsp/jstl/sql" %>
```

Following is the list of SQL JSTL Tags:

| Tag | Description |
|---|---|
| <sql:setDataSource> | Creates a simple DataSource suitable only for prototyping |
| <sql:query> | Executes the SQL query defined in its body or through the sql attribute. |
| <sql:update> | Executes the SQL update defined in its body or through the sql attribute. |
| <sql:param> | Sets a parameter in an SQL statement to the specified value. |
| <sql:dateParam> | Sets a parameter in an SQL statement to the specified java.util.Date value. |
| <sql:transaction > | Provides nested database action elements with a shared Connection, set up to execute all statements as one transaction. |

- **XML Tags**

The JSTL XML tags provide a JSP-centric way of creating and manipulating XML documents. Following is the syntax to include JSTL XML library in your JSP.

The JSTL XML tag library has custom tags for interacting with XML data. This includes parsing XML, transforming XML data, and flow control based on XPath expressions.

```
<%@ taglib prefix="x" uri="http://java.sun.com/jsp/jstl/xml" %>
```

Before you proceed with the examples, you would need to copy following two XML and XPath related libraries into your <Tomcat Installation Directory>\lib:

**xercesImpl.jar:** Download it from http://www.apache.org/dist/xerces/j/

**xalan.jar:** Download it from http://xml.apache.org/xalan-j/index.html

Following is the list of XML JSTL Tags:

| Tag | Description |
|---|---|
| <x:out> | Like <%= ... >, but for XPath expressions. |
| <x:parse> | Use to parse XML data specified either via an attribute or in the tag body. |
| <x:set > | Sets a variable to the value of an XPath expression. |
| <x:if > | Evaluates a test XPath expression and if it is true, it processes its body. If the test condition is false, the body is ignored. |
| <x:forEach> | To loop over nodes in an XML document. |
| <x:choose> | Simple conditional tag that establishes a context for mutually exclusive conditional operations, marked by <when> and <otherwise> |
| <x:when > | Subtag of <choose> that includes its body if its expression evalutes to 'true' |
| <x:otherwise > | Subtag of <choose> that follows <when> tags and runs only if all of the prior conditions evaluated to 'false' |
| <x:transform > | Applies an XSL transformation on a XML document |
| <x:param > | Use along with the transform tag to set a parameter in the XSLT stylesheet |

- **JSTL functions**

JSTL includes a number of standard functions, most of which are common string manipulation functions. Following is the syntax to include JSTL Functions library in your JSP:

```
<%@ taglib prefix="fn" uri="http://java.sun.com/jsp/jstl/functions" %>
```

Following is the list of JSTL Functions:

| Function | Description |
|---|---|
| fn:contains( ) | Tests if an input string contains the specified substring. |
| fn:containsIgnoreCase( ) | Tests if an input string contains the specified substring in a case insensitive way. |
| fn:endsWith( ) | Tests if an input string ends with the specified suffix. |
| fn:escapeXml( ) | Escapes characters that could be interpreted as XML markup. |
| fn:indexOf( ) | Returns the index withing a string of the first occurrence of a specified substring. |
| fn:join( ) | Joins all elements of an array into a string. |
| fn:length( ) | Returns the number of items in a collection, or the number of characters in a string. |
| fn:replace( ) | Returns a string resulting from replacing in an input string all occurrences with a given string. |
| fn:split( ) | Splits a string into an array of substrings. |
| fn:startsWith( ) | Tests if an input string starts with the specified prefix. |
| fn:substring( ) | Returns a subset of a string. |
| fn:substringAfter( ) | Returns a subset of a string following a specific substring. |
| fn:substringBefore( ) | Returns a subset of a string before a specific substring. |
| fn:toLowerCase( ) | Converts all of the characters of a string to lower case. |
| fn:toUpperCase( ) | Converts all of the characters of a string to upper case. |
| fn:trim( ) | Removes white spaces from both ends of a string. |

## 13.10 MVC in JSP

MVC stands for Model View and Controller. It is a design pattern that separates the business logic, presentation logic and data.

**Controller** acts as an interface between View and Model. Controller intercepts all the incoming requests.

**Model** represents the state of the application i.e. data. It can also have business logic.

**View** represents the presentation i.e. User Interface

There are two main advantages of using MVC architecture.

- Navigation Control is centralized
- Easy to maintain the large application

Refer following example, to understand MVC architecture, where we are using **servlet** as a *controller*, **jsp** as a *view* component, **JavaBean** class as a *model*.

In this example, we have created 5 pages:

- **index.jsp** a page that gets input from the user.
- **ControllerServlet.java** a servlet that acts as a controller.
- **loginSuccess.jsp** and **loginError.jsp** files acts as view components.
- **web.xml** file for mapping the servlet.

**File: index.jsp**

```
<form action="ControllerServlet" method="post">
Name:<input type="text" name="name"><br>
Password:<input type="password" name="password"><br>
<input type="submit" value="login">
</form>
```

**ControllerServlet.java**

```
package mvc.mvcdemo;
import java.io.IOException;
import java.io.PrintWriter;
import javax.servlet.RequestDispatcher;
import javax.servlet.ServletException;
import javax.servlet.http.HttpServlet;
import javax.servlet.http.HttpServletRequest;
import javax.servlet.http.HttpServletResponse;
public class ControllerServlet extends HttpServlet
{
   protected void doPost(HttpServletRequest request, HttpServletResponse response)
   throws ServletException, IOException
   {
      response.setContentType("text/html");
      PrintWriter out=response.getWriter( );
```

```
        String name=request.getParameter("name");
        String password=request.getParameter("password");
        LoginBean bean=new LoginBean( );
        bean.setName(name);
        bean.setPassword(password);
        request.setAttribute("bean",bean);
        boolean status=bean.validate( );
        if(status)
        {
            RequestDispatcher rd=request.getRequestDispatcher("login-success.jsp");
            rd.forward(request, response);
        }
        else
        {
            RequestDispatcher rd=request.getRequestDispatcher("login-error.jsp");
            rd.forward(request, response);
        }
    }   // end of doPost( )

    @Override
    protected void doGet(HttpServletRequest req, HttpServletResponse resp)
    throws ServletException, IOException
    {
      doPost(req, resp);
    }   // end of doGet( )
}       // end of class
```

**File: LoginBean.jsp**

```
package mvc.mvcdemo;
public class LoginBean
{
    private String name,password;
    public String getName( )
```

```
    {
        return name;
    }
    public void setName(String name)
    {
        this.name = name;
    }
    public String getPassword( )
    {
        return password;
    }
    public void setPassword(String password)
    {
        this.password = password;
    }
    public boolean validate( )
    {
        if(password.equals("admin"))
        {
            return true;
        }
        else
        {
            return false;
        }
    }
}
```

**File: LoginSuccess.jsp**

```
<%@page import="mvc.mvcdemo.LoginBean"%>


<p>You are successfully logged in!</p>
<%
LoginBean bean=(LoginBean)request.getAttribute("bean");
out.print("Welcome, "+bean.getName( ));
%>
```

**File: LoginError.java**

```
<p>Sorry! username or password error</p>
<%@ include file="index.jsp" %>
```

**File: web.xml**

```
<?xml version="1.0" encoding="UTF-8"?>
<web-app xmlns:xsi="http://www.w3.org/2001/XMLSchema-instance"
xmlns="http://java.sun.com/xml/ns/javaee" xmlns:web="http://java.sun.com/xml/ns/javaee/web-app_2_5.xsd"
xsi:schemaLocation="http://java.sun.com/xml/ns/javaee http://java.sun.com/xml/ns/javaee/web-app_3_0.xsd"
id="WebApp_ID" version="3.0">
 <servlet>
 <servlet-name>s1</servlet-name>
 <servlet-class> mvc.mvcdemo.ControllerServlet</servlet-class>
 </servlet>
 <servlet-mapping>
 <servlet-name>s1</servlet-name>
 <url-pattern>/ControllerServlet</url-pattern>
 </servlet-mapping>
</web-app>
```

The output of above program will be as shown in above screentshot.

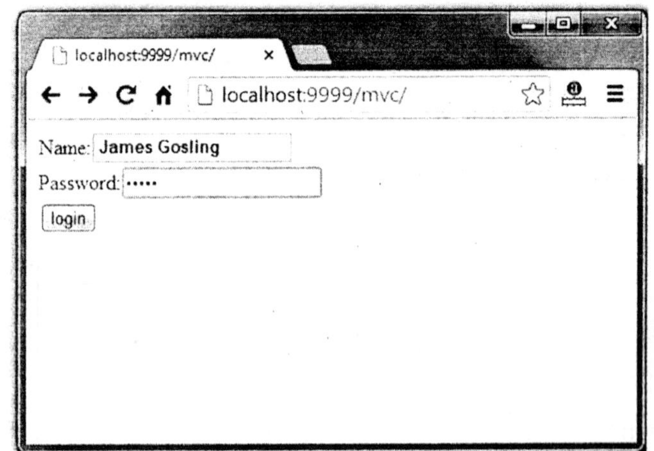


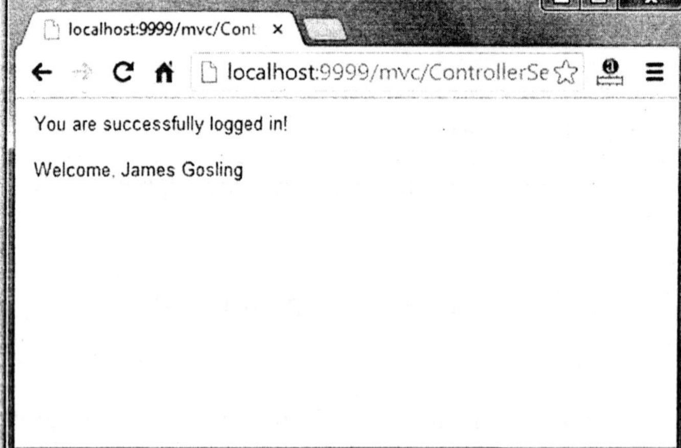


*****

# Chapter 14

# Struts

When Java servlets were first invented, many programmers quickly realized that they were a Good Thing. They were faster and more powerful that standard CGI, portable, and infinitely extensible. But writing HTML to send to the browser in endless println( ) statements was tiresome and problematic.

*The answer to that was JavaServer Pages, which turned Servlet writing into a new world. Now developers could easily mix HTML with Java code, and have all the advantages of servlets.* After that Java web applications quickly became "JSP-centric". Using JSP was not a Bad Thing at all, but it did require little more to resolve flow control issues and other problems endemic to web applications. So now another paradigm was needed that can overcome this problem of handling flow control.

Many clever developers realized that ***JavaServer Pages & servlets could be used together*** to deploy web applications. **The servlets could help with the control-flow, and the JSPs could focus on the nasty business of writing HTML**. With this using JSPs and servlets together became known as Model 2.

At that time many have been quick to point out that JSP's Model 2 follows the classic Model-View-Controller design pattern. This Model 2, following classic Model-View-Controller design pattern, was updated as Apache Struts project.

The Apache Struts Project was launched in May 2000 by Craig R. McClanahan to provide a standard MVC framework to the Java community. In July 2001, version 1.0 was released, and IOHO, Java Model 2 development has never been quite the same.

## 14.1 Introducing Struts2

Struts1 was the first version of the Struts framework. With the changing technology, the need for new enhancements and changes was felt in the original design of Struts1. These changes include development of new and lightweight MVC-based frameworks such as spring stripes, tapestry and many more, to enable rapid development of web applications. Therefore, it became necessary to modify the Struts framework.

Two new frameworks, **Shale** and **Struts Ti** were introduced in response to the growing need for rapid development of web applications. Then in March a2002, the WebWork framework was released. The WebWork includes new ideas, concepts and functionality with the original Struts code. In December 2005m *WebWorks* and *Struts Ti* merged and developed Struts2.

Struts2 has features similar to Struts1, but the Struts2 framework has some architectural differences as compare to Struts1. In general, the Struts2 framework implements MVC 2 architecture by centralizing the control using a front controller strategy similar to Struts1. However, the basic code of components and their configuration is quite different in Struts2.

## 14.2 Why Struts2?

Struts2 is created with the intention of streamlining the entire development life cycle of Web applications, which includes building, deploying and maintaining these Web applications. Each web application development framework has its own architecture; and the way the components are designed and configured using these frameworks is also different. What makes Struts2 better option amongst the other frameworks can be explained with the help of the features provided by Struts2.

Here are some of the great features that may force you to consider Struts2:

**POJO forms and POJO actions** - Struts2 has done away with the Action Forms that were an integral part of the Struts framework. With Struts2, you can use any POJO to receive the form input. Similarly, you can now see any POJO as an Action class.

**Tag support** - Struts2 has improved the form tags and the new tags allow the developers to write less code.

**AJAX support** - Struts2 has recognized the takeover by Web2.0 technologies, and has integrated AJAX support into the product by creating AJAX tags, that function very similar to the standard Struts2 tags.

**Easy Integration** - Integration with other frameworks like *Spring, Tiles* and *SiteMesh* is now easier with a variety of integration available with Struts2.

**Template Support** - Support for generating views using templates.

**Plug-in Support** - The core Struts2 behavior can be enhanced and augmented by the use of plug-ins. A number of plug-ins are available for Struts2.

**Profiling** - Struts2 offers integrated profiling to debug and profile the application. In addition to this, Struts also offers integrated debugging with the help of built in debugging tools.

**Easy to modify tags** - Tag markups in Struts2 can be tweaked using *Freemarker templates*. This does not require JSP or java knowledge. Basic HTML, XML and CSS knowledge is enough to modify the tags.

**Promote fewer configurations** - Struts2 promotes lesser configurations with the help of using default values for various settings. You don't have to configure something unless it deviates from the default settings set by Struts2.

## 14.3 MVC 2 architecture in Struts2

The Struts2 framework follows the MVC 2 design pattern, where Model, View and Controllers components are represented by Action, Result and FilterDispatcher classes, respectively. Following diagram shows the implementation of the MVC pattern by Struts2 components.

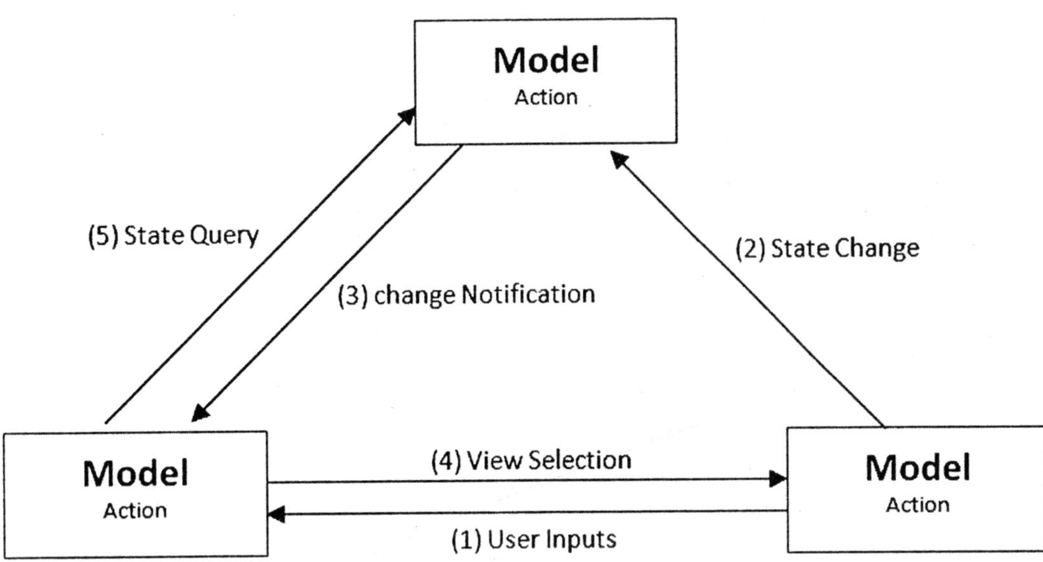


Following are the steps for the work flow in Struts2.

1. The user sends a request through a user interface provided by the view, which further passes this request to controller represented by *FilterDispatcher* class.
2. The controller servlet filter receives the input request coming from the user through the interface provided by the view, instantiates an object of the suitable action class, and executes different methods over this object.
3. If the state of model is changed, all the associated views are notified about the changes.
4. Then the controller selects the new view to be displayed according to the result code return by the action class.
5. The view presents the user interface. The view queries about the state of the model to show the current data, which is received from the action class.

## 14.4 Components of Struts2 based Application

Since Struts2 contains various framework components such as built-in classes, servlets and Struts tags. All framework components work together in a standard manner. The architecture of Struts2 based application defines the relationship and interaction between these framework components.

Following diagram shows the architecture of Struts2 based application.

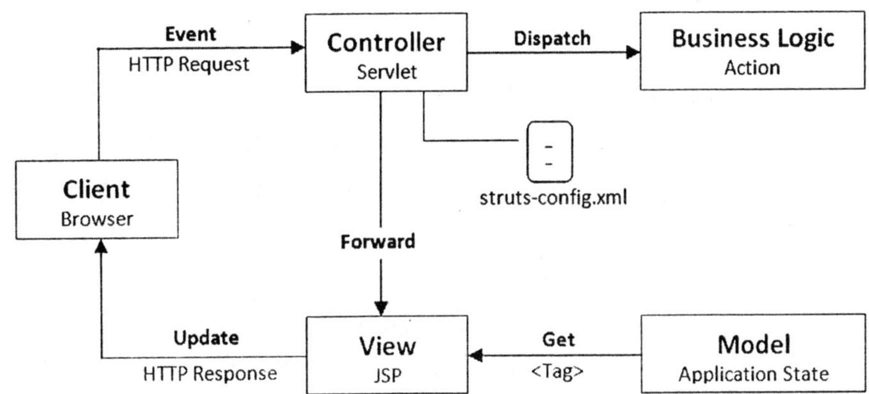

This architecture looks somewhat similar to the diagram shown in MVC architecture (section 14.3). But notice that a new group of components called Business Logic has been introduced. This can be seen as the separation of business logic from the model layer of the traditional MVC architecture. The business logic component allows the model layer to store only the state of a web application. *The components created as business logic group are known as action classes.*

Following is the list of different Struts2 components that performs specific task in Struts2 application.

- Controller
- The struts-config.xml File
- Action classes
- Model
- View

Let's discuss these components one by one.

**Controller**

The controller receives the requests from users and decides where to send the request. The main goal of the controller is to map the request URI to an action class using the mappings provided in the struts-config.xml file. There is a single controller servlet and all requests go through this servlet which is provided by the framework itself.

**The struts-config.xml File**

The struts-config.xml file contains the transformation and configuration information for the Struts application. It provides the information regarding various Struts resources, such as, action classes and interceptors.

**Action classes**

Action classes implements the business logic. They are basically responsible for executing the business service according to user requests.

**Model**

Model represents the data objects with the help of JavaBeans. In Struts2, the model is represented by *ActionForm* class, which provides the methods to get and set data fields with methods to validate the data.

**View**

The view represents a JSP or HTML page. The presentation semantics are encapsulated within a view. There is no business logic available in the view.

## 14.5 Struts2 Architecture / Request flow in Struts2

Apache Struts2 framework is a combined work of WebWork and Struts community. Previously it was known as webwork2 which later on named as Struts2. It uses Inversion of Control (IoC) and architectural MVC pattern, It also enables Aspect-Oriented Programming (AOP) using Interceptors. As Struts2 has built in support of AJAX, it is also ideally suitable for developing web 2.0 application.

The architecture of Struts2 combines the standard JEE technologies such as Java Filters, JavaBeans, ResourceBundles, Locales, XML etc in its architecture. Following diagram shows the Struts2 Architecture / Request flow in Struts2.

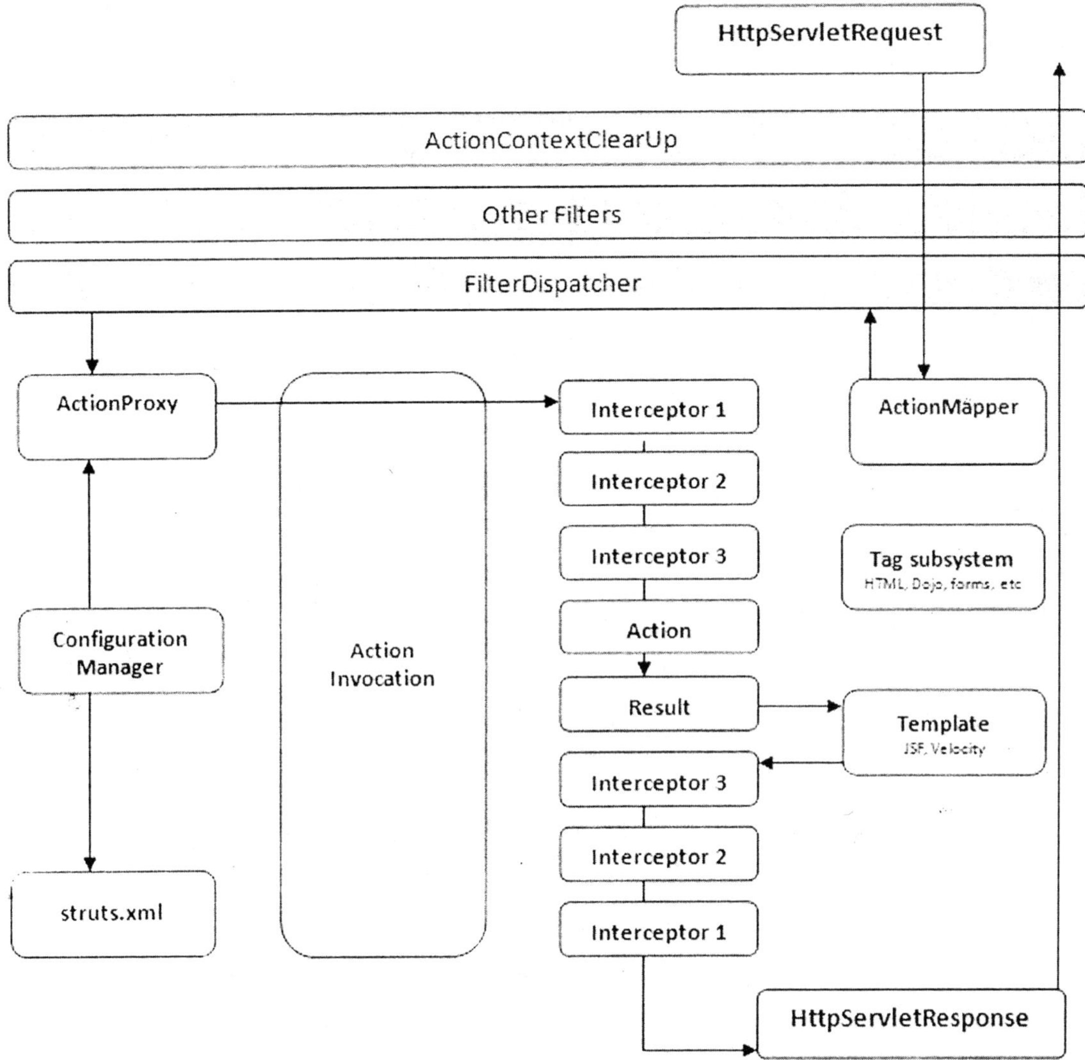


- Lifecycle begins with the request sent from User. Once this request reaches the ServetContainer container passes the request to Filter according to configuration defined in web.xml. If request need to forwarded to Struts2 Framework request will go to ***Filter*** (Struts2 provides *StrutsPrepareAndExecuteFilter* / *StrutsPrepareFilter* / *StrutsExecuteFilter*).
- Filter then called which consults the ***ActionMapper*** to determine whether an ***Action*** should be invoked or not.
- If ActionMapper finds an Action to be invoked, the FilterDispatcher delegates control to ***ActionProxy***.
- ActionProxy reads the configuration file such as struts.xml. ***ActionProxy*** creates an instance of ***ActionInvocation*** class and delegates the control.
- ***ActionInvocation*** is responsible for command pattern implementation. It invokes the ***Interceptors*** one by one (if required) and then invokes the Action.
- Once the Action returns, the ActionInvocation is responsible for looking up the proper result associated with the Action result code mapped in struts.xml.

- The result is then executed, which often involves a **template** written in JSP or FreeMarker to be rendered. While rendering, templates can use the Struts Tags provided by the framework. Some of those components will work with the ActionMapper to render proper URLs for additional requests.
- The Interceptors are executed again in reverse order and the response is returned to the Filter. And the result is then sent to the servlet container which in turns sends it back to client.
- If the ActionContextCleanUp filter is present, the FilterDispatcher will not clean up the ThreadLocal ActionContext. If the ActionContextCleanUp filter is not present, the FilterDispatcher will cleanup all ThreadLocals.

## 14.6 Struts2 Configuration Files

Struts 2 holds a set of configuration files for configuring a Web application. The files used to configure an application in Struts 2 are:

- web.xml file
- struts.xml file
- struts-config.xml file
- struts.properties

Honestly speaking we can survive using *web.xml* and *struts.xml* configuration files in any web application. Then also following sub-section explains all four configuration files.

**web.xml file:**

The web.xml configuration file is a J2EE configuration file that determines how elements of the HTTP request are processed by the servlet container. It is not strictly a Struts2 configuration file, but it is a file that needs to be configured for Struts2 to work.

As discussed earlier, this file provides an entry point for any web application. The entry point of Struts2 application will be a filter defined in deployment descriptor (web.xml). Hence we will define an entry of FilterDispatcher class in web.xml. The web.xml file needs to be created under the folder WebContent/WEB-INF.

This is the first configuration file we will need to configure if we start without the aid of a template or tool that generates it. Following is the example showing contents of web.xml file.

```
<?xml version="1.0" encoding="UTF-8"?>
<web-app xmlns:xsi="http://www.w3.org/2001/XMLSchema-instance"
  xmlns="http://java.sun.com/xml/ns/javaee"
  xmlns:web="http://java.sun.com/xml/ns/javaee/web-app_2_5.xsd"
  xsi:schemaLocation="http://java.sun.com/xml/ns/javaee
  http://java.sun.com/xml/ns/javaee/web-app_3_0.xsd"
  id="WebApp_ID" version="3.0">

  <display-name>Struts 2</display-name>
  <welcome-file-list>
    <welcome-file>index.jsp</welcome-file>
  </welcome-file-list>
```

```
<filter>
  <filter-name>struts2</filter-name>
  <filter-class>
    org.apache.struts2.dispatcher.FilterDispatcher
  </filter-class>
</filter>

<filter-mapping>
  <filter-name>struts2</filter-name>
  <url-pattern>/*</url-pattern>
</filter-mapping>
</web-app>
```

Note that we map the Struts 2 filter to /*, and not to /*.action which means that all urls will be parsed by the struts filter. We will cover this when we will go through the Annotations chapter.

**struts.xml file:**

The **struts.xml** file contains the configuration information that you will be modifying as actions are developed. This file can be used to override default settings for an application, for example*struts.devMode = false* and other settings which are defined in property file. This file can be created under the folder **WEB-INF/classes**.

Let us have a look at the struts.xml file.

```
<?xml version="1.0" encoding="UTF-8"?>
<!DOCTYPE struts PUBLIC
  "-//Apache Software Foundation//DTD Struts Configuration 2.0//EN"
  "http://struts.apache.org/dtds/struts-2.0.dtd">
<struts>
  <constant name="struts.devMode" value="true" />
  <package name="helloworld" extends="struts-default">

    <action name="hello"
        class="com.tutorialspoint.struts2.HelloWorldAction"
        method="execute">
        <result name="success">/HelloWorld.jsp</result>
    </action>
    <-- more actions can be listed here -->

  </package>
  <-- more packages can be listed here -->
</struts>
```

**struts-config.xml file:**

The struts-config.xml configuration file is a link between the View and Model components in the Web Client. For most of the projects, we never need to modify the contents of this file. Following is the sample struts-config.xml example.

```
<?xml version="1.0" encoding="ISO-8859-1" ?>
<!DOCTYPE struts-config PUBLIC
"-//Apache Software Foundation//DTD Struts Configuration 1.0//EN"
"http://jakarta.apache.org/struts/dtds/struts-config_1_0.dtd">

<struts-config>

  <!-- ========== Form Bean Definitions ============ -->
  <form-beans>
    <form-bean name="login" type="test.struts.LoginForm" />
  </form-beans>

  <!-- ========== Global Forward Definitions ========= -->
  <global-forwards>
  </global-forwards>

  <!-- ========== Action Mapping Definitions ======== -->
  <action-mappings>
    <action
      path="/login"
      type="test.struts.LoginAction" >

      <forward name="valid" path="/jsp/MainMenu.jsp" />
      <forward name="invalid" path="/jsp/LoginView.jsp" />
    </action>
  </action-mappings>

  <!-- ========== Controller Definitions ======== -->
  <controller
    contentType="text/html;charset=UTF-8"
    debug="3"
    maxFileSize="1.618M"
    locale="true"
    nocache="true"/>

</struts-config>
```

**struts.properties file**

This configuration file provides a mechanism to change the default behavior of the framework. Actually all of the properties contained within the struts.properties configuration file can also be configured in the web.xml using the init-param, as well using the constant tag in the struts.xml configuration file. But if you like to keep the things separate and more struts specific then you can create this file under the folder WEB-INF/classes.

```
### When set to true, Struts will act much more friendly for developers
struts.devMode = true

### Enables reloading of internationalization files
struts.i18n.reload = true

### Enables reloading of XML configuration files
struts.configuration.xml.reload = true

### Sets the port that the server is run on
struts.url.http.port = 8080
```

## 14.7 Struts Action classes

Action classes will be defined to handle requests. Actions exists **between the Model and View** of an application. This article will cover all of the standard actions and the helper methods of the Action class. The *struts-config.xml* file designates the Action classes that handle requests for various URLs. The Action objects do

- Invoke the appropriate business
- Data-access logic
- Store the results in beans
- Designate the type of situation (missing data, database error etc.)

The struts-config.xml file then decides which JSP page should apply to that situation. Generally Actions do

- Invoke business rules
- Return Model objects to the View to display.

Actions also prepare error messages to display in the View. We can also create utility actions. Utility actions can be linked to other actions using action chaining. This allows us to extend the behavior of an action without changing an action or having deeply nested class hierarchies of actions.

**Actions have a life cycle similar to servlets.** They are like servlets and they're **multithreaded**. We must be careful when working with member variables of an action because they are not thread safe. Struts has a servlet called the **ActionServlet**. The **ActionServlet** inspects the incoming request and delegates the request to an action based on the incoming request path. The object that relates the action to the incoming request path is the Action Mapping. Our actions are part of the Struts Controller.

As discussed above, we can create different action classes for different user cases. For every request, an action class mapping is searched and the associated class methods are invoked. Struts2 actions are not singletons; in other word, for each request, a different instance of the action class is created. Therefore, Struts2 action need not be thread-safe, as in case of Struts1 actions.

Now, the question arises, how can we access different objects to work with, such as request, response and session? The solution for this problem is Dependency Injection pattern.

The Dependency Injection pattern used in Struts2 is interface injection. This means that we can implement various interfaces that provide different methods to the action class. These implemented methods should be invoked in the predefined order, which is assured by the user of appropriate Interceptor configured for the action.

Let's now list the various interfaces and classes used to create, configure and execute the action class.

- Forward Action
- IncludeAction
- SwitchAction
- DispatchAction
- IncludeDispatchAction
- LookupDispatchAction

Let's discuss them one by one.

- **ForwardAction**

This is an Action that forwards to the context-relative URI specified by the parameter property of our associated ActionMapping. This can be used to integrate Struts with other business logic components that are implemented as servlets or JSP pages, but still take advantage of the Struts controller servlet's functionality such as processing of form beans. To configure the use of this Action in our struts-config.xml file, create an entry as follows.

```
<action
path="/saveSubscription"
type="org.apache.struts.actions.ForwardAction"
name="subscriptionForm"
scope="request"
input="/subscription.jsp"
parameter="/path to processing servlet" />
```

This one will forward control to the **context-relative URI** specified by the parameter attribute.

Steps to use ForwardAction:

- Using the **html:link** tag with the action attribute, add a link to the JSP page that points to the action.
- Create an **Action Mapping** in the Struts configuration file that uses the *ForwardAction* with the parameter attribute to specify the JSP path.

Let's consider, we have a JSP page that has a direct link to another JSP page:

```
<html:link page="/example.jsp">Home< /html:link>
```

Now we want to change the **html:link** tag to link to an action. Because we already have a link, simply change it as follows.

```
<html:link action="home">Home</html:link>
```

All we did is, removing the page attribute and adding an Action attribute that points to the home action. Now, we have to create the home action mapping. To add an action mapping to the home action that we referenced in our **html:link tag,** use this code.

```
<action path="/home" type="org.apache.struts.actions.ForwardAction" parameter="/example.jsp" />
```

Now let's see how to use forward attribute. *ForwardActions* get used quite a bit-so much so that the Struts configuration file includes support for them. So rather than doing this:

```
<action
path="/home"
type="org.apache.struts.actions.ForwardAction"
parameter="/ example.jsp"/>
```

We prefer to do this:

```
<action
path="/home"
forward="/example.jsp"/>
```

- **IncludeAction**

This is an Action that includes the context-relative URI specified by the parameter property of our associated *ActionMapping*. This can be used to integrate Struts with other business logic components that are implemented as servlets or JSP pages, but still take advantage of the Struts controller servlet's functionality such as processing of form beans. To configure the use of this Action in our struts-config.xml file, create an entry like this:

```
<action
path="/saveSubscription"
type="org.apache.struts.actions.IncludeAction"
name="subscriptionForm"
scope="request"
input="/subscription.jsp"
parameter="/path to processing servlet">
```

This will include the context-relative URI specified by the parameter attribute. This shorter form uses the include attribute:

```
<action
path="/legacy"
include="/legacy/roar"
input="/form/userForm2.jsp"
name="userForm"
parameter="/legacy/roar"
validate="true"
scope="request"/>
```

The difference between the *IncludeAction* and the *ForwardAction* is that we need to use the *IncludeAction* only if the action is going to be included by another action or JSP. Therefore, if we have code in our JSP that looks like this:

```
<jsp:include page="/someWebApp/ someModule/someAction.do " />
```

The action could not use a ForwardAction because it would forward control to the new action rather than including its output within the output of the JSP-or throw a nasty IllegalStateException if the output buffer was already committed.

- **SwitchAction**

This is a standard Action that switches to a new module and then forwards control to a URI within the new module. Valid request parameters for this Action are:

- **page**: Module-relative URI (beginning with "/") to which control should be forwarded after switching.
- **prefix**: The module prefix (beginning with "/") of the module to which control should be switched. Use a zero-length string for the default module. The appropriate ModuleConfig object will be stored as a request attribute, so any subsequent logic will assume the new module.

We have a web application that uses Struts. Struts has two modules: the default module and an admin module, both shown below.

```
<servlet>
<servlet-name>action</servlet-name>
<servlet-class>
org.apache.struts.action.ActionServlet
</servlet-class>
<init-param>
<param-name>config</param-name>
<param-value>/WEB-INF/struts-config.xml </param-value>
</init-param>
<init-param>
<param-name>config/admin</param-name>
<param-value>/WEB-INF/struts-config-admin.xml </param-value>
</init-param>
<load-on-startup>1</load-on-startup>
</servlet>
```

The **init parameter config/admin defines the admin module**. The *config* init parameter defines the default module. Now, let's say we have an action in the default module that edits users and we want to delegate the display of those users to an action in the admin module. Perform the following steps:

First, map a SwitchAction into the default moduleas shown here:

```
<action
path="/switch"
type="org.apache.struts.actions.SwitchAction">
</action>
```

Now, we can set up a forwardin the action that edits the users as follows:

```
<action
path="/userSubmit"
attribute="userForm"
input="/form/userForm.jsp"
name="userForm"
scope="request"
type="action.UserAction">
<forward name="success" path="/switch.do?page=/listUsers.do&prefix=/admin"/>
</action>
```

This forward passes two request parameters. The page parameter specifies the module relative action. The second parameter specifies the prefix of the module. We don't have to use forwards to use the SwitchAction; any JSP can link to the *SwitchAction* to move to any module. The listUser.do action is not defined in the default module; it's defined in the admin. The forward in this example forwards to the action at the path /admin/listUsers.do. The listUser.do is defined in /WEB-INF/struts-config-admin.xml, and the userSubmit. do action is defined in /WEB-INF/struts-config.xml.

- **DispatchAction**

This is an abstract Action that dispatches to a public method that is named by the request parameter whose name is specified by the parameter property of the corresponding ActionMapping. This Action is useful for developers who prefer to combine many similar actions into a single Action class, in order to simplify their application design. To configure the use of this action in our struts-config.xml file, create an entry like this:

```
<action
path="/saveSubscription"
type="org.apache.struts.actions.DispatchAction"
name="subscriptionForm"
scope="request"
input="/subscription.jsp"
parameter="method"/>
```

This will use the value of the request parameter named "method" to pick the appropriate "execute" method, which must have the same signature of the standard **Action.execute( )** method. For example, we might have the following three methods in the same action:

- **Public ActionForward delete(ActionMapping mapping, ActionForm form, HttpServletRequest request, HttpServletResponse response) throws Exception**
- **Public ActionForward insert(ActionMapping mapping, ActionForm form, HttpServletRequest request, HttpServletResponse response) throws Exception**
- **Public ActionForward update(ActionMapping mapping, ActionForm form, HttpServletRequest request, HttpServletResponse response) throws Exception**

and call one of the methods with a URL like this:

*http://localhost:8080/myapp/saveSubscription.do?method=update*

It should be noted that we don't have to use the *DispatchAction* to group multiple actions into one Action class. We could just use a hidden field that we inspect to delegate to member() methods inside of our action. On the other hand, we could use the action element's parameter attribute and decide which method to invoke based on the value of the parameter attribute.

The *DispatchAction* uses a hidden request parameter to determine which method to invoke. Thus, subclasses of the *DispatchAction* have many methods with the same signature of the **execute()** method. The name of the hidden request parameter specifies the name of the method to invoke. We specify the name of the hidden parameter by using the parameter attribute of the action element.

Rather than having a single **execute()** method, we have a method for each logical action. The *DispatchAction* dispatches to one of the logical actions represented by the methods. It picks a method to invoke based on an incoming request parameter. The value of the incoming request parameter is the name of the method that the *DispatchAction* will invoke.

All of the other mapping characteristics of this action must be shared by the various handlers. This places some constraints over what types of handlers may reasonably be packaged into the same *DispatchAction* subclass. If the value of the request parameter is empty, a method named unspecified is called. The default action is to throw an exception. If the request was cancelled, the custom handler cancelled, will be used instead. We can also override the **getMethodName( )** method to override the action's default handler selection. Here is an example that groups multiple actions into one action.

**Step 1:** Create an **action handlerclass** that subclasses *DispatchAction*:

```
public class UserRegistrationMultiAction extends DispatchAction { ... }
```

**Step 2:** Create a method to represent each logical related action:

```
public ActionForward processPage1(ActionMapping mapping, ActionForm form,
HttpServletRequest request, HttpServletResponse response) throws Exception
{
        ...
}
public ActionForward processPage2(ActionMapping mapping, ActionForm form,
HttpServletRequest request, HttpServletResponse response) throws Exception
{
        ...
}
```

These methods have the same signature other than the method name of the standard Action method.

**Step 3:** Create an Action Mapping for this action handler using the parameter attribute to specify the request parameter that carries the name of the method that we want to invoke:

```
<action
path="/userRegistrationMultiPage1"
type="strutsTutorial.UserRegistrationMultiAction"
name="userRegistrationForm"
attribute="user"
```

```
parameter="action"
input="/userRegistrationPage1.jsp">
...
</action>
<action
path="/userRegistrationMultiPage2"
type="strutsTutorial.UserRegistrationMultiAction"
name="userRegistrationForm"
attribute="user"
parameter="action"
input="/userRegistrationPage2.jsp">
...
</action>
```

Based on this code, the *DispatchAction* that we created uses the value of the request parameter named method to pick the appropriate method to invoke. The parameter attribute specifies the name of the request parameter that is inspected by the *DispatchAction*.

**Step 4:** Pass the action a request parameter that refers to the method we want to invoke. The userRegistrationPage1.jsp contains this hidden parameter.

```
<html:hidden property="action" value="processPage1"/>
```

while the userRegistrationPage2.jsp contains this hidden parameter:

```
<html:hidden property="action" value="processPage2"/>
```

This implementation sends a hidden field parameter instead that specifies which method to invoke.

- **LookupDispatchAction**

This is an abstract Action that dispatches to the subclass mapped execute method. This is useful in cases where an HTML form has multiple submit buttons with the same name. The button name is specified by the parameter property of the corresponding ActionMapping. To configure the use of this action in our struts-config.xml file, create an entry like this:

```
<action
path="/test"
type="org.example.MyAction"
name="MyForm"
scope="request"
input="/test.jsp"
parameter="method"/>
```

This will use the value of the request parameter named "method" to locate the corresponding key in *ApplicationResources*. For example, we might have the following ApplicationResources.properties:

```
button.add=Add Record
button.delete=Delete Record
```

And our JSP would have the following format for submit buttons:

```
<html:form action="/test">
<html:submit property="method">
<bean:message key="button.add"/>
</html:submit>
<html:submit property="method">
<bean:message key="button.delete"/>
</html:submit>
</html:form>
```

Our subclass must implement both **getKeyMethodMap( )** and the methods defined in the map. An example of such implementations are:

```
protected Map getKeyMethodMap( )
{
        Map map = new HashMap( );
        map.put("button.add", "add");
        map.put("button.delete", "delete");
        return map;
}
public ActionForward add(ActionMapping mapping, ActionForm form, HttpServletRequest request,
HttpServletResponse response) throws IOException, ServletException
{
        // do add
        return mapping.findForward("success");
}
public ActionForward delete(ActionMapping mapping, ActionForm form, HttpServletRequest request,
HttpServletResponse response) throws IOException, ServletException
{
        // do delete
        return mapping.findForward("success");
}
```

If duplicate values exist for the keys returned by getKeys, only the first one found will be returned. If no corresponding key is found then an exception will be thrown. We can override the method unspecified to provide a custom handler. If the **submit** was **cancelled**, the custom handler cancelled will be used instead.

For this example, we use the registration form to use the *LookupDispatchAction*. We will add two buttons. One button will be labeled Save; this button will save the user to the system. The second button will be called Remove to use the *LookupDispatchAction*, perform the following steps:

**Step 1:** Create an action handler class that subclasses LookupDispatchAction:

```
public class UserRegistrationAction extends LookupDispatchAction {...}
```

**Step 2:** Next, we create a method to represent each logical related action: save and remove:

```
public class UserRegistrationAction extends LookupDispatchAction
{
        private static Log log = LogFactory.getLog(UserRegistrationAction.class);
        public ActionForward remove( ActionMapping mapping, ActionForm form,
        HttpServletRequest request, HttpServletResponse response) throws Exception
        {
                log.debug("IN REMOVE METHOD");
                return mapping.findForward("success");
        }
        public ActionForward save(ActionMapping mapping, ActionForm form, HttpServletRequest request,
        HttpServletResponse response) throws Exception
        {
                /* Create a User DTO and copy the properties from the userForm */
                User user = new User( );
                BeanUtils.copyProperties(user, form);
                DataSource dataSource = getDataSource(request, "userDB");
                Connection conn = dataSource.getConnection();
                try
                {
                        /* Create UserDAO */
                        UserDAO dao = DAOFactory.createUserDAO(conn);
                        /* Use the UserDAO to insert the new user into the system */
                        dao.createUser(user);
                }
                finally
                {
                        conn.close( );
                }
                return mapping.findForward("success");
        }
}
```

The two action methods, save and remove, have identical signatures to the standard Action.execute() method except for the method name.

**Step 3:** Implement the getKeyMethodMap()method to map the resource keys to method names:

```
protected Map getKeyMethodMap( )
{
        Map map = new HashMap( );
        map.put("userRegistration.removeButton", "remove");
        map.put("userRegistration.saveButton", "save");
        return map;
}
```

**Step 4:** Create an action mapping for this action handler using the parameter attribute to specify the request parameter that carries the name of the method we want to invoke:

```
<action
path="/userRegistration"
type="strutsTutorial.UserRegistrationAction"
name="userRegistrationForm"
attribute="user"
input="/userRegistration.jsp"
parameter="action" >
...
<forward name="success" path="/regSuccess.jsp" />
<forward name="failure" path="/regFailure.jsp" />
</action>
```

Here we specify the parameter to the action. This has a similar meaning to the *DispatchAction*. Essentially, this means the *LookupDispatchAction* inspects the label of the button called action. The label will be looked up from the resource bundle, the corresponding key will be found, and the key will be used against the method map to find the name of the method to invoke.

**Step 5:** Set up the messages in the resource bundle for the labels and values of the buttons. Inside our resource bundle, add the following two entries:

```
userRegistration.removeButton=Remove
userRegistration.saveButton=Save
```

Here the keys are the same keys we used in the getKeyMethodMap.

**Step 6:** Use the **bean:messagetag** to display the labels of the button and associate the buttons with the name action:

```
<%@ taglib uri="/tags/struts-html" prefix="html"%>
<%@ taglib uri="/tags/struts-bean" prefix="bean"%>
...
<html:submit property="action">
<bean:message key="userRegistration.removeButton"/>
</html:submit>
...
<html:submit property="action">
<bean:message key="userRegistration.saveButton"/>
</html:submit>
...
```

- **Some more Actions and Action Helper Methods**

Some more actions are there. Those are

**BaseAction:** BaseAction is provided as an intermediate class for shared funtionality between Action and any stock implementation provided in this package.

**DownloadAction:** This is an abstract base class that minimizes the amount of special coding that needs to be written to download a file.

**EventDispatchAction:** An Action that dispatches to to one of the public methods that are named in the parameter attribute of the corresponding ActionMapping and matches a submission parameter.

**LocaleAction:** Implementation of Action that changes the user's Locale and forwards to a page, based on request level parameters that are set (language, country, & page).

**MappingDispatchAction:** An abstract Action that dispatches to a public method that is named by the parameter attribute of the corresponding ActionMapping.

The Action class contains many helper methods, which enable us to add advanced functionality to our Struts applications. Some of them are

**Action saveTokenand isTokenValid:** Make sure that a form is not submitted twice

**Action saveMessages and getResources:** Display dynamic messages that are i18n-enabled

**Action isCancelled:** Allow users to cancel an operation

**Action getLocale and setLocale:** Allow users to change their locale.

## 14.8 Interceptors

Interceptors are conceptually the same as servlet filters or the JDKs Proxy class. Interceptors allow for crosscutting functionality to be implemented separately from the action as well as the framework. We can achieve the following using interceptors:

- Providing pre-processing logic before the action is called.
- Providing post-processing logic after the action is called.
- Catching exceptions so that alternate processing can be performed.

Many of the features provided in the Struts2 framework are implemented using interceptors; examples include exception handling, file uploading, lifecycle callbacks and validation etc. In fact, as Struts2 bases much of its functionality on interceptors, it is not unlikely to have 7 or 8 interceptors assigned per action.

**Struts2 Framework Interceptors:**

Struts 2 framework provides a good list of out-of-the-box interceptors that come preconfigured and ready to use. Few of the important interceptors are listed below:

| Interceptor | Description |
|---|---|
| alias | Allows parameters to have different name aliases across requests. |
| checkbox | Assists in managing check boxes by adding a parameter value of false for check boxes that are not checked. |
| conversionError | Places error information from converting strings to parameter types into the action's field errors. |
| createSession | Automatically creates an HTTP session if one does not already exist. |
| debugging | Provides several different debugging screens to the developer. |

| | |
|---|---|
| execAndWait | Sends the user to an intermediary waiting page while the action executes in the background. |
| exception | Maps exceptions that are thrown from an action to a result, allowing automatic exception handling via redirection. |
| fileUpload | Facilitates easy file uploading. |
| i18n | Keeps track of the selected locale during a user's session. |
| logger | Provides simple logging by outputting the name of the action being executed. |
| params | Sets the request parameters on the action. |
| prepare | This is typically used to do pre-processing work, such as setup database connections. |
| profile | Allows simple profiling information to be logged for actions. |
| scope | Stores and retrieves the action's state in the session or application scope. |
| ServletConfig | Provides the action with access to various servlet-based information. |
| timer | Provides simple profiling information in the form of how long the action takes to execute. |
| token | Checks the action for a valid token to prevent duplicate formsubmission. |
| validation | Provides validation support for actions |

Please loook into Struts 2 documentation for complete detail on above mentioned interceptors. But I will show you how to use an interceptor in general in your Struts application.

**using Interceptors**

Let us see how to use an already existing interceptor to our program. We will use the timer interceptor whose purpose is to measure how long it took to execute an action method. Same time we are using params interceptor whose purpose is to send the request parameters to the action. We can try your example without using this interceptor and you will find that name property is not being set because parameter is not able to reach to the action.

```
<?xml version="1.0" encoding="UTF-8"?>
<!DOCTYPE struts PUBLIC
  "-//Apache Software Foundation//DTD Struts Configuration 2.0//EN"
  "http://struts.apache.org/dtds/struts-2.0.dtd">
<struts>
  <constant name="struts.devMode" value="true" />
  <package name="helloworld" extends="struts-default">
    <action name="hello"
      class="com.tutorialspoint.struts2.HelloWorldAction"
      method="execute">
      <interceptor-ref name="params"/>
      <interceptor-ref name="timer" />
      <result name="success">/HelloWorld.jsp</result>
    </action>
  </package>
</struts>
```

## Creating Custom Interceptors

Using custom interceptors in your application is an elegant way to provide cross-cutting application features. Creating a custom interceptor is easy; the interface that needs to be extended is the following Interceptor interface:

```
public interface Interceptor extends Serializable
{
  void destroy( );
  void init();
  String intercept(ActionInvocation invocation) throws Exception;
}
```

As the names suggest, the **init( )** method provides a way to initialize the interceptor, and the destroy() method provides a facility for interceptor cleanup. Unlike actions, interceptors are reused across requests and need to be thread-safe, especially the **intercept( )** method.

The ActionInvocation object provides access to the runtime environment. It allows access to the action itself and methods to invoke the action and determine whether the action has already been invoked.

If you have no need for initialization or cleanup code, the *AbstractInterceptor* class can be extended. This provides a default no-operation implementation of the **init( )** and **destroy( )** methods.

## Creating Interceptor class

```
package j2ee.web.struts2;

import java.util.*;
import com.opensymphony.xwork2.ActionInvocation;
import com.opensymphony.xwork2.interceptor.AbstractInterceptor;

public class MyInterceptor extends AbstractInterceptor {

  public String intercept(ActionInvocation invocation)throws Exception{

    /* let us do some pre-processing */
    String output = "Pre-Processing";
    System.out.println(output);

    /* let us call action or next interceptor */
    String result = invocation.invoke();

    /* let us do some post-processing */
    output = "Post-Processing";
    System.out.println(output);

    return result;
  }
}
```

As you notice, actual action will be executed using the interceptor by **invocation.invoke( )** call. So we can do some pre-processing and some post-processing based on your requirement.

The framework itself starts the process by making the first call to the ActionInvocation object's **invoke( )**. Each time **invoke( )** is called, ActionInvocation consults its state and executes whichever interceptor comes next. When all of the configured interceptors have been invoked, the **invoke( )** method will cause the action itself to be executed.

**Stacking multiple Interceptors**

As we can imagine, having to configure multiple interceptor for each action would quickly become extremely unmanageable. For this reason, interceptors are managed with interceptor stacks. Here is an example, directly from the struts-default.xml file:

```
<interceptor-stack name="basicStack">
  <interceptor-ref name="exception"/>
  <interceptor-ref name="servlet-config"/>
  <interceptor-ref name="prepare"/>
  <interceptor-ref name="checkbox"/>
  <interceptor-ref name="params"/>
  <interceptor-ref name="conversionError"/>
</interceptor-stack>
```

The above stake is called basicStack and can be used in your configuration as shown below. This configuration node is placed under the <package .../> node. Each <interceptor-ref .../> tag references either an interceptor or an interceptor stack that has been configured before the current interceptor stack. It is therefore very important to ensure that the name is unique across all interceptor and interceptor stack configurations when configuring the initial interceptors and interceptor stacks.

We have already seen how to apply interceptor to the action, applying interceptor stacks is no different. In fact, we use exactly the same tag:

```
<action name="hello" class=" package j2ee.web.struts2. MyInterceptor ">
  <interceptor-ref name="basicStack"/>
  <result>view.jsp</result>
</action>
```

The above registration of "basicStack" will register complete stake of all the six interceptors with hello action. This should be noted that interceptors are executed in the order, in which they have been configured. For example, in above case, exception will be executed first, second would be servlet-config and so on.

## 14.9 The ActionForm class

An *ActionForm* **is a JavaBean that extends** ***org.apache.struts.action.ActionForm***. *ActionForm* maintains the session state for web application and the *ActionForm* object is automatically populated on the server side with data entered from a form on the client side.

**Step 1:** We will first create the class *AddressForm* which extends the ActionForm class. Here is the code of the class:

**AddressForm.java**

```
package j2ee.web;

import javax.servlet.http.HttpServletRequest;
import org.apache.struts.action.*;

/**
 * Form bean for the Address Entry Screen.
*/

public class AddressForm extends ActionForm
{
        private String name=null;
        private String address=null;
        private String emailAddress=null;

        public void setName(String name)
        {
                this.name=name;
        }

        public String getName( )
        {
                return this.name;
        }

        public void setAddress(String address)
        {
                this.address=address;
        }

        public String getAddress( )
        {
                return this.address;
        }


        public void setEmailAddress(String emailAddress)
        {
                this.emailAddress=emailAddress;
        }

        public String getEmailAddress( )
        {
                return this.emailAddress;
```

```
    }

    /**
     * Reset all properties to their default values.
     * @param mapping The mapping used to select this instance
     * @param request The servlet request we are processing
     */

    public void reset(ActionMapping mapping, HttpServletRequest request)
    {
            this.name=null;
            this.address=null;
            this.emailAddress=null;
    }

    /**
     * Reset all properties to their default values.
     * @param mapping The mapping used to select this instance
     * @param request The servlet request we are processing
     * @return errors
     */

    public ActionErrors validate(ActionMapping mapping, HttpServletRequest request)
    {
            ActionErrors errors = new ActionErrors( );
            if( getName() == null || getName().length() < 1 )
            {
                    errors.add("name",new ActionMessage("error.name.required"));
            }
            if( getAddress() == null || getAddress().length() < 1 )
            {
                    errors.add("address",new ActionMessage("error.address.required"));
            }
             if( getEmailAddress() == null || getEmailAddress().length() < 1 )
            {
                    errors.add("emailaddress",new ActionMessage("error.emailaddress.required"));
            }
            return errors;
    }
}
```

The above class populates the Address Form data and validates it. The **validate( )** method is used to validate the inputs. If any or all of the fields on the form are blank, error messages are added to the *ActionMapping* object.

**Step 2:** Now we will create the Action class which is the model part of the application. Our action class simply forwards the request the **Success.jsp**. Here is the code of the *AddressAction* class:

***AddressAction.java***

```
package j2ee.web;

import javax.servlet.http.HttpServletRequest;
import javax.servlet.http.HttpServletResponse;
import org.apache.struts.action.Action;
import org.apache.struts.action.ActionForm;
import org.apache.struts.action.ActionForward;
import org.apache.struts.action.ActionMapping;

public class AddressAction extends Action
{
public ActionForward execute(ActionMapping mapping, ActionForm form, HttpServletRequest request,
        HttpServletResponse response) throws Exception
        {
                return mapping.findForward("success");
        }
}
```

**Step 3:** Now we have to create an entry for form bean in the *struts-config.xml*. Add the following lines in the *struts-config.xml* file:

**struts-config.xml**

```
<form-bean
name="AddressForm"
type="j2ee.web.AddressForm"/>
```

Add the following line in the struts-config.xml file for handling the action "/Address.do":

```
<action
  path="/Address"
  type=" j2ee.web.AddressAction"
  name="AddressForm"
  scope="request"
  validate="true"
  input="/pages/Address.jsp">
 <forward name="success" path="/pages/success.jsp"/>
</action>
```

**Step 4:** Now create Address.jsp, which is our form for entering the address details. Code for Address.jsp is as follows:

**Address.jsp**

```
<%@ taglib uri="/tags/struts-bean" prefix="bean" %>
  <%@ taglib uri="/tags/struts-html" prefix="html" %>
  <html:html locale="true">
  <head>
  <title><bean:message key="welcome.title"/></title>
```

```
<html:base/>
</head>
<body bgcolor="white">

<html:form action="/Address">
<html:errors/>
<table>
   <tr>
    <td align="center" colspan="2">
        <font size="4">Please Enter the Following Details</font>
   </tr>
   <tr>
    <td align="right">
     Name
    </td>
    <td align="left">
     <html:text property="name" size="30" maxlength="30"/>
    </td>
   </tr>
   <tr>
    <td align="right">
     Address
    </td>
    <td align="left">
     <html:text property="address" size="30" maxlength="30"/>
    </td>
   </tr>

   <tr>
    <td align="right">
     E-mail address
    </td>
    <td align="left">
     <html:text property="emailAddress" size="30" maxlength="30"/>
    </td>
   </tr>
   <tr>
    <td align="right">
     <html:submit>Save</html:submit>
    </td>
    <td align="left">
     <html:cancel>Cancel</html:cancel>
    </td>
   </tr>
</table>
</html:form>
</body>
</html:html>
```

User enter the values in the form and click on the submit form. The form validation is done on the server side and error message is displays on the JSP page. To display the error on the JSP page **<html:errors/>** tag is used. The **<html:errors/>** tag displays all the errors in one go. To create text box **<html:text .../>** is used in jsp page.

*<html:text property="address" size="30" maxlength="30"/>*

**Step 5:** Above tag creates text box for entering the address. The address is retrieved from and later stored in the property named address in the form-bean. The tag **<html:submit>Save</html:submit>** creates the submit button and the tag **<html:cancel>Cancel</html:cancel>** is used to create the Cancel button.

**Step 6:** Add the following line in the **index.jsp** to create a link for testing the Address.jsp form:

*<html:link page="/pages/Address.jsp">Test the Address Form</html:link>*

**Step 7:** Build the application and click on the ***Test the Address Form*** link on the index page to test the newly created screen.

## 14.10 Understanding Struts2 Tags

The 's' prefix has been used in JSP pages to implement Struts2 tags. The tags in Struts2 can be divided into two categories.

- Generic tags
- UI tags

Let's study these tags one by one.

- <u>Generic Tags</u>

Generic tags are used for controller the flow of data and data extraction from the value stack or other locations. In other words, the generic tags are developed to control the flow of execution in the page, and obtain & display data.

Similar to other tags, Generic tags are also contained in a tag library, which is a collection of predefined tags. We have been using Struts2 tag library in our previous applications and designed a number of JSP pages using them. Each tag has a specific work and many attributes. We can use these tags in our JSP page by simply importing a tag library in our JSP page, as follows:

*<%@ taglib prefix="s" uri="/struts-tags" %>*

We know that the <%@ %> directive identifies the URI defined in the previously listed <taglib> elements and states that all the tags should be prefixed with string 's'.

In Struts1 there are many tag libraries; whereas in Struts2 only one tag library is specified. The Generic tags are one of the most important tags of the Struts2 tag library. The Generic tags are specified in the ***/struts-tags*** tag library. There are two types of Generic tags.

- Control tags
- Data tags

**Control tags**

Control tags are used to control the behavior of data on a page. Control tags are designed to control the path of execution with the help of some decision making constructs. Following table shows the Control tags with description.

| Tag | Description | Attributes |
|---|---|---|
| if | Allow to implement the conditional flow of execution. 'If' tag could be used by itself or can be followed by zero or more 'Else if' Tags followed by zero or one 'Else' Tag. | - test |
| elseif | Allow to extend the decision making to a number of conditions, and is used along with *if tag.* | - test |
| else | Allow to provide alternate execution path if tests given in if tag are false. | |
| append | Allow to append iteratable lists together to form an appended iterator. | - id<br>- var |
| generator | Generates an iterator on the basis of a given value. | - converter<br>- count<br>- id<br>- separator<br>- val<br>- var |
| iterator | Allow to iterate over the given value. | - begin<br>- end<br>- id<br>- status<br>- step<br>- value<br>- var |
| merge | Allow to merge iteratable lists together to form a merged iterator. | - id<br>- var |
| sort | Allow to sort a given list. | - comparator<br>- id<br>- source<br>- var |
| subset | Accepts an iterator and provides output for its subset. | - count<br>- decider<br>- id<br>- source<br>- start<br>- var |

**Data tags**

Data tags are used for creating and manipulating data. These tags allow us to either get data out of the value stack or place variables and objects in the value stack. Following table shows the Data tags with description

| Tag | Description | Attributes |
|---|---|---|
| a | Helps to create hyperlink. | accesskey, action, encode, id, key, label, name, title, value, theme, tooltip, cssClass (and many more) |
| action | Helps to call actions directly from a page. | - executeResult<br>- flush<br>- id<br>- name<br>- namespace<br>- rethrowException<br>- var |
| bean | Helps to create an instance of a class, which is in agreement with JavaBean specification. | - id<br>- name<br>- var |
| date | Helps to format and display date objects in different ways. | - format<br>- id<br>- name<br>- nice<br>- timezone<br>- var |
| debug | Helps to create link, which can be clicked to view all value stack contents with different items available in the stack context. | |
| i18n | Helps to get a resource bundle and place it on value stack, so that in addition to the bundle associated with action, other resource bundles could be used. | - name |
| includes | Includes output of some Servlet or JSP page. | - value |
| param | Helps to define parameters to other tags. | - name<br>- supressEmptyParameters<br>- value |
| property | Helps to get the property of a value and returns the object from the top of the stack, by default | - default<br>- escape<br>- ecsapeCsv<br>- escapeHtml<br>- escapeJavaScript<br>- escapeXml<br>- value |
| push | Pushes the value into the stack. | - value |
| set | Helps to assign a value to a variable. It is similar to setting a variable with the given value. | - id<br>- name<br>- scope<br>- value<br>- var |
| text | Helps to render an internationalized message from the resource bundle. | - id<br>- name<br>- searchValueStack<br>- var |

| url | Helps to create a URL. | - anchor<br>- id<br>- method<br>- scheme<br>- value<br>- var (and many more) |
|---|---|---|

- **UI Tags**

The UI tags provide a way to create user interface components on the screen. The UI tags are basically used to design the web page with high quality UI components that may include a form with other individual components contained in it, such as textbox, combobox, submit buttons, radio buttons and checkboxes.

The UI tags represent the tags and generate the reusable HTML format. The UI tags work on the basis of templates. Templates again group together to form the themes, which are used to perform the actual operation. The UI tags are classified into the following three categories.

- Form tags
- Non-form tags
- Ajax tags

**Form tags**

Form tags allow the display of data in a simple and reusable format. These tags also include the HTML representation, which provides the features of reusability. These tags are used to create a basic HTML form and other form components. Following table lists the Form tags.

| checkbox | optgroup |
|---|---|
| checkboxlist | password |
| combobox | radio |
| doubleselect | reset |
| head | select |
| file | submit |
| form | textarea |
| hidden | textfield |
| label | token |
| optiontransferselect | updownselect |

These tags are already described in JSP, with all their syntaxes and attributes.

**Non-form tags**

The Non-form UI tags are used to display the output texts, such as action-level messages, action-level errors, and field-level errors. Following list shows the Non-form UI tags.

| actionerror | actionmessage | tabbedpanel |
|---|---|---|
| component | div | treenode |
| fielderror | table | tree |

**Ajax tags**

Struts uses the DOJO framework for the AJAX tag implementation. These Ajax tags are used for AJAX implementation to work with DOJO framework. Following table lists the Ajax tags.

| | | | |
|---|---|---|---|
| a | autocompleter | bind | datetimepicker |
| div | head | submit | tabbedpanel |
| textarea | tree | treenode | |

Remember, To use the AJAX tags we must:

- Include the Dojo Plugin distributed with Struts 2 in your /WEB-INF/lib folder.
- Add <%@ taglib prefix="sx" uri="/struts-dojo-tags" %> to your page.
- Include the head tag on the page, which can be configured for performance or debugging purposes.

## 14.11 Struts validator Framework

One of the important features of Struts framework is Struts Validation framework that performs validation on incoming form data. Validation framework was introduced by **David Winterfeldt** as an external plug-in to Struts framework. Its functionality has since been split so that validator can serve as the basis for an independent component and is now part of Jakarta Commons.

The Struts framework's simple validation interface alleviates much of the headache associated with handling data validation, allowing you to focus on validation code and not on the mechanics of capturing data and redisplaying incomplete or invalid data.

In order to do form validation without Validator framework, one has to use **validate( )** method of the form bean (ActionForm class) to perform this task. Also one has to handle error messages during manual validation.

Validation framework comes with set of useful routines to handle form validation automatically and it can handle both server side as well as client side form validation. If certain validation is not present, we can create our own validation logic and plug it into validation framework as a re-usable component.

**Validator uses two XML configuration files to determine which validation routines should be installed and how they should be applied for a given application, respectively.**

**The first configuration file, validator-rules.xml,** declares the validation routines that should be plugged into the framework and provides logical names for each of the validations. The validator-rules.xml file also defines client-side JavaScript code for each validation routine. Validator can be configured to send this JavaScript code to the browser so that validations are performed on the client side as well as on the server side.

**The second configuration file, validation.xml,** defines which validation routines should be applied to which Form Beans. The definitions in this file use the logical names of Form Beans from the struts-config.xml file along with the logical names of validation routines from the validator-rules.xml file to tie the two together.

The best way to understand about the Struts validator framework is create a simple application and walk through the validation works. Here's a simple user registration form to use the Struts validator framework to check the username, password and email.

**Step 1:** UserAction

Action class that forwards a success request.

```
package j2ee.struts2.action;

import javax.servlet.http.HttpServletRequest;
import javax.servlet.http.HttpServletResponse;
import org.apache.struts.action.Action;
import org.apache.struts.action.ActionForm;
import org.apache.struts.action.ActionForward;
import org.apache.struts.action.ActionMapping;

public class UserAction extends Action
{
        public ActionForward execute(ActionMapping mapping, ActionForm form,
                HttpServletRequest request, HttpServletResponse response) trows Exception
        {
                return mapping.findForward("success");
        }
}
```

**Step 2:** UserForm

UserForm class extends the ValidatorForm class.

```
package j2ee.struts2.user.form;
import org.apache.struts.validator.ValidatorForm;

public class UserForm extends ValidatorForm
{

        String username;
        String pwd;
        String pwd2;
        String email;
}
```

**Step 3:** Properties file

A properties file contains all the label and error messages.

**user.properties**

```
#user module label message
label.user.name = Name
label.user.username = UserName
label.user.pwd = Password
label.user.pwd2 = Confirm Password
label.user.email = Email

label.user.button.submit = Submit

#Error message
err.user.username.required = Username is required.<br/>
err.user.username.length = Username length should be between {0} and {1}.<br/>
err.user.username.invalid =
Username is invalid , it should be a-z, A-Z, 0-9, dash "-" or underscore "_".<br/>

err.user.pwd.required = Password is required.<br/>
err.user.pwd.length = Password length should be between {0} and {1}.<br/>
err.user.pwd.invalid = Password is invalid , it should be a-z, A-Z, 0-9.<br/>

err.user.pwd2.notmatch = Confirm password is not match.<br/>

err.user.email.required = Email is required.<br/>
err.user.email.invalid =  Email address is invalid.<br/>
```

**Step 4:** View Page (1)

A simple jsp page to create all require the text field, and a simple thank you page

**RegisterUser.jsp**

```
<%@taglib uri="http://struts.apache.org/tags-bean" prefix="bean"%>
<%@taglib uri="http://struts.apache.org/tags-logic" prefix="logic"%>
<%@taglib uri="http://struts.apache.org/tags-html" prefix="html"%>
<html>
<head>
</head>
<body>

<h2>Struts - Validator Example</h2>
RegisterUser.jsp
<b>User Registeration Form</b>
<br/><br/>
<font color="red">
<html:errors/>
</font>
```

```
<html:form action="/Register">
<br/>
<bean:message key="label.user.username" /> :
<html:text property="username" size="20"/>
<br/>
<bean:message key="label.user.pwd" /> :
<html:text property="pwd" size="20"/>
<br/>
<bean:message key="label.user.pwd2" /> :
<html:text property="pwd2" size="20"/>
<br/>
<bean:message key="label.user.email" /> :
<html:text property="email" size="20"/>
<br/><br/>
<html:submit>
<bean:message key="label.user.button.submit" />
</html:submit>
</html:form>
</body>
</html>
```

**Step 5:** View page (2)

**Thankyou.jsp**

```
<html>
<head>
</head>
<body>
<h2>Struts - Validator Example</h2>
Thank you for the registration
</body>
</html>
```

**Step 6:** Struts configuration

Configure action , form mappings and register the "ValidatorPlugIn" plug in.

**struts-connfig.xml**

```
<?xml version="1.0" encoding="UTF-8"?>
<!DOCTYPE struts-config PUBLIC
"-//Apache Software Foundation//DTD Struts Configuration 1.3//EN"
"http://jakarta.apache.org/struts/dtds/struts-config_1_3.dtd">

<struts-config>
```

```
<form-beans>
        <form-bean name="userForm" type="j2ee.struts2.user.form.UserForm" />
</form-beans>

<action-mappings>

                <action
                        path="/Register"
                        type="j2ee.struts2.user.action.UserAction"
                        name="userForm"
                        input="/pages/RegisterUser.jsp"
                        >

                        <forward name="success" path="/pages/ThanksYou.jsp"/>

                </action>

                <action
                        path="/RegisterUserPage"
                        type="org.apache.struts.actions.ForwardAction"
                        parameter="/pages/RegisterUser.jsp"/>

</action-mappings>

<message-resources
                parameter="j2ee.struts.user" />

<plug-in className="org.apache.struts.validator.ValidatorPlugIn" >
        <set-property property="pathnames"
        value="/WEB-INF/validator-rules.xml, /WEB-INF/validator-user.xml"/>
</plug-in>

</struts-config>
```

**Step 7:** validator-user.xml

Define the validator for the userForm's username, password and email property.

```
<!DOCTYPE form-validation PUBLIC
 "-//Apache Software Foundation
//DTD Commons Validator Rules Configuration 1.3.0//EN"
 "http://jakarta.apache.org/commons/dtds/validator_1_3_0.dtd">

<form-validation>
  <formset>
    <form name="userForm">
      <field property="username" depends="required,maxlength,minlength,mask">
```

```
<msg name="required" key="err.user.username.required" />
        <msg name="maxlength" key="err.user.username.length" />
        <msg name="minlength" key="err.user.username.length" />
        <msg name="mask" key="err.user.username.invalid" />

        <arg name="maxlength" key="${var:minlength}" position="0" resource="false"/>
 <arg name="maxlength" key="${var:maxlength}" position="1" resource="false"/>

     <arg name="minlength" key="${var:minlength}" position="0" resource="false"/>
 <arg name="minlength" key="${var:maxlength}" position="1" resource="false"/>

 <var>
     <var-name>minlength</var-name>
            <var-value>3</var-value>
        </var>
        <var>
               <var-name>maxlength</var-name>
               <var-value>15</var-value>
        </var>
 <var>
               <var-name>mask</var-name>
               <var-value>^[a-zA-Z0-9-_]*$</var-value>
        </var>
</field>

<field property="pwd" depends="required,maxlength,minlength,mask">

  <msg name="required" key="err.user.pwd.required" />
        <msg name="maxlength" key="err.user.pwd.length" />
        <msg name="minlength" key="err.user.pwd.length" />
        <msg name="mask" key="err.user.pwd.invalid" />

        <arg name="maxlength" key="${var:minlength}" position="0" resource="false"/>
 <arg name="maxlength" key="${var:maxlength}" position="1" resource="false"/>

        <arg name="minlength" key="${var:minlength}" position="0" resource="false"/>
 <arg name="minlength" key="${var:maxlength}" position="1" resource="false"/>

  <var>
      <var-name>minlength</var-name>
             <var-value>7</var-value>
        </var>
        <var>
               <var-name>maxlength</var-name>
               <var-value>15</var-value>
        </var>
  <var>
```

```
                    <var-name>mask</var-name>
                    <var-value>^[a-zA-Z0-9]*$</var-value>
            </var>
    </field>

    <field property="pwd2" depends="validwhen">

        <msg name="validwhen" key="err.user.pwd2.notmatch" />

            <var>
                    <var-name>test</var-name>
                    <var-value>
                            (pwd == *this*)
                    </var-value>
            </var>
        </field>

        <field property="email" depends="required,email">
                <msg name="required" key="err.user.email.required" />
                <msg name="email" key="err.user.email.invalid" />
        </field>

    </form>
  </formset>
</form-validation>
```

**Step 8:** deploy and run project.

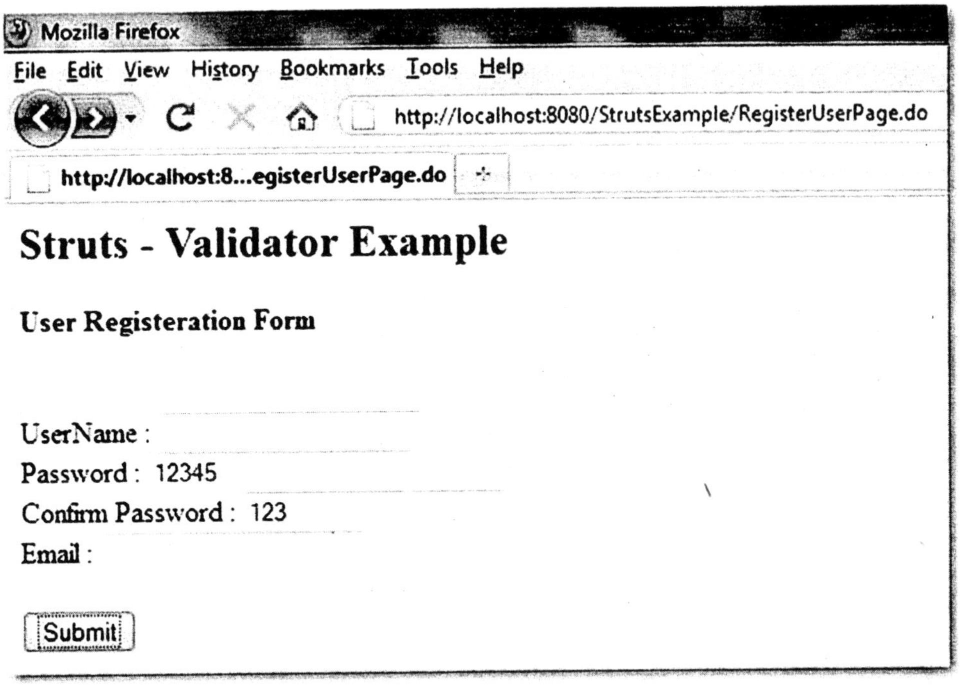

Mozilla Firefox

File Edit View History Bookmarks Tools Help

http://localhost:8080/StrutsExample/RegisterUserPage.do

http://localhost:8...egisterUserPage.do

# Struts - Validator Example

### User Registeration Form

UserName :

Password : 12345

Confirm Password : 123

Email :

Submit

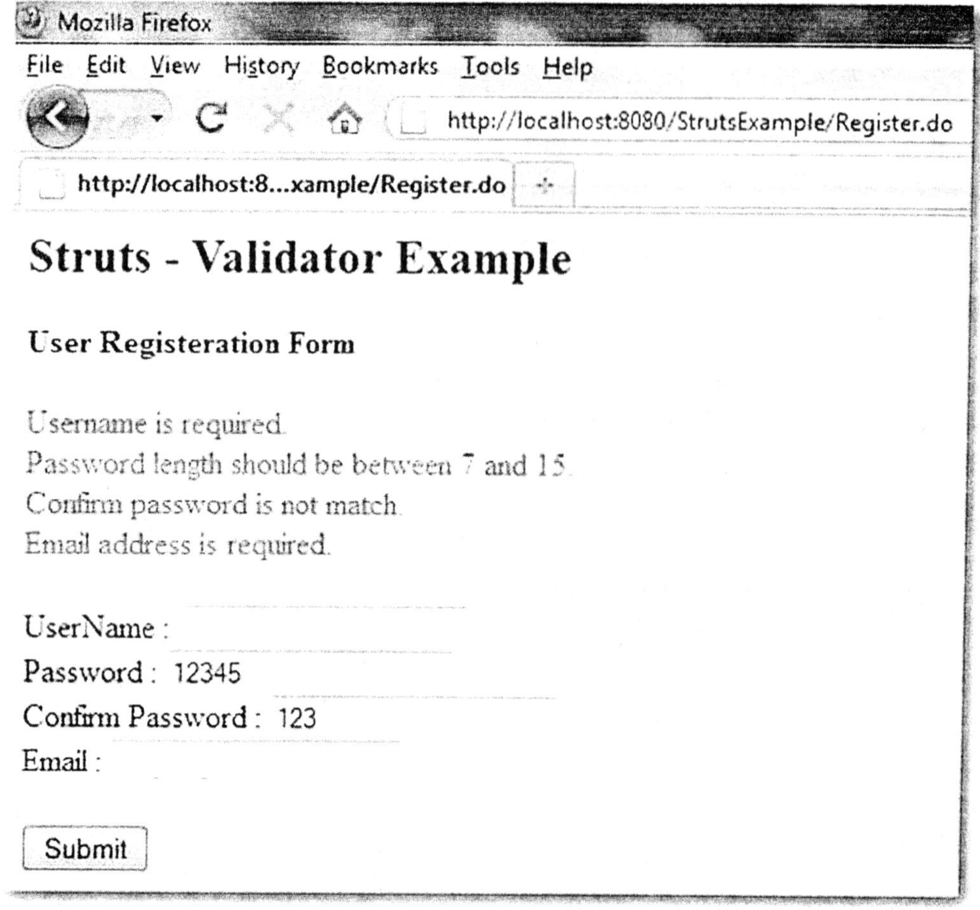


## 14.12 Custom validators

We can define our own validation logic (custom validation) in struts 2 by implementing the *Validateable* interface in the action class. The *workflow* interceptor is used to get information about the error messages defined in the action class.

**The *Workflow* Interceptor**

The workflow interceptor checks if there is any validation errors or not. It doesn't perform any validation. It is applied when action class implements the Validateable interface. The input is the default parameter for this interceptor that determines the result to be invoked for the action or field error.

It is found in the *defaultStack* so we don't need to define it explicitly. There is only 1 parameter defined for workflow interceptor. It is:

*inputResultName* : specifies the result name to be returned if field error or action error is found. It is set to input by default.

### The *Validateabale* interface

The Validateable interface must be implemented to perform validation logic in the action class. It contains only one method **validate( )** that must be overridden in the action class to define the validation logic. Signature of the validate method is:

*public void validate( );*

### The *ValidationAware* interface

The ValidationAware interface can accept the field level or action class level error messages. The field level messages are kept in Map and Action class level messages are kept in collection. It should be implemented by the action class to add any error message.

Following table shows the methods of *ValidationAware* interface.

| Method | Description |
|---|---|
| void addFieldError(String fieldName, String errorMessage) | Adds the error message for the specified field. |
| void addActionError(String errorMessage) | Adds an Action-level error message for this action. |
| void addActionMessage(String message) | Adds an Action-level message for this action. |
| void setFieldErrors(Map<String,List<String>> map) | Sets a collection of error messages for fields. |
| void setActionErrors(Collection<String> errorMessages) | Sets a collection of error messages for this action. |
| void setActionMessages(Collection<String> messages) | Sets a collection of messages for this action. |
| boolean hasErrors( ) | Checks if there are any field or action errors. |
| boolean hasFieldErrors( ) | Checks if there are any field errors. |
| boolean hasActionErrors( ) | Checks if there are any Action-level error messages. |
| boolean hasActionMessages( ) | Checks if there are any Action-level messages. |
| Map<String,List<String>> getFieldErrors( ) | Returns all the field level error messages. |
| Collection<String> getActionErrors( ) | Returns all the Action-level error messages. |
| Collection<String> getActionMessages( ) | Returns all the Action-level messages. |

### Steps to perform custom validation

The steps to perform custom validation are as follows:

Step 1: Create the form to get input from the user

Step 2: Define the validation logic in action class by extending the *ActionSupport* class and overriding the validate method

Step 3: Define result for the error message by the name input in struts.xml file

### Example to demonstrate custom validation

In this example, we are creating 4 files:

- **index.jsp** for input from the user.
- **RegisterAction.java** for defining the validation logic.
- **struts.xml** for defining the result and action.
- **welcome.jsp** for the view component.

**1) Create index.jsp for input**

*This JSP page creates a form using struts UI tags. It receives name, password and email id from the user.*

```
<%@ taglib uri="/struts-tags" prefix="s" %>
<s:form action="register">
<s:textfield name="name" label="Name"></s:textfield>
<s:password name="password" label="Password"></s:password>
<s:submit value="register"></s:submit>
</s:form>
```

**2) Create the action class (RegisterAction.java)**

This action class inherits the *ActionSupport* class and overrides the validate method to define the validation logic.

```
package j2ee.struts2;
import com.opensymphony.xwork2.ActionSupport;
public class RegisterAction extends ActionSupport
{
        private String name,password;
        public void validate( )
        {
                if(name.length( )<1)
                addFieldError("name","Name can't be blank");
                if(password.length()<6)
                addFieldError("password","Password must be greater than 5");
        }

        //getters and setters
        public String execute( )
        {
                //perform business logic here
                return "success";
        }
}
```

**3) Define input result in struts.xml**

This xml file defines an extra result by the name input, that will be invoked if any error message is found in the action class.

```
<?xml version="1.0" encoding="UTF-8" ?>
<!DOCTYPE struts PUBLIC "-//Apache Software Foundation//DTD Struts
 Configuration 2.1//EN" "http://struts.apache.org/dtds/struts-2.1.dtd">
<struts>
<package name="default" extends="struts-default">
<action name="register" class="com.javatpoint.RegisterAction">
<result>welcome.jsp</result>
<result name="input">index.jsp</result>
</action>
</package>
</struts>
```

**4) Create view component (welcome.jsp)**

The simple JSP file displaying the information of the user.

```
<%@ taglib uri="/struts-tags" prefix="s" %>
Name:<s:property value="name"/><br/>
Password:<s:property value="password"/><br/>
```

Deploy and execute above project and output will be as follows.

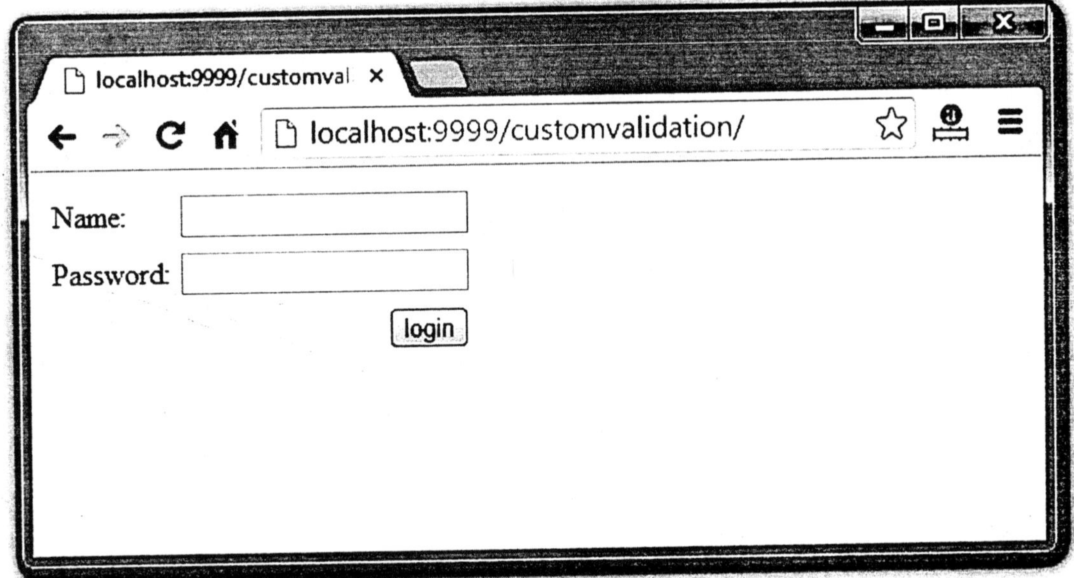


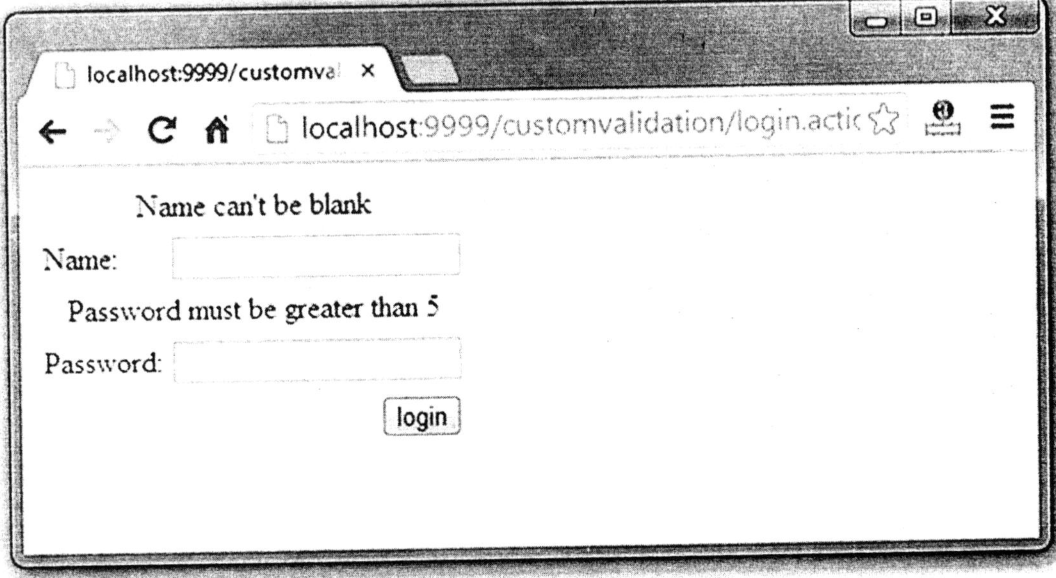


* * * * *

# Chapter 15

# Enterprise JavaBean

Developing enterprise applications has become a scary task. Enterprise applications are complex, used by different users, developed by multiple teams, and deployed on heterogeneous systems that might cover multiple environments. In addition, enterprise applications have to be distributed, secure, transactional, reliable, scalable, flexible, expandable, reusable, and manageable. Above all, enterprise applications must be integrated with existing systems, and subjective against the existing infrastructure.

Enterprise JavaBeans (EJB) is a server-side component-based architecture for developing, deploying, and managing reliable enterprise applications in production environments. EJB architecture is at the heart of the JavaEE platform. With the growth of the Web and the Internet, more and more enterprise applications are now Web based, including both intranet and internet applications. The use of EJB components helps in easy and fast development of distributed, transactional, secure and portable enterprise applications. Together, the J2EE and EJB architectures provide superior and unmatched support for Web-based enterprise applications.

The latest release of JavaBean is EJB 3.2 (on 28 May 2013). In this chapter we begin with knowing new features of EJB 3.2 and then start understanding JavaBeans and its types with examples.

## 15.1 Why JavaBeans?

Enterprise JavaBeans is a standard architecture used for enterprise level distributed applications that are object-oriented, transaction-oriented, distributed as well as secured. The implementation of enterprise bean means, creating the enterprise bean components that are managed by EJB container in the application server. The enterprise bean implements business logic, which can operate on enterprise data and is normally defined through some enterprise bean's specialized methods. These enterprise bean methods can be accessed and invoked by remote clients. The behavior of these enterprise beans can be customized at the time of their deployment by changing the entries in the deployment descriptor. The enterprise bean instance is created and managed by the EJB container where it is deployed. In addition to business logic, we can also provide service information by using annotations in the enterprise bean itself or declaratively in the deployment descriptor. The enterprise bean can use the container for all the services defined in the specification. We need to create a client view of the enterprise bean. The client view refers to creating another enterprise component or other Java program (such as applet and servlet) to access enterprise bean and its business method. The client view of the enterprise bean is independent of the type of container and server in which the enterprise bean is deployed.

EJB architecture is flexible and helps in implementing the enterprise bean in various scenarios as mentioned here:

- The enterprise bean can be used to provide all stateless services.
- The enterprise bean can be used as a web service endpoint that provides stateless service.
- The enterprise bean can be used to provide stateless service asynchronously with the arrival of some message.
- The enterprise bean can be used to provide stateful service, where the conversational state of a client is maintained.

- The enterprise bean can be used as an entity that represents a persistent object that is managed automatically for its persistence and relation with other entities.

There are different types of enterprise beans, which can be used in a web application, depending on the scenarios discussed earlier. Before we start discussing different types of bean, their implementation for business logic, their configuration, packaging and deployment; let's first discuss why EJB 3.2 is required and then discuss different EJB concepts and their architecture.

## 15.2 What is new in EJB 3.2 release?

The Enterprise JavaBeans 3.2 architecture extends Enterprise JavaBeans to include the following new functionality and simplifications to the earlier EJB APIs:

- Made support for the following features optional in this release and moved their description to a separate EJB Optional Features document:
  - EJB 2.1 and earlier Entity Bean Component Contract for Container-Managed Persistence
  - EJB 2.1 and earlier Entity Bean Component Contract for Bean-Managed Persistence
  - Client View of an EJB 2.1 and earlier Entity Bean
  - EJB QL: Query Language for Container-Managed Persistence Query Methods
  - JAX-RPC Based Web Service Endpoints
  - JAX-RPC Web Service Client View
- Enhanced message-driven beans contract with a no-methods message listener interface to expose all public methods as message listener methods.
- Defined the EJB API Groups with clear rules for an *EJB Lite* Container to support other API groups.
- Added container provided security role named "**" to indicate any authenticated caller independent of the actual role name.
- Extended the EJB Lite Group to include local asynchronous session bean invocations and non-persistent EJB Timer Service.
- Added an option for the lifecycle callback interceptor methods of stateful session beans to be executed in a transaction context determined by the lifecycle callback method's transaction attribute.
- Introduced an option to disable passivation of stateful session beans.
- Enhanced the *TimerService* API to access all active timers in the EJB module.
- Enhanced the embeddable *EJBContainer* to implement *AutoClosable* interface.
- Removed restrictions on *javax.ejb.Timer* and *javax.ejb.TimerHandle* that required references to be used only inside a bean.
- Relaxed default rules for a session bean to designate its implemented interfaces as local or as remote business interfaces.
- Enhanced the list of standard JMS MDB activation properties.
- Simplified requirements for definition of a security role using the ejb deployment descriptor.
- Removed restriction on obtaining the current class loader; replaced 'must not' with 'should exercise caution' when using the Java I/O package.

## 15.3 Enterprise Bean Architecture

The Enterprise JavaBeans architecture is a component architecture for the development and deployment of component-based distributed business applications. Applications written using the Enterprise JavaBeans architecture are scalable, transactional, and multi-user secure. These applications may be written once, and then deployed on any server platform that supports the Enterprise JavaBeans specification. The Enterprise JavaBeans architecture will make it easy to write applications: Application developers will not have to understand low-level transaction and state management details, multi-threading, connection pooling, and other complex low-level APIs.

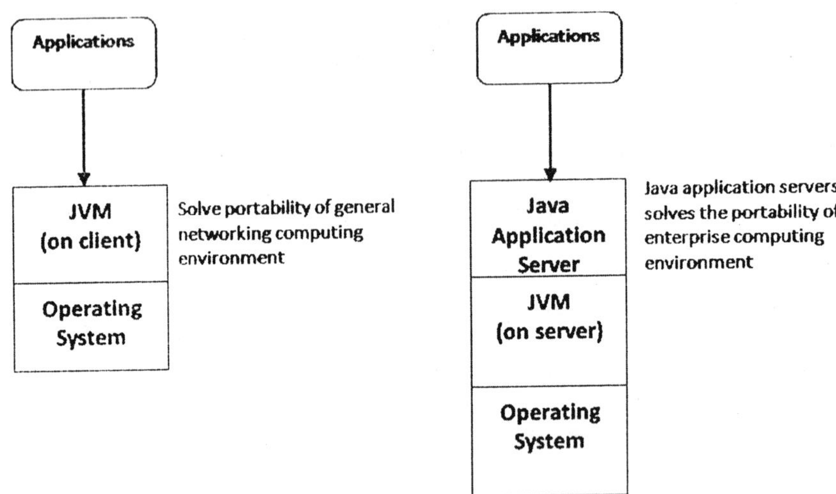


Above figure shows how Java benefits both the client and the server. The Java Virtual Machine (JVM) abstracts applications on the client from the underlying environment and operating systems. On the server side, the J2EE application server offers common infrastructure services to enterprise applications.

The J2EE architecture is a consolidation of standards, specifications, frameworks, and guidelines to provide Java capability on the server side for the enterprise. These standards and frameworks consist of classes and interfaces to be implemented by both service providers and developers. The EJB API is at the heart of the J2EE architecture. The other APIs are used as services to the EJB API. Many middleware vendors have been delivering implementations of the server-side APIs for the last few years.

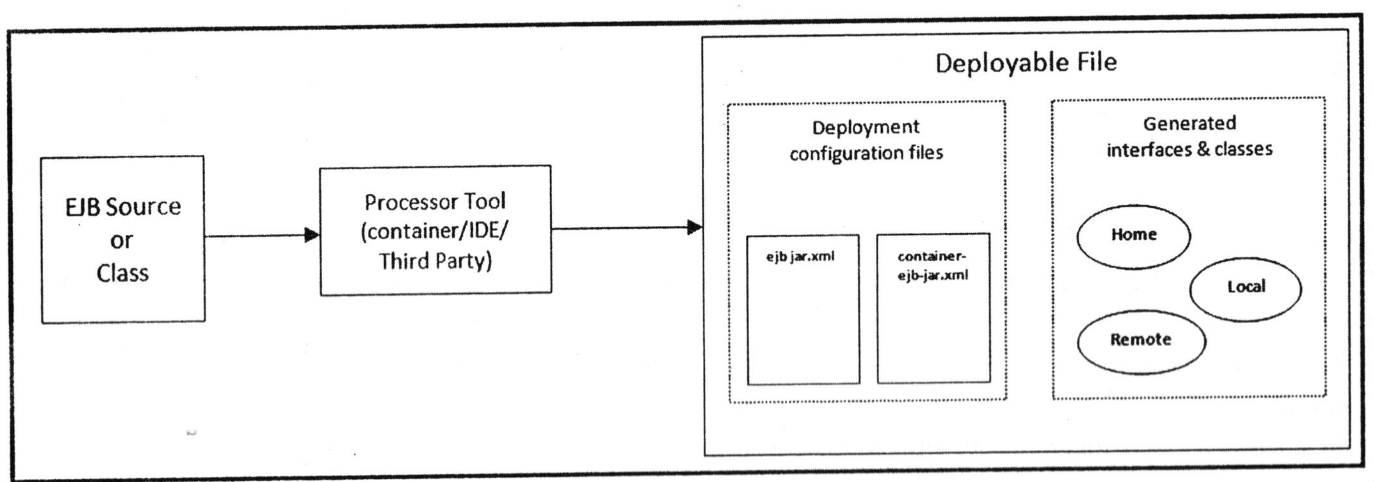


The EJB architecture comprises the EJB server, EJB container and EJB client. Let's discuss the EJB architecture by understanding EJB server, EJB container and EJB client as its important components.

**EJB server**

An EJB server is a high-level process or application that provides a run-time environment to support the execution of server applications that use enterprise beans. An EJB server provides a JNDI-accessible naming service, manages and coordinates the allocation of resources to client applications, provides access to system resources, and provides a transaction service.

In EJB architecture, servers are basically the resource managers. Every server manages the allocation of resources to the containers it controls. It is the resource manager that determines which and how many containers may run with in the memory of server (keeping in active or passive state).

The EJB container performs following functions.

- Manages all incoming client requests at the client level.
- Provides connections to clients, dispatching client requests to containers and routing response back to the clients.
- Manages the processing of resources that are available to the container at the container level.
- Verifies that the container has access to shared devices, such as a centralized security manager, a pool of JDBC drivers, a transaction service implementation, pool of active objects and response-ready methods and an asynchronous messaging service (using JMS).

We can run an EJB application on more than one server. Therefore the server must cooperate as a group to allocate resources efficiently across all the containers in a group.

EJB container

An Enterprise JavaBeans (EJB) container provides a run-time environment for enterprise beans within the application server. The container handles all aspects of an enterprise bean's operation within the application server and acts as an intermediary between the user-written business logic within the bean and the rest of the application server environment. One or more EJB modules, each containing one or more enterprise beans, can be installed in a single container.

The EJB container provides many services to the enterprise bean, such as:

- Beginning, committing, and rolling back transactions as necessary.
- Maintaining pools of enterprise bean instances ready for incoming requests and moving these instances between the inactive pools and an active state, ensuring that threading conditions within the bean are satisfied.
- Most importantly, automatically synchronizing data in an entity bean's instance variables with corresponding data items stored in persistent storage.

By dynamically maintaining a set of active bean instances and synchronizing bean state with persistent storage when beans are moved active or passive state, the container makes it possible for an application to manage many more bean instances than could otherwise simultaneously be held in the application server's memory. In this style, an EJB container provides services similar to virtual memory within an operating system.

EJB client

The client is the programming code written to execute business logic embedded in an enterprise bean and its methods. An EJB client can be a simple Java program or a web client. The end-user runs these clients to get results from the enterprise bean method invocation. The EJB client can use resource injection or JNDI service to access an enterprise bean. The EJB client can be a simple Java class, an applet, a POJO class, a servlet or JSP. An enterprise bean is looked up using resource injection or the lookup( ) method, irrespective of the different EJB clients.

## 15.4 Goals of EJB architecture

The Enterprise JavaBeans (EJB) architecture has the following goals:

- The Enterprise JavaBeans architecture will be the standard component architecture for building object-oriented business applications in the Java programming language.

- The Enterprise JavaBeans architecture will support the development, deployment, and use of distributed business applications in the Java programming language.
- The Enterprise JavaBeans architecture will support the development, deployment, and use of web services.
- The Enterprise JavaBeans architecture will make it easy to write applications: application developers will not have to understand low-level transaction and state management details, multi-threading, connection pooling, or other complex low-level APIs.
- Enterprise JavaBeans applications will follow the *Write Once, Run Anywhere* philosophy of the Java programming language. An enterprise bean can be developed once, and then deployed on multiple platforms without recompilation or source code modification.
- The Enterprise JavaBeans architecture will address the development, deployment, and runtime aspects of an enterprise application's life cycle.
- The Enterprise JavaBeans architecture will define the contracts that enable tools from multiple vendors to develop and deploy components that can interoperate at runtime.
- The Enterprise JavaBeans architecture will make it possible to build applications by combining components developed using tools from different vendors.
- The Enterprise JavaBeans architecture will provide interoperability between enterprise beans and Java Platform, Enterprise Edition (Java EE) components as well as non-Java programming language applications.
- The Enterprise JavaBeans architecture will be compatible with existing server platforms. Vendors will be able to extend their existing products to support Enterprise JavaBeans.
- The Enterprise JavaBeans architecture will be compatible with other Java programming language APIs.
- The Enterprise JavaBeans architecture will be compatible with the CORBA protocols.

## 15.5 Benefits of Enterprise Beans

The EJB architecture allows enterprise applications to be portable by running on a J2EE-compliant application server. An EJB application can be partitioned in a more usable, flexible, and expandable fashion. For example, new clients to access legacy systems can be easily built to meet user requirements. Moreover, the EJB architecture helps create a service-based model in which services are location-transparent components that can be delivered to their target clients. EJBs are highly reusable components, and represent the next step in the progression of Java technology for the development of application platforms capable of supporting mission-critical, component-based, enterprise applications. EJB components allow the development of business logic to be used across enterprise applications and to be portable across different platforms.

The EJB model is based on Java Remote Method Invocation (RMI) technology, which supports the separation of executable components across multiple tiers. This separation permits maximum implementation flexibility and high scalability. RMI allows access to remote components to appear as if it were local to the invoking client. In addition to that, the introduction of infrastructure services provided by the container helps to manage and offer such services to the deployed EJBs. These runtime services make it possible for the EJB developer to focus on writing robust and reliable applications.

The following summarizes the benefits gained by the enterprise and developers from using EJB technology:

**Simplicity**: The EJB architecture simplifies the development of complex enterprise applications by providing built-in common services. This allows an EJB application developer to access and utilize these services, and results in a reduction of the overall development effort.

**Application portability**: Portability can be accomplished by deploying an EJB application on any J2EE-compliant application server. Many Java application servers today implement all the services provided by J2EE-standard specifications.

**Component reusability**: An EJB is a highly reusable building block. J2EE applications can be composed of custom-based EJBs, off-the-shelf EJBs, or both. In addition, the application business logic of a certain EJB can be reused through Java sub-classing of the EJB class.

**Application partitioning**: The separation of an application's business logic from its presentation allows ease of development and helps business programmers to work independently from Web page designers. Again, the separation of the application's business logic from its data helps manage each team independently. Any change of a component hosted in one tier does not affect the other tiers.

**Distributed applications**: The EJB architecture helps to create distributed applications, which can span multiple environments. Each subsystem can work independently of the others, but still can interact with one another to deliver enterprise services to the target users. A user transaction, for example, can be executed across multiple servers within a single context, and will be perceived by the user as a single unit of work.

**Application interoperability**: The EJB architecture helps EJB components to access other components written in other component-based models, such as CORBA and .NET.

**Application integration**: One of the main objectives of the EJB architecture is to allow the integration of new applications with existing applications, such as legacy systems. Today, Enterprise Application Integration (EAI) is a hot topic for the corporate world. The related J2EE APIs, such as the J2EE Connector Architecture (JCA) and the Java Message Service (JMS) specification, make it possible to integrate enterprise bean applications with various non-Java applications, such as ERP systems or mainframe applications, in a standard way.

**Availability of Java application servers**: An enterprise has many J2EE-compliant application servers to choose from. Each application server provides J2EE services at a minimum, with the addition of other value-added services. A J2EE-compliant server can be selected to meet the customer's needs, which prevents vendor lock-in.

The most significant value provided by the EJB architecture is the separation of business logic programming from the challenge of integrating business logic with the complexities of enterprise-class server-side runtime environments. If the containers in which EJB components are deployed assume responsibility for managing runtime services such as persistence, transactions, and concurrent database access, bean developers are free to focus on developing software components that encapsulate business logic.

## 15.6 Types of Enterprise Bean

There are different situations in the enterprise application development where you need to implement different types of enterprise beans. Different enterprise beans provide different functionalities. Based on these functionalities there are three main types of Enterprise beans.

- Session Beans
- Message Driven Beans
- Entity Beans

Following diagram also represents the types of Enterprise bean along with its sub-types

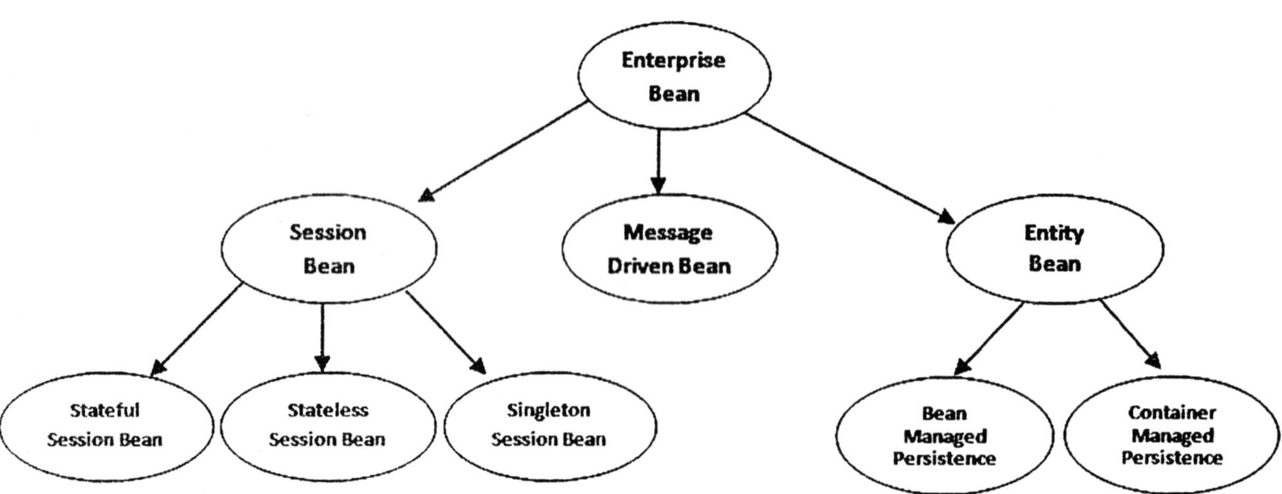


Let's talk about them in very brief.

*Session bean* is used to maintain the conversational state of the user.

*Message Driven bean* can be used only when a message is needed to pass to another client using Java Messaging Service (JMS).

*Entity bean* represents an object in a persistent state.

## 15.7 Understanding Session Bean

A session bean is a type of enterprise bean that exists only for the client and server sessions. A session bean generally created when a client requests a database with the help of a query to retrieve the required data. The bean exists till the client server session persists. Almost all the servers start with executing session beans, such as *LoginVerificationBean* and *ShoppingCartBean*. The session bean holds business processes, such as delivering an order and doing financial calculations for an application. These beans are reusable components, which provide methods that can be accessed by the client. All the services provided by the session bean are in the form of different methods.

As a session bean is never shared among multiple clients, the methods of a particular bean *can only be executed by a single client*. The length of a session determines the duration for which a session bean remains in use. This implies that a session bean is a *short-lived object*.

The actions performed using the methods of a session bean may lead to the change of data of an enterprise bean. This results in change in the state of enterprise bean that may be persistent or transient. A persistent change is available for the multiple sessions of a client. However, a transient change is available for a single session.

A typical session object has the following characteristics:

- Executes on behalf of a single client.
- Can be transaction-aware.
- Updates shared data in an underlying database.
- Does not represent directly shared data in the database, although it may access and update such data.
- May be relatively short-lived, or may have the same lifetime as that of the application.
- It is removed when the EJB container crashes. The client has to re-establish a new session object to continue computation.

A typical EJB container provides a scalable runtime environment to execute a large number of session objects concurrently.

There are three types of session beans that contain different APIs.

- stateful session bean
- stateless session bean
- singleton session bean

Now, before discussing more on session bean and its types, let's discuss some of the session bean concepts, such as *conversational state* as well as *state management of a session bean*.

**Conversational state**

An action performed by a method provided by the session bean may change the state of the bean instance. The state of a session bean instance is known as its conversational state. In other words, a conversational state can also be defined as the state of all the attributes of session bean instance, state of connection, and the reference to some other objects.

If the state of a session bean is stored for one client, then a different bean instance is needed for other clients. This may increase the number of session bean instance on the server. This can be avoided by the EJB container by writing the state of the stateful session bean to a secondary storage. This process of removing the session bean from the active storage is known as passivation – the reverse process of activation. The EJB container uses *serialization* and *deserialization* at the time of *passivation* and *activation* respectively. In this way the state can be preserved and the bean instances can be used to hold the new conversation with the new client.

**State management of session bean**

The word state refers to the state of all the attributes of a session bean class. The state of a bean is managed by the EJB container. The way the state of a session bean is maintained depends upon the type of the session bean.

In case of stateless bean, then it holds the state for a single method invocation. The next invocation of any method on the same instance of the bean does not need to know the past invocation results. In other words, there is no conversational state to be managed. All the clients inside the bean pool are equivalent and any client can be serviced by any other client.

In case of stateful bean, the new state of bean is decided by the action of the next method invoked and the result of the action performed by the last method call. The state of the bean is maintained across multiple method calls or transactions for a particular client, that is, for particular session. A single bean instance has a particular state for a particular client and thereby cannot be reassigned to another client. When the number of active beans allowed by the container exceeds, the container passivates those active beans which are not required and activates them again whenever they are required.

### ❖ Stateless session beans

The stateless session beans represent the session bean that does not need the state of a bean to be saved through multiple method invocations. A stateless session bean does not require its conversational state to be stored. The term stateless explains the fact that this type of session bean does not hold the state of a bean between different method calls.

In other words, a stateless session bean does not have any conversational state as the bean does not hold client details after a method call. The algorithm implemented by an EJB container decides whether the bean is to be destroyed or to be retained for reuse by some other client. The information held by a stateless session is not specific to any client.

**Skeleton of stateless session bean in NetBeans IDE**

```
package EJBDemo;

import javax.ejb.Stateless;

@Stateless
public class StatelessBean
{
        // Add business logic here.
}
```

**Life cycle of stateless session bean**

After having a brief discussion on session bean, let's now discuss life cycle of stateless session bean. The life cycle of stateless session bean can be described with various methods that re invoked throughout its life. A stateless session bean can be in one of the following two states.

- **Does Not Exist State**: Refers to the state in which bean is yet not instantiated.
- **Ready State**: Refers to the state in which bean is instantiated and tied to a particular client.

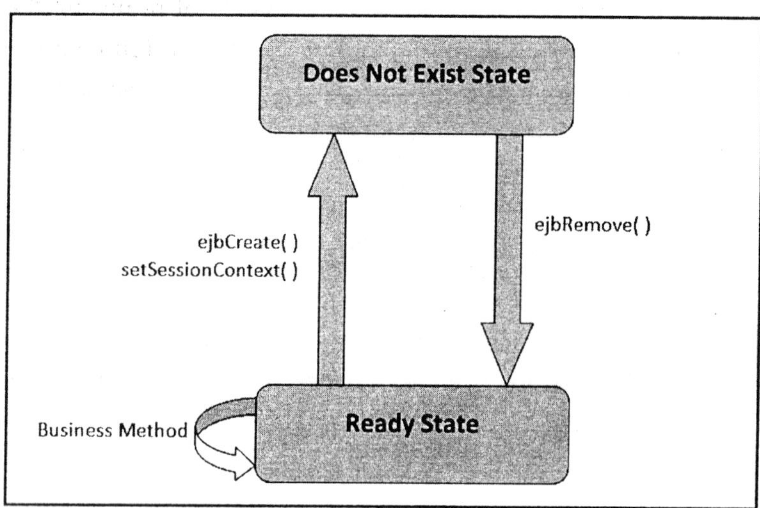


Above diagram shows that *ejbCreate( )* and *ejbRemove( )* methods are used to change the state of stateless session bean. We can see that, stateless session bean has two major transitions in its states. Let's explain these transitions in brief.

*Moving from Does Not Exist State to Ready State*

There are two methods that are used to change the state of stateless session bean from Does Not Exist State to Ready State. These methods are:

- *setSessionContext( )* – contains the reference of the session context. After creating a stateless session bean instance, the EJB container places it into the Ready state. This instance then invokes the *setSessionContext( )* method. The main purpose of calling this method is to associate a bean with a session context because the session context behaves as the gateway to interact with the container.
- *ejbCreate( )* – Refers to the method that is invoked only once during the lifetime of the session bean. After the *setSessionContext( )* method is called, the EJB container calls the *ejbCreate( )* method to initialize the beans. It is

important to remember that *ejbCreate( )* method is always called after the *setSessionContext( )* method, as the enterprise bean can be created only after the session context has been created.

When a bean instance is in the Ready state, it can service a client's request and invoke the business method. The EJB container uses the available bean instance to execute the business method. After the execution of the business method is finished, the session bean instance moves from ready state to Does Not Exist State.

*Moving from Ready State to Does Not Exist State*

Suppose the EJB container has a large number of session bean instances and one of these instances needs to access some resources or services of the container. In such a situation, the container needs to reduce the number of session bean instance that are in ready pool. To reduce the number of session bean instances, the EJB container calls the ejbRemove ( ) method on the session bean instance that are not in use. Using this method, the EJB container invalidates the reference to the bean instance that is in the ready pool state. It does not indicate that the bean has been destroyed; it only sets the status of the bean instance as an inactive one.

- **Stateful session bean**

When a business process needs to maintain the client's state, the stateful session bean should be used. The stateful session beans are basically used for the process in which the state of the bean should be retained to be used by the same client during further method invocation. One of the good examples of it is Shopping-cart. Each method call in a shopping cart needs to know the current state of the shopping cart i.e. number of items in the cart. If the state of the bean changes during the execution of the method, then the same changed state should be available to the same client on further method invocations.

The stateful session bean acts on behalf of a particular client, and maintains the client's particular information throughout the session. In order to understand it more clearly, let's make an example of Online Railway Reservation. Once the user logs in into IRCTC website with the account_id and password, the user can continue with any transactions, such as new ticket booking, previous booking history or cancelled tickets until either the user logs out or the session expires. All these transactions will be executed successfully. This is because during the login period of the user, the particular information of its account_id is being maintained across multiple transactions and across multiple web pages. So in this way, the stateful session bean creates a conversational state across multiple method calls and transactions.

**Skeleton of stateful session bean in NetBeans IDE**

```
package EJBDemo;

import javax.ejb.Stateful;
import javax.ejb.LocalBean;

@Stateful
@LocalBean
public class StatefulBean
{
        // Add business logic here.
}
```

**Life cycle of stateful session bean**

The life cycle of stateful session bean contains following states:

- **Does Not Exist State**: Refers to the state in which bean is yet not instantiated.
- **Ready State**: Refers to the state in which bean is instantiated and tied to a particular client.
- **Passive State**: Refers to the state in which the bean instance is passivated to optimize the resource utilization.

The different states as well as various methods that are available inside the life cycle of the stateful session bean are shown in following diagram.

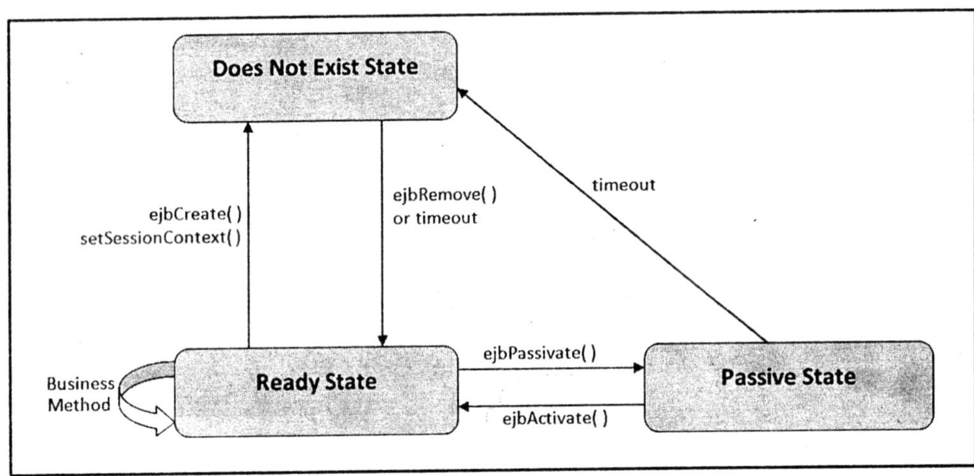


In above diagram, we can see three states of stateful session bean with methods that are responsible for moving from one state to another. Let's now discuss the four major transactions in states of stateful session bean.

*Moving from Does Not Exist State to Ready State*

This first state of stateful session bean is similar to that of stateless session bean. When there is interaction between the Does Not Exist State to Ready State, the following methods are used:

- *setSessionContext( )*
- *ejbCreate( )*

The functionality of both of these methods is similar as described in stateless session bean.

In ready state, the session bean instance is associated with a particular client for the duration of the conversation. During this duration, the instance executes the methods that are invoked by the client.

*Moving from Ready State to Passive State*

Suppose a client does not invoke a bean for a long time and lets it remain in memory. As it is not a good habit to keep the bean in the memory. Therefore, to save memory, the client performs the process of passivation. In the process of passivation, the bean instances, that are no longer used, are saved into a disk or in the same permanent storage device. The container performs this task by serializing the entire bean instance and then moving it into a permanent storage, such as database or a file. Activation is the opposite of the passivation stage. The activation stage is required when bean instance is needed again by the client. The container activates the bean instance by retrieving it from the permanent storage. It then deserializes the bean instance and sends it back to the memory for further use.

*Moving from Passive State to Ready State*

To perform the passivation task, the container calls the *ejbPassivate( )* method. After passivation, if the client wants to continue the conversation by invoking business methods, then it needs to reactivate the session bean instance by calling *ejbActivate( )* method.

*Moving from Ready State to Does Not Exist State*

When the client completes its task and logs out from the application, the session expires. Here the client invokes the *ejbRemove( )* method that removes the bean instance from the memory and sends the bean again to Does Not Exist State.

### ❖ Singleton session bean

A **singleton session bean** is instantiated once per application and exists for the lifecycle of the application. Singleton session beans are designed for circumstances in which a single enterprise bean instance is shared across and at the same time as accessed by clients.

Singleton session beans offer *similar functionality to stateless session beans* but differ from them in that there is only one singleton session bean per application, as opposed to a pool of stateless session beans, any of which may respond to a client request. Like stateless session beans, singleton session beans can implement web service endpoints.

Singleton session beans maintain their state between client invocations but are not required to maintain their state across server crashes or shutdowns.

Applications that use a singleton session bean may specify that the singleton should be instantiated upon application startup, which allows the singleton to perform initialization tasks for the application. The singleton may perform cleanup tasks on application shutdown as well, because the singleton will operate throughout the lifecycle of the application.

**Skeleton of singleton session bean in NetBeans IDE**

```
package EJBDemo;

import javax.ejb.Singleton;
import javax.ejb.LocalBean;

@Singleton
@LocalBean
public class SingletonBean
{
        // Add business logic here.
}
```

**Life cycle of singleton session bean**

Like a stateless session bean, a singleton session bean is never passivated and has only two states, non-existent and ready for the invocation of business methods. Following diagram shows the life cycle of singleton session bean containing two states.

- **Does Not Exist State**: Refers to the state in which bean is yet not instantiated.
- **Ready State**: Refers to the state in which bean is instantiated and tied to a particular client.

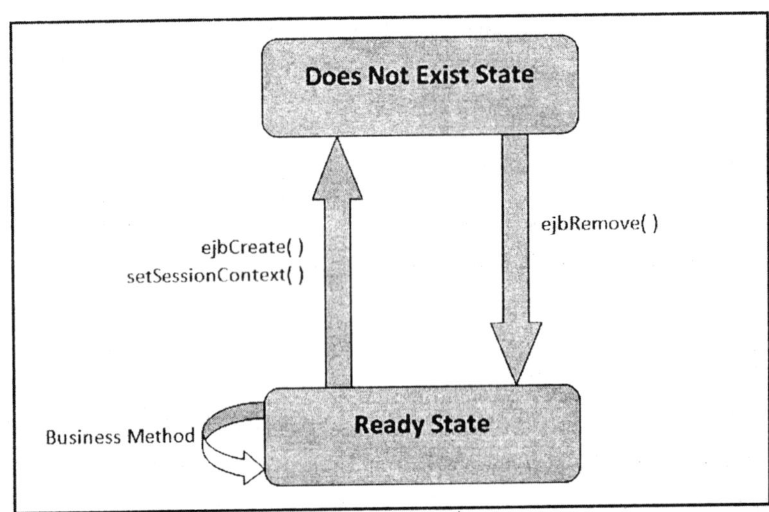


We can see that, there is no difference in life cycle of singleton session bean and stateless session bean. The singleton session bean has the same transition states as discussed in stateless session bean.

## 15.8 Understanding Message Driven Bean

The term Message Driven Bean (MDB) itself suggests that it is associated with some kind of messaging. This messaging is used to communicate among software components or application. By using this messaging service a client can send/receive messages to/from other clients. In case of MDBs, each client connects to a messaging agent that facilitates creating, sending, receiving and reading messages.

We know that, JMS is a core service provided by java EE application, which allows asynchronous invocation of different services via messaging. JMS clients send message to the **message queues,** which are maintained by the server.

A typical Message Driven object has the following characteristics:

- Executes upon receipt of a single client message.
- Is asynchronously invoked.
- Can be transaction-aware.
- May update shared data in an underlying database.
- Does not represent directly shared data in the database, although it may access and update such data.
- Is relatively short-lived.
- Is stateless.
- Is removed when the EJB container crashes. The container has to re-establish a new message-driven object to continue computation.

A typical EJB container provides a scalable runtime environment to execute a large number of message-driven objects concurrently.

**Skeleton of Message Driven Bean in NetBeans IDE**

```
package EJBDemo;
import javax.ejb.ActivationConfigProperty;
import javax.ejb.MessageDriven;
import javax.jms.Message;
import javax.jms.MessageListener;
```

```
@MessageDriven
(mappedName = "jms/servletdemo", activationConfig =
{
@ActivationConfigProperty(propertyName = "acknowledgeMode", propertyValue = "Auto-acknowledge"),
@ActivationConfigProperty(propertyName = "destinationType", propertyValue = "javax.jms.Queue")
}
)
public class NewMessageBean implements MessageListener
{
    public NewMessageBean( )
    {
        // define constructor here
    }
    @Override
    public void onMessage(Message message)
    {
        //This method is implemented from MessageListener interface
    }
}
```

**Life cycle of Message Driven Bean**

Life cycle of message-driven bean is exhibited through the following two states.

- Does Not Exist State
- Method – ready pool state

The message-driven bean is either in the Does Not Exist State or in the pooled state. When the container decides to insert a new instance to its pool, it creates a new instance and performs the required dependency injection. It performs all this by calling *setMessageDrivenContext( )* and *ejbCreate( )* methods.

The setMessageDrivenContext( ) provides access to the runtime message-driven context that the container provides for a message-driven enterprise bean instance. It is called by the container after creating the bean instance and it passes a reference to a MessageDrivenContext to an instance after the instance has been created. A message-driven bean can also acquire a reference to the MessageDrivenContext by using dependency injection by simply providing the *@Resource* annotation. The message-driven context remains associated with the corresponding instance as long as the instance is alive, i.e. throughout the life time. After creating the instance and getting MessageDrivenContext, message-driven bean is ready to receive the message. If any annotation, such as *@PostConstruct*, has been used to define a life-cycle call back method, then these methods are invoked here. According to the configuration, the application server will generate an initial pool of beans at the startup time. The size of this pool can be expanded as the size of message increases. When the bean instance is processing a JMS message, its *onMessage( )* method is invoked to perform the work. The container can destroy an instance by removing it from the pool in the container to conserve memory or to make the best utilization of the memory. To decrease the size of the pool, it needs to call the *ejbRemove( )* method, before the instance is ready for the garbage collection.

For taking an instance out of the bean pool, that container calls the *@PreDestroy( )* method. The diagrammatic representation of the life cycle of message-driven bean is shown in figure below.

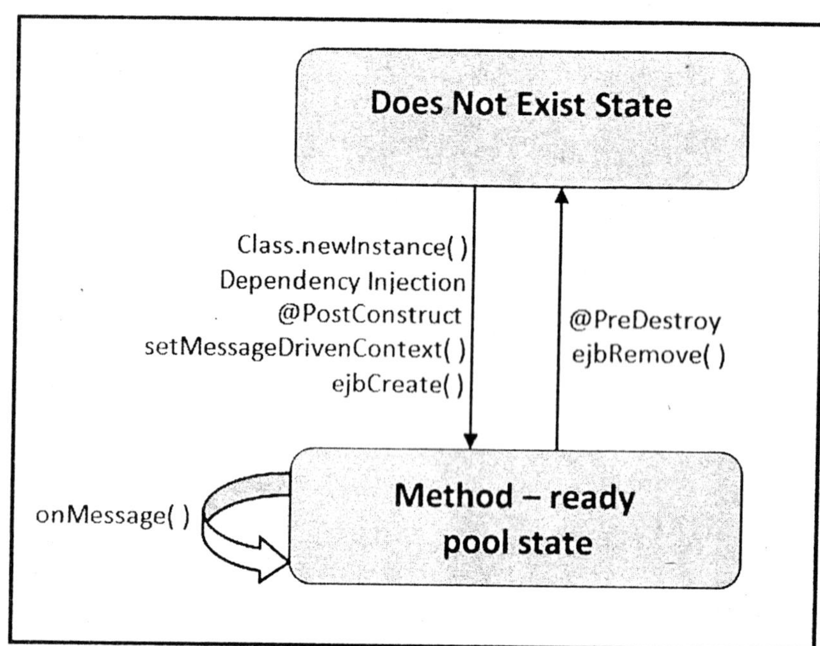


We can see that, the life cycle of stateless session bean described earlier is very much similar to that of the message-driven bean. Let's discuss the states of the message-driven bean.

- **Does Not Exist State**: when a message-driven bean instance is yet not instantiated.
- **Method-Ready Pool State**: As soon as the EJB server starts, it may create numbers of instance and sends into the method-ready pool. If the number of MDB instances is insufficient for handling incoming messages, more instances can be created into the pool.

Let's now discuss the three major transactions in the state of Message Driven beans.

*Moving from Does Not Exist State to Method-ready pool*

When a bean gets instantiated it performs following tasks:

1. The bean instance is instantiated when the container invokes the *newInstance( )* method on the MDB class.
2. The container injects the required resources. It injects the resources with the help of annotation or XML deployment descriptor.
3. *PostConstructor* callback is invoked by the container.

The bean class may or may not have a method that is annotated with *@javax.ejb.Postconstruct*. But in case it is present, this annotated method will be called by the container only after the bean is instantiated. The *@Postconstruct* annotated method can be of any name, but must of type *void* and without parameter list. The code block for using the *@PostConstruct* annotation would be as follows.

```
@MessageDriven
public class DemoBean implements MessageListener
{
        @PostConstruct
        public void myInit( )
        {
                // add code here.
        }
}
```

*Existence of MDB in Method-ready pool*

As soon as instance reaches to the method-ready pool state, it is ready to handle incoming messages. While a message is being forwarded to an MDB, it is delegated to any available instance in the method-ready pool. When an instance in MDB executing a request, it is unable to execute or process other messages. In such cases, MDB handles messages by delegating the responsibility of handling each message to a different MDB instance. While processing a message, once the instance has finished its work, it is immediately available to handle other new message that is present inside the message-driven bean.

*Removing MDB instance*

When the server does not need a bean instance, its state is changed from method-ready pool state to Does Not Exist State. This type of situation generally occurs when the server decides to decrease the total size of the method-ready pool. It is done by releasing one or more instances from memory. But before this, the container invokes another callback method annotated with @PreDestroy on the bean instance. At this time, the bean instance can perform any cleanup operation such as "closing available resources" by using the @PreDestroy annotation. The important point to be remember is that @PreDestroy callback method is invoked only once in the life cycle of MDB instance.

## 15.9 Understanding Entity Bean

If you've worked with databases, you're familiar with persistent data. Any change to the data will exist even after the database server is shut down. Entity beans are persistent objects. They typically represent business entities, such as customers, products, accounts, and orders. Normally, each entity bean has an underlying table in a relational database, and each instance of the bean corresponds to a row in that table. By persistence, we mean that the state of the entity bean in memory is synchronized with the data it represents in the database.

Multiple clients can share entity beans. Because those clients might want to change the same data, it's important that entity beans work within transactions.

Entity beans typically contain data-related logic that performs a task such as inserting, updating, or removing a customer record in the database.

*An entity bean is a server-side component that represents an object-oriented view of entities stored in persistent storage* (such as a database) or entities that are implemented by an existing enterprise application.

A typical entity object has the following characteristics:

- Is part of a domain model, providing an object view of data in the database.
- Can be long-lived (lives as long as the data in the database).
- The entity and its primary key survive the crash of the EJB container. If the state of an entity was being updated by a transaction at the time the container crashed, the entity's state is restored to the state of the last committed transaction when the entity is next retrieved.

Many students mystify the Entity bean with Session bean. But Entity beans differ from Session beans in several ways. Following shows the differences between session and entity beans.

| Session Bean | Entity Bean |
|---|---|
| Typically contains business process logic, such as sending an e-mail, looking up the stock price from a database, implementing compression and encryption algorithms. They also implement business logic such as workflow, algorithms, | Typically represents business entities, such as customers, products, accounts, and orders. |

| and business rules. | |
|---|---|
| Executes a particular business task on behalf of a single client during a single session. | Can be shared by multiple clients. |
| The state is not persistent. | The state is persistent. |
| Usually does not correspond directly to data. | Usually corresponds directly to data. |

**Life cycle of Entity Bean**

Life cycle of Entity bean is exhibited through the following three states.

- Does Not Exist State
- Pooled State
- Method – Ready State

When developing an Entity bean you can take advantage of the bean's relationship with the container to execute logic and optimizations outside the context of the bean's core logic. As the container creates and pools an instance, assigns data to it, executes bean methods, and eventually removes the instance, the container provides opportunities for your code to execute.

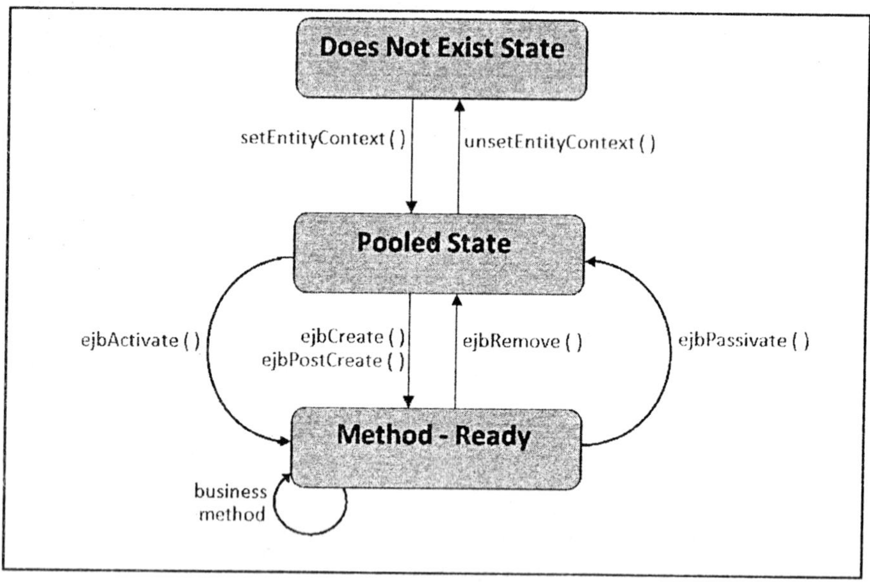


The above figure shows the life cycle of an Entity bean. An Entity bean has the following three states:

- **Does not Exist State**: In this state, the bean instance simply does not exist.
- **Pooled state**: When application server is first started, several bean instances are created and placed in the pool. A bean instance in the pooled state is not tied to particular data, that is, it does not correspond to a record in a database table. Additional bean instances can be added to the pool as needed, and a maximum number of instances can be set.
- **Ready state:** A bean instance in the ready state is tied to particular data, that is, it represents an instance of an actual business object.

The various state transitions available during the Entity bean states are discussed below.

*Moving from Does Not Exist State to Pooled State*

When application server creates a bean instance in the pool, it calls the callback method *setEntityContext( )*. This method has the parameter *javax.ejb.EntityContext*, which contains a reference to the entity context; i.e., the interface to the EJB container. The entity context contains a number of methods to self-reference the entity bean object, identify the caller of a method, and so forth.

When a bean instance is in the pooled state, it is not tied to any particular business object. When in the pooled state, the methods defined in the home interface can be invoked, effectively transitioning it from the pooled to the ready state, with the exception of *ejbHome( )* methods. When a home method is invoked, a result that is not bean instance specific is returned to the caller, and the bean instance remains in the pooled state. Home methods in turn often invoke *ejbSelect( )* methods to query bean instances.

*Moving from Pooled State to Mehod-Ready State*

The following methods move a bean instance from the pooled to the ready state to represent a business object:

- **ejbCreate( ) and ejbPostCreate( )**: When the create method is invoked on the bean's home interface, the *ejbCreate( )* and *ejbPostCreate( )* methods are invoked by the container. The bean instance moves to the ready state and represents this newly created business object. After creation, a (local or remote) reference to this object is returned to the caller, enabling the caller to invoke business methods on this instance. The ejbPostCreate( ) method is used to set references to other entity beans as part of the creation of a new bean instance.
- **findByPrimaryKey( ):** When this method is invoked on the bean's home interface with the (compound) primary key as the parameter, the bean instance moves to the ready state and represents the business object uniquely identified by the parameter. Also a (local or remote) reference to this object is returned to the caller, enabling the caller to invoke business methods on this instance.
- **Find( ) method:** When a find method is invoked on the bean's home interface, one or a set of references to objects matching the queries are returned to the caller. In many cases the corresponding bean instance(s) are not loaded with data and move to the ready state until at a later point when a business method is actually invoked on this object, a concept known as lazy loading.

*Moving from method-Ready State to Pooled State*

When a caller invokes a remove method to delete an entity bean instance and its underlying record in the database table, the EJB container will delete the bean instance. Just prior to deleting the instance, it will call the callback method *ejbRemove( )*. If your entity bean needs to execute some custom logic prior to deletion, you can implement it using this callback method. After the data is deleted, the bean instance returns to the pooled state. The bean instance is no longer tied to any particular business object, and can be used to execute a home method or one of the methods that will tie it to a new set of data and move it to the ready state.

*Moving from Pooled State to Does Not Exist State*

To more optimally manage resources, or when application server shuts down, the EJB container might remove a bean instance from the pooled state to the does not exist state, allowing it to be garbage collected. Just prior to its destruction, the callback method *unsetEntityContext( )* is invoked. If your entity bean needs to execute some cleanup prior to garbage collection, you can implement it using this callback method.

**Types of Entity bean Persistence**

Entity beans have two types of persistence:

- Bean-Managed Persistence (BMP)
- Container-Managed Persistence (CMP).

These two types are based on who is responsible for entity bean persistence bean provider or EJB provider. Let's discuss about these persistence in brief.

**Bean Managed Persistence (BMP)**

With bean-managed persistence, the entity bean code that you write contains the calls that access the database. The data access can be coded into the entity bean class or encapsulated in a data access object that is part of the entity bean. Following figure shows how bean-managed persistence works with database access.

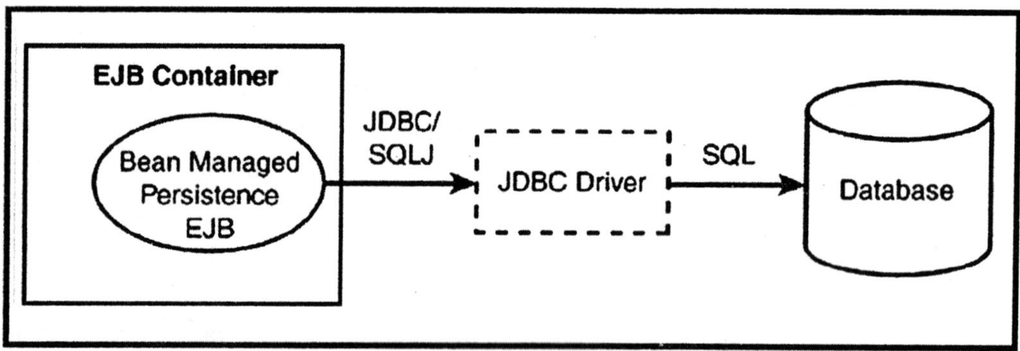


For example, as shown in the following snippet, the *StudentEJB*'s *ejbCreate( )* method contains the JBDC code to insert a student record into the students table:

```
public class StudentEJB implements EntityBean
{
   private String studentId;       // also the primary Key
   private String firstName;
   private String lastName;
   private String address;

  public String ejbCreate(String studentId, String firstName, String lastName, String address) throws
  CreateException
  {
      this.studentId = studentId;
      this.firstName = firstName;
      this.lastName = lastName;
      this.address = address;
      Connection con = null;
      PreparedStatement ps = null;
      try
      {
       con = getConnection( );
       ps = con.prepareStatement
       ("insert into students (student_id, "+" first_name, last_name, address) values(?, ?, ?, ?) ");
```

```
            ps.setString(1, studentId);
            ps.setString(1, firstName);
            ps.setString(1, lastName);
            ps.setString(1, address);
            if (ps.executeUpdate( ) != 1)
            {
              String error = "JDBC did not create any row";
              log(error);
              throw new CreateException (error);
              }
              return studentId;
            }
            catch (SQLException sqe)
            {
              ...
            }
            finally
            {
              cleanup(con, ps);
            }
        }
        ...
    }
```

Although writing this code is an additional responsibility, as an EJB developer, you'll have more control over how the entity bean accesses a database.

## Container Managed Persistence (CMP)

If your bean has container-managed persistence (CMP), the EJB container uses a persistence manager and automatically generates the necessary database access calls. The code that you write for the entity bean does not include these calls. The persistence manager is responsible for persistence of the entity bean, including creating, loading, and removing the entity bean instance in the database.

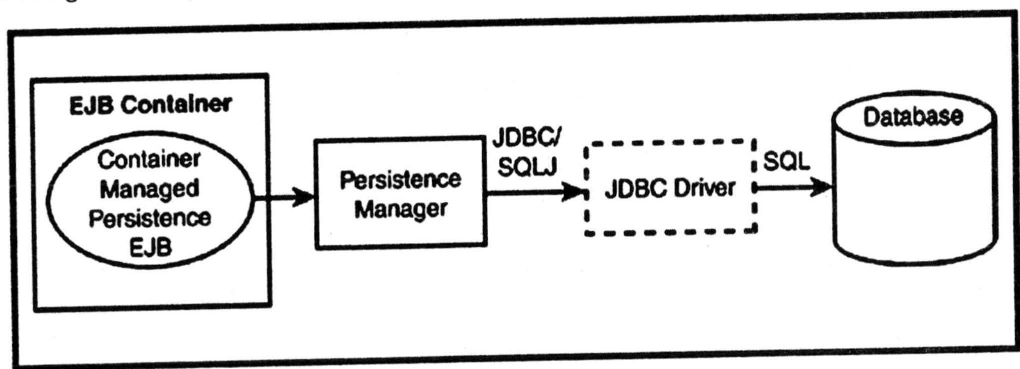


For example, as shown in the following listing, the *OrderEJB*'s *ejbCreate( )* method does not contain any JBDC code to insert order records into the orders table:

```
public abstract class OrderEJB implements EntityBean
{
    /* get and set methods for cmp fields */
    public abstract String getOrderId( );
    public abstract void setOrderId(String id);

    public abstract java.sql.Timestamp getOrderDate( );
    public abstract void setOrderDate(java.sql.Timestamp timestamp);

    public abstract String getStatus( );
    public abstract void setStatus(String status);

    public abstract double getAmount( );
    public abstract void setAmount(double amount);

    /* get and set methods for relationship fields */
    public abstract Collection getLineItems( );
    public abstract void setLineItems(Collection lineItems);

    public abstract StudentLocal getStudent( );
    public abstract void setStudent(StudentLocal student);

    public String ejbCreate(String orderId, StudentLocal student,String status,double amount) throws
    CreateException
    {
        setOrderId(orderId);
        setOrderDate(new java.sql.Timestamp(System.currentTimeMillis( )));
        setStatus(status);
        setAmount(amount);
        return null;
    }
 ...
}
```

You might wonder *how the EJB container is able to generate the database access code?* The answer is that you specify the persistence fields, relationship fields, schema, and queries in the deployment descriptor. Based on this information, the container tools generate data access calls corresponding to the underlying database, at deployment time.

*Remember that Entity beans with container-managed persistence are portable. Their code is not tied to a specific database.*

## 15.10 Working with Session Bean

In this section we will develop simple applications using all three types of session beans.

### 15.10.1 Developing Stateless session bean

With this example we are going to demonstrate how to create a simple Stateless Session Bean. A stateless session bean does not maintain state with the client. When a client invokes the methods of a stateless bean, the bean's instance variables may contain a state specific to that client, but only for the duration of the invocation. When the method is finished, the client-specific state should not be retained. Clients may, however, change the state of instance variables in pooled stateless beans, and this state is held over to the next invocation of the pooled stateless bean. Except during method invocation, all instances of a stateless bean are equivalent, allowing the EJB container to assign an instance to any client. That is, the state of a stateless session bean should apply across all clients.

**The EJB implementation class**

The *CalculatorService* is an EJB implementation class that is a stateless session bean that implements a few methods. It is annotated with the *javax.ejb.Stateless* annotation. The class must have a default public constructor.

```
package EE.EJB.stateless;
import javax.ejb.Stateless;
@Stateless
public class CalculatorService implements CalculatorServiceLocal, CalculatorServiceRemote
{
        public CalculatorService()
        { }
        @Override
        public long add(long i, long j)
        {
                return (i + j);
        }
        @Override
        public double divide(long i, long j)
        {
                return ((double)i / j);
        }
        @Override
        public long multiply(long i, long j)
        {
                return (i * j);
        }
        @Override
        public long subtract(long i, long j)
        {
                return (i - j);
        }
}
```

**The EJB local interface**

The local interface defines the bean's business and life cycle methods. To build an enterprise bean that allows only local access, you must annotate the business interface of the enterprise bean as a *@Local* interface.

```
package EE.EJB.stateless;
import javax.ejb.Local;
@Local
public interface CalculatorServiceLocal
{
        public long add(long i, long j);
        public long subtract(long i, long j);
        public long multiply(long i, long j);
        public double divide(long i, long j);
}
```

**The EJB remote interface**

A remote client of an enterprise bean can run on a different machine and a different Java virtual machine (JVM) than the enterprise bean it accesses. Create an enterprise bean that allows remote access, you must decorate the business interface of the enterprise bean with the *@Remote* annotation:

```
package EE.EJB.stateless;
import javax.ejb.Remote;
@Remote
public interface CalculatorServiceRemote
{
        public long add(long i, long j);
        public long subtract(long i, long j);
        public long multiply(long i, long j);
        public double divide(long i, long j);
}
```

**The application.xml file**

```
<?xml version="1.0" encoding="UTF-8"?>
<application version="1.4">
 <display-name>Calculator Application</display-name>
 <module>
        <ejb>calculatorServiceEJB3.jar</ejb>
 </module>
</application>
```

**Run the application using a client**

In *CalculatorServiceClient* we connect to JBoss naming service running on local host and on default port 1099. We use the Context to set the configuration for the *JBoss* server, such as *Context.INITIAL_CONTEXT_FACTORY*, *Context.PROVIDER_URL* and *Context.URL_PKG_PREFIXES*. We get the bean using the *lookup(name)* method of *Context* to invoke its methods.

```
package EE.EJB.stateless;
import java.util.Hashtable;
import javax.naming.Context;
import javax.naming.InitialContext;
public class CalculatorServiceClient
{
        public static void main(String ar[ ]) throws Exception
        {
                Hashtable env = new Hashtable();
                env.put(Context.INITIAL_CONTEXT_FACTORY, "org.jnp.interfaces.NamingContextFactory");
                env.put(Context.PROVIDER_URL, "jnp://localhost:1099");
                env.put(Context.URL_PKG_PREFIXES, "org.jboss.naming:org.jnp.interfaces");
                Context ctx = new InitialContext(env);
                CalculatorServiceRemote calculatorService = (CalculatorServiceRemote)
                ctx.lookup("calculatorApp/CalculatorService/remote");
                long i = 10;
                long j = 3;
                System.out.println(i+"+"+j+"="+calculatorService.add(i, j));
                System.out.println(i+"-"+j+"="+calculatorService.subtract(i, j));
                System.out.println(i+"*"+j+"="+calculatorService.multiply(i, j));
                System.out.println(i+"/"+j+"="+calculatorService.divide(i, j));
        }
}
```

**Output**

```
10+3=13
10-3=7
10*3=30
10/3=3.3333333333333335
```

### 15.10.2 Developing Stateful session bean

A stateful session bean maintains "conversational state" or instance data pertaining to 1 client between method calls. Each stateful session bean is associated with a particular client. It is not designed to be persistent. It maintains data that is transitional and relevant only for a particular session with a specific client. A stateful session bean instance typically cannot survive system failures and other destructive events. Some more important features of stateful session bean are:

- A stateful session bean holds the client session's state.
- A stateful session bean is an extension of the client that creates it.
- Its fields contain a conversational state on behalf of the session object's client. This state describes the conversation represented by a specific client/session object pair.
- It can read and update data in a database on behalf of the client. Within a transaction, some of this data may be cached in the instance.

- Its lifetime is controlled by the client.

Remember that, a stateful session Beans maintain conversational state across methods and transactions and as a result, the EJB server binds the Enterprise Bean instances to clients directly.

One more point on stateful session bean is that, it may use more resources. The reason for that is, to efficiently manage the size of its working set, a session bean container may need to temporarily transfer the state of an idle stateful session bean instance to some form of secondary storage. The transfer from the working set to secondary storage is called *instance passivation*. The transfer back is called activation. A container may only passivate a session bean instance when the instance is not in a transaction.

Now the point comes is when to use stateful bean? A business object should be modeled as a stateful session bean if it is:

- Client specific
- The bean's state must be initialized from input parameters when it is created.
- The bean needs to hold information about the client across method invocations.
- Non persistent
- Short lived (life of client session)
- Not shared among multiple clients
- Spanning multiple business concepts (not just request response service)

## 15.11 Interceptors

In the EJB, as the name suggests, Interceptors are used to intercept calls to EJB methods. If we declare an interceptor for a bean, every time a method of that bean is invoked, it will be intercepted with one method of the interceptor. That means the execution goes directly to the interceptor's method. The intercepting method then decides whether to call the intercepted EJB method or simply replace it.

Above discussion may make us think that the concept of interceptor may resemble the Aspect Oriented Programming philosophy. But the fact is that, we can combine these concepts of OOP and AOP for some purposes. For example, when we want to log something before or after a Beans method is executed or when we want to enforce a specific policy concerning method calls (Such as authentication, input checking, etc.) then an EJB can have a chain of Interceptors that will intercept the method in a specific order.

While defining an interceptor, we can define it either in a business method or in lifecycle event. An Interceptor that intercepts a business method is typically called an **AroundInvoke** method because it can be defined by annotating the method with **@AroundInvoke** annotation.

The AroundInvoke method can be defined either on Enterprise Bean class or on an Interceptor class. But it is a good habit to go with Interceptor classes. For Interceptor class, we do not need to extend or implement anything special, it is a simple Java class (As we have POJO classes).

**Creating an interceptor**

To create an interceptor, simple add a Java class to any project from the **ProjectPane**. See following class *EJBMethodTimer*.

```
package interceptor;
import javax.interceptor.AroundInvoke;
import javax.interceptor.InvocationContext;
public class EJBMethodTimer
{
        public EJBMethodTimer( )
        { }
        @AroundInvoke
        private object intercept(InvocationContext invCon) throws Exception
        {
                long t1 = System.nanoTime( );
                Object rslt = invCon.proceed( );
                long t2 = System.nanoTime( );
                System.out.println(" = " + invCon.getMethod( ).getName( ) + "( " + invCon.getParameters()[0] +
                " ) took : " + ((t2-t1)/1000.0) + " nano seconds");
                return rslt;
        }
}
```

The Interceptor methods must always call proceed( ) method. If the method is not called, no subsequent interceptor method, bean business method or lifecycle callback method will be invoked.

**Adding an interceptor to an Enterprise Bean**

First create a new Java class *Visitors* and to add an interceptor to an Enterprise Bean, simply add add @Interceptors annotation. Refer following class *Visitors.*

```
package enterprisebean;
import interceptor.EJBMethodTimer;
import javax.interceptor.Interceptors;
@Stateless
@Interceptors({EJBMethodTimer.class})
public class Visitors implements VisitorsStatRemote
{
        ...
        ...
        @PostConstruct
        public void connect( )
        {
                ...
                ...
        }
        @PreDestroy
        public void disconnect( )
        {
                ...
                ...
        }
        public void addVisitor(String host)
        {
                ...
                ...
```

```
        }
    }
```

Now compile and execute above class included web application. Whenever this page is visited, an entry appears in the output window.

## 15.12 Explaining EJB Timer Services [Dr. BAMU Nov/Dec 12; PUNE Uni. May/June 11 Nov/Dec 12; SRTMU May/June 12,14 Nov/Dec 11,12]

Applications that model business work flows often rely on timed notifications. The timer service of the enterprise bean container enables you to schedule timed notifications for all types of enterprise beans *except for stateful session beans*. You can schedule a timed notification to occur according to a calendar schedule, at a specific time, after duration of time, or at timed intervals. In other words, large organizations would perform these tasks at a particular point of time or within a period of time. This would become much clearer with the help of following situations.

- In customer care-center, all complaints are addressed and processed accordingly to the assigned batches. A batch can be the number of complaints received in one hour, a day, or at any fixed period. The complaints are grouped in batches so that necessary action can be promptly taken to resolve these complaints.
- In large scale enterprises, managers need to run specific reports on a daily basis. A scheduling system can help by running these reports automatically according to the scheduled time and deliver them as e-mail to the managers.
- In system dealing with finance, several different tasks need to be completed before a credit is closed. The processing of this job is time-bound and is, therefore, carried on schedule.
- A company with multiple job shifts needs to run the attendance report after the completion of the job shift. This is done on a regular basis to maintain a daily record of the employee attendance.
- A company may also need to clear up its temporary database at the end of day. This is also done on daily basis.
- The contracts table, charts, sheets, etc in a company needs to be updated every week, or hour, or minutes from a remote location.

All these operations require task scheduling. In order to implement task scheduling in Java EE applications, EJB 3.0 had introduced the Timer Service facility. Timer Services are available for building Java EE applications dependent on the time-based services.

Before the invention of Timer Services, the developers had to write code manually for building and deploying time-based workflows. However, with EJB 3.0 the task of creating such applications has been considerably simplified. Equipped with annotations and dependency injections, developers can use EJB 3.0 to build and deploy scheduled applications easily. The Timer Service facility of the EJB container provides the Timer Event API. The Timer Event API schedules the timer for a specific date, period and interval. As soon as the Timed Event API schedules the timer, the timer becomes associated with the enterprise bean responsible for setting it. The Timed Event API calls the *ejbTimeout( )* method of the enterprise bean as soon as the Timer object expires.

There are two types of timers.

- The Single Action Timer
- The Interval Timer

Let's understand about them in brief.

## The Single Action Timer

The single action timer expires only once, which means that there is no subsequent instantiation and expiration of this timer. A single action timer is also known as a single interval timer. EJB provides two ways for constructing a single action timer.

- one is to create a timer which expires at specific point of time, such as a specified date.
- second is to create a timer which expires after a certain period of time, such as 6 hours or 3 days.

After the time expires, the enterprise bean receives the notification. In other words, once the time expires, the container calls the *ejbTimeout( )* method or the method associated with @Timeout annotation to destroy the timer.

## The Interval Timer

The interval timer returns at multiple intervals of time and expires multiple times at regular intervals. As with the single action timer, there are two ways of constructing an interval timer.

- one is to create a timer having an initial expiration at a particular point of timer and succeeding expiration happening at specified intervals.
- Second is to create the timer having the initial expiration after a certain period of time and succeeding expiration happening after specified intervals.

Finally we can conclude that, Enterprise bean timers are either **programmatic timers** or **automatic timers.** **Programmatic timers** are set by explicitly calling one of the timer creation methods of the TimerService interface. **Automatic timers** are created upon the successful deployment of an enterprise bean that contains a method annotated with the java.ejb.Schedule or *java.ejb.Schedules* annotations.

### Creating Calendar-Based Timer Expressions

Timers can be set according to a calendar-based schedule, expressed using a syntax similar to the UNIX *cron* utility. Both programmatic and automatic timers can use calendar-based timer expressions. Following table shows the calendar-based timer attributes.

| Attribute | Description | Default Value | Allowable Values and Examples |
|---|---|---|---|
| second | *One or more seconds within a minute* | 0 | 0 to 59. For example: second="30". |
| minute | *One or more minutes within an hour* | 0 | 0 to 59. For example: minute="15". |
| hour | *One or more hours within a day* | 0 | 0 to 23. For example: hour="13". |
| dayOfWeek | *One or more days within a week* | * | 0 to 7 (both 0 and 7 refer to Sunday). For example: dayOfWeek="3".<br>Sun, Mon, Tue, Wed, Thu, Fri, Sat. For example: dayOfWeek="Mon". |
| dayOfMonth | *One or more days within a month* | * | 1 to 31. For example: dayOfMonth="15".<br>–7 to –1 (a negative number means the *n*th day or days before the end of the month). For |

| | | | |
|---|---|---|---|
| | | | example: dayOfMonth="–3".<br>Last. For example: dayOfMonth="Last".<br>[1st, 2nd, 3rd, 4th, 5th, Last]<br>[Sun, Mon, Tue, Wed, Thu, Fri, Sat]. For example: dayOfMonth="2nd Fri". |
| month | *One or more months within a year* | * | 1 to 12. For example: month="7".<br>Jan, Feb, Mar, Apr, May, Jun, Jul, Aug, Sep, Oct, Nov, Dec. For example: month="July". |
| year | A particular calendar year | * | A four–digit calendar year. For example: year="2011". |

**Specifying Multiple Values in Calendar Expressions**

You can specify multiple values in calendar expressions, as described in the following sections.

**Using Wildcards in Calendar Expressions**

Setting an attribute to an asterisk symbol (*) represents all allowable values for the attribute.

The following expression represents every minute:

*minute="*"*

The following expression represents every day of the week:

*dayOfWeek="*"*

**Specifying a List of Values**

To specify two or more values for an attribute, use a comma (,) to separate the values. A range of values is allowed as part of a list. Wildcards and intervals, however, are not allowed.

Duplicates within a list are ignored.

The following expression sets the day of the week to Tuesday and Thursday:

*dayOfWeek="Tue, Thu"*

The following expression represents 4:00 a.m., every hour from 9:00 a.m. to 5:00 p.m. using a range, and 10:00 p.m.:

*hour="4,9–17,22"*

**Specifying a Range of Values**

Use a dash character (–) to specify an inclusive range of values for an attribute. Members of a range cannot be wildcards, lists, or intervals. A range of the form x–x, is equivalent to the single-valued expression x. A range of the form x–y where x is greater than y is equivalent to the expression x–maximum value, minimum value–y. That is, the expression begins at x, rolls over to the beginning of the allowable values, and continues up to y.

The following expression represents 9:00 a.m. to 5:00 p.m.:

*hour="9–17"*

The following expression represents Friday through Monday:

*dayOfWeek="5–1"*

The following expression represents the twenty-fifth day of the month to the end of the month, and the beginning of the month to the fifth day of the month:

*dayOfMonth="25–5"*

It is equivalent to the following expression:

*dayOfMonth="25–Last,1–5"*

**Specifying Intervals**

The forward slash (/) constrains an attribute to a starting point and an interval and is used to specify every N seconds, minutes, or hours within the minute, hour, or day. For an expression of the form x/y, x represents the starting point and y represents the interval. The wildcard character may be used in the x position of an interval and is equivalent to setting x to 0.

Intervals may be set only for second, minute, and hour attributes.

The following expression represents every 10 minutes within the hour:

*minute="*/10"*

It is equivalent to:

*minute="0,10,20,30,40,50"*

The following expression represents every 2 hours starting at noon:

*hour="12/2"*

**Programmatic Timers**

When a programmatic timer expires (goes off), the container calls the method annotated @Timeout in the bean's implementation class. The @Timeout method contains the business logic that handles the timed event.

**The @Timeout Method**

Methods annotated @Timeout in the enterprise bean class must return void and optionally take a javax.ejb.Timer object as the only parameter. They may not throw application exceptions.

```
@Timeout
public void timeout(Timer timer)
{
  System.out.println("TimerBean: timeout occurred");
}
```

**Creating Programmatic Timers**

To create a timer, the bean invokes one of the create methods of the TimerService interface. These methods allow single-action, interval, or calendar-based timers to be created.

For single-action or interval timers, the expiration of the timer can be expressed as either duration or an absolute time. The duration is expressed as the number of milliseconds before a timeout event is triggered. To specify an absolute time, create a *java.util.Date* object and pass it to the *TimerService.createSingleActionTimer( )* or the *TimerService.createTimer( )* method.

The following code sets a programmatic timer that will expire in 1 minute (6,000 milliseconds):

```
long duration = 6000;
Timer timer = timerService.createSingleActionTimer(duration, new TimerConfig());
```

The following code sets a programmatic timer that will expire at 12:05 p.m. on May 1, 2010, specified as a java.util.Date:

```
SimpleDateFormatter formatter = new SimpleDateFormatter("MM/dd/yyyy 'at' HH:mm");
Date date = formatter.parse("05/01/2010 at 12:05");
Timer timer = timerService.createSingleActionTimer(date, new TimerConfig( ));
```

For calendar-based timers, the expiration of the timer is expressed as a *javax.ejb.ScheduleExpression* object, passed as a parameter to the *TimerService.createCalendarTimer( )* method. The *ScheduleExpression* class represents calendar-based timer expressions and has methods that correspond to the attributes described in Creating Calendar-Based Timer Expressions.

The following code creates a programmatic timer using the *ScheduleExpression* helper class:

```
ScheduleExpression schedule = new ScheduleExpression();
schedule.dayOfWeek("Mon");
schedule.hour("12-17, 23");
Timer timer = timerService.createCalendarTimer(schedule);
```

The bean described in The timersession Example creates a timer as follows:

```
Timer timer = timerService.createTimer(intervalDuration, "Created new programmatic timer");
```

In the timersession example, createTimer is invoked in a business method, which is called by a client.

Timers are persistent by default. If the server is shut down or crashes, persistent timers are saved and will become active again when the server is restarted. If a persistent timer expires while the server is down, the container will call the *@Timeout* method when the server is restarted.

Non-persistent programmatic timers are created by calling *TimerConfig.setPersistent(false)* and passing the *TimerConfig* object to one of the timer-creation methods.

The Date and long parameters of the *createTimer( )* methods represent time with the resolution of milliseconds. However, because the timer service is not intended for real-time applications, a callback to the *@Timeout* method might not occur with millisecond precision. The timer service is for business applications, which typically measure time in hours, days, or longer durations.

**Automatic Timers**

Automatic timers are created by the EJB container when an enterprise bean that contains methods annotated with the *@Schedule* or *@Schedules* annotations is deployed. An enterprise bean can have multiple automatic timeout methods, unlike a programmatic timer, which allows only one method annotated with the @Timeout annotation in the enterprise bean class.

Automatic timers can be configured through annotations or through the *ejb-jar.xml* deployment descriptor.

Adding a *@Schedule* annotation on an enterprise bean marks that method as a timeout method according to the calendar schedule specified in the attributes of *@Schedule*.

The *@Schedule* annotation has elements that correspond to the calendar expressions detailed in Creating Calendar-Based Timer Expressions and the persistent, info, and *timezone* elements.

The optional persistent element takes a Boolean value and is used to specify whether the automatic timer should survive a server restart or crash. By default, all automatic timers are persistent.

The optional *timezone* element is used to specify that the automatic timer is associated with a particular time zone. If set, this element will evaluate all timer expressions in relation to the specified time zone, regardless of the time zone in which the EJB container is running. By default, all automatic timers set are in relation to the default time zone of the server.

The optional info element is used to set an informational description of the timer. A timer's information can be retrieved later by using *Timer.getInfo*.

The following timeout method uses @Schedule to set a timer that will expire every Sunday at midnight:

```
@Schedule(dayOfWeek="Sun", hour="0")
public void cleanupWeekData() { ... }
```

The *@Schedules* annotation is used to specify multiple calendar-based timer expressions for a given timeout method.

The following timeout method uses the @Schedules annotation to set multiple calendar-based timer expressions. The first expression sets a timer to expire on the last day of every month. The second expression sets a timer to expire every Friday at 11:00 p.m.

```
@Schedules ({@Schedule(dayOfMonth="Last"), @Schedule(dayOfWeek="Fri", hour="23")})
public void doPeriodicCleanup( ) { ... }
```

**Canceling and Saving Timers**

Timers can be cancelled by the following events.

- When a single-event timer expires, the EJB container calls the associated timeout method and then cancels the timer.
- When the bean invokes the cancel method of the *Timer* interface, the container cancels the timer.

If a method is invoked on a cancelled timer, the container throws the *javax.ejb.NoSuchObjectLocalException*.

To save a *Timer* object for future reference, invoke its *getHandle( )* method and store the *TimerHandle* object in a database. To reinstantiate the Timer object, retrieve the handle from the database and invoke *getTimer( )* on the handle. A *TimerHandle* object cannot be passed as an argument of a method defined in a remote or web service interface. In other words, remote clients and web service clients cannot access a bean's *TimerHandle* object. Local clients, however, do not have this restriction.

### Getting Timer Information

In addition to defining the cancel and getHandle methods, the Timer interface defines methods for obtaining information about timers:

```
public long getTimeRemaining( );
public java.util.Date getNextTimeout( );
public java.io.Serializable getInfo( );
```

The *getInfo( )* method returns the object that was the last parameter of the *createTimer( )* invocation. For example, in the *createTimer* code snippet of the preceding section, this information parameter is a String object with the value created timer.

To retrieve all of a bean's active timers, call the *getTimers( )* method of the TimerService interface. The *getTimers( )* method returns a collection of Timer objects.

### Transactions and Timers

An enterprise bean usually creates a timer within a transaction. If this transaction is rolled back, the timer creation also is rolled back. Similarly, if a bean cancels a timer within a transaction that gets rolled back, the timer cancellation is rolled back. In this case, the timer's duration is reset as if the cancellation had never occurred.

In beans that use container-managed transactions, the *@Timeout* method usually has the *Required* or *RequiresNew* transaction attribute to preserve transaction integrity. With these attributes, the EJB container begins the new transaction before calling the *@Timeout* method. If the transaction is rolled back, the container will call the *@Timeout* method at least one more time.

### The timersession Example

*TimerSessionBean* is a singleton session bean that shows how to set both an automatic timer and a programmatic timer. In the source code listing of *TimerSessionBean* that follows, the *setTimer( )* and *@Timeout* methods are used to set a programmatic timer. A TimerService instance is injected by the container when the bean is created. Because it's a business method, *setTimer( )* is exposed to the local, no-interface view of *TimerSessionBean* and can be invoked by the client. In this example, the client invokes *setTimer( )* with an interval duration of 30,000 milliseconds. The *setTimer( )* method creates a new timer by invoking the *createTimer( )* method of TimerService. Now that the timer is set, the EJB container will invoke the programmatic *Timeout( )* method of *TimerSessionBean* when the timer expires, in about 30 seconds.

```
...
public void setTimer(long intervalDuration)
{
        logger.info("Setting a programmatic timeout for " + intervalDuration + " milliseconds from now.");
        Timer timer = timerService.createTimer(intervalDuration, "Created new programmatic timer");
}

@Timeout
public void programmaticTimeout(Timer timer)
{
        this.setLastProgrammaticTimeout(new Date());
        logger.info("Programmatic timeout occurred.");
}
...
```

TimerSessionBean also has an automatic timer and timeout method, automaticTimeout. The automatic timer is set to expire every 3 minutes and is set by using a calendar-based timer expression in the @Schedule annotation:

```
...
@Schedule(minute="*/3", hour="*")
public void automaticTimeout()
{
        this.setLastAutomaticTimeout(new Date());
        logger.info("Automatic timeout occured");
}
...
```

*TimerSessionBean* also has two business methods: getLastProgrammaticTimeout and getLastAutomaticTimeout. Clients call these methods to get the date and time of the last timeout for the programmatic timer and automatic timer, respectively.

Here's the source code for the *TimerSessionBean* class:

```
import java.util.Date;
import java.util.logging.Logger;
import javax.annotation.Resource;
import javax.ejb.Schedule;
import javax.ejb.Stateless;
import javax.ejb.Timeout;
import javax.ejb.Timer;
import javax.ejb.TimerService;

@Singleton
public class TimerSessionBean
{
        @Resource
        TimerService timerService;
        private Date lastProgrammaticTimeout;
        private Date lastAutomaticTimeout;
        private Logger logger =
        Logger.getLogger("com.sun.tutorial.javaee.ejb.timersession.TimerSessionBean");

        public void setTimer(long intervalDuration)
        {
            logger.info("Setting a programmatic timeout for " + intervalDuration + " milliseconds from now.");
           Timer timer = timerService.createTimer(intervalDuration, "Created new programmatic timer");
        }

        @Timeout
        public void programmaticTimeout(Timer timer)
        {
                this.setLastProgrammaticTimeout(new Date());
                logger.info("Programmatic timeout occurred.");
        }

        @Schedule(minute="*/3", hour="*")
        public void automaticTimeout()
```

```
    {
        this.setLastAutomaticTimeout(new Date());
        logger.info("Automatic timeout occured");
    }

    public String getLastProgrammaticTimeout( )
    {
        if (lastProgrammaticTimeout != null)
        {
            return lastProgrammaticTimeout.toString();
        }
        else
        {
            return "never";
        }
    }

    public void setLastProgrammaticTimeout(Date lastTimeout)
    {
        this.lastProgrammaticTimeout = lastTimeout;
    }

    public String getLastAutomaticTimeout( )
    {
        if (lastAutomaticTimeout != null)
        {
            return lastAutomaticTimeout.toString();
        }
        else
        {
            return "never";
        }
    }

    public void setLastAutomaticTimeout(Date lastAutomaticTimeout)
    {
        this.lastAutomaticTimeout = lastAutomaticTimeout;
    }
}
```

We can use either NetBeans IDE or Ant to build, package, deploy, and run above example.

*****

# Chapter 16

# Hibernating

Most significant development projects always involve a relational database. The foundation of most commercial applications is the large-scale storage of ordered information (such as: catalogs, customer lists, contract details, published text, and architectural designs, etc).

With the establishment of the World Wide Web, the demand for databases has increased. Though they may not know it, the customers of online bookshops and newspapers are using databases. Somewhere in the guts of the application a database is being queried and a response is offered.

While the demand for such applications have grown but their creation has not become visibly simpler. Some standardization has occurred; such as — the most successful **Enterprise JavaBeans (EJB) standards** of Java Enterprise Edition, which provides for container and bean-managed persistency of entity bean classes. Unfortunately, EJB and many other models had *suffered to one or more ways because of the mismatch between the relational model and the object-oriented model*. In short, database persistency was difficult.

There are solutions for which EJBs are appropriate, some for which some sort of **Object Relational Mapping (ORM)** like Hibernate is appropriate, and some for which the traditional approach of direct access via the **Java Database Connectivity (JDBC)** API is appropriate. We, personally, think that Hibernate represents a good first choice, as it does not stop the simultaneous use of these alternative approaches.

In this chapter we will study the strength of Hibernating with a small example and also study it in contrast with the traditional JDBC approach.

## 16.1 What is Hibernating?

Hibernate is a **lightweight Object Relational Mapping (ORM) framework** that is used to map an object oriented domain model to a relational database. Initially, the developers used Structured Query Language (SQL) to perform **CRUD** (Create, Read, Update and Delete) operations. But the main problem with such relational database is that, the developer need to provide additional Java code in the application to handle the resultsets containing data retrieved from the database.

With the introduction of the Hibernate framework, the JavaBean classes can now directly be mapped to the database tables, eliminating the need to provide the additional Java code in the application to handle query results.

The Hibernate framework automatically generates SQL calls and ensures that a web application is portable with all SQL supported databases. This framework also provides the persistence feature for Plain Old Java Objects (POJOs). You can use Hibernate framework on all type of Java's technological applications using servlet or EJB.

As discussed above, earlier JDBC and SQL were used to retrieve data from databases; however, writing queries using SQL for CRUD operations was time consuming process. This was simplified with the arrival of Hibernating. It provides HQL. As compare to SQL, in HQL, you do not need to write code to perform common data persistence related programming tasks.

The flexibility of Hibernate is because of its transparent programming model to map Java objects to the relational databases. To provide mapping for Java objects, you need to write a simple POJO class and create an XML mapping file. This XML file describes the relationship of the database with the class attributes and calls the Hibernate APIs to load and store the persistence objects.

Hibernate works efficiently with swings, servlets and EJB session beans. The developer does not need to implement interfaces or extend classes for persistence.

Hibernate is free open source software, and its support can be downloaded from www.hibernate.org. To download the latest Hibernate supporting JAR files, visit www.hibernate.org and then click the "download" link to go to download page. Click "Distribution bundles" link from the download page to download the latest release of hibernate. (You will get a zip file. Extract it to you Java or NetBeans directory for easy availibility).

## 16.2 Advantages of Hibernating over JDBC

The advantages of Hibernate over JDBC are:

- JDBC is database specific. **Whereas**
  Hibernate code will work well for all databases, for ex: Oracle, MySQL, etc.
- To work with JDBC, one needs to know SQL. **Whereas**
  No knowledge of SQL is needed because Hibernate is a set of objects and a table is treated as an object.
- In JDBC the query tuning is to be done by the database authors. **Whereas**
  Query tuning is not required in Hibernate. The query tuning is automatic in hibernate by using criteria queries, and the result of performance is at its best.
- In JDBC the java cache is to be implemented. **Whereas**
  With the support of cache of hibernate, the data can be placed in the cache for better performance.
- Developer has to write code in JDBC to map an object model's data representation to a relational data model and its corresponding database schema. **Whereas**
  Hibernate itself takes care of this mapping using XML files so developer does not need to write code for this.
- JDBC supports only native Structured Query Language (SQL). **Whereas**
  Hibernate provides Hibernate Query Language (HQL) which is similar to SQL syntax and supports polymorphic queries too. It also supports native SQL statements.
- The mapping of Java objects with database tables has to be taken care of in JDBC. **Whereas**
  Hibernate provides transparent persistence and therefore there is no need to map database tables tuples to application objects during interaction with RDBMS.
- With JDBC, caching needs to be manually maintained. **Whereas**
  Hibernate cache is set to application work space. Relational tuples are moved to this cache as a result of query. It improves performance during multiple writes for the same data.
- In JDBC there is no check that always every user has updated data. **Whereas**
  Hibernate enables definition of version type field to application, due to which Hibernate updates version field of database table every time relational tuple is updated in form of Java class object to that table.

## 16.3 Limitations of EJB over Hibernating

Truly speaking, an entity bean is permitted with two types of persistence in an EJB server: Bean Managed Persistence (BMP) and Container Managed Persistence (CMP). In BMP, the bean itself is responsible for carrying out all of the SQL associated with storing and retrieving its data—in other words, it requires the developer to create the appropriate JDBC logic. On the other hand, CMP requires the container to carry out the work of storing and retrieving the bean data. So why doesn't that solve the problem? Here are just a few of the reasons:

- Entity Beans have to follow naming conventions.
- Entity Beans require one-to-one mapping to database tables.
- EJB are comparatively slow.
- Someone has to determine which bean field maps to which table column in EJB.
- EJB require special method names. If these are not followed correctly, they will fail silently.
- Entity Beans have to reside within an EE application server environment.
- EJB cannot readily be extracted as "general purpose" components for other applications.
- EJB can't be serializable.
- EJB rarely exist as portable components to be dropped into a foreign application. (you generally have to roll your own EJB solution)

All above points are limitations or comparative disadvantages of EJB over use of hibernating.

## 16.4 What is new in Hibernate 3.5?

Hibernate 3.5 provides some new features that helps to develop more efficient hibernate applications. These features provides better support for JDBC 4.0, such as facilitating the use of annotations with EntityManager, providing support for column level read/write, and providing support for fetching profiles. Lets now discuss these features in detail.

- **Annotations with EntityManager**

  Hibernate 3.5 facilitates the developer to use annotations and EntityManager together in an application. In previous versions of Hibernate, it was not allowed.

- **Support for column level read/write**

  To update data in an application, you need to implement the read-write strategy in the application. Whenever serializable transaction isolation level is required then, read-write strategy should not be used. Whenever a cache is used in a JTA environment, then you have to define a value for the *hibernate.transaction.manager_lookup_class* property and also needed to specify a naming strategy that would be used to obtain the JTA transaction manager.

- **Support for fetching profiles**

  If the database supports ANSI, Oracle or Sybase style outer join, the use of outer joins to retrieve records often increases the execution performance by reducing the continuous flow of data to and from the database. The use of outer join allows you to use many-to-one, one-to-many, many-to-many and one-to-one associations to retrieve the records from the database in a single SQL SELECT query.

## 16.5 Features of Hibernating

After discussing about advantages of Hibernating, let's focus some of the features of hibernating which also adds some more flashlights on its impression.

- **Object/Relational Mapping**

Hibernate ORM enables developers to more easily write applications whose data outlives the application process. As an Object/Relational Mapping (ORM) framework, Hibernate is concerned with data persistence as it applies to relational databases (via JDBC).

- **JPA Provider**

In addition to its own "native" API, Hibernate is also an implementation of the Java Persistence API (JPA) specification. As such, it can be easily used in any environment supporting JPA including Java SE applications, Java EE application servers, Enterprise OSGi containers, etc.

- **Idiomatic persistence**

Hibernate enables you to develop persistent classes following natural Object-oriented idioms including inheritance, polymorphism, association, composition, and the Java collections framework. Hibernate requires no interfaces or base classes for persistent classes and enables any class or data structure to be persistent.

- **High Performance**

Hibernate supports lazy initialization, numerous fetching strategies and optimistic locking with automatic versioning and time stamping. Hibernate requires no special database tables or fields and generates much of the SQL at system initialization time instead of at runtime.

Hibernate consistently offers superior performance over straight JDBC code, both in terms of developer productivity and runtime performance.

- **Scalability**

Hibernate was designed to work in an application server cluster and deliver a highly scalable architecture. Hibernate scales well in any environment: Use it to drive your in-house Intranet that serves hundreds of users or for mission-critical applications that serve hundreds of thousands.

- **Reliable**

Hibernate is well known for its excellent stability and quality, proven by the acceptance and use by tens of thousands of Java developers.

- **Extensibility**

Hibernate is highly configurable and extensible.

## 16.6 Architecture of Hibernating

The architecture of hibernating includes many objects; such as persistent object, session factory, transaction factory, connection factory, session, transaction etc. All these objects have a particular role to play in hibernating.

There are 4 layers in hibernate architecture. They are

- Java application layer
- Hibernate framework layer
- Backend API layer and
- database layer

Let's see the diagram of hibernate architecture:

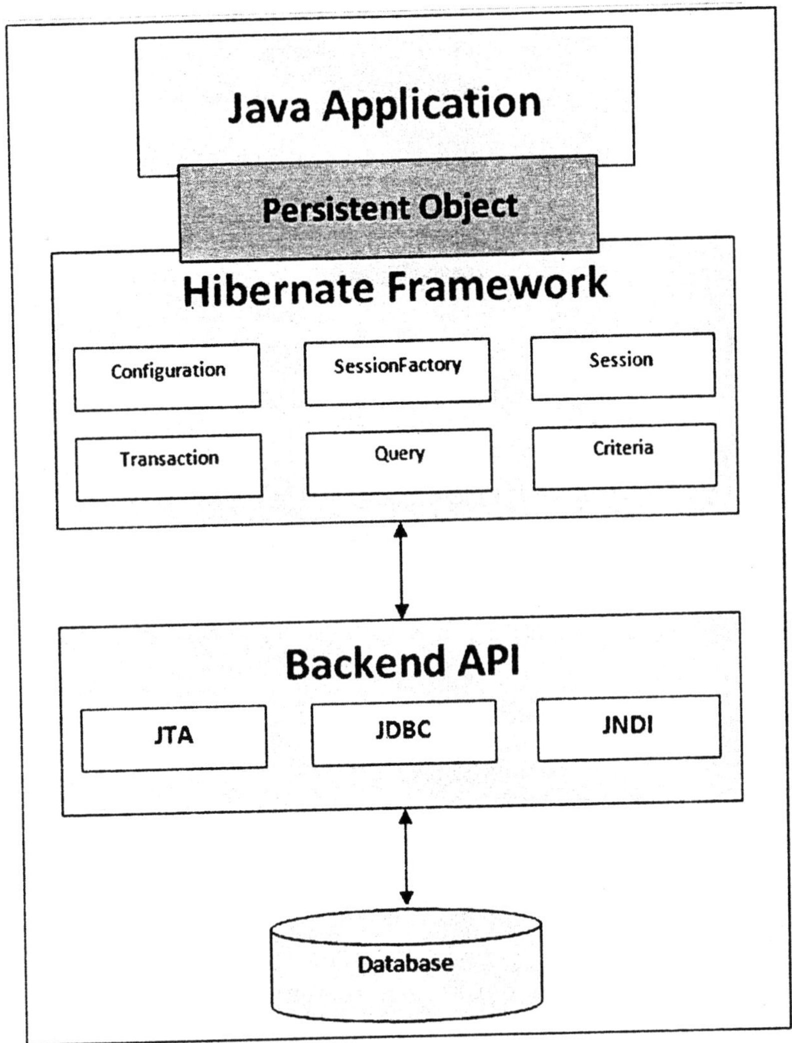


The above diagram shows a comprehensive architecture of Hibernate. In order to persist data to a database, Hibernate create an instance of entity class (Java class mapped with database table). This object is called Transient object as they are not yet associated with the session or not yet persisted to a database. To persist the object to database, the instance of *SessionFactory* interface is created. *SessionFactory* is a singleton instance which implements Factory design pattern. *SessionFactory* loads the Hibernate configuration file and with the help of *TransactionFactory* and *ConnectionProvider* implements all the configuration settings on a database.

Hibernate uses various existing Java APIs like **JDBC (Java Database Connectivity)**, **Java Transaction API (JTA)**, and **Java Naming and Directory Interface (JNDI)**. JDBC provides a rudimentary level of abstraction of functionality common to relational databases, allowing almost any database with a JDBC driver to be supported by Hibernate. JNDI and JTA allow Hibernate to be integrated with J2EE application servers.

Following section gives brief description of each of the class objects involved in Hibernate Framework layer.

**Configuration Object:**

The Configuration object is the first Hibernate object you create in any Hibernate application and usually created only once during application initialization. It represents a configuration or properties file required by the Hibernate. The Configuration object provides two keys components:

- **Database Connection**: This is handled through one or more configuration files supported by Hibernate. These files are *hibernate.properties* and *hibernate.cfg.xml.*
- **Class Mapping Setup**: This component creates the connection between the Java classes and database tables..

**SessionFactory Object:**

Configuration object is used to create a SessionFactory object which in-turn configures Hibernate for the application using the supplied configuration file and allows for a Session object to be instantiated. The SessionFactory is a thread safe object and used by all the threads of an application.

The SessionFactory is heavyweight object so usually it is created during application start up and kept for later use. You would need one SessionFactory object per database using a separate configuration file. So if you are using multiple databases then you would have to create multiple SessionFactory objects.

**Session Object:**

A Session is used to get a physical connection with a database. The Session object is lightweight and designed to be instantiated each time an interaction is needed with the database. Persistent objects are saved and retrieved through a Session object.

The session objects should not be kept open for a long time because they are not usually thread safe and they should be created and destroyed them as needed.

**Transaction Object:**

A Transaction represents a unit of work with the database and most of the RDBMS supports transaction functionality. Transactions in Hibernate are handled by an underlying transaction manager and transaction (from JDBC or JTA).

This is an optional object and Hibernate applications may choose not to use this interface, instead managing transactions in their own application code.

**Query Object:**

Query objects use SQL or Hibernate Query Language (HQL) string to retrieve data from the database and create objects. A Query instance is used to bind query parameters, limit the number of results returned by the query, and finally to execute the query.

**Criteria Object:**

Criteria object are used to create and execute object oriented criteria queries to retrieve objects.

## 16.7 Understanding Hibernate Query Language

Hibernate Query Language (HQL) is same as SQL (Structured Query Language) but it doesn't depends on the table of the database. Instead of table name, we use class name in HQL. So it is database independent query language.

There are many advantages of HQL. They are as follows:

- database independent
- supports polymorphic queries
- easy to learn for Java Programmer

HQL provides *a built-in interface* "**Query**" and it is an object oriented representation of Hibernate Query. The object of Query can be obtained by calling the createQuery( ) method Session interface.

The *Query interface* provides many methods. There is given commonly used methods:

- **public int executeUpdate(String query)** is used to fire the *update* or *delete* query.
- **public List list( )** returns the result of the relation as a list.
- **public Query setFirstResult(int rowno)** specifies the row number from where record will be retrieved.
- **public Query setMaxResult(int rowno)** specifies the no. of records to be retrieved from the relation (table).
- **public Query setParameter(int col_number, Object value)** it sets the value to the JDBC style query parameter.
- **public Query setParameter(String col_name, Object value)** it sets the value to a named query parameter.

Following subsection shows some of the examples of HQL queries using object of Query interface.

**Example of HQL to get all the records**

```
Query query=session.createQuery("from Emp");        //here persistent class name is Emp
List list=query.list( );
```

**Example of HQL to get records with pagination**

```
Query query=session.createQuery("from Emp");
query.setFirstResult(5);
query.setMaxResult(10);
List list=query.list();//will return the records from 5 to 10th number
```

**Example of HQL update query**

```
Transaction tx=session.beginTransaction( );
Query q=session.createQuery("update User set name=:n where id=:i");
q.setParameter("n","Udit Kumar");
q.setParameter("i",111);
int status=q.executeUpdate( );
System.out.println(status);
tx.commit( );
```

**Example of HQL delete query**

```
Query query=session.createQuery("delete from Emp where id=100"); //specifying class name (Emp) not tablename
query.executeUpdate();
```

**HQL's Aggregate functions**

*You may call avg( ), min( ), max( ) etc. aggregate functions by HQL. Let's see some common examples:*

**Example to get total salary of all the employees**

```
Query q=session.createQuery("select sum(salary) from Emp");
List<Emp> list=q.list( );
  Iterator<Emp> itr=list.iterator( );
  while(itr.hasNext( ))
  {
    System.out.println(itr.next( ));
  }
```

**Example to get maximum salary of employee**

```
Query q=session.createQuery("select max(salary) from Emp");
```

**Example to get minimum salary of employee**

*Query q=session.createQuery("select min(salary) from Emp");*

**Example to count total number of employee ID**

*Query q=session.createQuery("select count(id) from Emp");*

**Example to get average salary of each employees**

*Query q=session.createQuery("select avg(salary) from Emp");*

## 16.8 Understanding Hibernate O/R Mapping

ORM is a technique to map object-oriented data with the relational data. In other words, it is used to *convert the datatype supported in object-oriented programming language to a datatype supported by a database*. This facilitates the transfer of object oriented data to the database without the occurrence of an exception due to incompatibility of datatype.

ORM involves mapping of the object-oriented data to relational data. Mapping should be in a format that can define the mapping of the classes with tables, properties with columns, foreign keys with associations and SQL types with Java types. The document should be in such a mapping format that it can be easily read and edited. ORM is used to reduce programming code and map the object-oriented programming objects with the relational databases such as Oracle, DB2, MySQL, Sybase and any other relational database software. The programming code can be reduced through catching, and by using an embedded SQL or call-level interface, such as JDBC, XML documents are used to define O/R Mapping. They can be easily manipulated by version-control systems and text editors, and may be customized at development time or runtime. XML mapping document allows you to:

- Bridge the gap between object-oriented system and relational databases
- Define the object-relational mapping
- Help to generate and export database table
- Use XDoclet support that allows mapping to be generated from javadoc style source comments

In complex applications, a class can be inherited by other classes, which may lead to the problem of class mismatching. To overcome such problems, the following hierarchy approaches can be used:

- **table-per-class hierarchy:** Removes polymorphism and inheritance relationships completely from the relational model.
- **table-per-subclass hierarchy:** Denormalizes the relational model and enables polymorphism.
- **table-per-concreteclass hierarchy:** Represents inheritance relationships as foreign key relationships.

As discussed in many previous sections, mapping are done by using persistent class declarations but not by table declarations. The example of hibernate XML file is shown in following code block. [Create Hibernate Mapping file as directed in section 3.12]

```
<?xml version="1.0" encoding="utf-8"?>
<!DOCTYPE hibernate-mapping PUBLIC  "-//Hibernate/Hibernate Mapping DTD//EN"
"http://www.hibernate.org/dtd/hibernate-mapping-3.0.dtd">  // DTD declaration

<hibernate-mapping>
  <class name="Employee" table="EMPLOYEE">                    // class mapped to table
    <meta attribute="class-description">
      This class contains the employee detail.
    </meta>
```

```
    <id name="id" column="emp_id" type="int"></id>              // Identifier mapped (for primary key)
    <property name="firstName" column="emp_first_name" type="string"/>     // property 1 mapped
    <property name="lastName" column="emp_last_name" type="string"/>       // property 2 mapped
    <property name="salary" column="emp_salary" type="int"/>               // property 3 mapped
  </class>
</hibernate-mapping>
```

The above code block shows the Hibernate Mapping file in which **Employee class** is mapped with **EMPLOYEE table**. Following is a small explanation of tags and properties used in above file.

- **<DOCTYPE>** Refers to the Hibernate mapping Document Type Declaration (DTD) that should be declared in every mapping file for syntactic validation of the XML.
- **<hibernate-mapping>** It is the root element of the Hibernate mapping file. Inside this tag any numbers of class elements may be present. This tag has following important attributes.
  - schema (optional)
  - catalog (optional)
  - default-cascade (optional)
  - default-access (optional)
  - default-lazy (optional, by default true)
  - auto-import (optional, by default true)
  - package (optional)

The following code block shows all the attributes of <hibernate-mapping> tag.

```
<hibernate-mapping schema="Schema_Name" catalog="Catalog_Name" default-cascade="Cascade_Style" default-access="field | property | class" default-lazy="true | false" auto-import="true | false" package="Package_Name"/>
```

- **<class>** Maps a class object with its corresponding entity in the database. It also specifies the table name in the database that has to be accessed along with the column of the table. Within one <hibernate-mapping> tag, several <class> mappings are allowed. All attributes of the <class> tag is listed below.
  - name (optional)
  - table (optional)
  - discriminator-value (optional)
  - mutable (optional, by default true)
  - schema (optional)
  - catalog (optional)
  - proxy (optional)
  - dynamic-update (optional, by default false)
  - dynamic-insert (optional, by default false)
  - select-before-update (optional, by default false)
  - polymorphism (optional, by default implicit)
  - where (optional)
  - persister (optional)
  - batch-size (optional, by default 1)
  - optimistic-lock (optional)
  - entity-name (optional)

- check (optional)
- rowid (optional)
- subselect (optional)
- abstract (optional)

The following code block shows all the attributes of <class> tag.

```
<class name="Class_Name" table="Table_Name" discriminator-value="discriminator_value" mutable="true | false" schema="owner" catalog="Catalog" proxy="Proxy_Interface" dynamic-update="true | false" dynamic-insert="true | false" select-before-update="true | false" polymorphism="implicit | explicit" where="arbitrary sql where condition" persister="Persister_Class" batch-size="N" optimistic-lock="none | version | dirty | all" lazy="true | false" entity-name="Entity_Name" check="arbitrary sql check condition" rowid="row_ID" subselect="SQL expression" abstract="true | false" node="Element_Name"/>
```

- **<id>** Serves as a unique identifier used to map primary key column of database table. The attributes of <id> tag is listed below.
  - name (MANDATORY)
  - column (MANDATORY)
  - type (MANDATORY)
  - unsaved-value (optional)
  - access (optional)

The following code block shows all the attributes of <id> tag.

```
<id name= "Property_Name" column= "Column_Name" type= "Value_Type" unsaved-value= "null | any | none | undefined | id_value" access= "field | property | Class_Name" />
```

- **<property>** Defines standard Java attributes and their mapping into database schema. This element supports the column child element that specifies additional properties, such as the index name given on a column or a specified column type. The property name of the String type is mapped to a database column name. The attributes of <property> tag is listed below.
  - name
  - column
  - type
  - update
  - insert
  - formula (optional)
  - not-null (optional)
  - unique (optional)
  - lazy (optional, by default false)
  - access (optional)
- The following code block shows all the attributes of <property> tag.

```
<property name="Property_Name" column="Column_Name" type="Value_Type" update="true | false" insert="true | false" formula="arbitrary SQL expression" not-null="true | false" unique="true | false" lazy="true | false" access="field | property | Class_Name"/>
```

## 16.9 Complete Example using Hibernating

Let's consider a Hibernate example in which a JavaBean sets and retrieves the employee details from a database. For this example, lets create EMPLOYEE table to store employee details and configure the connection details, such as dialect, connection URL, username and password in *hibernate.cfg.xml* file. Then a JavaBean is created to set or retrieve the employee details from the database table. The EmployeeData.hbm.xml file is created to configure the EMPLOYEE table to the JavaBean. The following sets help in understanding and developing Hibernate application.

1. Create the java project
2. Add jar files for hibernate
3. Create the Persistent class (POJO class)
4. Create database table
5. Create the configuration file
6. Create the mapping file
7. Create the application class that retrieves or stores the persistent object
8. Compile and run the application

**Step 1:** Create a new Java project with required framework. (refer section 3.2)

**Step 2:** Add required jar files for hibernate. (refer section 3.11) Following diagram shows a list of required JAR files.

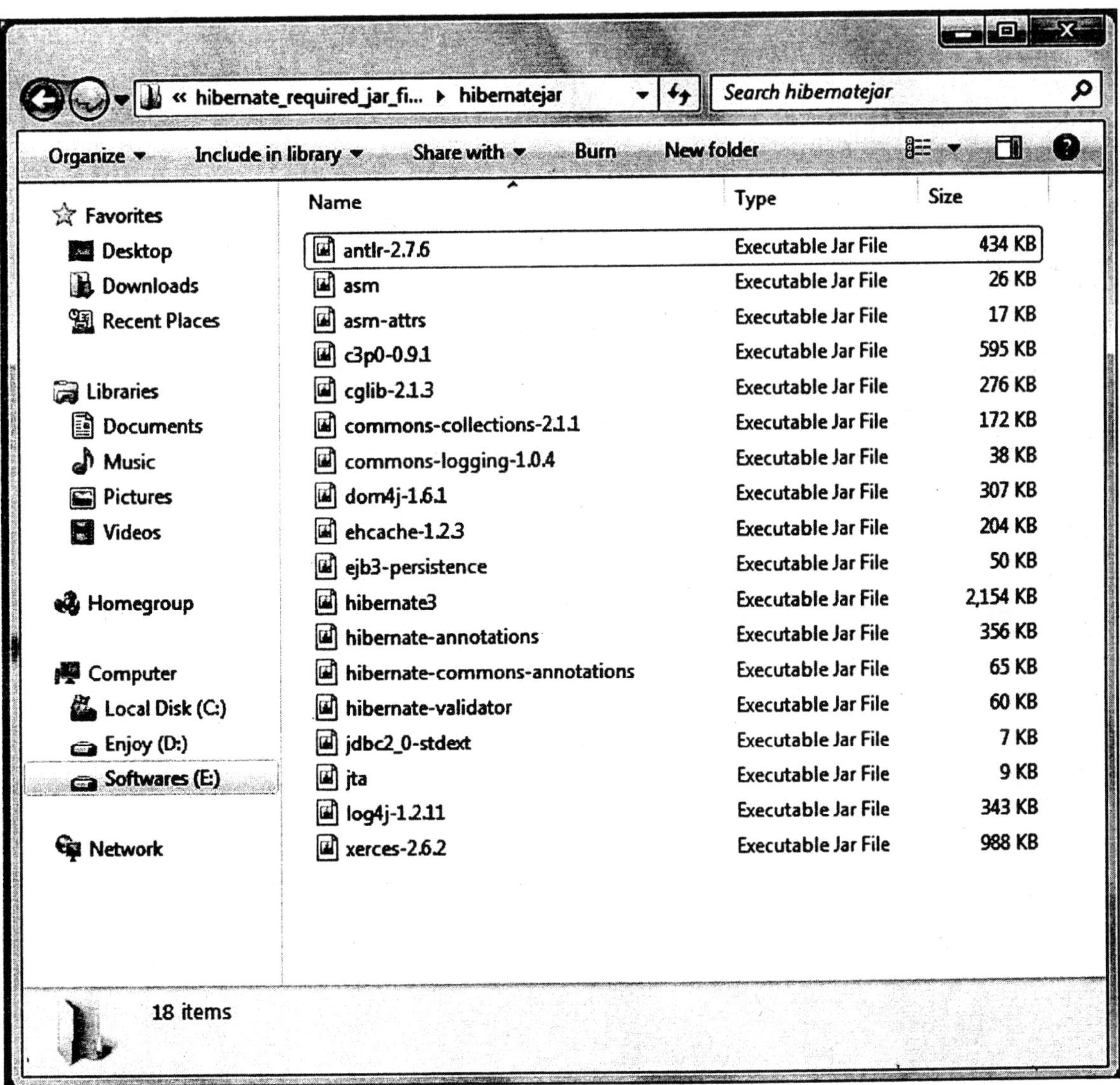

**Step 3:** Create a persistent class (POJO class)

The first step in creating an application is to build the Java POJO class or classes, depending on the application that will be persisted to the database. Let us consider our Employee class with some getter and setter methods to make it JavaBeans compliant class.

A POJO (Plain Old Java Object) is a Java object that doesn't extend or implement some specialized classes and interfaces respectively required by the EJB framework. All normal Java objects are POJO.

When you design a class to be persisted by Hibernate, it's important to provide JavaBeans compliant code as well as one attribute which would work as index like id attribute in the Employee class. Name this file as **Employee.java**

```
public class Employee
{
    private int id;
    private String firstName;
    private String lastName;
    private int salary;

    public Employee( )
    { }
    public Employee(String fname, String lname, int salary)
    {
      this.firstName = fname;
      this.lastName = lname;
      this.salary = salary;
    }
    public int getId( )
    {
      return id;
    }
    public void setId(int id)
    {
      this.id = id;
    }
    public String getFirstName( )
    {
      return firstName;
    }
    public void setFirstName(String first_name )
    {
      this.firstName = first_name;
    }
    public String getLastName( )
    {
      return lastName;
    }
```

```
        public void setLastName(String last_name )
        {
          this.lastName = last_name;
        }
        public int getSalary( )
        {
          return salary;
        }
        public void setSalary(int salary)
        {
          this.salary = salary;
        }
}
```

**Step 4:** Create database tables

Second step would be creating tables in your database. There would be one table corresponding to each object you are willing to provide persistence. Consider above objects need to be stored and retrieved into the following RDBMS table:

```
create table EMPLOYEE
(
  id INT NOT NULL auto_increment,
  first_name VARCHAR(20) default NULL,
  last_name  VARCHAR(20) default NULL,
  salary    INT  default NULL,
  PRIMARY KEY (id)
);
```

**Step 5:** Create the configuration file

Let's create the *hibernate.cfg.xml* file to configure Hibernate by declaring the environmental details. In the configuration file, you need to provide various details such as the table name that maps to a class and JavaBean properties mapping to column names of the specified table. This configuration file should be placed in \WEB-INF\classes directory of you application. The *hibernate.cfg.xml* file is shown in following code block.

```
<?xml version="1.0" encoding="utf-8"?>
<!DOCTYPE hibernate-mapping PUBLIC
"-//Hibernate/Hibernate Mapping DTD//EN"
"http://hibernate.sourceforge.net/hibernate-configuration-3.0.dtd">
<hibernate-configuration>
<session factory>

<!—setting properties-->
<property name= "connection.username">scott</property>
<property name= "connection.url">jdbc:oracle:thin:@192.168.1.123:1521:XE</property>
<property name= "dialect">org.hibernate.dialect.OracleDialect</property>
<property name= "connection.password">tiger</property>
```

```
<property name="connection.driver_class">oracle.jdbc.driver.OracleDriver</property>

<!—mapping files -->
<mapping resource = "EEApplication/hibernate/EmployeeData.hbm.xml"/>
</session factory>
</hibernate-configuration>
```

**Step 6:** Create the mapping file

This step is to create a mapping file that instructs Hibernate how to map the defined class or classes to the database tables. Name it as **EmployeeData.hbm.xml**

```
<?xml version="1.0" encoding="utf-8"?>
<!DOCTYPE hibernate-mapping PUBLIC
 "-//Hibernate/Hibernate Mapping DTD//EN"
 "http://www.hibernate.org/dtd/hibernate-mapping-3.0.dtd">

<hibernate-mapping>
  <class name="Employee" table="EMPLOYEE">
    <meta attribute="class-description">
      This class contains the employee detail.
    </meta>
    <id name="id" type="int" column="id">
      <generator class="native"/>
    </id>
    <property name="firstName" column="first_name" type="string"/>
    <property name="lastName" column="last_name" type="string"/>
    <property name="salary" column="salary" type="int"/>
  </class>
</hibernate-mapping>
```

You should save the mapping document in a file with the format *<classname>.hbm.xml.* We saved our mapping document in the file *EmployeeData.hbm.xml*. Let us see little detail about the mapping document:

- The mapping document is an XML document having <hibernate-mapping> as the root element which contains all the <class> elements.
- The **<class>** elements are used to define specific mappings from a Java classes to the database tables. The Java class name is specified using the name attribute of the class element and the database table name is specified using the table attribute.
- The **<meta>** element is optional element and can be used to create the class description.
- The <id> element maps the unique ID attribute in class to the primary key of the database table. The name attribute of the id element refers to the property in the class and the column attribute refers to the column in the database table. The type attribute holds the hibernate mapping type, this mapping types will convert from Java to SQL data type.
- The **<generator>** element within the id element is used to automatically generate the primary key values. Set the class attribute of the generator element is set to native to let hibernate pick up identity, sequence or HILO algorithm to create primary key depending upon the capabilities of the underlying database.

- The **<property>** element is used to map a Java class property to a column in the database table. The name attribute of the element refers to the property in the class and the column attribute refers to the column in the database table. The type attribute holds the hibernate mapping type, this mapping types will convert from Java to SQL data type.

There are other attributes and elements available which will be used in a mapping document and I would try to cover as many as possible while discussing other Hibernate related topics.

**Step 7:** Create application class

Finally, we will create our application class with the main( ) method to run the application. We will use this application to save few Employee's records and then we will apply CRUD operations on those records. Name it as **ManageEmployee.java**

```
import java.util.List;
import java.util.Date;
import java.util.Iterator;

import org.hibernate.HibernateException;
import org.hibernate.Session;
import org.hibernate.Transaction;
import org.hibernate.SessionFactory;
import org.hibernate.cfg.Configuration;

public class ManageEmployee
{
  private static SessionFactory factory;
  public static void main(String ar[ ])
  {
    try
    {
      factory = new Configuration( ).configure( ).buildSessionFactory( );
    }
    catch (Throwable ex)
    {
      System.err.println("Failed to create sessionFactory object." + ex);
      throw new ExceptionInInitializerError(ex);
    }
    ManageEmployee ME = new ManageEmployee( );

    /* Add few employee records in database */
    Integer empID1 = ME.addEmployee("Deepak", "Toshniwal", 1000);
    Integer empID2 = ME.addEmployee("Vijay", "Suryawanshi", 5000);
    Integer empID3 = ME.addEmployee("Rakesh", "Jain", 10000);

    /* List down all the employees */
    ME.listEmployees( );
```

```
    /* Update employee's records */
    ME.updateEmployee(empID1, 5000);

    /* Delete an employee from the database */
    ME.deleteEmployee(empID2);

    /* List down new list of the employees */
    ME.listEmployees( );
  }

  /* Method to CREATE an employee in the database */
  public Integer addEmployee(String fname, String lname, int salary)
  {
    Session session = factory.openSession( );
    Transaction tx = null;
    Integer employeeID = null;
    try
    {
      tx = session.beginTransaction( );
      Employee employee = new Employee(fname, lname, salary);
      employeeID = (Integer) session.save(employee);
      tx.commit( );
    }
    catch (HibernateException e)
    {
      if (tx!=null) tx.rollback();
      e.printStackTrace( );
    }
    finally
    {
      session.close( );
    }
    return employeeID;
  }


  /* Method to  READ all the employees */
  public void listEmployees( )
  {
    Session session = factory.openSession();
    Transaction tx = null;
    try
    {
      tx = session.beginTransaction( );
      List employees = session.createQuery("FROM Employee").list( );
```

```
        for (Iterator iterator = employees.iterator( ); iterator.hasNext( );)
        {
          Employee employee = (Employee) iterator.next( );
          System.out.print("First Name: " + employee.getFirstName( ));
          System.out.print("  Last Name: " + employee.getLastName( ));
          System.out.println("  Salary: " + employee.getSalary());
        }
        tx.commit( );
      }
      catch (HibernateException e)
      {
        if (tx!=null) tx.rollback( );
        e.printStackTrace();
      }
      finally
      {
        session.close( );
      }
    }


    /* Method to UPDATE salary for an employee */
    public void updateEmployee(Integer EmployeeID, int salary)
  {
      Session session = factory.openSession( );
      Transaction tx = null;
      try
      {
        tx = session.beginTransaction( );
        Employee employee = (Employee)session.get(Employee.class, EmployeeID);
        employee.setSalary( salary );
        session.update(employee);
        tx.commit( );
      }
      catch (HibernateException e)
      {
        if (tx!=null) tx.rollback( );
        e.printStackTrace( );
      }
      finally
      {
        session.close( );
      }
    }
```

```
/* Method to DELETE an employee from the records */
public void deleteEmployee(Integer EmployeeID)
{
  Session session = factory.openSession( );
  Transaction tx = null;
  try
  {
    tx = session.beginTransaction( );
    Employee employee = (Employee)session.get(Employee.class, EmployeeID);
    session.delete(employee);
    tx.commit( );
  }
  catch (HibernateException e)
  {
    if (tx!=null) tx.rollback( );
    e.printStackTrace( );
  }
  finally
  {
    session.close( );
  }
}
}
```

**Step 8:** Compile and Run project

After successful compilation, run the above project and you will get following records in EMPLOYEE table.

```
$java ManageEmployee
-----VARIOUS LOG MESSAGES WILL DISPLAY HERE-----

First Name: Deepak  Last Name: Toshniwal  Salary: 1000
First Name: Vijay  Last Name: Suryawanshi  Salary: 5000
First Name: Rakesh  Last Name: Jain  Salary: 10000
First Name: Deepak  Last Name: Toshniwal  Salary: 5000
First Name: Rakesh  Last Name: Jain  Salary: 10000
```

Note: If you check your EMPLOYEE table, you will get the record's entry.

*****

# Chapter 17

# Web Services and JavaMail

Web services are client and server applications that communicate over the World Wide Web's (WWW) HyperText Transfer Protocol (HTTP). As described by the World Wide Web Consortium (W3C), web services provide a standard means of interoperating between software applications running on a variety of platforms and frameworks. Web services are characterized by their great interoperability and extensibility, as well as their machine-processable descriptions, thanks to the use of XML. Web services can be combined in a loosely coupled way to achieve complex operations. Programs providing simple services can interact with each other to deliver sophisticated added-value services. JavaMail API is one of the most widely used facilities given by Java Web services.

JavaMail is one of the most important technologies introduced in Java EE. It is a platform and protocol independent technology used to build email applications. JavaMail provides JavaMail Application Program Interface (API), which is used to create Java based email client applications.

The JavaMail API is a set of classes and interfaces that help developers to create email client applications by using protocols, such as SMTP and IMAP. The SMTP protocol is a mail transfer protocol used for sending and receiving emails. These Java based email client applications provide various features, such as customized personal email applications and the ability to add email functionality to an enterprise application.

This chapter introduces Java's web services in brief along with JavaMail API, architecture and its components. This chapter later discusses important JavaMail classes and interfaces, along with sending and receiving text email, attachments and processing on HTML messages.

## 17.1 Introduction to web services

Web services are client and server applications that communicate over the World Wide Web's (WWW) HyperText Transfer Protocol (HTTP). As described by the World Wide Web Consortium (W3C), web services provide a standard means of interoperating between software applications running on a variety of platforms and frameworks. Web services are characterized by their great interoperability and extensibility, as well as their machine-processable descriptions, thanks to the use of XML. Web services can be combined in a loosely coupled way to achieve complex operations. Programs providing simple services can interact with each other to deliver sophisticated added-value services.

**Types of Web Services**

On the conceptual level, a service is a software component provided through a network-accessible endpoint. The service consumer and provider use messages to exchange invocation request and response information in the form of self-containing documents that make very few assumptions about the technological capabilities of the receiver.

On a technical level, web services can be implemented in various ways. The two types of web services discussed in this section can be distinguished as "big" web services and "RESTful" web services.

- **"Big" Web Services**

In Java EE 6, JAX-WS provides the functionality for "big" web services, which are described in Chapter 19, Building Web Services with JAX-WS. Big web services use XML messages that follow the Simple Object Access Protocol (SOAP) standard, an XML language defining a message architecture and message formats. Such systems often contain a machine-readable description of the operations offered by the service, written in the Web Services Description Language (WSDL), an XML language for defining interfaces syntactically.

The SOAP message format and the WSDL interface definition language have gained widespread adoption. Many development tools, such as NetBeans IDE, can reduce the complexity of developing web service applications.

A SOAP-based design must include the following elements.

- A formal contract must be established to describe the interface that the web service offers. WSDL can be used to describe the details of the contract, which may include messages, operations, bindings, and the location of the web service. You may also process SOAP messages in a JAX-WS service without publishing a WSDL.
- The architecture must address complex nonfunctional requirements. Many web service specifications address such requirements and establish a common vocabulary for them. Examples include transactions, security, addressing, trust, coordination, and so on.
- The architecture needs to handle asynchronous processing and invocation. In such cases, the infrastructure provided by standards, such as Web Services Reliable Messaging (WSRM), and APIs, such as JAX-WS, with their client-side asynchronous invocation support, can be leveraged out of the box.

- **RESTful Web Services**

In Java EE 6, JAX-RS provides the functionality for Representational State Transfer (RESTful) web services. REST is well suited for basic, ad hoc integration scenarios. RESTful web services, often better integrated with HTTP than SOAP-based services are, do not require XML messages or WSDL service–API definitions.

Project Jersey is the production-ready reference implementation for the JAX-RS specification. Jersey implements support for the annotations defined in the JAX-RS specification, making it easy for developers to build RESTful web services with Java and the Java Virtual Machine (JVM).

Because RESTful web services use existing well-known W3C and Internet Engineering Task Force (IETF) standards (HTTP, XML, URI, MIME) and have a lightweight infrastructure that allows services to be built with minimal tooling, developing RESTful web services is inexpensive and thus has a very low barrier for adoption. You can use a development tool such as NetBeans IDE to further reduce the complexity of developing RESTful web services.

A RESTful design may be appropriate when the following conditions are met.

- The web services are completely stateless. A good test is to consider whether the interaction can survive a restart of the server.
- A caching infrastructure can be leveraged for performance. If the data that the web service returns is not dynamically generated and can be cached, the caching infrastructure that web servers and other intermediaries inherently provide can be leveraged to improve performance. However, the developer must take care because such caches are limited to the HTTP GET method for most servers.
- The service producer and service consumer have a mutual understanding of the context and content being passed along. Because there is no formal way to describe the web services interface, both parties must agree out of band on the schemas that describe the data being exchanged and on ways to process it meaningfully. In the real world, most commercial applications that expose services as RESTful implementations also distribute so-called value-added toolkits that describe the interfaces to developers in popular programming languages.
- Bandwidth is particularly important and needs to be limited. REST is particularly useful for limited-profile devices, such as PDAs and mobile phones, for which the overhead of headers and additional layers of SOAP elements on the XML payload must be restricted.
- Web service delivery or aggregation into existing web sites can be enabled easily with a RESTful style. Developers can use such technologies as JAX-RS and Asynchronous JavaScript with XML (AJAX) and such

toolkits as Direct Web Remoting (DWR) to consume the services in their web applications. Rather than starting from scratch, services can be exposed with XML and consumed by HTML pages without significantly refactoring the existing web site architecture. Existing developers will be more productive because they are adding to something they are already familiar with rather than having to start from scratch with new technology.

## 17.2 Introducing JavaMail

JavaMail is the technology that provides a protocol independent framework for building Java based email client applications. JavaMail uses classes and interfaces of the JavaMail API to create email client applications, which supports various email protocols.

The JavaMail API is broadly divided into the following two parts:

- The first part of the API deals with how to send and receive messages independent of the providers and protocols.
- The second part of API deals with the protocol such as SMTP, POP, IMAP and NNTP used for transferring email.

For understanding JavaMail API in detail, let's first understand a few important terms related to email, which are described here.

- **Email client:** An email client is an application that is used to compose, read and send emails.
- **Mail server:** A mail server is an application that receives emails from email applications of other mail servers. It stores the user messages either permanently or until they are read by an email client. A computer that is used especially for running such applications is also called as mail servers. Some famous examples of mail servers are Eudora's mail server, Microsoft exchange server, Microsoft Windows POP3 service, and WinGate.
- **Messaging System:** It provides an electronic mail delivery system and is made up of Mail User Agent (MUA) and Message Transfer Agent (MTA).
    - **MUA** is the client email program that sends or receives a message from a mail server. User agents give the message to the transfer agent, which passes it onto another transfer agent.
    - **MTA** is responsible for the actual sending and delivering email messages between machines, as well as queuing of messages.
- **Message Delivery Agent:** This is used to store a message into a user's mailbox. When the message arrives at mail server, the final MTA gives the message to appropriate delivery agent, who then adds it to user's mailbox.
- Message Store (MS): Message store is the user mailbox that holds emails until it is read and deleted by the user.

In addition to this information, we must also be familiar with some of the protocols that performs major role in sending, delivering, transferring, reading and deleting an email. Following section explains the working and role of some of the most important protocols of JavaMail API.

## 17.3 Mail protocol

Before looking into the JavaMail API specifics, step back and take a look at the protocols used with the API. There are basically four that we will use.

- SMTP
- POP
- IMAP
- MIME

We will also run across NNTP and some others. Understanding the basics of all the protocols will help us to understand how to use the JavaMail API. While the API is designed to be protocol agnostic, we can't overcome the limitations of the underlying protocols. If a capability isn't supported by a chosen protocol, the JavaMail API doesn't magically add the capability on top of it. Following is the quick look on each of above protocols in very short.

**Simple Mail Transfer Protocol [SMTP]**

SMTP stands for Simple Mail Transfer Protocol. It's a set of communication guidelines that allow software to transmit email over the Internet. Most email software is designed to use SMTP for communication purposes when sending email and it only works for outgoing messages. When people set up their email programs, they will typically have to give the address of their Internet service provider's SMTP server for outgoing mail. There are two other protocols - POP3 and IMAP - that are used for retrieving and storing email.

The other purpose of SMTP is to set up communication rules between servers. For example, servers have a way of identifying themselves and announcing what kind of communication they are trying to perform. There are also ways to handle errors, including common things like incorrect email addresses. In a typical SMTP transaction, a server will identify itself, and announce the kind of operation it is trying to perform. The other server will authorize the operation, and the message will be sent. If the recipient address is wrong, or if there is some other problem, the receiving server may reply with an error message of some kind.

**Post Office Protocol [POP]**

POP stands for Post Office Protocol. POP is the mechanism most people on the Internet use to get their mail. It defines support for a single mailbox for each user. That is all it does, and that is also the source of most confusion. Much of what people are familiar with when using POP, like the ability to see how many new mail messages they have, are not supported by POP at all. These capabilities are built into programs like Microsoft Outlook, which remember things like the last mail received and calculate how many are new for a user.

POP3, which is an abbreviation for Post Office Protocol 3, is the third version of a widespread method of receiving email. Much like the physical version of a post office clerk, POP3 receives and holds email for an individual until they pick it up. And, much as the post office does not make copies of the mail it receives, in previous versions of POP3, when an individual downloaded email from the server into their email program, there were no more copies of the email on the server; POP automatically deleted them.

POP3 makes it easy for anyone to check their email from any computer in the world, provided they have configured their email program properly to work with the protocol.

**Internet Map Access Protocol [IMAP]**

IMAP is a more advanced protocol for receiving messages. IMAP stands for Internet Message Access Protocol, and is currently in version 4, also known as IMAP4. When using IMAP, your mail server must support the protocol. You can't just change your program to use IMAP instead of POP and expect everything in IMAP to be supported. Assuming your mail server supports IMAP, your JavaMail-based program can take advantage of users having multiple folders on the server and these folders can be shared by multiple users.

Due to the more advanced capabilities, you might think IMAP would be used by everyone. It isn't. It places a much heavier burden on the mail server, requiring the server to receive the new messages, deliver them to users when requested, and maintain them in multiple folders for each user. While this does centralize backups, as users' long-term mail folders get larger and larger, everyone suffers when disk space is exhausted. With POP, saved messages get offloaded from the mail server.

### Multipurpose Internet Mail Extension [MIME]

Short for Multipurpose Internet Mail Extensions, a specification for formatting non-ASCII messages so that they can be sent over the Internet. Many e-mail clients now support MIME, which enables them to send and receive graphics, audio, and video files via the Internet mail system. In addition, MIME supports messages in character sets other than ASCII.

There are many predefined MIME types, such as GIF graphics files and PostScript files. It is also possible to define your own MIME types.

In addition to e-mail applications, Web browsers also support various MIME types. This enables the browser to display or output files that are not in HTML format. The latest version, called S/MIME, supports encrypted messages.

## 17.4 JavaMail architecture

The JavaMail architectural components are layered as shown below:

- The Abstract Layer declares classes, interfaces and abstract methods intended to support mail handling functions that all mail systems support. API elements comprising the Abstract Layer are intended to be sub-classed and extended as necessary in order to support standard data types, and to interface with message access and message transport protocols as necessary.
- The internet implementation layer implements part of the abstract layer using internet standards - RFC822 and MIME.
- JavaMail uses the JavaBeans Activation Framework (JAF) in order to encapsulate message data, and to handle commands intended to interact with that data. Interaction with message data should take place via JAF-aware JavaBeans, which are not provided by the JavaMail API.

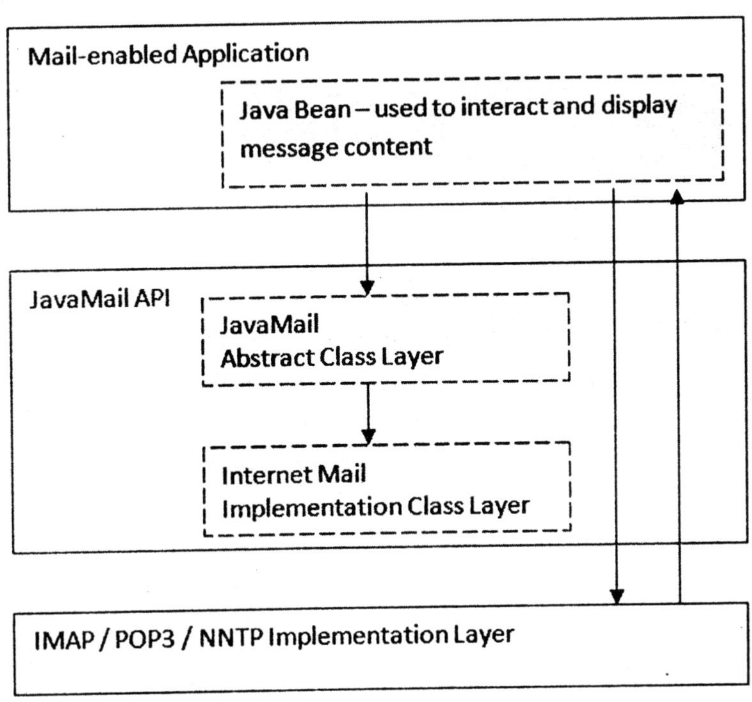


- JavaMail clients use the JavaMail API and Service Providers implement the JavaMail API. The layered design architecture allows clients to use the same JavaMail API calls to send, receive and store a variety of messages using different data-types from different message stores and using different message transport protocols

## 17.5 JavaMail Outline

The JavaMail API is intended to perform the following functions, which comprise the standard mail handling process for a typical client application:

- Create a mail message consisting of a collection of header attributes and a block of data of some known data type as specified in the Content-Type header field. JavaMail uses the Part interface and the Message class to define a mail message. It uses the JAF-defined DataHandler object to contain data placed in the message.
- Create a Session object, which authenticates the user, and controls access to the message store and transport.
- Send the message to its recipient list.
- Retrieve a message from a message store.
- Execute a high-level command on a retrieved message. High-level commands like view and print are intended to be implemented via JAF-Aware JavaBeans.

## 17.6 Components of JavaMail API

Before taking a how-to approach at looking at the JavaMail classes in depth, the following will take us through the core classes that make up the API: *Session*, *Message*, *Address*, *Authenticator*, *Transport*, *Store*, and *Folder*. All these classes are found in the top-level package for the JavaMail API: *javax.mail*.

**Session**

The Session class defines a basic mail session. It is through this session that everything else works. The Session object takes advantage of a *java.util.Properties* object to get information like mail server, username, password, and other information that can be shared across your entire application.

The constructors for the class are private. We can get a single default session that can be shared with the **getDefaultInstance()** method:

```
Properties props = new Properties();
// fill props with any information
Session session = Session.getDefaultInstance(props, null);
```

Or, we can create a unique session with **getInstance( )** method as:

```
Properties props = new Properties();
// fill props with any information
Session session = Session.getInstance(props, null);
```

In both cases here the null argument is an Authenticator object which is not being used at this time. In most cases, it is sufficient to use the shared session, even if working with mail sessions for multiple user mailboxes. You can add the username and password combination in at a later step in the communication process, keeping everything separate.

**Message**

Once we have your Session object, it is time to move on to creating the message to send. This is done with a type of *Message*. Being an abstract class, we must work with a subclass, in most cases *javax.mail.internet.MimeMessage*. A *MimeMessage* is a email message that understands MIME types and headers, as defined in the different RFCs. Message headers are restricted to US-ASCII characters only, though non-ASCII characters can be encoded in certain header fields.

To create a Message, pass along the Session object to the *MimeMessage* constructor:

```
MimeMessage message = new MimeMessage(session);
```

Once we have a message, we can set its parts, as Message implements the Part interface (with MimeMessage implementing MimePart). The basic mechanism to set the content is the **setContent( )** method, with arguments for the content and the mime type:

*message.setContent("Hello", "text/plain");*

If, however, we know that we are working with a *MimeMessage* and our message is plain text, we can use its **setText()** method which only requires the actual content, defaulting to the MIME type of text/plain:

*message.setText("Hello");*

For plain text messages, the latter form is the preferred mechanism to set the content. For sending other kinds of messages, like HTML messages, use the former.

For setting the subject, use the setSubject() method:

*message.setSubject("Subject Here");*

**Address**

Once we have created the Session and the Message, as well as filled the message with content, it is time to address a mail message with an Address. Like Message, Address is an abstract class. We use the *javax.mail.internet.InternetAddress* class.

To create an address with just the email address, pass the email address to the constructor:

*Address address = new InternetAddress("xyz@example.com");*

If we want a name to appear next to the email address, we can pass that along to the constructor, too:

*Address address = new InternetAddress("xyz@example.com", "James Gosling");*

We will need to create address objects for the message's from field as well as the to field. Unless a mail server prevents, there is nothing stopping us from sending a message that appears to be from anyone.

Once we've created the addresses, we connect them to a message in one of two ways. For identifying the sender, we use the **setFrom( )** and **setReplyTo( )** methods.

*message.setFrom(address)*

If a message needs to show multiple from addresses, use the **addFrom( )** method:

*Address addresses[ ] = {"xyz@example.com", "abx@example.com", "pqr@example.com"};*

*message.addFrom(addresses);*

For identifying the message recipients, we use the **addRecipient( )** method. This method requires a *Message.RecipientType* besides the address.

*message.addRecipient(type, address);*

The three predefined types of address are:

- Message.RecipientType.TO
- Message.RecipientType.CC
- Message.RecipientType.BCC

So, if the message was to go to the James Gosling, sending a carbon copy to the Patrick Naughton, the following would be appropriate:

```
Address toAddress = new InternetAddress("jamesgosling@example.com");
Address ccAddress = new InternetAddress("patricknaughton@example.com");
message.addRecipient(Message.RecipientType.TO, toAddress);
message.addRecipient(Message.RecipientType.CC, ccAddress);
```

The JavaMail API does not provide any mechanism to check for the validity of an email address. While we can program in support to scan for valid characters or verify the MX (mail exchange) record, programmatically.

**Authenticator**

Like the java.net classes, the JavaMail API can take advantage of an *Authenticator* to access protected resources via a username and password. For the JavaMail API, that resource is the mail server. The JavaMail Authenticator is found in the *javax.mail* package and is different from the java.net class of the same name. The two don't share the same Authenticator as the JavaMail API works with Java 1.1, which didn't have the java.net variety.

To use the Authenticator, we subclass the abstract class and return a *PasswordAuthentication* instance from the **getPasswordAuthentication( )** method. We must register the Authenticator with the session when created. Then, only an Authenticator will be notified when authentication is necessary. We could popup a window or read the username and password from a configuration file (though if not encrypted it is not secure), returning them to the caller as a PasswordAuthentication object.

```
Properties props = new Properties( );

//fill props with any information

Authenticator auth = new MyAuthenticator( );

Session session = Session.getDefaultInstance(props, auth);
```

**Transport**

The final part of sending a message is to use the Transport class. This class speaks the protocol-specific language for sending the message (usually SMTP). It's an abstract class and works something like Session. We can use the default version of the class by just calling the static send( ) method:

```
Transport.send(message);
```

Or, we can get a specific instance from the session for your protocol, pass along the username and password (blank if unnecessary), send the message, and close the connection:

```
message.saveChanges( ); // implicit with send( )

Transport transport = session.getTransport("smtp");

transport.connect(host, username, password);

transport.sendMessage(message, message.getAllRecipients( ));

transport.close( );
```

This latter way is best when we need to send multiple messages, as it will keep the connection with the mail server active between messages. The basic send( ) mechanism makes a separate connection to the server for each method call.

**Store and Folder**

Getting messages starts similarly to sending messages, with a Session. However, after getting the session, we connect to a Store, quite possibly with a username and password or Authenticator. Like Transport, we tell the Store what protocol to use:

```
// Store store = session.getStore("imap");
Store store = session.getStore("pop3");
store.connect(host, username, password);
```

After connecting to the Store, you can then get a Folder, which must be opened before you can read messages from it:

```
Folder folder = store.getFolder("INBOX");
folder.open(Folder.READ_ONLY);
Message message[ ] = folder.getMessages( );
```

For POP3, the only folder available is the INBOX. If you are using IMAP, you can have other folders available.

Once we have a Message to read, we can get its content with **getContent( )** or write its content to a stream with **writeTo( )**. The **getContent( )** method only gets the message content, while **writeTo( )** output includes headers.

```
System.out.println(((MimeMessage)message).getContent( ));
```

Once reading mail is done, close the connection to the folder and store.

```
folder.close(boolean value);
store.close( );
```

The boolean passed to the **close( )** method of folder states whether or not to update the folder by removing deleted messages.

## 17.7 Sending mail

Sending an email message involves getting a session, creating and filling a message, and sending it. We can specify an SMTP server by setting the *mail.smtp.host* property for the Properties object passed when getting the *Session*:

```
String host = ...;
String from = ...;
String to = ...;


// Get system properties
Properties props = System.getProperties( );


// Setup mail server
props.put("mail.smtp.host", host);


// Get session
Session session = Session.getDefaultInstance(props, null);
```

```
// Define message
MimeMessage message = new MimeMessage(session);
message.setFrom(new InternetAddress(from));
message.addRecipient(Message.RecipientType.TO, new InternetAddress(to));
message.setSubject("Hello JavaMail");
message.setText("Welcome to JavaMail");

// Send message
Transport.send(message);
```

Simply fill the required String variables and most importantly, place this code inside a try-catch block; because sending a message can throw exceptions.

## 17.8 Fetching mail

For reading mail, we get a session, get and connect to an appropriate store for your mailbox, open the appropriate folder, and get your message(s). Also, don't forget to close the connection when done.

```
String host = ...;
String username = ...;
String password = ...;

// Create empty properties
Properties props = new Properties( );

// Get session
Session session = Session.getDefaultInstance(props, null);

// Get the store
Store store = session.getStore("pop3");
store.connect(host, username, password);

// Get folder
Folder folder = store.getFolder("INBOX");
folder.open(Folder.READ_ONLY);

// Get directory
Message message[ ] = folder.getMessages( );

for (int i=0, n=message.length; i<n; i++)
{
System.out.println(i + ": " + message[i].getFrom( )[0] + "\t" + message[i].getSubject( ));
}

// Close connection
folder.close(false);
store.close( );
```

What to do with each message is up to a user. The above code block just displays who the message is from and the subject. Technically speaking, the list of from addresses could be empty and the **getFrom( )[0]** call could throw an exception.

To display the whole message, we can prompt the user after seeing the **from** and **subject** fields, and then call the message's **writeTo( )** method if they want to see it.

```
BufferedReader reader = new BufferedReader (new InputStreamReader(System.in));

// Get directory
Message message[ ] = folder.getMessages( );
for (int i=0, n=message.length; i<n; i++)
{
        System.out.println(i + ": " + message[i].getFrom( )[0] + "\t" + message[i].getSubject( ));
        System.out.println("Do you want to read message? " + "[YES to read/QUIT to end]");
        String line = reader.readLine( );
        if ("YES".equals(line))
        {
        message[i].writeTo(System.out);
                }
        else if ("QUIT".equals(line))
        {
                break;
        }
}
```

## 17.9 Deleting Messages and Flags

Deleting messages involves working with the Flags associated with the messages. There are different flags for different states, some system-defined and some user-defined. The predefined flags are defined in the inner class *Flags.Flag* and are listed below:

- Flags.Flag.ANSWERED
- Flags.Flag.DELETED
- Flags.Flag.DRAFT
- Flags.Flag.FLAGGED
- Flags.Flag.RECENT
- Flags.Flag.SEEN
- Flags.Flag.USER

Just because a flag exists doesn't mean the flag is supported by all mail servers/providers. For instance, besides deleting messages, the POP protocol supports none of them. Checking for new mail is not a POP task but one built into mail clients. To find out what flags are supported, ask the folder with **getPermanentFlags( )** method.

To delete messages, you set the message's DELETED flag:

```
message.setFlag(Flags.Flag.DELETED, true);
```

Open up the folder in READ_WRITE mode first though:

```
folder.open(Folder.READ_WRITE);
```

Then, when you are done processing all messages, close the folder, passing in a true value to expunge the deleted messages.

```
folder.close(true);
```

There is an **expunge( )** method of Folder that can be used to delete the messages. However, it doesn't work for Sun's POP3 provider. Other providers may or may not implement the capabilities. It will more than likely be implemented for IMAP providers. Because POP only supports single access to the mailbox, you have to close the folder to delete the messages with Sun's provider.

To unset a flag, just pass false to the **setFlag( )** method. To see if a flag is set, check with **isSet()** method.

## 17.10 Authenticating yourself

We previously learned that you can use an Authenticator to prompt for username and password when needed, instead of passing them in as strings. Here you'll actually see how to more fully use authentication.

Instead of connecting to the Store with the host, username, and password, you configure the Properties to have the host, and tell the Session about a custom Authenticator instance, as shown here:

```
// Setup properties
Properties props = System.getProperties( );
props.put("mail.pop3.host", host);

// Setup authentication, get session
Authenticator auth = new PopupAuthenticator( );
Session session = Session.getDefaultInstance(props, auth);

// Get the store
Store store = session.getStore("pop3");
store.connect( );
```

Then subclass the *Authenticator* and return a *PasswordAuthentication* object from the **getPasswordAuthentication( )** method. The following is one such implementation, with a single field for both. As this isn't a Project Swing tutorial, just enter the two parts in the one field, separated by a comma.

```
import javax.mail.*;
import javax.swing.*;
import java.util.*;

public class PopupAuthenticator extends Authenticator
{

        public PasswordAuthentication getPasswordAuthentication( )
        {
                String username, password;
                String result = JOptionPane.showInputDialog("Enter username, password'");
                StringTokenizer st = new StringTokenizer(result, ",");
                username = st.nextToken( );
                password = st.nextToken( );
                return new PasswordAuthentication(username, password);
        }
}
```

Since the *PopupAuthenticator* relies on Swing, it will start up the event-handling thread for AWT. This basically requires to add a call to **System.exit( )** in the code to stop the program.

## 17.11 Replying to Messages

The *Message* class includes a **reply( )** method to configure a new Message with the proper recipient and subject, adding "Re: " if not already there. This does not add any content to the message, only copying the *from* or *reply-to* header to the new recipient. The method takes a boolean parameter indicating whether to reply to only the sender (false) or reply to all (true).

```
MimeMessage reply = (MimeMessage)message.reply(false);
reply.setFrom(new InternetAddress("president@whitehouse.gov"));
reply.setText("Thanks");
Transport.send(reply);
```

To configure the *reply-to* address when sending a message, use the **setReplyTo( )** method.

### Forwarding Messages

Forwarding messages is a little more involved. There is no single method to call, and you build up the message to forward by working with the parts that make up a message.

A mail message can be made up of multiple parts. Each part is a *BodyPart*, or more specifically, a *MimeBodyPart* when working with MIME messages. The different body parts get combined into a container called *Multipart* or, again, more specifically a *MimeMultipart*. To forward a message, you create one part for the text of your message and a second part with the message to forward, and combine the two into a multipart. Then you add the multipart to a properly addressed message and send it.

That's essentially it. To copy the content from one message to another, just copy over its *DataHandler*, a class from the JavaBeans Activation Framework.

```
// Create the message to forward
Message forward = new MimeMessage(session);

// Fill in header
forward.setSubject("Fwd: " + message.getSubject());
forward.setFrom(new InternetAddress(from));
forward.addRecipient(Message.RecipientType.TO, new InternetAddress(to));

// Create your new message part
BodyPart messageBodyPart = new MimeBodyPart( );
messageBodyPart.setText("Here you go with the original message:\n\n");

// Create a multi-part to combine the parts
Multipart multipart = new MimeMultipart( );
multipart.addBodyPart(messageBodyPart);

// Create and fill part for the forwarded content
messageBodyPart = new MimeBodyPart( );
messageBodyPart.setDataHandler(message.getDataHandler( ));

// Add part to multi part
multipart.addBodyPart(messageBodyPart);

// Associate multi-part with message
forward.setContent(multipart);

// Send message
Transport.send(forward);
```

## 17.12 Working with Attachments

Attachments are resources associated with a mail message, usually kept outside of the message like a text file, spreadsheet, or image. As with common mail programs like Eudora and pine, you can attach resources to your mail message with the JavaMail API and get those attachments when you receive the message.

**Sending Attachments**

Sending attachments is quite like forwarding messages. We build up the parts to make the complete message. After the first part, your message text, you add other parts where the *DataHandler* for each is your attachment, instead of the shared handler in the case of a forwarded message. If you are reading the attachment from a file, your attachment data source is a *FileataSource*. Reading from a URL, it is a *URLDataSource*. Once you have your *DataSource*, just pass it on to the *DataHandler* constructor, before finally attaching it to the BodyPart with **setDataHandler( )**. Assuming you want to retain the original filename for the attachment, the last thing to do is to set the filename associated with the attachment with the **setFileName( )** method of BodyPart. All this is shown here:

```
// Define message
Message message = new MimeMessage(session);
message.setFrom(new InternetAddress(from));
message.addRecipient(Message.RecipientType.TO,
  new InternetAddress(to));
message.setSubject("Hello JavaMail Attachment");

// Create the message part
BodyPart messageBodyPart = new MimeBodyPart();

// Fill the message
messageBodyPart.setText("Pardon Ideas");

Multipart multipart = new MimeMultipart( );
multipart.addBodyPart(messageBodyPart);

// Part two is attachment
messageBodyPart = new MimeBodyPart( );
DataSource source = new FileDataSource(filename);
messageBodyPart.setDataHandler(new DataHandler(source));
messageBodyPart.setFileName(filename);
multipart.addBodyPart(messageBodyPart);

// Put parts in message
message.setContent(multipart);

// Send the message
Transport.send(message);
```

When including attachments with messages, if a program is a servlet, users must upload the attachment besides telling where to send the message. Uploading each file can be handled with a form encoding type of multipart/form-data.

```
<FORM ENCTYPE="multipart/form-data"
   method=post action="/myservlet">
 <INPUT TYPE="file" NAME="thefile">
 <INPUT TYPE="submit" VALUE="Upload">
</FORM>
```

**Getting attachment**

Getting attachments out of your messages is a little more involved than sending them, as MIME has no simple notion of attachments. The content of your message is a Multipart object when it has attachments. You then need to process each Part, to get the main content and the attachment(s). Parts marked with a disposition of **Part.ATTACHMENT** from **part.getDisposition( )** are clearly attachments. However, attachments can also come across with no disposition (and a non-text MIME type) or a disposition of Part.INLINE. When the disposition is either Part.ATTACHMENT or Part.INLINE, you can save off the content for that message part. Just get the original filename with getFileName() and the input stream with getInputStream( ).

```
Multipart mp = (Multipart)message.getContent( );
for (int i=0, n=multipart.getCount(); i<n; i++)
{
        Part part = multipart.getBodyPart(i));
        String disposition = part.getDisposition( );
        if ((disposition != null) && ((disposition.equals(Part.ATTACHMENT) || (disposition.equals(Part.INLINE)))
        {
                saveFile(part.getFileName(), part.getInputStream());
        }
}
```

The **saveFile( )** method just creates a File from the filename, reads the bytes from the input stream, and writes them off to the file. In case the file already exists, a number is added to the end of the filename until one is found that doesn't exist.

```
// from saveFile( )
File file = new File(filename);
for (int i=0; file.exists(); i++)
{
file = new File(filename+i);
}
```

The code above covers the simplest case where message parts are flagged appropriately. To cover all cases, handle when the disposition is null and get the MIME type of the part to handle accordingly.

```
if (disposition == null)
{
        // Check if plain
        MimeBodyPart mbp = (MimeBodyPart) part;
        if (mbp.isMimeType("text/plain"))
        {
                // Handle plain
        }
        else
        {
                // Special non-attachment cases here of
                // image/gif, text/html, ...
        }
        ...
}
```

## 17.13 Processing HTML Messages

Sending HTML-based messages can be a little more work than sending plain text messages, though it doesn't have to be that much more work. It all depends on your specific requirements.

### Sending HTML Messages

If all you need to do is send the equivalent of an HTML file as the message and let the mail reader worry about fetching any embedded images or related pieces, use the setContent() method of Message, passing along the content as a String and setting the content type to text/html.

```
String htmlText = "<H1>Hello</H1>" +
  "<img src=\"http://www.jguru.com/images/logo.gif\">";
message.setContent(htmlText, "text/html"));
```

On the receiving end, if you fetch the message with the JavaMail API, there is nothing built into the API to display the message as HTML. The JavaMail API only sees it as a stream of bytes. To display the message as HTML, you must either use the Swing JEditorPane or some third-party HTML viewer component.

```
if (message.getContentType().equals("text/html"))
{
        String content = (String)message.getContent( );
        JFrame frame = new JFrame( );
        JEditorPane text = new JEditorPane("text/html", content);
        text.setEditable(false);
        JScrollPane pane = new JScrollPane(text);
        frame.getContentPane().add(pane);
        frame.setSize(300, 300);
        frame.setDefaultCloseOperation(JFrame.DISPOSE_ON_CLOSE);
        frame.show( );
}
```

### Including Images with Your Messages

On the other hand, if you want your HTML content message to be complete, with embedded images included as part of the message, you must treat the image as an attachment and reference the image with a special cid URL, where the cid is a reference to the Content-ID header of the image attachment.

The process of embedding an image is quite similar to attaching a file to a message, the only difference is that you have to tell the MimeMultipart that the parts are related by setting its subtype in the constructor (or with setSubType()) and set the Content-ID header for the image to a random string which is used as the src for the image in the img tag. The following demonstrates this completely.

```
String file = ...;
// Create the message
Message message = new MimeMessage(session);

// Fill its headers
message.setSubject("Embedded Image");
message.setFrom(new InternetAddress(from));
message.addRecipient(Message.RecipientType.TO, new InternetAddress(to));
```

```
// Create your new message part
BodyPart messageBodyPart = new MimeBodyPart( );
String htmlText = "<H1>Hello</H1>" + "<img src=\"cid:memememe\">";
messageBodyPart.setContent(htmlText, "text/html");

// Create a related multi-part to combine the parts
MimeMultipart multipart = new MimeMultipart("related");
multipart.addBodyPart(messageBodyPart);

// Create part for the image
messageBodyPart = new MimeBodyPart( );

// Fetch the image and associate to part
DataSource fds = new FileDataSource(file);
messageBodyPart.setDataHandler(new DataHandler(fds));
messageBodyPart.setHeader("Content-ID","<memememe>");

// Add part to multi-part
multipart.addBodyPart(messageBodyPart);

// Associate multi-part with message
message.setContent(multipart);
```

*****

# Chapter 18

# Java Server Faces (JSF)

Before the introduction of JavaServer Faces (JSF), the developers had to manually code for defining the common user interface tasks to interact with the clients; such as validating user inputs and converting input string into required data type, implementing navigation rules, developing business logic to process data and many more.

JSF is a web application framework, which allows the developer to handle these tasks easily with the help of its APIs and tags and to design rich user interfaces with its components.

JSF can be defined as a framework that makes web application development easy by supporting different rich, powerful and ready to use User Interface (UI) components. JSF framework is based on MVC (Model-View-Controller) design pattern, which is one of the most popular design patterns available for implementing separate layers.

JSF reduces the effort in creating and maintaining applications which will run on a Java application server and will render application UI on to a target client. JSF facilitates Web application development by:

- providing reusable UI components
- making easy data transfer between UI components
- managing UI state across multiple server requests
- enabling implementation of custom components
- wiring client side event to server side application code

## 18.1 Overview of JSF

JavaServer Faces (JSF) is a Java-based web application framework intended to simplify development integration of web-based user interfaces. JavaServer Faces is a standardized display technology which was formalized in a specification through the Java Community Process (JCP).

From a web developer's point of view, creating a web application using JSF is a very simple and easy task. The standard and powerful features of JSF make it a preferred choice among all available Java technologies used for developing a web application.

JSF was developed by **Java Community Process (JCP)**. This is a community of web application experts. These experts are from different groups like Jakarta Struts, Oracle, Sun, IBM, ATG etc. They all collectively worked together to take the best from existing technologies and removed problems. So their collective effort brought a new technology named JavaServer Faces (JSF).

JavaServer Faces or JSF for short, is the standard framework to simplify the process of developing web application in java. It is a robust component framework, event driven programming model. It offers a set of UI components, extensible architecture, supports multiple client devices etc. Extensible means additional functionality can be given on the top of JSF core i.e. we can customize the functionality. JSF is vendor independent technology that is a standard to be supported by whole software industry.

One of the main features of JSF is that it has not only been designed for coding experts but for others also like:

- Page authors
- Application developers
- Component writers
- Application architects
- Tool developers and venders

In the past many web development frameworks came in to existence founded on servlet and jsp. Struts emerged as a standard web application framework. It became framework of choice because it came early in the market and provided necessary features at the time but competitors continued providing additional features that struts lacks. So it became necessary for java to advent new standard framework with a powerful component model. This was the reason for developing JSF technology. So main purpose of developing JSF was to create a collection of APIs for the UI components with the capacity to manage their states, handle events and validation.

Struts has an option to migrate to JSF. The simplest option is to use JSF components and rest as usual. This will enable them to take advantage of third party JSF components. Main feature of JSF is ease of use. Developing web applications is easier and faster than other frameworks like struts because JSF supports UI components and easy event handling. Taking advantages of third party components can reduce the cost of rewriting existing elements, minimize the time of development.

## 18.2 JSF features

We have many Java frameworks available that are used to develop web applications. Among all those, JSF is the most popular. It is one of the preferred choices for designing and managing UI components in web applications.

Following section lists the features of JSF. JSF 2.2 is the latest release of JSF.

- Inversion of Control (IoC), a methodology for leveraging Plain Old Java Objects (POJO).
- Template-based component system provides a means of creating composite component creation.
- Ajax support minimizes the requirement for JavaScript.
- Unified Expression Language (EL) which allows views to access Managed Bean properties and methods.
- A set of HTML and web-application specific UI components.
- A server-side event model for dispatching events and attaching listeners to system operations.
- State management for "request", "session", "application", "flash", and "view" scoped beans.
- XML-based tag libraries defining core and html functionality.
- JSF supports internationalization and enable displaying localized messages according to specified locale.
- Provides the developer with a way to link visual components to the controller or Model components without breaking layering.
- Allows configuration of application wide ResourceBundle to the EL using <resource-bundle> element in face-config.xml file.
- Along with these, JSF 2.2 also fixes some bugs from the previous releases of JSF.

## 18.3 JSF architecture

Similar to most of the popular Web application frameworks, JSF also implements Model – View – Controller design pattern. The implementation of MVC design patterns helps design different components separately, each of these components implement different types of logic.

For example, we can create **View** component with presentation logic and some **Model** component providing business logic implementation. A **Controller** controls the execution of various Model methods and navigation from one view to another in a web application. In JSF, we have a single front controller, which handles all JSF requests mapped to it. Following figure shows the MVC design pattern.

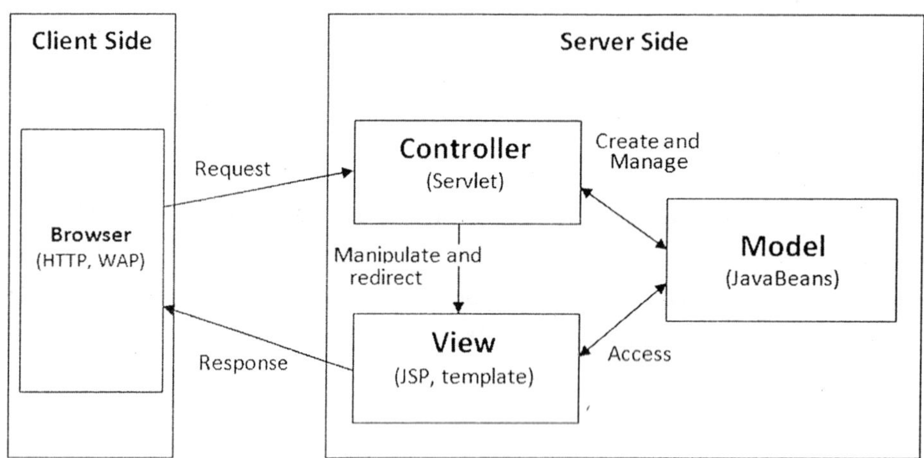


The controller part of JSF architecture consists of Front Controller Servlet, i.e. ***FacesServlet***, centralized configuration file (faces-config.xml) and a set of event handlers for the web application. The front controller servlet receives all the requests and manages the request processing life cycle of each request to generate response for the client. The *FacesServlet* is a Servlet that manages the request processing life cycle for configuring the application's settings pertaining to its use of JSF. In a JSF application, all requests are channeled through the *FacesServlet*. This is known as the *Front Controller Design pattern*. The *FacesServlet* knows how to route requests by referencing page-to-page mappings stored in a configuration file called *faces-config.xml*. Event listeners respond to component events, which perform some processing and general outcome to be used by *FacesServlet*.

The Model in JSF architecture is a set of server-side JavaBeans that holds the values and defines methods on these values. These JavaBeans may further be persisted in a database through an underlying persistence layer. This layer may include Java Data Objects, Enterprise JavaBeans or an Object Relational Mapping (ORM) implementation. The view in JSF architecture comprises the stateful user interface components.

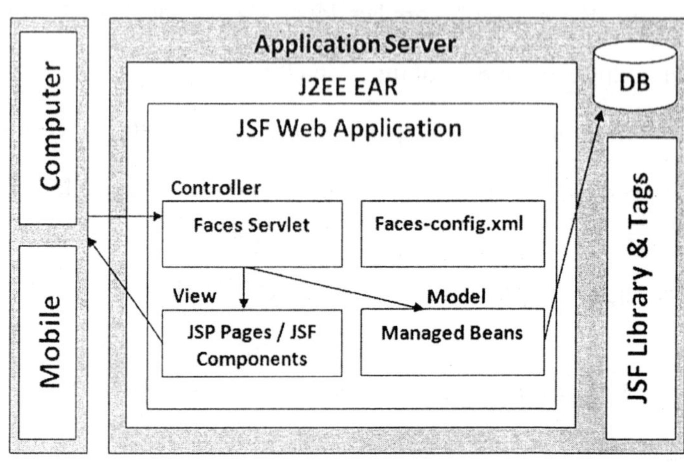

Components are rendered in different ways according to the type of the client. The view delegates this task to separate renders, each taking care of one specific output type, such as HTML or WML. Additional delegates are valuators and converts, which can be attached to specific components. Converters are used to validate and convert the values entered by the user. The client always submits strings as values for input fields that may required to be converted to a numeric data type, if these values have to be used in a calculation. The validators check if the values delivered by the client are syntactically correct or according to a specified format. The view also features resources, which may be used for localization of the web application.

## 18.4 Components of JSF application

JSF is a well-designed and easy-to-use component-based web framework. This component-based development model aligns perfectly with the lightweight POJO approach we are promoting. The development model is clean and simple. Following diagram shows the JSF components, such as UI components, validators, renderers and converter.

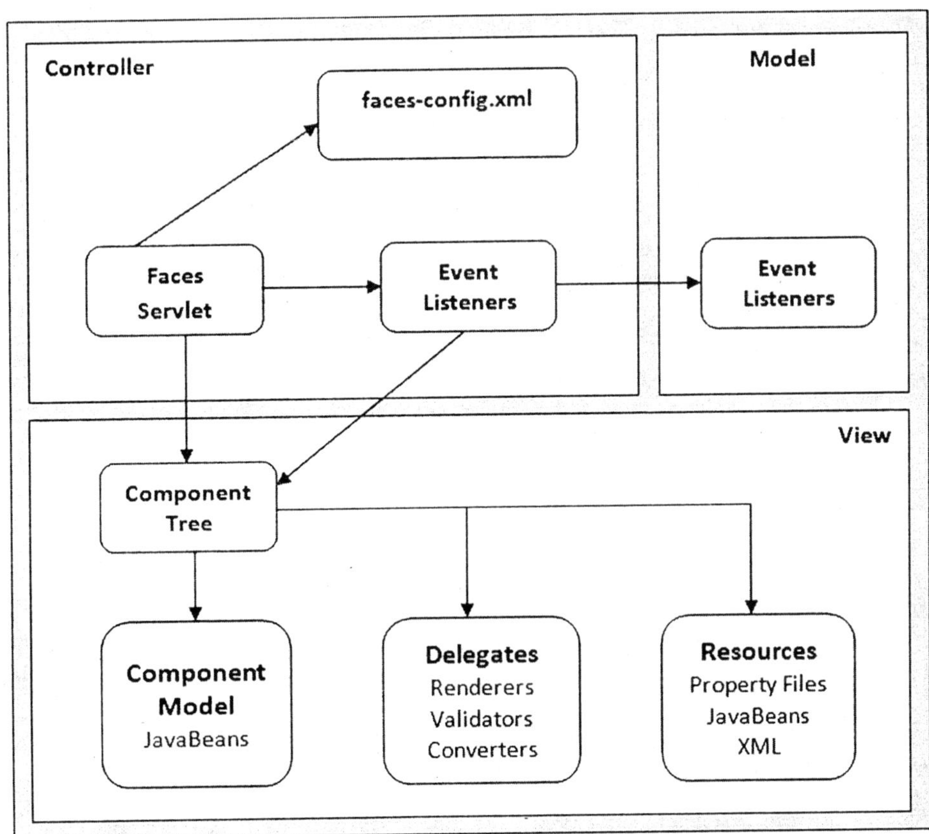


The following are the elements of JSF:

- UI Components
- Renderer
- Validator
- Backing Beans
- Converter
- Events and Listeners
- Message
- Navigation

Lets discuss all the JSF components and how they all are related to each other.

- **UI Components**

UI components are the basic reusable components, such as labels, text boxes, used for developing user interfaces. UI components are defined as stateful objects maintained on the server side. The server communicates with the clients through these UI components. The components are simple java beans containing properties, methods and events. The JSF UI components are also called *Web application user interface* components.

The UI Component tag inserts a new UI Component instance into the JSF component tree. Any components or content fragments outside this tag will be ignored by the Facelets view handler. Any components or content fragments within this tag will be added to the component tree as children of the UI Component instance. While using JSF UI components, we just need to assemble and configure them, instead of writing any code (html, java script or CSS) to make effective user interface components. For example,

```
<ui: component binding="#{myBean1.component}">
<div>Hello JavaServer Faces</div>
</ui: component>
```

- **Renderer**

Most web applications usually send a response to the web browser in the HTML format. Other client devices such as cell-phones or Personal Digital Assistants (PDA) do not provide HTML browsers. Therefore, web applications need to respond in another markup language. A JSF Renderer is responsible for two functions, rendering component as HTML markup and processing request attributes. While processing attributes in the code is usually simple, generating markup in the Java code may be cumbersome for big components. It is conceptually difficult to visualize the two-step process by which calls to a *ResponseWriter* are converted into HTML, and then the HTML and CSS are subsequently transformed into a visual representation. Also, each element and attribute require five times more characters than the generated string itself, this makes the renderer code much bigger than the original design. JSF 2.2 offers "*composite components*" for code reuse to ease some of these concerns, but developers or native component are still stuck writing dozens of *startElement/writeAttribute/writeText/endElement* calls.

There are two different rendering models supported by JSF:

**Direct Rendering Model:** In this model, the rendering logic is directly encapsulated into the UI components; therefore, there is no clear separation of functionality and presentation. This technique is used when we are sure that the component is being created for the particular client. The UI component is implemented in single class.

**Indirect Rendering Model:** This model uses a separate renderer for separator UI components. It's represented by the render class, does the work of encoding and decoding.

- **Validator**

UI components enable a client to interact with the server by giving some data entered by the client to the server. The data entered by the client must validate for its correctness. We use java script and java to write the validation logic. Validators can be specified using a component's Validator attribute or by nesting JSF provided tags. Validation can be performed only on UI Input components or components whose classes extend UI Input. Using the Validator attribute of a UI Input component allows you to specify a custom Validator or a validate method on a *managedBean*.

When using the standard Validator implementations, you don't need to write any code to perform validation. You simply nest the standard Validator tag of your choice inside a tag that represents a component of type UI Input and provide the necessary constraints. For example,

```
<h:inputText id="age" value="#{UserRegistration.user.age}">
<f:validate LongRange maximum="150" minimum="0"/>
</h:inputText>
```

- **Backing Beans**

In JSF applications, JavaBeans objects handle or store data between the business model and UI components at intermediate stage. These JavaBeans objects are known as Backing Beans or objects that handle the interaction between view and model are called backing beans in JSF.

- **Converter**

Web applications interact with clients through the http request and response mechanism. The values entered by the User in all cases will be in string format. Even, when asked to enter numerical values like age or salary whatever is being passed on to the Server end will still be in String format. So, there must be some intermediary who will do the job of converting the string values into the type that is appropriate for the particular field value. For example, if the User Form contains fields for name, age, salary and date of birth. Obviously, the model object for this form will contain string, integer, double and date data-types for storing name, age, salary and date of birth respectively. So the Converters do the job of converting the user input. JSF already comes with a bunch of Standard Converters for most of the common conversion process. If we can't find a suitable converter that is very specific to your Application, then we can define a Customized Converter that will do the job for us. For example,

```
<h:inputText id="name">
<f:converter converterId="javax.faces.Short"/>
</h:inputText>
```

- **Events and Listeners**

JSF implements an event driven processing, where events generated on different UI components can be mapped to the execution of some methods. A user can interact with a web application by generating different events on different UI components. The Event Handling Model in JavaServer Faces is very similar to Java Beans Event Handling Model. The types of Events emitted will fall either in Action Event, Value-Change Event or Phase Event.

- **Message**

These are the integral part of the JSF framework. These messages may be associated with some component or cab be used as application level messages. The message tag renders a message for a specific component. You can customize the message generated by this component by applying different CSS styles to the message depending on its severity as well as the detail level of the message itself. You can also customize the standard error messages by overriding specific JSF properties in your message bundle. For example,

```
<h:inputText id="username" required="#{true}"
value="#{userBean.user1.username}" errorStyle="color:pink" />
<h:message for="username" />
```

- **Navigation**

A Web application is a collection of web pages linked together in a specific order. The clients need to navigate from one page to the other and Web developer needs to implement this navigation logic. The JavaServer Faces (JSF) Navigation Framework provides navigation rules that allow to define navigation from view to view (mostly JSP pages) in a Web application. These navigation rules are defined in JSF configuration files along with other definitions for a JSF application. Usually, this file is named faces-config.xml. We can assign any other name and even use more than one file to store JSF configuration data. For example,

```
<navigation-rule>
<from-view-id>/pages/login.jsp</from-view-id>
```

```
<navigation-case>
<from-outcome>Hello</from-outcome>
<to-view-id>/pages/greeting.jsp</to-view-id>
</navigation-case>
<navigation-case>
<from-outcome>Goodday</from-outcome>
<to-view-id>/pages/goodday.jsp</to-view-id>
</navigation-case>
</navigation-rule>
```

## 18.5 JSF application lifecycle

The JSF application lifecycle, also known as standard request processing lifecycle, begins when the client makes an HTTP request for a page and ends when the server responds with the page, translated to HTML.

The lifecycle can be divided into two main phases, **execute** and **render**. The **execute** phase is further divided into sub-phases to support the sophisticated component tree. This structure requires that component data be converted and validated, component events be handled, and component data be propagated to beans in an orderly fashion.

A JavaServer Faces page is represented by a tree of components, called a view. During the lifecycle, the JavaServer Faces implementation must build the view while considering the state saved from a previous submission of the page. When the client requests a page, the JavaServer Faces implementation performs several tasks, such as validating the data input of components in the view and converting input data to types specified on the server side.

The JavaServer Faces implementation performs all these tasks as a series of steps in the Java Server Faces request-response lifecycle. Following figure illustrates these steps.

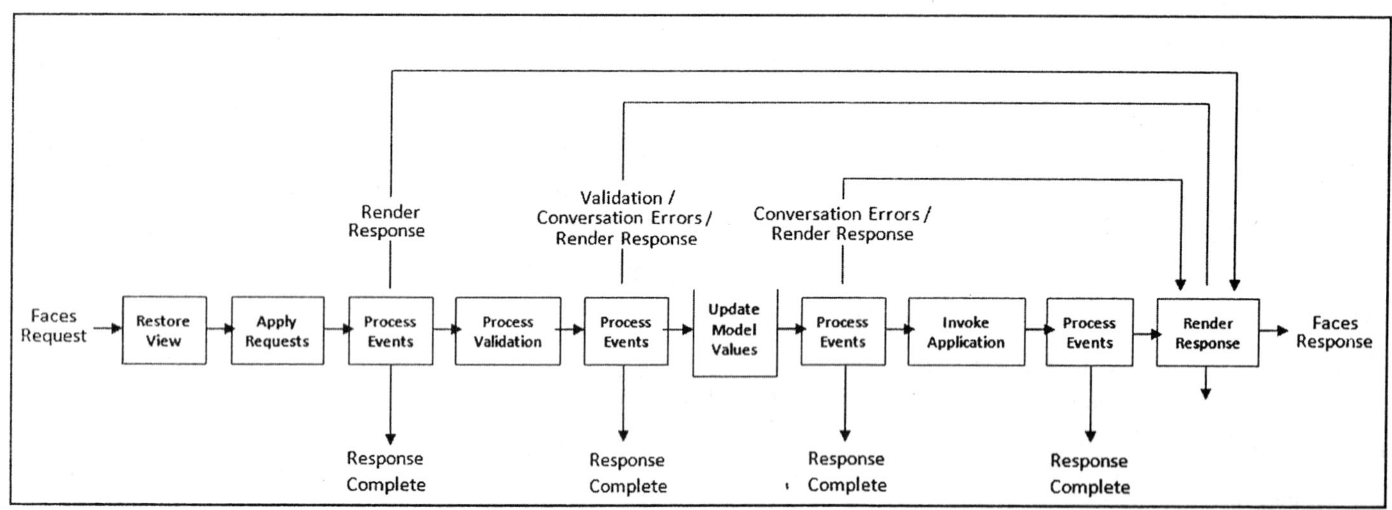


The request-response lifecycle handles two kinds of requests: initial requests and post-backs. An initial request occurs when a user makes a request for a page for the first time. A post-back request occurs when a user submits the form contained on a page that was previously loaded into the browser as a result of executing an initial request.

When the lifecycle handles an initial request, it executes only the Restore View and Render Response phases, because there is no user input or action to process. Conversely, when the lifecycle handles a postback, it executes all of the phases.

Usually, the first request for a JavaServer Faces page comes in from a client, as a result of clicking a link or button component on a JavaServer Faces page. To render a response that is another JavaServer Faces page, the application creates a new view and stores it in the *javax.faces.context.FacesContext* instance, which represents all of the information associated with processing an incoming request and creating a response. The application then acquires object references needed by the view and calls the *FacesContext.renderResponse* method, which forces immediate rendering of the view by skipping to the Render Response phase of the lifecycle, as is shown by the arrows labeled Render Response in the diagram.

Sometimes, an application might need to redirect to a different web application resource, such as a web service, or generate a response that does not contain JavaServer Faces components. In these situations, the developer must skip the Render Response phase by calling the **FacesContext.responseComplete( )** method. This situation is also shown in the diagram, with the arrows labeled Response Complete.

The most common situation is that a JavaServer Faces component submits a request for another JavaServer Faces page. In this case, the JavaServer Faces implementation handles the request and automatically goes through the phases in the lifecycle to perform any necessary conversions, validations, and model updates, and to generate the response.

The JavaServer Faces application lifecycle execute phase contains the following sub-phases:

- Phase 1: Restore View Phase
- Phase 2: Apply Request Values Phase
- Phase 3: Process Validations Phase
- Phase 4: Update Model Values Phase
- Phase 5: Invoke Application Phase
- Phase 6: Render Response Phase

The six phases shown here are in the order in which JSF processes a form. The list shows the phases in their likely order of execution with event processing at each phase.

**Phase 1: Restore view**

JSF begins the restore view phase as soon as a link or a button is clicked and JSF receives a request.

During this phase, the JSF builds the view, wires event handlers and Validators to UI components and saves the view in the FacesContext instance. The FacesContext instance will now contains all the information required to process a request.

**Phase 2: Apply request values**

After the component tree is created/restored, each component in component tree uses **decode( )** method to extract its new value from the request parameters. Component stores this value. If the conversion fails, an error message is generated and queued on FacesContext. This message will be displayed during the render response phase, along with any validation errors.

If any decode methods / event listeners called **renderResponse( )** on the current FacesContext instance, the JSF moves to the render response phase.

**Phase 3: Process validation**

During this phase, the JSF processes all Validators registered on component tree. It examines the component attribute rules for the validation and compares these rules to the local value stored for the component.

If the local value is invalid, the JSF adds an error message to the FacesContext instance, and the life cycle advances to the render response phase and display the same page again with the error message.

**Phase 4: Update model values**

After the JSF checks that the data is valid, it walks over the component tree and set the corresponding server-side object properties to the components' local values. The JSF will update the bean properties corresponding to input component's value attribute.

If any **updateModels( )** methods called **renderResponse( )** on the current FacesContext instance, the JSF moves to the render response phase.

**Phase 5: Invoke application**

During this phase, the JavaServer Faces implementation handles any application-level events, such as submitting a form or linking to another page.

At this point, if the application needs to redirect to a different web application resource or generate a response that does not contain any JavaServer Faces components, it can call the **responseComplete( )** method.

If the view being processed was reconstructed from state information from a previous request and if a component has fired an event, these events are broadcast to interested listeners.

Finally, the JavaServer Faces implementation transfers control to the Render Response phase.

**Phase 6: Render response**

During this phase, the JSF asks container/application server to render the page if the application is using JSP pages. For initial request, the components represented on the page will be added to the component tree as the JSP container executes the page. If this is not an initial request, the component tree is already built so components need not to be added again. In either case, the components will render themselves as the JSP container/Application server traverses the tags in the page.

After the content of the view is rendered, the response state is saved so that subsequent requests can access it and it is available to the restore view phase

## 18.6 JSF Tag library

We have already discussed that, JSF applications are designed by using different JSF UI components. The various UI components can be created easily by using tags defined in the JSF tag library. In addition to laying out different components in the page, designing a page in JSF application includes making provision in the page to use backing beans, validators, converters and other back-end objects associated with the components.

JSF 1.2 had given two different tag libraries – JSF HTML tag library and JSF Core Tag library. These tag libraries provide tags to create pages in JSF application with a rich set of UI components supporting event handling and input validation. For using JSF UI components in a JSP page, we must include these standard tag libraries.

- **JSF HTML tag library** defines the tags that represent general HTML user interface components. These HTML components include *HtmlInputText*, *HtmlInputTextarea*, *HtmlForm*, *HtmlCommandButton* and many more tags.

  This tag library is provided by using following *taglib directive* with proper URI and prefix.

  *<%@ taglib uri = http://java.sun.com/jsf/html prefix = "h" %>*

- **JSF Core tag library** defines the tags that perform core actions. This tag library does not depend upon specific render kit. This tag library is provided by using following *taglib directive* with proper URI and prefix.

  *<%@ taglib uri = http://java.sun.com/jsf/core prefix = "f" %>*

We know that, these taglib directives must be the first two lines in a JSP page in JSF based web application. Let's discuss all JSF HTML tags and JSF Core tags with their properties and description.

**JSF HTML tags**

The JSF HTML tag library contains JSF components tags for all UI components and HTML RenderKit Renderer combinations defined in the JavaServer Faces specification. It means that all the tags discussed for JSF HTML tag library will be rendering to some HTML response for the client browser. Each tag in JSF HTML tag library corresponds to a specific class of UI components present in the *javax.faces.component.html* package.

All HTML UI components created using the tags are defined in the JSF HTML tag library render to different common HTML tags. For example, <h:form> tags render to HTML <form> element. All JSF HTML tags support common HTML tag attributes, such as alt, style, tagindex and width. In addition, DHTML event attributes, such as onclick, ondbclick, onmouseover are also supported by JSF HTML tags. All JSF HTML tags have some common attributes, which have been listed in following table.

| Tag | Description |
|---|---|
| h:form | HTML form |
| h:inputText | Single-line text input control. |
| h:inputTextArea | Multiline text input control. |
| h:inputSecret | Password input control. |
| h:inputHidden | Hidden field |
| h:outputLabel | Label for another component for accessibility |
| h:outputLink | HTML anchor. |
| h:outputFormat | Like outputText, but formats compound messages |
| h:outputText | Single-line text output. |
| h:commandButton | Button: submit, reset, or pushbutton. |
| h:commandLink | Link that acts like a pushbutton. |
| h:message | Displays the most recent message for a component |
| h:messages | Displays all messages |
| h:grapicImage | Displays an image. |
| h:selectOneListbox | Single-select listbox. |
| h:selectOneMenu | Single-select menu. |
| h:selectOneRadio | Set of radio buttons. |
| h:selectBooleanCheckbox | Checkbox. |
| h:selectManyCheckbox | Set of checkboxes. |
| h:selectManyListbox | Multiselect listbox. |
| h:selectManyMenu | Multiselect menu. |
| h:panelGrid | HTML table |
| h:panelGroup | Two or more components that are laid out as one |
| h:dataTable | A feature-rich table control |
| h:column | Column in a dataTable |

Let's understand these tags in detail with their usage and important attributes.

**The <h:form> tag**

The form tag renders an HTML form element. JSF forms use the "post-back" technique to submit form data back to the page that contains the form.

The use of the POST method is also required and it is not possible to use the GET method for forms generated by this tag. If your application requires the use of the GET method for form submission, your options include using plain HTML forms, binding request parameters to backing bean properties, and using the outputLink tag to generate dynamic hyperlinks. Following table shows the important attributes of this tag.

| Attribute | Description |
|---|---|
| id | Identifier for a component |
| binding | Reference to the component that can be used in a backing bean |
| rendered | A boolean; false suppresses rendering |
| styleClass | Cascading stylesheet (CSS) class name |
| value | A component's value, typically a value binding |
| valueChangeListener | A method binding to a method that responds to value changes |
| converter | Converter class name |
| validator | Class name of a validator that's created and attached to a component |
| required | A boolean; if true, requires a value to be entered in the associated field |

JSF example,

```
<!DOCTYPE html PUBLIC "-//W3C//DTD XHTML 1.0 Transitional//EN"
"http://www.w3.org/TR/xhtml1/DTD/xhtml1-transitional.dtd">
<html xmlns="http://www.w3.org/1999/xhtml" xmlns:h="http://java.sun.com/jsf/html">
<h:head />
<body>
<h:form>
   <h:outputLabel value="Enter your name: " />
   <h:inputText value="#{customerController.customer.firstName}" />
</h:form>
</body>
</html>
```

**The <h:inputText> tag**

The inputText tag renders an HTML input element of the type "text". Following table shows the important attributes of this tag.

| Attribute | Description |
|---|---|
| immediate | Process validation early in the life cycle |
| required | Require input in the component when the form is submitted |
| valueChangeListener | A specified listener that's notified of value changes |

JSF example,

```
<!DOCTYPE html PUBLIC "-//W3C//DTD XHTML 1.0 Transitional//EN"
   "http://www.w3.org/TR/xhtml1/DTD/xhtml1-transitional.dtd">
<html xmlns="http://www.w3.org/1999/xhtml" xmlns:h="http://java.sun.com/jsf/html">
<h:head />
```

```
<body>
<h:form>
  <h:panelGrid>
    <h:outputLabel value="Username: " style="font-weight:bold" />
    <h:inputText value="#{userController.user.username}" />
    <h:outputLabel value="Password: " style="font-weight:bold" />
    <h:inputSecret value="#{userController.user.password}" />
    <h:commandButton value="Login" />
  </h:panelGrid>
</h:form>
</body>
</html>
```

**The <h:inputTextArea> tag**

The inputTextarea tag renders an HTML "textarea" element. Following table shows the important attributes of this tag.

| Attribute | Description |
|---|---|
| immediate | Process validation early in the life cycle |
| redisplay | For h:inputSecret only—when true, the input field's value is redisplayed when the web page is reloaded |
| required | Require input in the component when the form is submitted |
| rows | For h:inputTextarea only—number of rows |
| valueChangeListener | A specified listener that's notified of value changes |

JSF example,

```
<!DOCTYPE html PUBLIC "-//W3C//DTD XHTML 1.0 Transitional//EN"
  "http://www.w3.org/TR/xhtml1/DTD/xhtml1-transitional.dtd">
<html xmlns="http://www.w3.org/1999/xhtml" xmlns:h="http://java.sun.com/jsf/html">
<h:head />
<body>
<h:form>
  <h:panelGrid>
    <h:outputLabel value="Survey question: " />
    <h:inputTextarea value="#{surveyController.questions[1].comments}" />
  </h:panelGrid>
</h:form>
</body>
</html>
```

**The <h:inputSecret> tag**

The inputSecret tag renders an HTML input element of the type "password". Following table shows the important attributes of this tag.

| Attribute | Description |
|---|---|
| immediate | Process validation early in the life cycle |
| redisplay | For h:inputSecret only—when true, the input field's value is redisplayed when the web page is reloaded |
| required | Require input in the component when the form is submitted |
| valueChangeListener | A specified listener that's notified of value changes |

JSF example,

```
<!DOCTYPE html PUBLIC "-//W3C//DTD XHTML 1.0 Transitional//EN"
  "http://www.w3.org/TR/xhtml1/DTD/xhtml1-transitional.dtd">
<html xmlns="http://www.w3.org/1999/xhtml" xmlns:h="http://java.sun.com/jsf/html">
<h:head />
<body>
<h:form>
  <h:panelGrid>
    <h:outputLabel value="Username: " style="font-weight:bold" />
    <h:inputText value="#{userController.user.username}" />
    <h:outputLabel value="Password: " style="font-weight:bold" />
    <h:inputSecret value="#{userController.user.password}" />
    <h:commandButton value="Login" />
  </h:panelGrid>
</h:form>
</body>
</html>
```

**The <h:inputHidden> tag**

The inputHidden tag renders an HTML input element of the type "hidden". Following table shows the important attributes of this tag.

| Attribute | Description |
|---|---|
| immediate | Process validation early in the life cycle |
| required | Require input in the component when the form is submitted |
| valueChangeListener | A specified listener that's notified of value changes |

JSF example,

```
<!DOCTYPE html PUBLIC "-//W3C//DTD XHTML 1.0 Transitional//EN"
  "http://www.w3.org/TR/xhtml1/DTD/xhtml1-transitional.dtd">
<html xmlns="http://www.w3.org/1999/xhtml" xmlns:h="http://java.sun.com/jsf/html">
<h:head id="head_1"/>
<body>
<h:form id="form_1">
  <h:inputHidden value="123" id="inputHidden_1" />
</h:form>
</body>
</html>
```

**The <h:outputLabel> tag**

The outputLabel tag renders an HTML "label" element. It allows you to customize the appearance of the label using CSS styles. The outputLabel component is associated with another component via its "for" attribute.

The other component must be created before the outputLabel component when the JSF page is rendered. Note the use of the panelGroup container in the example below. The panelGroup component renders its children, allowing the outputLabel component to locate the inputText component at render time. Following table shows the important attributes of this tag.

| Attribute | Description |
|---|---|
| for | The ID of the component to be labeled. |

JSF example,

```
<!DOCTYPE html PUBLIC "-//W3C//DTD XHTML 1.0 Transitional//EN"
  "http://www.w3.org/TR/xhtml1/DTD/xhtml1-transitional.dtd">
<html xmlns="http://www.w3.org/1999/xhtml" xmlns:h="http://java.sun.com/jsf/html">
<h:head />
<body>
<h:form>
  <h:panelGroup>
    <h:outputLabel id="usernameLabel" for="username"
            value="#{messages.usernameLabel} " />
    <h:inputText id="username" value="#{userBean.user.username}" />
  </h:panelGroup>
</h:form>
</body>
</html>
```

**The <h:outputLink> tag**

The outputLink tag renders an HTML anchor tag with an "href" attribute.

The display value of the link can also be obtained from a message bundle to support internationalization (I18N). This tag facilitates the construction of HTML hyperlinks by allowing you to nest param tags to construct querystring arguments. You can place outputText or graphicImage tags, for example, within the outputLink tag to set the hyperlink text or image value. Following table shows the important attributes of this tag.

| Attribute | Description |
|---|---|
| id | Identifier for a component |
| binding | Reference to the component that can be used in a backing bean |
| rendered | A boolean; false suppresses rendering |
| styleClass | Cascading stylesheet (CSS) class name |
| value | A component's value, typically a value binding |
| layout | it is set with the type of layout markup used when rendering the component group. |
| style | It is used to set the CSS style to be applied when the component is rendered. |
| value | It is set for the linked resources name with its path. The value set for the value attribute here is set as the value for the href attribute of the rendered HTML anchor tag. |

JSF example,

```
<!DOCTYPE html PUBLIC "-//W3C//DTD XHTML 1.0 Transitional//EN"
  "http://www.w3.org/TR/xhtml1/DTD/xhtml1-transitional.dtd">
<html xmlns="http://www.w3.org/1999/xhtml" xmlns:f="http://java.sun.com/jsf/core"
   xmlns:h="http://java.sun.com/jsf/html">
<h:head />
<body>
<h:outputLink id="link1" value="http://www.mycompany.com">
  <f:param name="projectId" value="123" />
  <f:param name="userId" value="45" />
  <h:outputText value="Open Project" />
</h:outputLink>
</body>
</html>
```

**The <h:outputFormat> tag**

The outputFormat tag renders parameterized text and allows you to customize the appearance of this text using CSS styles. Parameterized text is compound text containing placeholder values to be replaced by actual values at rendering time. See also the param tag. Following table shows the important attributes of this tag.

| Attribute | Description |
|---|---|
| escape | if set to true, escape <,>,and & characters. Default value is false. |

JSF example,

```
<!DOCTYPE html PUBLIC "-//W3C//DTD XHTML 1.0 Transitional//EN"
  "http://www.w3.org/TR/xhtml1/DTD/xhtml1-transitional.dtd">
<html xmlns="http://www.w3.org/1999/xhtml" xmlns:f="http://java.sun.com/jsf/core"
   xmlns:h="http://java.sun.com/jsf/html">
<h:head />
<body>
<h:outputFormat value="Welcome, {0}. You have {1} new messages.">
  <f:param value="#{userController.user.firstName}" />
  <f:param value="#{userController.user.messageCount}" />
</h:outputFormat>
</body>
</html>
```

**The <h:outputText> tag**

The outputText tag renders basic text on your JSF page. You can customize the appearance of the text using CSS styles, in which case the generated text is wrapped in an HTML span element. You can also escape the rendered text if it contains sensitive HTML and XML characters. Following table shows the important attributes of this tag.

| Attribute | Description |
|---|---|
| escape | if set to true, escape <,>,and & characters. Default value is false. |

JSF example,

```
<!DOCTYPE html PUBLIC "-//W3C//DTD XHTML 1.0 Transitional//EN"
  "http://www.w3.org/TR/xhtml1/DTD/xhtml1-transitional.dtd">
<html xmlns="http://www.w3.org/1999/xhtml" xmlns:h="http://java.sun.com/jsf/html">
<h:head />
<body>
<h:outputText value="#{messages.welcomeMessage}" style="font-weight:bold" />
</body>
</html>
```

### The <h:commandButton> tag

The commandButton tag renders an HTML submit button that can be associated with a backing bean or ActionListener class for event handling purposes. The display value of the button can also be obtained from a message bundle to support internationalization. Following table shows the important attributes of this tag.

| Attribute | Description |
|---|---|
| action | If specified as a string: Directly specifies an outcome used by the navigation handler to determine the JSF page to load next as a result of activating the button or link If specified as a method binding; This method is defined as *String methodName( );* the string represents the outcome |
| actionListener | A method binding that refers to a method with this signature: *void methodName(ActionEvent)* |
| charset | For h:commandLink only—The character encoding of the linked reference |
| image | For h:commandButton only—A context-relative path to an image displayed in a button. If you specify this attribute, the HTML input's type will be image. |
| immediate | If false (the default), actions and action listeners are invoked at the end of the request life cycle; if true, actions and action listeners are invoked at the beginning of the life cycle. See Chapter 6 for more information about the immediate attribute. |
| type | For h:commandButton: The type of the generated input element: button, submit, or reset. The default, unless you specify the image attribute, is submit. For h:commandLink: The content type of the linked resource; for example, text/html, image/gif, or audio/basic |
| value | The label displayed by the button or link. You can specify a string or a value reference expression. |

JSF example,

```
<!DOCTYPE html PUBLIC "-//W3C//DTD XHTML 1.0 Transitional//EN"
  "http://www.w3.org/TR/xhtml1/DTD/xhtml1-transitional.dtd">
<html xmlns="http://www.w3.org/1999/xhtml" xmlns:h="http://java.sun.com/jsf/html">
<h:head/>
<body>
<h:form>
  <h:commandButton value="#{messages.checkoutLabel}"
             action="#{shoppingCartBean.checkout}" />
</h:form>
</body>
</html>
```

### The <h:commandLink> tag

The commandLink tag renders an HTML anchor tag that behaves like a form submit button and that can be associated with a backing bean or *ActionListener* class for event handling purposes. The display value of the link can also be obtained from a message bundle to support internationalization. Following table shows the important attributes of this tag.

| Attribute | Description |
|---|---|
| action | If specified as a string: Directly specifies an outcome used by the navigation handler to determine the JSF page to load next as a result of activating the button or link If specified as a method binding; This method is defined as *String methodName( );* the string represents the outcome |
| actionListener | A method binding that refers to a method with this signature: *void methodName(ActionEvent)* |
| charset | For h:commandLink only—The character encoding of the linked reference |
| image | For h:commandButton only—A context-relative path to an image displayed in a button. If you specify this attribute, the HTML input's type will be image. |
| immediate | If false (the default), actions and action listeners are invoked at the end of the request life cycle; if true, actions and action listeners are invoked at the beginning of the life cycle. See Chapter 6 for more information about the immediate attribute. |
| type | For h:commandButton: The type of the generated input element: button, submit, or reset. The default, unless you specify the image attribute, is submit. For h:commandLink: The content type of the linked resource; for example, text/html, image/gif, or audio/basic |
| value | The label displayed by the button or link. You can specify a string or a value reference expression. |

JSF example,

```
<!DOCTYPE html PUBLIC "-//W3C//DTD XHTML 1.0 Transitional//EN"
   "http://www.w3.org/TR/xhtml1/DTD/xhtml1-transitional.dtd">
<html xmlns="http://www.w3.org/1999/xhtml" xmlns:h="http://java.sun.com/jsf/html">
<h:head/>
<body>
<h:form>
   <h:commandLink value="#{messages.checkoutLabel}"
            action="#{shoppingCartBean.checkout}" />
</h:form>
</body>
</html>
```

**The <h:message> tag**

The message tag renders a message for a specific component. You can customize the message generated by this component by applying different CSS styles to the message depending on its severity (eg. red for error, green for information) as well as the detail level of the message itself. You can also customize the standard error messages by overriding specific JSF properties in your message bundle. Following table shows the important attributes of this tag.

| Attribute | Description |
|---|---|
| for | The ID of the component whose message is displayed—applicable only to h:message |
| errorClass | CSS class applied to error messages |
| errorStyle | CSS style applied to error messages |
| fatalClass | CSS class applied to fatal messages |
| fatalStyle | CSS style applied to fatal messages |
| globalOnly | Instruction to display only global messages—applicable only to *h:messages*. Default: false |
| infoClass | CSS class applied to information messages |
| infoStyle | CSS style applied to information messages |
| layout | Specification for message layout: table or list—applicable only to h:messages |
| showDetail | A *boolean* that determines whether message details are shown. Defaults are false for *h:messages*, true for h:message. |
| showSummary | A *boolean* that determines whether message summaries are shown. Defaults are true for *h:messages*, false for h:message. |
| tooltip | A boolean that determines whether message details are rendered in a tooltip; the tooltip is only rendered if *showDetail* and *showSummary* are true |
| warnClass | CSS class for warning messages |
| warnStyle | CSS style for warning messages |

For example,

```
<!DOCTYPE html PUBLIC "-//W3C//DTD XHTML 1.0 Transitional//EN"
  "http://www.w3.org/TR/xhtml1/DTD/xhtml1-transitional.dtd">
<html xmlns="http://www.w3.org/1999/xhtml" xmlns:h="http://java.sun.com/jsf/html">
<h:head />
<body>
<h:form>
  <h:message errorStyle="color:red; display:block" for="myInput" />
  <h:inputText id="myInput" required="true" label="My Input" />
  <h:commandButton value="Click" />
</h:form>
</body>
</html>
```

**The <h:messages> tag**

The messages tag renders all Faces messages for the current view. You can customize the messages generated by this component by applying different CSS styles depending on the severity level of the messages (eg. red for error, green for information) as well as changing the detail level of the messages. The messages tag supports two layouts for the generated messages:an HTML table or a bulleted list. The default layout is the list format. You can also customize the standard error messages by overriding specific JSF properties in your message bundle. Following table shows the important attributes of this tag.

| Attribute | Description |
|---|---|
| for | The ID of the component whose message is displayed—applicable only to h:message |
| errorClass | CSS class applied to error messages |
| errorStyle | CSS style applied to error messages |
| fatalClass | CSS class applied to fatal messages |
| fatalStyle | CSS style applied to fatal messages |
| globalOnly | Instruction to display only global messages—applicable only to *h:messages*. Default: false |
| infoClass | CSS class applied to information messages |
| infoStyle | CSS style applied to information messages |
| layout | Specification for message layout: table or list—applicable only to h:messages |
| showDetail | A *boolean* that determines whether message details are shown. Defaults are false for *h:messages*, true for h:message. |
| showSummary | A *boolean* that determines whether message summaries are shown. Defaults are true for *h:messages*, false for h:message. |
| tooltip | A boolean that determines whether message details are rendered in a tooltip; the tooltip is only rendered if *showDetail* and *showSummary* are true |
| warnClass | CSS class for warning messages |
| warnStyle | CSS style for warning messages |

For example,

```
<!DOCTYPE html PUBLIC "-//W3C//DTD XHTML 1.0 Transitional//EN"
  "http://www.w3.org/TR/xhtml1/DTD/xhtml1-transitional.dtd">
<html xmlns="http://www.w3.org/1999/xhtml" xmlns:h="http://java.sun.com/jsf/html">
<h:head />
<body>
<h:form>
  <h:messages errorStyle="color:red" />
  <h:inputText required="true" label="My Input" />
  <h:commandButton value="Click" />
</h:form>
</body>
</html>
```

**The <h:grapicImage> tag**

The graphicImage tag renders an HTML image tag. Following table shows the important attributes of this tag.

| Attribute | Description |
|---|---|
| id | Identifier for a component |
| binding | Reference to the component that can be used in a backing bean |
| rendered | A boolean; false suppresses rendering |
| styleClass | Cascading stylesheet (CSS) class name |

| | |
|---|---|
| value | A component's value, typically a value binding |
| value | It is set for the linked resources name with its path. The value set for the value attribute here is set as the value for the *href* attribute of the rendered HTML anchor tag. |
| alt | set with some textual description of the image |
| height | Used to set the height of the image. |
| style | Specifies the CSS style to be applied. |
| url | Set with context relative path for the resource image. It works as an alias for the value attribute. |
| width | Used to set the width of the image. |

JSF example,

```
<!DOCTYPE html PUBLIC "-//W3C//DTD XHTML 1.0 Transitional//EN"
  "http://www.w3.org/TR/xhtml1/DTD/xhtml1-transitional.dtd">
<html xmlns="http://www.w3.org/1999/xhtml" xmlns:h="http://java.sun.com/jsf/html">
<h:head />
<body>
<h:graphicImage value="/images/box_shot.gif" width="200" height="171" />
</body>
</html>
```

**The <h:selectOneListbox> tag**

The SelectOneListbox tag renders an HTML "select" element of any size without the "multiple" attribute. This component is designed for situations where you want to display a single-select list of options to the user in a list that displays several items at a time. If you do not specify the size, all the available options are shown. The main difference between select lists and menus in JSF is the "size" attribute. Menus always have a size of one, while lists can have a variable size. Following table shows the important attributes of this tag.

| Attribute | Description |
|---|---|
| id | Identifier for a component |
| binding | Reference to the component that can be used in a backing bean |
| rendered | A boolean; false suppresses rendering |
| styleClass | Cascading stylesheet (CSS) class name |
| value | A component's value, typically a value binding |
| valueChangeListener | A method binding to a method that responds to value changes |
| converter | Converter class name |
| validator | Class name of a validator that's created and attached to a component |
| required | A boolean; if true, requires a value to be entered in the associated field |

JSF example,

```
<!DOCTYPE html PUBLIC "-//W3C//DTD XHTML 1.0 Transitional//EN"
  "http://www.w3.org/TR/xhtml1/DTD/xhtml1-transitional.dtd">
```

```
<html xmlns="http://www.w3.org/1999/xhtml" xmlns:f="http://java.sun.com/jsf/core"
    xmlns:h="http://java.sun.com/jsf/html">
<h:head />
<body>
<h:form>
  <h:selectOneListbox id="subscriptions"
              value="#{subscriptionController.subscriptions}">
    <f:selectItem id="item1" itemLabel="News" itemValue="1" />
    <f:selectItem id="item2" itemLabel="Sports" itemValue="2" />
    <f:selectItem id="item3" itemLabel="Music" itemValue="3" />
    <f:selectItem id="item4" itemLabel="Java" itemValue="4" />
    <f:selectItem id="item5" itemLabel="Web" itemValue="5" />
  </h:selectOneListbox>
</h:form>
</body>
</html>
```

**The <h:selectOneMenu> tag**

The SelectOneMenu tag renders an HTML "select" element with a "size" of 1 without the "multiple" attribute. This component is designed for situations where you want to display a single-select list of options to the user in a menu that displays one item at a time. The main difference between select lists and menus in JSF is the "size" attribute. Menus always have a size of one, while lists can have a variable size. Following table shows the important attributes of this tag.

| Attribute | Description |
|---|---|
| disabledClass | CSS class for disabled elements—for h:selectOneRadio and h:selectManyCheckbox only |
| enabledClass | CSS class for enabled elements—for h:selectOneRadio and h:selectManyCheckbox only |
| layout | Specification for how elements are laid out: *lineDirection (horizontal)* or *pageDirection (vertical)*—for h:selectOneRadio and h:selectManyCheckbox only |
| converter | it is set with the converter instance registered with the component. |
| id | Identifier for a component |
| binding | Reference to the component that can be used in a backing bean |
| rendered | A boolean; false suppresses rendering |
| styleClass | Cascading stylesheet (CSS) class name |
| value | A component's value, typically, a value binding |
| valueChangeListener | A method binding to a method that responds to value changes |
| converter | Converter class name |
| validator | Class name of a validator that's created and attached to a component |
| required | A boolean; if true, requires a value to be entered in the associated field |
| immediate | it is set to true to process validation early in the life cycle. |

JSF example,

```
<!DOCTYPE html PUBLIC "-//W3C//DTD XHTML 1.0 Transitional//EN"
```

```
"http://www.w3.org/TR/xhtml1/DTD/xhtml1-transitional.dtd">
<html xmlns="http://www.w3.org/1999/xhtml" xmlns:f="http://java.sun.com/jsf/core"
    xmlns:h="http://java.sun.com/jsf/html">
<h:head />
<body>
<h:form>
   <h:selectOneMenu id="subscriptions"
            value="#{subscriptionController.subscriptions}">
      <f:selectItem id="item1" itemLabel="News" itemValue="1" />
      <f:selectItem id="item2" itemLabel="Sports" itemValue="2" />
      <f:selectItem id="item3" itemLabel="Music" itemValue="3" />
      <f:selectItem id="item4" itemLabel="Java" itemValue="4" />
      <f:selectItem id="item5" itemLabel="Web" itemValue="5" />
   </h:selectOneMenu>
</h:form>
</body>
</html
```

**The <h:selectOneRadio> tag**

The SelectOneRadio tag renders a table of HTML "input" elements of the type "radio". This component is designed for situations where you want to display a mutually exclusive list of options to the user as a set of radio buttons. Like the selectManyCheckbox tag, this tag supports two layout modes:lineDirection (horizontal, the default) and pageDirection (vertical). Following table shows the important attributes of this tag.

| Attribute | Description |
|---|---|
| disabledClass | CSS class for disabled elements—for h:selectOneRadio and h:selectManyCheckbox only |
| enabledClass | CSS class for enabled elements—for h:selectOneRadio and h:selectManyCheckbox only |
| layout | Specification for how elements are laid out: *lineDirection (horizontal)* or *pageDirection (vertical)*—for h:selectOneRadio and h:selectManyCheckbox only |
| converter | it is set with the converter instance registered with the component. |
| id | Identifier for a component |
| binding | Reference to the component that can be used in a backing bean |
| rendered | A boolean; false suppresses rendering |
| styleClass | Cascading stylesheet (CSS) class name |
| value | A component's value, typically a value binding |
| valueChangeListener | A method binding to a method that responds to value changes |
| converter | Converter class name |
| validator | Class name of a validator that's created and attached to a component |
| required | A boolean; if true, requires a value to be entered in the associated field |
| immediate | it is set to true to process validation early in the life cycle. |

JSF example,

```
<!DOCTYPE html PUBLIC "-//W3C//DTD XHTML 1.0 Transitional//EN"
  "http://www.w3.org/TR/xhtml1/DTD/xhtml1-transitional.dtd">
<html xmlns="http://www.w3.org/1999/xhtml" xmlns:f="http://java.sun.com/jsf/core"
   xmlns:h="http://java.sun.com/jsf/html">
<h:head />
<body>
<h:form>
  <h:selectOneRadio id="subscriptions"
          value="#{subscriptionController.subscriptions}">
    <f:selectItem id="item1" itemLabel="News" itemValue="1" />
    <f:selectItem id="item2" itemLabel="Sports" itemValue="2" />
    <f:selectItem id="item3" itemLabel="Music" itemValue="3" />
    <f:selectItem id="item4" itemLabel="Java" itemValue="4" />
    <f:selectItem id="item5" itemLabel="Web" itemValue="5" />
  </h:selectOneRadio>
</h:form>
</body>
</html
```

**The <h:selectBooleanCheckbox> tag**

The SelectBooleanCheckbox tag renders an HTML input element of the type "checkbox". This component is designed for situations where you want to display an option to the user that can be enabled or disabled, such as a "remember me" checkbox on a login form. Following table shows the important attributes of this tag.

| Attribute | Description |
|---|---|
| disabledClass | CSS class for disabled elements—for h:selectOneRadio and h:selectManyCheckbox only |
| enabledClass | CSS class for enabled elements—for h:selectOneRadio and h:selectManyCheckbox only |
| layout | Specification for how elements are laid out: *lineDirection (horizontal)* or *pageDirection (vertical)*—for h:selectOneRadio and h:selectManyCheckbox only |
| converter | it is set with the converter instance registered with the component. |
| id | Identifier for a component |
| binding | Reference to the component that can be used in a backing bean |
| rendered | A boolean; false suppresses rendering |
| styleClass | Cascading stylesheet (CSS) class name |
| value | A component's value, typically a value binding |
| valueChangeListener | A method binding to a method that responds to value changes |
| converter | Converter class name |
| validator | Class name of a validator that's created and attached to a component |
| required | A boolean; if true, requires a value to be entered in the associated field |
| immediate | it is set to true to process validation early in the life cycle. |

JSF example,

```
<!DOCTYPE html PUBLIC "-//W3C//DTD XHTML 1.0 Transitional//EN"
  "http://www.w3.org/TR/xhtml1/DTD/xhtml1-transitional.dtd">
<html xmlns="http://www.w3.org/1999/xhtml" xmlns:h="http://java.sun.com/jsf/html">
<h:head />
<body>
<h:form>
  <h:selectBooleanCheckbox id="remember" value="#{userController.user.remember}" />
  <h:outputLabel value="#{messages.rememberMeLabel}" for="remember" />
</h:form>
</body>
</html>
```

**The <h:selectManyCheckbox> tag**

The SelectManyCheckbox tag renders a list of HTML checkboxes. This component is designed for situations where you want to display a list of options to the user that are not mutually exclusive, such as a list of subscription choices. This component supports two layouts:"lineDirection" (horizontally, the default layout) and "pageDirection" (vertically). Following table shows the important attributes of this tag.

| Attribute | Description |
|---|---|
| disabledClass | CSS class for disabled elements—for h:selectOneRadio and h:selectManyCheckbox only |
| enabledClass | CSS class for enabled elements—for h:selectOneRadio and h:selectManyCheckbox only |
| layout | Specification for how elements are laid out: *lineDirection (horizontal)* or *pageDirection (vertical)*—for h:selectOneRadio and h:selectManyCheckbox only |
| converter | It is set with the converter instance registered with the component. |
| id | Identifier for a component |
| binding | Reference to the component that can be used in a backing bean |
| rendered | A boolean; false suppresses rendering |
| styleClass | Cascading stylesheet (CSS) class name |
| value | A component's value, typically a value binding |
| valueChangeListener | A method binding to a method that responds to value changes |
| converter | Converter class name |
| validator | Class name of a validator that's created and attached to a component |
| required | A boolean; if true, requires a value to be entered in the associated field |
| immediate | It is set to true to process validation early in the life cycle. |

JSF example,

```
<!DOCTYPE html PUBLIC "-//W3C//DTD XHTML 1.0 Transitional//EN"
  "http://www.w3.org/TR/xhtml1/DTD/xhtml1-transitional.dtd">
<html xmlns="http://www.w3.org/1999/xhtml" xmlns:f="http://java.sun.com/jsf/core"
   xmlns:h="http://java.sun.com/jsf/html">
<h:head />
<body>
<h:form>
  <h:selectManyCheckbox id="subscriptions"
                value="#{subscriptionController.subscriptions}"
                layout="pageDirection">
    <f:selectItem id="item1" itemLabel="News" itemValue="1" />
    <f:selectItem id="item2" itemLabel="Sports" itemValue="2" />
    <f:selectItem id="item3" itemLabel="Music" itemValue="3" />
    <f:selectItem id="item4" itemLabel="Java" itemValue="4" />
    <f:selectItem id="item5" itemLabel="Web" itemValue="5" />
  </h:selectManyCheckbox>
</h:form>
</body>
</html>
```

**The <h:selectManyListbox> tag**

The SelectManyListbox tag renders an HTML "select" list of any size with the "multiple" attribute present. This component is designed for situations where you want to display a list of options to the user that are not mutually exclusive, such as a list of subscription choices, within a multiple-select list element. The main difference between select lists and menus in JSF is the "size" attribute. Menus always have a size of one, while lists can have a variable size. Following table shows the important attributes of this tag.

| Attribute | Description |
|---|---|
| converter | It is set with the converter instance registered with the component. |
| id | Identifier for a component |
| binding | Reference to the component that can be used in a backing bean |
| rendered | A boolean; false suppresses rendering |
| styleClass | Cascading stylesheet (CSS) class name |
| value | A component's value, typically a value binding |
| valueChangeListener | A method binding to a method that responds to value changes |
| converter | Converter class name |
| validator | Class name of a validator that's created and attached to a component |
| required | A boolean; if true, requires a value to be entered in the associated field |
| immediate | It is set to true to process validation early in the life cycle. |

JSF example,

```
<!DOCTYPE html PUBLIC "-//W3C//DTD XHTML 1.0 Transitional//EN"
  "http://www.w3.org/TR/xhtml1/DTD/xhtml1-transitional.dtd">
<html xmlns="http://www.w3.org/1999/xhtml" xmlns:f="http://java.sun.com/jsf/core"
   xmlns:h="http://java.sun.com/jsf/html">
<h:head />
<body>
<h:form>
  <h:selectManyListbox id="subscriptions"
                  value="#{subscriptionController.subscriptions}">
    <f:selectItem id="item1" itemLabel="News" itemValue="1" />
    <f:selectItem id="item2" itemLabel="Sports" itemValue="2" />
    <f:selectItem id="item3" itemLabel="Music" itemValue="3" />
    <f:selectItem id="item4" itemLabel="Java" itemValue="4" />
    <f:selectItem id="item5" itemLabel="Web" itemValue="5" />
  </h:selectManyListbox>
</h:form>
</body>
</html>
```

**The <h:selectManyMenu> tag**

The SelectManyMenu tag renders an HTML "select" element with the "multiple" attribute present and the "size" attribute set to 1. This component is designed for situations where you want to display a list of menu items to the user that allows the selection of multiple options using a menu that displays one item at a time. The main difference between select lists and menus in JSF is the "size" attribute. Menus always have a size of one, while lists can have a variable size.

Note: This component is not rendered consistently across the major browsers. Internet Explorer displays a set of miniaturized arrow icons that allow the user to scroll up and down the menu list, however, Netscape/Mozilla browsers do not. Following table shows the important attributes of this tag.

| Attribute | Description |
|---|---|
| converter | It is set with the converter instance registered with the component. |
| id | Identifier for a component |
| binding | Reference to the component that can be used in a backing bean |
| rendered | A boolean; false suppresses rendering |
| styleClass | Cascading stylesheet (CSS) class name |
| value | A component's value, typically a value binding |
| valueChangeListener | A method binding to a method that responds to value changes |
| converter | Converter class name |
| validator | Class name of a validator that's created and attached to a component |
| required | A boolean; if true, requires a value to be entered in the associated field |
| immediate | It is set to true to process validation early in the life cycle. |

JSF example,

```
<!DOCTYPE html PUBLIC "-//W3C//DTD XHTML 1.0 Transitional//EN"
  "http://www.w3.org/TR/xhtml1/DTD/xhtml1-transitional.dtd">
<html xmlns="http://www.w3.org/1999/xhtml" xmlns:f="http://java.sun.com/jsf/core"
   xmlns:h="http://java.sun.com/jsf/html">
<h:head />
<body>
<h:form>
  <h:selectManyMenu id="subscriptions"
            value="#{subscriptionController.subscriptions}">
    <f:selectItem id="item1" itemLabel="News" itemValue="1" />
    <f:selectItem id="item2" itemLabel="Sports" itemValue="2" />
    <f:selectItem id="item3" itemLabel="Music" itemValue="3" />
    <f:selectItem id="item4" itemLabel="Java" itemValue="4" />
    <f:selectItem id="item5" itemLabel="Web" itemValue="5" />
  </h:selectManyMenu>
</h:form>
</body>
</html>
```

**The <h:panelGrid> tag**

The h:panelGrid tag renders an HTML4 compliant table element. The h:panelGrid component can be used as a layout manager for a grid-based user interface. It simplifies the task of constructing a layout table to hold form fields, labels, and buttons. The h:panelGrid component, like the h:dataTable component, can be customized extensively using Cascading Style Sheets (CSS). The h:panelGrid does not use an underlying data model to provide rows of data for rendering purposes. Rather, this component is a layout container that renders other JSF components in a grid of rows and columns. By default, a h:panelGrid component has only one column. Following table shows the important attributes of this tag.

| Attribute | Description |
|---|---|
| bgcolor | Background color for the table |
| border | Width of the table's border |
| cellpadding | Padding around table cells |
| cellspacing | Spacing between table cells |
| columnclasses | Comma-separated list of CSS classes for columns |
| columns | Number of columns in the table |
| footerclass | CSS class for the table footer |
| frame | Frame specification for sides of the frame surrounding the table that are to be drawn. |
| headerclass | CSS class for the table header |
| rowclasses | Comma-separated list of CSS classes for columns |
| rules | Specification for lines drawn between cells. |
| summary | Summary of the table's purpose and structure used for non-visual feedback, such as speech. |

JSF example,

```
<!DOCTYPE html PUBLIC "-//W3C//DTD XHTML 1.0 Transitional//EN"
  "http://www.w3.org/TR/xhtml1/DTD/xhtml1-transitional.dtd">
<html xmlns="http://www.w3.org/1999/xhtml" xmlns:f="http://java.sun.com/jsf/core"
   xmlns:h="http://java.sun.com/jsf/html">
<h:head />
<body>
<h:form id="form">
  <h:panelGrid id="panel" columns="2" border="1" cellpadding="0" cellspacing="2">
    <f:facet name="header">
      <h:outputText value="#{messages.signInMessage}"/>
    </f:facet>
    <h:outputLabel for="username" value="#{messages.usernameLabel}" />
    <h:inputText id="username" value="#{userController.user.username}" />
    <h:outputLabel for="password" value="#{messages.passwordLabel}" />
    <h:inputText id="password" value="#{userController.user.password}" />
    <f:facet name="footer">
      <h:panelGroup style="display:block; text-align:center">
        <h:commandButton id="submit" value="#{messages.submitLabel}" />
      </h:panelGroup>
    </f:facet>
  </h:panelGrid>
</h:form>
</body>
</html>
```

**The <h:panelGroup> tag**

The panelGroup tag is a container component that renders its child components. It is intended to be used in situations where it is desirable to include several components but when only one child component is allowed, such as within a panelGrid column or a facet component. The example below demonstrates the use of a panelGroup component to nest two components inside a single panelGrid column.

Without the panelGroup component, the two child components of the panelGrid would have been rendered in separate rows. Following table shows the important attributes of this tag.

| Attribute | Description |
|---|---|
| id | Identifier for a component |
| binding | Reference to the component that can be used in a backing bean |
| rendered | A boolean; false suppresses rendering |
| styleClass | Cascading stylesheet (CSS) class name |
| layout | It is set with the type of layout markup used when rendering the component group. |
| style | It is used to set the CSS style to be applied when the component is rendered. |

JSF example,

```
<!DOCTYPE html PUBLIC "-//W3C//DTD XHTML 1.0 Transitional//EN"
  "http://www.w3.org/TR/xhtml1/DTD/xhtml1-transitional.dtd">
<html xmlns="http://www.w3.org/1999/xhtml" xmlns:h="http://java.sun.com/jsf/html">
<h:head>
  <h:outputStylesheet library="styles" name="style.css" />
</h:head>
<body>
<h:form id="form">
  <h:panelGrid id="grid" columns="1">
    <h:panelGroup>
      <h:outputLabel value="#{messages.usernameLabel} " />
      <h:inputText label="#{messages.usernameLabel}" id="username"
              value="#{userController.user.username}" required="true" />
      <h:message for="username" errorClass="error" />
    </h:panelGroup>
    <h:panelGroup>
      <h:outputLabel value="#{messages.passwordLabel} " />
      <h:inputSecret label="#{messages.passwordLabel}" id="password"
              value="#{userController.user.username}" required="true" />
      <h:message for="password" errorClass="error" />
    </h:panelGroup>
    <h:commandButton id="submit" value="#{messages.submitLabel}" />
  </h:panelGrid>
</h:form>
</body>
</html>
```

**The <h:dataTable> tag**

The dataTable tag renders an HTML4 compliant table element that can be associated with a backing bean to obtain its data as well as for event handling purposes. The table can be customized extensively using cascading stylesheet (CSS) classes and definitions to enhance the appearance of the table's headers, footers, columns and rows. Common formatting techniques, such as alternating row colors, can be accomplished quite easily with this tag. The dataTable tag typically contains one or more column tags that define the columns of the table. A column component is rendered as a single "td" element. For more information about columns, see the column tag documentation. A dataTable tag can also contain header and footer facets. These are rendered as a single "th" element in a row at the top of the table and as a single "td" element in a row at the bottom of the table, respectively. Following table shows the important attributes of this tag.

| Attribute | Description |
|---|---|
| bgcolor | Background color for the table |
| border | Width of the table's border |
| cellpadding | Padding around table cells |
| cellspacing | Spacing between table cells |
| columnclasses | Comma-separated list of CSS classes for columns |

| | |
|---|---|
| columns | Number of columns in the table |
| footerclass | CSS class for the table footer |
| frame | Frame specification for sides of the frame surrounding the table that are to be drawn. |
| headerclass | CSS class for the table header |
| rowclasses | Comma-separated list of CSS classes for columns |
| rules | Specification for lines drawn between cells. |
| summary | Summary of the table's purpose and structure used for non-visual feedback, such as speech. |
| var | This is set with a string, which is taken as a variable representing current item in the value |

JSF example,

```
<!DOCTYPE html PUBLIC "-//W3C//DTD XHTML 1.0 Transitional//EN"
  "http://www.w3.org/TR/xhtml1/DTD/xhtml1-transitional.dtd">
<html xmlns="http://www.w3.org/1999/xhtml" xmlns:h="http://java.sun.com/jsf/html"
   xmlns:f="http://java.sun.com/jsf/core">
<h:head/>
<body>
<h:dataTable id="table1" value="#{shoppingCartBean.items}" var="item"
        border="1">
  <f:facet name="header">
    <h:outputText value="Your Shopping Cart" />
  </f:facet>
  <h:column>
    <f:facet name="header">
      <h:outputText value="Item Description" />
    </f:facet>
    <h:outputText value="#{item.description}" />
  </h:column>
  <h:column>
    <f:facet name="header">
      <h:outputText value="Price" />
    </f:facet>
    <h:outputText value="#{item.price}" />
  </h:column>
  <f:facet name="footer">
    <h:outputText value="Total: #{shoppingCartBean.total}" />
  </f:facet>
</h:dataTable>
</body>
</html>
```

**The <h:column> tag**

The column tag renders a single column of data within a data table component. A column of data can contain any number of rows depending on the length of the array or list associated with the data table. See the dataTable tag for more information. Following table shows the important attributes of this tag.

| Attribute | Description |
|---|---|
| id | Identifier for a component |
| binding | Reference to the component that can be used in a backing bean |
| rendered | A boolean; false suppresses rendering |
| footerClass | Space-separated list of CSS style class(es) that will be applied to any column footer generated for this table. |
| headerClass | Space-separated list of CSS style class(es) that will be applied to any column header generated for this table. |
| rowHeader | Flag indicating that this column is a row header column and therefore cells in this column should be rendered with "th" instead of "td" and must have the 'scope="row"' attribute |

JSF example,

```
<!DOCTYPE html PUBLIC "-//W3C//DTD XHTML 1.0 Transitional//EN"
  "http://www.w3.org/TR/xhtml1/DTD/xhtml1-transitional.dtd">
<html xmlns="http://www.w3.org/1999/xhtml" xmlns:h="http://java.sun.com/jsf/html">
<h:head/>
<body>
<h:dataTable value="#{itemBean.items}" var="item" border="1" cellspacing="2">
  <h:column>
    <h:outputText value="#{item}" />
  </h:column>
</h:dataTable>
</body>
</html>
```

## JSF Core tags

The JSF core tag library contains tags for different JSF custom actions that are independent of the particular render kit. The JSF core tags can be categorized to their usage in an application. For example, we have core tags to support event handling, to implement standard JSF validators and converters, and to create item(s) in a list. Following table shows the various JSF core tags.

| Tag | Description |
|---|---|
| f:view | Creates the top-level view |
| f:subview | Creates a subview of a view |
| f:facet | Adds a facet to a component |
| f:attribute | Adds an attribute (key/value) to a component |
| f:param | Constructs a parameter component |
| f:actionListener | Adds an action listener to a component |
| f:valueChangeListener | Adds a valuechange listener to a component |

| | |
|---|---|
| f:setPropertyActionListener | Adds an action listener to a component that sets a bean property to a given value. |
| f:converter | Adds an arbitrary converter to a component |
| f:convertDateTime | Adds a datetime converter to a component |
| f:convertNumber | Adds a number converter to a component |
| f:validator | Adds a validator to a component |
| f:validateDoubleRange | Validates a double range for a component's value |
| f:validateLength | Validates the length of a component's value |
| f:validateLongRange | Validates a long range for a component's value |
| f:loadBundle | Loads a resource bundle, stores properties as a Map |
| f:selectitems | Specifies items for a select one or select many component |
| f:selectitem | Specifies an item for a select one or select many component |
| f:verbatim | Adds markup to a JSF page |

Let's understand these tags with their important attributes

**The < f:actionListener> tag**

The ActionListener tag registers a javax.faces.event.ActionListener instance with the component. An ActionListener is an event handler interface for a class that can respond to user events in your JSF page.

When the button is clicked, JSF will invoke a method named "processAction" on the associated ActionListener object. The body content of this tag must be empty.

| Attribute | Description |
|---|---|
| type | Fully qualified Java class name of an *ActionListener* to be created and registered. |
| binding | Value binding expression that evaluates to an object that implements *javax.faces.event.ActionListener*. |
| for | If present, this attribute refers to the value of one of the exposed attached objects within the composite component inside of which this tag is nested. |

JSF example,

```
<!DOCTYPE html PUBLIC "-//W3C//DTD XHTML 1.0 Transitional//EN"
  "http://www.w3.org/TR/xhtml1/DTD/xhtml1-transitional.dtd">
<html xmlns="http://www.w3.org/1999/xhtml" xmlns:f="http://java.sun.com/jsf/core"
   xmlns:h="http://java.sun.com/jsf/html">
<h:head />
<body>
<h:form>
  <h:commandButton value="Click">
    <f:actionListener type="com.mycompany.MyActionListener" />
  </h:commandButton>
</h:form>
</body>
</html>
```

**The <f:subview> tag**

The Subview tag creates a naming container (a container component with a unique identifier) that contains all JavaServer Faces core and custom tags on a nested page via "jsp:include" or any tag that dynamically includes another page from the same web application, such as JSTL's "c:import".

The subview tag wraps JSF components contained in an included JSP or Facelets page that allows nested views. One advantage of this tag is that include files can be reused. Since JSF requires a unique ID for each component, the subview tag creates a unique "namespace" for child components.

| Attribute | Description |
|---|---|
| binding | Value binding expression to a backing bean property bound to the component instance for the UIComponent created by this custom action. |
| id | Component identifier of the UINamingContainer component to be created. |
| rendered | Flag indicating whether this component (and its children) should be rendered. Expressions must evaluate to a boolean. |

JSF example,

```
<!DOCTYPE html PUBLIC "-//W3C//DTD XHTML 1.0 Transitional//EN"
  "http://www.w3.org/TR/xhtml1/DTD/xhtml1-transitional.dtd">
<html xmlns="http://www.w3.org/1999/xhtml" xmlns:f="http://java.sun.com/jsf/core"
   xmlns:h="http://java.sun.com/jsf/html"
   xmlns:ui="http://java.sun.com/jsf/facelets">
<body>
<f:view>
  <h:form id="form_1">
    <h:outputLabel value="Home Address" id="outputLabel_1" style="font-weight:bold" />
    <f:subview id="subview_1">
      <ui:include src="/WEB-INF/includes/addressPanel.xhtml">
        <ui:param name="address" value="#{customerController.customer.homeAddress}" />
      </ui:include>
    </f:subview>
    <h:outputLabel value="Work Address" id="outputLabel_2" style="font-weight:bold" />
    <f:subview id="subview_2">
      <ui:include src="/WEB-INF/includes/addressPanel.xhtml">
        <ui:param name="address" value="#{customerController.customer.workAddress}" />
      </ui:include>
    </f:subview>
  </h:form>
</f:view>
</body>
</html>
```

**The <f:facet> tag**

The Facet tag registers a named facet on the component associated with the enclosing tag. A facet represents a named section within a container component. For example, you can create a header and a footer facet for a dataTable component.

| Attribute | Description |
|---|---|
| name | The name of the facet to be created. |

JSF example,

```
<!DOCTYPE html PUBLIC "-//W3C//DTD XHTML 1.0 Transitional//EN"
  "http://www.w3.org/TR/xhtml1/DTD/xhtml1-transitional.dtd">
<html xmlns="http://www.w3.org/1999/xhtml" xmlns:f="http://java.sun.com/jsf/core"
    xmlns:h="http://java.sun.com/jsf/html">
<body>
<f:view>
  <h:dataTable id="reportTable" value="#{reportController.dailyReport}"
          var="item" border="1">
    <h:column>
      <f:facet name="header">
        <h:outputText value="Daily Report" />
      </f:facet>
      <h:outputText value="#{item}" />
    </h:column>
  </h:dataTable>
</f:view>
</body>
</html>
```

**The <f:attribute> tag**

The Attribute tag is a name/value pair that sets the value of a named attribute on the component associated with the enclosing tag. The body content of this tag must be empty.

| Attribute | Description |
|---|---|
| name | The name of the component attribute to be set |
| value | The value of the component attribute to be set. |

JSF example,

```
<!DOCTYPE html PUBLIC "-//W3C//DTD XHTML 1.0 Transitional//EN"
  "http://www.w3.org/TR/xhtml1/DTD/xhtml1-transitional.dtd">
<html xmlns="http://www.w3.org/1999/xhtml" xmlns:f="http://java.sun.com/jsf/core"
    xmlns:h="http://java.sun.com/jsf/html">
<body>
<f:view>
  <h:form>
    <h:commandButton value="Click" actionListener="#{myBean.handleClick}">
      <f:attribute name="myAttribute" value="myValue" />
    </h:commandButton>
  </h:form>
</f:view>
</body>
</html>
```

**The <f:param> tag**

The Param tag sets a parameter for the component associated with the enclosing tag. You can use it to you build compound messages by replacing placeholder values in an outputFormat tag. The body content of the param tag must be empty. See also the HTML outputFormat tag.

| Attribute | Description |
|---|---|
| binding | ValueExpression to a backing bean property bound to the component instance for the UIComponent created by this custom action. |
| id | Component identifier of the UIParameter component to be created. |
| name | Name of the parameter to be created. |
| value | Value of the parameter to be set. |
| disable | Flag enabling or disabling the inclusion of the parameter. This flag is consulted by renderers that consider the UIParameter component associated with this *<f:param>* during their rendering. Such renderers include *javax.faces.Output javax.faces.Link* and *javax.faces.OutcomeTarget javax.faces.Link*. |

JSF example,

```
<!DOCTYPE html PUBLIC "-//W3C//DTD XHTML 1.0 Transitional//EN"
  "http://www.w3.org/TR/xhtml1/DTD/xhtml1-transitional.dtd">
<html xmlns="http://www.w3.org/1999/xhtml" xmlns:f="http://java.sun.com/jsf/core"
   xmlns:h="http://java.sun.com/jsf/html">
<h:head />
<body>
<h:outputFormat value="Welcome, {0}. You have {1} new messages.">
  <f:param value="#{userController.user.firstName}" />
  <f:param value="#{userController.user.messageCount}" />
</h:outputFormat>
</body>
</html>
```

**The <f:view> tag**

The View tag is the container for all JavaServer Faces component tags used on a page. You can wrap the root element of the structured markup language used in your document with this tag to ensure that all child tags are part of the same view. This tag is useful for internationalization purposes.

It provides you with several options for presenting your user with localized views of your application. By default the JSF framework will attempt to select the best view for your user based on the Accept-Language header sent to the server from the user's browser as part of the HTTP request for your page. If the locale requested by the user is not supported by your application, the JSF framework will use the default locale specified in your Faces configuration file. If you have not specified a default locale, JSF will use the default locale for the Java Virtual Machine serving your application.

| Attribute | Description |
|---|---|
| locale | Locale to use for localizing this page. Expressions must evaluate to a java.util.Locale or to a String that is converted to a Locale. |
| renderKitId | Identifier for the RenderKit to use for rendering this page. |

| | |
|---|---|
| contentType | Specifies the content-type of the response. |
| encoding | Specifies the character encoding that should be used for the response. |
| beforePhase | MethodBinding pointing to a method that takes a *javax.faces.event.PhaseEvent* and returns *void*. This method will be called before every phase except for restore view. |
| afterPhase | MethodBinding pointing to a method that takes a *javax.faces.event.PhaseEvent* and returns *void*. This method will be called after every phase except for restore view. |

JSF example,

```
<!DOCTYPE html PUBLIC "-//W3C//DTD XHTML 1.0 Transitional//EN"
  "http://www.w3.org/TR/xhtml1/DTD/xhtml1-transitional.dtd">
<html xmlns="http://www.w3.org/1999/xhtml" xmlns:f="http://java.sun.com/jsf/core"
   xmlns:h="http://java.sun.com/jsf/html">
<body>
<f:view locale="en">
  <f:loadBundle basename="com.mycompany.MessageBundle" var="bundle" />
  <h:outputText value="#{bundle.welcomeMessage}" />
</f:view>
</body>
</html>
```

**The <f:valueChangeListener> tag**

The ValueChangeListener tag registers a ValueChangeListener instance on the component associated with the enclosing tag. The ValueChangeListener interface should be implemented by classes that you want to register with components that publish value change events. Any component that receives user input, such as one of the HTML select or text input components, can publish value change events. A component fires a value change event when its input changes, but only if the new input is validated successfully. You can register several ValueChangeListeners with a component and they will be invoked in the order that they are registered.

An alternative to this tag is to use a method-binding expression pointing at a value change listener method of a backing bean on the component tag itself. Notice in the example below the use of the JavaScript onchange() event to trigger form submission when the list selection changes. Without this JavaScript event, the user must manually submit the form to invoke the ValueChangeListener.

| Attribute | Description |
|---|---|
| type | Fully qualified Java class name of an *ActionListener* to be created and registered. |
| binding | Value binding expression that evaluates to an object that implements *javax.faces.event.ActionListener*. |
| for | If present, this attribute refers to the value of one of the exposed attached objects within the composite component inside of which this tag is nested. |

JSF example,

```
<!DOCTYPE html PUBLIC "-//W3C//DTD XHTML 1.0 Transitional//EN"
  "http://www.w3.org/TR/xhtml1/DTD/xhtml1-transitional.dtd">
<html xmlns="http://www.w3.org/1999/xhtml" xmlns:f="http://java.sun.com/jsf/core"
   xmlns:h="http://java.sun.com/jsf/html">
<h:head />
<body>
<h:form>
  <h:selectOneMenu value="#{customerController.customer.homeAddress.country}"
            converter="countryConverter" id="countryList">
    <f:selectItems value="#{countryController.countries}" var="country"
              itemLabel="#{country.name}" itemValue="#{country}" />
    <f:valueChangeListener type="com.mycompany.MyValueChangeListener" />
    <f:ajax />
  </h:selectOneMenu>
</h:form>
</body>
</html>
```

### The <f:setPropertyActionListener> tag

The <f:setPropertyActionListener> tag creates a special ActionListener interface and registers it with associated ActionSource, such as HtmlCommandButton. This special ActionListener will set the bean property defined using a value expression for the target attribute with the value obtained from the evaluation of value expression for the value attribute.

| Attribute | Description |
|---|---|
| value | ValueExpression to be stored as the value of the target attribute. |
| target | ValueExpression that is the destination of the value attribute. |
| for | If present, this attribute refers to the value of one of the exposed attached objects within the composite component inside of which this tag is nested. |

JSF example,

```
<!DOCTYPE html PUBLIC "-//W3C//DTD XHTML 1.0 Transitional//EN"
  "http://www.w3.org/TR/xhtml1/DTD/xhtml1-transitional.dtd">
<html xmlns="http://www.w3.org/1999/xhtml" xmlns:f="http://java.sun.com/jsf/core"
   xmlns:h="http://java.sun.com/jsf/html">
<h:head />
<body>
<h:form>
<h:commanLink action= "#{student.delete}" value= "Delete">
        <f:setPropertyActionListener target="{student.roll}" value= "#{user.roll}"/>
</h:commandLink.
  <f:ajax />
  </h:selectOneMenu>
</h:form>
</body>
</html>
```

**The <f:converter> tag**

The Converter tag registers a Converter instance on the component associated with the enclosing tag. It takes one attribute:the converterId that you used to register your converter in your Faces configuration file. The Converter interface is implemented by classes that handle custom conversion of user input into a data type expected by the domain model of your JSF application, and vice versa. For example, you might have a select list of countries that your user can choose from. You could create a custom converter to handle converting the underlying Country objects in your list into strings to display to the user. When the user submits the form, your converter would also handle converting the selected country ID into the appropriate Country object expected by your domain model.

| Attribute | Description |
|---|---|
| converterId | Converter identifier of the Converter instance to be created and registered. |
| binding | A ValueExpression that evaluates to an object that implements *javax.faces.convert.Converter*. |
| for | If present, this attribute refers to the value of one of the exposed attached objects within the composite component inside of which this tag is nested. |

JSF example,

```
<!DOCTYPE html PUBLIC "-//W3C//DTD XHTML 1.0 Transitional//EN"
  "http://www.w3.org/TR/xhtml1/DTD/xhtml1-transitional.dtd">
<html xmlns="http://www.w3.org/1999/xhtml"
   xmlns:f="http://java.sun.com/jsf/core"
   xmlns:h="http://java.sun.com/jsf/html">
<h:head />
<body>
<h:form>
  <h:outputLabel value="Enter your country name: " />
  <h:inputText value="#{customerController.customer.homeAddress.country}">
    <f:converter converterId="countryConverter" />
  </h:inputText>
  <h:commandButton value="Submit" />
</h:form>
</body>
</html>
```

**The <f:convertDateTime> tag**

The ConvertDateTime tag is useful for converting a date into a human-readable format and supports a range of formatting options. You can use this tag to control the style and appearance of a date on your JSF page. The ConvertDateTime tag applies to the date value of the component associated with the enclosing tag. The body content of this tag must be empty.

| Attribute | Description |
|---|---|
| dateStyle | Predefined formatting style which determines how the date component of a date string is to be formatted and parsed. Applied only if type is "date" or "both". Valid values are "default", "short", "medium", "long", and "full". Default value is "default". |

| | |
|---|---|
| pattern | Custom formatting pattern which determines how the date/time string should be formatted and parsed. |
| timeStyle | Predefined formatting style which determines how the time component of a date string is to be formatted and parsed. Applied only if type is "time" or "both". Valid values are "default", "short", "medium", "long", and "full". Default value is "default". |
| timeZone | Time zone in which to interpret any time information in the date String. Value must be either a VB expression that evaluates to a *java.util.TimeZone* instance, or a String that is a timezone ID as described in the javadocs for *java.util.TimeZone.getTimeZone().* |
| type | Specifies what contents the string value will be formatted to include, or parsed expecting. Valid values are "date", "time", and "both". Default value is "date". |
| binding | A ValueExpression that evaluates to an instance of *javax.faces.convert.DateTimeConverter*. |
| for | If present, this attribute refers to the value of one of the exposed attached objects within the composite component inside of which this tag is nested. |

JSF example,

```
<!DOCTYPE html PUBLIC "-//W3C//DTD XHTML 1.0 Transitional//EN"
  "http://www.w3.org/TR/xhtml1/DTD/xhtml1-transitional.dtd">
<html xmlns="http://www.w3.org/1999/xhtml"
   xmlns:f="http://java.sun.com/jsf/core"
   xmlns:h="http://java.sun.com/jsf/html">
<body>
<f:view>
  <h:outputText value="#{dateBean.today}">
    <f:convertDateTime dateStyle="full" timeZone="EST" type="date" />
  </h:outputText>
</f:view>
</body>
</html>
```

**The <f:convertNumber> tag**

The ConvertNumber tag registers a NumberConverter instance on the component associated with the enclosing tag. A NumberConverter is a JSF converter class that handles the conversion of strings to numbers and vice versa. The convertNumber tag provides a range of options for customizing the appearance of numeric data. It is useful for converting floating-point and integer values from your domain model into a format that is appropriate for your users. The body content of this tag must be empty.

| Attribute | Description |
|---|---|
| currencyCode | ISO 4217 currency code, applied only when formatting currencies. |
| currencySymbol | Currency symbol, applied only when formatting currencies. |
| groupingUsed | Flag specifying whether formatted output will contain grouping separators. Expressions must evaluate to a boolean. Default value is true. |
| integerOnly | Flag specifying whether only the integer part of the value will be formatted and parsed. Expressions must evaluate to a boolean. Default value is false. |

| | |
|---|---|
| maxFractionDigits | Maximum number of digits that will be formatted in the fractional portion of the output. Expressions must evaluate to an int. |
| maxIntegerDigits | Maximum number of digits that will be formatted in the integer portion of the output. Expressions must evaluate to an int. |
| minFractionDigits | Minimum number of digits that will be formatted in the fractional portion of the output. Expressions must evaluate to an int. |
| minIntegerDigits | Minimum number of digits that will be formatted in the integer portion of the output. Expressions must evaluate to an int. |
| pattern | Custom formatting pattern which determines how the number string should be formatted and parsed. |
| type | Specifies how the number string will be formatted and parsed. Valid values are "number", "currency", and "percent". Default value is "number". |
| binding | A ValueExpression that evaluates to an instance of *javax.faces.convert.NumberConverter*. |
| for | If present, this attribute refers to the value of one of the exposed attached objects within the composite component inside of which this tag is nested. |

JSF example,

```
<!DOCTYPE html PUBLIC "-//W3C//DTD XHTML 1.0 Transitional//EN"
  "http://www.w3.org/TR/xhtml1/DTD/xhtml1-transitional.dtd">
<html xmlns="http://www.w3.org/1999/xhtml"
    xmlns:f="http://java.sun.com/jsf/core"
    xmlns:h="http://java.sun.com/jsf/html">
<body>
<h:outputText id="balance" value="#{accountBean.balance}">
  <f:convertNumber currencySymbol="$" groupingUsed="true"
            maxFractionDigits="2" type="currency" />
</h:outputText>
</body>
</html>
```

**The <f:validator> tag**

The Validator tag registers a named Validator instance on the component associated with the enclosing tag. The JavaServer Faces framework includes three standard validators (see the validateDoubleRange, validateLength, and validateLongRange tags) but the Validator interface can be implemented by classes that provide custom validation for your application. This tag accepts one value matching the validator ID you assigned to your validator class in your Faces configuration file. The body content of this tag must be empty.

| Attribute | Description |
|---|---|
| disabled | A boolean value enabling page level determination of whether or not this validator is enabled on the enclosing component. |
| binding | A ValueExpression that evaluates to an object that implements the *javax.faces.validator.Validator* interface. |
| for | If present, this attribute refers to the value of one of the exposed attached objects within the composite component inside of which this tag is nested. |
| validatorID | Validator identifier of the Validator to be created and registered. |

JSF example,

```
<!DOCTYPE html PUBLIC "-//W3C//DTD XHTML 1.0 Transitional//EN"
  "http://www.w3.org/TR/xhtml1/DTD/xhtml1-transitional.dtd">
<html xmlns="http://www.w3.org/1999/xhtml"
    xmlns:f="http://java.sun.com/jsf/core"
    xmlns:h="http://java.sun.com/jsf/html">
<h:head />
<body>
<h:form>
  <h:outputLabel value="Enter your email address: " for="emailAddress" />
  <h:inputText label="Email address" id="emailAddress" required="true"
        value="#{customerController.customer.emailAddress}">
    <f:validator validatorId="emailAddressValidator" />
  </h:inputText>
  <h:commandButton value="Submit" />
  <h:message for="emailAddress" errorStyle="color:red; display:block" />
</h:form>
</body>
</html>
```

**The <f:validateDoubleRange> tag**

The ValidateDoubleRange tag registers a DoubleRangeValidator instance on the component associated with the enclosing tag. This tag can be used to validate user input when the expected input is a floating-point value.

| Attribute | Description |
|---|---|
| disabled | A boolean value enabling page level determination of whether or not this validator is enabled on the enclosing component. |
| maximum | Maximum value allowed for this component. |
| minimum | Minimum value allowed for this component. |
| binding | A ValueExpression that evaluates to an instance of DoubleRangeValidator. |
| for | If present, this attribute refers to the value of one of the exposed attached objects within the composite component inside of which this tag is nested. |

JSF example,

```
<!DOCTYPE html PUBLIC "-//W3C//DTD XHTML 1.0 Transitional//EN"
  "http://www.w3.org/TR/xhtml1/DTD/xhtml1-transitional.dtd">
<html xmlns="http://www.w3.org/1999/xhtml"
    xmlns:f="http://java.sun.com/jsf/core"
    xmlns:h="http://java.sun.com/jsf/html">
<body>
<f:view>
  <h:inputText id="withdraw" value="#{accountBean.withdraw.amount}">
    <f:validateDoubleRange minimum="20.00" maximum="1000.00" />
  </h:inputText>
  <h:message for="withdraw" />
</f:view>
</body>
</html>
```

**The <f:validateLength> tag**

The ValidateLength tag registers a LengthValidator instance on the component associated with the enclosing tag. This tag can be used to validate user input when the expected value is a string of a specific length.

| Attribute | Description |
|---|---|
| disabled | A boolean value enabling page level determination of whether or not this validator is enabled on the enclosing component. |
| maximum | Maximum value allowed for this component. |
| minimum | Minimum value allowed for this component. |
| binding | A ValueExpression that evaluates to an instance of LengthValidator. |
| for | If present, this attribute refers to the value of one of the exposed attached objects within the composite component inside of which this tag is nested. |

For example,

```
<!DOCTYPE html PUBLIC "-//W3C//DTD XHTML 1.0 Transitional//EN"
  "http://www.w3.org/TR/xhtml1/DTD/xhtml1-transitional.dtd">
<html xmlns="http://www.w3.org/1999/xhtml"
    xmlns:f="http://java.sun.com/jsf/core"
    xmlns:h="http://java.sun.com/jsf/html">
<h:head />
<body>
<h:form>
   <h:outputLabel value="Enter your password: " for="password" />
   <h:inputSecret label="Password" id="password" redisplay="true"
            value="#{userController.user.password}">
      <f:validateLength minimum="8" maximum="16" />
   </h:inputSecret>
   <h:commandButton value="Sign In" />
   <h:message for="password" errorStyle="color:red; display:block" />
</h:form>
</body>
</html>
```

**The <f:validateLongRange> tag**

The ValidateLongRange tag registers a LongRangeValidator instance on the component associated with the enclosing tag. This tag can be used to validate user input when the expected value is a long integer that is greater than or less than another value or is between two values of the same data type.

| Attribute | Description |
|---|---|
| disabled | A boolean value enabling page level determination of whether or not this validator is enabled on the enclosing component. |
| maximum | Maximum value allowed for this component. |
| minimum | Minimum value allowed for this component. |
| binding | A ValueExpression that evaluates to an instance of LongRangeValidator. |
| for | If present, this attribute refers to the value of one of the exposed attached objects within the composite component inside of which this tag is nested. |

JSF example,

```
<!DOCTYPE html PUBLIC "-//W3C//DTD XHTML 1.0 Transitional//EN"
  "http://www.w3.org/TR/xhtml1/DTD/xhtml1-transitional.dtd">
<html xmlns="http://www.w3.org/1999/xhtml"
    xmlns:f="http://java.sun.com/jsf/core"
    xmlns:h="http://java.sun.com/jsf/html">
<h:head />
<body>
<h:form>
  <h:outputLabel value="Enter an amount to withdraw: " for="withdraw" />
  <h:inputText label="Amount" id="withdraw"
          value="#{accountBean.withdrawAmount}">
    <f:validateLongRange minimum="20" maximum="1000" />
  </h:inputText>
  <h:commandButton value="Withdraw" actionListener="#{accountBean.withdraw}" />
  <h:message for="withdraw" errorStyle="color:red; display:block" />
</h:form>
</body>
</html>
```

**The <f:loadBundle> tag**

The LoadBundle tag loads a resource bundle for the Locale of the current view and stores it as a Map in request scope. This tag is useful for internationalization (I18N) as it allows you to access your message bundle in your JSF page. The body content of this tag must be empty. Place this tag above any other component tags on your document (in the head section, for instance) and specify a variable name for the bundle.

| Attribute | Description |
|---|---|
| basename | Base name of the resource bundle to be loaded. |
| var | Name of a request scope attribute under which the resource bundle will be exposed as a Map. |

JSF example,

```
<!DOCTYPE html PUBLIC "-//W3C//DTD XHTML 1.0 Transitional//EN"
  "http://www.w3.org/TR/xhtml1/DTD/xhtml1-transitional.dtd">
<html xmlns="http://www.w3.org/1999/xhtml"
    xmlns:f="http://java.sun.com/jsf/core"
    xmlns:h="http://java.sun.com/jsf/html">
<body>
<f:view>
  <f:loadBundle basename="com.mycompany.MessageBundle" var="bundle" />
  <h:outputText value="#{bundle.welcomeMessage}" />
</f:view>
</body>
</html
```

**The <f:selectitem> tag**

The SelectItem tag adds a child UISelectItem component to the component associated with the enclosing tag. In the HTML renderkit, this creates a single element. It can be used with any of the select tags in the JSF HTML tag library. The body content of this tag must be empty.

| Attribute | Description |
|---|---|
| binding | Value binding expression to a backing bean property bound to the component instance for the UIComponent created by this custom action. |
| id | Component identifier of the UISelectItem component to be created. |
| itemDescription | Description of this option, for use in development tools. |
| itemDisabled | Flag indicating whether the option created by this component is disabled. Expressions must evaluate to a boolean. Default value is false. |
| itemLabel | Label to be displayed to the user for this option. |
| escapeItem | Flag indicating that characters that are sensitive in the value of the itemLabel attribute must be escaped. This flag is set to "true" by default. |
| itemValue | Value to be returned to the server if this option is selected by the user. |
| value | Value binding expression pointing at a SelectItem instance containing the information for this option. |
| noSelectionOption | Flag indicating whether the option created by this component represents the special "no selection" option. Expressions must evaluate to a boolean. Default value is false. |

JSF example,

```
<!DOCTYPE html PUBLIC "-//W3C//DTD XHTML 1.0 Transitional//EN"
  "http://www.w3.org/TR/xhtml1/DTD/xhtml1-transitional.dtd">
<html xmlns="http://www.w3.org/1999/xhtml"
   xmlns:f="http://java.sun.com/jsf/core"
   xmlns:h="http://java.sun.com/jsf/html">
<h:head />
<body>
<h:form>
  <h:selectOneMenu id="list1">
    <f:selectItem itemLabel="Option 1" itemValue="1" />
  </h:selectOneMenu>
</h:form>
</body>
</html>
```

**The <f:selectitems> tag**

The SelectItems tag adds a child UISelectItems component to the component associated with enclosing tag. You can use this tag to set a list of objects in your domain model as the options for a select component. The body content of this tag must be empty.

| Attribute | Description |
|---|---|
| binding | Value binding expression to a backing bean property bound to the component instance for the UIComponent created by this custom action. |
| id | Component identifier of the UISelectItem component to be created. |
| value | Value binding expression pointing at a SelectItem instance containing the information for this option. |
| var | Expose the value from the value attribute under this request scoped key so that it may be referred to in EL for the value of other attributes. |
| itemValue | Evaluates to a Collection, array, or Map from which the items to be shown will be rendered. |
| itemLabel | Evaluates to a String that will serve as the label to be shown for the item. |
| itemDescription | Evaluates to a String that will serve as the description to be shown for the item. |
| itemDisabled | Evaluates to a boolean that will determine if the item value is selectable or not. |
| itemLabelEscaped | Evaluates to a boolean that will determine if the rendered markup for the item receives normal JSF HTML escaping or not. |
| noSelectionValue | Is either an EL expression pointing to the element in the value collection whose value should be marked as a "no selection" item, or a literal string that exactly matches the value of the item in the collection that must be marked as the "no selection" item. If the user selects such an item and the field is marked as required, then it will not pass validation. |

JSF example,

```
<!DOCTYPE html PUBLIC "-//W3C//DTD XHTML 1.0 Transitional//EN"
  "http://www.w3.org/TR/xhtml1/DTD/xhtml1-transitional.dtd">
<html xmlns="http://www.w3.org/1999/xhtml"
   xmlns:f="http://java.sun.com/jsf/core"
   xmlns:h="http://java.sun.com/jsf/html">
<h:head />
<body>
<h:form id="form">
  <h:selectOneMenu value="#{customerController.customer.homeAddress.country}"
           converter="countryConverter" id="countryList">
    <f:selectItems value="#{countryController.countries}" var="country"
            itemLabel="#{country.name}" itemValue="#{country}" />
  </h:selectOneMenu>
  <h:commandButton value="Submit" id="button1" />
</h:form>
</body>
</html>
```

**The <f:verbatim> tag**

The Verbatim tag creates an output component as a child of the component associated with the enclosing tag. An output component renders the output contained in the body of this tag, such as HTML markup.

Note: this tag is more useful with JSP than with Facelets. This is because Facelets handles HTML mixed with JSF markup in a different way than JSP. For this reason, this tag is not necessary when using Facelets.

| Attribute | Description |
|---|---|
| escape | Flag indicating that generated markup must be escaped in a manner that is appropriate for the markup language to be rendered. Expressions must evaluate to a boolean. Default value is false. |
| rendered | Flag indicating whether or not this component should be rendered (during Render Response Phase), or processed on any subsequent form submit. The default value for this property is true. |

JSF example,

```
<!DOCTYPE html PUBLIC "-//W3C//DTD XHTML 1.0 Transitional//EN"
  "http://www.w3.org/TR/xhtml1/DTD/xhtml1-transitional.dtd">
<html>
<head>
</head>
<body>
<f:view>
   <f:verbatim escape="true">
      <span>This HTML will be escaped.</span>
   </f:verbatim>
</f:view>
</body>
</html>
```

## 18.7 understand patterns with JSF Facelets

In JavaServer Faces (JSF) 2.0, Facelets is the default *View Declaration Language (VDL)* instead of *JavaServer Pages (JSP)*. With Facelets, you don't need to configure a view handler as you used to do in JSF 1.2. Facelets is a JSF-centric view technology.

A "Facelet" is a reusable section of content or a sub-tree of components on a JSF page that can itself be composed of other Facelets. In this sense, a Facelet is a composite view element that can easily be combined with other Facelets to build a JSF view that will be rendered to the user.

Facelets is based on compositions. A composition defines a JSF UIComponents structure in a Facelets page. A Facelets application may consist of compositions defined in different Facelets pages and run as an application.

Facelets is a templating framework similar to Tiles. The advantage of Facelets over Tiles is that JSF UIComponents are pre-integrated with Facelets, and Facelets does not require a Facelets configuration file, unlike Tiles, which requires a Tiles configuration file.

JSF Validators and Converters may be added to Facelets. Facelets provides a complete expression language (EL) and *JavaServer Pages Standard Tag Library (JSTL)* support. Templating, re-use, and ease of development are some of the advantages of using Facelets in a Web application. Let's discuss more on JSF Facelets in following sub-sections.

### 18.7.1 Comparing Facelets with JSF

We recommend Facelets over JSP for JavaServer Faces. With a near-zero compile-time overhead, developing JSF applications with Facelets is simply faster.

Every time you edit, save and reload a JSP page, the server's JSP compiler generates Java servlet code and compiles it into a servlet. This is called the JSP translation process, and typically it costs between 1-2 seconds, depending on server performance.

Unlike JavaServer Pages, Facelets pages are not compiled into Servlets. Since Facelets pages are XML-compliant, the Facelets framework uses a fast SAX-based compiler to build your views. Also, Facelets can be configured to detect and render changes to your pages immediately, speeding up your JSF development cycle.

### 18.7.2 Facelets configuration

The Facelets view handler is a pluggable component that can be easily added to a Web application using the JavaServer Faces (JSF) framework. Facelets is capable of rendering JSF pages written in XML-compliant markup, and also builds a component tree for each view in a very flexible way.

To begin using Facelets, add the following to your Faces configuration file:

**faces-config.xml**

```
<application>
   <view-handler>com.sun.facelets.FaceletViewHandler</view-handler>
</application>
```

The Faces servlet can be mapped to any file extension, but we recommend the *.jsf extension. New Facelets XHTML pages created in Dreamweaver with Facelets Tools will use this file extension. The following example configures both the Faces servlet and Facelets to use the **.jsf* extension, and enables rapid application development features.

```
<!-- Web application context parameters -->
<context-param>
   <param-name>javax.faces.DEFAULT_SUFFIX</param-name>
   <param-value>.jsf</param-value>
</context-param>
<context-param>
   <param-name>javax.faces.STATE_SAVING_METHOD</param-name>
   <param-value>client</param-value></context-param>
<context-param>
   <param-name>facelets.DEVELOPMENT</param-name>
   <param-value>true</param-value>
</context-param>
<context-param>
   <param-name>facelets.REFRESH_PERIOD</param-name>
   <param-value>1</param-value>
</context-param>
<context-param>
   <param-name>facelets.SKIP_COMMENTS</param-name>
   <param-value>false</param-value>
</context-param>
<context-param>
   <param-name>facelets.VIEW_MAPPINGS</param-name>
   <param-value>*.jsf</param-value>
</context-param>

<!-- Faces servlet mapping -->
<servlet-name>Faces Servlet</servlet-name>
   <servlet-class>javax.faces.webapp.FacesServlet</servlet-class>
   <load-on-startup>0</load-on-startup>
</servlet>
<servlet-mapping>
   <servlet-name>Faces Servlet</servlet-name>
   <url-pattern>*.jsf</url-pattern>
</servlet-mapping>
```

### 18.7.3 Composite View Design Patterns

Facelets is based on the Composite View Design (CVD) pattern. This means that sections of a page or even pages themselves can be reused by other pages. The Sun Java Blueprints Catalogue defines a composite view as follows:

"A Composite View is a view built using other reusable sub-views. A single change to a sub-view is automatically reflected in every composite view that uses it. Furthermore, the composite view manages the layout of its sub-views and can provide a template, making consistent look and feel easier to achieve and modify across the entire application."

### 18.7.4 XML Markup Languages

One of the best things about Facelets is that it allows you to bind pages written in any XML markup language, such as XHTML, WML, or even XML itself, to JSF UI components, managed beans, and message bundles. It is very flexible, and renders dynamic XML documents based on any XML schema or DTD.

This makes Facelets an ideal choice for multi-client Web applications that present the same content to multiple browser technologies, from Internet browsers to mobile phones to handheld devices.

### 18.7.5 JSFC Attribute Feature

Facelets Tools Professional includes comprehensive support for the Facelets JSFC attribute feature and ships with an updated version of the standard HTML tag library for Dreamweaver that contains JSFC attributes for specific tags, as well as enumerated values and other enhancements to Dreamweaver's Code Hints feature for Facelets. It also provides JSF data-bound property inspectors and tag chooser dialogs for these tags.

Facelets Tools Professional also includes a powerful Facelets XML formatter and a Dreamweaver menu command with keyboard shortcut to power-clean and beautify whitespace in Facelets XHTML documents.

Since JSFC attributes and values are case-sensitive, this menu command also checks for and corrects any tag and attribute case issues in your documents, saving you much time and frustration by ensuring that your JSF markup is valid.

## 18.8 JSF standard UI component tags / Facelets Tags

JSF is a UI framework, implying that, it not only provide some tags to create and customize UI components on the page, but also enables programmers to access these components in the code. Therefore, all the UI components have their corresponding component classes, which can be created and manipulated with the code to provide logical behavior to the components on the page. While discussing different HTML tags and core JSF tags, the corresponding component classes have been specified, such as; HtmlInputText, HtmlInputTextarea, HtmlCommandButton. All JSF standard components can be categorized into different families according to the base class they inherit and how they behave. Following table shows all the base component classes and subsequently explains them.

| Facelets Tag | Description |
|---|---|
| The <ui:component> tag | Similar to ui:composition except adds a new UIComponent as the root component in the UIComponents structure. |
| The <ui:composition> tag | Defines a composition of UIComponents. A composition may consist of multiple UIComponents. Text not within ui:composition tags is not compiled in a Facelets page. |
| The <ui:debug> tag | The UI Debug tag allows you to display helpful information about the JSF component tree and scoped variables in your browser when we test a JSF pages. |
| The <ui:decorate> tag | Similar to ui:composition except that text not within the ui:decorate tags is included in the Facelets page |

| | |
|---|---|
| The <ui:define> tag | Used in a Facelets page to add content with a template. |
| The <ui:fragment> tag | A nontrimming tag for ui:component, similar to the ui:decorate tag for ui:composition. |
| The <ui:include> tag | Includes a Facelets page that defines a composition or a component in a Facelets page or the template page. |
| The <ui:insert> tag | Used in a template to define the layout of Facelets pages that use the template for defining UIComponents. A template client adds UIComponents to a Facelets page with corresponding ui:define tags |
| The <ui:param> tag | Specifies a variable when a Facelets page is included within a template or a Facelets page. |
| The <ui:remove> tag | The UI Remove tag is used to specify tags or blocks of content that should be removed from your page by the Facelets view handler at compile time. |
| The <ui:repeat> tag | The UI Repeat tag is used to iterate over a collection of objects exposed to the JSF page as a value-binding EL expression. |

Let's discuss these UI components in detail.

**The <ui:component> tag**

The UI Component tag inserts a new UIComponent instance into the JSF component tree. Any components or content fragments outside this tag will be ignored by the Facelets view handler. Any components or content fragments within this tag will be added to the component tree as children of the UIComponent instance.

JSF example,

```
<!DOCTYPE html PUBLIC "-//W3C//DTD XHTML 1.0 Transitional//EN"
  "http://www.w3.org/TR/xhtml1/DTD/xhtml1-transitional.dtd">
<html xmlns="http://www.w3.org/1999/xhtml"
   xmlns:h="http://java.sun.com/jsf/html"
   xmlns:ui="http://java.sun.com/jsf/facelets">
<h:head />
<body>
Text before will be ignored.
<ui:component binding="#{myController.component}">
  <div>
    Hello World!
  </div>
</ui:component>
Text after will be ignored.
</body>
</html>
```

**The <ui:composition> tag**

The UI Composition tag is a templating tag that wraps content to be included in another Facelet. Any content outside of the UI Composition tag will be ignored by the Facelets view handler. Any content inside of the UI Composition tag will be included when another Facelets page includes the page containing this UI Composition tag.

JSF example,

```
<!DOCTYPE html PUBLIC "-//W3C//DTD XHTML 1.0 Transitional//EN"
  "http://www.w3.org/TR/xhtml1/DTD/xhtml1-transitional.dtd">
<html xmlns="http://www.w3.org/1999/xhtml"
   xmlns:h="http://java.sun.com/jsf/html"
   xmlns:ui="http://java.sun.com/jsf/facelets">
<h:head />
<body>
<ui:composition template="template.xhtml">
  <ui:define name="title">
    Welcome
  </ui:define>
  <ui:define name="header">
    Hello World
  </ui:define>
  <ui:define name="message">
    How are you today?
  </ui:define>
</ui:composition>
</body>
</html>
```

**The <ui:debug> tag**

The UI Debug tag allows you to display helpful information about the JSF component tree and scoped variables in your browser when we test a JSF pages. The hotkey attribute specifies a key combination (CTRL + SHIFT + D is the default value) to display the popup window containing the information. The UI Debug tag can be enabled or disabled by setting the rendered attribute.

JSF example,

```
<!DOCTYPE html PUBLIC "-//W3C//DTD XHTML 1.0 Transitional//EN"
  "http://www.w3.org/TR/xhtml1/DTD/xhtml1-transitional.dtd">
<html xmlns="http://www.w3.org/1999/xhtml"
   xmlns:h="http://java.sun.com/jsf/html"
   xmlns:ui="http://java.sun.com/jsf/facelets">
<h:head>
<title><ui:insert name="title" /></title>
</h:head>
<body>
<h2>
  <ui:insert name="header" />
```

```
</h2>
<ui:insert name="message" />
<ui:debug rendered="#{initParam['javax.faces.PROJECT_STAGE'] eq 'Development'}"
      hotkey="0" />
</body>
</html>
```

**The <ui:decorate> tag**

The UI Decorate tag is a templating tag that decorates content included from another Facelet. Any content outside of the UI Decorate tag will be displayed by the Facelets view handler. Any content within the decorate tag will be passed to the associated template as parameters or simply ignored. You can use nested ui:define tags to pass named content to the associated template.

JSF example,

```
<!DOCTYPE html PUBLIC "-//W3C//DTD XHTML 1.0 Transitional//EN"
  "http://www.w3.org/TR/xhtml1/DTD/xhtml1-transitional.dtd">
<html xmlns="http://www.w3.org/1999/xhtml"
   xmlns:h="http://java.sun.com/jsf/html"
   xmlns:ui="http://java.sun.com/jsf/facelets">
<h:head />
<body>
<h:form>
  Text before will stay.
  <ui:decorate template="decorate-template.xhtml">
    <ui:define name="title">Our Products</ui:define>
    <ui:define name="body">
      <ul>
        <li>Apples</li>
        <li>Oranges</li>
        <li>Bananas</li>
      </ul>
    </ui:define>
  </ui:decorate>
  Text after will stay.
</h:form>
</body>
</html>
```

**The <ui:define> tag**

The Define tag is a templating tag that defines named content to be inserted into a template. The name attribute value must match that of a ui:insert tag in the target template for the named content to be included.

JSF example,

```
<!DOCTYPE html PUBLIC "-//W3C//DTD XHTML 1.0 Transitional//EN"
  "http://www.w3.org/TR/xhtml1/DTD/xhtml1-transitional.dtd">
<html xmlns="http://www.w3.org/1999/xhtml"
   xmlns:h="http://java.sun.com/jsf/html"
```

```
    xmlns:ui="http://java.sun.com/jsf/facelets">
<h:head />
<body>
<h:form>
  <ui:composition template="template.xhtml">
    <ui:define name="header">Hello World!</ui:define>
  </ui:composition>
</h:form>
</body>
</html>
```

**The <ui:fragment> tag**

The UI Fragment tag inserts a new UIComponent instance into the JSF component tree. Any components or content fragments outside this tag will be included by the Facelets view handler. Any components or content fragments within this tag will be added to the component tree as children of this component instance. See also ui:component.

JSF example,

```
<!DOCTYPE html PUBLIC "-//W3C//DTD XHTML 1.0 Transitional//EN"
  "http://www.w3.org/TR/xhtml1/DTD/xhtml1-transitional.dtd">
<html xmlns="http://www.w3.org/1999/xhtml"
    xmlns:h="http://java.sun.com/jsf/html"
    xmlns:ui="http://java.sun.com/jsf/facelets">
<h:head />
<body>
<h:form>
  This text will be included.
  <ui:fragment binding="#{myController.component}">
    <div id="message">
      Hello World!
    </div>
  </ui:fragment>
  This text will be included.
</h:form>
</body>
</html>
```

**The <ui:include> tag**

The UI Include tag is a server-side include tag for Facelets. It simply includes the document pointed to by the "src" attribute as part of the current JSF page. The included document should use a component or composition tag to trim unnecessary markup, or it may simply contain a fragment of XHTML or XML to be included.

JSF example,

```
<!DOCTYPE html PUBLIC "-//W3C//DTD XHTML 1.0 Transitional//EN"
  "http://www.w3.org/TR/xhtml1/DTD/xhtml1-transitional.dtd">
<html xmlns="http://www.w3.org/1999/xhtml"
    xmlns:f="http://java.sun.com/jsf/core"
    xmlns:h="http://java.sun.com/jsf/html"
```

```
    xmlns:ui="http://java.sun.com/jsf/facelets">
<h:head />
<body>
<f:view>
   <h:form>
      <ui:include src="header.xhtml" />
      Body text here.
   </h:form>
</f:view>
</body>
</html>
```

**The <ui:insert> tag**

The UI Insert tag is a templating tag that declares a named content element to be defined by another Facelet. It can be used effectively with the ui:define tag to pass values between Facelets.

JSF example,

```
<!DOCTYPE html PUBLIC "-//W3C//DTD XHTML 1.0 Transitional//EN"
   "http://www.w3.org/TR/xhtml1/DTD/xhtml1-transitional.dtd">
<html xmlns="http://www.w3.org/1999/xhtml"
    xmlns:h="http://java.sun.com/jsf/html"
    xmlns:ui="http://java.sun.com/jsf/facelets">
<h:head>
<title><ui:insert name="title" /></title>
</h:head>
<body>
<h2><ui:insert name="header" /></h2>
<ui:insert name="message" />
</body>
</html>
```

**The <ui:param> tag**

The UI Param tag is used to pass objects as named variables between Facelets. The name attribute of the UI Param tag should match the name attribute of a ui:define tag contained in a ui:composition or ui:decorate in the template page receiving the object. The UI Param tag can also be used to pass objects to another page by using the ui:include tag.

JSF example,

```
<!DOCTYPE html PUBLIC "-//W3C//DTD XHTML 1.0 Transitional//EN"
          "http://www.w3.org/TR/xhtml1/DTD/xhtml1-transitional.dtd">
<html xmlns="http://www.w3.org/1999/xhtml"
    xmlns:h="http://java.sun.com/jsf/html"
    xmlns:ui="http://java.sun.com/jsf/facelets">
<h:head />
<body>
<h:form>
          <ui:include src="hello.xhtml">
                    <ui:param name="greeting" value="#{messageController.message}"/>
```

```
        </ui:include>
    </h:form>
    </body>
    </html>
```

**The <ui:remove> tag**

The UI Remove tag is used to specify tags or blocks of content that should be removed from your page by the Facelets view handler at compile time. This tag has no attributes. You can use this tag within the "jsfc" attribute to indicate that a particular tag should be removed from the rendered page.

JSF example,

```
<!DOCTYPE html PUBLIC "-//W3C//DTD XHTML 1.0 Transitional//EN"
  "http://www.w3.org/TR/xhtml1/DTD/xhtml1-transitional.dtd">
<html xmlns="http://www.w3.org/1999/xhtml"
    xmlns:h="http://java.sun.com/jsf/html"
    xmlns:ui="http://java.sun.com/jsf/facelets">
<h:head />
<body>
<h:form>
  This text will be displayed.
  <ui:remove>
    This text will be removed.
  </ui:remove>
  This text will be displayed.
</h:form>
</body>
</html>
```

**The <ui:repeat> tag**

The UI Repeat tag is used to iterate over a collection of objects exposed to the JSF page as a value-binding EL expression. It is intended as a replacement for the c:forEach tag from the JSTL Core tag library.

JSF example,

```
<!DOCTYPE html PUBLIC "-//W3C//DTD XHTML 1.0 Transitional//EN"
  "http://www.w3.org/TR/xhtml1/DTD/xhtml1-transitional.dtd">
<html xmlns="http://www.w3.org/1999/xhtml"
    xmlns:h="http://java.sun.com/jsf/html"
    xmlns:ui="http://java.sun.com/jsf/facelets">
<h:head />
<body>
<h:form>
  <ul>
    <ui:repeat value="#{productController.products}" var="product">
      <li><h:outputText value="#{product.name}" /></li>
    </ui:repeat>
  </ul>
</h:form>
</body>
</html>
```

## 18.9 Adding JSF pages

To create a JSF page in a web application, follow the steps shown in section 4.10. Add the required file types; such as JSF pages, JSF managed beans and configuration file.

## 18.10 Configuring JSF Applications

Configuring a web application involves addition of different mappings in the configuration files. In a JSF application, the basic configuration starts with updating deployment descriptors to support the framework. In addition, the JSF application has its own configuration file which helps implementing various features of the framework in the application. So, configuring a JSF application includes setting *deployment descriptor (web.xml)* and *setting the JSF configuration file (faces-config.xml)*.

### Setting web.xml

In a web application the web.xml file is the file that defines everything about the application that a server needs to know. Servlets and other components like filters or listeners, initialization parameters, container-managed security constraints, resources, welcome pages, etc are set here. In a JFS application we need to define in web.xml file the *javax.faces.webapp.FacesServlet*, which is the class responsible for handling JSF applications. FacesServlet is the central controller for the JSF application. It receives all requests for the JSF application and initializes the JSF components before the JSP is displayed. So, web.xml file has an entry that defines the FacesServlet. It is the servlet entry. It also has a servlet-mapping entry in order to map all requests whose URL ends with *.xhtml* to be handled by the servlet.

```
<?xml version="1.0" encoding="UTF-8"?>
<web-app xmlns:xsi="http://www.w3.org/2001/XMLSchema-instance"
xmlns="http://java.sun.com/xml/ns/javaee" xmlns:web="http://java.sun.com/xml/ns/javaee/web-
app_2_5.xsd"
xsi:schemaLocation="http://java.sun.com/xml/ns/javaee
http://java.sun.com/xml/ns/javaee/web-app_3_0.xsd"
id="WebApp_ID" version="3.0">
<display-name>jsfexample</display-name>
<servlet>
<servlet-name>faces</servlet-name>
<servlet-class>javax.faces.webapp.FacesServlet</servlet-class>
<load-on-startup>1</load-on-startup>
</servlet>
<servlet-mapping>
<servlet-name>faces</servlet-name>
<url-pattern>*.xhtml</url-pattern>
</servlet-mapping>
</web-app>
```

### Setting faces-config.xml

Similar to other web application frameworks, the JSF configuration file provides essential mapping for the application. The configuration details, such as navigation rules, managed beans and internationalization settings are provides in the faces-config.xml file. In addition, we can configure customized validators, converters and components in this file.

Let's discuss most commonly used element in the faces-config.xml file., such as <application>, <managed-bean>, <referenced-bean> and <navigation-rule>.

The <application> element is used to declare supported locales to specify the location of resource bundle, and to define default render kit and other pluggable components. The <managed-bean> element implements the managed bean creation facility and helps create and manage different beans in given scopes. The <navigation-rule> element is used to define navigation rules to be followed in the application.

```
<?xml version="1.0" encoding="UTF-8"?>
<faces-config version="2.2" xmlns="http://xmlns.jcp.org/xml/ns/javaee"
xmlns:xsi="http://www.w3.org/2001/XMLSchema-instance"
        xsi:schemaLocation="http://xmlns.jcp.org/xml/ns/javaee http://xmlns.jcp.org/xml/ns/javaee/web-
facesconfig_2_2.xsd">

        <application>
                <message-bundle>i18nFaces</message-bundle>
                <resource-bundle>
                        <base-name>i18n</base-name>
                        <var>i18n</var>
                </resource-bundle>
        </application>
        <lifecycle>
                <phase-listener>com.liferay.faces.util.lifecycle.DebugPhaseListener</phase-listener>
                <phase-listener>com.liferay.faces.util.lifecycle.ViewScopePhaseListener</phase-listener>
        </lifecycle>
        <navigation-rule>
                <from-view-id>/views/portletViewMode.xhtml</from-view-id>
                <navigation-case>
                        <from-outcome>success</from-outcome>
                        <to-view-id>/views/confirmation.xhtml</to-view-id>
                </navigation-case>
        </navigation-rule>
</faces-config>
```

JSF framework can support multiple configuration files that can be easily defined by setting javax.faces.CONFIG_FILES context parameter in the deployment descriptor, web.xml. However, the faces-config.xml file need not to be configured in web.xml as it is by default found at WEB-INF/faces-config.xml file and is loaded automatically. The faces-config.xml file is the location where we place most of the application configuration details. We may need additional configuration files only when we are working on a large application divided into different modules.

## 18.11 Developing a JSF application

After adding required JSF components into a web application, following steps shows how to create a web application containing managed bean, JSP files and configuration files.

**Step 1: Create package and managed bean**

Create a package j2ee.jsf.helloworld in the source folder and create a Java file UserBean.java. Copy following content into UserBean.java.

```
package j2ee.jsf.helloworld;

public class UserBean
{
        private int id;
```

```
        private String name;

        //Action method to add user
        public String addUser()
        {
                return "success";
        }
        public int getId()
        {
                return id;
        }
        public void setId(int id)
        {
                this.id = id;
        }
        public String getName()
        {
                return name;
        }
        public void setName(String name)
        {
                this.name = name;
        }
}
```

Above Java class is a User bean that we will use to store our user's information. This class acts like a form bean and action class. The addUser() method will get called when we click Add button on our Add User page.

**Step 2: Create JSP file**

Create two JSP files: AddUser.jsp and ListUser.jsp in WebContent folder. Copy following content in each of these files.

AddUser.jsp

```
<%@taglib uri="http://java.sun.com/jsf/core" prefix="f"%>
<%@taglib uri="http://java.sun.com/jsf/html" prefix="h"%>
<html>
<head>
  <title>Add New User Form</title>
</head>
<body>
<f:view>
    <p>
      <h:message id="errors" for="User_ID" style="color:red"/>
    </p>
  <h:form>
    <h:panelGrid border="1" columns="2">
      <h:outputText value="ID"></h:outputText>
      <h:inputText id="User_ID" value="#{userBean.id}" required="true">
        <f:validateLongRange minimum="1" maximum="500"/>
      </h:inputText>
```

```
        <h:outputText value="Name"></h:outputText>
        <h:inputText value="#{userBean.name}"></h:inputText>
        <h:commandButton action="#{userBean.addUser}"
          value="Add Customer"></h:commandButton>
      </h:panelGrid>
    </h:form>
</f:view>
</body>
</html>
```

We have added a validation rule for ID using f:validateLongRange tag and required="true" attribute. The ID must be in between 1 and 500.

ListUser.jsp

```
<%@taglib uri="http://java.sun.com/jsf/core" prefix="f"%>
<%@taglib uri="http://java.sun.com/jsf/html" prefix="h"%>
<html>
<head>
  <title>List of Users</title>
</head>
<body>
<f:view>
  <h:form>
    <h:outputText value="User #{userBean.name} is added successfully.">
    </h:outputText>
  </h:form>
</f:view>
</body>
</html>
```

**Step 3: Modify faces-config.xml file**

Open faces-config.xml from WebContent -> WEB-INF folder and copy following content into it.

```
<?xml version="1.0" encoding="UTF-8"?>
<faces-config xmlns="http://java.sun.com/xml/ns/javaee"
  xmlns:xsi="http://www.w3.org/2001/XMLSchema-instance"
  xsi:schemaLocation="http://java.sun.com/xml/ns/javaee http://java.sun.com/xml/ns/javaee/web-
facesconfig_1_2.xsd"
  version="1.2">
  <managed-bean>
    <managed-bean-name>userBean</managed-bean-name>
    <managed-bean-class>
      net.viralpatel.jsf.helloworld.UserBean
```

```
    </managed-bean-class>
    <managed-bean-scope>session</managed-bean-scope>
  </managed-bean>
  <navigation-rule>
    <display-name>AddUser</display-name>
    <from-view-id>/AddUser.jsp</from-view-id>
    <navigation-case>
      <from-outcome>success</from-outcome>
      <to-view-id>/ListUser.jsp</to-view-id>
    </navigation-case>
  </navigation-rule>
</faces-config>
```

In faces çonfig we have defined a managed bean UserBean with scope session and mapping from AddUser.jsp to ListUser.jsp.

**Step 4: Execute and run the project**

Final step is to execute the project and view it in browser. For this, right click on Project Name in Project Explorer -> Run As -> Run on Server.

*****

# Chapter 19

# Remote Method Invocation (RMI)

Earlier, in many previous chapters we have discussed that *Java has great control and monitoring over its objects*. It can prove by **synchronized block** in multithreaded programming. The RMI is another example that can prove the same.

Remote Method Invocation (RMI) allows a Java object that executes on one machine to invoke a method of a Java object that executes on another machine. This is an important feature, because it allows you to build distributed applications. While a complete discussion of RMI is outside the scope of this book, the following simplified sections and examples describe the basic principles involved in RMI.

## 19.1 Introduction to RMI

RMI (Remote Method Invocation) is a way that a programmer can write object-oriented program in which objects on different computers can interact in a distributed network using the Java programming language and development environment. RMI is the Java version of what is generally known as a **Remote Procedure Call (RPC)**, but with the ability to pass one or more objects along with the request. The object can include information that will change the service that is performed in the remote computer. Sun Microsystems, the inventors of Java, calls this "moving behavior." ***For example***, *when a user at a remote computer fills out an expense account, the Java program interacting with the user could communicate, using RMI, with a Java program in another computer that always had the latest policy about expense reporting. In reply, that program would send back an object and associated method information that would enable the remote computer program to screen the user's expense account data in a way that was consistent with the latest policy. The user and the company both would save time by catching mistakes early. Whenever the company policy changed, it would require a change to a program in only one computer.*

Sun calls its object parameter-passing mechanism object serialization. An RMI request is a request to invoke the method of a remote object. The request has the same syntax as a request to invoke an object method in the same (local) computer. In general, RMI is designed to preserve the object model and its advantages across a network.

RMI is implemented as three layers:

- A stub program in the client side of the client/server relationship, and a corresponding skeleton at the server end. The stub appears to the calling program to be the program being called for a service. (Sun uses the term proxy as a synonym for stub.)
- A Remote Reference Layer that can behave differently depending on the parameters passed by the calling program. For example, this layer can determine whether the request is to call a single remote service or multiple remote programs as in a multicast.
- A Transport Connection Layer, which sets up and manages the request.

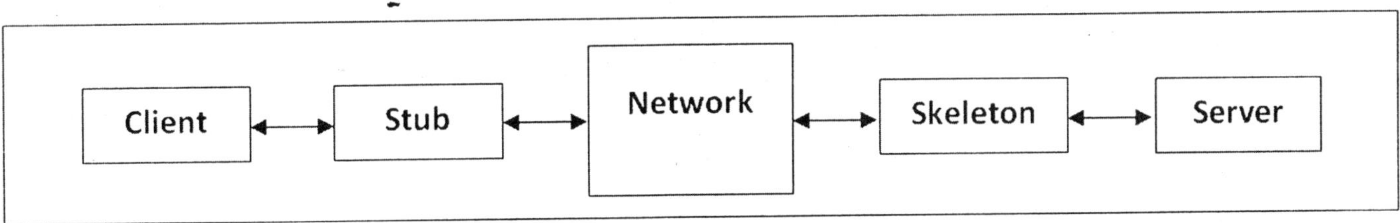


A single request travels down through the layers on one computer and up through the layers at the other end.

## 19.2 Serializable interface

Serializability of a class is enabled by implementing the *java.io.Serializable* interface. Classes that do not implement this interface will not have any of their state serialized or deserialized. All subtypes of a serializable class are themselves serializable. This interface is defined as:

```
public interface Serializable
```

The serialization interface has no methods or fields and serves only to identify the semantics of being serializable. To allow subtypes of non-serializable classes to be serialized, the subtype may assume responsibility for saving and restoring the state of the supertype's public, protected, and (if accessible) package fields. The subtype may assume this responsibility only if the class it extends has an accessible no-arg constructor to initialize the class's state. It is an error to declare a class Serializable if this is not the case. The error will be detected at runtime.

During deserialization, the fields of non-serializable classes will be initialized using the public or protected no-arg constructor of the class. A no-arg constructor must be accessible to the subclass that is serializable. The fields of serializable subclasses will be restored from the stream.

In many RMI applications, serialized objects are used to save its state and then on client side it needs to be serialized. The process of serialization and deserialization is frequently used. Hence it is necessary to understand the concept of Serializable interface.

Classes **ObjectInputStream** and **ObjectOutputStream** are high-level streams that contain the methods for serializing and deserializing an object.

The ObjectOutputStream class contains many write methods for writing various data types, but one method in particular is used often. It is:

```
public final void writeObject(Object x) throws IOException
```

The above method serializes an Object and sends it to the output stream. Similarly, the ObjectInputStream class contains the following method for deserializing an object:

```
public final Object readObject() throws IOException, ClassNotFoundException
```

This method retrieves the next Object out of the stream and deserializes it. The return value is Object, so you will need to cast it to its appropriate data type.

To demonstrate how serialization works in Java, I am going to use an **Employee** class.

```
public class Employee implements java.io.Serializable
{
        public String name;
        public String address;
        public transient int SSN;
        public int number;
        public void mailCheck( )
        {
                System.out.println("Mailing a check to " + name + " " + address);
        }
}
```

Notice that for a class to be serialized successfully, two conditions must be met:

- The class must implement the java.io.Serializable interface.
- All of the fields in the class must be serializable. If a field is not serializable, it must be marked transient.

If you are curious to know if a Java Standard Class is serializable or not, check the documentation for the class. The test is simple: If the class implements java.io.Serializable, then it is serializable; otherwise, it's not.

### 19.2.1 Serializing an object

The ObjectOutputStream class is used to serialize an Object. The following SerializeDemo program instantiates an Employee object and serializes it to a file.

When the program is done executing, a file named employee.ser is created. The program does not generate any output, but study the code and try to determine what the program is doing.

Note: When serializing an object to a file, the standard convention in Java is to give the file a .ser extension.

```
import java.io.*;
public class SerializeDemo
{
   public static void main(String ar[ ])
   {
     Employee e = new Employee( );
     e.name = "Ravi Majithia";
     e.address = "Aurangabad";
     e.SSN = 112233;
     e.number = 1010;
     try
     {
       FileOutputStream fileOut = new FileOutputStream("/tmp/employee.ser");
       ObjectOutputStream out = new ObjectOutputStream(fileOut);
       out.writeObject(e);
       out.close( );
       fileOut.close( );
       System.out.printf("Serialized data is saved in /tmp/employee.ser");
     }
     catch(IOException ioe)
     {
        ioe.printStackTrace( );
     }
   }
}
```

### 19.2.2 Deserializing an object

The following DeserializeDemo program deserializes the Employee object created in the above SerializeDemo program. Study the program and try to determine its output:

```
import java.io.*;
public class DeserializeDemo
{
  public static void main(String ar[ ])
  {
    Employee e = null;
    try
    {
      FileInputStream fileIn = new FileInputStream("/tmp/employee.ser");
      ObjectInputStream in = new ObjectInputStream(fileIn);
      e = (Employee) in.readObject( );
      in.close( );
      fileIn.close( );
    }
    catch(IOException ioe)
    {
      ioe.printStackTrace( );
      return;
    }catch(ClassNotFoundException c)
    {
      System.out.println("Employee class not found");
      c.printStackTrace( );
      return;
    }
    System.out.println("Deserialized Employee...");
    System.out.println("Name: " + e.name);
    System.out.println("Address: " + e.address);
    System.out.println("SSN: " + e.SSN);
    System.out.println("Number: " + e.number);
  }
}
```

This would produce the following result:

```
Deserialized Employee...
Name: Ravi Majithia
Address:Aurangabad
SSN: 0
Number:1010
```

Here are following important points to be noted:

- The try/catch block tries to catch a **ClassNotFoundException**, which is declared by the **readObject()** method. For a JVM to be able to deserialize an object, it must be able to find the bytecode for the class. If the JVM can't find a class during the deserialization of an object, it throws a **ClassNotFoundException**.
- Notice that the return value of **readObject( )** is cast to an Employee reference.

**Note: The value of the SSN field was 11122333 when the object was serialized, but because the field is transient, this value was not sent to the output stream. The SSN field of the deserialized Employee object is 0.**

## 19.3 RMI classes and interfaces

As now we know that RMI is the concept of writing an object-oriented program in which objects on different computers can interact in a distributed network using the Java programming language and development environment. During the Remote Programming following classes and interfaces are commonly necessary.

- java.rmi.Remote interface
- java.rmi.RemoteException class
- java.rmi.naming class class
- java.rmi.unicastremote class

**java.rmi.Remote interface**

The *Remote* interface serves to identify interfaces whose methods may be invoked from a non-local virtual machine. Any object that is a remote object must directly or indirectly implement this interface. Only those methods specified in a "remote interface", an interface that extends *java.rmi.Remote*, are available remotely.

This interface is defined as:

```
public interface Remote
```

Implementing classes can implement any number of remote interfaces and can extend other remote implementation classes also. RMI provides some other easy classes that remote object implementations can extend which also facilitates remote object creation. These classes are *java.rmi.server.UnicastRemoteObject* and *java.rmi.activation.Activatable.* For example,

```
public interface Hello extends Remote
{
        ...
        Declare remote methods here
        ...
}
```

As you can see here, interface *Hello* extending *Remote*. In this interface *Hello* we can declare user defined remote methods. But all those methods must throw *RemoteException.*

**java.rmi.RemoteException class**

The *RemoteException* is the common super-class for a number of communication related exceptions that may occur during the execution of a remote method call. As discussed above each method of a remote interface (above interface *Hello*), must throw *RemoteException*. This class is defined as:

```
public class RemoteException extends IOException
```

This exception class has two methods.

- Throwable getCause( ) : Returns the cause of the exception
- String getMessage( ) : Returns the detail message of exception

For example,

```
public interface Hello extends Remote
{
        String sayHello( ) throws RemoteException;
}
```

As you can see, above sayHello( ) method being part of a remote interface, must throw *RemoteException.*

### java.rmi.Naming class

The *Naming* class provides methods for storing and obtaining references to remote objects in a remote object registry. Each method of the Naming class takes as one of its arguments a name that is a String in URL format as:

*//host : port / name*

Here, *host* is the host (remote or local) where the registry is located; *port* is the port number on which the registry accepts calls, and where *name* is a simple string uninterpreted by the registry. Both *host* and *port* are optional. If *host* is omitted, the host defaults to the **local host**. If *port* is omitted, then the port defaults to **1099**.

This class is defined as:

```
public final class Naming extends Object
```

This class has total five methods. They are

| Method | Description |
|---|---|
| static void bind(String name, Remote obj) | Binds the specified name to a remote object. |
| static String[ ] list (String name) | Returns and array of names bound in the registry. |
| static Remote lookup(String name) | Returns a stub for the remote object associated with specified name |
| static void rebind(String name, Remote obj) | Rebinds the specified name to a new remote object. |
| static void unbind(String name) | Destroys the binding for the specified name that is associated with a remote object. |

### java.rmi.UnicastRemoteObject class

Used for exporting a remote object for obtaining a stub that communicates to the remote object. If the remote object is exported using the static *exportObject(Remote)* method of this class, then a stub class is loaded and an instance of that stub class gets constructed.

This class is defined as:

```
public class UnicastRemoteObject extends RemoteServer
```

This class has following important methods.

| Method | Description |
|---|---|
| Object clone( ) | Returns a clone of the remote object that is distinct from the original. |
| static RemoteStub exportObject(Remote obj) | Exports the remote object to make it available to receive incoming calls using an anonymous port. |
| static Remote exportObject(Remote obj, int port) | Exports the remote object to make it available to receive incoming calls, using the particular supplied port. |
| static Remote exportObject(Remote obj, int port, RMIClientSocketFactory csf, RMIServerSocketFactory ssf) | Exports the remote object to make it available to receive incoming calls, using a transport specified by the given socket factory. |
| static boolean unexportObject(Remote obj, boolean force) | Removes the remote object, obj, from the RMI runtime. |

Following sections has example programs that use classes and methods of above explained classes.

## 19.4 Programming a client

A remote object is an instance of a class that implements a Remote interface. A remote interface extends the interface java.rmi.Remote and declares a set of remote methods. Each remote method must throw java.rmi.RemoteException (or a superclass of RemoteException), in addition to any application-specific exceptions.

Here is the interface definition for the remote interface used in this example, example.hello.Hello. It declares just one method, sayHello, which returns a string to the caller:

```
package example.hello;
import java.rmi.Remote;
import java.rmi.RemoteException;
public interface Hello extends Remote
{
        String sayHello( ) throws RemoteException;
}
```

Remote method invocations can fail in many additional ways compared to local method invocations (such as network-related communication problems and server problems) and remote methods will report such failures by throwing a *java.rmi.RemoteException*.

## 19.5 Programming a server

A "server" class, in this context, is the class which has a main method that creates an instance of the remote object implementation, exports the remote object, and then binds that instance to a name in a Java RMI registry. The class that contains this main method could be the implementing class itself or another class entirely.

In this example, the main method for the server is defined in the class Server which also implements the remote interface Hello. The server's main method does the following:

- Create and export a remote object
- Register the remote object with a Java RMI registry

Here is the source code for the class Server. Descriptions for writing this server class follow the source code:

```
package example.hello;
import java.rmi.registry.Registry;
import java.rmi.registry.LocateRegistry;
import java.rmi.RemoteException;
import java.rmi.server.UnicastRemoteObject;
public class Serverr implements Hello
{
public Serverr( )
{ }
public String sayHello( ) throws RemoteException
{
        return "Hello, world!";
}
public static void main(String ar[ ])
{
        try
```

```
            {
                Serverr obj = new Serverr( );
                Hello stub = (Hello) UnicastRemoteObject.exportObject(obj, 0);

                // Bind the remote object's stub in the registry
                Registry registry = LocateRegistry.getRegistry( );
                registry.bind("Hello", stub);
                System.err.println("Server is ready");
            }
            catch(Exception e)
            {
                System.err.println("Server exception: " + e.toString( ));
                e.printStackTrace( );
            }
    }
}
```

The implementation class Server implements the remote interface Hello, providing an implementation for the remote method sayHello( ). The method sayHello( ) need to declare that it throws any exception because the method implementation itself throw *RemoteException*.

**Note: A class can define methods not specified in the remote interface, but those methods can only be invoked within the virtual machine running the service and cannot be invoked remotely.**

After you write these two programs compile both programs and execute the Serverr.java program and you will see the server saying "**Hello, world!**" as output.

May be above program will not create a great impression of RMI into your mind. But in these program only we have created a server and remote method to be executed from remote object to demonstrate different classes and methods of RMI.

Following section will show you another example and another way to understand, how exactly the RMI classes can be used for invoking remote methods using stub files.

## 19.6 Another example using stub files

This section provides step-by-step directions for building a simple client/server application by using RMI. The server receives a request from a client, processes it, and returns a result. In this example, the request specifies two numbers. The server adds these together and returns the sum.

- **Step 1: write source code**

Enter and Compile the Source Code This application uses four source files. The first file, *AddServerIntf.java*, de�nes the remote interface that is provided by the server. It contains one method that accepts two double arguments and returns their sum. All remote interfaces must extend the Remote interface, which is part of java.rmi.Remote de�nes no members. Its purpose is simply to indicate that an interface uses remote methods. All remote methods can throw *RemoteException*.

```
import java.rmi.*;
public interface AddServerIntf extends Remote
{
        double add(double d1, double d2) throws RemoteException;
}
```

The second source file, *AddServerImpl.java*, implements the remote interface. The implementation of the **add( )** method is straightforward. Remote objects typically extend **UnicastRemoteObject**, which provides functionality that is needed to make objects available from remote machines.

```
import java.rmi.*;
import java.rmi.server.*;
public class AddServerImpl extends UnicastRemoteObject implements AddServerIntf
{
        public AddServerImpl( ) throws RemoteException
        { }
        public double add(double d1, double d2) throws RemoteException
        {
                return d1 + d2;
        }
}
```

The third source file, *AddServer.java*, contains the main program for the server machine. Its *primary function is to update the RMI registry on that machine*. This is done by using the **rebind( )** method of the Naming class. That method associates name with an object reference. Note that the first argument to the **rebind( )** method is a string that names the server as "AddServer". Its second argument is a reference to an instance of AddServerImpl.

```
import java.net.*;
import java.rmi.*;
public class AddServer {
        public static void main(String ar[ ])
        {
                try
                {
                        AddServerImpl addServerImpl = new AddServerImpl( );
                        Naming.rebind("AddServer", addServerImpl);
                }
                catch(Exception e)
                {
                        System.out.println("Exception: " + e);
                }
        }
}
```

The fourth source file, *AddClient.java*, implements the client side of this distributed application. AddClient.java requires three command-line arguments.

- The first is the IP address or name of the server machine.
- The second and third arguments are the two numbers that are to be summed.

The application begins by forming a string that follows the URL syntax. This URL uses the RMI protocol. The string includes the IP address or name of the server and the string "AddServer". The program then invokes the **lookup( )** method of the Naming class. This method accepts the RMI URL, and returns a reference to an object of type AddServerIntf. All remote method invocations can then be directed to this object.

The program continues by displaying its arguments and then invokes the remote **add( )** method. The sum is returned from this method and is then printed.

```
import java.rmi.*;
public class AddClient
{
        public static void main(String ar[ ])
        {
                try
                {
                        String ServerURL = "rmi://" + args[0] + "/AddServer";

                        // creating connection and passing input IP
                        AddServerIntf addServerIntf = (AddServerIntf)Naming.lookup(ServerURL);

                        // accepting value into double variables
                        double d1 = Double.valueOf(args[1]).doubleValue( );
                        double d2 = Double.valueOf(args[2]).doubleValue( );

                        //displaying values
                        System.out.println("The first number is: " + d1);
                        System.out.println("The second number is: " + d2);

                        //calling and using remote add( ) method for sum
                        System.out.println("The sum is: " + addServerIntf.add(d1, d2));
                }
                catch(Exception e)
                {
                        System.out.println("Exception: " + e);
                }
        }
}
```

After you enter all the code, use *javac* to compile these four source file.

**Step 2: Manually Generate a Stub if Required**

In the context of RMI, a stub is a Java object that resides on the client machine. Its function is to present the same interfaces as the remote server. Remote method calls initiated by the client are actually directed to the stub. The stub works with the other parts of the RMI system to formulate a request that is sent to the remote machine.

A remote method may accept arguments that are simple types or objects. In the latter case, the object may have references to other objects. All of this information must be sent to the remote machine. That is, an object passed as an argument to a remote method call must be serialized and sent to the remote machine.

If a response must be returned to the client, the process works in reverse. Note that the serialization and deserialization facilities are also used if objects are returned to a client.

Prior to Java 5, stubs needed to be built manually by using *rmic* (one of the JDK tool). This step is not required for modern versions of Java. However, if you are working in a legacy environment, then you can use the rmic compiler, as shown here, to build a stub:

```
rmic AddServerImpl
```

This command generates the file *AddServerImpl_Stub.class*. When using rmic, be sure that CLASSPATH is set to include the current directory.

**Step 3: Install Files on the Client and Server Machines**

Copy

- AddClient.class
- AddServerImpl_Stub.class (if needed) and
- AddServerIntf.class

into a directory on the **client machine**.

Copy

- AddServerIntf.class
- AddServerImpl.class
- AddServerImpl_Stub.class (if needed) and
- AddServer.class

into a directory on the **server machine**

**Step 4: Start the RMI Registry on the Server Machine**

The JDK provides a program called RMI registry, which executes on the server machine. It maps names to object references. First of all, check that the CLASSPATH environment variable includes the directory in which your above copied files are located. Then, start the RMI Registry from the command line as:

```
start rmiregistry
```

When this command returns, you will see that a new window has been opened. You should keep this window open until you are done with the RMI example.

**Step 5: Start the Server**

The server code is started from the command line, as:

```
java AddServer
```

Here *AddServer* is the object name which gets registered above.

**Step 6: Start the Client**

The AddClient software requires three arguments: the name or IP address of the server machine and the two numbers that are to be summed together. You may invoke it from the command line by using one of the two formats shown here:

```
java AddClient  server1  8   9

java AddClient  11.12.13.14  8  9
```

In the first case, the server name is provided and in second case, IP address is provided.

You can try this example without actually having a remote server. To do so, simply install all of the programs on the same machine, start rmiregistry, start AddServer, and then execute AddClient using this command line:

```
java AddClient  127.0.0.1   8    9
```

Here, the address 127.0.0.1 is the "loop back" address for the local machine. Using this address allows you to exercise the entire RMI mechanism without actually having to install the server on a remote computer.

You execute this example with any of above two cases, you will get following output:

```
The first number is: 4.55
The second number is: 2.21
The sum is: 6.76
```

*****

# Part V
# Surplus to Java EE

- Java Collections Framework
- Java Naming and Directory Interface
- Java Security
- Java Design Patterns

# Chapter 20

# Java Collections Framework

Collections – sometimes called as containers – are Java's one of the most powerful and widely used sub-system. Collection is simply an object that groups multiple elements into a single unit. Collection is used to store, retrieve, manipulate and communicate collective data. Typically, they represent data items that are from a natural group such as a computer folder (a collection of different types of files), a mail box (a collection of letters) or a telephone directory (a mapping of names to numbers). If you are familiar with **.net framework** then for sure you are familiar with collections.

The collection is wide *group of classes and interfaces that support a broad range of functionality* and the collections framework is a *unified architecture for representing and manipulating collections*.

All these collections classes and interfaces are present in *java.util* package, along with many others. Following is the complete list of classes and interfaces, present under *java.util* package.

**classes under *java.util***

*AbstractCollection**
*AbstractList**
*AbstractMap*
*AbstractSequentialList**
*AbstractSet**
*ArrayList**
*Arrays*
*BitSet*
*Calendar*
*Collections*
*Currency*
*Date*
*Dictionary*
*EventListenerProxy*
*EventObject*
*GregorianCalendar*
*HashMap*
*HashSet**
*Hashtable*
*IdentityHashMap*
*LinkedHashMap*
*LinkedHashSet**
*LinkedList**
*ListResourceBundle*
*Locale*
*Observable*
*Properties*
*PropertyPermission*
*PropertyResourceBundle*
*Random*
*ResourceBundle*
*SimpleTimeZone*
*Stack*
*StringTokenizer*
*Timer*
*TimerTask*
*TimeZone*
*TreeMap*
*TreeSet**
*Vector*
*WeakHashMap*

<u>**interfaces under *java.util***</u>

| | | |
|---|---|---|
| *Collection** | *List** | *RandomAccess* |
| *Comparator* | *ListIterator* | *Set** |
| *Deque** | *Map* | *SortedMap* |
| *EventListener* | *Map.Entry* | *SortedSet** |
| *Enumeration* | *Observer* | |
| *Iterator* | *Queue** | |

**Note: The * marked classes and interfaces, belongs to collection framework.**

In addition to the collection interfaces, collections also use the *Comparator, Iterator, ListIterator* and *RandomAccess interfaces*, which are described in depth later in this chapter. Briefly speaking, **Comparator** defines how two objects are compared; **Iterator** and **ListIterator** enumerate the objects within a collection. By implementing **RandomAccess**, a list indicates that it supports efficient, random access to its elements.

## 20.1 Collections Framework overview

A collections framework is a unified architecture for representing and manipulating collections. All collections frameworks contain the following:

- **Interfaces**: Interfaces allow collections to be manipulated independently of the details of their representation.
- **Implementations**: These are the concrete implementations of the collection interfaces. Actually, they are reusable data structures.
- **Algorithms**: These are the methods that perform useful computations, such as searching and sorting, on objects that implement collection interfaces.

Apart from the Java Collections Framework, the best-known examples of collections frameworks are: the C++ Standard Template Library (STL) and Smalltalk's collection hierarchy. According to native languages, collections frameworks have been quite complex, which gave them a reputation for having a sharp learning curve.

In addition to collections, the framework defines several *map interfaces and classes. Maps* store key/value pairs. Although maps are not "collections" in the proper use of the term, they are fully integrated with collections. In the language of the collections framework, we can obtain a *collection-view* of a map. Such a view contains the elements from the map stored in a collection. Thus, we can process the contents of a map as a collection, if you choose.

In addition to collections, the framework also defines several map interfaces and classes which stores key/value pairs. In actual, maps are not collections, but they are designed in such a way that, they can be fully integrated with collections. The actual use of map is to obtain a collection-view.

The collections framework was mainly designed to meet several goals, which are discussed in following section.

## 20.2 Benefits of Java Collection Framework

The Java Collections Framework provides the following benefits:

- **Reduces programming effort**: By providing useful data structures and algorithms, the Collections Framework frees you to concentrate on the important parts of your program rather than on the low-level "plumbing" required to make it work. By facilitating interoperability among unrelated APIs, the Java Collections Framework frees you from writing adapter objects or conversion code to connect APIs.
- **Increases program speed and quality**: This Collections Framework provides high-performance, high-quality

implementations of useful data structures and algorithms. The various implementations of each interface are interchangeable, so programs can be easily tuned by switching collection implementations. Because you're freed from the drudgery of writing your own data structures, you'll have more time to devote to improving programs' quality and performance.

- **Allows interoperability among unrelated APIs**: The collection interfaces are the vernacular by which APIs pass collections back and forth. If my network administration API furnishes a collection of node names and if your GUI toolkit expects a collection of column headings, our APIs will interoperate seamlessly, even though they were written independently.
- **Reduces effort to learn and to use new APIs**: Many APIs naturally take collections on input and furnish them as output. In the past, each such API had a small sub-API devoted to manipulating its collections. There was little consistency among these ad hoc collections sub-APIs, so you had to learn each one from scratch, and it was easy to make mistakes when using them. With the advent of standard collection interfaces, the problem went away.
- **Reduces effort to design new APIs**: This is the flip side of the previous advantage. Designers and implementers don't have to reinvent the wheel each time they create an API that relies on collections; instead, they can use standard collection interfaces.
- **Fosters software reuse**: New data structures that conform to the standard collection interfaces are by nature reusable. The same goes for new algorithms that operate on objects that implement these interfaces.

## 20.3 The Collections Framework interfaces

The core collections framework interfaces encapsulate different types of collections, which are shown in the figure below. These interfaces allow collections to be manipulated independently of the details of their representation. As we can see in the following figure, the collection interface is the foundation interface, upon which the collections framework is built.

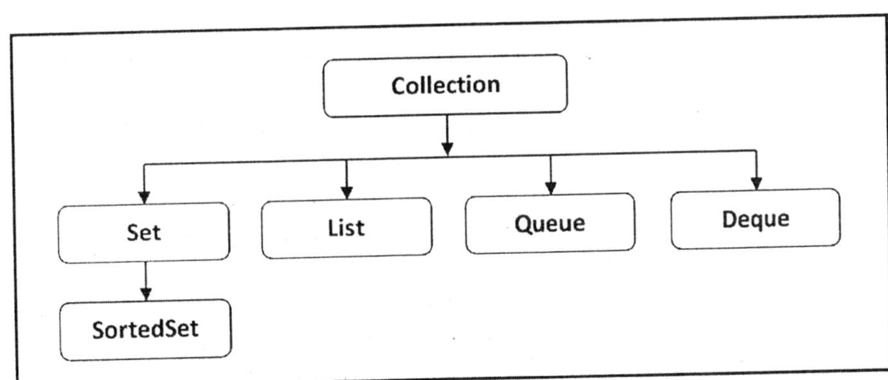


Let's enlist these interfaces with a small description on them.

| **Interface** | **Description** |
|---|---|
| *Collection* | Enables you to work with groups of objects; it is at the top of the collections hierarchy |
| *List* | Extends Collection to handle sequences (lists of objects) |
| *Set* | Extends Collection to handle sets, which must contain unique elements |
| *SortedSet* | Extends Set to handle sorted sets |
| *Queue* | Extends Collection to hold multiple elements prior to processing and can be used to order elements in a FIFO manner. |
| *Deque* | Extends Collection to hold multiple elements prior to processing and can be used to order elements in both, FIFO and LIFO, manner. |

**Note that all the core collection interfaces are generic**. For example, see the declaration of the Collection interface.

*public interface Collection<E>...*

The <E> syntax tells that the interface is generic. When we declare a Collection instance we should specify the type of object contained in the collection. Specifying the type allows the compiler to verify the type of object we put into the collection is correct, thus reducing errors at runtime.

At the end of this chapter, you will know most of what there is to know about the Java Collections Framework. This chapter discusses general guidelines for effective use of the interfaces, including when to use which interface.

## 20.3.1 Collection interface

This is the root interface in the Collections Framework hierarchy. A collection represents a group of objects, known as its elements. Some collections allow duplicate elements and others do not, some are ordered and others unordered. This interface is typically used to pass collections around and manipulate them where maximum simplification is required.

**Note: The JDK does not provide any direct implementations of this interface; whereas, it provides implementations of *Set* and *List*.**

This interface is defined as:

*public interface Collection<E> extends Iterable<E>*

Here, <E> tells that the interface is generic. Following table explains the methods concerned with this interface.

| Method | Description |
|---|---|
| boolean add(Object *obj*) | Adds *obj* to the invoking collection. Returns **true** if *obj* was added to the collection. Returns **false** if *obj* is already a member of the collection, or if the collection does not allow duplicates. |
| boolean addAll(Collection *c*) | Adds all the elements of c to the invoking collection. Returns true if the operation succeeded (i.e., the elements were added). Otherwise, returns false. |
| void clear( ) | Removes all of the elements from invoking collection. |
| boolean contains(Object *obj*) | Returns **true** if *obj* is an element of the invoking collection. Otherwise, returns **false**. |
| boolean containsAll(Collection *c*) | Returns **true** if the invoking collection contains all elements of *c*. Otherwise, returns **false**. |
| boolean equals(Object *obj*) | Returns **true** if the invoking collection and *obj* are equal. Otherwise, returns **false**. |
| int hashCode() | Returns the hash code value for invoking collection. |
| boolean isEmpty( ) | Returns **true** if the invoking collection is empty. Otherwise, returns **false**. |
| Iterator iterator() | Returns an iterator for the invoking collection. |
| boolean remove(Object *obj*) | Removes one instance of *obj* from the invoking collection. Returns **true** if the element was removed. Otherwise, returns **false**. |
| boolean removeAll(Collection c) | Removes all elements of *c* from the invoking collection. Returns **true** if the collection changed (i.e., elements were removed). Otherwise, returns **false**. |
| boolean retainAll(Collection *c*) | Removes all elements from the invoking collection except those in c. Returns **true** if the collection changed (i.e., elements were removed). Otherwise, returns **false**. |

| | |
|---|---|
| int size( ) | Returns the number of elements in invoking collection. |
| Object[ ] toArray( ) | Returns an array that contains all the elements stored in the invoking collection. The array elements are copies of the collection elements. |

Several of these methods can throw an **UnsupportedOperationException** or **ClassCastException**. A *UnsupportedOperationException* is generated if a collection cannot be modified and a *ClassCastException* is generated when one object is incompatible with another, such as when an attempt is made to add an incompatible object to a collection.

Above table, contains description of all important methods of Collection interface. A few of them are: **add( ), addAll( ), clear( ), remove( ), removeAll( ), retainAll( ),** and **toArray( ).**

To perform many collection related operations, we need to traverse through it. There are three ways to traverse collections:

- Using aggregate operations
- With the for-each construct and
- By using Iterators

Let's study them in short.

- **Using aggregate operations**

The preferred method of iterating over a collection is to obtain a stream and perform aggregate operations on it. Aggregate operations are often used in combination with lambda expressions to make programming more expressive, using less lines of code. The following code sequentially iterates through a collection of shapes and prints out the red objects:

```
myShapesCollection.stream( )
.filter(e -> e.getColor( ) == Color.RED)
.forEach(e -> System.out.println(e.getName( )));
```

- **With the for-each construct and**

The for-each construct allows to concisely traverse a collection or array using a for loop. The following code uses the *for-each construct* to print out each element of a collection on a separate line.

```
for(Object o : collection)
System.out.println(o);
```

- **By using Iterators**

An Iterator is an object that enables to traverse through a collection and to remove elements from the collection selectively, if desired. We get an Iterator for a collection by calling its iterator method. The following is the Iterator interface.

```
public interface Iterator<E>
{
boolean hasNext( );
E next( );
void remove( ); //optional
}
```

The *hasNext( )* method returns true if the iteration has more elements, and the *next( )* method returns the next element in the iteration. The *remove( )* method removes the last element that was returned by next from the underlying Collection. The *remove( )* method may be called only once per call to next and throws an exception if this rule is violated.

We will study the Iterator in detail later in this chapter.

## 20.3.2 List interface

List is an ordered collection. The user of this interface has precise control over where in the list each element is inserted. The user can access elements by their integer index, and search for elements in the list.

The List interface extends Collection and declares the behavior of a collection that stores a sequence of elements. See the following signature.

*public interface List<E> extends Collection<E>*

Here, <E> tells that the interface is generic.

Elements can be inserted or accessed by their position in the list, using a zero-based index. A list may contain duplicate elements. As it derives Collection interface, along with the methods of Collection interface, it also defines its own methods. Following table lists the methods of *List interface*.

| Method | Description |
|---|---|
| boolean add(Object *obj*) | Adds specified *obj* at the end of list. Returns **true** if inserted and returns **false** otherwise. |
| boolean add(int *index*, Object *obj*) | Inserts *obj* into the invoking list at the index passed in *index*. Any preexisting elements at or beyond the point of insertion are shifted up. Thus, no elements are overwritten. Returns **true** if the invoking list changes and returns **false** otherwise. |
| boolean addAll(int *index*, Collection *c*) | Inserts all elements of *c* into the invoking list at the index passed in *index*. Any preexisting elements at or beyond the point of insertion are shifted up. Thus, no elements are overwritten. Returns **true** if the invoking list changes and returns **false** otherwise. |
| Object get(int *index*) | Returns the object stored at the specified *index* within the invoking collection. |
| int indexOf(Object *obj*) | Returns the index of the first instance of *obj* in the invoking list. If *obj* is not an element of the list, –1 is returned. |
| int lastIndexOf(Object *obj*) | Returns the index of the last instance of *obj* in the invoking list. If *obj* is not an element of the list, –1 is returned. |
| ListIterator listIterator( ) | Returns an iterator to the start of the invoking list. |
| ListIterator listIterator(int *index*) | Returns an iterator to the invoking list that begins at the specified *index*. |
| Object remove(int *index*) | Removes the element at position index from the invoking list and returns the deleted element. And the indexes of successive elements are decremented by one. |
| Object set(int *index*, Object *obj*) | Assigns *obj* to the location specified by *index* within the invoking list. |
| List subList(int *start*, int *end*) | Returns a list that includes elements from start to end–1 in the invoking list. |
| boolean equals(Object *obj*) | Compares the specified object with this list for equality. |

| | |
|---|---|
| int hashCode( ) | Returns the hash code value for this list. |
| boolean isEmpty( ) | Returns **true** if this list contains no elements. |
| boolean removeAll(Collection c) | Removes from this list all of its elements that are contained in the specified collection. |
| Iterator<?> iterator( ) | Returns an iterator over the elements in this list in proper sequence. |
| int size( ) | Returns the number of elements in invoking list. |
| Object[ ] toArray( ) | Returns an array containing all of the elements in this list in proper sequence |

Several of these methods throws *UnsupportedOperationException* and *ClassCastException.* The if the ***UnsupportedOperationException*** will be throws if collection cannot be modified, and ***ClassCastException*** will be thrown when one object is incompatible with another, such as when an attempt is made to add an incompatible object to a collection.

The List interface provides four methods for positional (indexed) access to list elements. These methods are **add( ), addAll( ), get( ), set( )** and **subList( )**.

The List interface provides a special iterator, called a *ListIterator* that allows element insertion and replacement, and bidirectional access in addition to the normal operations that the Iterator interface provides. A method, **ListIterator( )** is provided to obtain a list iterator that starts at a specified position in the list.

The Java platform contains two general-purpose classes for List implementations: **ArrayList class**, which is usually the better-performing implementation and **LinkedList class**, which offers better performance under certain circumstances. These classes are described in following sections 20.4.4 and 20.4.5.

## 20.3.3 Set interface

As implied by its name, this interface models the mathematical set abstraction and does not allow duplicate elements. It extends Collection and declares the behavior of a collection that does not allow duplicate elements. The signature of this interface is

*public interface Set<E> extends Collection<E>*

Here, <E> tells that the interface is generic.

As it derives *Collection* interface, it uses the methods of *Collection* interface, but does not define any additional methods of its own. Hence, while studying *Collection* methods, also study them by keeping *Set* interface in mind.

The Set interface is derived into SortedSet interface. Hence, this creates a multilevel legacy. *The Set extends Collection and the SortedSet extends Set*. Therefore, all the methods of *Collection* are also available to *SortedSet*. The SortedSet interface is explained in next section with methods. Refer following example and output for more clear view about *Set*.

```
import java.util.Iterator;
import java.util.Set;
import java.util.TreeSet;
public class SetInterface
{
 public static void main(String args[])
  {
        Set s=new TreeSet();
        s.add(10);
        s.add(30);
```

```
        s.add(98);
        s.add(80);
        s.add(10); //duplicate value
        s.add(99);
        Iterator it=s.iterator( );
        while(it.hasNext( ))
        {
            System.out.println(it.next( ));
        }
        System.out.println("Size of Set is =  "+s.size( ));
        System.out.println("set is empty = "+s.isEmpty( ));
    }
}
```

Output of above program will be:

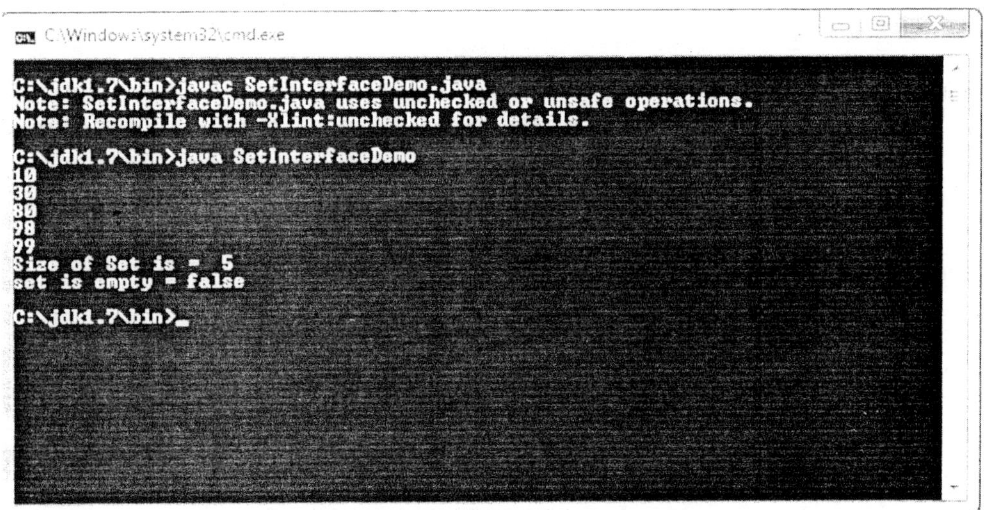


### 20.3.4 SortedSet interface

The SortedSet interface extends Set and declares the behavior of a set sorted in ascending order by default. Refer the following signature.

*public interface SortedSet<E> extends Set<E>*

We know that *Set* does not define any concrete method, but the *SortedSet* interface declares the methods summarized in following table.

| Method | Description |
|---|---|
| Comparator comparator( ) | Returns the invoking sorted set's comparator. If the natural ordering is used for this set, null is returned. |
| Object first( ) | Returns the first element in the invoking sorted set. |
| SortedSet headSet(Object *end*) | Returns a SortedSet containing those elements less than *end* that are contained in the invoking sorted set. |
| Object last( ) | Returns the last element in the invoking sorted set. |
| SortedSet subSet(Object *start*,Object *end*) | Returns a SortedSet that includes those elements between start and end –1. |
| SortedSet tailSet(Object *start*) | Returns a SortedSet that contains those elements greater than or equal to *start* that are contained in the sorted set. |

Several methods throws *NoSuchElementException,* when no items are contained in the invoking set and ***ClassCastException***, when an object is incompatible with the elements in a set. A ***NullPointerException*** is also sometimes thrown if an attempt is made to use a null object and null is not allowed in the set.

By studying above table we can find that there are several important *SortedSet* methods. Such as: **first( ), last( ), subset( ), headSet( )** and **tailSet( )**.

After studying this, if you found *SortedSet* as an important Collection Framework member then remember that this SortedSet also has its derived interface, which is **NavigableSet interface**. Its signature is:

*public interface NavigableSet<E> extends SortedSet<E>*

This interface also contains many concrete methods for comparison and sorting purposes. such as: **lower(Element *ele*)** returns elements less then specified *ele*, **floor(Element *ele*)** returns elements less than or equal to specified *ele*, **ceiling(Element ele)** returns elements greater than or equals to specified *ele*, and **higher(Element *ele*)** returns elements greater than specified *ele*.

### 20.3.5 Queue interface

A Queue interface is specially defined for holding elements earlier to processing. Following is the signature of this interface.

*public interface Queue<E> extends Collection<E>*

Along with all Collection operations, queue also provides additional operations such as insertion, removing, and searching operations. These operational methods are defined with two types of signatures, one is with exception handling mechanism and another is without exception handling mechanism. See following table.

| Operation | By throwing exception | Without throwing exception |
|---|---|---|
| *Insert* | *add(obj)* | *offer(obj)* |
| *Remove* | *remove( )* | *poll( )* |
| *Examine* | *element( )* | *peek( )* |

Following table shows the methods of Queue interface.

| Method | Description |
|---|---|
| boolean add(Object *obj*) throws *IllegalStateException* | Inserts the specified element into this queue if it is possible to do so immediately without violating capacity restrictions, returning true upon success and throwing an *IllegalStateException* if no space is currently available. |
| Object element( ) | Retrieves, but does not remove, the head of this queue. |
| boolean offer(Object *obj*) | Inserts the specified element into this queue if it is possible to do so immediately without violating capacity restrictions. |
| Object peek( ) | Retrieves, but does not remove, the head of this queue, or returns null if this queue is empty. |
| Object poll( ) | Retrieves and removes the head of this queue, or returns null if this queue is empty. |
| Object remove( ) | Retrieves and removes the head of this queue. |

Refer following program that demonstrates some of the basic methods of Queue.

```
import java.util.LinkedList;
import java.util.Queue;

public class QueueDemo
{
        public static void main(String ar[ ])
        {
                Queue queue = new LinkedList();
                queue.add("one");
                queue.add("two");
                queue.offer("three");
                queue.offer("four");
                System.out.println("Queue contains : \n" + queue);
                System.out.println("\nremove: " + queue.remove( ));
                System.out.println("\nelement: " + queue.element( ));
                System.out.println("\npoll: " + queue.poll( ));
                System.out.println("\npeek: " + queue.peek( ));
                System.out.println("\nNow Queue contains : \n" + queue);
```

See following output.

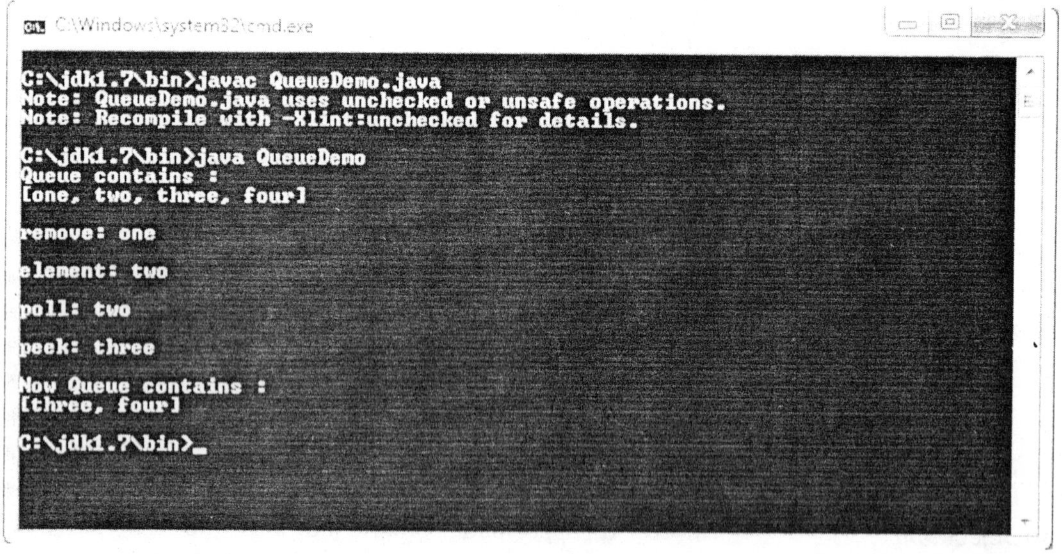

```
C:\Windows\system32\cmd.exe

C:\jdk1.7\bin>javac QueueDemo.java
Note: QueueDemo.java uses unchecked or unsafe operations.
Note: Recompile with -Xlint:unchecked for details.

C:\jdk1.7\bin>java QueueDemo
Queue contains :
[one, two, three, four]

remove: one

element: two

poll: two

peek: three

Now Queue contains :
[three, four]

C:\jdk1.7\bin>_
```

### 20.3.6 Deque interface

The Deque is the derived interface, extending Queue. The Deque provides a linear collection of elements that supports the insertion and removal operations at both ends. The Deque is the short form of "Double Ended Queue". As it is known that a Queue provides a dynamic sized list of elements, but this interface allows both, i.e. capacity-restricted Deque and dynamic sized Deque.

The signature of this interface is:

```
public interface Deque<E> extends Queue<E>
```

This interface defines the methods that help to perform insertion and removal from both the ends. Like we did in above section, following table summarize the Deque methods with and without exception.

**Methods that works on first element (Front)**

| Operation | By throwing exception | Without throwing exception |
|---|---|---|
| Insert | addFirst(*obj*) | offerFirst(*obj*) |
| Remove | removeFirst( ) | pollFirst( ) |
| Verify | getFirst( ) | peekFirst( ) |

**Methods that works for last element (Rear)**

| Operation | By throwing exception | Without throwing exception |
|---|---|---|
| Insert | addLast(*obj*) | offerLast(*obj*) |
| Remove | removeLast( ) | pollLast( ) |
| Verify | getLast( ) | peekLast( ) |

Following table explains the methods supported by Deque interface.

| Method | Description |
|---|---|
| void addFirst(Object obj) | Inserts the specified element at the front of this Deque. If it is possible to do so immediately throws *IllegalStateException*. |
| void addLast(Object obj) | Inserts the specified element at the end of this Deque. If it is possible to do so immediately throws *IllegalStateException*. |
| boolean offerFirst(Object *obj*) | Inserts the specified element at the front of this Deque unless it would violate capacity restrictions. |
| boolean offerLast(Object *obj*) | Inserts the specified element at the end of this Deque unless it would violate capacity restrictions. |
| Object pollFirst( ) | Retrieves and removes the first element of this Deque, or returns null if this Deque is empty. |
| Object pollLast() | Retrieves and removes the last element of this Deque, or returns null if this Deque is empty. |
| Object removeFirst( ) | Retrieves and removes the first element of this Deque. |
| Object removeLast( ) | Retrieves and removes the last element of this Deque. |
| Object getFirst( ) | Retrieves, but does not remove, the first element of this Deque. |
| object getLast( ) | Retrieves, but does not remove, the last element of this Deque. |
| OBject peekFirst( ) | Retrieves, but does not remove, the first element of this Deque, or returns null if this Deque is empty. |
| Object peekLast( ) | Retrieves, but does not remove, the last element of this Deque, or returns null if this Deque is empty. |
| int size( ) | Returns the number of elements in this Deque. |

Note: Deque implementations are not strictly required to prohibit the insertion of null elements, they are strongly encouraged to do so. It means, a user can insert *null*.

```
import java.util.Deque;
import java.util.LinkedList;
```

```
class DequeDemo
{
	public static void main(String ar[ ])
	{
		Deque deque=new LinkedList( );

		//Adding element to the Deque
		deque.add("This");
		deque.offer("test");
		deque.offerFirst("Hello");
		deque.addLast("Java");
		deque.offer(11);
		System.out.println("size of deque : "+deque.size());
		System.out.println("Elements in deque: "+deque);

		//Deleting element from deque
		deque.remove();
		deque.pollFirst();
		System.out.println("size of deque : "+deque.size());
		System.out.println("Elements in deque: "+deque);
		System.out.println("Last element in deque: "+deque.peekLast());
		System.out.println("Top element of deque : "+deque.element());
	}
}
```

Output of above program will be:

```
C:\Windows\system32\cmd.exe

C:\jdk1.7\bin>javac DequeDemo.java
Note: DequeDemo.java uses unchecked or unsafe operations.
Note: Recompile with -Xlint:unchecked for details.

C:\jdk1.7\bin>java DequeDemo
size of deque : 5
Elements in deque: [Hello, This, test, Java, 11]
size of deque : 3
Elements in deque: [test, Java, 11]
Last element in deque: 11
Top element of deque : test

C:\jdk1.7\bin>_
```

## 20.4 The Collections Framework classes

At this stage, we are now familiar with Collection interfaces. Now this is the time to study the core collections framework classes. Some of the collection classes are abstract and some are not. Most importantly noticeable point is that, these collection classes do not support synchronization, but we can manually achieve synchronization in it. Following is the list of collection classes with a small verdict talk on it.

| Class | Description |
|---|---|
| *AbstractCollection* | *Implements most of the Collection interface* |
| *AbstractList* | *Extends AbstractCollection and implements most of the List interface* |
| *AbstractSequentialList* | *Extends AbstractList for use by a collection that uses sequential rather than random access of its elements* |
| *LinkedList* | *Implements a linked list by extending AbstractSequentialList* |
| *ArrayList* | *Implements a dynamic array by extending AbstractList* |
| *AbstractSet* | *Extends AbstractCollection and implements most of the Set interface* |
| *HashSet* | *Extends AbstractSet for use with a hash table* |
| *LinkedHashSet* | *Extends HashSet to allow insertion-order iterations* |
| *TreeSet* | *Implements a set stored in a tree. Extends AbstractSet* |

Along with these classes, the *java.util* package provides some more important classes **Vector**, **Stack** and **Hashtable.** These have been reengineered specially for the purpose of supporting above collection classes. Following sub-section explains above listed collection classes.

### 20.4.1 AbstractCollection class

This abstract class by default *provides a non-changeable collection*. A programmer who wants to use a non-changeable collection, simply need to extend this class. This class implements Collection interface which provide implementations permission for the iterator and size methods. Following is the signature of this class.

*public abstract class AbstractCollection<E> extends Object implements Collection<E>*

In case if a programmer wants changeable (variable) collection, then additionally programmer has to override Collection interface's **add( )** method in this class. Otherwise the program will throw UnsupportedOperationException. Following table shows the methods of this class.

| Method | Description |
|---|---|
| boolean add(Object *obj*) | Ensures that this collection contains the specified element. |
| boolean addAll(Collection *c*) | Adds all of the elements in the specified collection to this collection. |
| void clear( ) | Removes all of the elements from this collection. |
| boolean contains(Object *obj*) | Returns true if this collection contains the specified element. |
| boolean containsAll(Collection *c*) | Returns true if this collection contains all of the elements in the specified collection. |
| boolean isEmpty( ) | Returns true if this collection contains no elements. |
| abstract Iterator iterator( ) | Returns an iterator over the elements contained in this collection. |
| boolean remove(Object *obj*) | Removes a single instance of the specified element from this collection, if it is present. |
| boolean removeAll(Collection *c*) | Removes all of this collection's elements that are also contained in the specified collection. |
| boolean retainAll(Collection *c*) | Retains only the elements in this collection that are contained in the |

| | |
|---|---|
| | specified collection. |
| abstract int size( ) | Returns the number of elements in this collection. |
| Object[ ] toArray( ) | Returns an array containing all of the elements in this collection. |
| String toString( ) | Returns a string representation of this collection. |

### 20.4.2 AbstractList class

This abstract class implements List interface to minimize the efforts required to provide a *random access* data, like an array. The signature of this class is:

*public abstract class AbstractList<E> extends AbstractCollection<E> implements List<E>*

To implement an non-changeable list, the programmer needs only to extend this class and provide implementations for the **get( )** and **size( )** methods.

To implement a changeable (variable) list, the programmer must additionally override the **set( )** method, otherwise throws an *UnsupportedOperationException*. The following table shows the methods of this class.

| Method | Description |
|---|---|
| boolean add(Object *obj*) | Appends the specified *obj* to the end of this list. |
| void add(int *index*, Object *obj*) | Inserts the specified *obj* at the specified *index* in this list. |
| boolean addAll(int *index*, Collection *c*) | Inserts all of the elements of Collection *c* into this list at the specified *index*. |
| void clear( ) | Removes all of the elements from this list. |
| boolean equals(Object *obj*) | Compares the specified *obj* with this list for equality. |
| abstract Object get(int *index*) | Returns the element at the specified *index* in this list. |
| int hashCode( ) | Returns the hash code value for this list. |
| int indexOf(Object *obj*) | Returns the index of the first occurrence of the specified *obj* in this list, or -1 if this list does not contain the element. |
| Iterator iterator( ) | Returns an iterator over the elements in this list in proper sequence. |
| int lastIndexOf(Object *obj*) | Returns the index of the last occurrence of the specified *obj* in this list, or -1 if this list does not contain the element. |
| ListIterator listIterator( ) | Returns a list iterator over the elements in this list. |
| ListIterator listIterator(int *index*) | Returns a list iterator over the elements in this list, starting at the specified position in the list. |
| Object remove(int *index*) | Removes the element at the specified *index* in this list. |
| void removeRange(int *start*, int *end*) | Removes from this list all of the elements whose index is *start* to *end*-1. |
| Object set(int *index*, Object *obj*) | Replaces the *obj* at the specified *index* in this list with the specified *obj*. |
| List subList(int *start*, int *end*) | Returns a view of the portion of this list between the specified *start* to *end*-1 |

We can see that, all the methods that are available in AbstractCollection and List are also available in this class.

### 20.4.3 AbstractSequentialList class

For sequential access data (such as a linked list), AbstractSequentialList should be used in preference to this class.

This *abstract* class extends *AbstractList* to minimize the efforts required to provide a *sequential access data*, like a linked list. The signature of this class is:

*public abstract class AbstractSequentialList<E> extends AbstractList<E>*

To obtain an implementation of list the programmer needs only to extend this class and provide implementations for the **ListIterator( )** and **size( )** methods.

For an non-changeable list, the programmer need only implement the list iterator's hasNext( ), next( ), hasPrevious( ), previous( ) and index( ) methods.

For a changeable list the programmer should additionally implement the list iterator's set( ) method.

Following table shows the methods of AbstractSequentialList class.

| Method | Description |
|---|---|
| void add(int index, Object *obj*) | Inserts the specified *obj* at the specified *index* in this list. |
| boolean addAll(int index, Collection *c*) | Inserts all of the elements in the specified collection into this list at the specified *index*. |
| Object get(int *index*) | Returns the element at the specified *index* in this list. |
| Iterator iterator( ) | Returns an iterator over the elements in this list. |
| abstract ListIterator listIterator(int *index*) | Returns a list iterator over the elements in this list. |
| Object remove(int *index*) | Removes the element at the specified *index* in this list. |
| Object set(int *index*, Object *obj*) | Replaces the element at the specified *index* in this list with the specified *obj*. |

The programmer should provide a void and collection constructor, as discussed in the Collection interface specification.

**20.4.4 LinkedList class**

The LinkedList class is provides a linked-list data structure. It extends AbstractSequentialList and implements the List interface. This class is defined as:

*public class LinkedList<E> extends AbstractSequentialList<E> implements List<E>, Deque<E>, Cloneable, Serializable*

This class also automatically grows and shrinks. This class defines following overloaded constructors.

*LinkedList( )*

*LinkedList(Collection c)*

The first constructor builds an empty linked list. The second constructor builds a LinkedList instance that is initialized with the elements of the collection c.

Following table shows the methods of this class.

| Method | Description |
|---|---|
| boolean add(Object *obj*) | Appends the specified *obj* to the end of this list. |
| void add(int index, Object *obj*) | Inserts the specified *obj* at the specified position in this list. |
| boolean addAll(Collection *c*) | Appends all of the elements in the specified collection to the end of this list. |
| void addFirst(Object *obj*) | Inserts the specified *obj* at the beginning of this list. |
| void addLast(Object *obj*) | Appends the specified *obj* to the end of this list. |
| void clear( ) | Removes all of the elements from this list. |
| Object clone( ) | Returns a shallow copy of this LinkedList. |
| boolean contains(Object *obj*) | Returns **true** if this list contains the specified element. |
| Object get(int *index*) | Returns the element at the specified *index* in this list. |
| Object getFirst( ) | Returns the first element in this list. |
| Object getLast( ) | Returns the last element in this list. |

| | |
|---|---|
| int indexOf(Object *obj*) | Returns the index of the first occurrence of the specified element in this list, or -1 if this list does not contain the element. |
| int lastIndexOf(Object *obj*) | Returns the index of the last occurrence of the specified element in this list, or -1 if this list does not contain the element. |
| ListIterator listIterator(int *index*) | Returns a list-iterator of the elements in this list (in proper sequence), starting at the specified *index* in the list. |
| boolean offerFirst(Object *obj*) | Inserts the specified *obj* at the front of this list. |
| boolean offerLast(Object *obj*) | Inserts the specified *obj* at the end of this list. |
| Object remove( ) | Retrieves and removes the head (first element) of this list. |
| Object remove(int *index*) | Removes the element at the specified *index* in this list. |
| boolean remove(Object *obj*) | Removes the first occurrence of the specified *obj* from this list, if it is present. |
| Object removeFirst( ) | Removes and returns the first element from this list. |
| Object removeLast( ) | Removes and returns the last element from this list. |
| int size( ) | Returns the number of elements in this list. |
| Object[ ] toArray( ) | Returns an array containing all of the elements in this list in proper sequence. |

From above table **get( )**, **set( )**, **addFirst( )**, **addLast( )**, **getFirst( )**, **getLast( )**, **removeFirst( )** and **removeLast( )** are commonly used. Following is the program to demonstrate the use of these methods in LinkedList instance.

```
import java.util.*;
class LinkedListDemo
{
        public static void main(String ar[ ])
        {
                // create a linked list
                LinkedList list = new LinkedList( );
                // add elements to the linked list
                list.add("one");
                list.add("two");
                list.add("three");
                list.add("four");
                list.add("five");
                list.addLast("six");
                list.addFirst("seven");
                list.add(1, "eight");
                System.out.println("Original contents of list: " + list);

                // remove elements from the linked list
                list.remove("Five");
                list.remove(2);
                System.out.println("\nContents of list after deletion: " + list);

                // removing first and last elements
                list.removeFirst( );
                list.removeLast( );
```

```
            System.out.println("\nlist after deleting first and last: " + list);

            // get and set a value
            Object val = list.get(2);
            list.set(2, (String) val + " Changed");
            System.out.println("\nlist after change: " + list);
        }
    }
```

Output of above program will be:

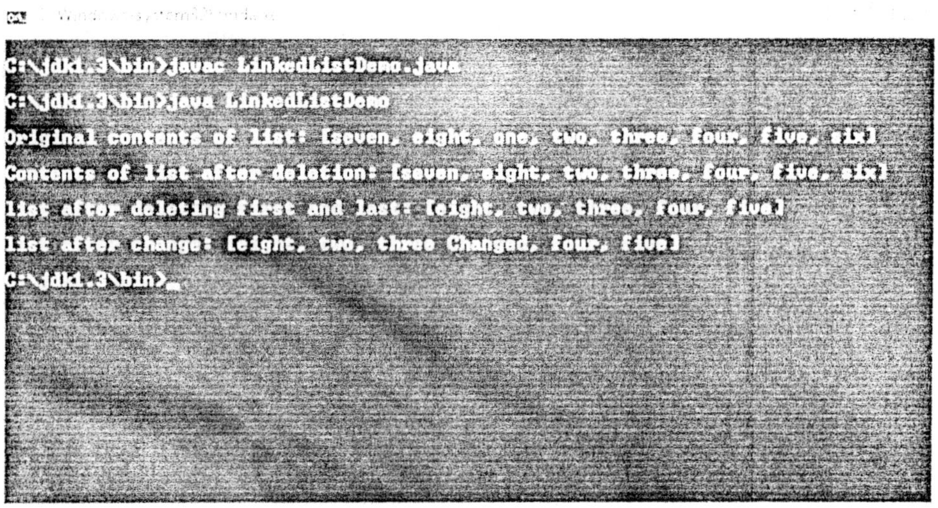

```
C:\jdk1.3\bin>javac LinkedListDemo.java
C:\jdk1.3\bin>java LinkedListDemo
Original contents of list: [seven, eight, one, two, three, four, five, six]
Contents of list after deletion: [seven, eight, two, three, four, five, six]
list after deleting first and last: [eight, two, three, four, five]
list after change: [eight, two, three Changed, four, five]
C:\jdk1.3\bin>_
```

### 20.4.5 ArrayList class

In Java, standard array is a static entity, i.e. once declared; it cannot grow or shrink as required. But, sometimes, we may not know until run time precisely how large of an array we need. To handle this situation, the collections framework defines *ArrayList*.

An instance of *ArrayList* supports dynamic array that can grow as needed. The *ArrayList* class extends *AbstractList* and implements the List interface. It is defined as:

*public class ArrayList<E> extends AbstractList<E> implements List<E>, RandomAccess, Cloneable, Serializable*

In essence, an *ArrayList* is a variable-length array of object references. That is, an *ArrayList* can dynamically increase or decrease in size. *ArrayList* instances are created with an initial size. When this size is exceeded, the collection is automatically enlarged. When objects are removed, the array gets shrunk.

Java also provides support for dynamic array by the class Vector, which is described later in this chapter.

Following is the list of overloaded constructors of ArrayList.

*ArrayList( )*
*ArrayList(Collection c)*
*ArrayList(int capacity)*

The first constructor builds an empty ArrayList instance with default size *zero*. The second constructor builds an ArrayList instance that is initialized with the elements of the collection *c*. The third constructor builds an ArrayList instance that has the specified initial capacity. The capacity is the size of the underlying array that is used to store the elements. In all three constructors, the capacity grows automatically as elements are added to an array list.

Following table shows the methods of this class.

| Method | Description |
|---|---|
| boolean add(E e) | Appends the specified element to the end of this list. |
| void add(int index, E element) | Inserts the specified element at the specified position in this list. |
| boolean addAll(Collection *c*) | Appends all of the elements in the specified collection to the end of this list, in the order that they are returned by the specified collection's Iterator. |
| boolean addAll(int index,Collection c) | Inserts all of the elements in the specified collection into this list, starting at the specified position. |
| void clear( ) | Removes all of the elements from this list. |
| Object clone( ) | Returns a shallow copy of this ArrayList instance. |
| boolean contains(Object *obj*) | Returns true if this list contains the specified element *obj*. |
| void ensureCapacity(int minCapacity) | Increases the capacity of this ArrayList instance, if necessary, to ensure that it can hold at least the number of elements specified by the minimum capacity argument. |
| Object get(int index) | Returns the element at the specified position in this list. |
| int indexOf(Object o) | Returns the index of the first occurrence of the specified element in this list, or -1 if this list does not contain the element. |
| boolean isEmpty( ) | Returns true if this list contains no elements. |
| Iterator iterator( ) | Returns an iterator over the elements in this list in proper sequence. |
| int lastIndexOf(Object *obj*) | Returns the index of the last occurrence of the specified *obj* in this list, or -1 if this list does not contain the element. |
| ListIterator listIterator( ) | Returns a list iterator over the elements in this list. |
| ListIterator listIterator(int index) | Returns a list iterator over the elements in this list, starting at the specified position in the list. |
| Object remove(int index) | Removes the element at the specified position in this list. |
| boolean remove(Object o) | Removes the first occurrence of the specified element from this list, if it is present. |
| boolean removeAll(Collection c) | Removes from this list all of its elements that are contained in the specified collection. |
| void removeRange(int start, int end) | Removes from this list all of the elements whose index is between start to end-1. |
| boolean retainAll(Collection c) | Retains only the elements in this list that are contained in the specified collection *c*. |
| Object set(int index, Object *element*) | Replaces the element at the specified position in this list with the specified element. |
| int size( ) | Returns the number of elements in this list. |
| List subList(int *start*, int *end*) | Returns a view of the portion of this list between the specified *from to end-1*. |
| Object[ ] toArray( ) | Returns an array containing all of the elements in this list in proper sequence. |
| void trimToSize( ) | Trims the capacity of this ArrayList instance to be the list's current size. |

Following program demonstrates the simple use of ArrayList.

```
// Demonstrate ArrayList.
import java.util.*;
class ArrayListDemo
```

```
    public static void main(String ar[ ])
    {
            // create an array list
            ArrayList list = new ArrayList( );
            System.out.println("\nInitilist size of list: " + list.size( ));

            // add elements to the array list
            list.add("first");
            list.add("second");
            list.add("three");
            list.add("four");
            list.add("five");
            list.add("six");
            list.add(1, "seven");
            System.out.println("\nSize of list after additions: " + list.size( ));

            // display the array list
            System.out.println("\nContents of list: " + list);
            // Remove elements from the array list
            list.remove("Five");
            list.remove(2);
            System.out.println("\nSize of list after deletions: " + list.size( ));
            System.out.println("\nContents of list: " + list);
    }
}
```

This program creates an empty ArrayList instance "**list**" and adds String instances by using **add( )** method. The initial size of **list** is zero and automatically gets expanded when elements are added. Then desired elements are removed by using **remove( )** method. The output of above program will be:

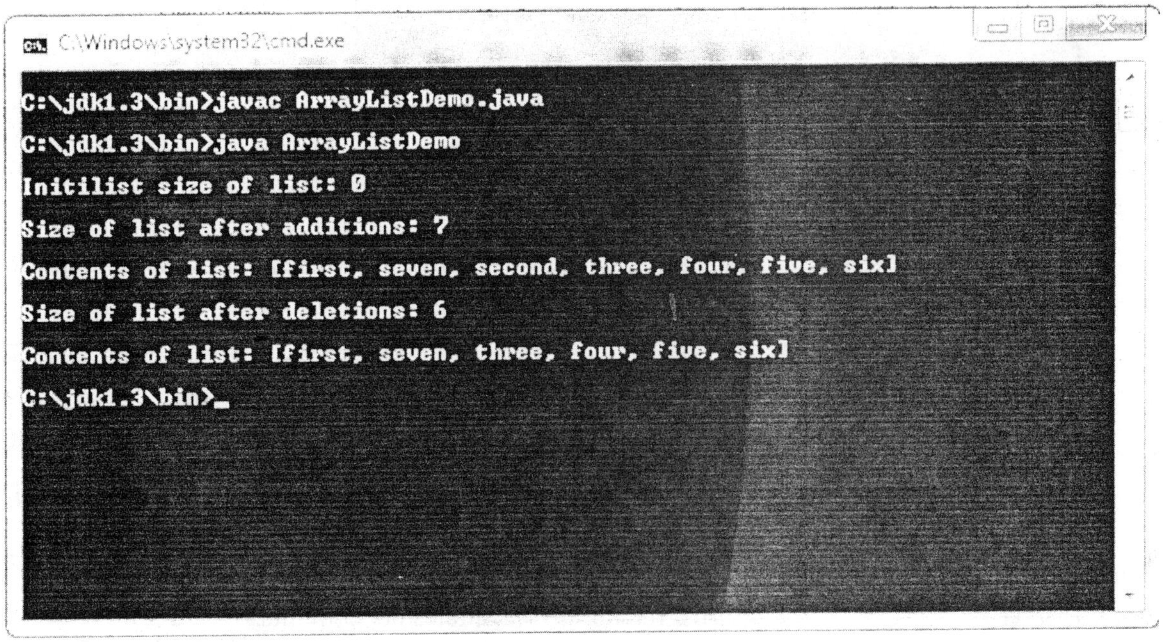

```
C:\Windows\system32\cmd.exe

C:\jdk1.3\bin>javac ArrayListDemo.java
C:\jdk1.3\bin>java ArrayListDemo
Initilist size of list: 0
Size of list after additions: 7
Contents of list: [first, seven, second, three, four, five, six]
Size of list after deletions: 6
Contents of list: [first, seven, three, four, five, six]
C:\jdk1.3\bin>_
```

## 20.4.6 AbstractSet class

This class implements Set interface to minimize the efforts required to implement a Set instance. This class is defined as:

*public abstract class AbstractSet<E> extends AbstractCollection<E> implements Set<E>*

The process of using this class is easier than using AbstractCollection class. But the condition is that, all the methods and constructors of extending class must follow the restrictions imposed by Set interface.

Following table shows the methods provided in this class.

| Method | Description |
|---|---|
| boolean equals(Object *obj*) | Compares the specified *obj* with this set for equality. |
| int hashCode( ) | Returns the hash code value for this set. |
| boolean removeAll(Collection *c*) | Removes from this set all of its elements that are contained in the specified collection *c*. |

Note that this class does not override any of the implementations from the *AbstractCollection* class. It just adds implementations for **equals( )** and **hashCode( )**.

## 20.4.7 HashSet class

This class extends AbstractSet and implements Set. It creates a collection that uses hash-table for storage. As we are already familiar with that hash-table stores information by using a mechanism called *hashing*. See following signature of this class.

*public class HashSet<E>extends AbstractSet<E>implements Set<E>, Cloneable, Serializable*

This class does not guarantee that the order will remain, during storage or during iterator assignment, constant over time. This class permits the null element. This class is not abstract hence contains constructors. The following list shows the overloaded constructor definitions of this class.

*HashSet( )*
*HashSet(Collection c)*
*HashSet(int capacity)*
*HashSet(int capacity, float fillRatio)*

The **first** form constructs a default hash set. The **second** form initializes the hash set by using the elements of *c*. The third form defines a hash set that is initial of specified *capacity*. The **fourth** form initializes both the *capacity* and the *fillratio* of the hash set from its arguments. The *fillratio* must be between 0.0 and 1.0. It determines how full the hash set can be before it is resized upward. For first three constructors, default *fillratio* is 0.75.

HashSet does not define any additional methods beyond those provided by its super-classes and interfaces. Following is the list of methods that can be used with the instance of this class.

| Method | Description |
|---|---|
| boolean add(Object obj) | Adds the specified element to this set if it is not already present. |
| void clear( ) | Removes all of the elements from this set. |
| Object clone( ) | Returns a shallow copy of this HashSet instance: the elements themselves are not cloned. |
| boolean contains(Object obj) | Returns true if this set contains the specified element. |
| boolean isEmpty( ) | Returns true if this set contains no elements. |

| | |
|---|---|
| Iterator iterator( ) | Returns an iterator over the elements in this set. |
| boolean remove(Object obj) | Removes the specified element from this set if it is present. |
| int size( ) | Returns the number of elements in this set. |

The advantage of hashing is that it allows the execution time of basic operations, such as **add( ), contains( ), remove(), and size( )**, to remain constant even for large sets. Importantly, note that a hash set does not guarantee the order of its elements, because the process of hashing doesn't usually lend itself to the creation of sorted sets. If you need sorted storage, then another collection, such as TreeSet, is a better choice. Following is the example of HashSet instance.

```
import java.util.*;
class HashSetDemo
{
        public static void main(String ar[ ])
        {
                // create a hash set
                HashSet hs = new HashSet( );

                // add elements to the hash set
                hs.add("one");
                hs.add("two");
                hs.add("three");
                hs.add("four");
                hs.add("five");
                hs.add("six");
                System.out.println(hs);
        }
}
```

Output of above program will be:

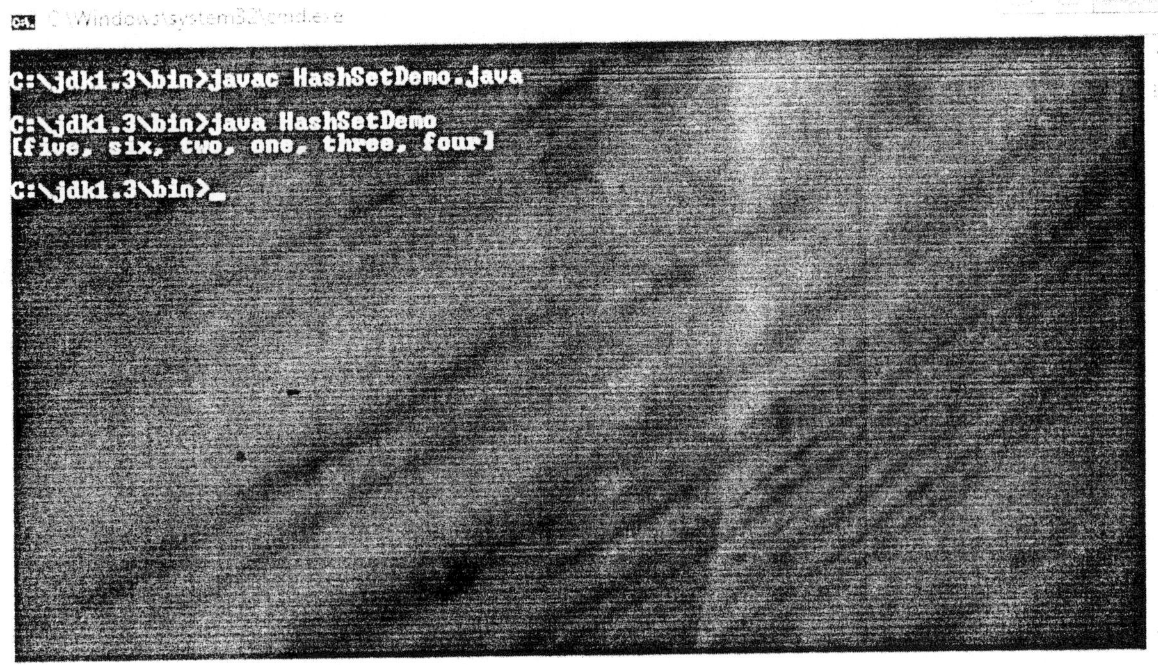

## 20.4.8 LinkedHashSet class

This class is the derived class of HashSet and **do not contain any concrete methods**. See following signature.

*public class LinkedHashSet<E> extends HashSet<E> implements Set<E>, Cloneable, Serializable*

This implementation differs from implementation of *HashSet*. This maintains a doubly-linked list running through all of its entries and this linked list also defines the iteration ordering, which is the order in which elements were inserted into the set.

To create instance of this class, we have following constructors.

*LinkedHashSet( )*
*LinkedHashSet(Collection c)*
*LinkedHashSet(int initialCapacity)*
*LinkedHashSet(int initialCapacity, float loadFactor)*

The **first** constructor constructs a new, empty linked hash set with the default initial capacity 16 and load factor 0.75. **Second** constructor constructs a new linked hash set with the same elements as the specified collection. **Third** constructor constructs a new, empty linked hash set with the specified initial capacity and the default load factor 0.75. **Fourth** constructor constructs a new, empty linked hash set with the specified initial capacity and load factor.

This class provides all of the optional Set operations, and permits null elements. Like HashSet, it provides constant-time performance for the basic operations such as add, contains and remove.

We will simply modify above *HashSetDemo.java* program with only one statement. See following program.

```
import java.util.*;
class LinkedHashSetDemo
{
        public static void main(String ar[ ])
        {
                // create a hash set
                LinkedHashSet lhs = new LinkedHashSet( );
                //Set lhs = new LinkedHashSet( ); will also work.

                // add elements to the hash set
                lhs.add("one");
                lhs.add("two");
                lhs.add("three");
                lhs.add("four");
                lhs.add("five");
                lhs.add("six");
                System.out.println(lhs);
        }
}
```

As discussed above, this program maintains the order in which they are entered into the set. The output of above program will be:

*[one, two, three, four, five, six]*

Note that this class implementation is **not synchronized.** Hence, if multiple threads are running and access a linked hash set at the same time, and one of the thread modifies the set, then it affects the execution of other threads and may throws exception. The better way is to synchronize at least a few objects that naturally encapsulates this set instance.

### 20.4.9 TreeSet class

This class extends AbstractSet and implements *NavigableSet* interface. Following is the signature of this class.

*public class TreeSet<E> extends AbstractSet<E> implements NavigableSet<E>, Cloneable, Serializable*

This class provides an implementation of the Set interface that uses a tree style for storing elements. Objects are by default stored in sorted, ascending order. Access and retrieval times are quite fast, which makes TreeSet an excellent choice when storing large amounts of sorted information that must be found quickly. Following are the overloaded constructors that are used to instantiate the TreeSet class.

*TreeSet( )*
*TreeSet(Collection c)*
*TreeSet(Comparator comp)*
*TreeSet(SortedSet ss)*

**First** constructor constructs a new, empty tree set, sorted according to the natural ordering of its elements. **Second** constructor constructs a new tree set containing the elements in the specified collection, sorted according to the natural ordering of its elements. **Third** constructor constructs a new tree set containing the elements in the specified collection, sorted according to the natural ordering of its elements. **Fourth** constructor constructs a new, empty tree set, sorted according to the specified comparator. **Fifth** constructor constructs a new tree set containing the same elements and using the same ordering as the specified sorted set.

Along with base class, this class also contains some concrete methods. Following table shows the commonly used methods of this class.

| Method | Description |
|---|---|
| boolean add(Object *obj*) | Adds the specified *obj* to this set if it is not already present. |
| boolean addAll(Collection *c*) | Adds all of the elements in the specified collection to this set. |
| Object ceiling(Object *obj*) | Returns the least element in this set greater than or equal to the given *obj*, or null if there is no such element. |
| void clear( ) | Removes all of the elements from this set. |
| Object clone( ) | Returns a shallow copy of this TreeSet instance. |
| Comparator comparator( ) | Returns the comparator used to order the elements in this set, or null if this set uses the natural ordering of its elements. |
| boolean contains(Object *obj*) | Returns true if this set contains the specified *obj*. |
| Iterator descendingIterator( ) | Returns an iterator over the elements in this set in descending order. |
| NavigableSet descendingSet( ) | Returns a reverse order view of the elements contained in this set. |
| Object first( ) | Returns the first (lowest) element currently in this set. |
| Object floor(Object *obj*) | Returns the greatest element in this set less than or equal to the given *obj*, or null if there is no such element. |
| SortedSet headSet(Object *ele*) | Returns a view of the portion of this set whose elements are strictly less than *ele*. |
| NavigableSet headSet(Object *ele*, | Returns a view of the portion of this set whose elements are less than or |

| | |
|---|---|
| boolean *inclusive*) | equal to *ele*. |
| Object higher(Object *obj*) | Returns the least element in this set strictly greater than the given *obj*, or null if there is no such element. |
| boolean isEmpty( ) | Returns true if this set contains no elements. |
| Iterator iterator( ) | Returns an iterator over the elements in this set in ascending order. |
| Object last( ) | Returns the last (highest) element currently in this set. |
| Object lower(Object *obj*) | Returns the greatest element in this set strictly less than the given *obj*, or null if there is no such element. |
| Object pollFirst( ) | Retrieves and removes the first (lowest) element, or returns null if this set is empty. |
| Object pollLast( ) | Retrieves and removes the last (highest) element, or returns null if this set is empty. |
| boolean remove(Object *obj*) | Removes the specified *obj* from this set if it is present. |
| int size( ) | Returns the number of elements in this set. |
| NavigableSet subSet(Object fromEle, boolean fromInclusive, Object toEle, boolean toInclusive) | Returns a view of the portion of this set whose elements range from *fromEle* to *toEle*. |
| SortedSet subSet(Object *fromEle*, Object *toEle*) | Returns a view of the portion of this set whose elements range from *fromEle*, to *toEle-1*. |
| SortedSet tailSet(Object *fromEle*) | Returns a view of the portion of this set whose elements are greater than or equal to *fromEle*. |
| NavigableSet tailSet(Object *fromEle*, boolean *inclusive*) | Returns a view of the portion of this set whose elements are greater than or equal to *fromEle*. |

Following program demonstrates the TreeSet class.

```
import java.util.*;

public class TreeSetDemo
{
        public static void main(String ar[ ])
        {
                System.out.println("Tree Set Example!\n");
                TreeSet <Integer>tree = new TreeSet<Integer>( );
                tree.add(12);
                tree.add(23);
                tree.add(34);
                tree.add(45);
                Iterator iterator;
                iterator = tree.iterator( );
                System.out.print("Tree set data: ");

                //Displaying the Tree set data
                 while (iterator.hasNext( ))
                {
                        System.out.print(iterator.next( ) + " ");
                }
```

```
        //Check empty or not
        if (tree.isEmpty( ))
        {
                System.out.print("\nTree Set is empty.");
        }
        else
        {
                System.out.println("\nTree Set size: " + tree.size());
        }

        //Retrieve first data from tree set
        System.out.println("First data: " + tree.first( ));

        //Retrieve last data from tree set
        System.out.println("Last data: " + tree.last( ));
        if (tree.remove(30))
        {
        System.out.println("Data is removed from tree set");
        }
        else
        {
                System.out.println("Data doesn't exist!");
        }
        System.out.print("Now the tree set contain: ");
        iterator = tree.iterator( );

        //Displaying the Tree set data
        while (iterator.hasNext( ))
        {
                System.out.print(iterator.next() + " ");
        }
        System.out.println("\nNow the size of tree set: " + tree.size( ));

        //Remove all
        tree.clear( );
        if (tree.isEmpty( ))
        {
                System.out.print("Tree Set is empty.");
        }
        else
        {
                System.out.println("Tree Set size: " + tree.size( ));
        }
    }
}
```

Output of above program will be:

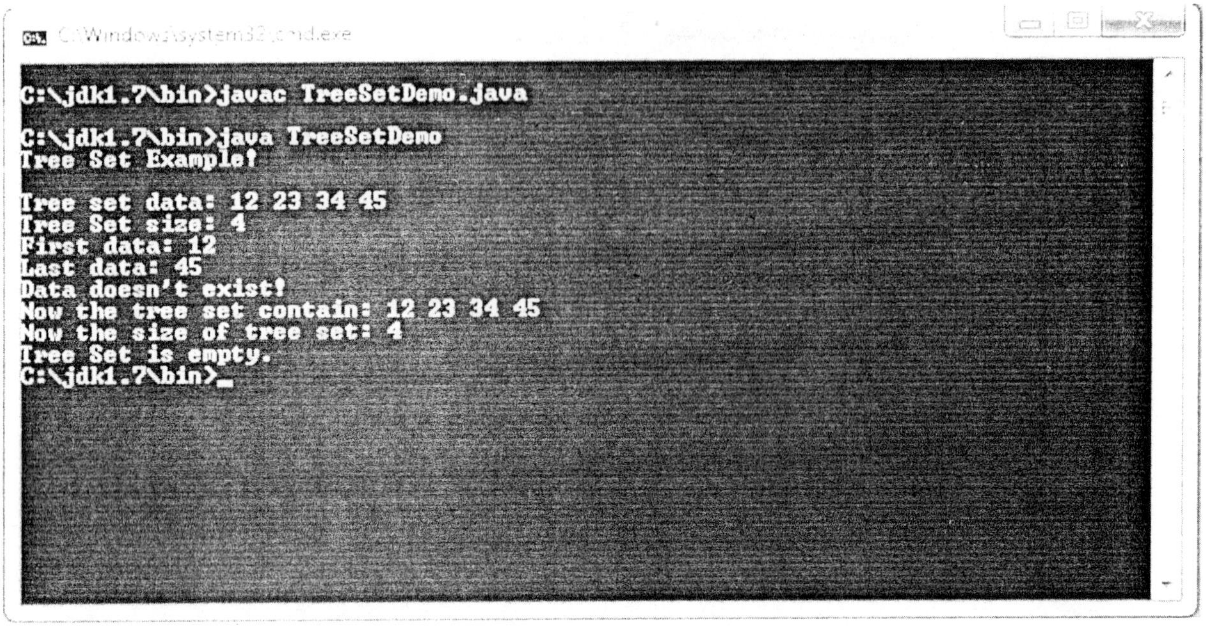

```
C:\Windows\system32\cmd.exe
C:\jdk1.7\bin>javac TreeSetDemo.java

C:\jdk1.7\bin>java TreeSetDemo
Tree Set Example!

Tree set data: 12 23 34 45
Tree Set size: 4
First data: 12
Last data: 45
Data doesn't exist!
Now the tree set contain: 12 23 34 45
Now the size of tree set: 4
Tree Set is empty.
C:\jdk1.7\bin>_
```

## 20.5 Using an Iterator

The term iterator and loop might sound same, but they are not. The working of iterator is very much similar to loop. Both are used to cycle through the elements, but loop is used to cycle through an array or a logical statement block whereas an iterator is used to cycle through a collection. In many of above example programs, we have used iterator instances, to display elements of a list or a collection.

Using an iterator is the easiest way to cycle through a collection. An iterator is actually an object, which can be obtained by implementing **Iterator** or **ListIterator** interface. The applications of both these interfaces are same but they differ in one characteristic i.e. an **Iterator** enables you to cycle through a collection, obtaining or removing elements, whereas a **ListIterator** extends Iterator to allow bidirectional traversal of a list, and the modification of elements.

Note that, each of collection class contains a method called **iterator( )** method. This method returns the *Iterator* instance, by using which we can invoke methods of *Iterator* or *ListIterator*.

Following table shows the methods declared in Iterator interface.

| Method | Description |
|---|---|
| boolean hasNext( ) | Returns true if there are more elements. Otherwise, returns false. |
| Object next( ) | Returns the next element. Throws *NoSuchElementException* if there is not a next element. |
| void remove( ) | Removes the current element. Throws IllegalStateException if an attempt is made to call **remove( )** that is not preceded by a call to **next( )**. |

Following table shows the methods of ListIterator. Remember that, **the *ListIterator* is available only to those collections that have implemented the *List* interface.**

| Method | Description |
|---|---|
| void add(Object *obj*) | Inserts *obj* into the list in front of the element that will be returned by the next call to **next( )**. |
| boolean hasNext( ) | Returns true if there is a next element. Otherwise, returns false. |

| | |
|---|---|
| boolean hasPrevious( ) | Returns true if there is a previous element. Otherwise, returns false. |
| Object next( ) | Returns the next element. A *NoSuchElementException* is thrown if there is not a next element. |
| int nextIndex( ) | Returns the index of the next element. If there is not a next element, returns the size of the list. |
| Object previous( ) | Returns the previous element. A *NoSuchElementException* is thrown if there is not a previous element. |
| int previousIndex( ) | Returns the index of the previous element. If there is not a previous element, returns –1. |
| void remove( ) | Removes the current element from the list. An *IllegalStateException* is thrown if **remove( )** is calledbefore **next( )** or **previous( )** is invoked. |
| void set(Object *obj*) | Assigns *obj* to the current element. This is the element last returned by a call to either **next( )** or **previous( )**. |

Many inquisitive people wonder, an Iterator or ListIterator can cycle through the collection or list, only one element at each cycle. Generally, following steps are needs to be taken if you want to iterate through, using an Iterator.

1. Obtain an iterator by calling the collection's **iterator( )** method.

2. Define a loop that makes a call to **hasNext( )** till it is returning **true**. *(see Iterator method table for signature)*

3. Inside the loop, obtain each element by calling **next( )**. *(see Iterator method table for signature)*

As explained earlier, each collection that implements *List* interface contains **listIterator( )** method. We can also obtain a ListIterator by calling this method. As explained, a list iterator gives you the ability to access the collection in either the forward or backward direction and lets you modify an element. Otherwise, ListIterator is used just like Iterator.

Check any of above collection programs that use Iterator. Following program also demonstrates the use of Iterator and ListIterator interfaces.

```
import java.util.*;

class IteratorsDemo
{
        public static void main(String ar[ ])
        {
                // create an array list
                ArrayList arlist = new ArrayList( );

                // add elements to the array list
                arlist.add("one");
                arlist.add("two");
                arlist.add("three");
                arlist.add("four");
                arlist.add("five");
                arlist.add("six");

                // use Iterator to display contents of arlist
                System.out.print("Original contents of arlist: ");
                Iterator itr = arlist.iterator( );
                while(itr.hasNext( ))
                {
```

```
                Object element = itr.next( );
                System.out.print(element + " ");
        }

        // modify objects being iterated
        ListIterator litr = arlist.listIterator( );
        while(litr.hasNext( ))
        {
                Object element = litr.next( );
                litr.set(element + ",");
        }
        System.out.print("\nModified contents of arlist: ");
        itr = arlist.iterator( );
        while(itr.hasNext( ))
        {
        Object element = itr.next( );
        System.out.print(element + " ");
        }

        // now, display the list backwards
        System.out.print("\nModified list backwards: ");
        while(litr.hasPrevious( ))
        {
                Object element = litr.previous( );
                System.out.print(element + " ");
        }
    }
}
```

Refer following output.

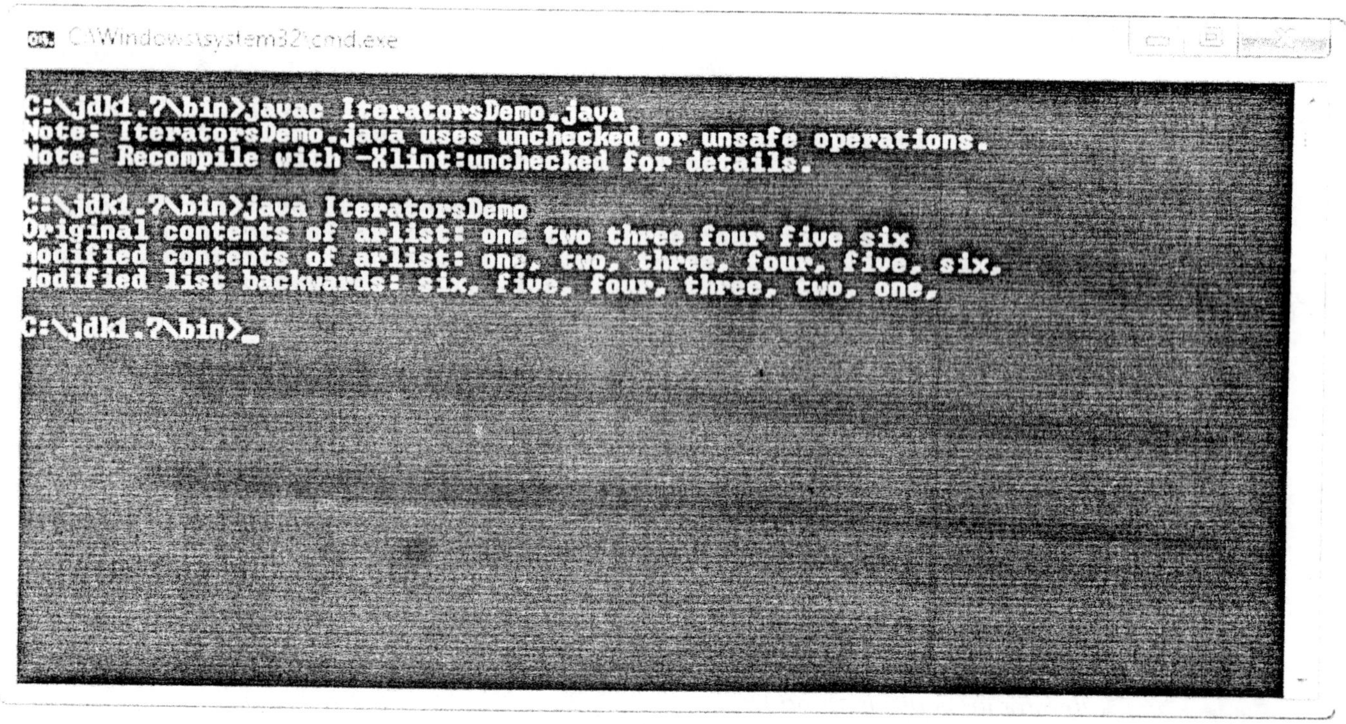

```
C:\Windows\system32\cmd.exe

C:\jdk1.7\bin>javac IteratorsDemo.java
Note: IteratorsDemo.java uses unchecked or unsafe operations.
Note: Recompile with -Xlint:unchecked for details.

C:\jdk1.7\bin>java IteratorsDemo
Original contents of arlist: one two three four five six
Modified contents of arlist: one, two, three, four, five, six,
Modified list backwards: six, five, four, three, two, one,

C:\jdk1.7\bin>_
```

## 20.6 RandomAccess interface

This interface is another member of Java Collections Framework. This standalone class does not extend or implement any class or interface. This class is defined as:

*public interface RandomAccess*

This interface does not contain any members. This class is used to **access the members of list** (as Iterators do), but instead this class provides faster random access, as compare to Iterators. Even the collections can also support *RandomAccess* interface, but it might not work so efficiently in collections as it works for lists.

The primary purpose of this interface is to allow generic algorithms to alter their behavior to provide good performance when applied to either random or sequential access lists.

This interface is more suitable, while working with lists containing large numbers of elements. In case of networked applications (uses RMI or networking concepts), a client application can determine whether the source class has implemented this interface or not (by using *instanceof* operator). And if the source has implemented this interface, then the client can take benefit of this and cycle through a list or collection, faster.

The best algorithms for manipulating random access lists (such as ArrayList) can produce quadratic behavior when applied to sequential access lists (such as LinkedList). Generic list algorithms are encouraged to check whether the given list is an instanceof this interface before applying an algorithm that would provide poor performance if it were applied to a sequential access list, and to alter their behavior if necessary to guarantee acceptable performance.

This class **does not have any methods** to override in implementing class. To use this class, a list or collection class has to implement this interface. For example,

```
class SampleClass1 implements Collection, RandomAccess
{
        ...
}
```

***or***

```
class SampleClass2 implements List,RandomAccess
{
        ...
}
```

These classes, *SampleClass1* and *SampleClass2,* implements *RandomAccess*. The class SampleClass1 can create a Collection supporting RandomAccess. The class SampleClass2 can create a List supporting RandomAccess.

## 20.7 Working with Maps

Map is an object that stores **the association of a *value* and a *key***. If key is provided, we can find its concern value. Actually both, the *key* and the *value*, are objects (Generally of String type).

Simply for more ease to deal with keys and values, simply consider the association of index and value, in array. **The index in array is as key in Map and value in Array is as value Map.** The key must be unique but value can be duplicate. In Java there are some classes and interface the characteristics and nature of Map. Following sections describes the class and interfaces of Map.

### 20.7.1 map interfaces

The map interfaces defines the characteristics and nature of a map. Hence, let's start this discussion with interfaces. Following is the list and brief description of map interfaces.

| **Interface** | **Description** |
|---|---|
| *Map* | Maps unique keys to values. |
| Map.Entry | Describes an element (a key/value pair) in a map. This is an inner class of Map. |
| *SortedMap* | Extends Map so that the keys are maintained in ascending order. |

Let's study these interfaces in detail.

#### 20.7.1.1 Map interface

The Map interface ties a key to a value. The mapping concept is completely dependent upon a key and its value. Both are objects that we store. By providing a key, we can obtain its value. This interface is defined as:

*public interface Map<K,V>*

Where, *K* is the **key** object and *V* is the **value** object.

The methods declared by Map are summarized in following table.

| Method | Description |
|---|---|
| void clear( ) | Removes all key/value pairs from the invoking map. |
| boolean containsKey(Object *key*) | Returns **true** if the invoking map contains *key* as key. Otherwise, returns **false**. |
| boolean containsValue(Object *val*) | Returns **true** if the map contains *val* as a value. Otherwise, returns **false**. |
| Set entrySet( ) | Returns a Set that contains the entries in the map. The set contains objects of type *Map.Entry* |
| boolean equals(Object *obj*) | Returns **true** if *obj* is a Map and contains the same entries. Otherwise, returns false. |
| Object get(Object *key*) | Returns the value associated with the key *key*. |
| int hashCode( ) | Returns the hash code for the invoking map. |
| boolean isEmpty( ) | Returns **true** if the invoking map is empty. Otherwise, returns **false**. |
| Set keySet( ) | Returns a Set that contains the keys in the invoking map. This method provides a set-view of the keys in the invoking map. |
| Object put(Object *key*, Object *val*) | Puts an entry in the invoking map, overwriting any previous value associated with the key. The key and value are *key* and *val*, respectively. Returns null if the key did not already exist. Otherwise, the previous value linked to the key is returned. |
| void putAll(Map *m*) | Puts all the entries from *m* into this map. |
| Object remove(Object *key*) | Removes the entry whose key equals *key*. |
| int size( ) | Returns the number of key/value pairs in the map. |
| Collection values( ) | Returns a collection containing the values in the map. This method provides a collection-view of the values in the map. |

Several methods throw several exceptions. A **NoSuchElementException** when no items exist in the invoking map. A **ClassCastException** is thrown when an object is incompatible with the elements in a map. A **NullPointerException** is thrown if an attempt is made to use a null object and null is not allowed in the map. An **UnsupportedOperationException** is thrown when an attempt is made to change an unmodifiable map.

### 20.7.1.2 Map.Entry interface

The *Map.Entry* interface enables you to work with a map entry. Many of the methods of map classes returns *Map.Entry* instance. This interface is defined as:

*public static interface Map.Entry<K,V>*

This interface defines following methods.

| Method | Description |
|---|---|
| boolean equals(Object *obj*) | Compares the specified *obj* with this entry for equality. |
| Object getKey( ) | Returns the key corresponding to this entry. |
| Object getValue( ) | Returns the value corresponding to this entry. |
| int hashCode( ) | Returns the hash code value for this map entry. |
| Object setValue(Object *val*) | Replaces the value corresponding to this entry with the specified *val*. |

The only way to obtain a reference to a map entry is from the iterator of this collection-view.

```
import java.util.*;

public class MapEntryDemo
{
	public static void main(String ar[])
	{
		// Create a hash map
		HashMap hm = new HashMap( );
		// Put elements to the map
		hm.put("Deepak Toshniwal", new Double(3434.34));
		hm.put("Kaushik Deoda", new Double(2123.22));
		hm.put("Kartik Khanapurkar", new Double(1378.00));
		hm.put("Rakesh Jain", new Double(1999.22));

		// Get a set of the entries
		Set set = hm.entrySet( );

		// Get an iterator
		Iterator i = set.iterator( );
		// Display elements
		while(i.hasNext( ))
		{
			Map.Entry me = (Map.Entry)i.next();
			System.out.print(me.getKey( ) + ": ");
			System.out.println(me.getValue( ));
		}

		// Deposit 1000 into Deepak Toshniwal's account
		double balance = ((Double)hm.get("Deepak Toshniwal")).doubleValue();
		hm.put("Deepak Toshniwal", new Double(balance + 1000));
		System.out.println("\nDeepak Toshniwal's new balance: " + hm.get("Deepak Toshniwal"));
	}
}
```

Output of above program will be:

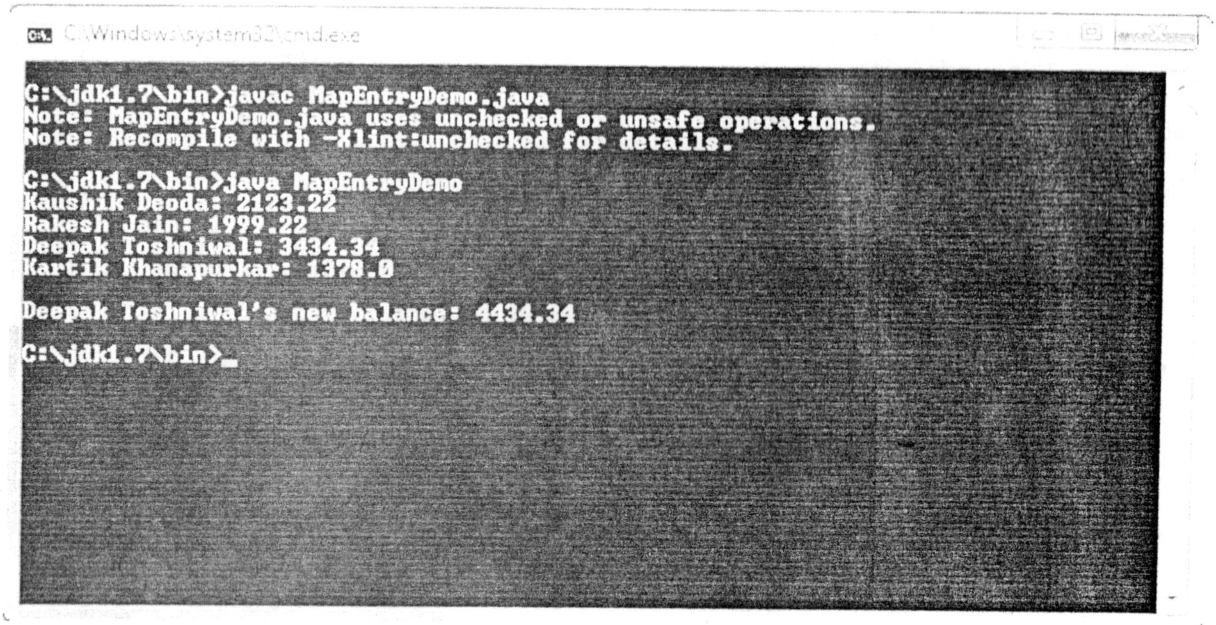

```
C:\jdk1.7\bin>javac MapEntryDemo.java
Note: MapEntryDemo.java uses unchecked or unsafe operations.
Note: Recompile with -Xlint:unchecked for details.

C:\jdk1.7\bin>java MapEntryDemo
Kaushik Deoda: 2123.22
Rakesh Jain: 1999.22
Deepak Toshniwal: 3434.34
Kartik Khanapurkar: 1378.0

Deepak Toshniwal's new balance: 4434.34

C:\jdk1.7\bin>_
```

### 20.7.1.3 SortedMap interface

The SortedMap interface extends Map. It ensures that the entries are maintained in ascending key order. Signature of this interface is:

*public interface SortedMap<K,V> extends Map<K,V>*

This map is ordered according to the natural ordering of its keys, or by a *Comparator* typically provided at sorted map creation time.

Following table lists the methods defined by this interface.

| Method | Description |
|---|---|
| Comparator comparator( ) | Returns the invoking sorted map's comparator. If the natural ordering is used for the invoking map, null is returned. |
| Object firstKey( ) | Returns the first key in the invoking map. |
| SortedMap headMap(Object *end*) | Returns a sorted map for those map entries with keys that are less than *end*. |
| Object lastKey( ) | Returns the last key in the invoking map. |
| SortedMap subMap(Object *start*, Object *end*) | Returns a map containing those entries with keys that are greater than or equal to *start* and less than *end*. |
| SortedMap tailMap(Object *start*) | Returns a map containing those entries with keys that are greater than or equal to *start*. |

Several methods throw several exceptions. A **NoSuchElementException** when no items are in the invoking map. A **ClassCastException** is thrown when an object is incompatible with the elements in a map. A **NullPointerException** is thrown if an attempt is made to use a null object when null is not allowed in the map.

### 20.7.2 map classes

There are some classes that provides implementation of the map interfaces. These classes are listed here.

| Class | Description |
|---|---|
| *AbstractMap* | Implements most of the Map interface and base class of all map classes. |
| *HashMap* | Extends AbstractMap to use a hash table. |
| *TreeMap* | Extends AbstractMap to use a tree. |
| *WeakHashMap* | Extends AbstractMap to use a hash table with weak keys. |
| *LinkedHashMap* | Extends HashMap to allow insertion-order iterations. |
| *IdentityHashMap* | Extends AbstractMap and uses reference equality when comparing documents. |

Let's study these classes on detail.

#### 20.7.2.1 AbstractMap class

This class is an abstract class and implements Map interface, to minimize the efforts required to implement this interface. Following is the signature of AbstractMap class.

*public abstract class AbstractMap<K,V> extends Object implements Map<K,V>*

As this class is an abstract class, this class cannot be directly instantiated, but instead the developer needs to extend this class to any of the user defined class.

This class contains two static inner classes, **AbstractMap.SimpleEntry<K,V>** and **AbstractMap.SimpleImmutableEntry<K,V>** and one default argument constructor.

Following table shows the methods included in this class.

| Method | Description |
|---|---|
| void clear( ) | Removes all of the mappings from this map. |
| protected Object clone( ) | Returns a shallow copy of this AbstractMap instance: the keys and values themselves are not cloned. |
| boolean containsKey(Object *key*) | Returns **true** if this map contains a mapping for the specified *key*. |
| boolean containsValue(Object *value*) | Returns **true** if this map maps one or more keys to the specified *value*. |
| abstract Set entrySet( ) | Returns a Set view of the mappings contained in this map. |
| boolean equals(Object *obj*) | Compares the specified *obj* with this map for equality. |
| Object get(Object *key*) | Returns the value to which the specified key is mapped, or null if this map contains no mapping for the *key*. |
| int hashCode( ) | Returns the hash code value for this map. |
| boolean isEmpty( ) | Returns true if this map contains no key-value mappings. |
| Set keySet( ) | Returns a Set view of the keys contained in this map. |
| Object put(Object *key*, Object *value*) | Associates the specified *value* with the specified *key* in this map. |
| void putAll(Map *m*) | Copies all of the mappings from the specified map to this map. |
| Object remove(Object *key*) | Removes the mapping for a *key* from this map if it is present. |
| int size( ) | Returns the number of key-value mappings in this map. |
| String toString( ) | Returns a string representation of this map. |
| Collection values( ) | Returns a Collection view of the values contained in this map. |

To implement a non-changeable map, the programmer needs only to extend this class and provide an implementation for the **entrySet( )** method, which returns a set-view of the map's mappings. Typically, the returned set will, in turn, be implemented atop AbstractSet. This set should not support the **add( )** or **remove( )** methods, and its iterator should not support the remove method.

To implement a changeable map, the programmer must additionally override this class's **put( )** method, which otherwise throws an **UnsupportedOperationException**, and the iterator returned by **entrySet( ).iterator( )** must additionally implement its **remove( )** method.

### 20.7.2.2 HashMap class

Provides Hashtable based implementation of the Map interface, and also provides all of the optional map operations, and permits *null* values and the *null* key. Signature of this class is:

*public class HashMap<K,V> extends AbstractMap<K,V> implements Map<K,V>, Cloneable, Serializable*

From above implementation we can say that, the basic **get( )** and **put( )** methods. The instances of this class requires two properties. One is *initial_capacity* that specifies the size of map, when it is created. Second is *load_factor* is the measure of how full Hashtable is allowed to get before its capacity is automatically gets increased.

Following are the constructors of HashMap class.

*HashMap( )*
*HashMap(Map m)*
*HashMap(int capacity)*
*HashMap(int capacity, float load_factor)*

**First** constructor creates an empty HashMap instance. **Second** constructor creates a HashMap instance initialized with the elements of specified Map *m*. **Third** constructor creates a HashMap instance with specified initial capacity. **Fourth** constructor creates a HashMap instance with specified capacity and *load_factor*.

This class extends *AbstractMap* class and implements *Map* interface. This class does not define any concrete methods on its own. All the basic methods of AbstractMap and Map interface are usable here.

```
import java.util.*;

class HashMapDemo
{
        public static void main(String ar[ ])
        {
                // Create a hash map
                HashMap hm = new HashMap( );

                // Put elements to the map
                hm.put("Rakesh Jain", new Double(3434.34));
                hm.put("Deepak Toshniwal", new Double(123.22));
                hm.put("Kartik Khanapurkar", new Double(1378.00));
                hm.put("Kaushik Deoda", new Double(99.22));

                // Get a set of the entries
                Set set = hm.entrySet( );

                // Get an iterator
                Iterator i = set.iterator( );
```

```
                // Display elements
                while(i.hasNext( ))
                {
                Map.Entry me = (Map.Entry)i.next( );
                System.out.print(me.getKey( ) + ": ");
                System.out.println(me.getValue( ));
                }

                // Deposit 1000 into Rakesh Jain's account
                double balance = ((Double)hm.get("Rakesh Jain")).doubleValue( );
                hm.put("Rakesh Jain", new Double(balance + 1000));
                System.out.println("\nRakesh Jain's new balance: " + hm.get("Rakesh Jain"));
        }
}
```

Output of above program will be:

```
C:\Windows\system32\cmd.exe

C:\jdk1.7\bin>javac HashMapDemo.java
Note: HashMapDemo.java uses unchecked or unsafe operations.
Note: Recompile with -Xlint:unchecked for details.

C:\jdk1.7\bin>java HashMapDemo
Kaushik Deoda: 99.22
Rakesh Jain: 3434.34
Deepak Toshniwal: 123.22
Kartik Khanapurkar: 1378.0

Rakesh Jain's new balance: 4434.34

C:\jdk1.7\bin>_
```

From above output, note that a hash map **does not guarantee the order** of its elements. Therefore, the order in which elements are added to a hash map is not necessarily the order in which they are read by an iterator.

### 20.7.2.3 TreeMap class

The TreeMap class also provides an efficient means of storing key/value pairs in sorted order, and allows rapid retrieval. The signature of this class is given here.

*public class TreeMap<K,V> extends AbstractMap<K,V> implements NavigableMap<K,V>, Cloneable, Serializable*

This class extends AbstractMap and implements *NavigableMap*; hence it defines a tree map, that guarantees the order of its elements. I.e. elements will be sorted in ascending key order.

Following are the overloaded constructors of this class.

```
TreeMap( )
TreeMap(Comparator comp)
TreeMap(Map m)
TreeMap(SortedMap sm)
```

**First** constructor constructs a new, empty tree map, using the natural ordering of its keys. **Second** constructor constructs a new, empty tree map, ordered according to the given comparator. **Third** constructor constructs a new tree map containing the same mappings as the given map, ordered according to the natural ordering of its keys. **Fourth** constructor constructs a new tree map containing the same mappings and using the same ordering as the specified sorted map.

TreeMap implements *NavigableMap* and extends *AbstractMap*. This class does not define any additional concrete methods of its own.

The following program reworks the preceding example so that it uses TreeMap:

```
import java.util.*;

class TreeMapDemo
{
        public static void main(String ar[ ])
        {

                // Create a tree map
                TreeMap tm = new TreeMap( );

                // Put elements to the map
                tm.put("Rakesh Jain", new Double(3434.34));
                tm.put("Deepak Toshniwal", new Double(123.22));
                tm.put("Kartik Khanapurkar", new Double(1378.00));
                tm.put("Kaushik Deoda", new Double(99.22));

                // Get a set of the entries
                Set set = tm.entrySet();

                // Get an iterator
                Iterator i = set.iterator();

                // Display elements
                while(i.hasNext( ))
                {
                Map.Entry me = (Map.Entry)i.next( );
                System.out.print(me.getKey( ) + ": ");
                System.out.println(me.getValue( ));
                }

                // Deposit 1000 into Rakesh Jain's account
                double balance = ((Double)tm.get("Rakesh Jain")).doubleValue( );
                tm.put("Rakesh Jain", new Double(balance + 1000));
                System.out.println("\nRakesh Jain's new balance: " +
                tm.get("Rakesh Jain"));
        }
}
```

The output of above program will be:

```
C:\Windows\system32\cmd.exe

C:\jdk1.7\bin>javac TreeMapDemo.java
Note: TreeMapDemo.java uses unchecked or unsafe operations.
Note: Recompile with -Xlint:unchecked for details.

C:\jdk1.7\bin>java TreeMapDemo
Deepak Toshniwal: 123.22
Kartik Khanapurkar: 1378.0
Kaushik Deoda: 99.22
Rakesh Jain: 3434.34

Rakesh Jain's new balance: 4434.34

C:\jdk1.7\bin>_
```

From above output, note that the tree map guarantee the order of its elements, it is in ascending order. Therefore, elements are added into a tree map is ordered and they are read by an iterator in same stored sequence.

#### 20.7.2.4 WeakHashMap class

This is a really interesting map class, as compare to other hash table based map classes. The signature of this class is:

*public class WeakHashMap<K,V> extends AbstractMap<K,V> implements Map<K,V>*

This class provides hash table based implementation of the Map interface, with *weak keys*. An element in a WeakHashMap will automatically be removed when its key is no longer in ordinary use. (Remembered Circular Queue)

Let's talk more accurately. A key is made finalizable, finalized, and then broken from the map. When a key has been discarded its entry is effectively removed from the map by **garbage collector**.

Following is the list of constructors of this class.

*WeakHashMap( )*
*WeakHashMap(int initialCapacity)*
*WeakHashMap(int initialCapacity, float loadFactor)*
*WeakHashMap(Map m)*

**First** constructor constructs a new, empty WeakHashMap with the default initial capacity (16) and load factor (0.75). **Second** constructor constructs a new, empty WeakHashMap with the given initial capacity and the default load factor (0.75). **Third** constructor constructs a new, empty WeakHashMap with the given initial capacity and the given load factor. **Fourth** constructor constructs a new WeakHashMap with the same mappings as the specified map.

| Method | Description |
|---|---|
| void clear( ) | Removes all of the mappings from this map. |
| boolean containsKey(Object key) | Returns true if this map contains a mapping for the specified key. |
| boolean containsValue(Object value) | Returns true if this map maps one or more keys to the specified value. |
| Set entrySet( ) | Returns a Set view of the mappings contained in this map. |

| | |
|---|---|
| object get(Object key) | Returns the value to which the specified key is mapped, or null if this map contains no mapping for the key. |
| boolean isEmpty( ) | Returns true if this map contains no key-value mappings. |
| Set keySet( ) | Returns a Set view of the keys contained in this map. |
| Object put(K key, V value) | Associates the specified value with the specified key in this map. |
| void putAll(Map m) | Copies all of the mappings from the specified map to this map. |
| Object remove(Object key) | Removes the mapping for a key from this weak hash map if it is present. |
| int size( ) | Returns the number of key-value mappings in this map. |
| Collection values( ) | Returns a Collection view of the values contained in this map. |

Following is the example that demonstrates WeakHashMap class.

```
import java.util.WeakHashMap;

public class WeakHashMapDemo
{
        public static void main(String ar[ ])
        {
                // Fill a weak hash map with one entry
                WeakHashMap<Data, String> map = new WeakHashMap<Data, String>( );
                Data DataObj = new Data("Demo");
                map.put(DataObj, DataObj.value);
                System.out.println("map contains DataObj ? " + map.containsKey(DataObj));

                //now make DataObj elligible for garbage collection...
                DataObj = null;
                for (int i = 0; i < 10000; i++)
                {
                        if (map.size( ) != 0)
                        {
                                System.out.println("At iteration " + i + " the map still holds the reference on
                                DataObj");
                        }
                        else
                        {
                                System.out.println("somDataObject has finally been garbage collected at
                                iteration " + i + ", hence the map is now empty");
                                break;
                        }
                }
        }

        static class Data
        {
                String value;
                Data(String value)
                {
                        this.value = value;
                }
        }
}
```

### 20.7.2.5 LinkedHashMap class

This class extends HashMap. Following is the signature of this class.

*public class LinkedHashMap<K,V> extends HashMap<K,V> implements Map<K,V>*

LinkedHashMap maintains a linked list of the entries in the map, in the order in which they were inserted. This allows insertion-order iteration over the map. That is, when iterating a LinkedHashMap, the elements will be returned in the order in which they were inserted. You can also create a LinkedHashMap that returns its elements in the order in which they were last accessed. LinkedHashMap defines the following constructors.

*LinkedHashMap( )*
*LinkedHashMap(Map m)*
*LinkedHashMap(int capacity)*
*LinkedHashMap(int capacity, float fillRatio)*
*LinkedHashMap(int capacity, float fillRatio, boolean Order)*

**First** constructor constructs an empty insertion-ordered LinkedHashMap instance with the default initial capacity (16) and load factor (0.75). **Second** constructor constructs an insertion-ordered LinkedHashMap instance with the same mappings as the specified map. **Third** constructor constructs an empty insertion-ordered LinkedHashMap instance with the specified initial capacity and a default load factor (0.75). **Fourth** constructor constructs an empty insertion-ordered LinkedHashMap instance with the specified initial capacity and load factor. **Fifth** constructor constructs an empty LinkedHashMap instance with the specified initial capacity, load factor and ordering mode.

This class uses all the methods defined by HashMap, and adds only one concrete method to its own. This method is **removeEldestEntry( )**. This method is defined as:

*protected boolean removeEldestEntry(Map.Entry e)*

This method is called by **put( )** and **putAll( )**. The oldest entry is passed to *e* as argument. By default, this method returns false and does nothing. However, if we override this method, then we can have the *LinkedHashMap* remove the oldest entry in the map. To do this, have your override return true. To keep the oldest entry, return false.

### 20.7.2.6 IdentityHashMap class

All previous map classes, compares keys and values using object-equality. This class *compares keys and values using reference-equality*. This class is defined as:

*public class IdentityHashMap<K,V> extends AbstractMap<K,V> implements Map<K,V>, Serializable, Cloneable*

Following is the list of overloaded constructors of this class.

*IdentityHashMap( )*
*IdentityHashMap(int expectedMaxSize)*
*IdentityHashMap(Map m)*

**First** constructor constructs a new, empty identity hash map with a default expected maximum size (21). **Second** constructor constructs a new, empty map with the specified expected maximum size. **Third** constructor constructs a new identity hash map containing the keys-value mappings in the specified map.

Following is the list of methods available in this class.

| Method | Description |
|---|---|
| void clear( ) | Removes all of the mappings from this map. |
| Object clone( ) | Returns a shallow copy of this identity hash map: the keys and values |

| | |
|---|---|
| | themselves are not cloned. |
| boolean containsKey(Object *key*) | Tests whether the specified object reference is a key in this identity hash map. |
| boolean containsValue(Object *value*) | Tests whether the specified object reference is a value in this identity hash map. |
| Set entrySet( ) | Returns a Set view of the mappings contained in this map. |
| boolean equals(Object *obj*) | Compares the specified object with this map for equality. |
| Object get(Object *key*) | Returns the value to which the specified key is mapped, or null if this map contains no mapping for the key. |
| int hashCode( ) | Returns the hash code value for this map. |
| boolean isEmpty( ) | Returns true if this identity hash map contains no key-value mappings. |
| Set keySet( ) | Returns an identity-based set view of the keys contained in this map. |
| Object put(Object *key*, Object *value*) | Associates the specified value with the specified key in this identity hash map. |
| void putAll(Map *m*) | Copies all of the mappings from the specified map to this map. |
| Object remove(Object *key*) | Removes the mapping for this key from this map if present. |
| int size( ) | Returns the number of key-value mappings in this identity hash map. |
| Collection values( ) | Returns a Collection view of the values contained in this map. |

## 20.8 Arrays class

No developer likes to work with a large array and to use loops to cycle through an array to perform different operations (such as; display, binary search, fill, compare, sort, etc.) on it.

This class *Arrays* is added by Java 2, containing different **overloaded static methods** to work with an array. It is not the part of collections framework but help to fill the gap between collections and array. Following is the list of methods that are provided by this class, we will see their overloaded versions later in this section.

***static List asList( )***
***static int binarySearch( )***
***static boolean equals( )***
***static void fill( )***
***static void sort( )***

This is simply a list of methods that are overloaded in this class, **except asList( )** method**.** Straight point is, we provide any array as parameters to these overloaded methods, and that array will be **controlled by Arrays class' methods** to perform different operations. Now, let's study and see the role of these methods, individually.

The **asList( ) method** returns a *List* that is flipped by a specified array. Very simply we can say that the array is returned as a List object. It has the following signature:

*static List asList(Object arr[ ])*

Here, *arr[ ]* is the array that contains the data.

The **binarySearch( ) method** used to find specific value. This method must apply only to sorted arrays. Following are the overloaded forms of this method.

*static int binarySearch(byte arr[ ], byte val)*

*static int binarySearch(char arr[ ], char val)*
*static int binarySearch(double arr[ ], double val)*
*static int binarySearch(float arr[ ], float val)*
*static int binarySearch(int arr[ ], int val)*
*static int binarySearch(long arr[ ], long val)*
*static int binarySearch(short arr[ ], short val)*
*static int binarySearch(Object arr[ ], Object val) throws ClassCastException*
*static int binarySearch(Object[ ] array, Object value, Comparator c) throws ClassCastException*

Here, *arr[ ]* is the name of array in which binary search is to be made and *val* is the value that is to be searched.

The **equals( ) method** equates two arrays. If they are totally equal then returns **true** otherwise returns **false**. This method has following overloaded forms.

*static boolean equals(boolean arr1[ ], boolean arr2[ ])*
*static boolean equals(byte arr1[ ], byte arr2[ ])*
*static boolean equals(char arr1[ ], char arr2[ ])*
*static boolean equals(double arr1[ ], double arr2[ ])*
*static boolean equals(float arr1[ ], float arr2[ ])*
*static boolean equals(int arr1[ ], int arr2[ ])*
*static boolean equals(long arr1[ ], long arr2[ ])*
*static boolean equals(short arr1[ ], short arr2[ ])*
*static boolean equals(Object arr1[ ], Object arr2[ ])*

Here, arr1 and arr2 are the arrays to that are to be checked for equality.

The **fill( ) method** fills an array with a value. This fill( ) method has two editions. First one fills the entire array with specified value. See following overloaded signatures of fill( ) method.

*static void fill(boolean arr[ ], boolean val)*
*static void fill(byte arr[ ], byte val)*
*static void fill(char arr[ ], char val)*
*static void fill(double arr[ ], double val)*
*static void fill(float arr[ ], float val)*
*static void fill(int arr[ ], int val)*
*static void fill(long arr[ ], long val)*
*static void fill(short arr[ ], short val)*
*static void fill(Object arr[ ], Object val)*

Here, *arr* is the array name and *val* is the value to be filled.

Second edition of this method works on range, i.e. specified *start_index* to *end_index* – 1. See following signatures.

*static void fill(boolean arr[ ], int start_index, int end_index, boolean val)*
*static void fill(byte arr[ ], int start_index, int end_index, byte val)*
*static void fill(char arr[ ], int start_index, int end_index, char val)*
*static void fill(double arr[ ], int start_index, int end_index, double val)*
*static void fill(float arr[ ], int start_index, int end_index, float val)*
*static void fill(int arr[ ], int start_index, int end_index, int val)*
*static void fill(long arr[ ], int start_index, int end_index, long val)*

*static void fill(short arr[ ], int start_index, int end_index, short val)*
*static void fill(Object arr[ ], int start_index, int end_index, Object val)*

Here, *arr* is the array name, *start_index* and *end_index* are the range, *val* is the value to be filled. Here, all the methods throws **IllegalArgumentException** if *start_index* is greater than *end_index* and **ArrayIndexOutOfBoundsException** if start_index and end_index are out of sizes.

The **sot( ) method** sorts an array into ascending order. Following are the overloaded signatures of sort( ) method.

*static void sort(byte arr[ ])*
*static void sort(char arr[ ])*
*static void sort(double arr[ ])*
*static void sort(float arr[ ])*
*static void sort(int arr[ ])*
*static void sort(long arr[ ])*
*static void sort(short arr[ ])*
*static void sort(Object arr[ ]) throws ClassCastException*
*static void sort(Object arr[ ], Comparator c) throws ClassCastException*

Here, *arr* is the name of array to be sorted. This sort( ) method also has second edition, where we can provide *start_index* and *end_index* as range. Sorting will be performed between these ranges only.

Following program, demonstrates the role of static methods of this class.

```
import java.io.*;
import java.util.*;
class ArraysDemo
{
        public static void main(String ar[ ]) throws Exception
        {
                int array[ ] = new int[10];
                DataInputStream dis = new DataInputStream(System.in);

                // accepting array
                System.out.println("Enter array contents");
                for(int i = 0; i <=9; i++)
                array[i] = Integer.parseInt(dis.readLine( ));

                // displaying original contents
                System.out.print("Original contents:\n");
                display(array);

                //sorting and displaying contents
                Arrays.sort(array);
                System.out.print("\n\nSorted contents:\n");
                display(array);

                //filling indexed part and display
                Arrays.fill(array, 2, 6, 55);
```

```
        System.out.print("\n\nAfter fill( ) method is invoked:\n");
        display(array);

        // again sorting after filling and display
        Arrays.sort(array);
        System.out.print("\n\nAfter sorting again:\n");
        display(array);

        // binary search for content
        System.out.println("\n\nEnter element to be searched : ");
        int n = Integer.parseInt(dis.readLine( ));
        int ind = Arrays.binarySearch(array, n);
        System.out.print("\n\nDesired value is at location " + ind);
    }

    static void display(int arr[ ])
    {
        for(int i = 0; i < arr.length; i++)
        System.out.print(arr[i] + " ");
    }
}
```

Output of above program will be:

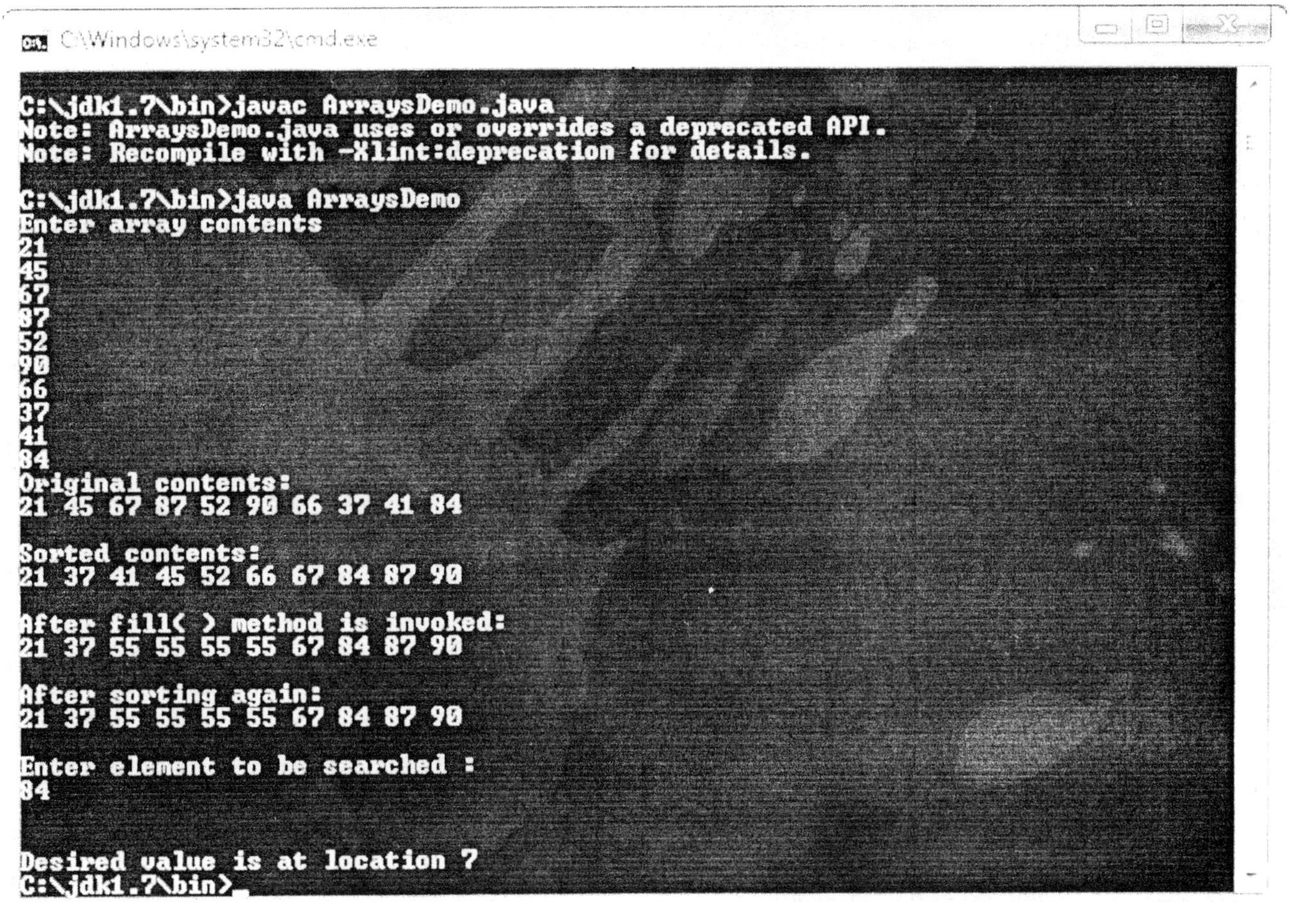

```
C:\Windows\system32\cmd.exe

C:\jdk1.7\bin>javac ArraysDemo.java
Note: ArraysDemo.java uses or overrides a deprecated API.
Note: Recompile with -Xlint:deprecation for details.

C:\jdk1.7\bin>java ArraysDemo
Enter array contents
21
45
67
87
52
90
66
37
41
84
Original contents:
21 45 67 87 52 90 66 37 41 84

Sorted contents:
21 37 41 45 52 66 67 84 87 90

After fill( ) method is invoked:
21 37 55 55 55 55 67 84 87 90

After sorting again:
21 37 55 55 55 55 67 84 87 90

Enter element to be searched :
84


Desired value is at location 7
C:\jdk1.7\bin>_
```

## 20.9 The legacy classes and interfaces

All above classes and interface are **part of Java Collection Framework, except Arrays class**. *None of the collection classes are synchronized.* But during many development situations we required synchronized objects. This gap is fulfilled by a small group of classes and interfaces, called as **legacy classes and interfaces**.

These legacy classes and interfaces are reengineered during Java 2 release and supports synchronization and all collection interfaces. This legacy classes and interfaces are included in *java. util* and they are listed below.

- Enumeration interface
- Vector class
- Stack class
- Dictionary class
- Hashtable class
- Properties class

Let's study these legacy classes and interfaces in detail.

### 20.9.1 Enumeration Interface

In all above examples we have used Iterator to cycle through a list instance. The Enumeration interface is also used for same purpose, but the difference is that the Enumeration interface obtains only one element at a time, i.e. provide enumeration.

The Enumeration interface is replaced by the Iterator and the use of Enumeration gets reduced. But still, Enumeration is used by several methods defined by the legacy classes such as Vector and Properties, is used by several other API classes, and is currently in widespread use in application code.

This interface is defined with following two methods.

| Method | Description |
|---|---|
| boolean hasMoreElements( ) | When implemented, it must return **true** while there are still more elements to retrieve, and **false** when all the elements have been retrieved. |
| Object nextElement( ) | This returns the next object in the enumeration as a generic Object reference. |

Following program demonstrates the use of Enumeration interface to display elements of a Vector.

```
import java.util.Vector;
import java.util.Enumeration;

public class EnumerationDemo
{
        public static void main(String ar[ ])
        {
                Enumeration days;
                Vector dayNames = new Vector( );
                dayNames.add("Sunday");
                dayNames.add("Monday");
                dayNames.add("Tuesday");
                dayNames.add("Wednesday");
                dayNames.add("Thursday");
```

```
            dayNames.add("Friday");
            dayNames.add("Saturday");
            days = dayNames.elements( );
            while (days.hasMoreElements( ))
            {
                    System.out.println(days.nextElement( ));
            }
        }
    }
```

Output of above program will be:

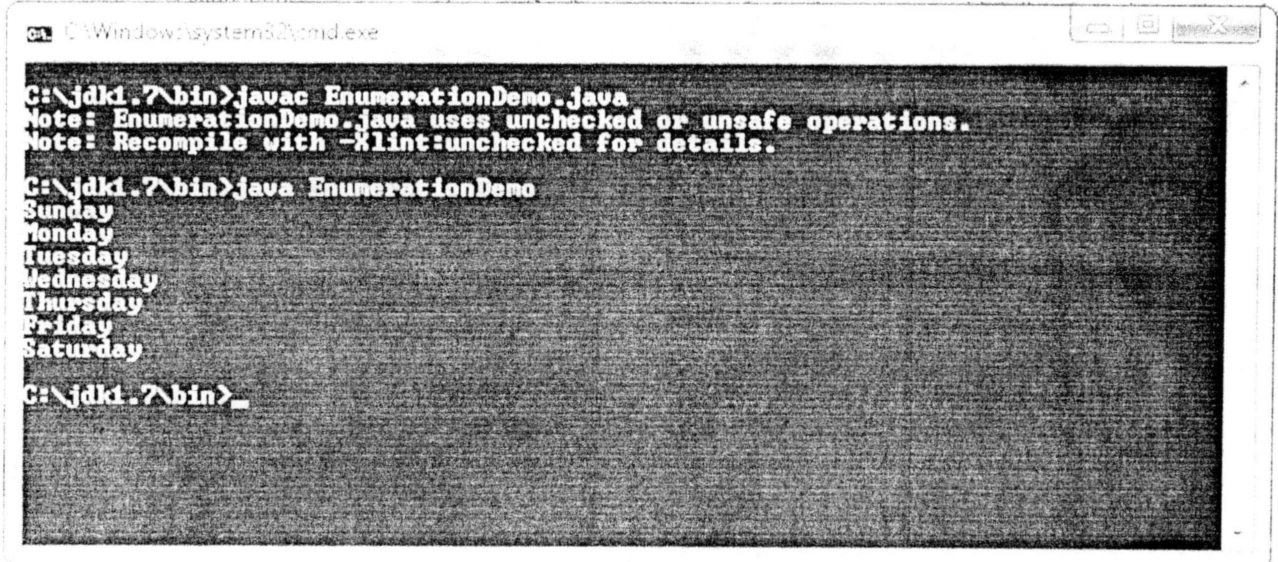

```
C:\jdk1.7\bin>javac EnumerationDemo.java
Note: EnumerationDemo.java uses unchecked or unsafe operations.
Note: Recompile with -Xlint:unchecked for details.

C:\jdk1.7\bin>java EnumerationDemo
Sunday
Monday
Tuesday
Wednesday
Thursday
Friday
Saturday

C:\jdk1.7\bin>_
```

### 20.9.2 Vector class

A vector is a legacy class which provides dynamic array implementation; same as ArrayList class (refer section 20.4.5). But Vector differs from ArrayList in two ways. One Vector is synchronized and second Vector contains many legacy methods that are not available in ArrayList. Following is the signature of Vector class.

*public class Vector<E> extends AbstractList<E> implements List<E>, RandomAccess, Cloneable, Serializable*

We have already discussed that legacy classes were reengineered by Java 2. Previously Vector class was not compatible with collections, because previously it was not extending AbstractList and implementing List. But now it is fully compatible with collections.

Let's discuss one important characteristic of vector. All vectors start with an initial capacity. After a vector is filled up to this initial capacity, the next time when we attempt to store an object in the vector, the vector automatically allocates space for that object, along with extra spaces for additional objects. This additional space is actually the double of initial capacity of vector. This always results as extra space allocation during program execution. For example, a vector of initial capacity 10, if gets filled, allocates new 10 spaces to store next single object. This can be controlled by third constructor specified below.

Following are the constructors of Vector.

*Vector( )*
*Vector(int size)*
*Vector(int size, int incr)*
*Vector(Collection c)*

**First** form creates a default vector with initial size of 10. **Second** form creates a vector with specified size. **Third** form creates a vector with initial *size* whose increment is specified by *incr*. **Fourth** constructor creates a vector and initialize it with specified collection elements.

Vector class defines following data members as protected.

*int capacityIncrement*
*int elementCount*
*Object[ ] elementData*

The increment value is stored in **capacityIncrement**. The number of elements currently in the vector is stored in **elementCount**. The array that holds the vector is stored in **elementData**.

In addition to these data members, this class also defines several methods. These methods are explained in following table.

| Method | Description |
|---|---|
| void addElement(Object *ele*) | The object specified by *ele* is added to the vector. |
| int capacity( ) | Returns the capacity of the vector. |
| Object clone( ) | Returns a duplicate of the invoking vector. |
| boolean contains(Object *ele*) | Returns **true** if *ele* is contained by the vector, and returns **false** if it is not. |
| void copyInto(Object arr[ ]) | The elements contained in the invoking vector are copied into the array specified by arr. |
| Object elementAt(int *index*) | Returns the element at the location specified by index. |
| Enumeration elements( ) | Returns an enumeration of the elements in the vector. |
| void ensureCapacity(int *size*) | Sets the minimum capacity of the vector to size. |
| Object firstElement( ) | Returns the first element in the vector. |
| int indexOf(Object *ele*) | Returns the index of the first occurrence of *ele*. If the object is not in the vector, –1 is returned. |
| int indexOf(Object *ele*, int *start*) | Returns the index of the first occurrence of *ele* at or after *start*. If the object is not in that portion of the vector, –1 is returned. |
| void insertElementAt(Object *ele*, int *index*) | Adds *ele* to the vector at the location specified by *index*. |
| boolean isEmpty( ) | Returns true if the vector is empty and returns false if it contains one or more elements. |
| Object lastElement( ) | Returns the last element in the vector. |
| int lastIndexOf(Object *ele*) | Returns the index of the last occurrence of *ele*. If the object is not in the vector, –1 is returned. |
| int lastIndexOf(Object *ele*, int *start*) | Returns the index of the last occurrence of *ele* before *start*. If the object is not in that portion of the vector, –1 is returned. |
| void removeAllElements( ) | Empties the vector. After this method executes, the size of the vector is zero. |
| boolean removeElement(Object *ele*) | Removes *ele* from the vector. If more than one instance of the specified object exists in the vector, then it is the first one that is removed. Returns true if successful and false if the object is not found. |
| void removeElementAt(int *index*) | Removes the element at the location specified by *index*. |
| void setElementAt(Object *ele*, *int* index) | The location specified by *index* is assigned *ele*. |

| | |
|---|---|
| void setSize(int *size*) | Sets the number of elements in the vector to *size*. If the new size is less than the old size, elements are lost. If the new size is larger than the old size, null elements are added. |
| int size( ) | Returns the number of elements currently in the vector. |
| String toString( ) | Returns the string equivalent of the vector. |
| void trimToSize( ) | Sets the vector's capacity equal to the number of elements that it currently holds. |

The following program demonstrates the legacy methods of Vector and stores various types of numeric objects.

```
import java.util.*;

public class VectorDemo
{
        public static void main(String ar[ ])
        {
                // initial size is 3, increment is 2
                Vector v = new Vector(3, 2);
                System.out.println("Initial size: " + v.size( ));
                System.out.println("Initial capacity: " + v.capacity( ));
                v.addElement(new Integer(1));
                v.addElement(new Integer(2));
                v.addElement(new Integer(3));
                v.addElement(new Integer(4));
                System.out.println("Capacity after four additions: " + v.capacity( ));
                v.addElement(new Double(5.45));
                System.out.println("Current capacity: " + v.capacity( ));
                v.addElement(new Double(6.08));
                v.addElement(new Integer(7));
                System.out.println("Current capacity: " + v.capacity( ));
                v.addElement(new Float(9.4));
                v.addElement(new Integer(10));
                System.out.println("Current capacity: " + v.capacity( ));
                v.addElement(new Integer(11));
                v.addElement(new Integer(12));
                System.out.println("First element: " + (Integer)v.firstElement( ));
                System.out.println("Last element: " + (Integer)v.lastElement( ));
                if(v.contains(new Integer(3)))
                System.out.println("Vector contains 3.");
                // use an iterator to display contents
                Iterator itr = v.iterator( );
                System.out.println("\nElements in vector:");
                while(itr.hasNext( ))
                System.out.print(vItr.next( ) + " ");
        }
}
```

The output of above program will be:

```
C:\jdk1.7\bin>javac VectorDemo.java
Note: VectorDemo.java uses unchecked or unsafe operations.
Note: Recompile with -Xlint:unchecked for details.

C:\jdk1.7\bin>java VectorDemo
Initial size: 0
Initial capacity: 3
Capacity after four additions: 5
Current capacity: 5
Current capacity: 7
Current capacity: 9
First element: 1
Last element: 12
Vector contains 3.

Elements in vector:
1 2 3 4 5.45 6.08 7 9.4 10 11 12

C:\jdk1.7\bin>_
```

### 20.9.3 Stack class

Stack is a subclass of Vector and implements the standard stack characteristic LIFO (Last-in First-out). The signature of this class is:

*public class Stack<E> extends Vector<E>*

This class has only one constructor, i.e. its default constructor that creates an empty stack. Along with Vector methods, this class also adds several methods; such as **push( )** and **pop( )**. Following table explains the methods of this class.

| Method | Description |
|---|---|
| boolean empty( ) | Returns true if the stack is empty, and returns false if the stack contains elements. |
| Object peek( ) | Returns the element on the top of the stack, but does not remove it. |
| Object pop( ) | Returns the element on the top of the stack, removing it in the process. |
| Object push(Object *ele*) | Pushes *ele* onto the stack. Same element is also returned. |
| int search(Object *ele*) | Searches for *ele* in the stack. If found, its offset from the top of the stack is returned. Otherwise, –1 is returned. |

Following program demonstrates several methods that are provided by this class.

```
import java.util.*;

public class StackDemo
{
public static void main(String ar[ ])
{
```

```
        Stack st = new Stack( );
        System.out.println("initially stack elements are : " + st);
        st.push(new Integer(42));
        System.out.println("Element 42 is pushed");
        st.push(new Integer(66));
        System.out.println("Element 66 is pushed");
        st.push(new Integer(99));
        System.out.println("Element 99 is pushed");
        System.out.println("Afeter three push operations, stack elements are : " + st);
        System.out.println("Now performing pop operations");
        System.out.println("Popped element : " + st.pop( ));
        System.out.println("Popped element : " + st.pop( ));
        System.out.println("Popped element : " + st.pop( ));
        System.out.println("Afeter three pop operations, stack elements are : " + st);
        try
        {
           showpop(st);
        }
        catch (EmptyStackException e)
        {
          System.out.println("empty stack");
        }
      }
    }
```

Output of above program will be:

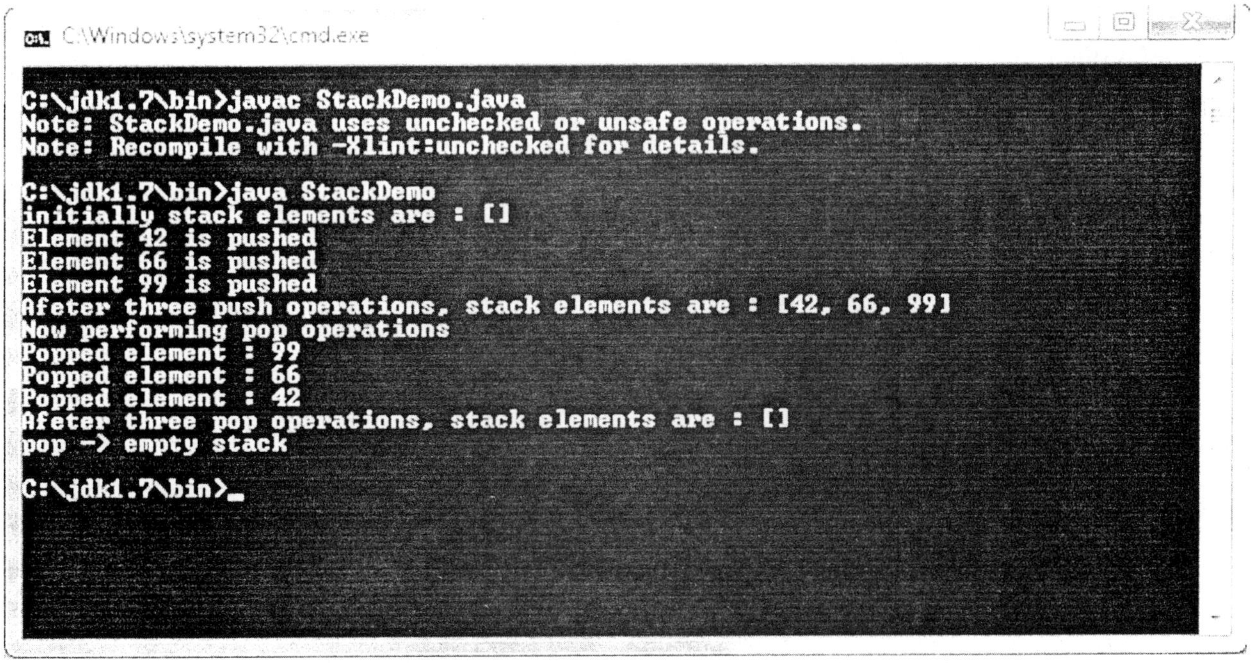

```
C:\Windows\system32\cmd.exe

C:\jdk1.7\bin>javac StackDemo.java
Note: StackDemo.java uses unchecked or unsafe operations.
Note: Recompile with -Xlint:unchecked for details.

C:\jdk1.7\bin>java StackDemo
initially stack elements are : []
Element 42 is pushed
Element 66 is pushed
Element 99 is pushed
Afeter three push operations, stack elements are : [42, 66, 99]
Now performing pop operations
Popped element : 99
Popped element : 66
Popped element : 42
Afeter three pop operations, stack elements are : []
pop -> empty stack

C:\jdk1.7\bin>_
```

### 20.9.4 Dictionary class

Dictionary is an abstract class that operates much like a Map and stores key/value. Following is the signature of this class.

*public abstract class Dictionary<K,V> extends Object*

Here, K represents key and V represents value.

Once the value is stored as an object at specified key, we can retrieve that value it by using same key. Although, Dictionary class is not that much preferred, because it is out of date and replaced by Map. Still Dictionary interface is still in use, with its abstract methods. Following is the list of abstract methods of this class.

| Method | Description |
|---|---|
| Enumeration elements( ) | Returns an enumeration of the values contained in the dictionary. |
| Object get(Object *key*) | Returns the object that contains the value associated with key. If key is not in the dictionary, a null object is returned. |
| boolean isEmpty( ) | Returns true if the dictionary is empty, and returns false if it contains at least one key. |
| Enumeration keys( ) | Returns an enumeration of the keys contained in the dictionary. |
| Object put(Object *key*, Object *value*) | Inserts a *key* and its *value* into the dictionary. Returns null if key is not already in the dictionary; returns the previous value associated with key if key is already in the dictionary. |
| Object remove(Object *key*) | Removes key and its value. Returns the value associated with key. If key is not in the dictionary, a null is returned. |
| int size( ) | Returns the number of entries in the dictionary. |

Following program demonstrates the use of this class in coordination with *Hashtable* (refer section 20.9.5) for *Hashtable*.

```
import java.util.*;
public class DictionaryDemo
{
        public static void main(String ar[ ])
        {
                Dictionary d=new Hashtable( );
                d.put("1", "Dictionary1");
                d.put("2","Dictionary2" );
                d.put("3","Dictionary3" );
                d.put("4","Dictionary4" );
                d.put("10","Dictionary5" );
                System.out.println(d.get("4"));
                System.out.println(d.remove("4")+"  has been removed");
                System.out.println("the  value of key 4 = " +d.get("4"));
                for(Enumeration e = d.keys( ); e.hasMoreElements( );)
                System.out.println(e.nextElement( ));
                System.out.println(e.nextElement( ));
        }
}
```

Output of above program will be:

*Dictionary1*
*Dictionary1 has been removed*
*the value of key 4 = null*
*1*
*2*
*3*
*10*

### 20.9.5 Hashtable class

In Java 2, the Hashtable class was reengineered and implemented Map interface and obtained support for key/value. Following is the signature of this class.

*public class Hashtable<K,V> extends Dictionary<K,V> implements Map<K,V>, Cloneable, Serializable*

When using a Hashtable, simply specify an object that is used as a key, and the value that you want linked to that key. The key is then hashed, and the resulting hash code is used as the index at which the value is stored within the table. The most common type of Hashtable uses a String object as the key.

The Hashtable constructors are shown here:

*Hashtable( )*
*Hashtable(int size)*
*Hashtable(int size, float load_factor)*
*Hashtable(Map m)*

First constructor constructs a new, empty Hashtable instance with a default initial capacity (11) and load factor (0.75). Second constructor constructs a new, empty Hashtable instance with the specified initial size and default load factor (0.75). Third constructor constructs a new, empty Hashtable instance with the specified initial size and the specified *load_factor*. Fourth constructor constructs a new Hashtable instance with the same mappings as the given Map *m*.

Refer following methods of Hashtable class.

| Method | Description |
|---|---|
| void clear( ) | Resets and empties the hash table. |
| Object clone( ) | Returns a duplicate of the invoking object. |
| boolean contains(Object *val*) | Returns **true** if some *val* equal to value exists within the hash table. Returns **false** if the value isn't found. |
| boolean containsKey(Object *key*) | Returns **true** if some *key* equal to key exists within the hash table. Returns **false** if the key isn't found. |
| boolean containsValue(Object *val*) | Returns **true** if some *val* equal to value exists within the hash table. Returns **false** if the value isn't found. |
| Enumeration elements( ) | Returns an enumeration of the values contained in the hash table. |
| Object get(Object *key*) | Returns the object that contains the value associated with *key*. If key is not in the hash table, a null object is returned. |
| boolean isEmpty( ) | Returns **true** if the hash table is empty; returns **false** if it contains at least one key. |
| Enumeration keys( ) | Returns an enumeration of the keys contained in the hash table. |
| Object put(Object *key*, Object *val*) | Inserts a *key* and a *val* into the hash table. |

| | |
|---|---|
| void rehash( ) | Increases the size of the hash table and rehashes all of its keys. |
| Object remove(Object *key*) | Removes key and its value. Returns the value associated with specified *key*. If key is not in the hash table, a null object is returned. |
| int size( ) | Returns the number of entries in the hash table. |
| String toString( ) | Returns the string equivalent of a hash table. |

Remember, if many entries are to be made into a Hashtable, creating it with a sufficiently large capacity may allow the entries to be inserted more efficiently than letting it perform automatic rehashing as needed to grow the table.

Refer following example.

```
import java.util.*;

public class HashtableDemo
{
        public static void main(String ar[ ])
        {
                // Create a hash map
                Hashtable balance = new Hashtable( );
                Enumeration names;
                String str;
                double bal;

                // filling balance
                balance.put("Deepak", new Double(14345.34));
                balance.put("Rakesh", new Double(12312.22));
                balance.put("Nitin", new Double(13478.00));
                balance.put("Kaushik", new Double(1299.22));
                balance.put("Kartik", new Double(1420.08));

                // Show all balances in hash table.
                names = balance.keys( );
                while(names.hasMoreElements( ))
                {
                        str = (String) names.nextElement( );
                        System.out.println(str + " : " + balance.get(str));
                }

                // Deposit 1000 into Kartik's account
                bal = ((Double)balance.get("Nitin")).doubleValue( );
                balance.put("Kartik", new Double(bal+1000));
                System.out.println("Kartik's new balance: " + balance.get("Kartik"));
        }
}
```

Output of above program will be:

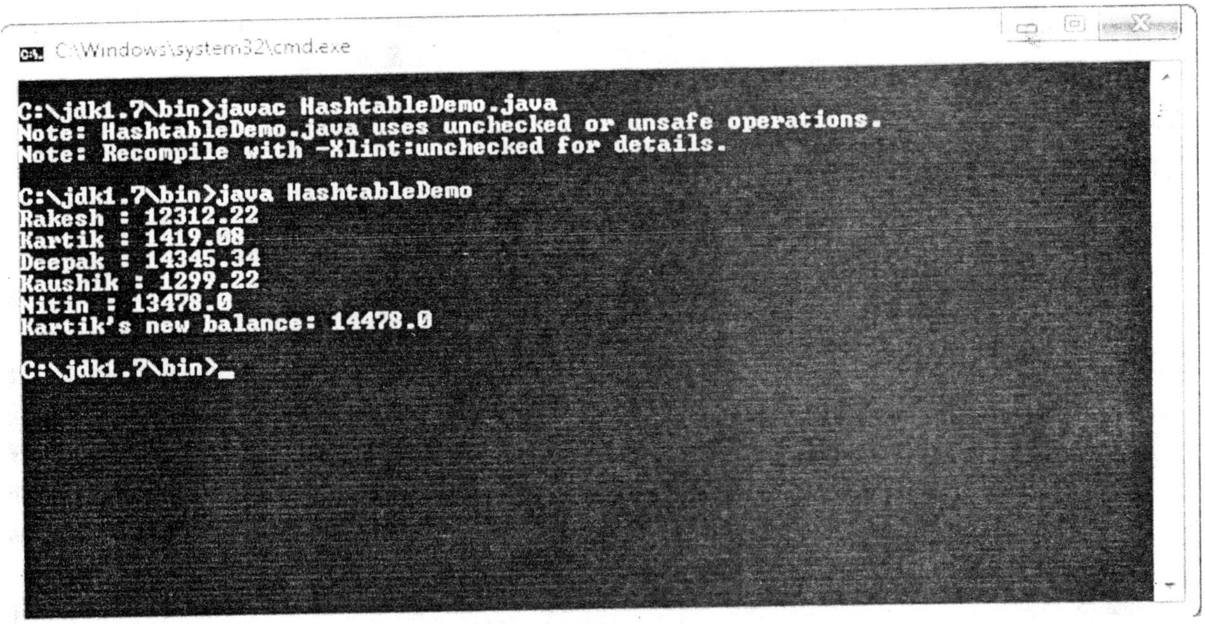

```
C:\Windows\system32\cmd.exe

C:\jdk1.7\bin>javac HashtableDemo.java
Note: HashtableDemo.java uses unchecked or unsafe operations.
Note: Recompile with -Xlint:unchecked for details.

C:\jdk1.7\bin>java HashtableDemo
Rakesh : 12312.22
Kartik : 1419.08
Deepak : 14345.34
Kaushik : 1299.22
Nitin : 13478.0
Kartik's new balance: 14478.0

C:\jdk1.7\bin>_
```

In above program, the elements of Hashtable are displayed by using Enumeration, but same can be done by using Iterator also. Refer following replacement.

```
Iterator itr = set.iterator( );
while(itr.hasNext( ))
{
        str = (String) itr.next( );
        System.out.println(str + ": " + balance.get(str));
}
```

This will also display the same output.

**20.9.6 Properties class**

This class is the derived class of Hashtable class. It is defined as follows.

*public class Properties extends Hashtable<Object,Object>*

This class is used to maintain lists of values in which the key and value, both are String instances. The Properties class is used by many other Java classes. For example, it is the type of object returned by **System.getProperties( )** when obtaining environmental values. Similarly in *Servlet* also, **request.getProperty( )** method is used that returns the value of *specified_property* name. Where, *property_name* is the *key*.

Following are the overloaded constructors of this class.

*Properties( )*
*Properties(Properties propDefault)*

**First** constructor creates an empty property list with no default values. **Second** constructor creates an empty property list with the specified defaults.

This class also defines one protected data member;

*Properties defaults;*

This data member holds the *default* values for any keys not found in this property list.

This class extends *Hashtable* class. Along with the methods of Hashtable, this class also defines its concrete methods. These methods are listed in following table.

| Method | Description |
|---|---|
| String getProperty(String *key*) | Returns the value associated with key. A null object is returned if key is neither in the list nor in the default property list. |
| String getProperty(String *key*, String *defaultProperty*) | Returns the value associated with key. defaultProperty is returned if key is neither in the list nor in the default property list. |
| void list(PrintStream *streamOut*) | Sends the property list to the output stream linked to streamOut. |
| void list(PrintWriter *streamOut*) | Sends the property list to the output stream linked to streamOut. |
| void load(InputStream *streamIn*) throws IOException | Inputs a property list from the input stream linked to streamIn. |
| Enumeration propertyNames( ) | Returns an enumeration of the keys. This includes those keys found in the default property list, too. |
| Object setProperty(String *key*, String *value*) | Associates value with key. Returns the previous value associated with key, or returns null if no such association exists. |
| void store(OutputStream *streamOut*, String *description*) | After writing the string specified by description, the property list is written to the output stream linked to streamOut. |

Let's study one example that demonstrates the simple methods of this class.

```
import java.util.*;
class PropertiesDemo
{
        public static void main(String ar[ ])
        {
                Properties propList = new Properties();
                propList.put("Gujarat", "Gandhinagar");
                propList.put("Maharashtra", "Mumbai");
                Properties statecapitals = new Properties(propList);
                Set states;
                String str;
                statecapitals.put("Bihar", "Patna");
                statecapitals.put("Punjab", "Chandigarh");
                statecapitals.put("Tamil Nadu", "Chennai");
                statecapitals.put("Karnataka", "Bengaluru");
                statecapitals.put("Rajasthan", "Jaipur");

                // Show all states and capitals in hashtable.
                states = statecapitals.keySet( );
                Iterator itr = states.iterator( );
                while(itr.hasNext( ))
                {
                        str = (String) itr.next( );
```

```
            System.out.println("The capital of " + str + " is " + statecapitals.getProperty(str) + ".");
        }

        // Bihar will now be found in the default list.
        str = statecapitals.getProperty("Bihar");
        System.out.println("\nThe capital of Bihar is " + str + ".");
    }
}
```

The output of above program will be:

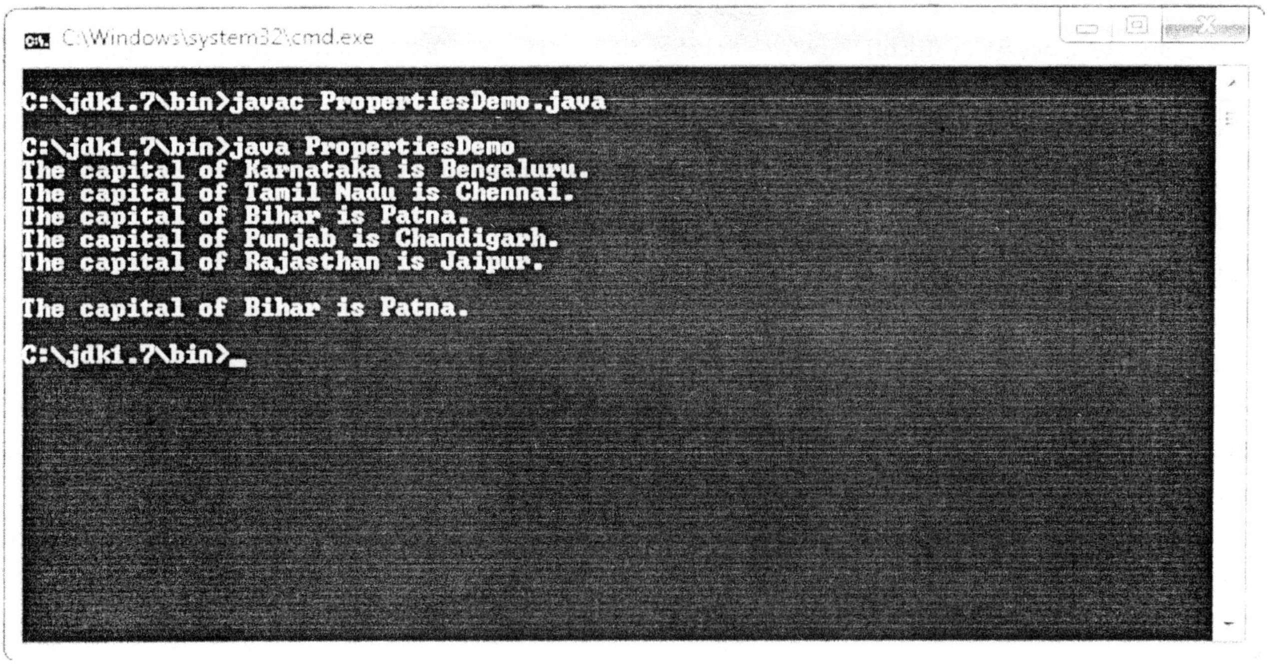

```
C:\Windows\system32\cmd.exe

C:\jdk1.7\bin>javac PropertiesDemo.java

C:\jdk1.7\bin>java PropertiesDemo
The capital of Karnataka is Bengaluru.
The capital of Tamil Nadu is Chennai.
The capital of Bihar is Patna.
The capital of Punjab is Chandigarh.
The capital of Rajasthan is Jaipur.

The capital of Bihar is Patna.

C:\jdk1.7\bin>_
```

* * * * *

# Chapter 21

# Java Naming and Directory Interface

JNDI is an enterprise Java API that provides naming and directory functionality using a common set of classes and interfaces that are independent of a specific naming and directory service implementation. A standard extension to the Java platform, some developers consider its use to be limited to interfacing with directory services such as **LDAP (Lightweight Directory Access Protocol)**. However, this lightweight concept fails to fully justify its flexibility and power. JNDI is a particularly important J2EE API given its pervasive use among other important enterprise Java APIs such as **EJB (Enterprise Java Bean)**, **JDBC (Java Database Connectivity)** and **JMS (Java Message Service)**. This chapter introduces JNDI as a common framework for locating enterprise computing components using enterprise Java APIs such as EJB and JMS.

## 21.1 What is naming and directory services?

Before discussing JNDI, let's have a quick overview of some naming and directory service terminology that might be helpful. Although there are a number of existing naming and directory services, they all share some **common concepts and terms** that are helpful in understanding the flexibility of JNDI. Here's a list of some well-known naming and directory services:

- **LDAP (Lightweight Directory Access Protocol):** A directory services protocol that enables clients to manage and query a hierarchical repository of entries and attributes. For example, LDAP can be used to locate information that belongs to users (e.g., X.509 certificates) and network resources (e.g., available printers).
- **NIS (Network Information System):** A naming service, formerly known as yp, developed by Sun. It allows users to access systems on other hosts with a single user ID and password.
- **COS Naming Service:** The CORBA naming service that enables CORBA clients to locate CORBA server objects using names.
- **DNS (Domain Name Service):** A distributed naming service that allows users to refer to hosts using easily remembered names (e.g., Anthony) instead of IP addresses.

### 21.1.1 Naming service

**A naming service** can be described as *a mechanism that associates names with objects and provides a way to find an object, based on a given name*. A binding can be described as an association of a name with an object. A file name is associated with a reference that an application can use to access a file. A binding is defined relative to a context. A context comprises a set of bindings. For example, /home, the UNIX file directory, is a context comprising a set of bindings pertaining to files and directories. The process of finding an object in a context, based on its name is known as **resolution**. This would be fairly similar to finding phone number of a person by referring his name.

All objects in a context are named using a specific naming convention. Thus a naming system can be described as a set of contexts with the same naming convention. For example, in file systems a name in the DOS file system (c:\boot.ini) has a different naming syntax than a name in the UNIX file system (/etc/gated.conf). In opposite way, LDAP's naming syntax reads names from right to left.

When discussing naming systems, we need to describe different types of names. An atomic name is simply an indivisible component of a name. For example, in the directory name */etc/mail*, mail is an atomic name. A compound name is a sequence of atomic names that conforms to a specific naming convention. For example, */var/adm* is a compound name. Composite names span multiple naming systems. For example, a URL such as http:*//www.computerworld.ind.in/contact.html* spans different naming systems such as DNS (Domain Name Service), and the UNIX file system. Namespace is a term used to describe the collection of names in a naming system

### 21.1.2 Directory service

**A directory service** is an extension of the naming service. A directory is typically used to associate attributes with objects. For example, a user object could have attributes such as the user's name, phone number, e-mail address and fax number. Directory services provide functionality for evaluating and modifying attributes attached to contexts and the ability to search a context using those attributes as a filter.

Although naming and directory services such as LDAP, NIS and DNS vary in their exact implementation from one service to the next, JNDI provides a common framework for accessing existing mixed naming and directory services in a way that hides their protocol and implementation details

## 21.2 JNDI architecture

The JNDI architecture can be described in terms of three main layers. JNDI's layered architecture enables clients to use a common API to work with different naming and directory services (Such as DNS, LDAP, COS Naming).

The top layer is the application layer that uses the JNDI API. The middle layer is the JNDI API that defines a set of classes and interfaces for supporting common naming and directory service functionality. This is the layer that frees a developer from having to deal with specific naming and directory service complexities. It relies on concrete implementations of naming and directory services.

The bottom layer is the implementation layer. Since the JNDI API is independent of specific naming and directory services, it's up to service providers to provide implementations using the JNDI **Service Provider Interface (SPI),** which can access different naming and directory services. These service provider implementations can easily be plugged in to the JNDI architecture, thus enabling the application layer to access their services using the JNDI API. Following figure shows an overview of the JNDI architecture.

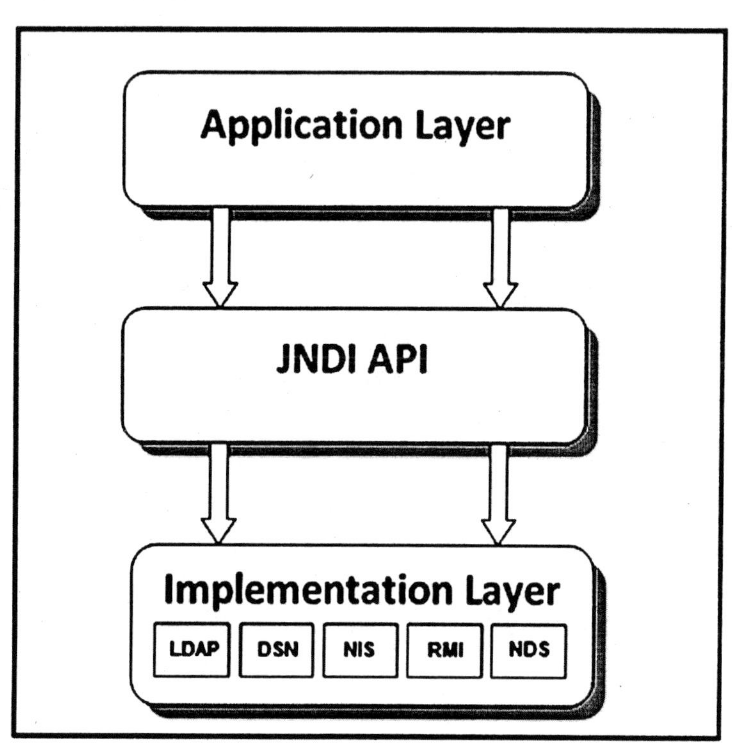

The JNDI API includes number of packages. To provide a more concrete description of the JNDI architecture, the main JNDI packages are explained below.

- **javax.naming:** Defines classes (e.g., *Binding*) and interfaces (e.g., *Name*) for accessing naming services.
- **javax.naming.directory:** The *javax.naming.directory* package extends the *javax.naming* package to provide functionality for accessing directory services in addition to naming services. This package allows applications to retrieve attributes associated with objects stored in the directory and to search for objects using specified attributes. Defines classes (e.g., *InitialDirContext*) and interfaces (e.g., *Attribute*) for accessing directory services
- **javax.naming.event:** Defines classes (e.g., *NamingEvent*) and interfaces (e.g., *NamingListener*) for event notification while accessing naming and directory services
- **javax.naming.ldap:** Defines classes (e.g., *InitialLdapContext*) and interfaces (e.g., *ExtendedRequest*) to provide support for LDAPv3 extended operations and controls.
- **javax.naming.spi:** Defines classes (e.g., *NamingManager*) and interfaces (e.g., *InitialContextFactory*) used to access existing naming and directory services using JNDI's SPI

## 21.3 Resources and JNDI naming

In a distributed application, components need to access other components and resources, such as databases. For example, a servlet might invoke remote methods on an enterprise bean that retrieves information from a database.

In the Java EE platform, the **Java Naming and Directory Interface (JNDI)** naming service enables components to locate other components and resources.

A **resource** is a program object that provides connections to systems, such as database servers and messaging systems.

**Note: data source is a good example of commonly used JDBC resource.**

Each resource object is identified by a unique, people-friendly name, called the JNDI name. For example, the JNDI name of the JDBC resource for the Java DB database that is shipped with the GlassFish Server is jdbc/__default.

An administrator creates resources in a JNDI namespace. In the *GlassFish* Server, we can use either the Administration Console or the as *admin* command to create resources. Applications then use annotations to inject the resources. If an application uses resource injection, the GlassFish Server invokes the JNDI API, and the application is not required to do so. However, it is also possible for an application to locate resources by making direct calls to the JNDI API.

A resource object and its JNDI name are bound together by the naming and directory service. To create a new resource, a new name/object binding is entered into the JNDI namespace. We inject resources by using the @Resource annotation in an application.

We can use a deployment descriptor to override the resource mapping that we specify in an annotation. Using a deployment descriptor allows us to change an application by repackaging it rather than by both recompiling the source files and repackaging. However, for most applications, a deployment descriptor is not necessary.

## 21.4 Resource Injection

The *javax.annotation.Resource* annotation is used to declare a reference to a resource; *@Resource* can decorate a class, a field, or a method. The container will inject the resource referred to by *@Resource* into the component either at runtime or when the component is initialized; depending on whether field/method injection or class injection is used (*refer sections 21.4.1, 21.4.2 and 21.4.3*). With field-based and method-based injection, the container will inject the resource when the application is initialized. For class-based injection, the resource is looked up by the application at runtime.

The @Resource annotation has the following elements:

- *name*: The JNDI name of the resource
- *type*: The Java language type of the resource
- *authenticationType*: The authentication type to use for the resource
- *shareable*: Indicates whether the resource can be shared
- *mappedName*: A non-portable, implementation-specific name to which the resource should be mapped
- *description*: The description of the resource

Let's discuss these elements in brief.

**The *name* element** is the JNDI name of the resource and is optional for field-based and method-based injection. For field-based injection, the default *name* is the field name qualified by the class name. For method-based injection, the default *name* is the *JavaBeans* property name, based on the method qualified by the class name. The name element must be specified for class-based injection.

**The *type* element** is determined by one of the following:

- The type of the field the @Resource annotation is decorating for field-based injection
- The type of the JavaBeans property the @Resource annotation is decorating for method-based injection
- The type element of @Resource

**Note: For class-based injection, the type element is required.**

**The *authenticationType* element** is used only for connection factory resources, such as the resources of a connector, also called the resource adapter, or data source. This element can be set to one of the *javax.annotation.Resource.AuthenticationType* enumerated type values: *CONTAINER*, the *default*, and *APPLICATION*.

**The *shareable* element** is used only for Object Resource Broker (ORB) instance resources or connection factory resource. This *element* indicates whether the resource can be shared between this component and other components and may be set to *true*, the *default*, or *false*.

**The *mappedName* element** is a non-portable, implementation-specific name to which the resource should be mapped. Because the name element, when specified or defaulted, is local only to the application, many Java EE servers provide a way of referring to resources across the application server. This is done by setting the mappedName element. Use of the mappedName element is nonportable across Java EE server implementations.

**The *description* element** is the description of the resource, typically in the default language of the system on which the application is deployed. This element is used to help identify resources and to help application developers choose the correct resource.

As we have mentioned the names of injection types, let's briefly discuss these injection types.

### 21.4.1 Field-Based Injection

To use field-based resource injection, declare a field and decorate it with the @Resource annotation. The container will infer the name and type of the resource if the name and type elements are not specified. If you do specify the type element, it must match the field's type declaration.

In the following code, the container infers the name of the resource, based on the class name and the field name: *javaEE.chapter21.SomeClass/myDB*. The inferred type is javax.sql.DataSource.class:

```
package javaEE.chapter20;
public class SomeClass
{
@Resource
private javax.sql.DataSource myDB;
...
}
```

In the following code, the JNDI name is *customerDB*, and the inferred type is *javax.sql.DataSource.class*:

```
package javaEE.chapter20;
public class SomeClass
{
@Resource(name = "customerDB")
private javax.sql.DataSource myDB;
...
}
```

**21.4.2 Method-Based Injection**

To use method-based injection, declare a setter method and decorate it with the @Resource annotation. The container will infer the name and type of the resource if the name and type elements are not specified. The setter method must follow the JavaBeans conventions for property names: The method name must begin with set, have a void return type, and only one parameter. If you do specify the type element, it must match the field's type declaration.

In the following code, the container infers the name of the resource based on the class name and the field name: com.example.SomeClass/myDB. The inferred type is javax.sql.DataSource.class:

```
package javaEE.chapter20;
public class SomeClass
{
        private javax.sql.DataSource myDB;
        ...
        @Resource
        private void setMyDB(javax.sql.DataSource ds)
        {
                myDB = ds;
        }
        ...
}
```

In the following code, the JNDI name is *customerDB*, and the inferred type is *javax.sql.DataSource.class*:

```
package javaEE.chapter20;
public class SomeClass
{
        private javax.sql.DataSource myDB;
        ...
        @Resource(name="customerDB")
        private void setMyDB(javax.sql.DataSource ds)
        {
                myDB = ds;
        }
        ...
}
```

### 21.4.3 Class-Based Injection

To use class-based injection, decorate the class with a @Resource annotation, and set the required name and type elements:

```
@Resource(name="myMessageQueue", type="javax.jms.ConnectionFactory")
public class SomeMessageBean
{
        ...
}
```

The @Resources annotation is used to group together multiple @Resource declarations for class-based injection. The following code shows the @Resources annotation containing two @Resource declarations. One is a Java Message Service message queue, and the other is a JavaMail session:

```
@Resources({
@Resource(name="myMessageQueue", type="javax.jms.ConnectionFactory"),
@Resource(name="myMailSession", type="javax.mail.Session")
})
public class SomeMessageBean
{
        ...
}
```

## 21.5 Portable JNDI syntax

There are three JNDI namespaces used for portable JNDI lookups: java:global, java:module, and java:app.

**The *java:global JNDI namespace*** is the portable way of finding remote enterprise beans using JNDI lookups. JNDI addresses are of the following form:

*java:global[/application name]/module name/enterprise bean name[/interface name]*

Application name and module name default to the name of the application and module minus the file extension. Application names are only required if the application is packaged within an EAR. The interface name is only required if the enterprise bean implements more than one business interface.

**The *java:module JNDI namespace*** is used to lookup local enterprise beans within the same module. JNDI addresses using the java:module namespace are of the following form:

*java:module/enterprise bean name/[interface name]*

The interface name is only required if the enterprise bean implements more than one business interface.

**The *java:app JNDI namespace*** is used to lookup local enterprise beans packaged within the same application. That is, the enterprise bean is packaged within an EAR file containing multiple Java EE modules. JNDI addresses using the java:app namespace are of the following form:

*java:app[/module name]/enterprise bean name[/interface name]*

The module name is optional. The interface name is only required if the enterprise bean implements more than one business interface.

*****

# Chapter 22

# Java Security

In today's world, every organization faces the plentiful security threats that can expose the confidential information of the organization to unauthorized access. These threats may occur due to system failure, lake of availability of resources, access to data by unauthorized users and many more. Because of the security threats, an organization can feel the threats of disclosure of confidential information, modification or destruction of information, misappropriation protected resources, compromise on accountability and modification of access protocols. These security threats may appear depending upon the environment in which enterprise application is running.

Therefore, every organization must take required steps to identify these possibilities of threats and take necessary action to eliminate them. Java EE platform provides various security mechanisms, such as authentication, authorization, encryption and auditing, which allow you to expose data only to the authorized users.

In this chapter, we will discuss about the concept of security in Java EE. Along with this we will discuss about different security mechanisms, including implementing security on application servers. Further we will discuss about making secure enterprise beans and application clients.

## 22.1 The original *Sandbox* Model

The original security model provided by the Java platform is known as the sandbox model, which existed in order to provide a very restricted environment in which to run untrusted code obtained from the open network. The essence of the sandbox model is that local code is trusted to have full access to vital system resources (such as the file system) while downloaded remote code (an applet) is not trusted and can access only the limited resources provided inside the sandbox. This sandbox model is illustrated in the figure below.

**JDK 1.0 Security Model**

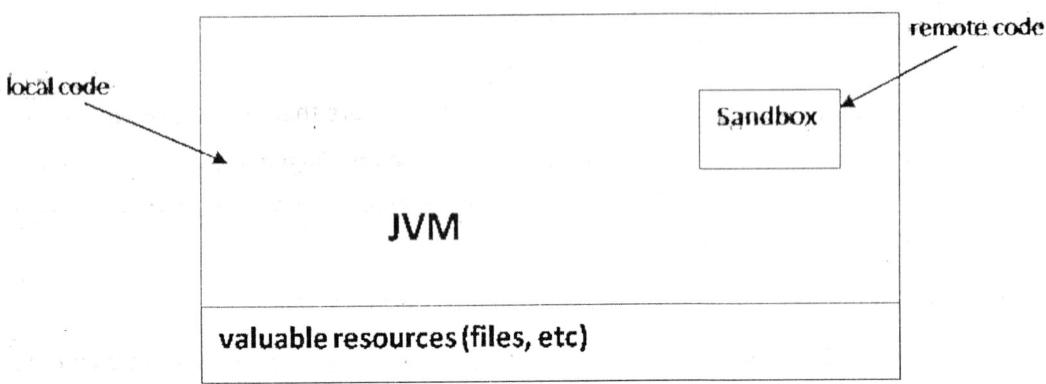


The sandbox model was deployed through the Java Development Kit (JDK), and was generally adopted by applications built with JDK 1.0, including Java enabled web browsers.

Overall security is enforced through a number of mechanisms. First of all, the language is designed to be type-safe and easy to use. The hope is that the burden on the programmer is such that the likelihood of making subtle mistakes is lessened compared with using other programming languages such as C or C++. Language features such as automatic memory management, garbage collection, and range checking on strings and arrays are examples of how the language helps the programmer to write safe code.

Second, compilers and a bytecode verifier ensure that only legitimate Java bytecodes are executed. The bytecode verifier, together with the Java Virtual Machine, guarantees language safety at run time. Moreover, a classloader defines a local name space, which can be used to ensure that an untrusted applet cannot interfere with the running of other programs.

Finally, access to crucial system resources is mediated by the Java Virtual Machine and is checked in advance by a *SecurityManager* class that restricts the actions of a piece of untrusted code to the bare minimum.

**JDK 1.1 Security Model**

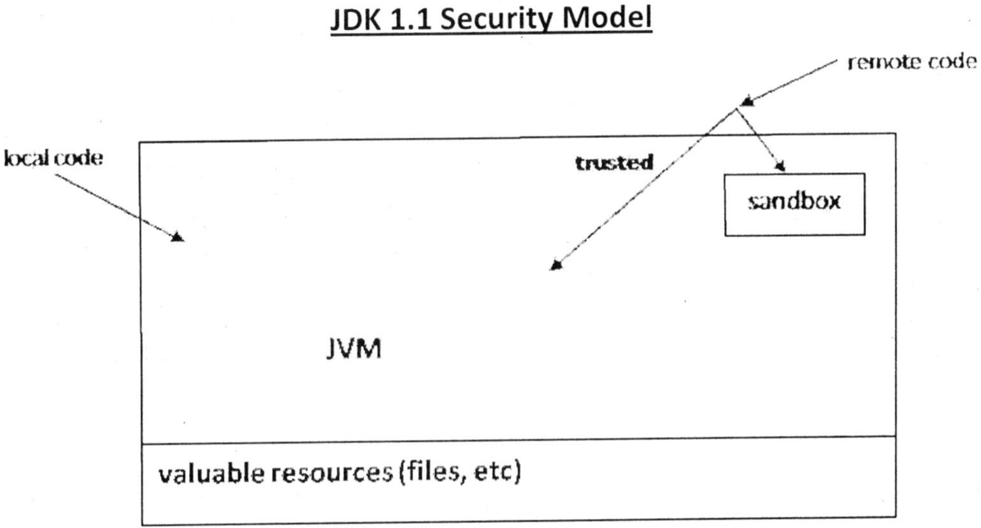


JDK 1.1 introduced the concept of a "signed applet", as illustrated by the figure below. In that release, a correctly digitally signed applet is treated as if it is trusted local code if the signature key is recognized as trusted by the end system that receives the applet. Signed applets, together with their signatures, are delivered in the JAR (Java Archive) format. In JDK 1.1, unsigned applets still run in the sandbox.

## 22.2 Evolving the Sandbox Model

The new Java 2 Platform Security Architecture, illustrated in the figure below, is introduced primarily for the following purposes.

**Java 2 Platform Security Model**

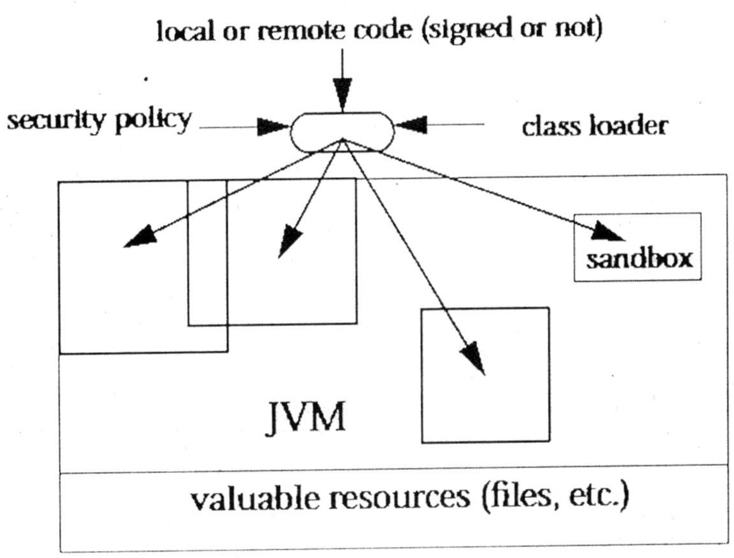


codes run with different permissions, no built-in notion of trusted code

- **Fine-grained access control**

This capability existed in the JDK from the beginning, but to use it, the application writer had to do substantial programming (e.g., by sub-classing and customizing the SecurityManager and ClassLoader classes). The **HotJava** browser 1.0 is such an application, as it allows the browser user to choose from a small number of different security levels. However, such programming is extremely security-sensitive and requires sophisticated skills and in-depth knowledge of computer security. The new architecture will make this procedure simpler and safer.

- **Easily configurable security policy**

Once again, this capability existed previously in the JDK but was not easy to use. Moreover, writing security code is not straightforward, so it is desirable to allow application builders and users to configure security policies without having to program.

- **Easily extensible access control structure**

Up to JDK 1.1, in order to create new access permission, you had to add a new check method to the SecurityManager class. The new architecture allows typed permissions (each representing an access to a system resource) and automatic handling of all permissions (including yet-to-be-defined permissions) of the correct type. No new method in the SecurityManager class needs to be created in most cases.

- **Extension of security checks to all Java programs, including applications as well as applets.**

There is no longer a built-in concept that all local code is trusted. Instead, local code is subjected to the same security control as applets, although it is possible, if desired, to declare that the policy on local code or remote code be the most liberal, thus enabling such code to effectively run as totally trusted. The same principle applies to signed applets and any Java application. Finally, an implicit goal is to make internal adjustment to the design of security classes to reduce the risks of creating subtle security holes in future programming.

## 22.3 New Protection Mechanism - Overview

We now go over, in some detail, the new protection architecture and give a brief explanation of its functionality. We start with an overview of the basic concepts behind the new architecture. We then introduce the major new classes in a natural order, starting with permission specifications, going on to the policy and related features, followed by access control and its usage, and then covering secure class loading and resolution.

A fundamental concept and important building block of system security is the protection domain. A domain can be scoped by the set of objects that are currently directly accessible by a principal, where a principal is an entity in the computer system to which permissions (and as a result, accountability) are granted. The sandbox utilized in JDK 1.0 is one example of a protection domain with a fixed boundary.

The protection domain concept serves as a convenient mechanism for grouping and isolation between units of protection. For example, it is possible (but not yet provided as a built-in feature) to separate protection domains from interacting with each other so that any permitted interaction must be either through trusted system code or explicitly allowed by the domains concerned. Note that *existing object accessibility rules remain valid under the new security architecture*.

Protection domains generally fall into two distinct categories: system domain and application domain. It is important that all protected external resources, such as the file system, the networking facility, and the screen and keyboard, be accessible only via system domains. The figure below illustrates the domain composition of a Java application environment.

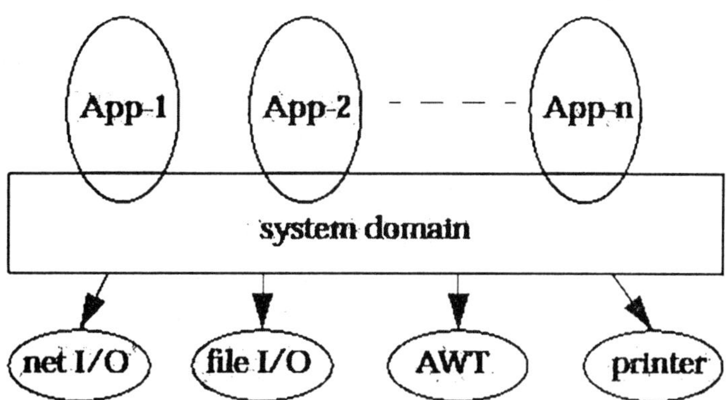


A domain conceptually encloses a set of classes whose instances are granted the same set of permissions. Protection domains are determined by the policy currently in effect. The Java application environment maintains a mapping from code (classes and instances) to their protection domains and then to their permissions, as illustrated by the figure below.

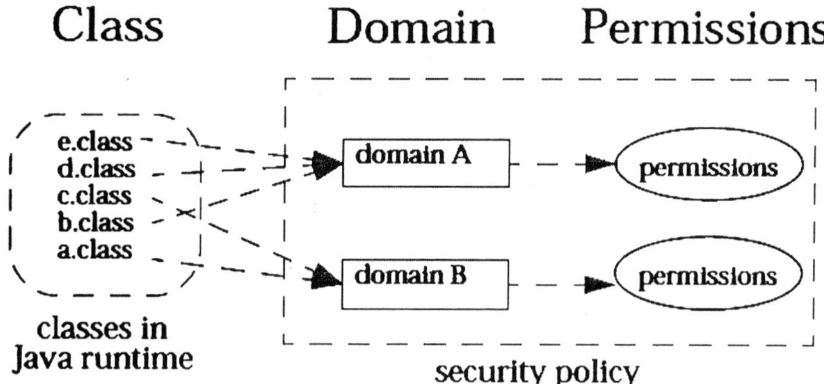


A thread of execution (which is often, but not necessarily tied to, a single Java thread, which in turn is not necessarily tied to the thread concept of the underlying operation system) may occur completely within a single protection domain or may involve an application domain and also the system domain. For example, an application that prints a message out will have to interact with the system domain that is the only access point to an output stream. In this case, it is crucial that at any time the application domain does not gain additional permissions by calling the system domain. Otherwise, there can be serious security implications.

In the reverse situation where a system domain invokes a method from an application domain, such as when the AWT system domain calls an applet's paint method to display the applet, it is again crucial that at any time the effective access rights are the same as current rights enabled in the application domain.

In other words, a less "powerful" domain cannot gain additional permissions as a result of calling or being called by a more powerful domain.

This discussion of one thread involving two protection domains naturally generalizes to a thread that traverses multiple protection domains. A simple and prudent rule of thumb for calculating permissions is the following:

- The permission set of an execution thread is considered to be the intersection of the permissions of all protection domains traversed by the execution thread.
- When a piece of code calls the **doPrivileged( )** method, the permission set of the execution thread is considered to include a permission if it is allowed by the said code's protection domain and by all protection domains that are called or entered directly or indirectly subsequently.

As you can see, the **doPrivileged( )** method enables a piece of trusted code to temporarily enable access to more resources than are available directly to the application that called it. This is necessary in some situations. For example, an application may not be allowed direct access to files that contain fonts, but the system utility to display a document must obtain those fonts, on behalf of the user. We provide the **doPrivileged( )** method for the system domain to deal with this situation, and the method is in fact available to all domains.

During execution, when access to a critical system resource (such as, file I/O and network I/O) is requested, the resource-handling code directly or indirectly invokes a special *AccessController* class method that evaluates the request and decides if the request should be granted or denied.

Such an evaluation follows and generalizes the "rule of thumb" given above. The actual way in which the evaluation is conducted can vary between implementations. The basic principle is to examine the call history and the permissions granted to the relevant protection domains, and to return silently if the request is granted or throw a security exception if the request is denied.

Finally, each domain (system or application) may also implement additional protection of its internal resources within its own domain boundary. For example, a banking application may need to support and protect internal concepts such as checking accounts, deposits and withdrawals. Because the semantics of such protection is unlikely to be predictable or enforceable by the Java 2 SDK, the protection system at this level is best left to the system or application developers. Nevertheless, whenever appropriate, we provide helpful primitives to simplify developers' tasks.

## 22.4 Introducing Security in Java EE

The Java EE applications consist of web components, such as servlet and JSP pages. These components are deployed in different web containers to build an enterprise application. After creating an enterprise application, you need to consider various security issues so that the data in the system can be protected from unauthorized access. In a Java EE application, a security mechanism is configured to allow only authenticated user to access functions and data of the application. Java EE uses the Java EE container to supply low level platform specific functionality to the web components. The java EE container provides the following two types of security.

**Declarative Security:** It refers to the type of security provided to the web components by using the deployment descriptor, which is an XML file that explains the deployment of web and enterprise applications. The deployment descriptor includes the mapping for applications specific components, which provides security roles, users and policies to protect the web applications and enterprise application components from unauthorized and unauthenticated access.

**Programmatic Security:** It refers to the type of security that is embedded in an application and is used to make security decisions, such as determining whether or not a user is authorized to access a resource. Programmatic security defines the security model of the application.

## 22.5 Security Mechanisms

The Java EE security mechanisms are easier to implement and configure. These mechanisms provide fine access control to data and functions available in Java EE application. In Java EE application, a user interacts with enterprise resources within the web or enterprise JavaBean through the client container.

Java EE security services are very much different from the security mechanisms of the operating system. Java EE security services are provided by the component container and can be implemented by using declarative or programmatic techniques (section 22.1). Java EE security services provide a **robust** and **easily configured** security mechanism for **authenticating** and **authorizing** user access to the **application functions** and **data** at many different layers. In this section, the security mechanism is discussed in context of the following three layers of security.

- Application layer security
- Transport layer security
- Message layer security

Now let's discuss these security layers in detail with its advantages and disadvantages.

**Application layer security**

In Java EE, component containers are responsible for providing application-layer security, security services for a specific application type tailored to the needs of the application. At the application layer, application firewalls can be used to enhance application protection by protecting the communication stream and all associated application resources from attacks.

Java EE security is easy to implement and configure. It can offer great access control to application functions and data. However, as is inherent to security applied at the application layer, security properties are not transferable to applications running in other environments and protect data only while it is residing in the application environment. In the context of a traditional enterprise application, this is not necessarily a problem, but when applied to a web services application, in which data often travels across several mediators, *we would need to use the Java EE security mechanisms along with transport layer security and message layer security for a complete security solution.*

**Advantages of using application layer security**

- Security is uniquely suited to the needs of the application.
- Security is fine grained, with application-specific settings.

**Disadvantages of using application layer security**

- The application is dependent on security attributes that are not transferable between application types.
- Support for multiple protocols makes this type of security vulnerable.
- Data is close to or contained within the point of vulnerability.

**Transport layer security**

Transport-layer security is provided by the transport mechanisms used to transmit information over the physical wire between clients and providers; thus, transport layer security relies on **secure HTTP (HTTPS) transport** using **Secure Sockets Layer (SSL)**. Transport security is a point-to-point security mechanism that can be used for authentication, message integrity, and confidentiality. When running over an SSL-protected session, the server and client can authenticate each other and negotiate an encryption algorithm and cryptographic keys before the application protocol transmits or receives its first byte of data. Security is active from the time the data leaves the client until it arrives at its destination, or vice versa, even across intermediaries. The problem is that the data is not protected once it gets to the destination. One solution is to encrypt the message before sending.

Transport-layer security is performed in three stages, as follows.

- The client and server agree on an appropriate algorithm.
- A key is exchanged using public-key encryption and certificate-based authentication.
- A symmetric cipher is used during the information exchange.

Digital certificates are necessary when running HTTPS using SSL. The HTTPS service of most web servers will not run unless a digital certificate has been installed. Digital certificates have already been created for the **GlassFish Server**.

**Advantages of using transport layer security**

- It is relatively simple, well-understood, standard technology.
- It applies to both a message body and its attachments.

**Disadvantages of using transport layer security**

- It is tightly coupled with the transport-layer protocol.
- It represents an all-or-nothing approach to security. This implies that the security mechanism is unaware of message contents, so that you cannot selectively apply security to portions of the message as you can with message-layer security.
- Protection is transient. The message is protected only while in transit. Protection is removed automatically by the endpoint when it receives the message.
- It is not an end-to-end solution, simply point-to-point.

**Message layer security**

In message-layer security, security information is contained within the SOAP message and/or SOAP message attachment, which allows security information to travel along with the message or attachment. For example, a portion of the message may be signed by a sender and encrypted for a particular receiver. When sent from the initial sender, the message may pass through intermediate nodes before reaching its intended receiver. In this scenario, the encrypted portions continue to be opaque to any intermediate nodes and can be decrypted only by the intended receiver. For this reason, message layer security is also sometimes referred to as **end-to-end security**.

**Advantages of message layer security**

- Security stays with the message over all hops and after the message arrives at its destination.
- Security can be selectively applied to different portions of a message and, if using XML Web Services Security, to attachments.
- Message security can be used with intermediaries over multiple hops.
- Message security is independent of the application environment or transport protocol.

**Disadvantage of using message-layer security**

- It is relatively complex and adds some overhead to processing.

Note: The **GlassFish** Server supports message security using Metro. Metro is a web services stack that uses **Web Services Security (WSS)** to secure messages.

## 22.6 Implementing security on an application server

The deployment of a web application on an application server offers highly secure, interoperable and distributed component computing based on the Java EE security model. The security model is supported by the application server. The application server can be configured to perform the following tasks:

- Adding, deleting and modifying authorized users.
- Configuring the HTTP and internet Inter-ORB protocol (IIOP) listeners.
- Configuring the Java Management Extensions (JMX) connectors.
- Adding, modifying and deleting existing realms.
- Defining an interface using Java Authorization Contract for Containers (JACC) for the pluggable authorization providers.

- Setting and changing an application's policy permissions.

To implement the security on the application server, it must be ensured that only authorized users are given access to the resources. Controlled access to protected resources is made possible with the help of authorization. Authorization is based on two concepts, i.e. **identification** and **authentication**.

**Identification** is technique using which a system can recognize an entity.

**Authentication** is a process with the help of which it is possible to verify the user's identity.

You must perform the following steps to authenticate a user:

1. Write the code to prompt the users for their username and password.
2. Provide information in the Deployment Descriptor to establish security for the application.
3. Set authorized users and groups on the application server
4. Map the application's security roles (to users or groups) and principals on the application server.

Prior to creating an application that implements security, you need to understand how to work with realms, users, groups and roles.

**Realms**

In terms of Java EE application security, a realm is a database of users and groups that is used to identify valid users of a web application. The authentication services available in Java EE manage the realms available in an application server. In the application server, the *admin-realms file* and *certificate realm* are configured.

**In the file realm**, the server stores information of files in a file name *keyfile*. The file realm is used to check the authentication mechanism for entities. It is used for authenticating all clients, except the web browser client containing the HTTP protocol and certificate.

**In case of certificate realm**, the server stores user's information in a certificate database. The application server uses the HTTP protocol and the certificates to authenticate clients.

**User**

A user is an individual identity defined by the application server. It can have multiple roles corresponding with that identity. These multiple roles helps the user to access all resources protected by the roles. The users can be related to a group. Note that a user in Java EE is same as a user in an operating system, but the security mechanism involved in both cases are different.

**Group**

A group is collection of authentication users, which have common traits specified in an application server. A Java EE user, who is also the user of the file realm, can belong to an application server group. An application server group is a category of user's type identified by the common file traits, such as job title or customer profile. For example, it may be possible that majority of customers of an e-commerce application are associated with the CUSTOMER group, while the more profitable customers are associated with the PREFERRED group. In such situations, to manage and control the access of large numbers of users, classifying users into groups is a good strategy. It makes it easier to control the access of application components by the large numbers of users.

**Role**

To grant permission to access a particular collection of resources in an application, an abstract name called role is provided. A role may be considered as a key that is capable of opening a lock. Various users might possess a copy of the key, needed to open a lock; or the role, needed to access the application resources. An application's resources can be accessed by the original or the copy of the role.

## 22.7 Securing Enterprise Beans

Enterprise beans are Java EE components that implement EJB technology. Enterprise beans run in the EJB container, a runtime environment within the GlassFish Server. Although transparent to the application developer, the EJB container provides system-level services, such as transactions and security to its enterprise beans, which form the core of transactional Java EE applications.

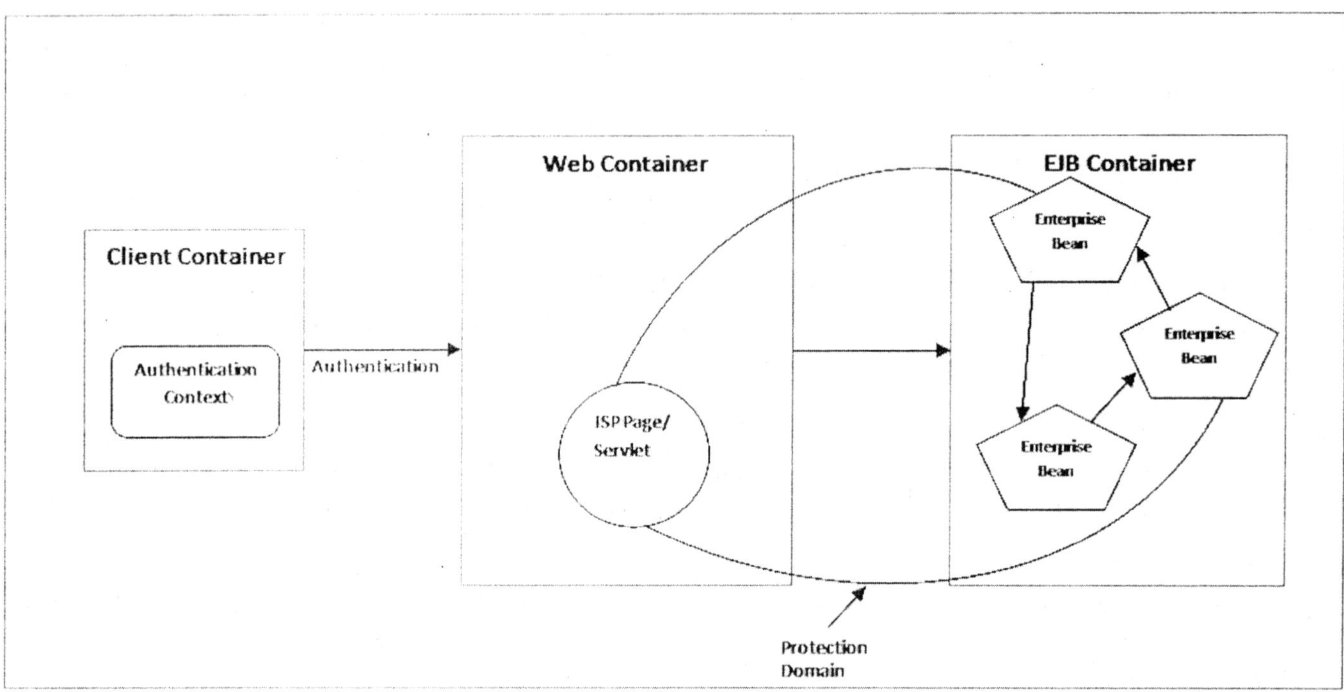


Enterprise bean methods can be secured in either of the following ways:

- Declarative security
- Programmatic security

Let's discuss these in details with propagating security identity and deployment of secured beans.

❖ <u>Declarative security (mostly preferred)</u>

Declarative security enables the application developer to specify which users are authorized to access which methods of the enterprise beans and to authenticate these users with basic, or username-password, authentication. Frequently, the person who is developing an enterprise application is not the same person who is responsible for deploying the application. An application developer who uses declarative security to define method permissions and authentications mechanisms is passing along to the deployer a security view of the enterprise beans contained in the EJB JAR. When a security view is passed on to the deployer, he or she uses this information to define method permissions for security roles. If you don't define a security view, the deployer will have to determine what each business method does to determine which users are authorized to call each method.

A security view consists of a set of security roles, a semantic grouping of permissions that a given type of users of an application must have to successfully access the application. Security roles are meant to be logical roles, representing a type of user. You can define method permissions for each security role. The method permission is a permission to invoke a specified group of methods of an enterprise bean's business interface, home interface, component interface, and/or web service endpoints. After method permissions are defined, user name/password authentication will be used to verify the identity of the user.

It is important to keep in mind that security roles are used to define the logical security view of an application. They should not be confused with the user groups, users, principals, and other concepts that exist in the GlassFish Server. An additional step is required to map the roles defined in the application to users, groups, and principals that are the components of the user database in the file realm of the GlassFish Server.

The following sections show how an application developer uses declarative security to either secure an application or to create a security view to pass along to the deployer.

**Specifying Authorized Users by Declaring Security Roles**

The method permissions can be specified on the class, the business methods of the class, or both. Method permissions can be specified on a method of the bean class to override the method permissions value specified on the entire bean class. The following annotations are used to specify method permissions:

***@DeclareRoles***

Specifies all the roles that the application will use, including roles not specifically named in a *@RolesAllowed* annotation. The set of security roles the application uses is the total of the security roles defined in the *@DeclareRoles* and *@RolesAllowed* annotations.

The *@DeclareRoles* annotation is specified on a bean class, where it serves to declare roles that can be tested (for example, by calling isCallerInRole) from within the methods of the annotated class. When declaring the name of a role used as a parameter to the isCallerInRole(String roleName) method, the declared name must be the same as the parameter value.

The following example code demonstrates the use of the *@DeclareRoles* annotation:

```
@DeclareRoles("BusinessAdmin")
public class Calculator
{
   .....
}
```

The syntax for declaring more than one role is as shown in the following example:

```
@DeclareRoles({"Administrator", "Manager", "Employee"})
```

***@RolesAllowed***

Specifies the security roles permitted to access methods in an application. This annotation can be specified on a class or on one or more methods. When specified at the class level, the annotation applies to all methods in the class. When specified on a method, the annotation applies to that method only and overrides any values specified at the class level.

To specify that no roles are authorized to access methods in an application, use the *@DenyAll* annotation. To specify that a user in any role is authorized to access the application, use the *@PermitAll* annotation.

When used in conjunction with the *@DeclareRoles* annotation, the combined set of security roles is used by the application.

The following example code demonstrates the use of the *@RolesAllowed* annotation:

```
@DeclareRoles({"Administrator", "Manager", "Employee"})
public class Calculator
{
 @RolesAllowed("Administrator")
```

```
        public void setNewRate(int rate)
        {
            ...
        }
    }
```

***@PermitAll***

Specifies that all security roles are permitted to execute the specified method or methods. The user is not checked against a database to ensure that he or she is authorized to access this application.

This annotation can be specified on a class or on one or more methods. Specifying this annotation on the class means that it applies to all methods of the class. Specifying it at the method level means that it applies to only that method.

The following example code demonstrates the use of the *@PermitAll* annotation:

```
import javax.annotation.security.*;
@RolesAllowed("RestrictedUsers")
public class Calculator
{
    @RolesAllowed("Administrator")
    public void setNewRate(int rate)
    {
        .....
    }
    @PermitAll
    public long convertCurrency(long amount)
    {
        .....
    }
}
```

***@DenyAll***

Specifies that no security roles are permitted to execute the specified method or methods. This means that these methods are excluded from execution in the Java EE container.

The following example code demonstrates the use of the *@DenyAll* annotation:

```
import javax.annotation.security.*;
    @RolesAllowed("Users")
    public class Calculator
    {
        @RolesAllowed("Administrator")
        public void setNewRate(int rate)
        {
            .....
        }
        @DenyAll
```

```
    public long convertCurrency(long amount)
    {
        .....
    }
}
```

The following code snippet demonstrates the use of the @DeclareRoles annotation with the isCallerInRole method. In this example, the @DeclareRoles annotation declares a role that the enterprise bean PayrollBean uses to make the security check by using isCallerInRole("payroll") to verify that the caller is authorized to change salary data:

```
@DeclareRoles("payroll")
@Stateless public class PayrollBean implements Payroll
{
    @Resource SessionContext ctx;
        public void updateEmployeeInfo(EmplInfo info)
        {
            oldInfo = ...                  // read from database;
            // The salary field can be changed only by callers
            // who have the security role "payroll"
            Principal callerPrincipal = ctx.getCallerPrincipal( );
            if (info.salary != oldInfo.salary && !ctx.isCallerInRole("payroll"))
            {
                throw new SecurityException(...);
            }
            ...
        }
    ...
}
```

The following example code illustrates the use of the @RolesAllowed annotation:

```
@RolesAllowed("admin")
public class SomeClass
{
    public void aMethod ( ) {...}
    public void bMethod ( ) {...}
    ...
}
@Stateless public class MyBean extends SomeClass implements A
{
    @RolesAllowed("HR")
    public void aMethod ( ) {...}
    public void cMethod ( ) {...}
    ...
}
```

In this example, assuming that *aMethod*, *bMethod*, and *cMethod* are methods of business interface A, the method permissions values of methods *aMethod* and *bMethod* are *@RolesAllowed("HR")* and *@RolesAllowed("admin")*, respectively. The method permissions for method *cMethod* have not been specified.

To clarify, the annotations are not inherited by the subclass itself. Instead, the annotations apply to methods of the superclass that are inherited by the subclass.

**Specifying an Authentication Mechanism and Secure Connection**

When method permissions are specified, basic user name/password authentication will be invoked by the GlassFish Server.

To use a different type of authentication or to require a secure connection using SSL, specify this information in an application deployment descriptor.

- **Programmatic Security**

Programmatic security, code that is embedded in a business method, is used to access a caller's identity programmatically and uses this information to make security decisions within the method itself.

**Accessing an Enterprise Bean Caller's Security Context**

In general, security management should be enforced by the container in a manner that is transparent to the enterprise bean's business methods. The security API described in this section should be used only in the less frequent situations in which the enterprise bean business methods need to access the security context information, such as when you want to restrict access to a particular time of day.

The *javax.ejb.EJBContext* interface provides two methods that allow the bean provider to access security information about the enterprise bean's caller:

- **getCallerPrincipal( )**

It allows the enterprise bean methods to obtain the current caller principal's name. The methods might, for example, use the name as a key to information in a database.

The following code sample illustrates the use of the getCallerPrincipal method:

```
@Stateless public class EmployeeServiceBean implements EmployeeService
{
    @Resource SessionContext ctx;
    @PersistenceContext EntityManager em;
    public void changePhoneNumber(...)
    {
        ...
        // obtain the caller principal.
        callerPrincipal = ctx.getCallerPrincipal( );

        // obtain the caller principal's name.
        callerKey = callerPrincipal.getName( );

        // use callerKey as primary key to find EmployeeRecord
        EmployeeRecord myEmployeeRecord = em.find(EmployeeRecord.class, callerKey);
```

```
            // update phone number
            myEmployeeRecord.setPhoneNumber(...);
            ...
        }
    }
```

In this example, the enterprise bean obtains the principal name of the current caller and uses it as the primary key to locate an *EmployeeRecord* entity. This example assumes that application has been deployed such that the current caller principal contains the primary key used for the identification of employees (for example, employee number).

- ***isCallerInRole( )***

The enterprise bean code can use to allow the bean provider/application developer to code the security checks that cannot be easily defined using method permissions. Such a check might impose a role-based limit on a request, or it might depend on information stored in the database.

The enterprise bean code can use the *isCallerInRole* method to test whether the current caller has been assigned to a given security role. Security roles are defined by the bean provider or the application assembler and are assigned by the deployer to principals or principal groups that exist in the operational environment.

The following code sample illustrates the use of the *isCallerInRole* method:

```
@Stateless public class PayrollBean implements Payroll
{
    @Resource SessionContext ctx;
    public void updateEmployeeInfo(EmplInfo info)
    {
        oldInfo = ... read from database;
        // The salary field can be changed only by callers
        // who have the security role "payroll"
        if (info.salary != oldInfo.salary &&!ctx.isCallerInRole("payroll"))
        {
            throw new SecurityException(...);
        }
        ...
    }
    ...
}
```

You would use programmatic security in this way to dynamically control access to a method, for example, when you want to deny access except during a particular time of day.

❖ **Configuring a Component's Propagated Security Identity**

You can configure an enterprise bean's run-as, or propagated, security identity by using the *@RunAs* annotation, which defines the role of the application during execution in a Java EE container. The annotation can be specified on a class, allowing developers to execute an application under a particular role. The role must map to the user/group information in the container's security realm. The *@RunAs* annotation specifies the name of a security role as its parameter.

Here is a sample code that demonstrates the use of the *@RunAs* annotation.

```
@RunAs("Admin")
public class Calculator
{
  //....
}
```

You will have to map the run-as role name to a given principal defined on the GlassFish Server if the given roles are associated with more than one user principal.

❖ **Deploying Secure Enterprise Beans**

The deployer is responsible for ensuring that an assembled application is secure after it has been deployed in the target operational environment. If a security view has been provided to the deployer through the use of security annotations and/or a deployment descriptor, the security view is mapped to the mechanisms and policies used by the security domain in the target operational environment, which in this case is the GlassFish Server. If no security view is provided, the deployer must set up the appropriate security policy for the enterprise bean application.

**Note: Generally the deployment information is web server or application server specific.**

## 22.8 Securing application client

The Java EE authentication requirements for application clients are the same as for other Java EE components, and the same authentication techniques can be used as for other Java EE application components. No authentication is necessary when accessing unprotected web resources.

When accessing protected web resources, the usual varieties of authentication can be used: HTTP basic authentication, HTTP login-form authentication, or SSL client authentication. Specifying an Authentication Mechanism in the Deployment Descriptor describes how to specify HTTP basic authentication and HTTP login-form authentication. Client Authentication describes how to specify SSL client authentication.

Authentication is required when accessing protected enterprise beans. The authentication mechanisms for enterprise beans are discussed in Securing Enterprise Beans. (Section 22.4)

An application client makes use of an authentication service provided by the application client container for authenticating its users. The container's service can be integrated with the native platform's authentication system so that a single sign-on capability is used. The container can authenticate the user either when the application is started or when a protected resource is accessed.

An application client can provide a class, called a login module, to gather authentication data. If so, the *javax.security.auth.callback.CallbackHandler* interface must be implemented, and the class name must be specified in its deployment descriptor. The application's callback handler must fully support Callback objects specified in the *javax.security.auth.callback* package.

**Using Login Module**

An application client can use the Java Authentication and Authorization Service (JAAS) to create login modules for authentication. A JAAS-based application implements the javax.security.auth.callback.CallbackHandler interface so that it can interact with users to enter specific authentication data, such as user names or passwords, or to display error and warning messages.

Applications implement the CallbackHandler interface and pass it to the login context, which forwards it directly to the underlying login modules. A login module uses the callback handler both to gather input, such as a password or smart card PIN, from users and to supply information, such as status information, to users. Because the application specifies the callback handler, an underlying login module can remain independent of the various ways applications interact with users.

For example, the implementation of a callback handler for a GUI application might display a window to solicit user input, or the implementation of a callback handler for a command-line tool might simply prompt the user for input directly from the command line.

The login module passes an array of appropriate callbacks to the callback handler's handle method, such as a *NameCallback* for the user name and a *PasswordCallback* for the password; the callback handler performs the requested user interaction and sets appropriate values in the callbacks. For example, to process a *NameCallback*, the *CallbackHandler* might prompt for a name, retrieve the value from the user, and call the *setName* method of the *NameCallback* to store the name.

**Using Programmatic Login**

Programmatic login enables the client code to supply user credentials. If you are using an EJB client, you can use the *com.sun.appserv.security.ProgrammaticLogin* class with its convenient login and logout methods. Programmatic login is specific to a server.

## 22.9 Implementing security in web applications using JAAS

The **Java Authentication and Authorization Service (JAAS)** was introduced as an optional package (extension) to the Java 2 SDK, Standard Edition (J2SDK), v 1.3. JAAS was integrated into the J2SDK 1.4.

JAAS can be used for two purposes:

- for authentication of users, to reliably and securely determine who is currently executing Java code, regardless of whether the code is running as an application, an applet, a bean, or a servlet; and
- for authorization of users to ensure they have the access control rights (permissions) required to do the actions performed.

JAAS implements a Java version of the standard **Pluggable Authentication Module (PAM) framework**. Traditionally Java has provided *codesource*-based access controls (access controls based on where the code originated from and who signed the code). It lacked, however, the ability to additionally enforce access controls based on who runs the code. JAAS provides a framework that augments the Java security architecture with such support.

JAAS authentication is performed in a pluggable fashion. This permits applications to remain independent from underlying authentication technologies. New or updated authentication technologies can be plugged under an application without requiring modifications to the application itself. Applications enable the authentication process by instantiating a *LoginContext* object, which in turn references a Configuration to determine the authentication *technology*(ies), or *LoginModule*(s), to be used in performing the authentication. Typical *LoginModules* may prompt for and verify a username and password. Others may read and verify a voice or fingerprint sample.

Once the user or service executing the code has been authenticated, the JAAS authorization component works in conjunction with the core Java SE access control model to protect access to sensitive resources. Unlike in the J2SDK 1.3 and earlier, where access control decisions are based solely on code location and code signers (a *CodeSource*), in the J2SDK 1.4 access control decisions are based both on the executing code's *CodeSource* and on the user or service running the code, who is represented by a Subject object. The Subject is updated by a *LoginModule* with relevant Principals and credentials if authentication succeeds.

<u>Core classes and interfaces used in JAAS</u>

The JAAS-related core classes and interfaces can be broken into three categories: Common, Authentication, and Authorization.

- **Common classes:** *Subject, Principal, Credential*
- **Authentication classes and interfaces:** *LoginContext, LoginModule, CallbackHandler, Callback*
- **Authorization classes:** *Policy, AuthPermission, PrivateCredentialPermission*

Now, let's discuss about these classes and interfaces in detail.

### ❖ Common classes

Common classes are those shared by both the JAAS authentication and authorization components.

The key JAAS class is *javax.security.auth.Subject*, which represents a grouping of related information for a single entity such as a person. It encompasses the entity's Principals, public credentials, and private credentials.

#### 1. *javax.security.auth.Subject class:*

To authorize access to resources, applications first need to authenticate the source of the request. The JAAS framework defines the term subject to represent the source of a request. A subject may be any entity, such as a person or a service. Once the subject is authenticated, a *javax.security.auth.Subject* is populated with associated identities, or *Principals*.

A *Subject* may also own security-related attributes, which are referred to as credentials. Sensitive credentials that require special protection, such as private cryptographic keys, are stored within a private credential Set. Credentials intended to be shared, such as public key certificates, are stored within a public credential Set. Different permissions are required to access and modify the different credential Sets.

Subjects are created using these constructors:

*public Subject( );*
*public Subject(boolean readOnly, Set principals, Set pubCredentials, Set privCredentials);*

The first constructor creates a Subject with empty (non-null) *Sets* of *Principals* and credentials. The second constructor creates a *Subject* with the specified *Sets* of *Principals* and credentials. It also has a boolean argument which can be used to make the *Subject* **read-only**. In a read-only *Subject*, the *Principal* and *credential Sets* are immutable.

An application writer does not have to instantiate a *Subject*. If the application instantiates a *LoginContext* and does not pass a Subject to the *LoginContext* constructor, the *LoginContext* instantiates a new empty Subject.

If a Subject was not instantiated to be in a read-only state, it can be set read-only by calling the following method:

*public void setReadOnly( );*

A *javax.security.auth.AuthPermission* with target "**setReadOnly**" is required to invoke this method. Once in a read-only state, any attempt to add or remove *Principals* or credentials will result in an *IllegalStateException* being thrown.

#### 2. *java.security.Principal interface:*

As mentioned previously, Principals may be associated with a Subject if authentication is successful. Principals represent Subject identities, and must implement the *java.security.Principal* and *java.io.Serializable* interfaces. The *Subject* section describes ways to update the *Principals* associated with a Subject.

#### 3. *Credentials [javax.security.auth.Refreshable and javax.security.auth.Destroyable interfaces]:*

Public and private credential classes are not part of the core JAAS class library. Any class can represent a credential. Developers may elect to have their *credential classes implement two interfaces* related to credentials: *Refreshable* and *Destroyable*.

- **Refreshable interface**

The *javax.security.auth.Refreshable* interface provides the capability for a credential to refresh itself. For example, a credential with a particular time-restricted lifespan may implement this interface to allow callers to refresh the time period for which it is valid. The interface has two abstract methods:

*boolean isCurrent( );*

*void refresh( ) throws RefreshFailedException;*

*isCurrent( )* method determines whether the credential is current or valid.

*refresh( )* updates or extends the validity of the credential. The method implementation should perform an AuthPermission("refreshCredential") security check to ensure the caller has permission to refresh the credential.

- **Destroyable interface**

The javax.security.auth.Destroyable interface provides the capability of destroying the contents within a credential. The interface has two abstract methods:

*boolean isDestroyed();*

*void destroy() throws DestroyFailedException;*

*isDestroyed( )* method determines whether the credential has been destroyed.

*destroy( )* method destroys and clears the information associated with this credential. Subsequent calls to certain methods on this credential will result in an IllegalStateException being thrown. The method implementation should perform an AuthPermission("destroyCredential") security check to ensure the caller has permission to destroy the credential.

❖ **Authentication classes and interfaces**

The authentication classes are described below.

**1. *javax.security.auth.login.LoginContext class***

The *javax.security.auth.login.LoginContext* class provides the basic methods used to authenticate subjects, and provides a way to develop an application independent of the underlying authentication technology. The *LoginContext* consults a *Configuration* to determine the authentication services, or *LoginModule(s),* configured for a particular application. Therefore, different *LoginModules* can be plugged in under an application without requiring any modifications to the application itself.

*LoginContext* offers four constructors from which to choose:

*public LoginContext(String name) throws LoginException;*

*public LoginContext(String name, Subject subject) throws LoginException;*

*public LoginContext(String name, CallbackHandler callbackHandler) throws LoginException*

*public LoginContext(String name, Subject subject, CallbackHandler callbackHandler) throws LoginException*

All of the constructors share a common parameter: name. This argument is used by the *LoginContext* as an index into the login Configuration to determine which *LoginModules* are configured for the application instantiating the *LoginContext*. The constructors that do not take a Subject as an input parameter instantiate a new Subject. Null inputs are disallowed for all constructors. Callers require an *AuthPermission* with target "*createLoginContext.*<name>" to instantiate a *LoginContext*. Here, <name> refers to the name of the login configuration entry that the application references in the name parameter for the *LoginContext* instantiation.

*public void login( ) throws LoginException;*

*public Subject getSubject( );*

*public void logout( ) throws LoginException;*

*login( )* method is responsible for actual authentication occurance.

*getSubject( )* returns the subject.

*logout( )* method is used to logout a Subject and remove its authenticated Principals and credentials.

**2. *javax.security.auth.login.LoginModule interface***

The *LoginModule* interface gives developers the ability to implement different kinds of authentication technologies that can be plugged in under an application. For example, one type of *LoginModule* may perform a username/ password- based form of authentication. Other LoginModules may interface to hardware devices such as smart cards or biometric devices.

**Note: If you are an application writer, you do not need to understand the workings of *LoginModules*. All you have to know is how to write your application and specify configuration information, such as in a login configuration file, such that the application will be able to utilize the *LoginModule* specified by the configuration to authenticate the user.**

If, on the other hand, you are a programmer who wishes to write a *LoginModule* implementing an authentication technology, see the JAAS *LoginModule* Developer's Guide for detailed step-by-step instructions.

**3. *javax.security.auth.callback.CallbackHandler interface***

In some cases a *LoginModule* must communicate with the user to obtain authentication information. *LoginModules* use a *javax.security.auth.callback.CallbackHandler* for this purpose. Applications implement the *CallbackHandler* interface and pass it to the LoginContext, which forwards it directly to the underlying LoginModules. A *LoginModule* uses the *CallbackHandler* both to gather input from users and to supply information to users. By allowing the application to specify the *CallbackHandler*, underlying *LoginModules* can remain independent of the different ways applications interact with users. For example, the implementation of a *CallbackHandler* for a GUI application might display a window to solicit input from a user. On the other hand, the implementation of a *CallbackHandler* for a non-GUI tool might simply prompt the user for input directly from the command line.

CallbackHandler is an interface with one method to implement:

*void handle(Callback[ ] callbacks) throws java.io.IOException, UnsupportedCallbackException;*

The *LoginModule* passes the *CallbackHandler* handle method an array of appropriate *Callbacks*, for example a *NameCallback* for the user name and a *PasswordCallback* for the password, and the *CallbackHandler* performs the requested user interaction and sets appropriate values in the *Callbacks*. For example, to process a *NameCallback*, the CallbackHandler may prompt for a name, retrieve the value from the user, and call the *NameCallback's* **setName( )** method to store the name.

**4. *javax.security.auth.callback interface***

The *javax.security.auth.callback* package contains the *Callback* interface as well as several implementations. *LoginModules* may pass an array of *Callbacks* directly to the handle method of a *CallbackHandler*.

## ❖ Authorization classes

To make JAAS authorization take place, granting access control permissions based not just on what code is running but also on who is running it, the following is required:

- The user must be authenticated, as described in the LoginContext section.
- The Subject that is the result of authentication must be associated with an access control context, as described in the Subject section.
- Principal-based entries must be configured in the security policy, as described below.

The *Policy* abstract class and the authorization-specific classes *AuthPermission* and *PrivateCredentialPermission* are described below.

### 1. *java.security.Policy class*

The *java.security.Policy* class is an abstract class for representing the system-wide access control policy. The *Policy* API was upgraded in the J2SDK 1.4 to support Principal-based queries.

As a default, the J2SDK provides a file-based subclass implementation, which was upgraded to support Principal-based grant entries in policy files.

### 2. *javax.security.auth.AuthPermission class*

The javax.security.auth.AuthPermission class encapsulates the basic permissions required for JAAS. An AuthPermission contains a name (also referred to as a "target name") but no actions list; you either have the named permission or you don't.

In addition to its inherited methods (from the *java.security.Permission* class), an *AuthPermission* has two public constructors:

*public AuthPermission(String name);*

*public AuthPermission(String name, String actions);*

The first constructor creates a new *AuthPermission* with the specified name. The second constructor also creates a new *AuthPermission* object with the specified name, but has an additional actions argument which is currently unused and should be **null**. This constructor exists solely for the *Policy* object to instantiate new *Permission* objects. For most other code, the first constructor is appropriate.

### 3. *javax.security.auth.PrivateCredentialPermission class*

The *javax.security.auth.PrivateCredentialPermission* class protects access to a Subject's private credentials and provides one public constructor:

*public PrivateCredentialPermission(String name, String actions);*

*****

# Chapter 23

# Java Design Patterns

Suppose you are working on an enterprise application and you come across some error and you are not able to find any proper solution for it. Now you have decided to ask to another developer for help (either personally or on blog). The first question that developer will ask is *"Which design pattern you have used in your project?"*. It is because most of the time the solution depends on the designing pattern you have used.

The design patterns are some standard designing scenarios that are knowingly or unknowingly followed by every developer. In this chapter we will discuss about different Java design patterns and some most important characteristics them.

## 23.1 Why design patterns?

Design patterns have been evolved over a long period of time and they provide best solutions to certain problems faced during software development. Learning these patterns helps un-experienced developers to learn software design in an easy and faster way

Success of any enterprise application depends on its design i.e. an enterprise application designed effectively will have following benefits.

- Design Patterns are already defined and provides industry standard approach to solve a recurring problem, so it saves time if we sensibly use the design pattern.
- Using design patterns promotes reusability that leads to more robust and highly maintainable code. It helps in reducing total cost of ownership (TCO) of the software product.
- Since design patterns are already defined, it makes our code easy to understand and debug. It leads to faster development and new members of team understand it easily.

Design patterns provide a standard terminology and are specific to particular scenario. For example, a *singleton design* pattern signifies use of single object so all developers familiar with single design pattern will make use of single object and they can tell each other that program is following a singleton pattern.

## 23.2 Different Design Patterns

Design patterns are a popular topic in software development. A design pattern is a common, well-described solution to a common software problem. Sensible use of design patterns results in increased code maintainability, since in addition to being a good solution to a common problem, design patterns can be recognized by other developers, thus reducing the learning curve when dealing with a particular piece of code.

Java Design Patterns are divided into three categories – creational, structural, and behavioral design patterns.

- <u>Creational Design Patterns</u>

Creational design patterns provide solution to instantiate an object in the best possible way for specific situations.

1. **Singleton Pattern**

   Singleton pattern restricts the instantiation of a class and ensures that only one instance of the class exists in the

Java Virtual Machine. It seems to be a very simple design pattern but when it comes to implementation, it comes with a lot of implementation concerns. The implementation of Singleton pattern has always been a controversial topic among developers.

2. **Factory Pattern**

   Factory design pattern is used when we have a super class with multiple sub-classes and based on input, we need to return one of the sub-class. This pattern takes out the responsibility of instantiation of a class from client program to the factory class. We can apply Singleton pattern on Factory class or make the factory method static.

3. **Abstract Factory Pattern**

   Abstract Factory pattern is similar to Factory pattern and its factory of factories. If you are familiar with factory design pattern in java, you will notice that we have a single Factory class that returns the different sub-classes based on the input provided and factory class uses if-else or switch statement to achieve this.

   In Abstract Factory pattern, we get rid of if-else block and have a factory class for each sub-class and then an Abstract Factory class that will return the sub-class based on the input factory class.

4. **Builder Pattern**

   This pattern was introduced to solve some of the problems with Factory and Abstract Factory design patterns when the Object contains a lot of attributes. Builder pattern solves the issue with large number of optional parameters and inconsistent state by providing a way to build the object step-by-step and provide a method that will actually return the final Object.

5. **Prototype Pattern**

   Prototype pattern is used when the Object creation is a costly affair and requires a lot of time and resources and you have a similar object already existing. So this pattern provides a mechanism to copy the original object to a new object and then modify it according to our needs. This pattern uses java cloning to copy the object.

   Prototype design pattern mandates that the Object which you are copying should provide the copying feature. It should not be done by any other class. However whether to use shallow or deep copy of the Object properties depends on the requirements and it's a design decision.

- **Structural Design Patterns**

Structural patterns provide different ways to create a class structure, for example using inheritance and composition to create a large object from small objects.

1. **Adapter Pattern**

   Adapter design pattern is one of the structural design patterns and it's used so that two unrelated interfaces can work together. The object that joins these unrelated interfaces is called an Adapter.

   As a real life example, we can think of a mobile charger as an adapter because mobile battery needs 3 volts to charge but the normal socket produces either 120V (US) or 240V (India). So the mobile charger works as an adapter between mobile charging socket and the wall socket.

2. **Composite Pattern**

   Composite pattern is one of the structural design patterns and is used when we have to represent a part-whole hierarchy. When we need to create a structure in a way that the objects in the structure have to be treated the same way, we can apply composite design pattern.

   Let's understand it with a real life example – A diagram is a structure that consists of Objects such as Circle, Lines, Triangle etc and when we fill the drawing with color (say Red), the same color also gets applied to the Objects in the drawing. Here drawing is made up of different parts and they all have same operations.

3. **Proxy Pattern**

   Proxy pattern intent is to "Provide a surrogate or placeholder for another object to control access to it". The definition itself is very clear and proxy pattern is used when we want to provide controlled access of functionality.

   Let's say we have a class that can run some command on the system. Now if we are using it, its fine but if we want to give this program to a client application, it can have severe issues because client program can issue command to delete some system files or change some settings that you don't want.

4. **Flyweight Pattern**

   Flyweight design pattern is used when we need to create a lot of Objects of a class. Since every object consumes memory space that can be crucial for low memory devices, such as mobile devices or embedded systems, flyweight design pattern can be applied to reduce the load on memory by sharing objects. String Pool implementation in java is one of the best example of Flyweight pattern implementation

5. **Facade Pattern**

   Facade Pattern is used to help client applications to easily interact with the system. Suppose we have an application with set of interfaces to use MySql/Oracle database and to generate different types of reports, such as HTML report, PDF report etc. So we will have different set of interfaces to work with different types of database. Now a client application can use these interfaces to get the required database connection and generate reports. But when the complexity increases or the interface behavior names are confusing, client application will find it difficult to manage it. So we can apply Facade pattern here and provide a wrapper interface on top of the existing interface to help client application.

6. **Bridge Pattern**

   When we have interface hierarchies in both interfaces as well as implementations, then builder design pattern is used to decouple the interfaces from implementation and hiding the implementation details from the client programs. Like Adapter pattern, it's one of the Structural design patterns. The implementation of bridge design pattern follows the notion to prefer Composition over inheritance.

7. **Decorator Pattern**

   Decorator design pattern is used to modify the functionality of an object at runtime. At the same time other instances of the same class will not be affected by this, so individual object gets the modified behavior. Decorator design pattern is one of the structural design patterns (such as Adapter Pattern, Bridge Pattern, Composite Pattern) and uses abstract classes or interface with composition to implement.

   We use inheritance or composition to extend the behavior of an object but this is done at compile time and it's applicable to all the instances of the class. We can't add any new functionality of remove any existing behavior at runtime – this is when Decorator pattern comes into picture.

- **Behavioral Design Patterns**

Behavioral patterns provide solution for the better interaction between objects and how to provide lose coupling and flexibility to extend easily.

1. **Template Method Pattern**

   Template Method is a behavioral design pattern and it's used to create a method stub and deferring some of the steps of implementation to the subclasses. Template method defines the steps to execute an algorithm and it can provide default implementation that might be common for all or some of the subclasses.

   Suppose we want to provide an algorithm to build a house. The steps need to be performed to build a house are – building foundation, building pillars, building walls and windows. The important point is that we can't change the order of execution because we can't build windows before building the foundation. So in this case we can create a template method that will use different methods to build the house.

2. **Mediator Pattern**

Mediator design pattern is used to provide a centralized communication medium between different objects in a system. Mediator design pattern is very helpful in an enterprise application where multiple objects are interacting with each other. If the objects interact with each other directly, the system components are tightly-coupled with each other that make maintainability cost higher and not flexible to extend easily. Mediator pattern focuses on provide a mediator between objects for communication and help in implementing lose-coupling between objects.

Air traffic controller is a great example of mediator pattern where the airport control room works as a mediator for communication between different flights. Mediator works as a router between objects and it can have its own logic to provide way of communication.

3. **Chain of Responsibility Pattern**

Chain of responsibility pattern is used to achieve lose coupling in software design where a request from client is passed to a chain of objects to process them. Then the object in the chain will decide themselves who will be processing the request and whether the request is required to be sent to the next object in the chain or not.

We know that we can have multiple catch blocks in a try-catch block code. Here every catch block is kind of a processor to process that particular exception. So when any exception occur in the try block, its send to the first catch block to process. If the catch block is not able to process it, it forwards the request to next object in chain i.e. next catch block. If even the last catch block is not able to process it, the exception is thrown outside of the chain to the calling program.

4. **Observer Pattern**

Observer design pattern is useful when you are interested in the state of an object and want to get notified whenever there is any change. In observer pattern, the objects that watch on the state of another object are called Observer and the object that is being watched is called Subject.

Java provides inbuilt platform for implementing Observer pattern through *java.util.Observable* class and *java.util.Observer* interface. However it's not widely used because the implementation is really simple and most of the times we don't want to end up extending a class just for implementing Observer pattern as java doesn't provide multiple inheritance in classes.

**Java Message Service (JMS)** uses Observer pattern along with Mediator pattern to allow applications to subscribe and publish data to other applications.

5. **Strategy Pattern**

Strategy pattern is used when we have multiple algorithms for a specific task and client decides the actual implementation to be used at runtime.

Strategy pattern is also known as Policy Pattern. We define multiple algorithms and let client application pass the algorithm to be used as a parameter. One of the best example of this pattern is *Collections.sort( )* method that takes Comparator parameter. Based on the different implementations of Comparator interfaces, the Objects are getting sorted in different ways.

6. **Command Pattern**

Command Pattern is used to implement lose coupling in a request-response model. In command pattern, the request is send to the invoker and invoker passes it to the encapsulated command object. Command object passes the request to the appropriate method of Receiver to perform the specific action.

Let's say we want to provide a File System utility with methods to open, write and close file and it should support multiple operating systems such as *Windows* and *Unix*.

To implement our File System utility, first of all we need to create the receiver classes that will actually do all the work. Since we code in terms of java interfaces, we can have *FileSystemReceiver* interface and its implementation classes for different operating system flavors such as Windows, Unix, Solaris etc.

7. **State Pattern**

   State design pattern is used when an Object change its behavior based on its internal state. If we have to change the behavior of an object based on its state, we can have a state variable in the Object and use if-else condition block to perform different actions based on the state. State pattern is used to provide a systematic and lose-coupled way to achieve this through Context and State implementations.

8. **Visitor Pattern**

   Visitor pattern is used when we have to perform an operation on a group of similar kind of Objects. With the help of visitor pattern, we can move the operational logic from the objects to another class.

   For example, think of a Shopping cart where we can add different type of items (Elements), when we click on checkout button, it calculates the total amount to be paid. Now we can have the calculation logic in item classes or we can move out this logic to another class using visitor pattern. Let's implement this in our example of visitor pattern.

9. **Interpreter Pattern**

   Interpreter pattern is used to define a grammatical representation for a language and provides an interpreter to deal with this grammar.

   The best example of this pattern is java compiler that interprets the java source code into byte code that is understandable by JVM. Google Translator is also an example of interpreter pattern where the input can be in any language and we can get the output interpreted in another language.

10. **Iterator Pattern**

    Iterator pattern in one of the behavioral pattern and it's used to provide a standard way to traverse through a group of Objects. Iterator pattern is widely used in Java Collection Framework where Iterator interface provides methods for traversing through a collection.

    Iterator pattern is not only about traversing through a collection, but we can provide different kind of iterators based on our requirements. Iterator pattern hides the actual implementation of traversal through the collection and client programs just use iterator methods.

11. **Memento Pattern**

    Memento design pattern is used when we want to save the state of an object so that we can restore later on. Memento pattern is used to implement this in such a way that the saved state data of the object is not accessible outside of the object; this protects the integrity of saved state data.

    Memento pattern is implemented with two objects – Originator and Caretaker. Originator is the object whose state needs to be saved and restored and it uses an inner class to save the state of Object. The inner class is called Memento and its private, so that it can't be accessed from other objects.

## 23.3 Design Patterns in depth

In previous section we have discussed the design patterns in very brief. Let's now expand above section and discuss on each of the design pattern with more discussion and a program with design.

### 23.3.1 Creational Design patterns

#### 1. Singleton pattern

Singleton pattern is one of the simplest design patterns in Java. This type of design pattern comes under creational pattern as this pattern provides one of the best ways to create an object.

This pattern involves a single class which is responsible to creates own object while making sure that only single object get created. This class provides a way to access its only object which can be accessed directly without need to instantiate the object of the class.

**Implementation**

We're going to create a *SingleObject* class. *SingleObject* class have its constructor as private and have a static instance of itself.

*SingleObject* class provides a static method to get its static instance to outside world. Our demo class, *SingletonPatternDemo*, will use *SingleObject* class to get a *SingleObject* object.

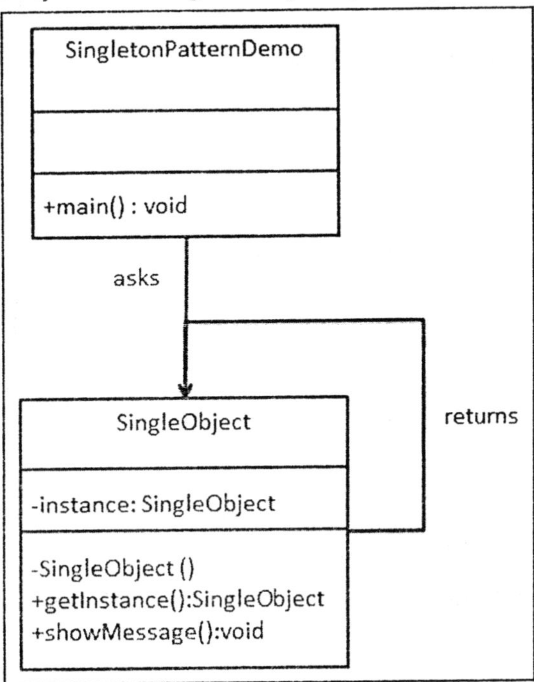


**Step 1:** Create a singleton class. Name it as **SingleObject.java**

```
public class SingleObject
{
  //create an object of SingleObject
  private static SingleObject instance = new SingleObject( );

  //make the constructor private so that this class cannot be instantiated
  private SingleObject( )
  { }
  //Get the only object available
  public static SingleObject getInstance( )
  {
     return instance;
  }
   public void showMessage( )
  {
     System.out.println("Hello World!");
  }
}
```

**Step 2:** Get the only object in main class from the singleton class. Name it as **SingletonPatternDemo.java**

```
public class SingletonPatternDemo
{
  public static void main(String ar[ ])
  {
    //illegal construct
    //Compile Time Error: The constructor SingleObject( ) is not visible
    //SingleObject object = new SingleObject( );

    //Get the only object available
    SingleObject object = SingleObject.getInstance( );

    //show the message
    object.showMessage( );
  }
}
```

**Step 3:** Verify Output

```
Hello World!
```

**2. Factory pattern**

Factory pattern is one of most used design pattern in Java. This type of design pattern comes under creational pattern as this pattern provides one of the best ways to create an object.

In Factory pattern, we create object without exposing the creation logic to the client and refer to newly created object using a common interface.

**Implementation**

We're going to create a Shape interface and concrete classes implementing the Shape interface. A factory class *ShapeFactory* is defined as a next step.

*FactoryPatternDemo*, our demo class will use *ShapeFactory* to get a Shape object. It will pass information (CIRCLE / RECTANGLE / SQUARE) to *ShapeFactory* to get the type of object it needs.

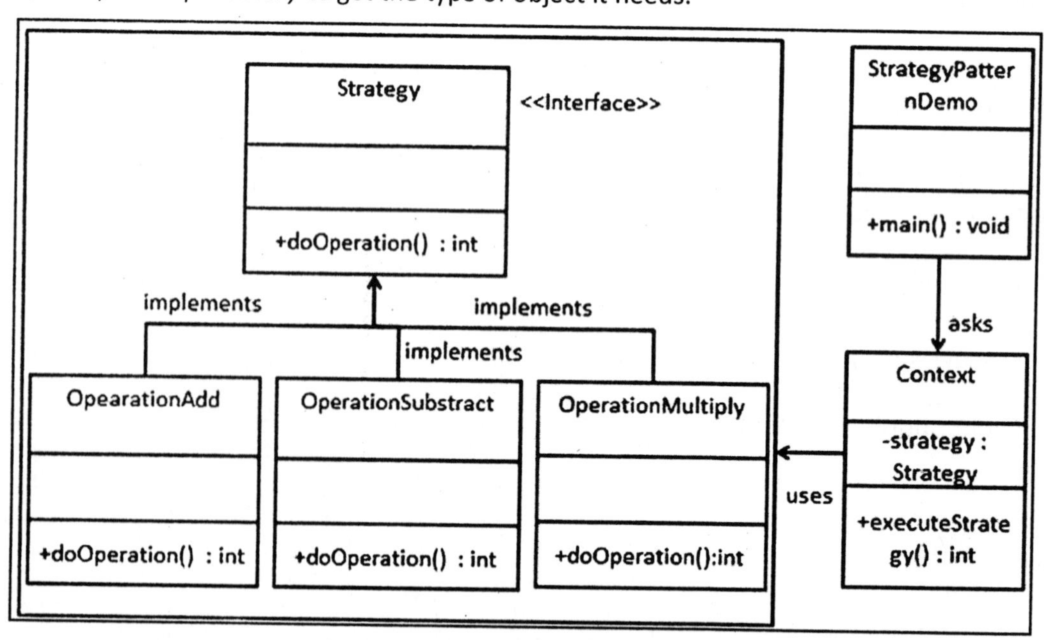

**Step 1:** Create an interface. Name it **Shape.java**

```
public interface Shape
{
   void draw( );
}
```

**Step 2:** Create classes, implementing the interface Shape.

**Rectangle.java**

```
public class Rectangle implements Shape
{
  @Override
  public void draw( )
  {
    System.out.println("Inside Rectangle::draw() method.");
  }
}
```

**Square.java**

```
public class Square implements Shape
{
  @Override
  public void draw( )
  {
    System.out.println("Inside Square::draw() method.");
  }
}
```

**Circle.java**

```
public class Circle implements Shape
{
  @Override
  public void draw( )
  {
    System.out.println("Inside Circle::draw() method.");
  }
}
```

**Step 3:** Create a Factory to generate object of concrete class based on given information. Name it **ShapeFactory.java**

```
public class ShapeFactory
{
  //use getShape method to get object of type shape
  public Shape getShape(String shapeType)
  {
    if(shapeType == null)
    {
     return null;
    }
    if(shapeType.equalsIgnoreCase("CIRCLE"))
    {
     return new Circle( );
    }
```

```
        else if(shapeType.equalsIgnoreCase("RECTANGLE"))
        {
          return new Rectangle( );
        }
        else if(shapeType.equalsIgnoreCase("SQUARE"))
        {
          return new Square( );
        }
        return null;
      }
    }
```

Step 4: Use the Factory to get object of concrete class by passing information such as type. Name it **FactoryPatternDemo.java**

```
public class FactoryPatternDemo
{
  public static void main(String ar[ ])
  {
    ShapeFactory shapeFactory = new ShapeFactory( );

    //get an object of Circle and call its draw method.
    Shape shape1 = shapeFactory.getShape("CIRCLE");

    //call draw method of Circle
    shape1.draw( );

    //get an object of Rectangle and call its draw method.
    Shape shape2 = shapeFactory.getShape("RECTANGLE");

    //call draw method of Rectangle
    shape2.draw( );

    //get an object of Square and call its draw method.
    Shape shape3 = shapeFactory.getShape("SQUARE");

    //call draw method of circle
    shape3.draw( );
  }
}
```

**Step 5:** Verify output

```
Inside Circle::draw() method.
Inside Rectangle::draw() method.
Inside Square::draw() method.
```

**3. Abstract Factory pattern**

Abstract Factory patterns works around a super-factory which creates other factories. This factory is also called as Factory of factories. This type of design pattern comes under creational pattern as this pattern provides one of the best ways to create an object.

In Abstract Factory pattern an interface is responsible for creating a factory of related objects, without explicitly specifying their classes. Each generated factory can give the objects as per the Factory pattern.

**Implementation**

We're going to create a Shape and Color interfaces and concrete classes implementing these interfaces. We create an abstract factory class *AbstractFactory* as next step. Factory classes *ShapeFactory* and *ColorFactory* are defined where each factory extends *AbstractFactory*. A factory creator/generator class *FactoryProducer* is created.

*AbstractFactoryPatternDemo*, our demo class uses *FactoryProducer* to get a *AbstractFactory* object. It will pass information (CIRCLE / RECTANGLE / SQUARE for Shape) to *AbstractFactory* to get the type of object it needs. It also passes information (RED / GREEN / BLUE for Color) to *AbstractFactory* to get the type of object it needs.

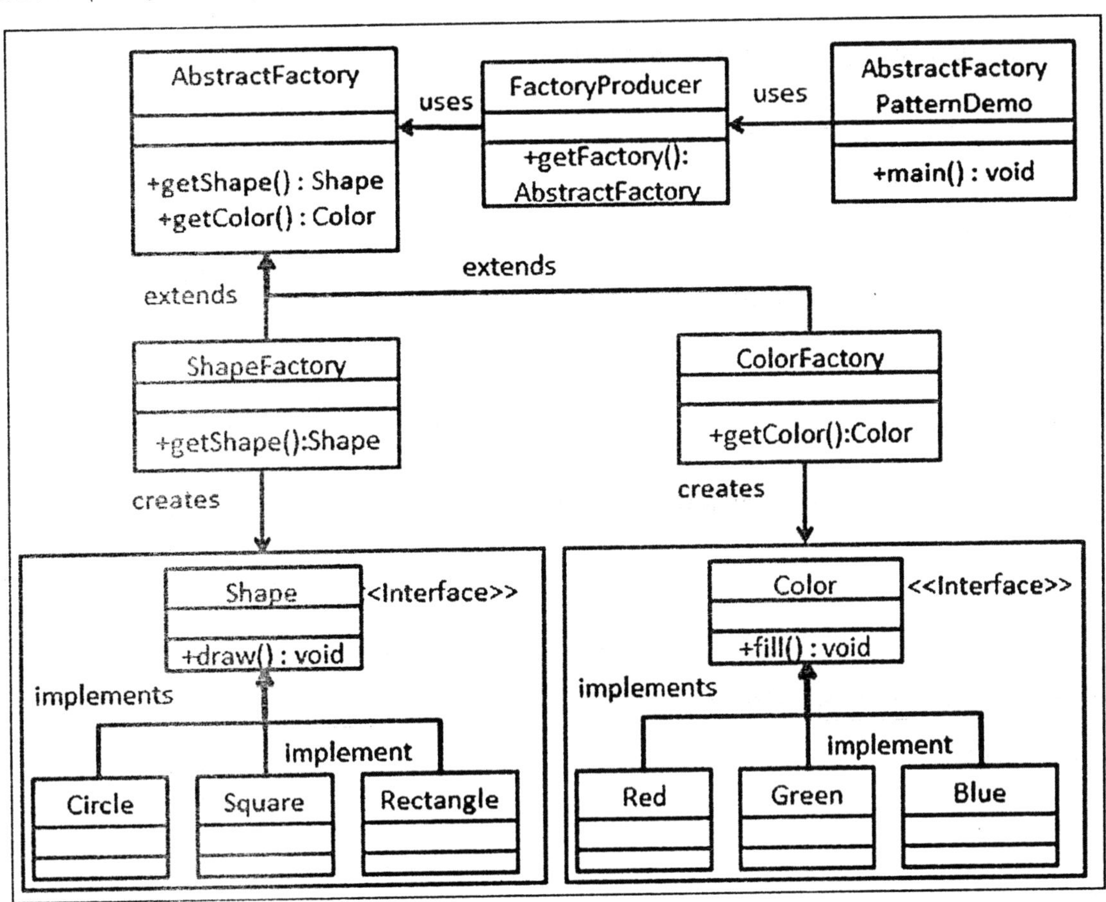


**Step 1:** Create an interface for Shapes. Name it **Shape.java**

```
public interface Shape
{
  void draw( );
}
```

**Step 2:** Create classes implementing the same interface.

**Rectangle.java**

```
public class Rectangle implements Shape
{
  @Override
  public void draw( )
  {
```

```
    System.out.println("Inside Rectangle::draw() method.");
  }
}
```

**Square.java**

```
public class Square implements Shape
{
  @Override
  public void draw( )
  {
    System.out.println("Inside Square::draw() method.");
  }
}
```

**Circle.java**

```
public class Circle implements Shape
{
  @Override
  public void draw( )
  {
    System.out.println("Inside Circle::draw() method.");
  }
}
```

**Step 3:** Create an interface for Colors. Name it Color.java

```
public interface Color
{
  void fill( );
}
```

**Step 4:** Create classes implementing the same interface.

**Red.java**

```
public class Red implements Color
{
  @Override
  public void fill( )
  {
    System.out.println("Inside Red::fill() method.");
  }
}
```

**Green.java**

```
public class Green implements Color
{
  @Override
  public void fill( )
  {
    System.out.println("Inside Green::fill() method.");
  }
}
```

**Blue.java**

```
public class Blue implements Color
{
  @Override
  public void fill( )
  {
    System.out.println("Inside Blue::fill() method.");
  }
}
```

**Step 5:** Create an Abstract class to get factories for Color and Shape Objects. Name it **AbstractFactory.java**

```
public abstract class AbstractFactory
{
   abstract Color getColor(String color);
   abstract Shape getShape(String shape) ;
}
```

**Step 6:** Create classes extending *AbstractFactory* to generate object of concrete class based on given information.

**ShapeFactory.java**

```
public class ShapeFactory extends AbstractFactory
{
  @Override
  public Shape getShape(String shapeType)
  {
    if(shapeType == null)
    {
      return null;
    }
    if(shapeType.equalsIgnoreCase("CIRCLE"))
    {
     return new Circle( );
```

```
    }
    else if(shapeType.equalsIgnoreCase("RECTANGLE"))
    {
     return new Rectangle( );
    }
    else if(shapeType.equalsIgnoreCase("SQUARE"))
    {
     return new Square( );
    }
    return null;
  }


  @Override
  Color getColor(String color)
  {
    return null;
  }
}
```

**ColorFactory.java**

```
public class ColorFactory extends AbstractFactory
{
  @Override
  public Shape getShape(String shapeType)
  {
    return null;
  }

  @Override
  Color getColor(String color)
  {
    if(color == null)
    {
      return null;
    }
    if(color.equalsIgnoreCase("RED"))
    {
      return new Red( );
    }
    else if(color.equalsIgnoreCase("GREEN"))
    {
      return new Green( );
    }
    else if(color.equalsIgnoreCase("BLUE"))
    {
      return new Blue( );
    }
    return null;
  }
}
```

**Step 7:** Create a Factory generator/producer class to get factories by passing information such as Shape or Color. **Name** it **FactoryProcedures.java**

```
public class FactoryProducer
{
  public static AbstractFactory getFactory(String choice)
  {
    if(choice.equalsIgnoreCase("SHAPE"))
    {
      return new ShapeFactory( );
    }
    else if(choice.equalsIgnoreCase("COLOR"))
    {
      return new ColorFactory( );
    }
     return null;
  }
}
```

**Step 8:** Use the *FactoryProducer* to get *AbstractFactory* in order to get factories of concrete classes by passing information such as type.

```
public class AbstractFactoryPatternDemo
{
    public static void main(String ar[ ])
    {
        //get shape factory
        AbstractFactory shapeFactory = FactoryProducer.getFactory("SHAPE");

        //get an object of Shape Circle
        Shape shape1 = shapeFactory.getShape("CIRCLE");

        //call draw method of Shape Circle
        shape1.draw( );

        //get an object of Shape Rectangle
        Shape shape2 = shapeFactory.getShape("RECTANGLE");

        //call draw method of Shape Rectangle
        shape2.draw( );

        //get an object of Shape Square
        Shape shape3 = shapeFactory.getShape("SQUARE");

        //call draw method of Shape Square
        shape3.draw( );
```

```
            //get color factory
            AbstractFactory colorFactory = FactoryProducer.getFactory("COLOR");

            //get an object of Color Red
            Color color1 = colorFactory.getColor("RED");

            //call fill method of Red
            color1.fill( );

            //get an object of Color Green
            Color color2 = colorFactory.getColor("Green");

            //call fill method of Green
            color2.fill( );

            //get an object of Color Blue
            Color color3 = colorFactory.getColor("BLUE");

            //call fill method of Color Blue
            color3.fill( );
        }
    }
```

**Step 9:** Verify the output

```
Inside Circle::draw() method.
Inside Rectangle::draw() method.
Inside Square::draw() method.
Inside Red::fill() method.
Inside Green::fill() method.
Inside Blue::fill() method.
```

**4. Builder pattern**

Builder pattern builds a complex object using simple objects and using a step by step approach. This type of design pattern comes under creational pattern as this pattern provides one of the best ways to create an object.

A Builder class builds the final object step by step. This builder is independent of other objects.

**Implementation**

We've considered a business case of fast-food restaurant where a typical meal could be a burger and a cold drink. Burger could be either a Veg Burger or Chicken Burger and will be packed by a wrapper. Cold drink could be either a Coke or Pepsi and will be packed in a bottle.

We're going to create an Item interface representing food items such as burgers and cold drinks and concrete classes implementing the Item interface and a Packing interface representing packaging of food items and concrete classes implementing the Packing interface as burger would be packed in wrapper and cold drink would be packed as bottle.

We then create a Meal class having *ArrayList* of Item and a *MealBuilder* to build different types of Meal object by combining Item. *BuilderPatternDemo*, our demo class will use *MealBuilder* to build a Meal.

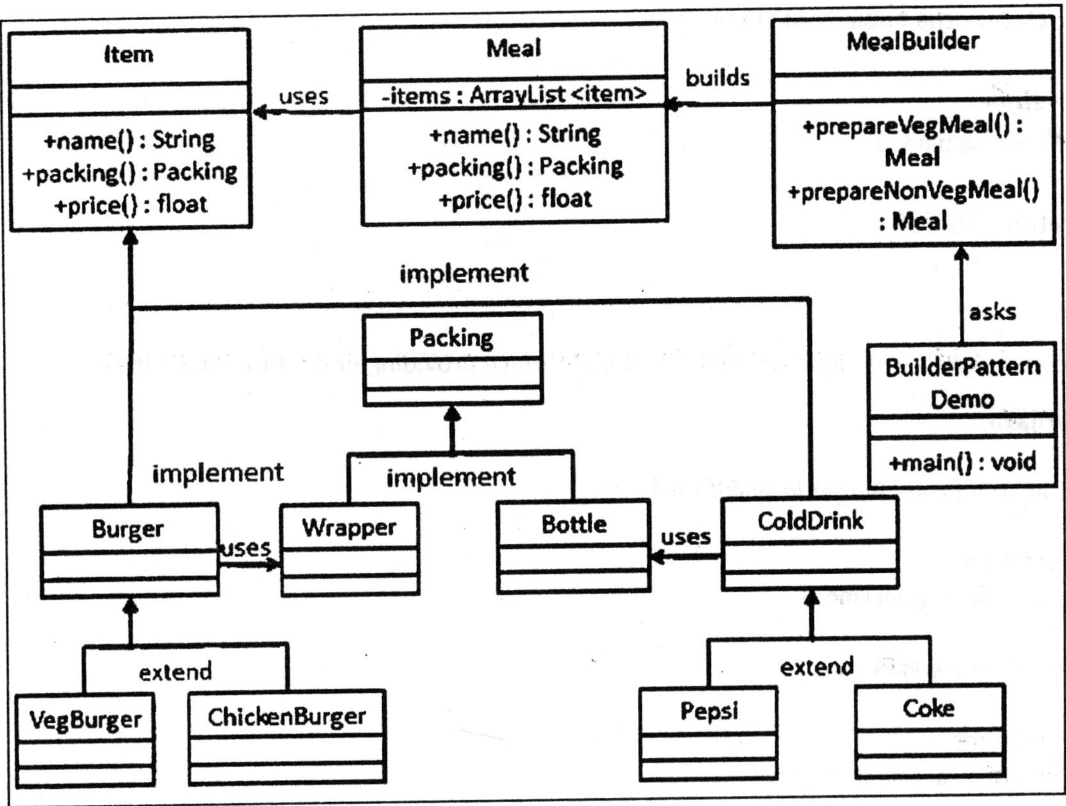


**Step 1:** Create an interface Item representing food item and packing.

**item.java**

```
public interface Item
{
   public String name( );
   public Packing packing( );
   public float price( );
}
```

**Packing.java**

```
public interface Packing
{
   public String pack( );
}
```

**Step 2:** Create classes implementing the Packing interface.

**Wrapper.java**

```
public class Wrapper implements Packing
{
  @Override
  public String pack( )
  {
     return "Wrapper";
  }
}
```

**Bottle.java**

```
public class Bottle implements Packing
{
  @Override
  public String pack( )
  {
     return "Bottle";
  }
}
```

**Step 3:** Create abstract classes implementing the item interface providing default functionalities.

**Burger.java**

```
public abstract class Burger implements Item
{
    @Override
    public Packing packing( )
    {
      return new Wrapper( );
    }
    @Override
    public abstract float price( );
}
```

**ColdDrink.java**

```
public abstract class ColdDrink implements Item
{
    @Override
    public Packing packing( )
    {
        return new Bottle( );
    }
    @Override
    public abstract float price( );
}
```

**Step 4:** Create concrete classes extending Burger and ColdDrink classes

**VegBurger.java**

```
public class VegBurger extends Burger
{
  @Override
  public float price()
  {
    return 25.0f;
```

```
  }

  @Override
  public String name( )
  {
     return "Veg Burger";
  }
}
```

**ChickenBurger.java**

```
public class ChickenBurger extends Burger
{
  @Override
  public float price( )
  {
     return 50.5f;
  }

  @Override
  public String name( )
  {
     return "Chicken Burger";
  }
}
```

**Coke.java**

```
public class Coke extends ColdDrink
{
  @Override
  public float price( )
  {
     return 30.0f;
  }

  @Override
  public String name( )
  {
     return "Coke";
  }
}
```

**Pepsi.java**

```
public class Pepsi extends ColdDrink
{
   @Override
   public float price( )
   {
      return 35.0f;
```

```
    }

    @Override
    public String name( )
    {
       return "Pepsi";
    }
}
```

**Step 5:** Create a Meal class having Item objects defined above. Name it **Meal.java**

```
import java.util.ArrayList;
import java.util.List;

public class Meal
{
    private List<Item> items = new ArrayList<Item>( );
    public void addItem(Item item)
    {
       items.add(item);
    }

    public float getCost( )
    {
        float cost = 0.0f;
        for (Item item : items)
        {
           cost += item.price( );
        }
        return cost;
    }

    public void showItems( )
    {
        for (Item item : items)
        {
           System.out.print("Item : "+item.name( ));
           System.out.print(", Packing : "+item.packing( ).pack( ));
           System.out.println(", Price : "+item.price( ));
        }
    }
}
```

**Step 6:** Create a *MealBuilder* class, the actual builder class responsible to create Meal objects. Name it **MealBuilder.java**

```
public class MealBuilder
{
    public Meal prepareVegMeal( )
    {
```

```
        Meal meal = new Meal( );
        meal.addItem(new VegBurger( ));
        meal.addItem(new Coke( ));
        return meal;
    }

    public Meal prepareNonVegMeal( )
    {
        Meal meal = new Meal( );
        meal.addItem(new ChickenBurger( ));
        meal.addItem(new Pepsi( ));
        return meal;
    }
}
```

**Step 7:** BuiderPatternDemo uses MealBuider to demonstrate builder pattern. Name it **BuilderPatternDemo.java**

```
public class BuilderPatternDemo
{
  public static void main(String ar[ ])
  {
      MealBuilder mealBuilder = new MealBuilder();
      Meal vegMeal = mealBuilder.prepareVegMeal();
      System.out.println("Veg Meal");
      vegMeal.showItems();
      System.out.println("Total Cost: " +vegMeal.getCost());
      Meal nonVegMeal = mealBuilder.prepareNonVegMeal();
      System.out.println("\n\nNon-Veg Meal");
      nonVegMeal.showItems();
      System.out.println("Total Cost: " +nonVegMeal.getCost());
  }
}
```

**Step 8:** Verify the output.

```
Veg Meal
Item : Veg Burger, Packing : Wrapper, Price : 25.0
Item : Coke, Packing : Bottle, Price : 30.0
Total Cost: 55.0

Non-Veg Meal
Item : Chicken Burger, Packing : Wrapper, Price : 50.5
Item : Pepsi, Packing : Bottle, Price : 35.0
Total Cost: 85.5
```

**5. Prototype pattern**

Prototype pattern refers to creating duplicate object while keeping performance in mind. This type of design pattern comes under creational pattern as this pattern provides one of the best ways to create an object.

This pattern involves implementing a prototype interface which tells to create a clone of the current object. This pattern is used when creation of object directly is costly. For example, a object is to be created after a costly database operation. We can cache the object, returns its clone on next request and update the database as as and when needed thus reducing database calls.

**Implementation**

We're going to create an abstract class Shape and concrete classes extending the Shape class. A class *ShapeCache* is defined as a next step which stores shape objects in a *Hashtable* and returns their clone when requested.

*PrototypPatternDemo*, our demo class will use *ShapeCache* class to get a Shape object.

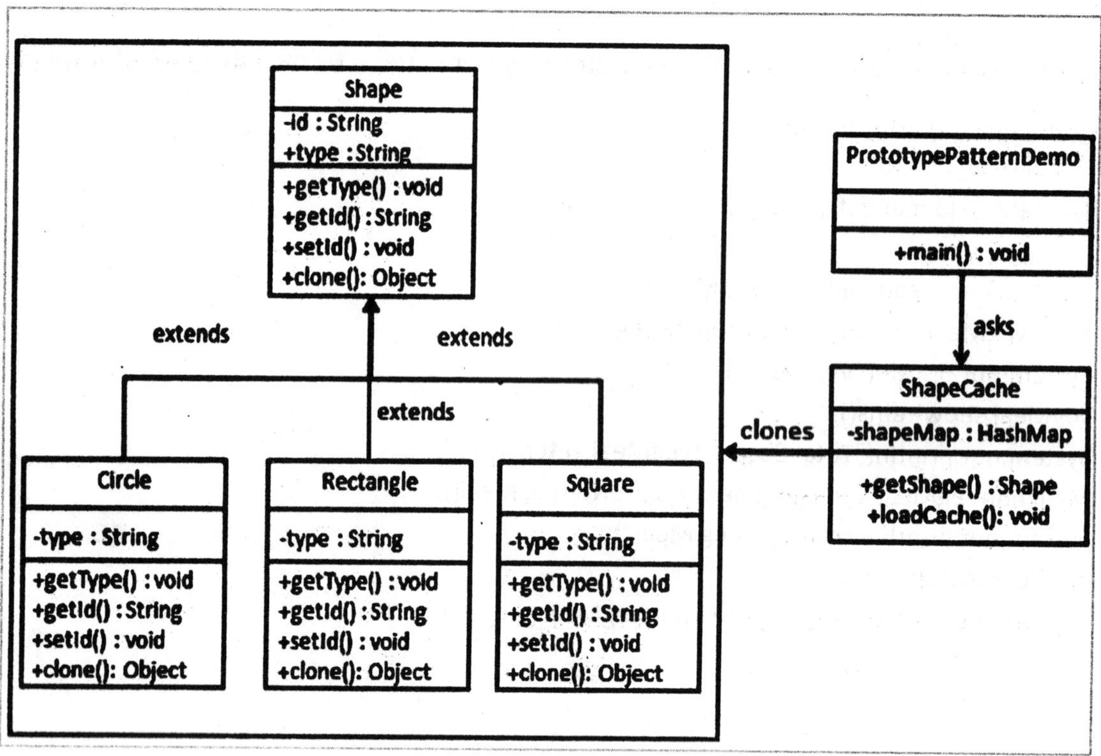


**Step 1:** Create an abstract class implementing *Clonable* interface.

```
public abstract class Shape implements Cloneable
{
   private String id;
   protected String type;
   abstract void draw( );

   public String getType( )
   {
      return type;
   }

   public String getId( )
   {
```

```
        return id;
    }

    public void setId(String id)
    {
        this.id = id;
    }

    public Object clone( )
    {
      Object clone = null;
      try
      {
        clone = super.clone( );
      }
      catch (CloneNotSupportedException e)
      {
        e.printStackTrace( );
      }
      return clone;
    }
}
```

**Step 2:** Create classes extending the above class.

**Rectangle.java**

```
public class Rectangle extends Shape
{
     public Rectangle( )
     {
        type = "Rectangle";
     }
    @Override
    public void draw( )
    {
        System.out.println("Inside Rectangle::draw() method.");
    }
}
```

**Square.java**

```
public class Square extends Shape
{
    public Square( )
    {
        type = "Square";
    }
    @Override
    public void draw( )
    {
        System.out.println("Inside Square::draw() method.");
```

```
    }
}
```

**Circle.java**

```
public class Circle extends Shape
{
    public Circle( )
    {
        type = "Circle";
    }
    @Override
    public void draw( )
    {
        System.out.println("Inside Circle::draw() method.");
    }
}
```

**Step 3:** Create a class to get concreate classes from database and store them in a *Hashtable*. Name it **ShapeCache.java**

```
import java.util.Hashtable;
public class ShapeCache
{
    private static Hashtable<String, Shape> shapeMap = new Hashtable<String, Shape>( );

    public static Shape getShape(String shapeId)
    {
        Shape cachedShape = shapeMap.get(shapeId);
        return (Shape) cachedShape.clone();
    }

    // for each shape run database query and create shape
    // shapeMap.put(shapeKey, shape);
    // for example, we are adding three shapes
    public static void loadCache()
    {
        Circle circle = new Circle();
        circle.setId("1");
        shapeMap.put(circle.getId(),circle);

        Square square = new Square( );
        square.setId("2");
        shapeMap.put(square.getId(),square);

        Rectangle rectangle = new Rectangle( );
        rectangle.setId("3");
        shapeMap.put(rectangle.getId(),rectangle);
    }
}
```

**Step 4:** *PrototypePatternDemo* uses *ShapeCache* class to get clones of shapes stored in a *Hashtable*. Name it **PrototypePatternDemo.java**

```
public class PrototypePatternDemo
{
    public static void main(String ar[ ])
    {
        ShapeCache.loadCache( );
        Shape clonedShape = (Shape) ShapeCache.getShape("1");
        System.out.println("Shape : " + clonedShape.getType( ));
        Shape clonedShape2 = (Shape) ShapeCache.getShape("2");
        System.out.println("Shape : " + clonedShape2.getType( ));
        Shape clonedShape3 = (Shape) ShapeCache.getShape("3");
        System.out.println("Shape : " + clonedShape3.getType( ));
    }
}
```

**Step 5:** Verify the output.

```
Shape : Circle
Shape : Square
Shape : Rectangle
```

### 23.3.2 Structural Design patterns

**1. Adapter pattern**

Adapter pattern works as a bridge between two incompatible interfaces. This type of design pattern comes under structural pattern as this pattern combines the capability of two independent interfaces.

This pattern involves a single class which is responsible to join functionalities of independent or incompatible interfaces. A real life example could be a case of card reader which acts as an adapter between memory card and a laptop. You plugins the memory card into card reader and card reader into the laptop so that memory card can be read via laptop.

We are demonstrating use of Adapter pattern via following example in which an audio player device can play mp3 files only and wants to use an advanced audio player capable of playing vlc and mp4 files.

**Implementation**

We've an interface *MediaPlayer* interface and a concrete class *AudioPlayer* implementing the *MediaPlayer* interface. *AudioPlayer* can play mp3 format audio files by default.

We're having another interface *AdvancedMediaPlayer* and concrete classes implementing the *AdvancedMediaPlayer* interface. These classes can play **vlc** and **mp4** format files.

We want to make *AudioPlayer* to play other formats as well. To attain this, we've created an adapter class *MediaAdapter* which implements the *MediaPlayer* interface and uses *AdvancedMediaPlayer* objects to play the required format.

*AudioPlayer* uses the adapter class *MediaAdapter* passing it the desired audio type without knowing the actual class which can play the desired format. *AdapterPatternDemo*, our demo class will use *AudioPlayer* class to play various formats.

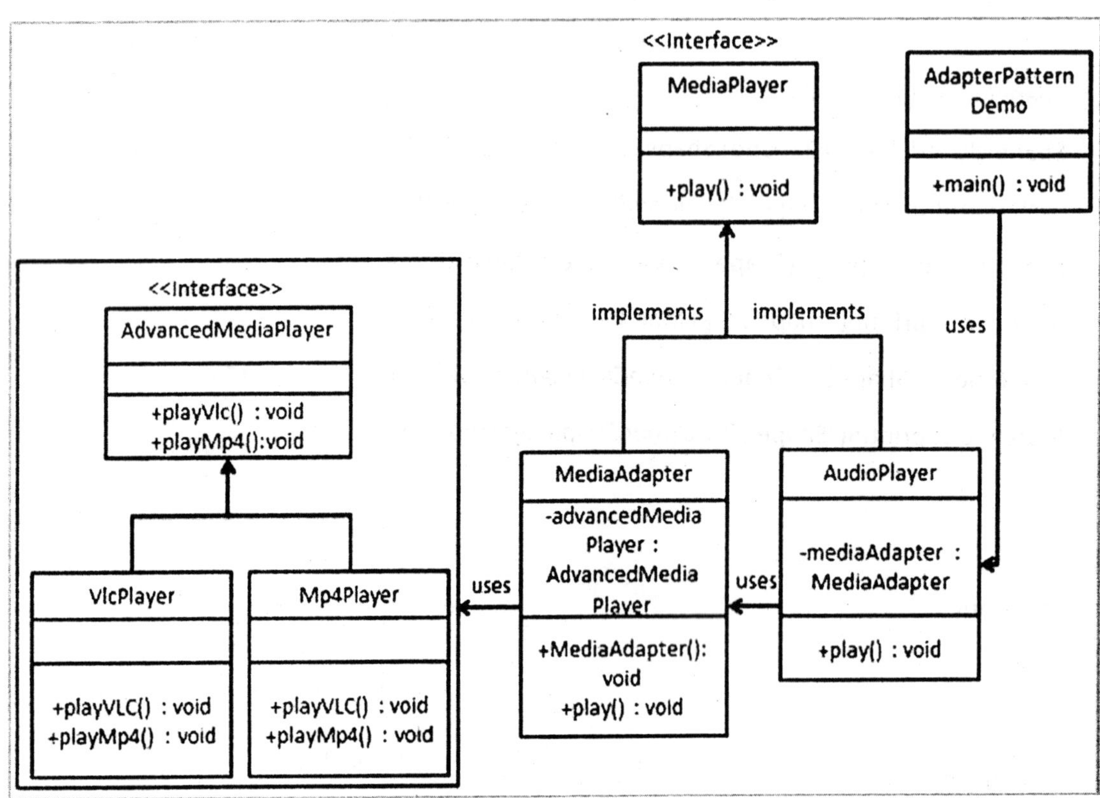


**Step 1:** Create interfaces for Media Player and Advanced Media Player.

**MediaPlayer.java**

```
public interface MediaPlayer
{
   public void play(String audioType, String fileName);
}
```

**AdvancedMediaPlayer.java**

```
public interface AdvancedMediaPlayer
{
   public void playVlc(String fileName);
   public void playMp4(String fileName);
}
```

**Step 2:** Create classes implementing the *AdvancedMediaPlayer* interface.

**VlcPlayer.java**

```
public class VlcPlayer implements AdvancedMediaPlayer
```

```
{
    @Override
    public void playVlc(String fileName)
    {
       System.out.println("Playing vlc file. Name: "+ fileName);
    }
    @Override
    public void playMp4(String fileName)
    {
       //do nothing
    }
}
```

**Mp4Player.java**

```
public class Mp4Player implements AdvancedMediaPlayer
{
    @Override
    public void playVlc(String fileName)
    {
       //do nothing
    }
    @Override
    public void playMp4(String fileName)
    {
       System.out.println("Playing mp4 file. Name: "+ fileName);
    }
}
```

**Step 3:** Create adapter class implementing the *MediaPlayer* interface. Name it **MediaAdapter.java**

```
public class MediaAdapter implements MediaPlayer
{
     AdvancedMediaPlayer advancedMusicPlayer;
     public MediaAdapter(String audioType)
     {
        if(audioType.equalsIgnoreCase("vlc"))
        {
            advancedMusicPlayer = new VlcPlayer( );
        }
        else if (audioType.equalsIgnoreCase("mp4"))
        {
           advancedMusicPlayer = new Mp4Player( );
        }
      }
     @Override
     public void play(String audioType, String fileName)
     {
         if(audioType.equalsIgnoreCase("vlc"))
         {
            advancedMusicPlayer.playVlc(fileName);
```

```
            }
            else if(audioType.equalsIgnoreCase("mp4"))
            {
               advancedMusicPlayer.playMp4(fileName);
            }
        }
    }
```

**Step 4:** Create concrete class implementing the MediaPlayer interface. Name it **AudioPlayer.java**

```
public class AudioPlayer implements MediaPlayer
{
    MediaAdapter mediaAdapter;
    @Override
    public void play(String audioType, String fileName)
    {
        //inbuilt support to play mp3 music files
        if(audioType.equalsIgnoreCase("mp3"))
        {
          System.out.println("Playing mp3 file. Name: "+ fileName);
        }

        //mediaAdapter is providing support to play other file formats
        else if(audioType.equalsIgnoreCase("vlc") || audioType.equalsIgnoreCase("mp4"))
        {
          mediaAdapter = new MediaAdapter(audioType);
          mediaAdapter.play(audioType, fileName);
        }
        else
        {
          System.out.println("Invalid media. "+
            audioType + " format not supported");
        }
    }
}
```

**Step 5:** Use the *AudioPlayer* to play different types of audio formats. Name it **AdapterPatternDemo.java**

```
public class AdapterPatternDemo
{
    public static void main(String ar[ ])
    {
        AudioPlayer audioPlayer = new AudioPlayer( );
        audioPlayer.play("mp3", "beyond the horizon.mp3");
        audioPlayer.play("mp4", "alone.mp4");
        audioPlayer.play("vlc", "far far away.vlc");
        audioPlayer.play("avi", "mind me.avi");
    }
}
```

**Step 6:** Verify the output.

```
Playing mp3 file. Name: beyond the horizon.mp3
Playing mp4 file. Name: alone.mp4
Playing vlc file. Name: far far away.vlc
Invalid media. avi format not supported
```

### 2. Composite pattern

Composite pattern is used where we need to treat a group of objects in similar way as a single object. Composite pattern composes objects in term of a tree structure to represent part as well as whole hierarchy. This type of design pattern comes under structural pattern as this pattern creates a tree structure of group of objects.

This pattern creates a class contains group of its own objects. This class provides ways to modify its group of same objects.

We are demonstrating use of Composite pattern via following example in which show employees hierarchy of an organization.

**Implementation**

We've a class Employee which acts as composite pattern actor class. *CompositePatternDemo*, our demo class will use Employee class to add department level hierarchy and print all employees.

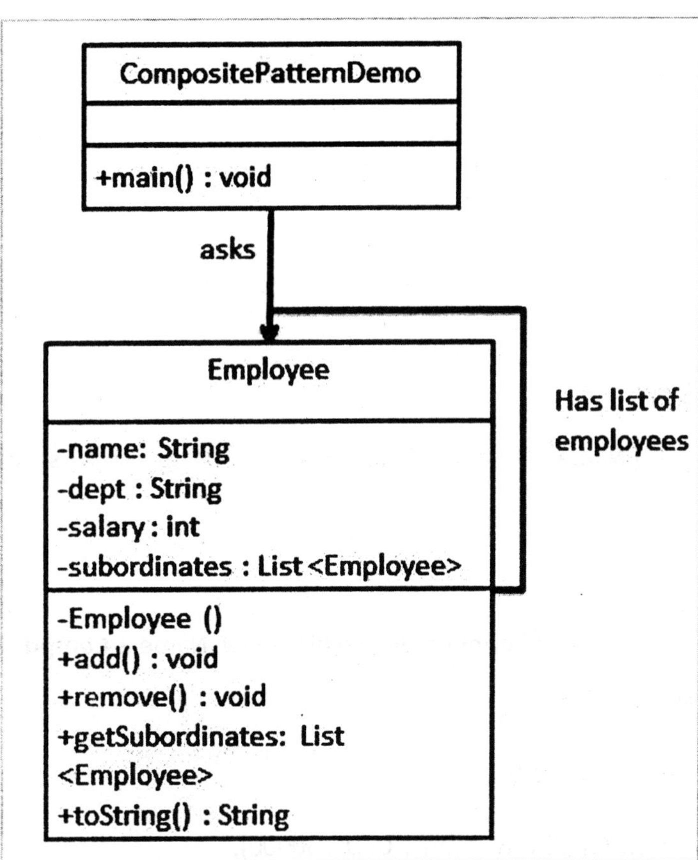


**Step 1:** Create Employee class having list of Employee objects. Name it **Employee.java**

```
import java.util.ArrayList;
import java.util.List;
```

```
public class Employee
{
    private String name;
    private String dept;
    private int salary;
    private List<Employee> subordinates;

    // constructor
    public Employee(String name,String dept, int sal)
    {
        this.name = name;
        this.dept = dept;
        this.salary = sal;
        subordinates = new ArrayList<Employee>();
    }

    public void add(Employee e)
    {
        subordinates.add(e);
    }

    public void remove(Employee e)
    {
        subordinates.remove(e);
    }

    public List<Employee> getSubordinates()
    {
        return subordinates;
    }


    public String toString( )
    {
        return ("Employee :[ Name : "+ name +", dept : "+ dept + ", salary :" + salary+" ]");
    }
}
```

**Step 2:** Use the Employee class to create and print employee hierarchy. Name it **CompositePatternDemo.java**

```
public class CompositePatternDemo
{
    public static void main(String ar[ ])
    {
        Employee CEO = new Employee("John","CEO", 30000);
        Employee headSales = new Employee("Robert","Head Sales", 20000);
        Employee headMarketing = new Employee("Michel","Head Marketing", 20000);
        Employee clerk1 = new Employee("Laura","Marketing", 10000);
        Employee clerk2 = new Employee("Bob","Marketing", 10000);
        Employee salesExecutive1 = new Employee("Richard","Sales", 10000);
        Employee salesExecutive2 = new Employee("Rob","Sales", 10000);
```

```
            CEO.add(headSales);
            CEO.add(headMarketing);

            headSales.add(salesExecutive1);
            headSales.add(salesExecutive2);

            headMarketing.add(clerk1);
            headMarketing.add(clerk2);

            //print all employees of the organization
            System.out.println(CEO);
            for (Employee headEmployee : CEO.getSubordinates( ))
            {
               System.out.println(headEmployee);
               for (Employee employee : headEmployee.getSubordinates( ))
               {
                  System.out.println(employee);
               }
            }
        }
    }
```

**Step 3:** Verify the output.

```
Employee :[ Name : John, dept : CEO, salary :30000 ]

Employee :[ Name : Robert, dept : Head Sales, salary :20000 ]

Employee :[ Name : Richard, dept : Sales, salary :10000 ]

Employee :[ Name : Rob, dept : Sales, salary :10000 ]

Employee :[ Name : Michel, dept : Head Marketing, salary :20000 ]

Employee :[ Name : Laura, dept : Marketing, salary :10000 ]

Employee :[ Name : Bob, dept : Marketing, salary :10000 ]
```

**3. Proxy pattern**

In Proxy pattern, a class represents functionality of another class. This type of design pattern comes under structural pattern.

In Proxy pattern, we create object having original object to interface its functionality to outer world.

**Implementation**

We're going to create a Image interface and concrete classes implementing the Image interface. *ProxyImage* is a a proxy class to reduce memory footprint of *RealImage* object loading.

*ProxyPatternDemo*, our demo class will use ProxyImage to get a Image object to load and display as it needs.

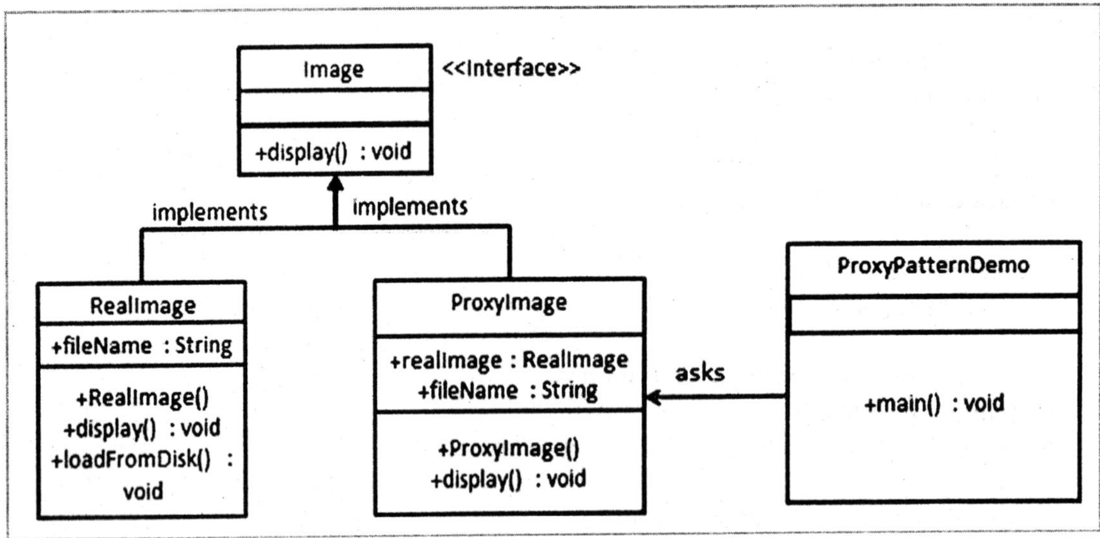


**Step 1:** Create an interface. Name it **Image.java**

```
public interface Image
{
   void display( );
}
```

**Step 2:** Create classes implementing the same interface.

**RealImage.java**

```
public class RealImage implements Image
{
    private String fileName;
    public RealImage(String fileName)
    {
       this.fileName = fileName;
       loadFromDisk(fileName);
    }
    @Override
    public void display( )
    {
       System.out.println("Displaying " + fileName);
    }

    private void loadFromDisk(String fileName)
    {
       System.out.println("Loading " + fileName);
    }
}
```

**ProxyImage.java**

```
public class ProxyImage implements Image
{
   private RealImage realImage;
```

```
    private String fileName;
    public ProxyImage(String fileName)
    {
        this.fileName = fileName;
    }

    @Override
    public void display( )
    {
        if(realImage == null)
        {
            realImage = new RealImage(fileName);
        }
        realImage.display();
    }
}
```

**Step 3:** Use the ProxyImage to get object of RealImage class when required. Name it **ProxyPatternDemo.java**

```
public class ProxyPatternDemo
{
    public static void main(String ar[ ])
    {
        Image image = new ProxyImage("test_10mb.jpg");
        //image will be loaded from disk
        image.display( );
        System.out.println("");
        //image will not be loaded from disk
        image.display( );
    }
}
```

**Step 4:** Verify the output.

```
Loading test_10mb.jpg
Displaying test_10mb.jpg
Displaying test_10mb.jpg
```

**4. Flyweight pattern**

Flyweight pattern is primarily used to reduce the number of objects created, to decrease memory footprint and increase performance. This type of design pattern comes under structural pattern as this pattern provides ways to decrease objects count thus improving application required objects structure.

Flyweight pattern try to reuse already existing similar kind objects by storing them and creates new object when no matching object is found. We'll demonstrate this pattern by drawing 20 circles of different locations but we'll creating only 5 objects. Only 5 colors are available so color property is used to check already existing Circle objects.

**Implementation**

We're going to create a Shape interface and concrete class Circle implementing the Shape interface. A factory class *ShapeFactory* is defined as a next step.

*ShapeFactory* have a *HashMap* of Circle having key as color of the Circle object. Whenever a request comes to create a circle of particular color to *ShapeFactory*, it checks the circle object in its *HashMap*, if object of Circle found, that object is returned otherwise a new object is created, stored in *hashmap* for future use and returned to client.

*FlyWeightPatternDemo*, our demo class will use *ShapeFactory* to get a Shape object. It will pass information (red / green / blue/ black / white) to *ShapeFactory* to get the circle of desired color it needs.

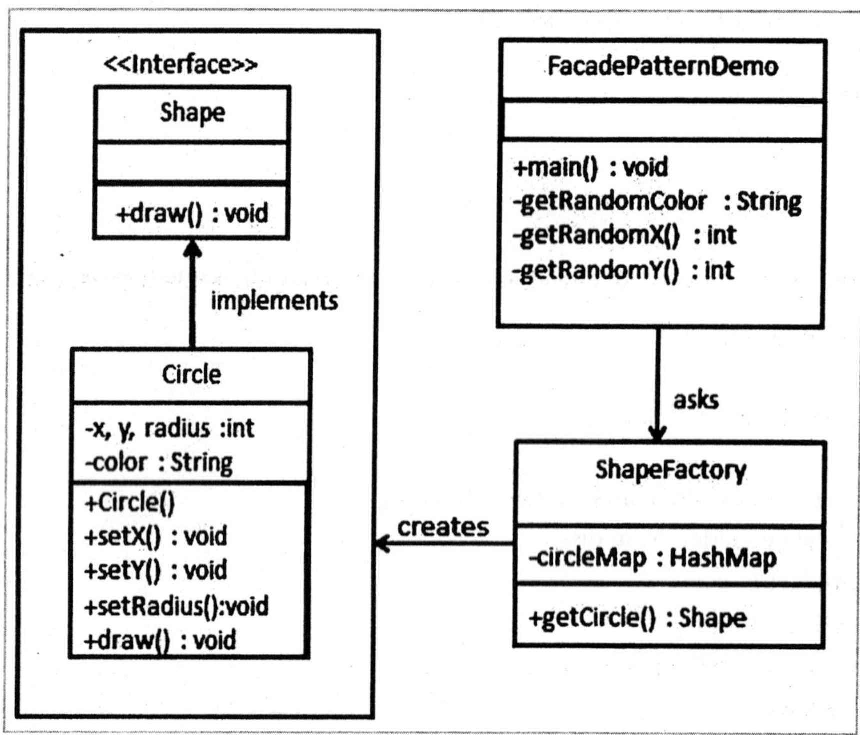


**Step 1:** Create an interface. Name it **Shape.java**

```
public interface Shape
{
    void draw( );
}
```

**Step 2:** Create concrete class implementing the same interface. Name it **Circle.java**

```
public class Circle implements Shape
{
    private String color;
    private int x;
    private int y;
    private int radius;

    public Circle(String color)
    {
        this.color = color;
```

```
    }
    public void setX(int x)
    {
        this.x = x;
    }
    public void setY(int y)
    {
        this.y = y;
    }
    public void setRadius(int radius)
    {
        this.radius = radius;
    }
    @Override
    public void draw( )
    {
        System.out.println("Circle: Draw() [Color : " + color +", x : " + x +", y :" + y +", radius :" + radius);
    }
}
```

**Step 3:** Create a Factory to generate object of concrete class based on given information. Name it **ShapeFactory.java**

```
import java.util.HashMap;
public class ShapeFactory
{
    private static final HashMap<String, Shape> circleMap = new HashMap( );
    public static Shape getCircle(String color)
    {
        Circle circle = (Circle)circleMap.get(color);
        if(circle == null)
        {
            circle = new Circle(color);
            circleMap.put(color, circle);
            System.out.println("Creating circle of color : " + color);
        }
        return circle;
    }
}
```

**Step 4:** Use the Factory to get object of concrete class by passing an information such as color. Name it

**FlyweightPatternDemo.java**

```
public class FlyweightPatternDemo
{
    private static final String colors[ ] = { "Red", "Green", "Blue", "White", "Black" };
    public static void main(String ar[ ])
    {
        for(int i=0; i < 20; ++i)
        {
```

```
            Circle circle = (Circle)ShapeFactory.getCircle(getRandomColor( ));
            circle.setX(getRandomX( ));
            circle.setY(getRandomY( ));
            circle.setRadius(100);
            circle.draw( );
        }
    }
    private static String getRandomColor( )
    {
        return colors[(int)(Math.random()*colors.length)];
    }
    private static int getRandomX( )
    {
        return (int)(Math.random( )*100 );
    }
    private static int getRandomY( )
    {
        return (int)(Math.random( )*100);
    }
}
```

**Step 5:** Verify the output.

```
Creating circle of color : Black
Circle: Draw() [Color : Black, x : 36, y :71, radius :100
Creating circle of color : Green
Circle: Draw() [Color : Green, x : 27, y :27, radius :100
Creating circle of color : White
Circle: Draw() [Color : White, x : 64, y :10, radius :100
Creating circle of color : Red
Circle: Draw() [Color : Red, x : 15, y :44, radius :100
Circle: Draw() [Color : Green, x : 19, y :10, radius :100
Circle: Draw() [Color : Green, x : 94, y :32, radius :100
Circle: Draw() [Color : White, x : 69, y :98, radius :100
Creating circle of color : Blue
Circle: Draw() [Color : Blue, x : 13, y :4, radius :100
Circle: Draw() [Color : Green, x : 21, y :21, radius :100
Circle: Draw() [Color : Blue, x : 55, y :86, radius :100
Circle: Draw() [Color : White, x : 90, y :70, radius :100
Circle: Draw() [Color : Green, x : 78, y :3, radius :100
Circle: Draw() [Color : Green, x : 64, y :89, radius :100
Circle: Draw() [Color : Blue, x : 3, y :91, radius :100
Circle: Draw() [Color : Blue, x : 62, y :82, radius :100
Circle: Draw() [Color : Green, x : 97, y :61, radius :100
Circle: Draw() [Color : Green, x : 86, y :12, radius :100
Circle: Draw() [Color : Green, x : 38, y :93, radius :100
Circle: Draw() [Color : Red, x : 76, y :82, radius :100
Circle: Draw() [Color : Blue, x : 95, y :82, radius :100
```

## 5. Facade pattern

Facade pattern hides the complexities of the system and provides an interface to the client using which the client can access the system. This type of design pattern comes under structural pattern as this pattern adds an interface to exiting system to hide its complexities.

This pattern involves a single class which provides simplified methods which are required by client and delegates calls to existing system classes' methods.

### Implementation

We're going to create a Shape interface and concrete classes implementing the Shape interface. A facade class *ShapeMaker* is defined as a next step.

*ShapeMaker* class uses the concrete classes to delegate user calls to these classes. *FacadePatternDemo*, our demo class will use *ShapeMaker* class to show the results.

**Step 1:** Create an interface. Name it **Shape.java**

```
public interface Shape
{
   void draw( );
}
```

**Step 2:** Create classes implementing the same interface.

**Rectangle.java**

```
public class Rectangle implements Shape
{
    @Override
    public void draw( )
    {
      System.out.println("Rectangle::draw()");
    }
}
```

**Square.java**

```
public class Square implements Shape
{
    @Override
    public void draw( )
    {
       System.out.println("Square::draw()");
    }
}
```

**Circle.java**

```
public class Circle implements Shape
{
    @Override
    public void draw( )
    {
        System.out.println("Circle::draw()");
    }
}
```

**Step 3:** Create a facade class. Name it **ShapeMaker.java**

```
public class ShapeMaker
{
    private Shape circle;
    private Shape rectangle;
    private Shape square;

    public ShapeMaker( )
    {
        circle = new Circle( );
        rectangle = new Rectangle( );
        square = new Square( );
    }

    public void drawCircle( )
    {
        circle.draw( );
    }
    public void drawRectangle( )
    {
        rectangle.draw( );
    }
    public void drawSquare( )
    {
        square.draw( );
    }
}
```

**Step 4:** Use the facade to draw various types of shapes. Name it **FacadePatternDemo.java**

```
public class FacadePatternDemo
{
    public static void main(String ar[ ])
    {
        ShapeMaker shapeMaker = new ShapeMaker( );
        shapeMaker.drawCircle( );
```

```
        shapeMaker.drawRectangle( );
        shapeMaker.drawSquare( );
    }
}
```

**Step 5:** Verify the output.

```
Circle::draw()
Rectangle::draw()
Square::draw()
```

### 6. Bridge pattern

Bridge is used where we need to decouple an abstraction from its implementation so that the two can vary independently. This type of design pattern comes under structural pattern as this pattern decouples implementation class and abstract class by providing a bridge structure between them.

This pattern involves an interface which acts as a bridge which makes the independent functionality of concrete classes from interface implementer classes. Both types of classes can be altered structurally without affecting each other.

#### Implementation

We've an interface *DrawAPI* interface which is acting as a bridge implementer and concrete classes *RedCircle*, *GreenCircle* implementing the *DrawAPI* interface. Shape is an abstract class and will use object of *DrawAPI*. *BridgePatternDemo*, our demo class will use Shape class to draw different colored circle.

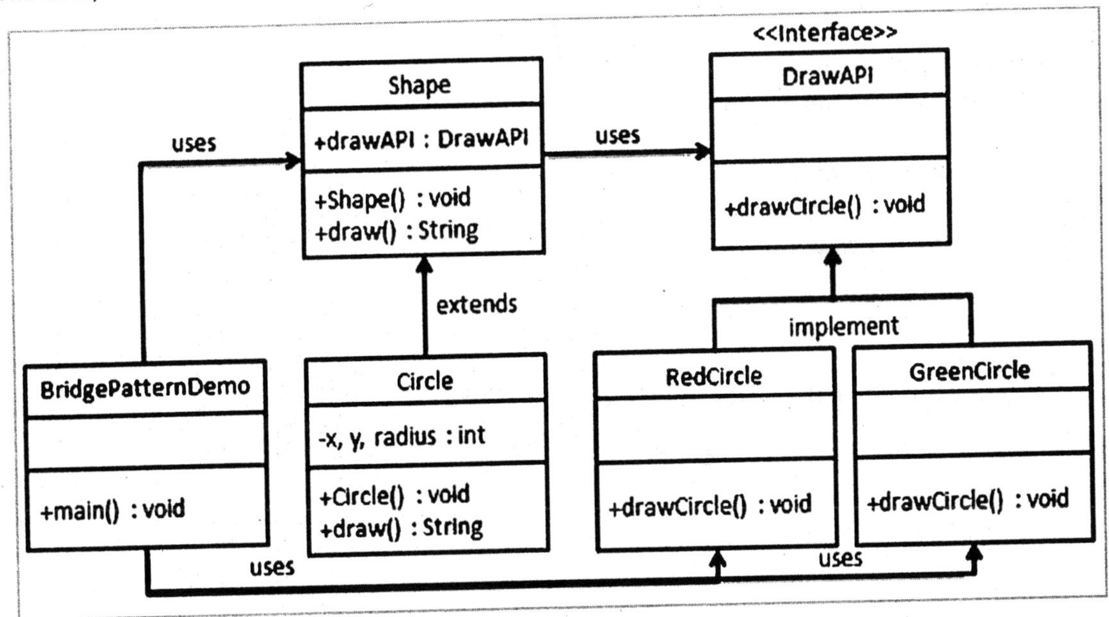


**Step 1:** Create bridge implementer interface. Name it **DrawAPI.java**

```
public interface DrawAPI
{
    public void drawCircle(int radius, int x, int y);
}
```

**Step 2:** Create bridge implementer classes implementing the *DrawAPI* interface.

**RedCircle.java**

```
public class RedCircle implements DrawAPI
{
    @Override
    public void drawCircle(int radius, int x, int y)
    {
        System.out.println("Drawing Circle[ color: red, radius: " + radius +", x: " +x+", "+ y +"]");
    }
}
```

**GreenCircle.java**

```
public class GreenCircle implements DrawAPI
{
    @Override
    public void drawCircle(int radius, int x, int y)
    {
        System.out.println("Drawing Circle[ color: green, radius: " + radius +", x: " +x+", "+ y +"]");
    }
}
```

**Step 3:** Create an abstract class Shape using the *DrawAPI* interface. Name it **Shape.java**

```
public abstract class Shape
{
    protected DrawAPI drawAPI;
    protected Shape(DrawAPI drawAPI)
    {
        this.drawAPI = drawAPI;
    }
    public abstract void draw( );
}
```

**Step 4:** Create a class implementing the Shape interface.

Circle.java

```
public class Circle extends Shape
{
    private int x, y, radius;
    public Circle(int x, int y, int radius, DrawAPI drawAPI)
    {
        super(drawAPI);
        this.x = x;
        this.y = y;
        this.radius = radius;
    }
```

```
    public void draw()
    {
       drawAPI.drawCircle(radius,x,y);
    }
}
```

**Step 5:** Use the Shape and DrawAPI classes to draw different colored circles. Name it **BridgePatternDemo.java**

```
public class BridgePatternDemo
{
    public static void main(String ar[ ])
    {
        Shape redCircle = new Circle(100,100, 10, new RedCircle( ));
        Shape greenCircle = new Circle(100,100, 10, new GreenCircle( ));
        redCircle.draw( );
        greenCircle.draw( );
    }
}
```

**Step 6:** Verify the output.

```
Drawing Circle[ color: red, radius: 10, x: 100, 100]

Drawing Circle[  color: green, radius: 10, x: 100, 100]
```

**7. Decorator pattern**

Decorator pattern allows to add new functionality an existing object without altering its structure. This type of design pattern comes under structural pattern as this pattern acts as a wrapper to existing class.

This pattern creates a decorator class which wraps the original class and provides additional functionality keeping class methods signature intact.

We are demonstrating use of Decorator pattern via following example in which we'll decorate a shape with some color without alter shape class.

**Implementation**

We're going to create a Shape interface and concrete classes implementing the Shape interface. We then create an abstract decorator class *ShapeDecorator* implementing the Shape interface and having Shape object as its instance variable.

*RedShapeDecorator* is concrete class implementing *ShapeDecorator*.

*DecoratorPatternDemo*, our demo class will use *RedShapeDecorator* to decorate Shape objects.

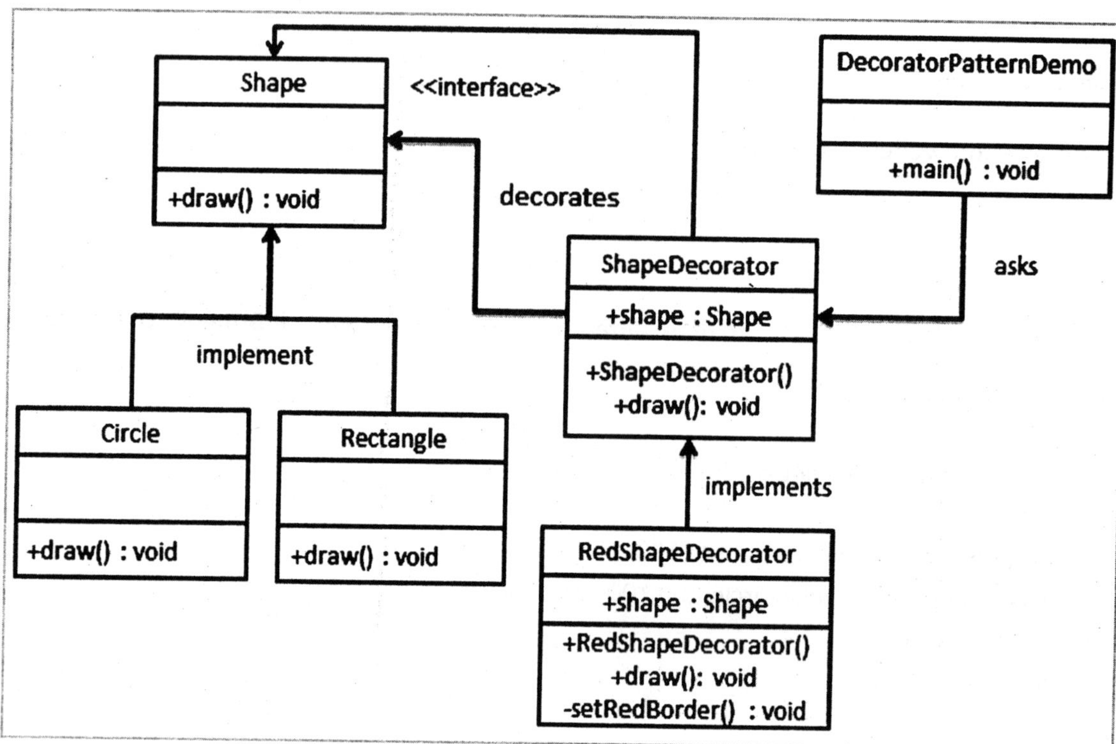


**Step 1:** Create an interface. Name it **Shape.java**

```
public interface Shape
{
   void draw( );
}
```

**Step 2:** Create classes implementing the same interface.

**Rectangle.java**

```
public class Rectangle implements Shape
{
    @Override
    public void draw( )
    {
       System.out.println("Shape: Rectangle");
    }
}
```

**Circle.java**

```
public class Circle implements Shape
{

    @Override
    public void draw( )
    {
       System.out.println("Shape: Circle");
    }
}
```

**Step 3:** Create abstract decorator class implementing the Shape interface. Name it **ShapeDecorator.java**

```
public abstract class ShapeDecorator implements Shape
{
    protected Shape decoratedShape;

    public ShapeDecorator(Shape decoratedShape)
    {
       this.decoratedShape = decoratedShape;
    }

    public void draw( )
    {
       decoratedShape.draw( );
    }
}
```

**Step 4:** Create concrete decorator class extending the ShapeDecorator class. Name it **RedShapeDecorator.java**

```
public class RedShapeDecorator extends ShapeDecorator
{
    public RedShapeDecorator(Shape decoratedShape)
    {
       super(decoratedShape);
    }
    @Override
    public void draw( )
    {
       decoratedShape.draw( );
       setRedBorder(decoratedShape);
    }
    private void setRedBorder(Shape decoratedShape)
    {
       System.out.println("Border Color: Red");
    }
}
```

**Step 5:** Use the RedShapeDecorator to decorate Shape objects. Name it **DecoratorPatternDemo.java**

```
public class DecoratorPatternDemo
{
    public static void main(String ar[ ])
    {
        Shape circle = new Circle( );
        Shape redCircle = new RedShapeDecorator(new Circle( ));

        Shape redRectangle = new RedShapeDecorator(new Rectangle());
        System.out.println("Circle with normal border");
        circle.draw( );

        System.out.println("\nCircle of red border");
        redCircle.draw( );
```

```
        System.out.println("\nRectangle of red border");
        redRectangle.draw( );
    }
}
```

**Step 6:** Verify the output.

```
Circle with normal border
Shape: Circle

Circle of red border
Shape: Circle
Border Color: Red

Rectangle of red border
Shape: Rectangle
Border Color: Red
```

### 23.3.3 Behavioural Design patterns

#### 1. Template Method pattern

In Template pattern, an abstract class exposes defined way(s)/template(s) to execute its methods. Its subclasses can overrides the method implementations as per need basis but the invocation is to be in the same way as defined by an abstract class. This pattern comes under behavior pattern category.

**Implementation**

We're going to create a Game abstract class defining operations with a template method set to be final so that it cannot be overridden. Cricket and Football are concrete classes extend Game and override its methods.

*TemplatePatternDemo*, our demo class will use Game to demonstrate use of template pattern.

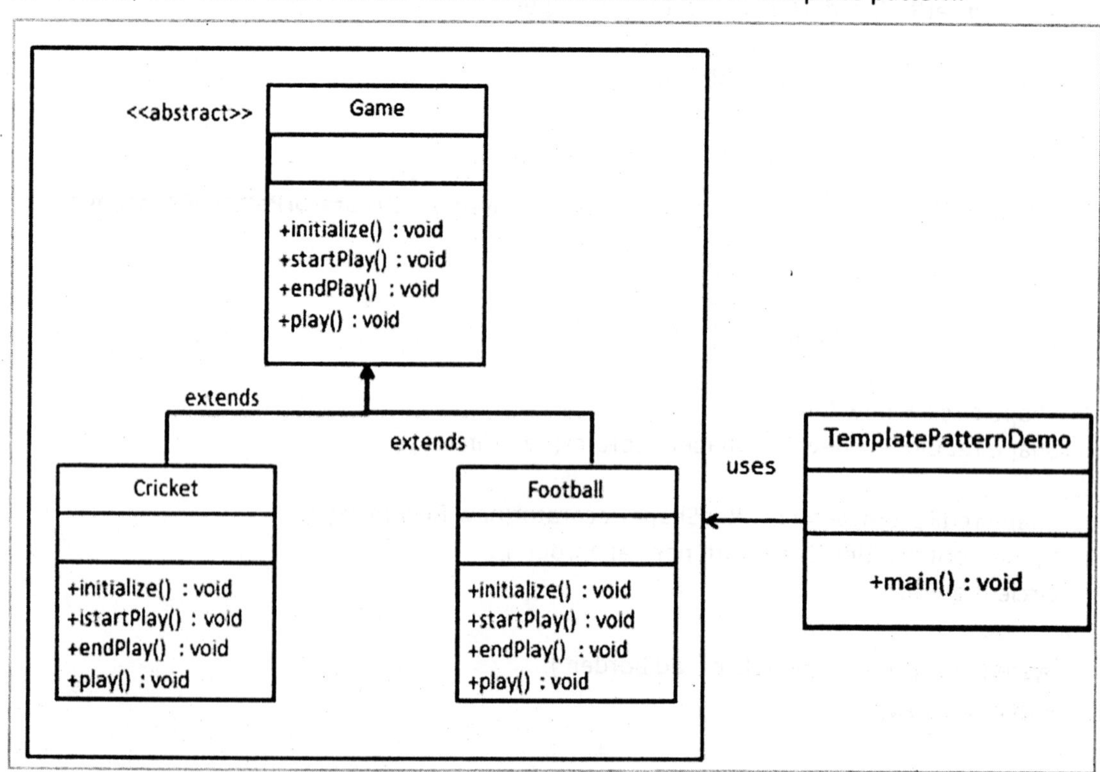

**Step 1:** Create an abstract class with a template method being final. Name it **Game.java**

```
public abstract class Game
{
    abstract void initialize( );
    abstract void startPlay( );
    abstract void endPlay( );

    //template method
    public final void play( )
    {
      //initialize the game
      initialize( );

      //start game
      startPlay( );

      //end game
      endPlay( );
    }
}
```

**Step 2:** Create concrete classes extending the above class.

**Cricket.java**

```
public class Cricket extends Game
{
    @Override
    void endPlay( )
    {
       System.out.println("Cricket Game Finished!");
    }
    @Override
    void initialize( )
    {
       System.out.println("Cricket Game Initialized! Start playing.");
    }
    @Override
    void startPlay( )
    {
       System.out.println("Cricket Game Started. Enjoy the game!");
    }
}
```

**Football.java**

```
public class Football extends Game
{
    @Override
    void endPlay( )
```

```
        {
            System.out.println("Football Game Finished!");
        }
        @Override
        void initialize( )
        {
            System.out.println("Football Game Initialized! Start playing.");
        }
        @Override
        void startPlay()
        {
            System.out.println("Football Game Started. Enjoy the game!");
        }
    }
```

**Step 3:** Use the Game's template method play( ) to demonstrate a defined way of playing game. Name it **TemplatePatternDemo.java**

```
public class TemplatePatternDemo
{
    public static void main(String ar[ ])
    {
        Game game = new Cricket();
        game.play( );
        System.out.println( );
        game = new Football( );
        game.play( );
    }
}
```

**Step 4:** Verify the output.

```
Cricket Game Initialized! Start playing.
Cricket Game Started. Enjoy the game!
Cricket Game Finished!

Football Game Initialized! Start playing.
Football Game Started. Enjoy the game!
Football Game Finished!
```

**2. Mediator pattern**

Mediator pattern is used to reduce communication complexity between multiple objects or classes. This pattern provides a mediator class which normally handles all the communications between different classes and supports easy maintainability of the code by loose coupling. Mediator pattern falls under behavioral pattern category.

**Implementation**

We're demonstrating mediator pattern by example of a Chat Room where multiple users can send message to Chat Room and it is the responsibility of Chat Room to show the messages to all users. We've created two classes *ChatRoom* and User. User objects will use *ChatRoom* method to share their messages.

*MediatorPatternDemo*, our demo class will use User objects to show communication between them.

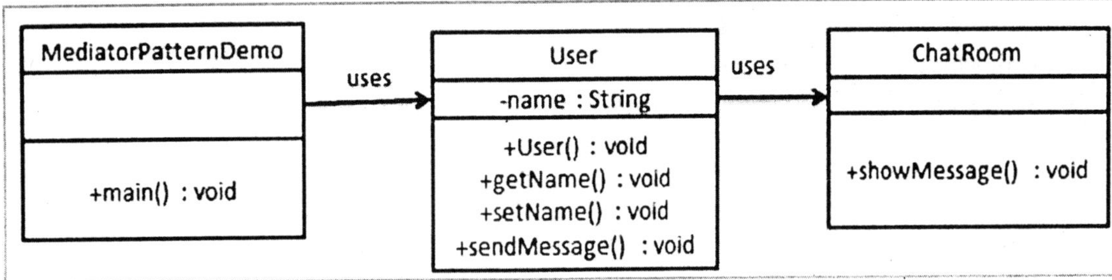


**Step 1:** Create mediator class. Name it **ChatRoom.java**

```
import java.util.Date;
public class ChatRoom
{
    public static void showMessage(User user, String message)
    {
        System.out.println(new Date().toString( ) + " [" + user.getName( ) +"] : " + message);
    }
}
```

**Step 2:** Create user class. Name it **User.java**

```
public class User
{
    private String name;
    public String getName( )
    {
        return name;
    }
    public void setName(String name)
    {
        this.name = name;
    }
    public User(String name)
    {
        this.name  = name;
    }
    public void sendMessage(String message)
    {
        ChatRoom.showMessage(this,message);
    }
}
```

**Step 3:** Use the User object to show communications between them. Name it **MediatorPatternDemo.java**

```
public class MediatorPatternDemo
{
  public static void main(String ar[ ])
    {
        User ravi = new User("Ravi");
```

```
            User kalpesh = new User("Kalpesh");
            ravi.sendMessage("Hi! Ravi!");
            kalpesh.sendMessage("Hello! Kalpesh!");
        }
    }
```

**Step 4:** Verify the output.

```
Thu Apr 17 16:05:46 IST 2014 [Ravi] : Hi! Ravi!
Thu Apr 17 16:05:46 IST 2014 [Kalpesh] : Hello! Kalpesh!
```

### 3. Chain of Responsibility pattern

As the name suggest, the chain of responsibility pattern creates a chain of receiver objects for a request. This pattern decouples sender and receiver of a request based on type of request. This pattern comes under behavioral patterns.

In this pattern, normally each receiver contains reference to another receiver. If one object cannot handle the request then it passes the same to the next receiver and so on.

#### Implementation

We've created an abstract class *AbstractLogger* with a level of logging. Then we've created three types of loggers extending the *AbstractLogger*. Each logger checks the level of message to its level and print accordingly otherwise does not print and pass the message to its next logger.

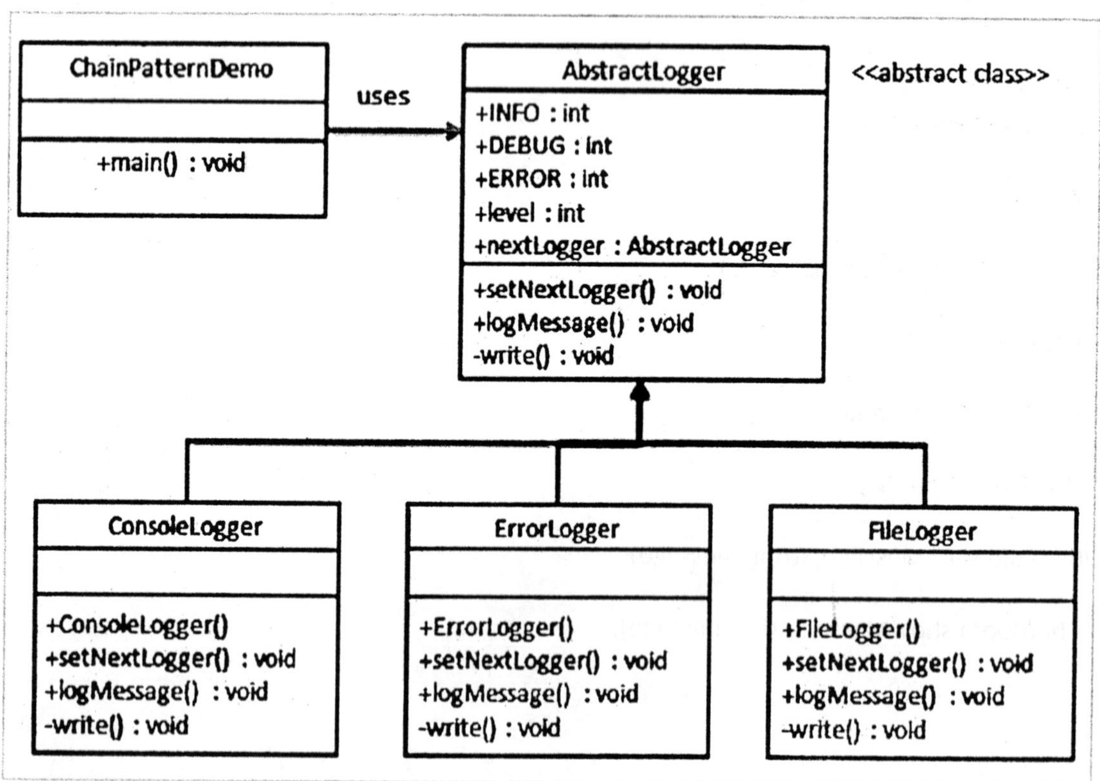


**Step 1:** Create an abstract logger class. Name it **AbstractLogger.java**

```
public abstract class AbstractLogger
{
    public static int INFO = 1;
    public static int DEBUG = 2;
    public static int ERROR = 3;
    protected int level;
```

```
    //next element in chain or responsibility
    protected AbstractLogger nextLogger;

    public void setNextLogger(AbstractLogger nextLogger)
    {
       this.nextLogger = nextLogger;
    }
    public void logMessage(int level, String message)
    {
       if(this.level <= level)
       {
          write(message);
       }
      if(nextLogger !=null)
      {
         nextLogger.logMessage(level, message);
      }
    }
    abstract protected void write(String message);
}
```

**Step 2:** Create concrete classes extending the logger.

**ConsoleLogger.java**

```
public class ConsoleLogger extends AbstractLogger
{
  public ConsoleLogger(int level)
  {
     this.level = level;
  }
  @Override
  protected void write(String message)
  {
     System.out.println("Standard Console::Logger: " + message);
  }
}
```

**ErrorLogger.java**

```
public class ErrorLogger extends AbstractLogger
{
    public ErrorLogger(int level)
    {
      this.level = level;
    }
    @Override
    protected void write(String message)
    {
```

```
        System.out.println("Error Console::Logger: " + message);
    }
}
```

**FileLogger.java**

```
public class FileLogger extends AbstractLogger
{
    public FileLogger(int level)
    {
        this.level = level;
    }
    @Override
    protected void write(String message)
    {
        System.out.println("File::Logger: " + message);
    }
}
```

**Step 3:** Create different types of loggers. Assign them error levels and set next logger in each logger. Next logger in each logger represents the part of the chain. Name it **ChainPatternDemo.java**

```
public class ChainPatternDemo
{
    private static AbstractLogger getChainOfLoggers( )
    {
        AbstractLogger errorLogger = new ErrorLogger(AbstractLogger.ERROR);
        AbstractLogger fileLogger = new FileLogger(AbstractLogger.DEBUG);
        AbstractLogger consoleLogger = new ConsoleLogger(AbstractLogger.INFO);
        errorLogger.setNextLogger(fileLogger);
        fileLogger.setNextLogger(consoleLogger);
        return errorLogger;
    }

    public static void main(String ar[ ])
    {
        AbstractLogger loggerChain = getChainOfLoggers( );
        loggerChain.logMessage(AbstractLogger.INFO, "This is an information.");
        loggerChain.logMessage(AbstractLogger.DEBUG, "This is an debug level information.");
        loggerChain.logMessage(AbstractLogger.ERROR, "This is an error information.");
    }
}
```

**Step 4:** Verify the output.

```
Standard Console::Logger: This is an information.
File::Logger: This is an debug level information.
Standard Console::Logger: This is an debug level information.
Error Console::Logger: This is an error information.
File::Logger: This is an error information.
Standard Console::Logger: This is an error information.
```

### 4. Observer pattern

Observer pattern is used when there is one to many relationship between objects such as if one object is modified, its dependent objects are to be notified automatically. Observer pattern falls under behavioral pattern category.

#### Implementation

Observer pattern uses three actor classes: Subject, Observer and Client. Subject is an object having methods to attach and de-attach observers to a client object. We've created classes Subject, Observer abstract class and concrete classes extending the abstract class the Observer.

*ObserverPatternDemo*, our demo class will use Subject and concrete class objects to show observer pattern in action.

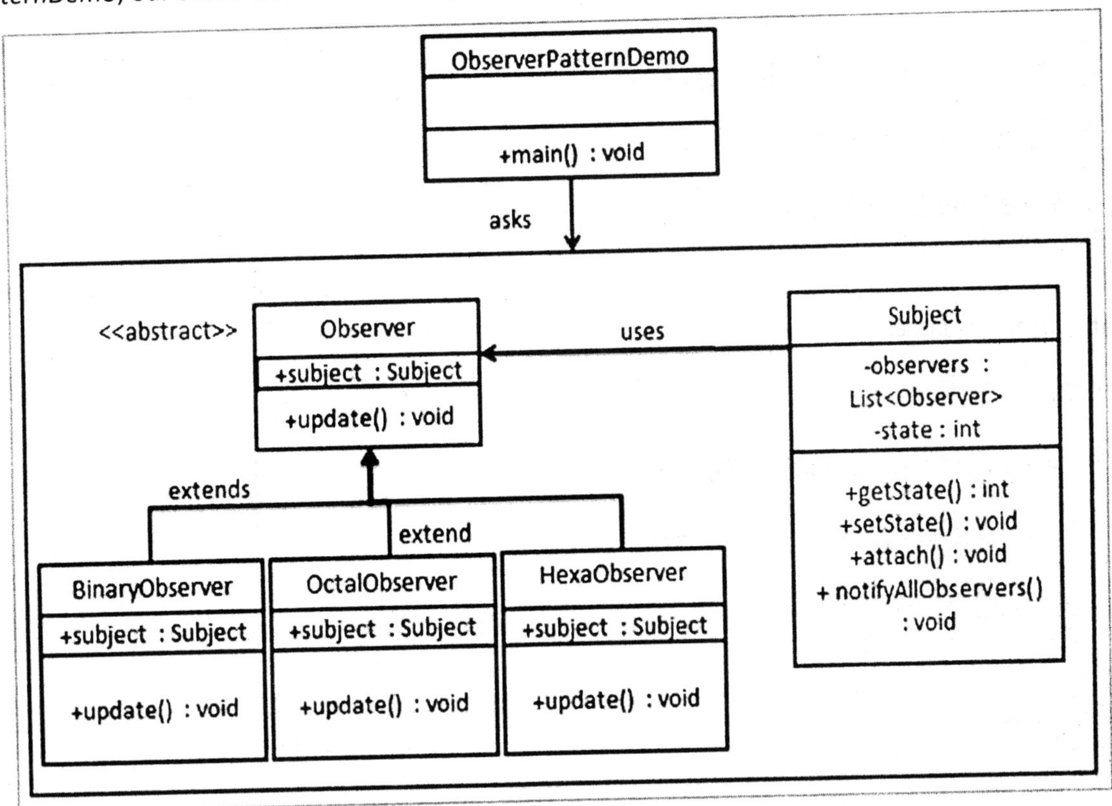


**Step 1:** Create Subject class. Name it **Subject.java**

```
import java.util.ArrayList;
import java.util.List;

public class Subject
{
    private List<Observer> observers = new ArrayList<Observer>( );
    private int state;
    public int getState( )
    {
        return state;
    }
    public void setState(int state)
    {
        this.state = state;
        notifyAllObservers();
    }
```

```
    public void attach(Observer observer)
    {
        observers.add(observer);
    }
    public void notifyAllObservers( )
    {
        for (Observer observer : observers)
        {
            observer.update();
        }
    }
}
```

**Step 2:** Create Observer class. Name it **Observer.java**

```
public abstract class Observer
{
    protected Subject subject;
    public abstract void update( );
}
```

**Step 3:** Create observer classes

**BinaryObserver.java**

```
public class BinaryObserver extends Observer
{
    public BinaryObserver(Subject subject)
    {
        this.subject = subject;
        this.subject.attach(this);
    }
    @Override
    public void update( )
    {
        System.out.println( "Binary String: " + Integer.toBinaryString( subject.getState( )) );
    }
}
```

**OctalObserver.java**

```
public class OctalObserver extends Observer
{
    public OctalObserver(Subject subject)
    {
        this.subject = subject;
        this.subject.attach(this);
    }
    @Override
    public void update( )
    {
        System.out.println( "Octal String: " + Integer.toOctalString( subject.getState( )));
    }
```

```
}
```

**HexaObserver.java**

```
public class HexaObserver extends Observer
{
    public HexaObserver(Subject subject)
    {
        this.subject = subject;
        this.subject.attach(this);
    }
    @Override
    public void update( )
    {
        System.out.println( "Hex String: " + Integer.toHexString( subject.getState() ).toUpperCase( ));
    }
}
```

**Step 4:** Use Subject and concrete observer objects. Name it **ObserverPatternDemo.java**

```
public class ObserverPatternDemo
{
    public static void main(String ar[ ])
    {
        Subject subject = new Subject();
        new HexaObserver(subject);
        new OctalObserver(subject);
        new BinaryObserver(subject);
        System.out.println("First state change: 15");
        subject.setState(15);
        System.out.println("Second state change: 10");
        subject.setState(10);
    }
}
```

**Step 5:** Verify the output.

```
First state change: 15
Hex String: F
Octal String: 17
Binary String: 1111
Second state change: 10
Hex String: A
Octal String: 12
Binary String: 1010
```

**5. Strategy pattern**

In Strategy pattern, a class behavior or its algorithm can be changed at run time. This type of design pattern comes under behavior pattern.

In Strategy pattern, we create objects which represent various strategies and a context object whose behavior varies as per its strategy object. The strategy object changes the executing algorithm of the context object.

**Implementation**

We're going to create a Strategy interface defining a action and concrete strategy classes implementing the Strategy interface. Context is a class which uses a Strategy.

*StrategyPatternDemo*, our demo class will use Context and strategy objects to demonstrate change in Context behavior based on strategy it deploys or uses.

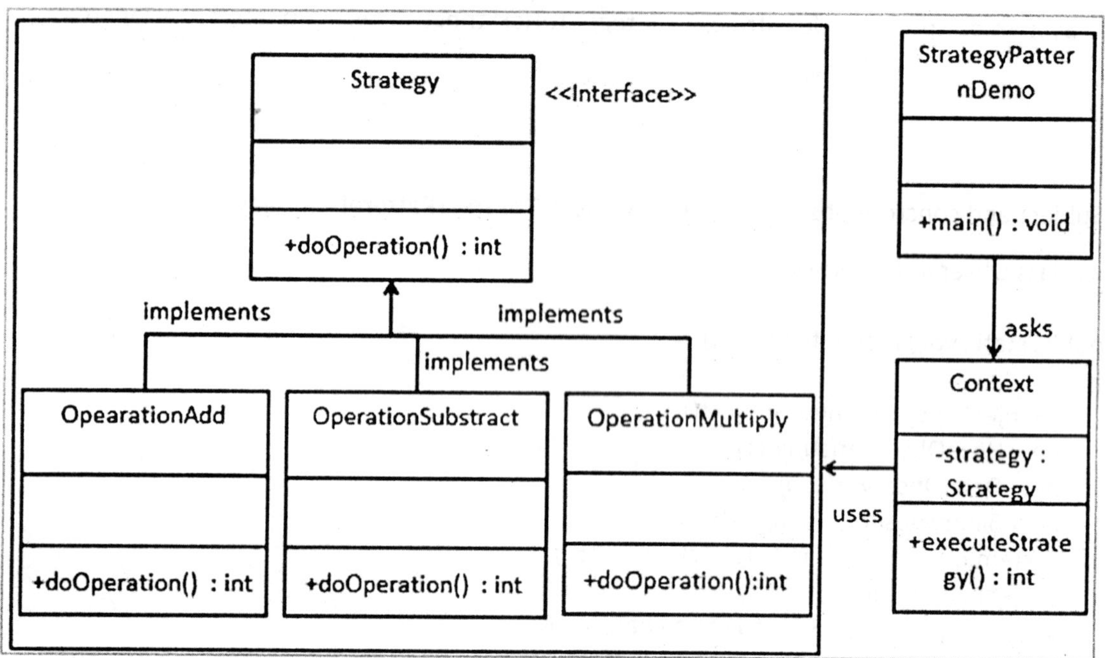


**Step 1:** Create an interface. Name it **Strategy.java**

```
public interface Strategy
{
   public int doOperation(int num1, int num2);
}
```

**Step 2:** Create concrete classes implementing the same interface.

**OperationAdd.java**

```
public class OperationAdd implements Strategy
{
    @Override
    public int doOperation(int num1, int num2)
    {
        return num1 + num2;
    }
}
```

**OperationSubstract.java**

```
public class OperationSubstract implements Strategy
{
    @Override
    public int doOperation(int num1, int num2)
    {
      return num1 - num2;
    }
}
```

**OperationMultiply.java**

```
public class OperationMultiply implements Strategy
{
    @Override
    public int doOperation(int num1, int num2)
    {
       return num1 * num2;
    }
}
```

**Step 3:** Create Context Class. Name it **Context.java**

```
public class Context
{
    private Strategy strategy;
    public Context(Strategy strategy)
    {
       this.strategy = strategy;
    }

    public int executeStrategy(int num1, int num2)
    {
       return strategy.doOperation(num1, num2);
    }
}
```

**Step 4:** Use the Context to see change in behaviour when it changes its Strategy.

StatePatternDemo.java

```
public class StrategyPatternDemo
{
    public static void main(String ar[ ])
    {
        Context context = new Context(new OperationAdd());
        System.out.println("10 + 5 = " + context.executeStrategy(10, 5));
        context = new Context(new OperationSubstract( ));
        System.out.println("10 - 5 = " + context.executeStrategy(10, 5));
        context = new Context(new OperationMultiply( ));
        System.out.println("10 * 5 = " + context.executeStrategy(10, 5));
    }
}
```

**Step 5:** Verify the output.

10 + 5 = 15

10 - 5 = 5

10   5 = 50

**6. Command pattern**

Command pattern is a data driven design pattern and falls under behavioral pattern category. A request is wrapped under a object as command and passed to invoker object. Invoker object looks for the appropriate object which can handle this command and pass the command to the corresponding object and that object executes the command.

**Implementation**

We've created an interface Order which is acting as a command. We've created a *Stock* class which acts as a request. We've concrete command classes *BuyStock* and *SellStock* implementing Order interface which will do actual command processing. A class *Broker* is created which acts as an invoker object. It can take order and place orders.

Broker object uses command pattern to identify which object will execute which command based on type of command. *CommandPatternDemo*, our demo class will use Broker class to demonstrate command pattern.

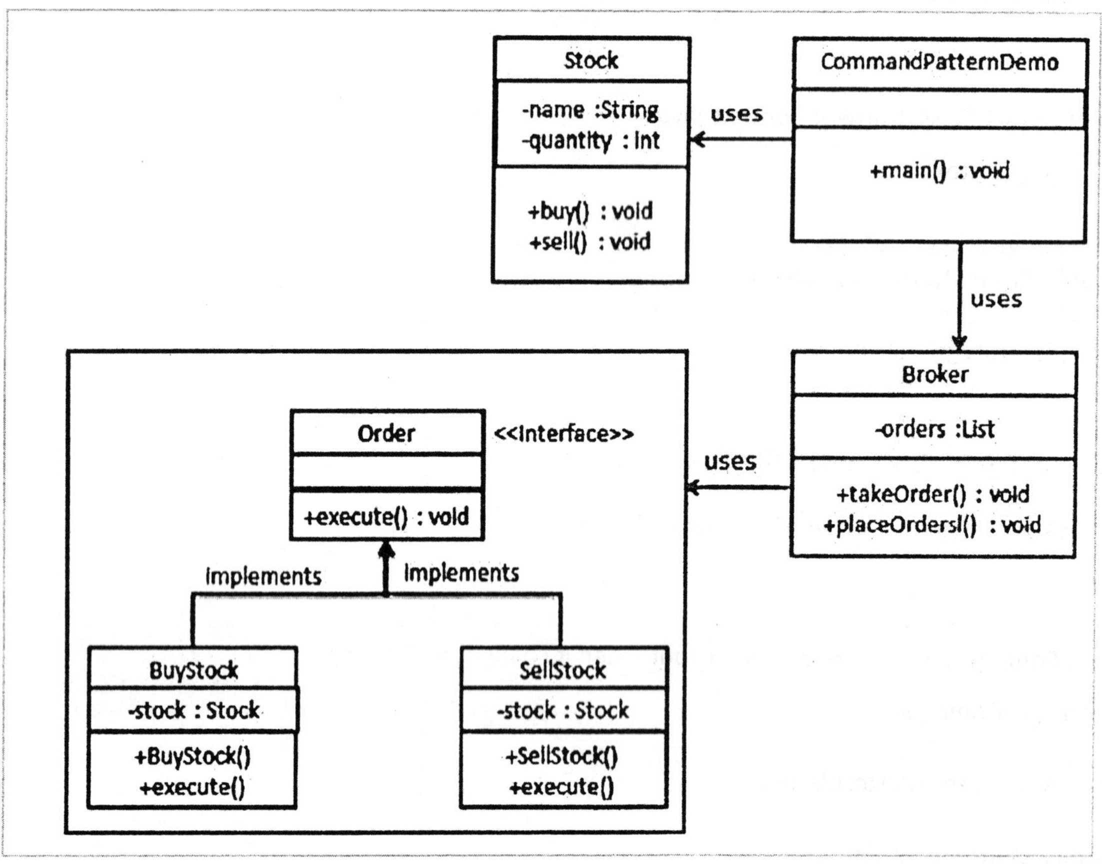


**Step 1:** Create a command interface. Name it **Order.java**

```
public interface Order
{
   void execute( );
}
```

**Step 2:** Create a request class. Name it **Stock.java**

```
public class Stock
{
    private String name = "ABC";
    private int quantity = 10;
    public void buy( )
    {
       System.out.println("Stock [ Name: "+name+", Quantity: " + quantity +" ] bought");
    }
    public void sell( )
    {
       System.out.println("Stock [ Name: "+name+", Quantity: " + quantity +" ] sold");
    }
}
```

**Step 3:** Create classes implementing the Order interface.

**BuyStock.java**

```
public class BuyStock implements Order
{
    private Stock abcStock;
    public BuyStock(Stock abcStock)
    {
       this.abcStock = abcStock;
    }
    public void execute( )
    {
       abcStock.buy();
    }
}
```

**SellStock.java**

```
public class SellStock implements Order
{
    private Stock abcStock;
    public SellStock(Stock abcStock)
    {
       this.abcStock = abcStock;
    }
    public void execute( )
    {
       abcStock.sell( );
    }
}
```

**Step 4:** Create command invoker class. Name it **Broker.java**

```
import java.util.ArrayList;
import java.util.List;

public class Broker
{
   private List<Order> orderList = new ArrayList<Order>( );
   public void takeOrder(Order order)
   {
      orderList.add(order);
   }
   public void placeOrders( )
   {
      for (Order order : orderList)
      {
        order.execute( );
      }
      orderList.clear();
   }
}
```

**Step 5:** Use the Broker class to take and execute commands. Name it **CommandPatternDemo.java**

```
public class CommandPatternDemo
{
     public static void main(String ar[ ])
     {
          Stock abcStock = new Stock( );
          BuyStock buyStockOrder = new BuyStock(abcStock);
          SellStock sellStockOrder = new SellStock(abcStock);
          Broker broker = new Broker( );
          broker.takeOrder(buyStockOrder);
          broker.takeOrder(sellStockOrder);
          broker.placeOrders( );
     }
}
```

**Step 6:** Verify the output.

```
Stock [ Name: ABC, Quantity: 10 ] bought
Stock [ Name: ABC, Quantity: 10 ] sold
```

**7. State pattern**

In State pattern a class behavior changes based on its state. This type of design pattern comes under behavior pattern.

In State pattern, we create objects which represent various states and a context object whose behavior varies as its state object changes.

**Implementation**

We're going to create a State interface defining a action and concrete *state* classes implementing the State interface. *Context* is a class which carries a State.

*StatePatternDemo*, our demo class will use Context and state objects to demonstrate change in Context behavior based on type of state it is in.

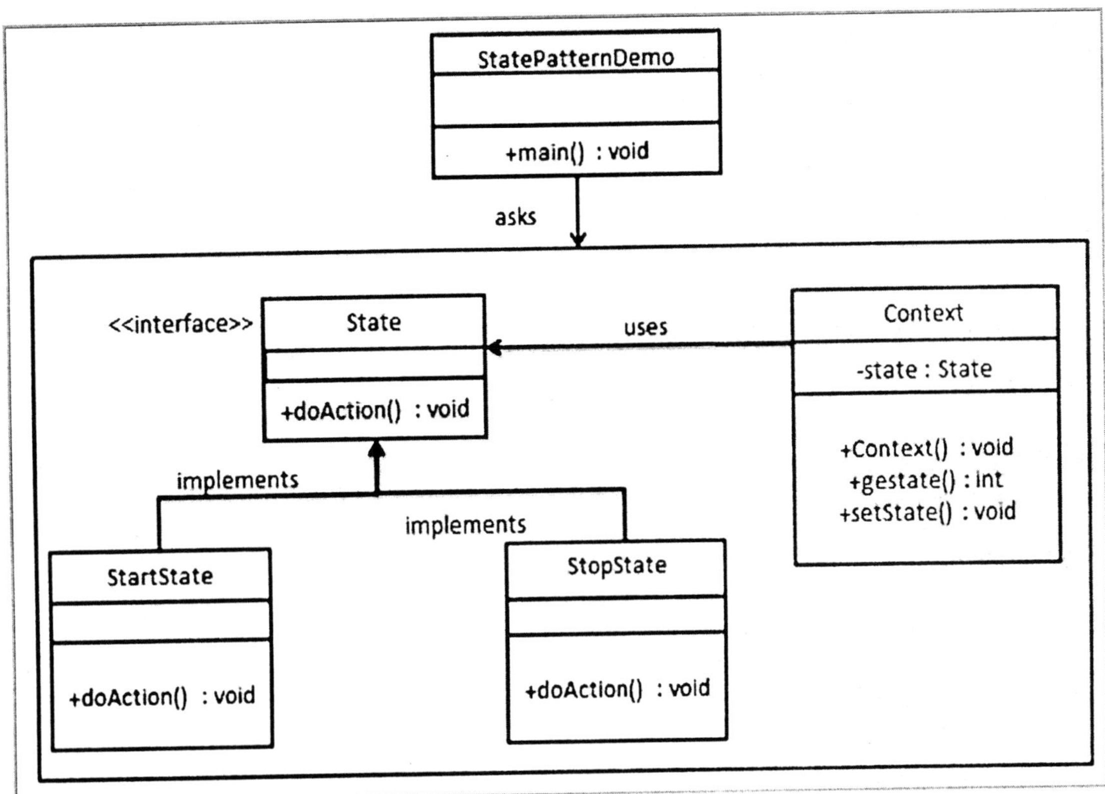


**Step 1:** Create an interface. Name it **Image.java**

```
public interface State
{
   public void doAction(Context context);
}
```

**Step 2:** Create classes implementing the same interface.

**StartState.java**

```
public class StartState implements State
{
    public void doAction(Context context)
    {
       System.out.println("Player is in start state");
       context.setState(this);
    }

    public String toString( )
    {
       return "Start State";
    }
}
```

**StopState.java**

```
public class StopState implements State
{
    public void doAction(Context context)
    {
       System.out.println("Player is in stop state");
```

```
            context.setState(this);
        }

        public String toString( )
        {
            return "Stop State";
        }
    }
```

**Step 3:** Create Context Class. Name it **Context.java**

```
public class Context
{
    private State state;
    public Context( )
    {
        state = null;
    }
    public void setState(State state)
    {
        this.state = state;
    }
    public State getState( )
    {
        return state;
    }
}
```

**Step 4:** Use the Context to see change in behavior when State changes. Name it **StatePatternDemo.java**

```
public class StatePatternDemo
{
    public static void main(String ar[ ])
    {
        Context context = new Context( );
        StartState startState = new StartState( );
        startState.doAction(context);
        System.out.println(context.getState().toString( ));
        StopState stopState = new StopState( );
        stopState.doAction(context);
        System.out.println(context.getState().toString( ));
    }
}
```

**Step 5:** Verify the output.

```
Player is in start state
Start State
Player is in stop state
Stop State
```

**8. Visitor pattern**

In Visitor pattern, we use a visitor class which changes the executing algorithm of an element class. By this way, execution algorithm of element can varies as visitor varies. This pattern comes under behavior pattern category. As per the pattern, element object has to accept the visitor object so that visitor object handles the operation on the element object.

**Implementation**

We're going to create a *ComputerPart* interface defining accepts operation. Keyboard, Mouse, Monitor and Computer are concrete classes implementing *ComputerPart* interface. We'll define another interface *ComputerPartVisitor* which will define visitor class operations. Computer uses concrete visitor to do corresponding action.

*VisitorPatternDemo*, our demo class will use Computer, *ComputerPartVisitor* classes to demonstrate use of visitor pattern.

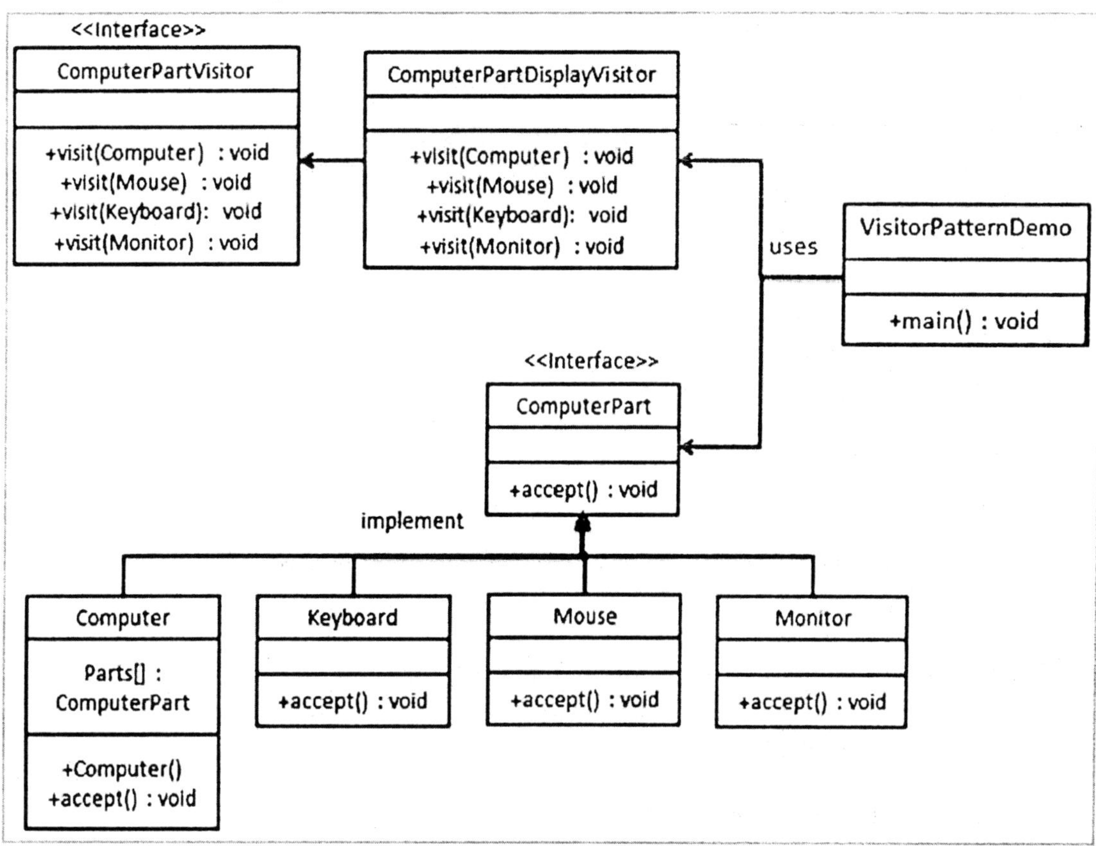


<u>**Step 1:**</u> Define an interface to represent element. Name it **ComputerPart.java**

```
public interface class ComputerPart
{
   public void accept(ComputerPartVisitor computerPartVisitor);
}
```

<u>**Step 2:**</u> Create classes extending the above class.

**Keyboard.java**

```
public class Keyboard  implements ComputerPart
{
    @Override
    public void accept(ComputerPartVisitor computerPartVisitor)
    {
       computerPartVisitor.visit(this);
    }
}
```

**Monitor.java**

```
public class Monitor  implements ComputerPart
{
    @Override
    public void accept(ComputerPartVisitor computerPartVisitor)
    {
       computerPartVisitor.visit(this);
    }
}
```

**Mouse.java**

```
public class Mouse  implements ComputerPart
{
    @Override
    public void accept(ComputerPartVisitor computerPartVisitor)
    {
      computerPartVisitor.visit(this);
    }
}
```

**Computer.java**

```
public class Computer implements ComputerPart
{
    ComputerPart[ ] parts;
    public Computer( )
    {
       parts = new ComputerPart[ ] {new Mouse( ), new Keyboard( ), new Monitor( )};
    }
    @Override
    public void accept(ComputerPartVisitor computerPartVisitor)
    {
       for (int i = 0; i < parts.length; i++)
       {
          parts[i].accept(computerPartVisitor);
       }
       computerPartVisitor.visit(this);
    }
}
```

<u>Step 3:</u> Define an interface to represent visitor. Name it **ComputerPartVisitor.java**

```
public interface ComputerPartVisitor
{
  public void visit(Computer computer);
  public void visit(Mouse mouse);
  public void visit(Keyboard keyboard);
  public void visit(Monitor monitor);
}
```

<u>Step 4:</u> Create visitor implementing the above class. Name it **ComputerPartDisplayVisitor.java**

```
public class ComputerPartDisplayVisitor implements ComputerPartVisitor
{
    @Override
    public void visit(Computer computer)
```

```
        {
            System.out.println("Displaying Computer.");
        }
        @Override
        public void visit(Mouse mouse)
        {
            System.out.println("Displaying Mouse.");
        }
        @Override
        public void visit(Keyboard keyboard)
        {
            System.out.println("Displaying Keyboard.");
        }
        @Override
        public void visit(Monitor monitor)
        {
            System.out.println("Displaying Monitor.");
        }
    }
```

**Step 5:** Use the ComputerPartDisplayVisitor to display parts of Computer. Name it **VisitorPatternDemo.java**

```
public class VisitorPatternDemo
{
    public static void main(String ar[ ])
    {
        ComputerPart computer = new Computer( );
        computer.accept(new ComputerPartDisplayVisitor( ));
    }
}
```

**Step 6:** Verify the output.

```
Displaying Mouse.
Displaying Keyboard.
Displaying Monitor.
Displaying Computer.
```

### 9. Interpreter pattern

Interpreter pattern provides way to evaluate language grammar or expression. This type of pattern comes under behavioral patterns. This pattern involves implementing a expression interface which tells to interpret a particular context. This pattern is used in SQL parsing, symbol processing engine etc.

### Implementation

We're going to create an interface *Expression* and concrete classes implementing the Expression interface. A class *TerminalExpression* is defined which acts as a main interpreter of context in question. Other classes Or Expression, *AndExpression* are used to create combinational expressions.

*InterpreterPatternDemo*, our demo class will use Expression class to create rules and demonstrate parsing of expressions.

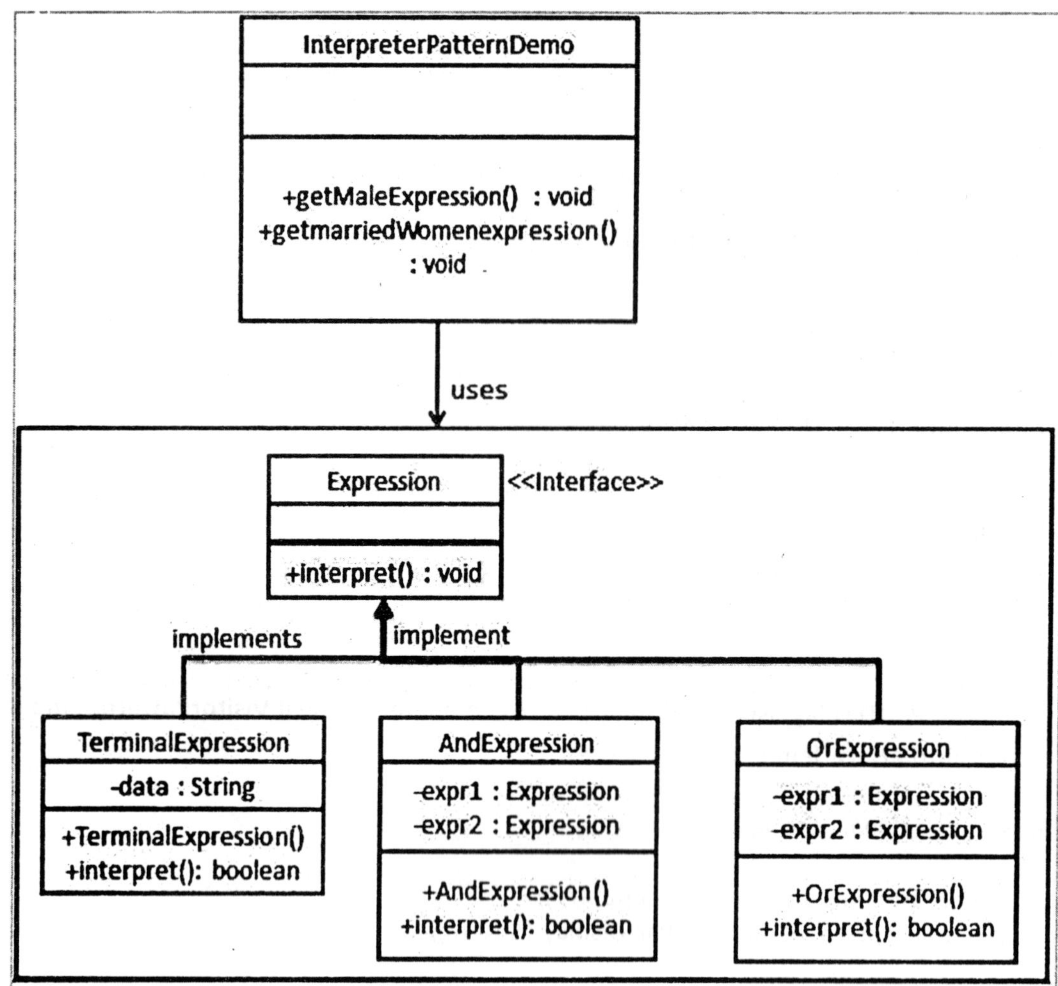


**Step 1:** Create an expression interface. Name it **Expression.java**

```
public interface Expression
{
   public boolean interpret(String context);
}
```

**Step 2:** Create classes implementing the above interface.

**TerminalExpression.java**

```
public class TerminalExpression implements Expression
{
    private String data;
    public TerminalExpression(String data)
    {
       this.data = data;
    }
    @Override
    public boolean interpret(String context)
    {
       if(context.contains(data))
       {
          return true;
```

```
        }
        return false;
    }
}
```

**OrExpression.java**

```
public class OrExpression implements Expression
{
    private Expression expr1 = null;
    private Expression expr2 = null;
    public OrExpression(Expression expr1, Expression expr2)
    {
        this.expr1 = expr1;
        this.expr2 = expr2;
    }
    @Override
    public boolean interpret(String context)
    {
        return expr1.interpret(context) || expr2.interpret(context);
    }
}
```

**AndExpression.java**

```
public class AndExpression implements Expression
{
    private Expression expr1 = null;
    private Expression expr2 = null;
    public AndExpression(Expression expr1, Expression expr2)
    {
        this.expr1 = expr1;
        this.expr2 = expr2;
    }
    @Override
    public boolean interpret(String context)
    {
        return expr1.interpret(context) && expr2.interpret(context);
    }
}
```

**<u>Step 3:</u>** InterpreterPatternDemo uses Expression class to create rules and then parse them. Name it

**InterpreterPatternDemo.java**

```
public class InterpreterPatternDemo
{
    //Rule: Robert and John are male
    public static Expression getMaleExpression( )
    {
```

```
        Expression robert = new TerminalExpression("Robert");
        Expression john = new TerminalExpression("John");
        return new OrExpression(robert, john);
    }

    //Rule: Julie is a married women
    public static Expression getMarriedWomanExpression( )
    {
        Expression julie = new TerminalExpression("Julie");
        Expression married = new TerminalExpression("Married");
        return new AndExpression(julie, married);
    }

    public static void main(String[] args)
    {
        Expression isMale = getMaleExpression( );
        Expression isMarriedWoman = getMarriedWomanExpression( );
        System.out.println("John is male? " + isMale.interpret("John"));
        System.out.println("Julie is a married women? " + isMarriedWoman.interpret("Married Julie"));
    }
}
```

**Step 4:** Verify the output.

```
John is male? true

Julie is a married women? true
```

**10. Iterator pattern**

Iterator pattern is very commonly used design pattern in Java and .Net programming environment. This pattern is used to get a way to access the elements of a collection object in sequential manner without any need to know its underlying representation.

Iterator pattern falls under behavioral pattern category.

**Implementation**

We're going to create an *Iterator* interface which narrates navigation method and a Container interface which returns the Iterator. Concrete classes implementing the Container interface will be responsible to implement Iterator interface and use it

*IteratorPatternDemo*, our demo class will use *NamesRepository*, a concrete class implementation to print a Names stored as a collection in *NamesRepository*.

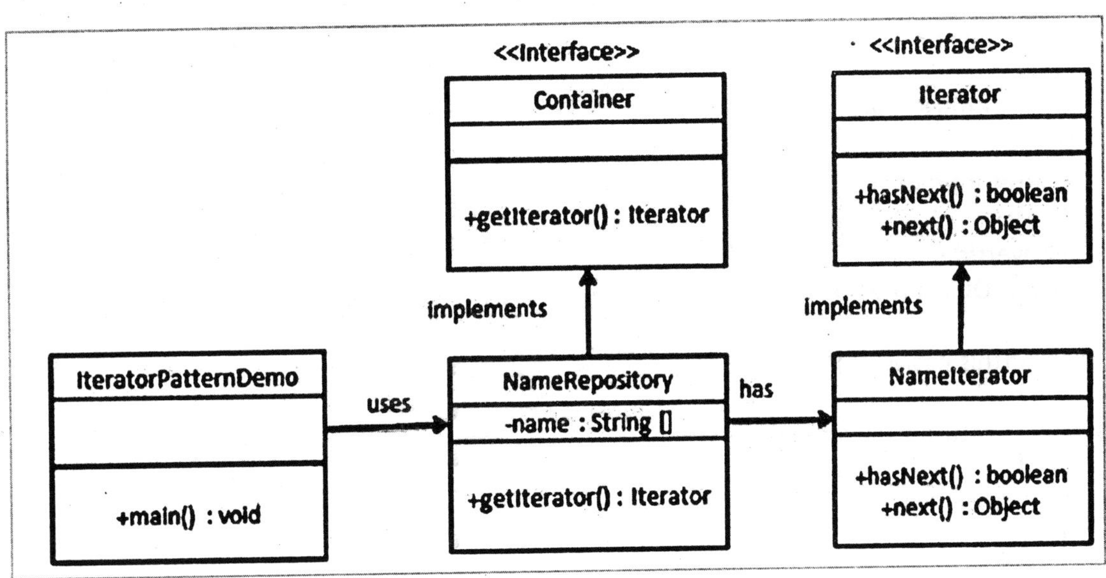


**Step 1:** Create interfaces. Name it

**Iterator.java**

```
public interface Iterator
{
   public boolean hasNext( );
   public Object next( );
}
```

**Container.java**

```
public interface Container
{
   public Iterator getIterator( );
}
```

**Step 2:** Create concrete class implementing the Container interface. This class has inner class NameIterator implementing the Iterator interface. Name it **NameRepository.java**

```
public class NameRepository implements Container
{
    public String names[ ] = {"Robert" , "John" ,"Julie" , "Lora"};

    @Override
    public Iterator getIterator( )
    {
       return new NameIterator( );
    }

    private class NameIterator implements Iterator
    {
        int index;
        @Override
        public boolean hasNext( )
        {
```

```
                if(index < names.length)
                {
                    return true;
                }
                return false;
            }
            @Override
            public Object next( )
            {
                if(this.hasNext( ))
                {
                    return names[index++];
                }
                return null;
            }
        }
    }
```

**Step 3:** Use the NameRepository to get iterator and print names. Name it **IteratorPatternDemo.java**

```
public class IteratorPatternDemo
{
    public static void main(String ar[ ])
    {
        NameRepository namesRepository = new NameRepository( );
        for(Iterator iter = namesRepository.getIterator(); iter.hasNext( );)
        {
            String name = (String)iter.next( );
            System.out.println("Name : " + name);
        }
    }
}
```

**Step 4:** Verify the output.

```
Name : Robert
Name : John
Name : Julie
Name : Lora
```

**11. Memento pattern**

Memento pattern is used to reduce where we want to restore state of an object to a previous state. Memento pattern falls under behavioral pattern category.

**Implementation**

Memento pattern uses three actor classes. Memento contains state of an object to be restored. Originator creates and stores states in Memento objects and Caretaker object which is responsible to restore object state from Memento. We've created classes Memento, Originator and CareTaker.

*MementoPatternDemo*, our demo class will use *CareTaker* and Originator objects to show restoration of object states.

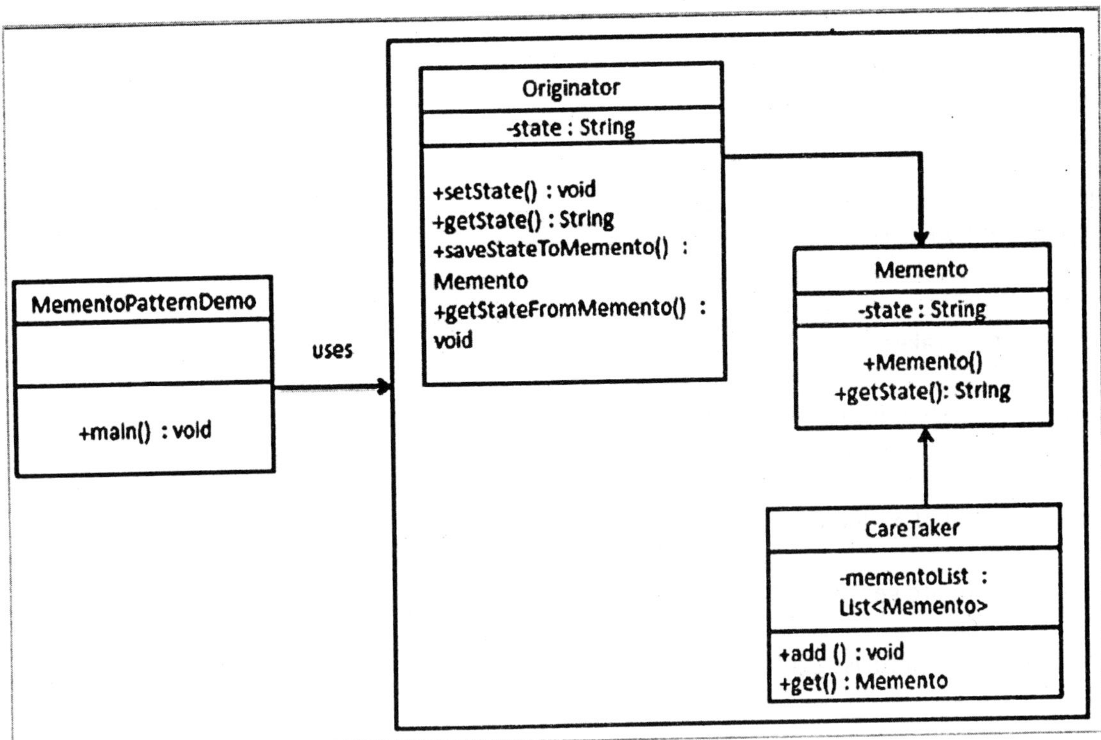


**Step 1:** Create Memento class. Name it **Memento.java**

```
public class Memento
{
    private String state;
    public Memento(String state)
    {
        this.state = state;
    }

    public String getState( )
    {
        return state;
    }
}
```

**Step 2:** Create Originator class. Name it **Originator.java**

```
public class Originator
{
    private String state;
    public void setState(String state)
    {
        this.state = state;
    }
    public String getState( )
    {
        return state;
    }
    public Memento saveStateToMemento( )
    {
        return new Memento(state);
    }
    public void getStateFromMemento(Memento Memento)
```

```
        {
            state = Memento.getState();
        }
    }
```

**Step 3:** Create CareTaker class. Name it **CareTaker.java**

```
import java.util.ArrayList;
import java.util.List;

public class CareTaker
{
    private List<Memento> mementoList = new ArrayList<Memento>( );
    public void add(Memento state)
    {
        mementoList.add(state);
    }
    public Memento get(int index)
    {
        return mementoList.get(index);
    }
}
```

**Step 4:** Use CareTaker and Originator objects. Name it **MementoPatternDemo.java**

```
public class MementoPatternDemo
{
    public static void main(String ar[ ])
    {
        Originator originator = new Originator();
        CareTaker careTaker = new CareTaker();
        originator.setState("State #1");
        originator.setState("State #2");
        careTaker.add(originator.saveStateToMemento());
        originator.setState("State #3");
        careTaker.add(originator.saveStateToMemento());
        originator.setState("State #4");
        System.out.println("Current State: " + originator.getState());
        originator.getStateFromMemento(careTaker.get(0));
        System.out.println("First saved State: " + originator.getState());
        originator.getStateFromMemento(careTaker.get(1));
        System.out.println("Second saved State: " + originator.getState());
    }
}
```

**Step 5:** Verify the output.

```
Current State: State #4
First saved State: State #2
Second saved State: State #3
```

*****

# Part VI
# Farewell

- Concise Talk on J2ME
- Sample Projects

# Chapter 24

# Concise talk on J2ME

Throughout this book we discussed about computers, computers, computers and only computers along with the famous Java EE platform to prepare enterprise applications. When we talk about "computer" we imagine about desktops, laptops and huge servers. These words are sufficient to portray a computer, but it is not up to that. There are many more computers that are different from computer shape but contain all basic characteristics found in a desktops and laptops. Cell phones, digital set-top box for cable television, car navigation system, pager, PDA are all computers. These computers are used to control the operations of automobiles, industrial equipments, house hold equipments and appliances. These new division of computers is called as *small computing devices*. These new division of computers are easily distinguishable from traditional computers by their reduced resource availability. These resources such as memory, permanent storage and power are very much valuable.

Now along with this new division, a new Java programming platform had arrived, on which developers can build and implement programs to control these small computing devices. This platform is called as **Java 2 Micro Edition (J2ME)**. In this chapter you will be introduced with J2ME platform.

## 24.1 Birth of J2ME?

Remember that Java began as a programming language to create programs for embedded systems—microcomputers found in consumer electronic devices. The development team at Sun worked on Java in the early 1990s to tackle the programming needs of the embedded computer market, but that effort was abstracted by gripping opportunities presented by the Internet.

When those internet related opportunities were addressed, meanwhile a new division of portable communication devices was opening its doors for upcoming century. These portable communication devices such as cell phones, PDAs, car navigation devices, pagers and many more were ready to turn the whole world around in new digital era. The cell phones were expanded from a simple voice communication device to a voice, text and digital communication devices. Pocket telephone directories were changed to PDAs. The digital chipmakers were releasing new chips and ICs to transfer computer power into these small computing devices.

The time was right for next evolution of Java. This time, instead of updating existing Java with new APIs and JVM, they decided to originate a completely new APIs and JVM that requires minimum coding to provide intelligence to embedded systems and micro computer devices. This new origination was required because of the completely different hardware designs of these devices. The result of their efforts is J2ME. Hence the J2ME is the compact version of Java APIs and virtual machine that is specially designed to operate with these devices with tiny resources (memory, permanent storage and power).

## 24.2 How J2ME is organized

Now finally we came to know that these new division of portable communication devices has arrived and grabbing the communication market all over the world. These computing devices lack hardware configuration continuity among devices. But some devices don't have display, permanent storage, memory, keyboard or mouse.

This lack of uniform hardware configuration in these small computing devices creates a terrifying challenge for the Java Community Process Program, which is charged with developing standards for the JVM and the J2ME for small computing devices.

J2ME must service many different kinds of small computing devices, including screen-phones, digital set-top boxes used for cable television, cell phones, and personal digital assistants. The challenge for the Java Community Process Program is to develop a Java standard that can be implemented on small computing devices that have nonstandard hardware configurations.

The Java Community Process Program has used a dual approach to handle the needs of small computing devices.

***J2ME configuration***: A configuration defines the JVM and core API classes (collectively called as JVM) that can operate on each device. (There are two configurations, one for handheld devices and other for plug-in devices.)

***J2ME profile***: A profile consists of classes that enable developers to implement features found on a related group of small computing devices.

Let's discuss about them in detail.

- **J2ME configuration**

There are two configurations for J2ME as of this writing. These are **Connected Limited Device Configuration (CLDC)** and the **Connected Device Configuration (CDC)**.

The CLDC is designed for 16-bit or 32-bit small computing devices with limited amounts of memory. CLDC devices usually have between 160KB and 512KB of available memory and are battery powered. They also use an inconsistent, small-bandwidth network wireless connection and may not have a user interface. CLDC devices use the **KJava Virtual Machine (KVM)** implementation, which is a tiny version of the JVM. *CLDC devices include pagers, personal digital assistants, cell phones, dedicated terminals, and handheld consumer devices.*

CDC devices use a 32-bit architecture, have at least two megabytes of memory available, and implement a complete functional JVM. *CDC devices include digital set-top boxes, home appliances, navigation systems, point-of-sale terminals, and smart phones.*

- **J2ME profile**

A profile consists of Java classes that enable implementation of features for either a particular small computing device or for a class of small computing devices. Small computing technology continues to evolve, and with that, there is an ongoing process of defining J2ME profiles. Seven profiles have been defined as of this writing. These are:

- **Foundation Profile:** used with the CDC configuration and is the core for nearly all other profiles used with the CDC configuration because the Foundation Profile contains core Java classes.
- **Game Profile:** used with the CDC configuration and contains the necessary classes for developing game applications for any small computing device that uses the CDC configuration.
- **Mobile Information Device Profile (MIDP):** used with the CLDC configuration and contains classes that provide local storage, a user interface, and networking capabilities to an application that runs on a mobile computing device such as Palm OS devices. MIDP is used with wireless Java applications.
- **PDA Profile:** used with the CLDC configuration and contains classes that utilize sophisticated resources found on personal digital assistants. These features include better displays and larger memory than similar resources found on MIDP mobile devices (such as cell phones).

- **Personal Profile:** used with the CDC configuration and the Foundation Profile and contains classes to implement a complex user interface. The Foundation Profile provides core classes, and the Personal Profiles provide classes to implement a sophisticated user interface, which is a user interface that is capable of displaying multiple windows at a time.
- **Personal Basis Profile:** is similar to the Personal Profile in that it is used with the CDC configuration and the Foundation Profile. However, the Personal Basis Profile provides classes to implement a simple user interface, which is a user interface that is capable of displaying one window at a time.
- **RMI Profile:** used with the CDC configuration and the Foundation Profile to provide Remote Method Invocation classes to the core classes contained in the Foundation Profile.

There will likely be many profiles as the production of small computing devices continues. Industry groups within the Java Community Process Program define profiles. Each group establishes the standard profile used by small computing devices manufactured by that industry.

| *Visit: java.sun.com/aboutjava/communityprocess for information on latest profiles* |
|---|

## 24.3 J2ME and wireless devices

With the dramatic increase and sophistication of mobile communications devices such as cell phones; came demand for applications that can run on those devices. Consumers and corporations want to expand mobile communications devices *from voice communications to applications* that are mostly found on laptops and PCs. They want to send and receive email, store and retrieve personal information, perform sophisticated calculations, and play games.

Developers, mobile communications device manufacturers, and mobile network providers are worried to plug this need, but there is a serious difficulty: *an application written for one device cannot run on another device, without alteration in the code.* Mobile communications devices do not have a standard application platform and operating system, and this has made developing applications for mobile devices a risky gamble.

Frankly speaking, the "*lack of principles*" situation is nothing new to computing technology. The **Wireless Application Protocol (WAP)** became the initial trade that set out to create standards for wireless technology. *Ericsson, Motorola, Nokia, and Unwired Planet* formed the WAP forum in 1997, and it has since grown to include nearly all mobile device manufacturers, mobile network providers, and developers. The WAP forum created mobile communications device standards referred to as the **WAP standard**.

The *WAP standard is an enhancement of HTML, XML, and TCP/IP*. One element of this standard is the **Wireless Markup Language (WML)** specification, which consists of a blend of HTML and XML. It is widely used by developers to create documents that can be displayed by a micro-browser.

The WAP standard also includes specifications for a **Wireless Telephony Application Interface (WTAI)** specification and the WML-Script specification. **WTAI** is used to create an interface for applications that run on a mobile communications device. WML-Script is a stripped-down version of JavaScript.

While the WAP forum provided the framework within which developers can build mobile communications device applications, they still had to overcome a common difficulty found in every rapidly developing technology. The sophistication of mobile communications devices, phenomenal growth of the market, and high demand for industrial-strength mobile communications applications out-paced the ability to define and implement new mobile communications device standards.

Many sophisticated applications designed for mobile communications devices require the device to process information beyond the capabilities of the WAP specification. J2ME provided the standard to fill this gap. For example, a businessman wants to check available flights and hotel accommodations, purchase an airline ticket, book the hotel and car rental, and then send the schedule to a client, all while sitting in a taxi in traffic. The businessman also wants to store the schedule on the mobile device and retrieve it any time during the trip.

J2ME applications referred to as a **MIDlet** can run on practically any mobile communications device that implements a JVM and MIDP. This encourages developers to invest time and money in building applications for mobile communications devices without the risk that the application is device dependent. However, J2ME isn't seen as a replacement for the WAP specification because both are balancing technologies.

From the above discussion we came to two conclusions about wireless applications.

1. The developers whose applications are light and client based continue to use WML and WML-Script.
2. The developers whose applications are heavier and require sophisticated processing on the mobile communications devices has turned to J2ME platform.

## 24.4 Small Computing Device Requirements

There are minimum resource requirements for a small computing device to run a J2ME application.

- First the device must have a minimum of 96 × 54 pixel display that can handle bitmapped graphics and have a way for users to input information (such as a keypad, keyboard, or touch screen).
- At least 128 kilobytes (KB) of nonvolatile memory is necessary to run Mobile Information Device (MID), and 8KB of nonvolatile memory is needed for storage of persistent application data. To run JVM, 32KB of volatile memory must be available.
- The device must also provide two-way network connectivity.
- A native operating system; that must implement exception handling, process interrupts, be able to run the JVM, and provide schedule capabilities.
- Most importantly, all user input to the operating system must be forwarded to the JVM; otherwise the device cannot run a J2ME application.

**Note: Although the native operating system doesn't need to implement a file system to run a J2ME application, it must be able to write and read persistent data (i.e. the data retained when the device is powered down) to nonvolatile memory.**

## 24.5 J2ME architecture

J2ME is "a highly optimized Java run-time environment targeting a wide range of consumer products, including pagers, cellular phones, screen-phones, digital set-top boxes and car navigation systems."

J2ME uses configurations and profiles to customize the Java Runtime Environment (JRE). As a complete JRE, J2ME is comprised of a *configuration* (which determines the JVM used) and a *profile* (which defines the application by adding domain-specific classes.) The configuration defines the basic run-time environment as a set of core classes and a specific JVM that run on specific types of devices. The profile defines the application; specifically, it adds domain-specific classes to the J2MEconfiguration to define certain uses for devices. The following graphic depicts the relationship between the different virtual machines, configurations, and profiles. It also draws a parallel with the J2SE API and its Java virtual machine. While the J2SE virtual machine is generally referred to as a JVM, the J2ME virtual machines, KVM and CVM, are subsets of JVM. Both KVM and CVM can be thought of as a kind of Java virtual machine — it's just that they are shrunken versions of the J2SE JVM and are specific to J2ME.

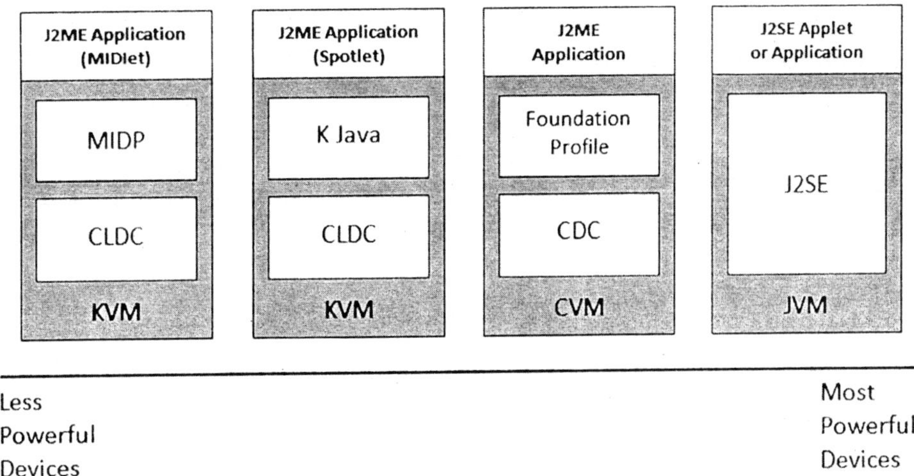


The configuration defines the basic run-time environment as a set of core classes and a specific JVM that run on specific types of devices. Currently, two configurations exist for J2ME, though others may be defined in the future:

**Configurations overview**

*Connected Limited Device Configuration (CLDC)* is used specifically with the KVM for 16-bit or 32-bit devices with limited amounts of memory. This is the configuration (and the virtual machine) used for developing small J2ME applications. Its size limitations make CLDC more interesting and challenging (from a development point of view) than CDC. CLDC is also the configuration that we will use for developing our drawing tool application. An example of a small wireless device running small applications is a Palm hand-held computer.

*Connected Device Configuration (CDC)* is used with the C virtual machine (CVM) and is used for 32-bit architectures requiring more than 2 MB of memory. An example of such a device is a Net TV box.

**Profile overview**

The profile defines the type of devices supported by your application. Specifically, it adds domain-specific classes to the J2ME configuration to define certain uses for devices. Profiles are built on top of configurations. Two profiles have been defined for J2ME and are built on CLDC: KJava and **Mobile Information Device Profile (MIDP)**. These profiles are geared toward smaller devices. A skeleton profile on which you create your own profile, the Foundation Profile, is available for CDC.

## 24.6 J2ME profiles – KJava and MIDP

As we mentioned earlier, a profile defines the type of device supported. The Mobile Information Device Profile (MIDP), for example, defines classes for cellular phones. It adds domain-specific classes to the J2ME configuration to define uses for similar devices.

Two profiles have been defined for J2ME and are built upon CLDC: KJava and MIDP. Both KJava and MIDP are associated with CLDC and smaller devices. Profiles are built on top of configurations. Because profiles are specific to the amount of memory of the device on which an application runs, certain profiles are associated with certain configurations.

A skeleton profile upon which you can create your own profile, the Foundation Profile, is available for CDC. However, for this tutorial and this section, we will focus only on the KJava and MIDP profiles built on top of CLDC.

**Profile 1: KJava**

KJava is Sun's proprietary profile and contains the KJava API. The KJava profile is built on top of the CLDC configuration. The KJava virtual machine, KVM, accepts the same bytecodes and class file format as the classic J2SE virtual machine.

KJava contains a Sun-specific API that runs on the Palm OS. The KJava API has a great deal in common with the J2SE Abstract Windowing Toolkit (AWT). However, because it is not a standard J2ME package, its main package is *com.sun.kjava*.

**Profile 2: MIDP**

MIDP is geared toward mobile devices such as cellular phones and pagers. The MIDP is also built upon CLDC and provides a standard run-time environment that allows new applications and services to be deployed dynamically on end-user devices.

MIDP is a common, industry-standard profile for mobile devices that is not dependent on a specific vendor. It is a complete and supported foundation for mobile application development.

MIDP contains the following packages, the first three are core CLDC packages and next three are MIDP-specific packages.

- *java.lang*
- *java.io*
- *java.util*
- *javax.microedition.io*
- *javax.microedition.lcdui*
- *javax.microedition.midlet*
- *javax.microedition.rms*

## 24.7 Other Java platforms for Small Computing Devices

J2ME isn't the only Java platform designed for small computing devices. Other Java platforms—EmbeddedJava, JavaCard, and PersonalJava—predate J2ME.

**EmbeddedJava** is the Java platform used for small computing devices that are dedicated to one purpose and have a 32-bit processor and 512KB of ROM and RAM. EmbeddedJava is based on JDK 1.1 and is being replaced by the CDLC configuration

**JavaCard** is the Java platform used for smart cards, the smallest computing device that supports Java. The JavaCard VM runs on small computing devices that have 16KB of nonvolatile memory and 512 bytes of volatile memory. However, unlike the EmbeddedJava platform, there isn't any movement to replace JavaCard with J2ME because of the resource constraints of the current generation of smart cards. Future smart card generations will probably have great resources available and be compatible with the CDLC configuration.

**PersonalJava** is the Java platform used for small computing devices that have a maximum of 2MB of ROM and a minimum of 1MB of RAM, such as large PDAs and mobile communications devices. PersonalJava uses JDK 1.1.8 and the JVM and will be replaced by the CDC configuration and the Personal Basis Profile and Personal Profile.

*****

# Chapter 25

# Sample Java Projects

In this last chapter, we are going to study some small Java projects that will inspire and sharpen your java skills. Most of these projects are simple and can run on Java NetBeans IDE.

**Project 1: Simple Calculator in Java Source Code**

```
//mathServer//
import java.rmi.*;
import java.rmi.Naming.*;
import java.rmi.server.*;
import java.rmi.registry.*;
import java.net.*;
import java.util.*;

interface mathInterface extends Remote
{
 public int add(int a,int b) throws RemoteException;
 public int subt(int a,int b) throws RemoteException;
 public int mult(int a,int b) throws RemoteException;
 public int div(int a,int b) throws RemoteException;
}

public class mathServer extends UnicastRemoteObject implements mathInterface

{
          public mathServer( ) throws RemoteException
          {
                    System.out.println("Initializing Server");
  }
  public int add(int a,int b)
  {
                    return(a+b);
          }
          public int subt(int a,int b)
            {
                              return(a-b);
          }
          public int mult(int a,int b)
            {
```

```
                        return(a*b);
        }
        public int div(int a,int b)
          {
                        return(a/b);
        }
        public static void main(String args[])
        {
                try
                {
                mathServer ms=new mathServer();
                java.rmi.Naming.rebind("MathServ",ms);
                System.out.println("Server Ready");
          }
          catch(RemoteException RE)
          {
                        System.out.println("Remote Server Error:"+ RE.getMessage());
                        System.exit(0);
                }
                catch(MalformedURLException ME)
                {
                        System.out.println("Invalid URL!!");
                }
        }
}
```

```
//mathClient//
import java.rmi.*;
import java.rmi.registry.*;
import java.awt.*;
import java.awt.event.*;
public class mathClient extends Frame implements ActionListener
{
        Button B1=new Button("Sum");
        Button B2=new Button("Subtract");
        Button B3=new Button("Multiply");
        Button B4=new Button("Divide");
        Label l1=new Label("Number 1");
        Label l2=new Label("Number 2");
        Label l3=new Label("Result");
        TextField t1=new TextField(20);
        TextField t2=new TextField(20);
        TextField t3=new TextField(20);
        public mathClient()
```

```
{
        super("Calculator");
        setLayout(null);
        l1.setBounds(20,50,55,25);
        add(l1);
        l2.setBounds(20,100,55,25);
        add(l2);
        l3.setBounds(20,150,55,25);
        add(l3);
        t1.setBounds(150,50,100,25);
        add(t1);
        t2.setBounds(150,100,100,25);
        add(t2);
        t3.setBounds(150,150,100,25);
        add(t3);
        B1.setBounds(20,200,80,25);
        add(B1);
        B2.setBounds(100,200,80,25);
        add(B2);
        B3.setBounds(180,200,80,25);
        add(B3);
        B4.setBounds(260,200,80,25);
        add(B4);
        B1.addActionListener(this);
        B2.addActionListener(this);
        B3.addActionListener(this);
        B4.addActionListener(this);
        addWindowListener(
                new WindowAdapter()
                        {
                                public void windowClosing(WindowEvent e)
                                {
                                        System.exit(0);
                                }
                        }
        );
}
public void actionPerformed(ActionEvent AE)
{
                if(AE.getSource()==B1)
                {
                        sum();
                }
                else if(AE.getSource()==B2)
                {
```

```
                subt();
        }
        else if(AE.getSource()==B3)
        {
                mult();
        }
        else if(AE.getSource()==B4)
                {
                                div();
        }
}
public void sum()
{
        int i=Integer.parseInt(t1.getText());
        int j=Integer.parseInt(t2.getText());
        int val;
        try
        {
                String ServerURL="MathServ";
                mathInterface MI=(mathInterface)Naming.lookup(ServerURL);
                val=MI.add(i,j);
                t3.setText(""+val);
        }
        catch(Exception ex)
        {
                System.out.println("Exception:"+ex);
        }
}
public void subt()
{
        int i=Integer.parseInt(t1.getText());
        int j=Integer.parseInt(t2.getText());
        int val;
        try
        {
                String ServerURL="MathServ";
                mathInterface MI=(mathInterface)Naming.lookup(ServerURL);
                val=MI.subt(i,j);
                t3.setText(""+val);
        }
        catch(Exception ex)
        {
                System.out.println("Exception:"+ex);
        }
}
```

```
        public void mult()
        {
                int i=Integer.parseInt(t1.getText());
                int j=Integer.parseInt(t2.getText());
                int val;
                try
                {
                        String ServerURL="MathServ";
                        mathInterface MI=(mathInterface)Naming.lookup(ServerURL);
                        val=MI.mult(i,j);
                        t3.setText(""+val);
                }
                catch(Exception ex)
                {
                        System.out.println("Exception:"+ex);
                }
        }
        public void div()
        {
                int i=Integer.parseInt(t1.getText());
                int j=Integer.parseInt(t2.getText());
                int val;
                try
                {
                        String ServerURL="MathServ";
                        mathInterface MI=(mathInterface)Naming.lookup(ServerURL);
                        val=MI.div(i,j);
                        t3.setText(""+val);
                }
                catch(Exception ex)
                {
                        System.out.println("Exception:"+ex);
                }
        }
        public static void main(String args[])
        {
                mathClient MC=new mathClient();
                MC.setVisible(true);
                MC.setSize(600,500);
        };
}
```

**Project 2: Text Editor in Java Source Code**

This small project will create simple text editor in Java can perform following simple tasks.

- New

- Open
- Save
- Save As
- Page Setup
- Print
- Exit
- Delete
- Cut
- Copy
- Paste
- Find Next
- Replace
- Go To
- Select All

This project mainly developed using event handling concepts. Simply open NetBeans IDE and create a simple class and apply following code in it.

```
import java.awt.*;
import java.awt.event.*;
import java.io.*;
import java.util.*;

//Texteditor class starts here
class Texteditor extends Frame implements ActionListener
{
        TextArea ta=new TextArea( );
        int i,len1,len,pos1;
        String str="",s3="",s2="",s4="",s32="",s6="",s7="",s8="",s9="";
        String months[] = {"January","February","March","April","May","June","July","August","September",
        "October","November","December"};
CheckboxMenuItem chkb=new CheckboxMenuItem("Word Wrap");
public Texteditor( )
{
MenuBar mb=new MenuBar();
setLayout(new BorderLayout());
add("Center",ta);
setMenuBar(mb);
Menu m1=new Menu("File");
Menu m2=new Menu("Edit");
Menu m3=new Menu("Tools");
Menu m4=new Menu("Help");
mb.add(m1);
mb.add(m2);
mb.add(m3);
mb.add(m4);
```

```
MenuItem mi1[ ]={
new MenuItem("New"),new MenuItem("Open"),new MenuItem("Save")
,new MenuItem("Save As"),new MenuItem("Page Setup")
,new MenuItem("Print"),new MenuItem("Exit")
};
MenuItem mi2[ ]={new MenuItem("Delete"),new MenuItem("Cut"),
new MenuItem("Copy"),new MenuItem("Paste"),new MenuItem("Find"),
new MenuItem("Find Next"),new MenuItem("Replace"),
new MenuItem("Go To"),new MenuItem("Select All"),
new MenuItem("Time Stamp")};
MenuItem mi3[]={new MenuItem("Choose Font"),new MenuItem("Compile"),
new MenuItem("Run")};
MenuItem mi4[]={new MenuItem("Help Topics"),
new MenuItem("About Texteditor")};
for(int i=0;i<len1;i++ )="" <br="">{
m1.add(mi1[i]);
mi1[i].addActionListener(this);
}
for(int i=0;i<len1;i++) {="" <br=""> m2.add(mi2[i]);
mi2[i].addActionListener(this);
}
m3.add(chkb);
chkb.addActionListener(this);
for(int i=0;i<len1;i++ )="" <br="">{
m3.add(mi3[i]);
mi3[i].addActionListener(this);
}
for(int i=0;i<len1;i++) <br="">{
m4.add(mi4[i]);
mi4[i].addActionListener(this);
}
MyWindowsAdapter mw=new MyWindowsAdapter(this);
addWindowListener(mw);
setSize(500,500);
setTitle("untitled notepad");
setVisible(true);
}
public void actionPerformed(ActionEvent ae)
{
String arg=(String)ae.getActionCommand();
if(arg.equals("New"))
{ dispose();
Texteditor t11=new Texteditor();
t11.setSize(500,500);
t11.setVisible(true);
```

```
}
try {
if(arg.equals("Open"))
{
FileDialog fd1=new FileDialog(this,"Select File",FileDialog.LOAD);
fd1.setVisible(true);
String s4="";
s2=fd1.getFile();
s3=fd1.getDirectory();
s32=s3+s2;
File f=new File(s32);
FileInputStream fii=new FileInputStream(f);
len=(int)f.length();
for(int j=0;j<len1;j++ )="" <br="">{
char s5=(char)fii.read();
s4=s4 + s5;
}
ta.setText(s4);
}
}
catch(IOException e)
{
}
try
{
if(arg.equals("Save As"))
{
FileDialog dialog1=new FileDialog(this,"Save As",FileDialog.SAVE);
dialog1.setVisible(true);
s7=dialog1.getDirectory();
s8=dialog1.getFile();
s9=s7+s8+".txt";
s6=ta.getText();
len1=s6.length();
byte buf[]=s6.getBytes();
File f1=new File(s9);
FileOutputStream fobj1=new FileOutputStream(f1);
for(int k=0;k<len1;k++) <br="">{
fobj1.write(buf[k]);
}
fobj1.close();
}
this.setTitle(s8 +" Texteditor File");
}
catch(IOException e){}
```

```
if(arg.equals("Exit"))
{
System.exit(0);
}
if(arg.equals("Cut"))
{
str=ta.getSelectedText();
i=ta.getText().indexOf(str);
ta.replaceRange(" ",i,i+str.length());
}
if(arg.equals("Copy"))
{
str=ta.getSelectedText();
}
if(arg.equals("Paste"))
{
pos1=ta.getCaretPosition();
ta.insert(str,pos1);
}
if(arg.equals("Delete"))
{
String msg=ta.getSelectedText();
i=ta.getText().indexOf(msg);
ta.replaceRange(" ",i,i+msg.length());
msg="";
}
if(arg.equals("Select All"))
{
String strText=ta.getText();
int strLen=strText.length();
ta.select(0,strLen);
}
if(arg.equals("Time Stamp"))
{
GregorianCalendar gcalendar=new GregorianCalendar();
String h=String.valueOf(gcalendar.get(Calendar.HOUR));
String m=String.valueOf(gcalendar.get(Calendar.MINUTE));
String s=String.valueOf(gcalendar.get(Calendar.SECOND));
String date=String.valueOf(gcalendar.get(Calendar.DATE));
String mon=months[gcalendar.get(Calendar.MONTH)];
String year=String.valueOf(gcalendar.get(Calendar.YEAR));
String hms="Time"+" - "+h+":"+m+":"+s+" Date"+" - "+date+" "+mon+" "+year+" ";
int loc=ta.getCaretPosition();
ta.insert(hms,loc);
}
```

```
if(arg.equals("About Texteditor"))
{
AboutDialog d1=new AboutDialog(this,"About Texteditor");
d1.setVisible(true);
setSize(500,500);
}
}//Action pereformed end
public class MyWindowsAdapter extends WindowAdapter
{
Texteditor tt;
public MyWindowsAdapter(Texteditor ttt)
{
tt=ttt;
}
public void windowClosing(WindowEvent we)
{
tt.dispose();
}
}//Inner class winadapter end....
}//End of Texteditor class
public class balls
{ public static void main(String args[])
{
Texteditor to=new Texteditor();
}
}
class AboutDialog extends Dialog implements ActionListener
{
AboutDialog(Frame parent,String title)
{
super(parent,title,false);
this.setResizable(false);
setLayout(new FlowLayout(FlowLayout.LEFT));
setSize(500,300);
}
public void actionPerformed(ActionEvent ae)
{
dispose();
}
}
```

**Project 3: LAN chat and file sharing Java Source Code**

***Login.jsp***

```
<%@ page language="java" contentType="text/html; charset=ISO-8859-1"
```

```
        pageEncoding="ISO-8859-1" import="java.util.*,java.text.*"%>
<!DOCTYPE html PUBLIC "-//W3C//DTD HTML 4.01 Transitional//EN"
"http://www.w3.org/TR/html4/loose.dtd">
<html>
<head>
<meta http-equiv="Content-Type" content="text/html; charset=ISO-8859-1">
<title>Insert title here</title>
</head>
<body>
<table width=700>
        <tr>
                <td width=200><%@ include file="menu.jsp"%></td>

                <td>   
                <div><font color=000033 size=20>      
                <%
if("admin".equals(request.getParameter("type")))
{
        out.print("Admin Console</font>");
}
else
{
        out.print("User Console</font>");
}
DateFormat df=new SimpleDateFormat("EEEE, dd MMMM, yyyy ");
String date=df.format(new Date());
out.print("<br>");
for(int i=0;i<37;i++)
        out.print(" ");
out.print("<font size=3 color=3300FF>"+date+"</font>");
%> </font></div>
                </td>
        </tr>

        <tr>
                <td></td>
                <td>
                <form action=loginhandler.jsp method=post>
                <table align=center cellpadding=5>
                        <tr>
                                <td>UserName</td>
                                <td><input type=text name=userName></td>
                        </tr>
                        <tr>
                                <td>Password</td>
```

```
                <td><input type=password name=password></td>
            </tr>
            <tr>
                <td>Type</td>
                <td><label><%= request.getParameter("type") %></label></td>
            </tr>
            <tr>
                <td><input type=hidden name=type
                    value=<%= request.getParameter("type") %>></td>
            </tr>
            <tr>
                <td></td>
                <td align=center><input type=submit value=Submit></td>
            </tr>
        </table>
        </form>
        </td>
    </tr>

</table>
</body>
</html>
```

**Adminchatservlet**

```
package chat;

import java.io.*;
import javax.servlet.*;
import javax.servlet.http.HttpServletRequest;
import javax.servlet.http.HttpServletResponse;
import java.util.*;
import java.sql.*;

/**
 * Servlet implementation class for Servlet: AdminChatServlet
 *
 */
public class AdminChatServlet extends javax.servlet.http.HttpServlet implements javax.servlet.Servlet {
  static final long serialVersionUID = 1L;

  /* (non-Java-doc)
        * @see javax.servlet.http.HttpServlet#HttpServlet()
        */
```

```
	public AdminChatServlet() {
		super();
	}

	/* (non-Java-doc)
	 * @see javax.servlet.http.HttpServlet#doGet(HttpServletRequest request, HttpServletResponse
response)
	 */
	protected void doGet(HttpServletRequest request, HttpServletResponse response) throws
ServletException, IOException {
		// TODO Auto-generated method stub
		doPost(request,response);
	}

	/* (non-Java-doc)
	 * @see javax.servlet.http.HttpServlet#doPost(HttpServletRequest request, HttpServletResponse
response)
	 */
	protected void doPost(HttpServletRequest request, HttpServletResponse response) throws
ServletException, IOException {
		// TODO Auto-generated method stub

		//adding rooms
		String roomname=request.getParameter("roomname");
		String roomdesc=request.getParameter("roomdesc");

		if(roomname!=null&&roomname.length()>0)
		{	try
			{
				Class.forName("sun.jdbc.odbc.JdbcOdbcDriver");
				Connection con=DriverManager.getConnection("jdbc:odbc:abc");
				String query="insert into chatrooms values(?,?)";
				PreparedStatement stmt=con.prepareStatement(query);
				stmt.setString(1, roomname);
				stmt.setString(2, roomdesc);
				stmt.execute();
			}catch(Exception e)
			{
				System.out.print(e);
			}
		}
		//removing rooms
		String[] remove=request.getParameterValues("remove");
		if(remove!=null)
		{
```

```
                    try
                    {
                            Class.forName("sun.jdbc.odbc.JdbcOdbcDriver");
                            Connection con=DriverManager.getConnection("jdbc:odbc:abc");
                            String query="delete from chatrooms where roomname=?";
                            PreparedStatement stmt=con.prepareStatement(query);
                            for(int i=0;i<remove.length;i++)
                            {
                                    stmt.setString(1, remove[i]);
                                    stmt.execute();
                            }
                    }catch(Exception e)
                    {
                            System.out.print(e);
                    }
            }
            RequestDispatcher rd=request.getRequestDispatcher("adminchatservlet.jsp");
            rd.forward(request,response);
        }
}
```

**Chatroomservlet**

```
package chat;

import java.io.*;
import javax.servlet.*;
import javax.servlet.http.*;
import java.text.*;
import java.util.*;
import java.sql.*;

/**
 * Servlet implementation class for Servlet: ChRoomServlet
 *
 */
public class ChRoomServlet extends javax.servlet.http.HttpServlet implements javax.servlet.Servlet {
  static final long serialVersionUID = 1L;

  /* (non-Java-doc)
        * @see javax.servlet.http.HttpServlet#HttpServlet()
        */

  public ChRoomServlet() {
                super();
```

```
	}
	/* (non-Java-doc)
	 * @see javax.servlet.http.HttpServlet#doGet(HttpServletRequest request, HttpServletResponse
response)
	 */
	protected void doGet(HttpServletRequest request, HttpServletResponse response) throws
ServletException, IOException {
		// TODO Auto-generated method stub
		response.setContentType("text/html");
		PrintWriter out=response.getWriter();
		ChatRooms chatroom=getRoom(request,response);
		if(chatroom==null)
		{
			return;
		}
		String s=request.getParameter("list");
		if(s!=null&s.equals("true"))
			writeMessage(out,chatroom,getProfileName(request));
		else
		{
			out.println("<html><head>");
			out.print("<script language=javascript>");
		out.print("function fun1(e){");

		out.print("if(e.keyCode==13)");
		out.print("document.form1.submit();}");

		out.print("</script></head>");

			out.println("<body>");
			out.println("<form method=post action=ChRoomServlet target=_parent>");
			out.println("<table align=center width=100%>");
			out.println("<tr><td><font color=#476BC0>Your message</font></td></tr>");
			out.println("<tr><td><textarea name=msg cols=50 rows=3
class=smalltext></textarea></td></tr>");
			out.println("<tr><td><input type=submit value=Send class=smalltext
onkeydown=fun1(event) ></td></tr>");
			out.println("</table></form>");
			out.println("<form action="+response.encodeURL("/chat/roomlist.jsp")+"
target=_parent>");
			out.println("<center><input type=submit value='Exit from Chat Room'
class=smalltext>");
			out.println("</center></form>");
			out.println("<form action=logout.jsp method=get target=_parent>");
			out.println("<center><input type=submit value='Logout' class=smalltext>");
```

```
                out.println("</center></form>");
                out.println("</body></html>");
            }
            out.close();
        }

        /* (non-Java-doc)
         * @see javax.servlet.http.HttpServlet#doPost(HttpServletRequest request, HttpServletResponse
response)
         */
        protected void doPost(HttpServletRequest request, HttpServletResponse response) throws
ServletException, IOException {
            // TODO Auto-generated method stub
            response.setContentType("text/html");
            ChatRooms chatroom=getRoom(request,response);
            if(chatroom==null)
            {
                return;
            }

            String s=getProfileName(request);
            String s1=request.getParameter("msg");

            if(s1!=null&&s1.length()!=0)
            {
                DateFormat d=new SimpleDateFormat("hh:mm");
                String time=d.format(new java.util.Date());
                s1="[ "+time+" ] "+s1;
                chatroom.joinChatEntry(new ChatRoomEntry(s,s1));
            }

            messageFrame(response,chatroom);
        }

        private String getProfileName(HttpServletRequest request)
        {
            HttpSession httpsession=request.getSession(true);
            String s=(String)httpsession.getAttribute("profileName");

            if(s==null)
            {
                s=request.getParameter("profileName");
                if(s==null||s.length()==0)
                {
                    s="Anonymous";
```

```
            }
            httpsession.setAttribute("profileName", s);
        }
        else
        {
            String s1=request.getParameter("profileName");
            if(s1!=null&&s1.length()>0&& !s.equals(s1))
            {
                s=s1;
                httpsession.setAttribute("profileName", s);
            }
        }

        return s;
    }

    private ChatRooms getRoom(HttpServletRequest request, HttpServletResponse response) throws
ServletException, IOException
    {
        HttpSession httpsession=request.getSession(true);
        PrintWriter out=response.getWriter();
        String s=(String)httpsession.getAttribute("roomName");

        if(s==null)
        {
            s=request.getParameter("roomName");
            if(s==null||s.length()==0)
            {
                error(request,response);
            }
            httpsession.setAttribute("roomName", s);
        }
        else
        {
            String s1=request.getParameter("roomName");
            if(s1!=null&&s1.length()>0&& !s.equals(s1))
            {
                s=s1;
                httpsession.setAttribute("roomName", s);
            }
        }

        HashMap hashmap=(HashMap)getServletContext().getAttribute("roomList");
        ChatRooms chatroom=(ChatRooms)hashmap.get(s);
```

```
            if(chatroom==null)
            {
                    error(request,response);
                    return null;
            }
            else
            {
                    return chatroom;
            }
    }

    private void error(HttpServletRequest request, HttpServletResponse response) throws ServletException,
IOException
    {

    }

    private void messageFrame(HttpServletResponse response,ChatRooms chatroom) throws
ServletException, IOException
    {
            PrintWriter out=response.getWriter();
            out.println("<html>");
            out.println("<head><title>"+chatroom.getName()+"</title></head>");
            out.println("<frameset rows='320,180'>");
            out.println("<frame src=ChRoomServlet?list=true name=list SCROLLING=AUTO>");
            out.println("<frame src=ChRoomServlet?list=false name=form SCROLLING=no>");

            out.println("</frameset>");
            out.println("</html>");
    }

    private void writeMessage(PrintWriter out,ChatRooms chatroom,String s)
    {
            StringBuffer stringbuffer=new StringBuffer();
            out.println("<html>");
            out.println("<head><meta http-equiv=refresh content=1></head>");

            out.println("<body marginheight=0 marginwidth=0>");
            out.println("<table align=center bgcolor=#476BC0 width=100% height=100%>");
            out.println("<tr><td valign=top>");
            out.println("Chat-Room Name: "+chatroom.getName()+"<br>You are: "+s+"<br><br><br>");

            if(chatroom.size()==0)
            {
                    out.print("<font color=red>No messages available in this room</font>");
```

```
            }
            else
            {
                for(Iterator iterator=chatroom.iterator();iterator.hasNext();)
                {
                    ChatRoomEntry chatentry=(ChatRoomEntry)iterator.next();
                    if(chatentry!=null)
                    {
                        String s1=chatentry.getProfileName();

                        if(s1.equals(s))
                            out.println("<font color=yellow>");
                        out.println(s1+" : "+chatentry.getMsg()+"<br>");

                        if(s1.equals(s))
                            out.println("</font>");

                    }
                }
            }
            out.println("</td></tr></table>");
            out.print("</body></html>");
        }

        public void destroy()
        {
            System.out.print("chroomservlet");
        }

}
```

***UPLOAD SERVLET***

```
package chat;

import java.io.*;
import java.util.*;

import javax.servlet.RequestDispatcher;
import javax.servlet.ServletConfig;
import javax.servlet.ServletException;
import javax.servlet.http.*;

import org.apache.commons.fileupload.*;
import org.apache.commons.fileupload.disk.*;
```

```
import org.apache.commons.fileupload.servlet.*;
import org.apache.commons.io.*;
import java.sql.*;

public class UploadServlet extends HttpServlet {

  //private boolean isMultipart;

  private int maxMemorySize = 50 * 1024;
  private int maxRequestSize = 300 * 1024;
  private File tempDirectory;

  public void init( ){
   }
  public void doPost(HttpServletRequest request,HttpServletResponse response)
         throws ServletException, java.io.IOException {
           //check for file upload request
          // boolean isMultipart=ServletFileUpload.isMultipartContent(request);
           //response.getWriter().print(isMultipart);


           // Create a factory for disk-based file items
           DiskFileItemFactory factory = new DiskFileItemFactory();

           // Set factory constraints
           factory.setSizeThreshold(maxMemorySize);
           factory.setRepository(tempDirectory);

           // Create a new file upload handler
           ServletFileUpload upload = new ServletFileUpload(factory);

           // Set overall request size constraint
           upload.setSizeMax(maxRequestSize);

           // Parse the request
           try
           {
                   List items = upload.parseRequest(request);

           // Process the uploaded items
           Iterator iter = items.iterator();
           while (iter.hasNext()) {
              FileItem item = (FileItem) iter.next();

              if (item.isFormField()) {
```

```
} else {
                        //response.getWriter().println("a file is uploaded");
        String fieldName = item.getFieldName();
        String fileName=item.getName();
        //response.getWriter().println(fileName.lastIndexOf('/')+1);
        // fileName = fileName.substring(fileName.lastIndexOf('/')+1);
        fileName = fileName.substring(fileName.lastIndexOf('\\')+1);

        String contentType = item.getContentType();
        boolean isInMemory = item.isInMemory();
        long sizeInBytes = item.getSize();

        InputStream uploadedStream = item.getInputStream();

        item.write(new File("D:\\PROJECT\\chat\\WebContent\\"+fileName));
        uploadedStream.close();

        int x=contentType.indexOf('/');
        contentType=contentType.substring(0, x);

        Class.forName("sun.jdbc.odbc.JdbcOdbcDriver");
            Connection con=DriverManager.getConnection("jdbc:odbc:abc");
            String query="insert into sharedfiles values(?,?,?)";
            PreparedStatement pstmt=con.prepareStatement(query);

            HttpSession httpsession=request.getSession();
            String loginid=(String)httpsession.getAttribute("login");

            pstmt.setString(1,fileName);
            pstmt.setString(2,contentType);
            pstmt.setString(3,loginid);

            pstmt.execute();

  }
}
}catch(Exception e)
{
        response.getWriter().println(e);
}
RequestDispatcher view=request.getRequestDispatcher("viewfiles.jsp");
      view.forward(request,response);

}
public void doGet(HttpServletRequest request,HttpServletResponse response)
```

```
    throws ServletException, java.io.IOException {

        doPost(request,response);

    }
}
```

***IMAGE DOWNLOADER***

```
package chat;

import java.io.BufferedInputStream;
import java.io.IOException;
import java.io.InputStream;
import java.net.URL;
import java.net.URLConnection;

import javax.servlet.*;
import javax.servlet.ServletOutputStream;
import javax.servlet.http.HttpServletRequest;
import javax.servlet.http.HttpServletResponse;

/**
 * Servlet implementation class for Servlet: imageDownloader2
 *
 */
public class imageDownloader2 extends javax.servlet.http.HttpServlet implements javax.servlet.Servlet {
  static final long serialVersionUID = 1L;

  /* (non-Java-doc)
        * @see javax.servlet.http.HttpServlet#HttpServlet()
        */
        public imageDownloader2() {
                super();
        }

        /* (non-Java-doc)
        * @see javax.servlet.http.HttpServlet#doGet(HttpServletRequest request, HttpServletResponse
response)
        */
        protected void doGet(HttpServletRequest request, HttpServletResponse response) throws
ServletException, IOException {
                // TODO Auto-generated method stub
        }
```

```
        /* (non-Java-doc)
         * @see javax.servlet.http.HttpServlet#doPost(HttpServletRequest request, HttpServletResponse
response)
         */
        protected void doPost(HttpServletRequest request, HttpServletResponse response) throws
ServletException, IOException {
                // TODO Auto-generated method stub
                try
                {
                        String filename2=request.getParameter("filename");
                        URL u=new URL("http://localhost:8080/chat/"+filename2);
                        //URL u=new URL("http://www.aitpune.com/directorpage.asp");

                        URLConnection uc=u.openConnection();
                        String contentType=uc.getContentType();
                        int contentLength=uc.getContentLength();
                        System.out.print(contentLength);
                        System.out.print(contentType);
                        InputStream raw=uc.getInputStream();
                        InputStream buffer=new BufferedInputStream(raw);
                        String filename=u.getFile();
                        filename=filename.substring(filename.lastIndexOf('/')+1);
                        ServletOutputStream stream = null;
                        stream = response.getOutputStream();
                        response.setContentType(contentType);

                response.addHeader("Content-Disposition","attachment; filename="+filename );

                response.setContentLength( contentLength );
                int readBytes = 0;

                while((readBytes = buffer.read()) != -1)
                        stream.write(readBytes);
                RequestDispatcher view=request.getRequestDispatcher("viewfiles.jsp");
                                view.forward(request,response);
                }catch(Exception e){
                        response.getWriter().print(e);
                }
        }
}
```

**DELETE USER:**

```
<%@ page language="java" contentType="text/html; charset=ISO-8859-1"
        pageEncoding="ISO-8859-1" import="java.sql.*"%>
```

```
<%
String[] users=request.getParameterValues("loginid");
try
{
        Class.forName("sun.jdbc.odbc.JdbcOdbcDriver");
        Connection con=DriverManager.getConnection("jdbc:odbc:abc");
        String query="delete from login where loginid=?";
        PreparedStatement stmt=con.prepareStatement(query);
        for(int i=0;i<users.length;i++)
        {
                stmt.setString(1,users[i]);
                stmt.execute();
        }
        RequestDispatcher rd=request.getRequestDispatcher("viewuser.jsp");
        rd.forward(request,response);

}catch(Exception e)
{
        out.print(e);
}
%>
<!DOCTYPE html PUBLIC "-//W3C//DTD HTML 4.01 Transitional//EN"
"http://www.w3.org/TR/html4/loose.dtd">
<html>
<head>
<meta http-equiv="Content-Type" content="text/html; charset=ISO-8859-1">
<title>Insert title here</title>
</head>
<body>

</body>
</html>
```

**ADD USER :**

```
<%@ page language="java" contentType="text/html; charset=ISO-8859-1"
        pageEncoding="ISO-8859-1"%>
<!DOCTYPE html PUBLIC "-//W3C//DTD HTML 4.01 Transitional//EN"
"http://www.w3.org/TR/html4/loose.dtd">
<html>
<head>
<meta http-equiv="Content-Type" content="text/html; charset=ISO-8859-1">
<title>Java Chat-Admin Console-Add User</title>
</head>
<body>
```

```
<table width=700>
        <tr>
                <td width=300><%@ include file="menu.jsp"%></td>
                <td>
                <div align=center>
                <table>
                        <tr>
                                <td align=center height=30 width=200 bgcolor=red><a
                                        href=adduser.jsp>Add Users</a></td>
                                <td align=center height=30 width=200 bgcolor=CCCCFF><a
                                        href=viewuser.jsp>View Users</a></td>
                                <td align=center height=30 width=200 bgcolor=CCFFFF><a
                                        href=AdminChatServlet>Configure Rooms</a></td>
                                <td align=center height=30 width=200 bgcolor=9966FF><a
                                        href=logout.jsp>Logout</a></td>
                        </tr>
                </table>
                <br>
                <br>
                <font size=5 color=000033>Enter New User Information</font></div>
        </tr>

        <tr>
                <td></td>
                <td>
                <form action=adduserhandler.jsp method=post>
                <table align=center cellpadding=5>
                        <tr>
                                <td>Name</td>
                                <td><input type=text name=name></td>
                        </tr>
                        <tr>
                                <td>Email</td>
                                <td><input type=text name=email></td>
                        </tr>
                        <tr>
                                <td>Loginid</td>
                                <td><input type=text name=loginid></td>
                        </tr>
                        <tr>
                                <td>Password</td>
                                <td><input type=password name=password></td>
                        </tr>
                        <tr>
                                <td>Type</td>
```

```
                        <td><select name=type>
                                <option value=admin>admin</option>
                                <option value=user>user</option>
                        </select></td>
                <tr>
                        <td></td>
                        <td align=center><input type=submit value=Submit></td>
                </tr>
        </table>
        </form>
        </td>
    </tr>
</table>
</body>
</html>
```

**CHAT CLIENT :**

```
import java.awt.*;
import java.awt.event.*;
import java.net.*;
import java.io.*;

public class ChatClient extends Frame implements ActionListener,Runnable {

  private Button button1, button2;
  private TextArea textarea1, textarea2;
  private TextField textfield1;
  private Label label1, label2, label3;
  Socket socket;
  Thread thread;

  InputStream in;
  OutputStream out;
 // PrintWriter out;

  public static void main(String[] args)
  {
    new ChatClient();
  }

  public ChatClient()
  {
    setLayout(null);
```

```
label1 = new Label("Server IP address:");
label1.setBounds(35, 80, 105, 20);
add(label1);

textfield1 = new TextField("127.0.0.1");
textfield1.setBounds(145, 80, 100, 20);
add(textfield1);

button1 = new Button("Connect");
button1.setBounds(255, 80, 80, 20);
add(button1);
button1.addActionListener(this);

button2 = new Button("Send");
button2.setBounds(160, 390, 60, 20);
add(button2);
button2.addActionListener(this);

textarea1 = new TextArea("", 7, 45, TextArea.SCROLLBARS_VERTICAL_ONLY);
textarea1.setBounds(20, 110, 340, 120);
add(textarea1);

label2 = new Label();
label2.setBounds(20, 240, 100, 20);
label2.setText("Type here:");
add(label2);

textarea2 = new TextArea("", 7, 45,
   TextArea.SCROLLBARS_VERTICAL_ONLY);
textarea2.setBounds(20, 260, 340, 120);
textarea2.setForeground(Color.RED);
add(textarea2);

label3 = new Label("Chat Client");
label3.setFont(new Font("Times New Roman", Font.BOLD, 36));
label3.setBounds(100, 35, 200, 30);
add(label3);

setSize(400, 430);

setTitle("Chat Client");
setVisible(true);
//textarea2.requestFocus();

this.addWindowListener(new WindowAdapter(){
```

```
    public void windowClosing(
      WindowEvent e){
        System.exit(0);
      }
    }
  );


}
public void actionPerformed(ActionEvent event)
{
      if(event.getSource()==button1)
      {
            String hostname=textfield1.getText();
            try
            {
                  socket = new Socket(hostname, 13);

                  in=socket.getInputStream();
                  out=socket.getOutputStream();

                  textarea1.setText("you are now connected");

                  thread=new Thread(this);
                  thread.start();


            }catch (UnknownHostException e)
            {
                  textarea1.setText(e.getMessage());
            }catch (IOException e)
            {
                  textarea1.setText(e.getMessage());
            }


      }

            if(event.getSource()==button2)
            {
                  try
                  {
                        String str = textarea2.getText() + "\n";
           byte buffer[] = str.getBytes();
           out.write(buffer);
```

```
            textarea1.setForeground(Color.RED);
            textarea1.append(str+"\n");
            textarea2.setText("");
            textarea2.requestFocus();
          }catch(Exception e){}
            }

  }

      public void run()
      {
              String instring;
    try {

      BufferedReader in = new BufferedReader (new InputStreamReader(socket.getInputStream()));

      textarea1.setForeground(Color.BLUE);
      while((instring = in.readLine()) != null){
        textarea1.append(instring + "\n");
      }

    }catch (Exception e)
    {
      textarea1.setText(e.getMessage());
    }

      }

}
```

**CHAT SERVER :**

```
import java.awt.*;
import java.awt.event.*;
import java.net.*;
import java.util.Date;
import java.io.*;

public class ChatServer2 extends Frame implements ActionListener,Runnable {

      private Label label1,label2;
      private Button button1;
      private TextArea textarea1,textarea2;
      ServerSocket socket;
```

```
    Socket insocket;
    int port=13;
    Thread thread;

    ServerSocket server;
    Socket connection=null;

    InputStream in;
    OutputStream out;


    public static void main(String[] arg)
    {
            new ChatServer2();
    }
    public ChatServer2()
    {
            setLayout(null);

            label2=new Label("Chat Server");
            label2.setBounds(100,35,200,30);
            label2.setFont(new Font("Times New Roman",Font.BOLD,36));
add(label2);

            setSize(400,400);
setVisible(true);
setTitle("Chat Server");

button1 = new Button("Send");
button1.setBounds(160, 360, 60, 20);
add(button1);
button1.addActionListener(this);

textarea1 = new TextArea("", 7, 45, TextArea.SCROLLBARS_VERTICAL_ONLY);
textarea1.setBounds(20, 80, 340, 100);
//textarea1.setText("hi");
add(textarea1);

label1=new Label();
label1.setBounds(20,210,100,20);
label1.setText("Type Here");
add(label1);

textarea2 = new TextArea("", 7, 45, TextArea.SCROLLBARS_VERTICAL_ONLY);
textarea2.setBounds(20, 230, 340, 120);
```

```
    textarea2.setForeground(Color.RED);
    add(textarea2);

    this.addWindowListener(new WindowAdapter()
    {
        public void windowClosing(WindowEvent e)
        {
                System.exit(0);
                try
                {
                        socket.close();
                }catch(Exception ex){}
        }
    });

    try
        {
                socket = new ServerSocket(port);
                insocket = null;

                        try {
                                insocket = socket.accept( );
                                //OutputStreamWriter out = new
OutputStreamWriter(connection.getOutputStream( ));
                                in=insocket.getInputStream();
                                out=insocket.getOutputStream();

                                thread=new Thread(this);
                                thread.start();

                        }catch (IOException e) {}

        }catch (IOException e)
        {
                System.err.println(e);
        }
        }

        public void actionPerformed(ActionEvent event)
  {
                if(event.getSource()==button1)
                {
                        try
                        {
                                String str = textarea2.getText() + "\n";
```

```
                byte buffer[] = str.getBytes();
                out.write(buffer);
                textarea1.setForeground(Color.RED);
                textarea1.append(str+"\n");
                textarea2.setText("");
                textarea2.requestFocus();
                        }catch(Exception e){}
                 }

    }

        public void run()
        {
                String instring;
      try {

         BufferedReader in = new BufferedReader (new InputStreamReader(insocket.getInputStream()));

         textarea1.setForeground(Color.BLUE);

         while((instring = in.readLine()) != null)
          {
           textarea1.append(instring + "\n");
          }

      }catch (Exception e)
      {
         textarea1.setText(e.getMessage());
      }

          }
  }
```

**Project 4: Simple Search Engine in JAVA Servlets**

**Part 1: Search.java**

```
import java.io.*;
import java.util.Enumeration;

import javax.servlet.*;
import javax.servlet.http.*;

import java.sql.*;
import java.net.*;
import java.util.*;
```

```
public class search extends HttpServlet{
	//Connection object
	Connection theConnection;

	//Change StringdbURL according to your database url.

	//private  String dbURL = "jdbc:mysql://127.0.0.1:3306/roseindia_net?user=root&password=";

	private  String dbURL = "jdbc:mysql://10.0.0.1/javadevelopers?user=abc&password=abc";


	//private String servletURL="/servlet";
	private String servletURL="http://www.webappcabaret.com/javadevelopers";


	//private String image="/images/open.gif";
	private String image="http://www.roseindia.net/images/open.gif";

 public void init() throws ServletException{
	makeConnection();
 }

 public void makeConnection(){
      //System.out.println("Opening db connection");
				try
				{
				   Class.forName("org.gjt.mm.mysql.Driver").newInstance();
					theConnection = DriverManager.getConnection(dbURL);
				}
				catch (Exception e)
				{
				//	System.out.println(e.getMessage());
				}
     // System.out.println("Connected to the database");

 }
 public void destory(){
	try{
	theConnection.close();
	}catch(Exception e){}
 }

 public void service (HttpServletRequest req, HttpServletResponse res)
  throws ServletException, IOException
  {
```

```
  //Get the session object
  HttpSession session = req.getSession(true);
  res.setContentType("text/html");
  PrintWriter out = res.getWriter();

 writeHead(out);

 String strSection = req.getParameter("section");
 String strCategory = req.getParameter("category");
 String strUnder = req.getParameter("under");
 String strLink = req.getParameter("link");
 String straddnew = req.getParameter("addnew");
 String striunder = req.getParameter("iunder");
 String strilink = req.getParameter("ilink");
 String strserno = req.getParameter("serno");
 String modifylink= req.getParameter("modifylink");
 String validate= req.getParameter("validate");
 String updatemodified = req.getParameter("updatemodified");
 String placelinks = req.getParameter("placelinks");
 String item= req.getParameter("item");


 if ( item!= null)
         searchitems(out,item);


 else if ( placelinks != null)
         placelinks(out);

 else if (updatemodified!= null)
         updateModified(out,req);

 else if (validate!= null)
         validateLogin(out,req);

 else if (modifylink!= null)
         displayLoginForm(out);
 else if (strserno != null)
         displayFinalResult(out,strserno);
 else if (straddnew != null && striunder != null && strilink!=null)
         updatenewEntry(out,straddnew,striunder,strilink,req);
 else if (strSection != null)
         displayCategories(out,strSection);
 else if (strCategory!= null)
         displayListings(out,strCategory);
```

```
else if (strUnder!= null)
        addListings(out,strUnder,strLink);
else

 displaySections(out);

 writeBottom(out);
 out.close();
}


public void searchitems(PrintWriter pr,String item){

        Statement theStatement;
        ResultSet theResult;
    pr.println("<tr>");
     pr.println("<td width=\"100%\" align=\"center\"><font color=\"#000080\" size=\"5\">Search
results:</font></td>");
    pr.println("</tr>");
    pr.println("<tr>");
     pr.println("<td width=\"100%\" align=\"center\">");
      pr.println("<div align=\"center\">");
       pr.println("<table border=\"1\" cellpadding=\"0\" cellspacing=\"0\" width=\"91%\"
bgcolor=\"#FFFFFF\" bordercolor=\"#C6FFFF\">");


        String sql;
        sql="select serno,caption,descp from listings where caption like '%" + item + "%' or descp like
'%" + item + "%'";

        try{
        if(theConnection == null) makeConnection();

        theStatement=theConnection.createStatement();
    theResult=theStatement.executeQuery(sql);

        int i;
        i=0;

//      i=theResult.getFetchSize();


   pr.println("<tr>");
    pr.println("<td width=\"100%\" align=\"center\">");
     pr.println("<b>");
```

```
pr.println("This Page Will Show You The Final Hit.</font>");
pr.println("</b>");
pr.println("</td>");


pr.println("<tr>");
pr.println("<td width=\"100%\" align=\"center\">");
pr.println("<div align=\"center\">");
pr.println("<table border=\"0\" cellpadding=\"0\" cellspacing=\"0\" width=\"91%\"
bgcolor=\"#FFFFFF\" bordercolor=\"#C6FFFF\" height=\"1\">");

while(theResult.next()) //Fetch all the records
{
i++;
pr.println("<tr>");
pr.println("<td width=\"5%\" valign=\"top\" height=\"1\" bgcolor=\"#FFFFCC\">" +
String.valueOf(i) + "</td>");
pr.println("<td width=\"95%\" valign=\"top\" height=\"1\" bgcolor=\"#FFFFCC\"><a href=\"" +
servletURL + "/search?serno=" + theResult.getString(1) + "\"><font color=\"#CC3300\" size=\"3\">" +
theResult.getString(2) + "</font></a></td>");
pr.println("</tr>");
pr.println("<tr>");
pr.println("<td width=\"5%\" valign=\"top\" height=\"1\" bgcolor=\"#FFFFF0\"><font
color=\"#CC3300\" size=\"4\"> </font></td>");
pr.println("<td width=\"95%\" valign=\"top\" height=\"1\" bgcolor=\"#FFFFF0\"><font
color=\"#000080\" size=\"2\">" + theResult.getString(3) + "</font></td>");
pr.println("</tr>");
}



/*      pr.println("<tr>");
pr.println("<td colspan=2 bgcolor=\"#FFFFF0\"><font color=\"#CC3300\" size=\"4\"><a href=\"" +
servletURL + "/search?under=" + strCategory + "\">Add Link</a></font></td>");
pr.println("</tr>");
*/
pr.println("</table>");
pr.println("</div>");
pr.println("</td>");
pr.println("</tr>");


theResult.close();//Close the result set
theStatement.close();//Close statement
}catch (Exception e){
```

```
                    pr.println(e.getMessage());
            }


        }

        public void placelinks(PrintWriter out){

        out.println("<tr>");
         out.println("<td width=\"100%\" align=\"center\">");
          out.println("<div align=\"center\">");
           out.println("<table border=\"0\" cellpadding=\"0\" cellspacing=\"0\" width=\"88%\"
bgcolor=\"#FFFFFF\" bordercolor=\"#C6FFFF\" height=\"1\">");
            out.println("<tr>");
             out.println("<td width=\"100%\" valign=\"top\" height=\"2\" bgcolor=\"#FFFFCC\">");

              out.println("<h2>Please be more specific!</h2>");
              out.println("<p>Please find a more specific sub-category for your entry and resubmit your request
there. ");
              out.println("<p>Return to <a href=\"" + servletURL + "/search\">Java Search</a></p>");
              out.println("<p>  ");
             out.println("</td>");
            out.println("</tr>");
           out.println("</table>");
          out.println("</div>");
         out.println("</td>");
        out.println("</tr>");

        }


        public void updateModified(PrintWriter out,HttpServletRequest req){

         //Get the session object
         HttpSession session = req.getSession(true);
      String username = (String) session.getValue ("user");

        //out.println(username);

        String address = req.getParameter("address");
                if(address==null) address="";
                        else address = change(address);
        String city= req.getParameter("city");
                if(city==null) city="";
                        else city = change(city);
```

```
String state= req.getParameter("state");
        if(state==null) state="";
                else state= change(state);
String zip= req.getParameter("zip");
        if(zip==null) zip="";
                else zip= change(zip);
String country= req.getParameter("country");
        if(country==null) country="";
                else country= change(country);
String phone= req.getParameter("phone");
        if(phone==null) phone="";
                else phone= change(phone);
String email= req.getParameter("email");
String url= req.getParameter("url");
String caption= req.getParameter("caption");
        if(caption==null) caption="";
                else caption= change(caption);
String description= req.getParameter("description");
        if(description==null) description="";
                else description= change(description);
String mail= req.getParameter("mail");

String sql;
sql="update listings set street='" + address + "', city='" + city + "', state='" + state + "', zip='" + zip + "',
country='" + country + "', telephone='" + phone + "', email='" + email + "', url='" + url + "', caption='" + caption +
"', descp='" + description + "', mailing_list='" + mail + "' where login='" + username + "'";

try{
Statement theStatement;
theStatement=theConnection.createStatement();
theStatement.executeUpdate(sql);
theStatement.close();
out.println("<tr>");
out.println("<td width=\"100%\" align=\"center\"><font color=\"#FF0000\" size=\"5\">Database
successfully updated.</font></td>");
out.println("</tr>");
out.println("<tr>");

}catch(Exception e){}

}

public void validateLogin(PrintWriter pr,HttpServletRequest req){
String login= req.getParameter("login");
String password = req.getParameter("password");
```

```
int serno;
serno=0;

String s1,s2,s3,s4,s5,s6,s7,s8,s9,s10,s11,s12,s13,s14,s15,s16;
s1="";
s2="";
s3="";
s4="";
s5="";
s6="";
s7="";
s8="";
s9="";
s10="";
s11="";
s12="";
s13="";
s14="";
s15="";
s16="";

try{

Statement theStatement;
ResultSet theResultset;


theStatement=theConnection.createStatement();
theResultset=theStatement.executeQuery("select * from listings where login='" + login + "' and
password='" + password + "'");
        while(theResultset.next()){
        serno++;
        //create a session for user
        HttpSession session = req.getSession(true);
    session.putValue ("user", login);
        s1=theResultset.getString(1);
        s2=theResultset.getString(2);
        s3=theResultset.getString(3);
        s4=theResultset.getString(4);
        s5=theResultset.getString(5);
        s6=theResultset.getString(6);
        s7=theResultset.getString(7);
        s8=theResultset.getString(8);
        s9=theResultset.getString(9);
        s10=theResultset.getString(10);
```

```
                s11=theResultset.getString(11);
                s12=theResultset.getString(12);
                s13=theResultset.getString(13);
                s14=theResultset.getString(14);
                s15=theResultset.getString(15);
                }
        theResultset.close();
        theStatement.close();

if(serno==0){
        pr.println("<tr>");
         pr.println("<td width=\"100%\" align=\"center\">");
          pr.println("<div align=\"center\">");
           pr.println("<table border=\"0\" cellpadding=\"0\" cellspacing=\"0\" width=\"83%\"
bgcolor=\"#FFFFFF\" bordercolor=\"#C6FFFF\" height=\"1\">");
            pr.println("<tr>");
             pr.println("<td width=\"100%\" valign=\"top\" height=\"2\" bgcolor=\"#FFFFCC\">");
              pr.println("<form method=\"POST\" action=\"" + servletURL + "/search\">");
               pr.println("<input type=hidden name=validate value=1>");
               pr.println("<p><br>");
               pr.println("<font color=\"#800000\">  <font size=\"4\">Invalid user ID or Password! Try
again!</font></font><br>");
               pr.println("   <font
color=\"#FF0000\">Login: </font>       ");
               pr.println("<input type=\"text\" name=\"login\" size=\"20\"><br>");
               pr.println("   <font color=\"#FF0000\">Password: </font>");
               pr.println("<input type=\"password\" name=\"password\" size=\"20\"></p>");

pr.println("<p>             &nb
sp;       ");
               pr.println("<input type=\"submit\" value=\"Submit\" name=\"B1\"></p>");
              pr.println("</form>");
             pr.println("</td>");
            pr.println("</tr>");
           pr.println("</table>");
          pr.println("</div>");
         pr.println("</td>");
        pr.println("</tr>");


return;
}


        pr.println("<script language=javascript>");
```

```
pr.println("function validate1(){");

        pr.println("if(window.document.f2.address.value.length==0){");
                pr.println("alert (\"Re enter your address.\");");
                pr.println("window.document.f2.address.focus();");
                pr.println("return false;");
                pr.println("}");


        pr.println("if(window.document.f2.city.value.length==0){");
                pr.println("alert (\"Re enter your city.\");");
                pr.println("window.document.f2.city.focus();");
                pr.println("return false;");
                pr.println("}");

        pr.println("if(window.document.f2.state.value.length==0){");
                pr.println("alert (\"Re enter your state.\");");
                pr.println("window.document.f2.state.focus();");
                pr.println("return false;");
                pr.println("}");

        pr.println("if(window.document.f2.country.value.length==0){");
                pr.println("alert (\"Re enter your country.\");");
                pr.println("window.document.f2.country.focus();");
                pr.println("return false;");
      pr.println("}");

        pr.println("if(window.document.f2.email.value.length==0){");
                pr.println("alert (\"Re enter your email.\");");
                pr.println("window.document.f2.email.focus();");
                pr.println("return false;");
                pr.println("}");


pr.println("// FOR EMAIL ");

    pr.println("if(window.document.f2.email.value.length)");
    pr.println("{     var Ename = document.f2.email.value = document.f2.email.value.toLowerCase();");
        pr.println("var sLength =  Ename.length;");

        pr.println("//Validate the login name");
        pr.println("if (isWhitespace(Ename))");
                pr.println("{");
                pr.println("alert (\"You can't leave this field blank\")");
    pr.println("window.document.f2.email.focus();");
```

```
pr.println("return false;");
pr.println("}");
pr.println("else if ( !isCharsInBag( Ename, \"abcdefghijklmnopqrstuvwxyz0123456789.-_@\"
))");
pr.println("{");
pr.println("alert( \"Email ID may only contain the following
characters:\\nabcdefghijklmnopqrstuvwxyz0123456789.-_@\" );");
pr.println("window.document.f2.email.focus();");
pr.println("return false;");
pr.println("}");
pr.println("else if ( !isCharsInBag( Ename.charAt(Ename.length - 1),
\"abcdefghijklmnopqrstuvwxyz0123456789\") )");
pr.println("{");
pr.println("alert( \"Email ID must end in an alphanumeric character.\");");
pr.println("window.document.f2.email.focus();");
pr.println("return false;");
pr.println("}");
pr.println("else if ( !isCharsInBag( Ename.charAt(0),
\"abcdefghijklmnopqrstuvwxyz0123456789\") )");
pr.println("{");
pr.println("alert( \"Email ID must start with an alphanumeric character.\");");
pr.println("window.document.f2.email.focus();");
pr.println("return false;");
pr.println("}");

pr.println("else if ( Ename.length < 3 )");
pr.println("{");
pr.println("alert( \"Email ID must be 3 or more characters.\" );");
pr.println("window.document.f2.email.focus();");
pr.println("return false;");
pr.println("}");
pr.println("// look for @");
pr.println("else if (Ename.indexOf(\"@\") == -1)");
pr.println("{");
pr.println("alert(\"Your Email ID must contain @ sign\") ");
pr.println("window.document.f2.email.focus();");

pr.println("return false;");
pr.println("}");
pr.println("// look for .");
pr.println("else if (Ename.indexOf(\".\") == -1)");
pr.println("{");
pr.println("alert(\"Your Email ID must contain . sign\")");
pr.println("window.document.f2.email.focus();");
```

```
        pr.println("return false;");
        pr.println("}");
    pr.println("// return true;");
        pr.println("}");


                        pr.println("////EMAIL");



                pr.println("if(window.document.f2.url.value.length==0 ||
window.document.f2.url.value==\"http://\"){");
                        pr.println("alert (\"Re enter your web url.\");");
                        pr.println("window.document.f2.url.focus();");
                        pr.println("return false;");
                        pr.println("}");


                pr.println("if(window.document.f2.caption.value.length==0){");
                        pr.println("alert (\"Re enter caption of your page.\");");
                        pr.println("window.document.f2.caption.focus();");
                        pr.println("return false;");
                        pr.println("}");

                pr.println("if(window.document.f2.description.value.length==0){");
                        pr.println("alert (\"Re enter description.\");");
                        pr.println("window.document.f2.description.focus();");
                        pr.println("return false;");
                        pr.println("}");

        pr.println("return true;");
        pr.println("}");


pr.println("</script>");


        pr.println("<tr>");
        pr.println("<td width=\"100%\" align=\"center\"><font color=\"#000080\" size=\"5\">Modify Your
Link</font></td>");
        pr.println("</tr>");
        pr.println("<tr>");
        pr.println("<td width=\"100%\" align=\"center\">");
```

```
pr.println("<table border=\"0\" width=\"95%\" cellpadding=\"0\" cellspacing=\"0\" bgcolor=\"#FFFFDB\">");
pr.println("<form name=\"f2\" method=\"post\" action=\"" + servletURL + "/search\" onsubmit=\"return validate1();\">");

pr.println("<input type=\"hidden\" name=\"updatemodified\" value=Y>");


  pr.println("<tr>");
    pr.println("<td width=\"5%\"> </td>");
    pr.println("<td width=\"39%\">   </td>");
    pr.println("<td width=\"89%\">   </td>");
  pr.println("</tr>");

  pr.println("<tr>");
    pr.println("<td width=\"5%\"> </td>");
    pr.println("<td width=\"39%\"><b>Address<font color=\"#FF0000\">*</font></b></td>");
    pr.println("<td width=\"89%\"><textarea rows=\"4\" name=\"address\" cols=\"22\" maxlength=200>" + s4 + "</textarea></td>");
  pr.println("</tr>");
  pr.println("<tr>");
    pr.println("<td width=\"5%\"> </td>");
    pr.println("<td width=\"39%\"><b>City<font color=\"#FF0000\">*</font></b></td>");
    pr.println("<td width=\"89%\"><input type=\"text\" name=\"city\" size=\"20\" maxlength=30 value=\"" + s5 + "\" ></td>");
  pr.println("</tr>");
  pr.println("<tr>");
    pr.println("<td width=\"5%\"> </td>");
    pr.println("<td width=\"39%\"><b>State<font color=\"#FF0000\">*</font></b></td>");
    pr.println("<td width=\"89%\"><input type=\"text\" name=\"state\" size=\"20\" maxlength=30 value=\"" + s6 + "\"></td>");
  pr.println("</tr>");
  pr.println("<tr>");
    pr.println("<td width=\"5%\"> </td>");
    pr.println("<td width=\"39%\"><b>Zip</b></td>");
    pr.println("<td width=\"89%\"><input type=\"text\" name=\"zip\" size=\"20\" maxlength=10 value=\"" + s7 + "\"></td>");
  pr.println("</tr>");
  pr.println("<tr>");
    pr.println("<td width=\"5%\"> </td>");
    pr.println("<td width=\"39%\"><b>Country<font color=\"#FF0000\">*</font></b></td>");
    pr.println("<td width=\"89%\"><input type=\"text\" name=\"country\" size=\"20\" maxlength=30 value=\"" + s8 + "\"></td>");
  pr.println("</tr>");
  pr.println("<tr>");
    pr.println("<td width=\"5%\"> </td>");
```

```
    pr.println("<td width=\"39%\"><b>Phone</b></td>");
    pr.println("<td width=\"89%\"><input type=\"text\" name=\"phone\" size=\"20\" maxlength=30 value=\"" + 
s9 + "\"></td>");
  pr.println("</tr>");
  pr.println("<tr>");
    pr.println("<td width=\"5%\"> </td>");
    pr.println("<td width=\"39%\"><b>E-mail<font color=\"#FF0000\">*</font></b></td>");
    pr.println("<td width=\"89%\"><input type=\"text\" name=\"email\" size=\"20\" maxlength=50 value=\"" + 
s10 + "\"></td>");
  pr.println("</tr>");
  pr.println("<tr>");
    pr.println("<td width=\"5%\"> </td>");
    pr.println("<td width=\"39%\"><b>URL<font color=\"#FF0000\">*</font></b></td>");
    pr.println("<td width=\"89%\"><input type=\"text\" name=\"url\" size=\"20\" value=\"" + s11 + "\" 
maxlength=100 > </td>");
  pr.println("</tr>");
  pr.println("<tr>");
    pr.println("<td width=\"5%\"> </td>");
    pr.println("<td width=\"39%\"><b>Caption<font color=\"#FF0000\">*</font></b></td>");
    pr.println("<td width=\"89%\"><input type=\"text\" name=\"caption\" size=\"20\" maxlength=100 
value=\"" + s13 + "\"> </td>");
  pr.println("</tr>");
  pr.println("<tr>");
    pr.println("<td width=\"5%\"> </td>");
    pr.println("<td width=\"39%\"><b>Description<font color=\"#FF0000\">*</font></b></td>");
    pr.println("<td width=\"89%\"><input type=\"text\" name=\"description\" size=\"35\" maxlength=\"200\" 
value=\"" + s14 + "\"> </td>");
  pr.println("</tr>");
  pr.println("<tr>");
    pr.println("<td width=\"5%\"> </td>");
    pr.println("<td width=\"39%\"><b>Add me to mailing list</b></td>");
    pr.println("<td width=\"89%\"><input type=\"checkbox\" name=\"mail\" value=\"Y\" checked> </td>");
  pr.println("</tr>");
  pr.println("<tr>");
    pr.println("<td width=\"5%\"> </td>");
    pr.println("<td width=\"39%\">  </td>");
    pr.println("<td width=\"89%\">   </td>");
  pr.println("</tr>");
  pr.println("<tr>");
    pr.println("<td width=\"133%\" colspan=\"3\" align=\"center\"><input type=\"submit\" value=\"Submit\" 
name=\"B1\"> ");
      pr.println("<input type=\"reset\" value=\"Reset\" name=\"B2\"></td>");
  pr.println("</tr>");
  pr.println("<tr>");
    pr.println("<td width=\"5%\"> </td>");
```

```
    pr.println("<td width=\"39%\"> </td>");
    pr.println("<td width=\"89%\">    </td>");
   pr.println("</tr>");
  pr.println("</table>");


}catch(Exception e){}



        }

        public void displayLoginForm(PrintWriter out){

       out.println("<tr>");
        out.println("<td width=\"100%\" align=\"center\">");
         out.println("<div align=\"center\">");
          out.println("<table border=\"0\" cellpadding=\"0\" cellspacing=\"0\" width=\"83%\"
bgcolor=\"#FFFFFF\" bordercolor=\"#C6FFFF\" height=\"1\">");
           out.println("<tr>");
            out.println("<td width=\"100%\" valign=\"top\" height=\"2\" bgcolor=\"#FFFFCC\">");
             out.println("<form method=\"POST\" action=\"" + servletURL + "/search\">");
              out.println("<input type=hidden name=validate value=1>");
              out.println("<p><br>");
              out.println("<font color=\"#800000\">  <font size=\"4\">Please login to modify your
listings.</font></font><br>");
              out.println("   <font
color=\"#FF0000\">Login: </font>       ");
              out.println("<input type=\"text\" name=\"login\" size=\"20\"><br>");
              out.println("   <font color=\"#FF0000\">Password: </font>");
              out.println("<input type=\"password\" name=\"password\" size=\"20\"></p>");

out.println("<p>             &n
bsp;       ");
              out.println("<input type=\"submit\" value=\"Submit\" name=\"B1\"></p>");
             out.println("</form>");
            out.println("</td>");
           out.println("</tr>");
          out.println("</table>");
         out.println("</div>");
        out.println("</td>");
       out.println("</tr>");

        }
```

```
public void updatenewEntry(PrintWriter out,String straddnew,String striunder,String
strilink,HttpServletRequest req){

    int serno;
    serno=1;

    try{

    String strregid = req.getParameter("regid");
        if(strregid==null) strregid="";
            else strregid = change(strregid);



    Statement theStatement;
    ResultSet theResultset;


    theStatement=theConnection.createStatement();
    theResultset=theStatement.executeQuery("select * from listings where login='" + strregid + "'");
        while(theResultset.next()){

    out.println("<tr>");
    out.println("<td width=\"100%\" align=\"center\"><font color=\"#FF0000\" size=\"5\">Registration ID
already exists! Please hit your browsers back button and select another Registration ID.</font></td>");
    out.println("</tr>");
    out.println("<tr>");
        return;

        }
    theResultset.close();
    theStatement.close();


    theStatement=theConnection.createStatement();
    theResultset=theStatement.executeQuery("select max(serno) from listings");
        while(theResultset.next()){
            serno=theResultset.getInt(1)+1;
        }
    theResultset.close();
    theStatement.close();

    String password = req.getParameter("pass1");
        if(password==null) password="";
            else password = change(password);
```

```
String address = req.getParameter("address");
        if(address==null) address="";
                else address = change(address);

String city= req.getParameter("city");
        if(city==null) city="";
                else city = change(city);


String state= req.getParameter("state");
        if(state==null) state="";
                else state= change(state);


String zip= req.getParameter("zip");
        if(zip==null) zip="";
                else zip= change(zip);

String country= req.getParameter("country");
        if(country==null) country="";
                else country= change(country);

String phone= req.getParameter("phone");
        if(phone==null) phone="";
                else phone= change(phone);

String email= req.getParameter("email");
String url= req.getParameter("url");
String category= req.getParameter("iunder");
String caption= req.getParameter("caption");
        if(caption==null) caption="";
                else caption= change(caption);
String description= req.getParameter("description");
        if(description==null) description="";
                else description= change(description);
String mail= req.getParameter("mail");


        String sql="insert into listings values('" + String.valueOf(serno) + "','" + strregid + "','" + password + "','"
+ address + "','" + city + "','" + state + "','" + zip + "','" + country + "','" + phone + "','"  + email + "','" + url + "','" +
category + "','" + caption + "','" + description + "','" + mail + "',now())";

theStatement=theConnection.createStatement();
theStatement.executeUpdate(sql);
theStatement.close();
```

```
        out.println("<tr>");
          out.println("<td width=\"100%\" align=\"center\"><font color=\"#000080\" size=\"5\">Thank you for
adding your link.</font></td>");
        out.println("</tr>");
        out.println("<tr>");


          }
          catch(Exception e){
        out.println("<tr>");
          out.println("<td width=\"100%\" align=\"center\"><font color=\"#FF0000\" size=\"5\">" +
e.getMessage() + "</font></td>");
        out.println("</tr>");
        out.println("<tr>");


          }

                //out.println("Adding new Entry");


          }


 public String change(String  str){

           String st;
           st="";

   StringTokenizer t=new StringTokenizer(str,"'");
   if(str==null)
          {
                  st="";
          }
          else
          {
           int i =t.countTokens();
           while(t.hasMoreTokens()){
                  if(st.compareTo("")==0)
                  st=t.nextToken();
                  else
                          st=st + "\\'" + t.nextToken();

           }
          }
```

```
 return st;
 }


        //Displays the form, which allows to add new entry.

        public void addListings(PrintWriter pr,String strUnder,String strLink){

       pr.println("<script language=javascript>");

pr.println("function validate1(){");
              pr.println("if(window.document.f2.regid.value.length==0){");
                     pr.println("alert (\"Please enter a login.\");");
                     pr.println("window.document.f2.regid.focus();");
                     pr.println("return false;");
                     pr.println("}");

              pr.println("if(window.document.f2.pass1.value.length==0){");
                     pr.println("alert (\"Please enter your password.\");");
                     pr.println("window.document.f2.pass1.focus();");
                     pr.println("return false;");
                     pr.println("}");

              pr.println("if(window.document.f2.pass2.value.length==0){");
                     pr.println("alert (\"Re enter your password.\");");
                     pr.println("window.document.f2.pass2.focus();");
                     pr.println("return false;");
                     pr.println("}");


              pr.println("if(window.document.f2.pass2.value != window.document.f2.pass1.value){");
                     pr.println("alert (\"Password does not match. Re-enter password!\");");
                     pr.println("window.document.f2.pass1.focus();");
                     pr.println("return false;");
                     pr.println("}");

              pr.println("if(window.document.f2.address.value.length==0){");
                     pr.println("alert (\"Re enter your address.\");");
                     pr.println("window.document.f2.address.focus();");
                     pr.println("return false;");
                     pr.println("}");


              pr.println("if(window.document.f2.city.value.length==0){");
                     pr.println("alert (\"Re enter your city.\");");
```

```
                pr.println("window.document.f2.city.focus();");
                pr.println("return false;");
                pr.println("}");

        pr.println("if(window.document.f2.state.value.length==0){");
                pr.println("alert (\"Re enter your state.\");");
                pr.println("window.document.f2.state.focus();");
                pr.println("return false;");
                pr.println("}");

        pr.println("if(window.document.f2.country.value.length==0){");
                pr.println("alert (\"Re enter your country.\");");
                pr.println("window.document.f2.country.focus();");
                pr.println("return false;");
      pr.println("}");

        pr.println("if(window.document.f2.email.value.length==0){");
                pr.println("alert (\"Re enter your email.\");");
                pr.println("window.document.f2.email.focus();");
                pr.println("return false;");
                pr.println("}");


pr.println("// FOR EMAIL ");

    pr.println("if(window.document.f2.email.value.length)");
    pr.println("{     var Ename = document.f2.email.value = document.f2.email.value.toLowerCase();");
        pr.println("var sLength =  Ename.length;");

        pr.println("//Validate the login name");
        pr.println("if (isWhitespace(Ename))");
            pr.println("{");
            pr.println("alert (\"You can't leave this field blank\")");
     pr.println("window.document.f2.email.focus();");
            pr.println("return false;");
            pr.println("}");
        pr.println("else if ( !isCharsInBag( Ename, \"abcdefghijklmnopqrstuvwxyz0123456789.-_@\"
))");
        pr.println("{");
        pr.println("alert( \"Email ID may only contain the following
characters:\\nabcdefghijklmnopqrstuvwxyz0123456789.-_@\" );");
        pr.println("window.document.f2.email.focus();");
        pr.println("return false;");
     pr.println("}");
```

```
pr.println("else if ( !isCharsInBag( Ename.charAt(Ename.length - 1),
\"abcdefghijklmnopqrstuvwxyz0123456789\") )");
pr.println("{");
pr.println("alert( \"Email ID must end in an alphanumeric character.\");");
pr.println("window.document.f2.email.focus();");
pr.println("return false;");
pr.println("}");
pr.println("else if ( !isCharsInBag( Ename.charAt(0),
\"abcdefghijklmnopqrstuvwxyz0123456789\") )");
pr.println("{");
pr.println("alert( \"Email ID must start with an alphanumeric character.\");");
pr.println("window.document.f2.email.focus();");
pr.println("return false;");
pr.println("}");

pr.println("else if ( Ename.length < 3 )");
pr.println("{");
pr.println("alert( \"Email ID must be 3 or more characters.\" );");
pr.println("window.document.f2.email.focus();");
pr.println("return false;");
pr.println("}");
pr.println("// look for @");
pr.println("else if (Ename.indexOf(\"@\") == -1)");
pr.println("{");
pr.println("alert(\"Your Email ID must contain @ sign\") ");
pr.println("window.document.f2.email.focus();");

pr.println("return false;");
pr.println("}");
pr.println("// look for .");
pr.println("else if (Ename.indexOf(\".\") == -1)");
pr.println("{");
pr.println("alert(\"Your Email ID must contain . sign\")");
pr.println("window.document.f2.email.focus();");

pr.println("return false;");
pr.println("}");
pr.println("// return true;");
pr.println("}");


pr.println("////EMAIL");
```

```
            pr.println("if(window.document.f2.url.value.length==0 ||
window.document.f2.url.value==\"http://\"){");
                    pr.println("alert (\"Re enter your web url.\");");
                    pr.println("window.document.f2.url.focus();");
                    pr.println("return false;");
                    pr.println("}");


            pr.println("if(window.document.f2.caption.value.length==0){");
                    pr.println("alert (\"Re enter caption of your page.\");");
                    pr.println("window.document.f2.caption.focus();");
                    pr.println("return false;");
                    pr.println("}");

            pr.println("if(window.document.f2.description.value.length==0){");
                    pr.println("alert (\"Re enter description.\");");
                    pr.println("window.document.f2.description.focus();");
                    pr.println("return false;");
                    pr.println("}");

        pr.println("return true;");
        pr.println("}");


pr.println("</script>");


        pr.println("<tr>");
         pr.println("<td width=\"100%\" align=\"center\"><font color=\"#000080\" size=\"5\">Place Your
Link</font></td>");
        pr.println("</tr>");
        pr.println("<tr>");
         pr.println("<td width=\"100%\" align=\"center\">");


 pr.println("<table border=\"0\" width=\"95%\" cellpadding=\"0\" cellspacing=\"0\" bgcolor=\"#FFFFDB\">");
 pr.println("<form name=\"f2\" method=\"post\" action=\"" + servletURL + "/search\" onsubmit=\"return
validate1();\">");

 pr.println("<input type=\"hidden\" name=\"addnew\" value=Y>");
 pr.println("<input type=\"hidden\" name=\"iunder\" value=" + strUnder + ">");
 pr.println("<input type=\"hidden\" name=\"ilink\" value=" + strLink + ">");
```

```
pr.println("<tr>");
 pr.println("<td width=\"5%\"> </td>");
 pr.println("<td width=\"39%\">   </td>");
 pr.println("<td width=\"89%\">   </td>");
pr.println("</tr>");
pr.println("<tr>");
 pr.println("<td width=\"5%\"> </td>");
 pr.println("<td width=\"39%\"><b>Select Registration ID<font color=\"#FF0000\">*</font></b></td>");
 pr.println("<td width=\"89%\"><input type=\"text\" name=\"regid\" size=\"20\" maxlength=15></td>");
pr.println("</tr>");
pr.println("<tr>");
 pr.println("<td width=\"5%\"> </td>");
 pr.println("<td width=\"39%\"><b>Enter Password<font color=\"#FF0000\">*</font></b></td>");
 pr.println("<td width=\"89%\"><input type=\"password\" name=\"pass1\" size=\"20\"
maxlength=15></td>");
pr.println("</tr>");
pr.println("<tr>");
 pr.println("<td width=\"5%\"> </td>");
 pr.println("<td width=\"39%\"><b>Re -Enter Password<font color=\"#FF0000\">*</font></b></td>");
 pr.println("<td width=\"89%\"><input type=\"password\" name=\"pass2\" size=\"20\"
maxlength=15></td>");
pr.println("</tr>");
pr.println("<tr>");
 pr.println("<td width=\"5%\"> </td>");
 pr.println("<td width=\"39%\"><b>Address<font color=\"#FF0000\">*</font></b></td>");
 pr.println("<td width=\"89%\"><textarea rows=\"4\" name=\"address\" cols=\"22\"
maxlength=200></textarea></td>");
pr.println("</tr>");
pr.println("<tr>");
 pr.println("<td width=\"5%\"> </td>");
 pr.println("<td width=\"39%\"><b>City<font color=\"#FF0000\">*</font></b></td>");
 pr.println("<td width=\"89%\"><input type=\"text\" name=\"city\" size=\"20\" maxlength=30></td>");
pr.println("</tr>");
pr.println("<tr>");
 pr.println("<td width=\"5%\"> </td>");
 pr.println("<td width=\"39%\"><b>State<font color=\"#FF0000\">*</font></b></td>");
 pr.println("<td width=\"89%\"><input type=\"text\" name=\"state\" size=\"20\" maxlength=30></td>");
pr.println("</tr>");
pr.println("<tr>");
 pr.println("<td width=\"5%\"> </td>");
 pr.println("<td width=\"39%\"><b>Zip</b></td>");
 pr.println("<td width=\"89%\"><input type=\"text\" name=\"zip\" size=\"20\" maxlength=10></td>");
pr.println("</tr>");
pr.println("<tr>");
 pr.println("<td width=\"5%\"> </td>");
```

```
    pr.println("<td width=\"39%\"><b>Country<font color=\"#FF0000\">*</font></b></td>");
    pr.println("<td width=\"89%\"><input type=\"text\" name=\"country\" size=\"20\" maxlength=30></td>");
   pr.println("</tr>");
   pr.println("<tr>");
    pr.println("<td width=\"5%\"> </td>");
    pr.println("<td width=\"39%\"><b>Phone</b></td>");
    pr.println("<td width=\"89%\"><input type=\"text\" name=\"phone\" size=\"20\" maxlength=30></td>");
   pr.println("</tr>");
   pr.println("<tr>");
    pr.println("<td width=\"5%\"> </td>");
    pr.println("<td width=\"39%\"><b>E-mail<font color=\"#FF0000\">*</font></b></td>");
    pr.println("<td width=\"89%\"><input type=\"text\" name=\"email\" size=\"20\" maxlength=50></td>");
   pr.println("</tr>");
   pr.println("<tr>");
    pr.println("<td width=\"5%\"> </td>");
    pr.println("<td width=\"39%\"><b>URL<font color=\"#FF0000\">*</font></b></td>");
    pr.println("<td width=\"89%\"><input type=\"text\" name=\"url\" size=\"20\" value=\"http://\"
maxlength=100> </td>");
   pr.println("</tr>");
   pr.println("<tr>");
    pr.println("<td width=\"5%\"> </td>");
    pr.println("<td width=\"39%\"><b>Caption<font color=\"#FF0000\">*</font></b></td>");
    pr.println("<td width=\"89%\"><input type=\"text\" name=\"caption\" size=\"20\" maxlength=100>
</td>");
   pr.println("</tr>");
   pr.println("<tr>");
    pr.println("<td width=\"5%\"> </td>");
    pr.println("<td width=\"39%\"><b>Description<font color=\"#FF0000\">*</font></b></td>");
    pr.println("<td width=\"89%\"><input type=\"text\" name=\"description\" size=\"35\" maxlength=\"200\">
</td>");
   pr.println("</tr>");
   pr.println("<tr>");
    pr.println("<td width=\"5%\"> </td>");
    pr.println("<td width=\"39%\"><b>Add me to mailing list</b></td>");
    pr.println("<td width=\"89%\"><input type=\"checkbox\" name=\"mail\" value=\"Y\" checked> </td>");
   pr.println("</tr>");
   pr.println("<tr>");
    pr.println("<td width=\"5%\"> </td>");
    pr.println("<td width=\"39%\">  </td>");
    pr.println("<td width=\"89%\">   </td>");
   pr.println("</tr>");
   pr.println("<tr>");
    pr.println("<td width=\"133%\" colspan=\"3\" align=\"center\"><input type=\"submit\" value=\"Submit\"
name=\"B1\"> ");
     pr.println("<input type=\"reset\" value=\"Reset\" name=\"B2\"></td>");
```

```
pr.println("</tr>");
pr.println("<tr>");
  pr.println("<td width=\"5%\"> </td>");
  pr.println("<td width=\"39%\"> </td>");
  pr.println("<td width=\"89%\">    </td>");
pr.println("</tr>");
pr.println("</table>");


        }//end of addListings


        public void displayFinalResult(PrintWriter pr,String strserno){

                Statement theStatement;
                ResultSet theResult;
        pr.println("<tr>");
         pr.println("<td width=\"100%\" align=\"center\"><font color=\"#000080\" size=\"5\">Search
results:</font></td>");
        pr.println("</tr>");


                String sql;
                sql="select * from listings where serno=" + strserno;

                try{
                if(theConnection == null) makeConnection();

                theStatement=theConnection.createStatement();
            theResult=theStatement.executeQuery(sql);


        pr.println("<tr>");
         pr.println("<td width=\"100%\" align=\"center\">");
          pr.println("<b>");
          pr.println("This Page Will Show You The Final Hit.</font>");
          pr.println("</b>");
         pr.println("</td>");
                 pr.println("</tr>");

                while(theResult.next()) //Fetch all the records
                {
         pr.println("<td width=\"100%\" align=\"center\">");
          pr.println("<div align=\"center\">");
```

```
            pr.println("<table border=\"2\" cellpadding=\"0\" cellspacing=\"1\" width=\"91%\"
bgcolor=\"#FFFFFF\" bordercolor=\"#C6FFFF\" height=\"1\">");
              pr.println("<tr>");
               pr.println("<td width=\"100%\" valign=\"top\" height=\"1\" bgcolor=\"#000066\"
align=\"center\"><font size=\"4\" color=\"#FFFFFF\">" + theResult.getString(13) + "</font></td>");
              pr.println("</tr>");
              pr.println("<tr>");
               pr.println("<td width=\"100%\" valign=\"top\" height=\"1\" bgcolor=\"#FFFFF0\"><b><font
color=\"#000080\">Description:<br>");
                pr.println("</font></b>&quot;" + theResult.getString(14) + "&quot;<br>");
                pr.println("  <br>");
                pr.println("<font color=\"#000080\"><b>Contact</b></font><font color=\"#000080\"><b>");
                pr.println("Address:<br>");
                pr.println("</b></font><font face=\"Arial\" size=\"2\">" + theResult.getString(4) + "<br>");
                pr.println(theResult.getString(5) + "<br>");
                pr.println(theResult.getString(6) + "<br>");
                pr.println(theResult.getString(7) + "<br>");
                pr.println(theResult.getString(8) + "<br>");
                pr.println(" <br>");
                pr.println("<font color=\"#008000\">Tel: </font> " + theResult.getString(9) + "<br>");

                                                String em;
                                                em=theResult.getString(10);

               pr.println("<font color=\"#008000\">Email:</font> <a href=\"mailto:" + em + "\">" + em +
"<br>");
               pr.println("</a><font color=\"#008000\">Web: </font><a href=\"" + theResult.getString(11) +
"\">Visit at our web site.</a> <br>");
              pr.println("   </font></td>");
             pr.println("</tr>");
            pr.println("</table>");
           pr.println("</div>");
          pr.println("</td>");
         pr.println("</tr>");
               }

        theResult.close();//Close the result set
        theStatement.close();//Close statement
               }catch (Exception e){
                      pr.println(e.getMessage());
               }


       }
```

```
//displays add links
public void displayListings(PrintWriter pr,String strCategory){


        Statement theStatement;
        ResultSet theResult;
    pr.println("<tr>");
     pr.println("<td width=\"100%\" align=\"center\"><font color=\"#000080\" size=\"5\">Search
results:</font></td>");
    pr.println("</tr>");
    pr.println("<tr>");
     pr.println("<td width=\"100%\" align=\"center\">");
      pr.println("<div align=\"center\">");
       pr.println("<table border=\"1\" cellpadding=\"0\" cellspacing=\"0\" width=\"91%\"
bgcolor=\"#FFFFFF\" bordercolor=\"#C6FFFF\">");


        String sql;
        sql="select serno,caption,descp from listings where category=" + strCategory;

        try{
        if(theConnection == null) makeConnection();

        theStatement=theConnection.createStatement();
      theResult=theStatement.executeQuery(sql);

        int i;
        i=0;

//      i=theResult.getFetchSize();


    pr.println("<tr>");
     pr.println("<td width=\"100%\" align=\"center\">");
      pr.println("<b>");
      pr.println("This Page Will Show You The Final Hit.</font>");
      pr.println("</b>");
     pr.println("</td>");


    pr.println("<tr>");
     pr.println("<td width=\"100%\" align=\"center\">");
      pr.println("<div align=\"center\">");
       pr.println("<table border=\"0\" cellpadding=\"0\" cellspacing=\"0\" width=\"91%\"
bgcolor=\"#FFFFFF\" bordercolor=\"#C6FFFF\" height=\"1\">");
```

```
            while(theResult.next()) //Fetch all the records
            {
                        i++;
        pr.println("<tr>");
         pr.println("<td width=\"5%\" valign=\"top\" height=\"1\" bgcolor=\"#FFFFCC\">" +
String.valueOf(i) + "</td>");
         pr.println("<td width=\"95%\" valign=\"top\" height=\"1\" bgcolor=\"#FFFFCC\"><a href=\"" +
servletURL + "/search?serno=" + theResult.getString(1) + "\"><font color=\"#CC3300\" size=\"3\">" +
theResult.getString(2) + "</font></a></td>");
        pr.println("</tr>");
        pr.println("<tr>");
         pr.println("<td width=\"5%\" valign=\"top\" height=\"1\" bgcolor=\"#FFFFF0\"><font
color=\"#CC3300\" size=\"4\"> </font></td>");
         pr.println("<td width=\"95%\" valign=\"top\" height=\"1\" bgcolor=\"#FFFFF0\"><font
color=\"#000080\" size=\"2\">" + theResult.getString(3) + "</font></td>");
        pr.println("</tr>");
            }


        pr.println("<tr>");
         pr.println("<td colspan=2 bgcolor=\"#FFFFF0\"><font color=\"#CC3300\" size=\"4\"><a href=\"" +
servletURL + "/search?under=" + strCategory + "\">Add Link</a></font></td>");
        pr.println("</tr>");

                        pr.println("</table>");
      pr.println("</div>");
     pr.println("</td>");
    pr.println("</tr>");


    theResult.close();//Close the result set
    theStatement.close();//Close statement
            }catch (Exception e){
                        pr.println(e.getMessage());
            }


    }//end of displayListings


    public void displayCategories(PrintWriter pr,String strSection){

            Statement theStatement;
            ResultSet theResult;
```

```
pr.println("<tr>");
  pr.println("<td width=\"100%\" align=\"center\"><font color=\"#000080\"
size=\"5\">Categories</font></td>");
pr.println("</tr>");
pr.println("<tr>");
  pr.println("<td width=\"100%\" align=\"center\">");
    pr.println("<div align=\"center\">");
      pr.println("<table border=\"1\" cellpadding=\"0\" cellspacing=\"0\" width=\"91%\"
bgcolor=\"#FFFFFF\" bordercolor=\"#C6FFFF\">");


            String sql;
            sql="select serno,description from categories where section_code=" + strSection;

            try{
            if(theConnection == null) makeConnection();

            theStatement=theConnection.createStatement();
        theResult=theStatement.executeQuery(sql);
            while(theResult.next()) //Fetch all the records
            {

        pr.println("<tr>");
          pr.println("<td width=\"7%\" valign=\"top\" height=\"1\"><font face=\"arial\"
size=\"3\"><b><small><img border=\"0\" src=\"" + image + "\" width=\"24\"
height=\"24\"></small></b></font></td>");
          pr.println("<td width=\"42%\" valign=\"top\" height=\"1\"><font face=\"arial\" size=\"3\"><a
href=\"" + servletURL + "/search?category=" + String.valueOf(theResult.getInt(1)) + "\">" +
theResult.getString(2)+ "</a></font></td>");

                        if(theResult.next()){


          pr.println("<td width=\"7%\" valign=\"top\" height=\"1\"><font face=\"arial\"
size=\"3\"><b><small><img border=\"0\" src=\""+ image +"\" width=\"24\"
height=\"24\"></small></b></font></td>");
          pr.println("<td width=\"44%\" valign=\"top\" height=\"1\"><font face=\"arial\" size=\"3\"><a
href=\"" + servletURL + "/search?category=" + theResult.getString(1) + "\">" + theResult.getString(2)+
"</a></font></td>");
                    }else{
          pr.println("<td width=\"7%\" valign=\"top\" height=\"1\"> </td>");
          pr.println("<td width=\"44%\" valign=\"top\" height=\"1\"> </td>");

                    }
```

```
            pr.println("</tr>");

                }
        theResult.close();//Close the result set
        theStatement.close();//Close statement
                }catch (Exception e){
                        pr.println(e.getMessage());
                }

        }

        public void displaySections(PrintWriter pr){

                Statement theStatement;
                ResultSet theResult;

        pr.println("<tr>");
          pr.println("<td width=\"100%\" align=\"center\"><font color=\"#000080\"
size=\"5\">Sections</font></td>");
        pr.println("</tr>");
        pr.println("<tr>");
          pr.println("<td width=\"100%\" align=\"center\">");
            pr.println("<div align=\"center\">");
              pr.println("<table border=\"1\" cellpadding=\"0\" cellspacing=\"0\" width=\"91%\"
bgcolor=\"#FFFFFF\" bordercolor=\"#C6FFFF\">");

                String sql;
                sql="select * from section";
                try{
                if(theConnection == null) makeConnection();

                theStatement=theConnection.createStatement();
            theResult=theStatement.executeQuery(sql);
                while(theResult.next()) //Fetch all the records
                {
            pr.println("<tr>");
              pr.println("<td width=\"50%\" valign=\"top\"><small><font face=\"arial\" size=\"3\"><a href=\"" +
servletURL + "/search?section=" + theResult.getString(1) + "\"><b>" + theResult.getString(2) +
"</b></a></font></small><font face=\"arial\" size=\"2\"><br>");
                pr.println(theResult.getString(3) + "</font></td>");
                                if(theResult.next()){
                        pr.println("<td width=\"50%\" valign=\"top\"><small><font face=\"arial\"
size=\"3\"><a href=\"" + servletURL + "/search?section=" + theResult.getString(1) + "\"><b>" +
theResult.getString(2) + "</b></a></font></small><font face=\"arial\" size=\"2\"><br>");
                pr.println(theResult.getString(3) + "</font></td>");
```

```
                        }
                        else pr.println("<td width=\"50%\" valign=\"top\"> </td>");
        pr.println("</tr>");

                }
        theResult.close();//Close the result set
        theStatement.close();//Close statement
                }catch (Exception e){
                        pr.println(e.getMessage());
                }
        }

        public void writeHead(PrintWriter pr){


pr.println("<html>");

pr.println("<head>");
pr.println("<title>Welcome to Java Developers paradise!</title>");
pr.println("<meta content=\"Welcome to Java Developers paradise! We are totally devoted to Java server side ,
servlets, JSP, JDBC, EJB, XML,MySql\"name=\"description\">");
pr.println("<meta content=\"JAVA, JSP, Servlets, Servlet, Search Engine, Directory, Jserv, Apache, JDBC, EJB,
programming, developer, news, intranet, internet, Web, http, cgi alternatives, jdbc servlets, links,
help\"name=\"keywords\">");

pr.println("<script language=javascript>");


pr.println("var whitespace=\"/t/n/r\"");

pr.println("function isEmpty(s)");
        pr.println("{ return ");
        pr.println("((s == null) || (s.length == 0))");
        pr.println("}");

        pr.println("function isWhitespace (s)");
        pr.println("{ var i;");
        pr.println(" // Is s empty?");
         pr.println("if (isEmpty(s)) ");
         pr.println("return true;");

         pr.println("// Search through string's characters one by one");
         pr.println("// until we find a non-whitespace character.");
        pr.println(" // When we do, return false; if we don't, return true.");
         pr.println("for (i = 0; i < s.length; i++)");
```

```
pr.println("{  ");
  pr.println("// Check that current character isn't whitespace.");
  pr.println("var c = s.charAt(i);");

  pr.println("if (whitespace.indexOf(c) == -1)");
  pr.println("return false;");
pr.println("}");

pr.println("// All characters are whitespace.");
pr.println(" return true;");
pr.println("}");

pr.println("function isCharsInBag (s, bag)");
pr.println("{  ");
 pr.println("var i;");
 pr.println("// Search through string's characters one by one.");
 pr.println("// If character is in bag, append to returnString.");

 pr.println("for (i = 0; i < s.length; i++)");
 pr.println("{  ");
   pr.println("// Check that current character isn't whitespace.");
   pr.println("var c = s.charAt(i);");
   pr.println("if (bag.indexOf(c) == -1) return false;");
 pr.println("}");
 pr.println("return true;");
pr.println("}");


pr.println("function validate(){");

pr.println("if(window.document.f1.name.value.length==0){");
        pr.println("alert(\"Please enter your name\");");
        pr.println("window.document.f1.name.focus();");
        pr.println("return false;");
        pr.println("}");
pr.println("if(window.document.f1.email.value.length==0){");
        pr.println("alert(\"Please enter your email\");");
        pr.println("window.document.f1.email.focus();");
        pr.println("return false;");
        pr.println("}");

pr.println("//  FOR EMAIL ");

        pr.println("if(window.document.f1.email.value.length)");
        pr.println("{     var Ename = document.f1.email.value = document.f1.email.value.toLowerCase();");
```

```
pr.println("var sLength =  Ename.length;");

pr.println("//Validate the login name");
pr.println("if (isWhitespace(Ename))");
        pr.println("{");
        pr.println("alert (\"You can't leave this field blank\")");
pr.println("window.document.f1.email.focus();");
        pr.println("return false;");
        pr.println("}");
pr.println("else if ( !isCharsInBag( Ename, \"abcdefghijklmnopqrstuvwxyz0123456789.-_@\"
))");
pr.println("{");
pr.println("alert( \"Email ID may only contain the following
characters:\\nabcdefghijklmnopqrstuvwxyz0123456789.-_@\" );");
pr.println("window.document.f1.email.focus();");
pr.println("return false;");
pr.println("}");
pr.println("else if ( !isCharsInBag( Ename.charAt(Ename.length - 1),
\"abcdefghijklmnopqrstuvwxyz0123456789\") )");
pr.println("{");
pr.println("alert( \"Email ID must end in an alphanumeric character.\");");
pr.println("window.document.f1.email.focus();");
pr.println("return false;");
pr.println("}");
pr.println("else if ( !isCharsInBag( Ename.charAt(0),
\"abcdefghijklmnopqrstuvwxyz0123456789\") )");
pr.println("{");
pr.println("alert( \"Email ID must start with an alphanumeric character.\");");
pr.println("window.document.f1.email.focus();");
pr.println("return false;");
pr.println("}");

pr.println("else if ( Ename.length < 3 )");
pr.println("{");
pr.println("alert( \"Email ID must be 3 or more characters.\" );");
pr.println("window.document.f1.email.focus();");
pr.println("return false;");
pr.println("}");
pr.println("// look for @");
pr.println("else if (Ename.indexOf(\"@\") == -1)");
pr.println("{");
pr.println("alert(\"Your Email ID must contain @ sign\") ");
pr.println(" window.document.f1.email.focus();");

pr.println("return false;");
```

```
pr.println("}");
pr.println("// look for .");
pr.println("else if (Ename.indexOf(\".\") == -1)");
pr.println("{");
pr.println("alert(\"Your Email ID must contain . sign\")");
pr.println("window.document.f1.email.focus();");

pr.println("return false;");
pr.println("}");
pr.println("// return true;");
pr.println("}");

pr.println("return true;");
pr.println("}");

pr.println("</script>");

pr.println("</head>");

pr.println("<body bgcolor=\"#c6ffff\">");


pr.println("<div align=\"center\">");
pr.println("<center>");
pr.println("<table border=\"0\" cellpadding=\"0\" cellspacing=\"0\" width=\"99%\">");
pr.println("<tr>");
pr.println("<td width=\"100%\" colspan=\"2\" bgcolor=\"#FFCCFF\"><a
href=http://www.roseindia.net><img border=\"0\" src=\"http://www.roseindia.net/images/paradise.gif\"
width=\"420\" height=\"60\" alt=\"Welcome to Java Developers Paradise\"></a>");

pr.println("</td>");
pr.println("</tr>");
pr.println("<tr>");
pr.println("<td width=\"23%\" valign=\"top\">");
pr.println("<div align=\"center\">");
pr.println("<table border=\"1\" cellpadding=\"0\" cellspacing=\"0\" width=\"99%\"
bordercolor=\"#FFFF00\">");
pr.println("<tr>");
pr.println("<td width=\"100%\" bgcolor=\"#FFFFFF\">");
pr.println("<p align=\"center\"><font color=\"#000080\" size=\"3\">Features</font></td>");
pr.println("</tr>");
pr.println("<tr>");
pr.println("<td width=\"100%\">");
pr.println("<p align=\"center\"><font color=\"#FF0000\" face=\"Times New Roman\" size=\"4\">Have
tutorials?</font><font size=\"1\"><br>            </font><a
```

```
href=\"http://www.roseindia.net/subscription/addsite.htm\"><font size=\"2\">Add your tutorial to our Java
Resource and get tons of hits.</font></a><font size=\"2\"><br>We offer <b>free hosting</b> for your tutorials.
and exposure for thousands of readers. drop a mail</font><font face=\"MS Sans serif\" size=\"-2\"><a
href=\"mailto:deepak@roseindia.net\"><font
color=\"maroon\"><br>deepak@roseindia.net<br></font></a>   ");
            pr.println(" </font></td>");
          pr.println("</tr>");
          pr.println("<tr>");
           pr.println("<td width=\"100%\" align=\"center\" bgcolor=\"#FFFFFF\">");
            pr.println("<font color=\"#000080\" size=\"3\">Search Options</font></td>");
          pr.println("</tr>");
          pr.println("<tr>");
           pr.println("<td width=\"100%\" align=\"center\">");
            pr.println("<form method=\"POST\" action=\"" + servletURL + "/search\">");

              pr.println("<p><input type=\"text\" name=\"item\" size=\"20\"><br>");
              pr.println("<input type=\"submit\" value=\"Search\" name=\"B1\"></p>");
            pr.println("</form>");
           pr.println("</td>");
          pr.println("</tr>");
          pr.println("<tr>");
           pr.println("<td width=\"100%\" align=\"center\" bgcolor=\"#FFFFFF\">");
            pr.println("<p align=\"center\"><font color=\"#000080\" size=\"3\">Link Options</font></td>");
          pr.println("</tr>");
          pr.println("<tr>");
           pr.println("<td width=\"100%\" align=\"center\">");
            pr.println("<font color=\"#000080\" size=\"2\"><a href=\"" + servletURL +
"/search?placelinks=y\">Place Links</a></font></td>");
          pr.println("</tr>");
          pr.println("<tr>");
           pr.println("<td width=\"100%\" align=\"center\">");
            pr.println("<font color=\"#000080\" size=\"2\"><a href=\"" + servletURL +
"/search?modifylink=y\">Modify Links</a></font></td>");
          pr.println("</tr>");

          pr.println("<tr>");
           pr.println("<td width=\"100%\" bgcolor=\"#FFCCFF\" align=\"center\">");
            pr.println("<p align=\"center\"><a href=\"http://www.roseindia.net/jsp/jsp.htm\" style=\"color:
#800000\"><font face=\"Times New Roman\" color=\"#800000\" size=\"2\">Java Server Pages</font></a>");
           pr.println("</td>");
          pr.println("</tr>");
          pr.println("<tr>");
           pr.println("<td width=\"100%\" bgcolor=\"#FFCCFF\" align=\"center\">");
```

```
pr.println("<p align=\"center\"><a style=\"color: #800000\"
href=\"http://www.roseindia.net/rmi/rmi.htm\"><font face=\"Times New Roman\" color=\"#800000\"
size=\"2\">RMI</font></a>");
pr.println("</p>");
pr.println("</td>");
pr.println("</tr>");
pr.println("<tr>");
pr.println("<td width=\"100%\" bgcolor=\"#FFCCFF\" align=\"center\">");

pr.println("<p align=\"center\"><a style=\"color: #800000\"
href=\"http://www.roseindia.net/javabeans/javabeans.htm\"><font face=\"Times New Roman\"
color=\"#800000\" size=\"2\">Java Beans</font></a>");

pr.println("</td>");
pr.println("</tr>");
pr.println("<tr>");
pr.println("<td width=\"100%\" bgcolor=\"#FFCCFF\" align=\"center\">");
pr.println("<p align=\"center\"><a style=\"color: #800000\"
href=\"http://www.roseindia.net/jdbc/jdbc.htm\"><font face=\"Times New Roman\" color=\"#800000\"
size=\"2\">JDBC</font></a>");
pr.println("</p>");
pr.println("</td>");
pr.println("</tr>");
pr.println("<tr>");
pr.println("<td width=\"100%\" bgcolor=\"#FFCCFF\" align=\"center\">");
pr.println("<p align=\"center\"><a style=\"color: #800000\"
href=\"http://www.roseindia.net/mysql/mysql.htm\"><font face=\"Times New Roman\" color=\"#800000\"
size=\"2\">MySQL</font></a>");
pr.println("</p>");
pr.println("</td>");
pr.println("</tr>");
pr.println("<tr>");
pr.println("<td width=\"100%\" bgcolor=\"#FFCCFF\" align=\"center\">");
pr.println("<p align=\"center\"><a style=\"color: #800000\"
href=\"http://www.roseindia.net/servlets/servlets.htm\"><font face=\"Times New Roman\" color=\"#800000\"
size=\"2\">Java Servlets</font></a>");
pr.println("</td>");
pr.println("</tr>");
pr.println("<tr>");
pr.println("<td width=\"100%\" bgcolor=\"#FFCCFF\" align=\"center\">");
pr.println("<p align=\"center\"><a style=\"color: #800000\" href=\"" + servletURL + "/search\"><font
face=\"Times New Roman\" color=\"#800000\" size=\"2\">Home</font></a></td>");
pr.println("</tr>");
pr.println("<tr>");
pr.println("<td width=\"100%\">");
```

```
        pr.println("<form name=\"f1\" method=\"post\"
action=\"http://www.roseindia.net/subscription/subscribe.php3\" onsubmit=\"return validate()\">");
       pr.println("<P align=center><font color=\"#FF0000\" size=\"3\">Join Now For Free</font><FONT size=4
color=\"#000080\"></FONT><font color=\"#800000\"> <font size=\"2\"> Weekly newsletter about latest in
java. <br>");
       pr.println("Your Name</font> <input type=\"text\" name=\"name\" size=\"20\"><br>");
       pr.println("<font size=\"2\">Your E-mail <br></font></font><INPUT id=text2 size=13
name=email><br><INPUT align=absMiddle alt=Join border=0 name=I2
src=\"http://www.roseindia.net/images/blue_submit.gif\" type=image value=Join width=\"94\" height=\"26\"
></P>");
    pr.println("</form>");

        pr.println("</td>");
       pr.println("</tr>");
      pr.println("</table>");
    pr.println("</div>");
   pr.println("</td>");
   pr.println("<td width=\"77%\" valign=\"top\">");
    pr.println("<div align=\"center\">");
      pr.println("<center>");
      pr.println("<table border=\"0\" width=\"100%\" cellpadding=\"0\" cellspacing=\"0\">");
       pr.println("<tr>");
        pr.println("<td width=\"100%\" bgcolor=\"#FFFFFF\"><font size=\"3\"><a
href=\"http://www.roseindia.net/sourcecode/searchengine\">Download</a> the source code of java search
engine.</font></td>");
       pr.println("</tr>");
       pr.println("<tr>");
        pr.println("<td width=\"100%\">   </td>");
       pr.println("</tr>");

        }

public void writeBottom(PrintWriter pr){

          pr.println("</table>");
         pr.println("</div>");
        pr.println("</td>");
       pr.println("</tr>");
      pr.println("</table>");
      pr.println("</center>");
     pr.println("</div>");
    pr.println("</td>");
   pr.println("</tr>");
  pr.println("</table>");
  pr.println("</center>");
```

```
pr.println("</div>");
pr.println("<p align=\"center\"> <font color=\"#800000\">Copyright 2000, by Java Developers
Paradise.<br>All rights reserved.<br>");
   pr.println("</font> ");

pr.println("</p>");
pr.println("<p> </p>");
pr.println("</body>");
pr.println("</html>");
}
```

## Part 2 creating tables

**Scripts to create the tables necessary for search engines.**

**Run all these queries on your MySQL Database server.**

```
create table section(serno int, head char(40) primary key,description char(100))

insert into section values(1,'Arts and Humanities','Artists, Literature, Arts'),(2,'Business and Economy','Employment and careers, finance'),(3,'Careers and Employment','Computers, Information technology'),(4,'Computers and Internet','Free stuff, hardware, software'),(5,'Entertainment','Humor, Jokes, Movies and Film'),(6,'Free Stuff','Games and Downloads'),(7,'Health','Disease and symptoms, First aid'),(8,'News and Current Events','Government, Lottery, Radio, Weather'),(9,'Opportunities','Aids, Franchises, Home-based'),(10,'Recreation and Leisure','Fitness, Shopping, Sports, Travel'),(11,'Reference','Religion and Encyclopedia'),(12,'Shopping and Services','Classifieds, Footwear, Gift ideas'),(13,'Science','Biology, Chemistry, Education and employment'),(14,'Wealth Development','Bonds, Collectables, Commodities');

create table categories(serno int primary key,description char(50),section_code int);

insert into categories values(1,'Art History',1),(2,'Artists',1),(3,'Awards',1),(4,'Books',1),(5,'Censorship',1),(6,'Criticism and Theory',1),(7,'Culture and Groups',1),(8,'Design Arts',1),(9,'Education',1),(10,'Employment',1),(11,'Events',1),(12,'Institutes',1),(13,'Literature',1),(14,'Museums and Galleries',1),(15,'News and Media',1),(16,'Performing Arts',1),(17,'Photography',1),(18,'Prints and Paintings',1),(19,'Reference',1);

insert into categories values(20,'Classifieds',2),(21,'Companies',2),(22,'Conventions and Conferences',2),(23,'Education',2),(24,'Electronic Commerce',2),(25,'Employment',2),(26,'Entrepeneurs',2),(27,'Finance',2),(28,'Franchises',2),(29,'Free Stuff',2),(30,'Home Business',2),(31,'International',2),(32,'Investments',2),(33,'Magazine',2),(34,'Mail Order',2),(35,'Marketing',2),(36,'MLM',2),(37,'Network Marketing',2),(38,'Online Malls',2),(39,'Real Estate',2),(40,'Small Business',2),(41,'Product and Services',2);

insert into categories values(42,'Accounting',3),(43,'Arts',3),(44,'Biology',3),(45,'Business',3),(46,'Chemistry',3),(47,'Computers',3),(48,'Cooking',3),(49,'Denisty',3),(50,'Engineering',3),(51,'Health',3),(52,'Information Technology',3),(53,'Management',3),(54,'Mathematics',3),(55,'Medicine',3),(56,'Nursing',3),(57,'Physics',3),(58,'Science ',3),(59,'Web Design',3);
```

insert into categories values(60,'Communications',4),(61,'Companies',4),(62,'Contests and prizes',4),(63,'Discussion Forum',4),(64,'Employment',4),(65,'FAQ',4),(66,'Free Stuff',4),(67,'Games',4),(68,'Hardware',4),(69,'Help Desk',4),(70,'Information and Reviews',4),(71,'Mobile Computing',4),(72,'Networking',4),(73,'Online Gaming',4),(74,'Operating Systems',4),(75,'Security and Encryption',4),(76,'Software',4),(77,'Tech Support',4),(78,'TECH talk',4),(79,'Training and Certification',4),(80,'Utilities',4),(81,'Web Development',4),(82,'World Wide Web',4);

insert into categories values(83,'Actors and Actresses',5),(84,'Bestsellers',5),(85,'Books and Magazines',5),(86,'Comics and Cartoon',5),(87,'Companies',5),(88,'Computer',5),(89,'Employment',5),(90,'Humor, Jokes and Laugh',5),(91,'Movies and Film',5),(92,'Music',5),(93,'Party Games',5),(94,'Music',5),(95,'Party Games',5),(96,'Radio',5),(97,'Reviews',5),(98,'Space',5),(99,'Talk Show',5),(100,'Television',5),(101,'Trivia',5);

insert into categories values(102,'Antivirus',6),(103,'Communication & Email',6),(104,'Compression',6),(105,'Contest',6),(106,'Desktop Themes',6),(107,'Educational',6),(108,'Fragmentation',6),(109,'Game and Downloads',6),(110,'Graphics and Video',6),(111,'Hobbies',6),(112,'Macintosh',6),(113,'Money',6),(114,'Music',6),(115,'Programming',6),(116,'Screen Savers',6),(117,'Simulators',6),(118,'Utilities and Applications',6),(119,'Webs and internet',6);

insert into categories values(120,'Babies and Pregnancy',7),(121,'Children',7),(122,'Dentistry',7),(123,'Diseases and Symptoms',7),(124,'Doctors',7),(125,'Education',7),(126,'Employment',7),(127,'First Aid',7),(128,'Fitness and Weight',7),(129,'Health Care',7),(130,'Insurance',7),(131,'Mail Order',7),(132,'Medicine',7),(133,'Nursing',7),(134,'Nutrition',7),(135,'Pharmacology',7),(136,'Psychiatrist',7),(137,'Wo men',7);

insert into categories values(138,'Arts and Humanities',8),(139,'Automotive',8),(140,'College and University',8),(141,'Commercial Services',8),(142,'Crime',8),(143,'Employment',8),(144,'Entertainment',8),(145,'Government',8),(146,'Health',8),(147,'Jo urnals and Newspaper',8),(148,'Legal Aid',8),(149,'Lottery',8),(150,'Music',8),(151,'Politics',8),(152,'Radio',8),(153,'Sports',8),(154,'Taxes',8),(155,'Technology' ,8),(156,'Television',8),(157,'Travel',8),(158,'Weather',8);

insert into categories values(159,'Aids',9),(160,'Franchises',9),(161,'Home based',9),(162,'Internet',9),(163,'Investments',9),(164,'Mail Order',9),(165,'Network Marketing',9),(166,'World Wide Investments',9)

insert into categories values(167,'Amusement and Theme Parks',10),(168,'Cars',10),(169,'Cooking',10),(170,'Dance',10),(171,'Dating',10),(172,'Fitness',10),(173,'Gambling',10),(1 74,'Games',10),(175,'Home and Garden',10),(176,'Pets',10),(177,'Shopping',10),(178,'Sports',10),(179,'Stamps',10),(180,'Television',10),(181,'Toys',10),( 182,'Travel',10),(183,'Wine',10);

insert into categories values(184,'Religion',11),(185,'Biblography',11),(186,'Calender',11),(187,'Dictionaries & Thesauri',11),(188,'Encyclopedia',11),(189,'Health Jourmnals',11),(190,'Maps',11),(191,'Music',11),(192,'Quotations',11),(193,'Research Papers',11),(194,'Time',11);

insert into categories values(195,'Art and Painting',12),(196,'Books and Magazines',12),(197,'Classifieds',12),(198,'Computer',12),(199,'Cooking',12),(200,'Electronics',12),(201,'Fashion and Clothing',12),(202,'Florist',12),(203,'Footwear',12),(204,'Furniture',12),(205,'Gift Ideas',12),(206,'Health',12),(207,'Help Wanted',12),(208,'Insurance',12),(209,'Jewelry',12),(210,'Music',12),(211,'Perfume',12),(212,'Toys',12),(213,'Wedding', 12);;

insert into categories values(214,'Aeronautics and Aviation',13),(215,'Agriculture',13),(216,'Astrology',13),(217,'Others',13);

insert into categories values(218,'Bonds',14),(219,'Collectables',14),(220,'Commodities',14),(221,'Currency',14),(222,'Stocks',14),(223,'Tax Free',14)

create table listings (serno int,login char(15) primary key,password char(15),address char(200),city char(30),state char(30),zip char(10),country char(30),telephone char(30),email char(50),url char(100),category int,caption char(100),descp char(200),mailing_list char(1),posted_on datetime)

create table listings(serno int,login char(15) primary key,password char(15) not null,street char(100),city char(30),state char(30),zip char(10),country char(30),telephone char(30),email char(50),url char(100),category int,caption char(100),descp char(200),mailing_list char(1),posted_on datetime)

*****